THE KARIYE DJAMI

VOLUME 4 *of the publication*

of an archaeological project of

THE BYZANTINE INSTITUTE, INC.

† PAUL A. UNDERWOOD, Editor

Otto Demus
Sirarpie Der Nersessian
André Grabar
Jacqueline Lafontaine-Dosogne
John Meyendorff
Ihor Ševčenko
Paul A. Underwood

THE KARIYE DJAMI

Volume 4 Studies in the Art of
the Kariye Djami and
Its Intellectual Background

ROUTLEDGE & KEGAN PAUL · LONDON

ISBN   0 7100 6932 4

Manufactured in the United States of America

BASED ON THE ORIGINAL DESIGN BY ANDOR BRAUN

Paul A. Underwood, 1902–1968

Paul A. Underwood, Professor of Byzantine Architecture and Archaeology at Dumbarton Oaks Center for Byzantine Studies of Harvard University, died on September 22nd, 1968, in Knoxville, Tennessee. At the time of his death he had completed his own study for, and carried far his work as Editor of, this fourth volume of *The Kariye Djami*.

Professor Underwood was born in 1902 at Aguadilla, Puerto Rico. In 1925 he received a Bachelor of Science degree in architecture, and in 1928 the degree of Master of Fine Arts in Architecture, from Princeton University. After several years of practicing architecture in New York, he spent three years in Greece traveling and studying classical sites. From 1935 to 1938 he studied again at Princeton University, in the Department of Art and Archaeology. From 1938 to 1943 he was a member of the faculty of Cornell University. He went to Dumbarton Oaks as a Fellow in 1943, joined the faculty there in 1946, and became a full professor in 1960. In 1950 he became Field Director of the Byzantine Institute and continued to direct the archaeological and restoration projects in Istanbul and Cyprus when these were taken over by Dumbarton Oaks.

In May of 1960 Professor Underwood directed a symposium at Dumbarton Oaks on "The Mosaics and Frescoes of the Kariye Djami," which was the foundation of the present volume. In 1966 Bollingen Foundation published the first three volumes of his work on the Kariye Djami, which received the Charles Rufus Morey citation of the College Art Association, awarded for the most distinguished work of scholarship for the year in the field of the history of art.

In addition to his major work, *The Kariye Djami*, Professor Underwood published many papers in the Byzantine field, including an iconographic study, "The Fountain of Life in Manuscripts of the Gospels," a number of articles on the mosaics and frescoes of the Kariye Djami and of St. Sophia, and reports on the field activities of the Byzantine Institute and Dumbarton Oaks.

FROM ITS INCEPTION the plan for the publication of the series of volumes on the representational arts of the Kariye Djami (the church of the monastery of Chora) included this fourth volume entitled *Studies in the Art of the Kariye Djami*, a collaborative work by seven authors. Of necessity it has been preceded by two volumes of plates, illustrating the entire repertory of the mosaics and frescoes still existing in the church, and by their accompanying text volume.[1] The main purpose of the earlier volumes was to provide the factual and illustrative "source material" on the monument. In citing works in the Kariye Djami the authors of this volume will refer by plate or subject number to the illustrations in Volumes 2 and 3, or by page or subject number to material contained in Volume 1.[2]

With the view to exploring what the content and approach should be for a volume of special studies that would best exploit the potentials of the material, it was thought that one of the Dumbarton Oaks symposia might well be devoted to the art of the church of the Chora and the intellectual and spiritual milieu of which it was an expression. With the generous assistance of the Bollingen Foundation such a symposium was presented in May of 1960 under the direction of the editor of this volume. Although most of the studies published herein are an outgrowth and further development of lectures presented on that occasion, they are not merely refinements of those lectures; some changes of topic have been made and each author has entered more deeply and critically into his subject.

The original proposal to present discussions of the social, intellectual, and spiritual background in Constantinople in the period with which we are dealing has been retained in this volume. Thus, the work opens with three studies directed to matters of that nature. The first, by Professor Grabar, is a sketch summarizing, without reference to specific works in the Chora or other monuments, some of the historical and cultural conditions under which Palaeologan art developed and was adopted far and wide by the politically hostile and independent neighbors of the greatly diminished Byzantine state who nevertheless professed the Orthodox faith of Byzantium and acknowledged its leadership in religious and ecclesiastical matters. Most appropriately, Professor Ševčenko has given us a short but penetrating insight into the character of Theodore Metochites, the extraordinary and learned personage who was responsible for the

---

1 Paul A. Underwood, *The Kariye Djami*, Vols. 1–3 (Bollingen Series LXX; New York, 1966): Vol. 1, Text; Vol. 2, The Mosaics, Plates 1–334; Vol. 3, The Frescoes, Plates 335–553.
2 A reference in this volume to a scene or detail in the Kariye Djami illustrated in Volume 2 or 3 is indicated either by plate number, or by subject number enclosed in square brackets, thus [ ]. Illustrations in Volume 4, all of which depict works in other monuments and are reproduced for purposes of comparison, are referred to as Fig.

restoration of the Chora monastery and its decoration, and his role in the intellectual life of the early fourteenth century. Professor Ševčenko's contribution is made all the more valuable by the publication, in appendices, of hitherto unpublished and practically unknown texts of Metochites' writings which are pertinent to the subject of the paper. While Metochites' career represented a number of facets of the cultural life of the day, these are complemented in Professor Meyendorff's study on the equally important religious, or spiritual, climate of the time. Despite the secular, humanistic interests displayed by the learned circles of the city, it must not be assumed that they directly affected in a tangible way or to a marked degree the traditional Christian piety of Byzantium or the outlook of the artists, who continued to regard their works as religious expressions and in them sustained much of the spirit and the basic content of the slowly evolving Byzantine art.

To lead off the specifically art historical studies and to place our monument in its proper relation to the development of Byzantine style, Professor Demus presents an analysis of the stylistic characteristics of the mosaics and paintings in the Kariye Djami and traces the development of Palaeologan style from its antecedents at the end of the Comnene period to a point even later than the Kariye Djami itself. The remaining four studies are concerned mainly with the iconographic programs of the Chora. They take up, in turn, the three existing cycles in the mosaics of the narthexes of the church and the independent program depicted in the frescoes of the parecclesion. Because of the chronological disposition of the cycles in the narthexes, the iconography of the Life of the Virgin in the inner narthex is discussed first, by Mme. Jacqueline Lafontaine-Dosogne. Because of her extensive studies of the subject, now published in a two-volume monograph, she was eminently equipped to discuss the most celebrated example of such a cycle—that of the Chora. She is also the author of the sixth essay which deals with the iconography of the Infancy of Christ. A study of the third of the cycles in the narthexes, that of Christ's Ministry, is presented by the present writer. Too extensive to be analyzed iconographically in its totality and because a Ministry cycle poses interesting and special problems that are not encountered in other Christological cycles, the treatment of the subject is not restricted to iconographic questions in the usual sense but includes an attempt to discover the bases for the layouts of a number of Ministry cycles in Byzantine art and the ways whereby some were given iconological content and meanings over and above those of simple narration. Finally, the study by Professor Der Nersessian on the paintings in the parecclesion is another in which considerable attention is given to the themes and content of the program, which, though not entirely unique, are perhaps most clearly developed in the Kariye Djami.

The art historical studies take the Kariye Djami as their point of departure, but widening their scope they take into account the broader field of Byzantine art, paying special attention to that of the Palaeologan era, which until recent years has been generally neglected. Far from being a sterile or degenerate extension of Byzantine art, the Palaeologan works will appear in the course of these studies to have possessed vitality and originality in synthesizing into new forms and meanings much from their long and ancient heritage.

P.A.U.

Dumbarton Oaks
Washington, D.C.
August 1968

viii

Editorial Note

After the death of Professor Underwood in September 1968, editorial responsibility for the present volume was in the hands of Messrs. William McGuire and George Robinson, with the assistance of Mrs. Pauline Batchelder, on behalf of Bollingen Series and Princeton University Press. At various stages aid and advice were given by Professor Ernst Kitzinger. A great deal of the editorial work was done by Mrs. Fanny Bonajuto, of Dumbarton Oaks. The essays written by André Grabar and Jacqueline Lafontaine-Dosogne were translated from the French by Willard R. Trask.

Contents

List of Illustrations

Jacqueline Lafontaine-Dosogne

Paul A. Underwood

LIST OF ILLUSTRATIONS

Sirarpie Der Nersessian

1. Mount Sinai, monastery of St. Catherine, icon. Enthroned Virgin and Child Surrounded by Prophets (courtesy Michigan-Princeton-Alexandria Expedition to Mount Sinai)
2. Prizren, church of the Bogorodica Ljeviška, outer narthex, north bay, lunette. Jacob's Vision of the Ladder and Jacob Wrestling with the Angel (photo T. Dobać, Zagreb)
3. Salonika, church of the Holy Apostles, outer narthex, east bay, north lunette. The Tabernacle of Moses (courtesy Thalia Peterson)
4. Staro Nagoričino, church of St. George, iconostasis. The Virgin Pelagonitissa (from G. Millet and A. Frolow, *La peinture du Moyen Âge en Yougoslavie*, III, PL. 1191)
5. Studenica, church of Sts. Joachim and Anne, nave, north wall, tympanum, east half. The Anastasis (photo D. Tasić, Belgrade)
6. Kalenić, monastery church, nave, west wall. The Raising of the Widow's Son (photo D. Tasić, Belgrade)
7. Kalenić, monastery church, south apse, west side. The Raising of Jairus' Daughter
8. Athens, Byzantine Museum, icon no. 2162. The Archangel Michael (photo Hirmer Fotoarchiv, Munich)
9. Cyprus, monastery of St. Neophytos, bema. Neophytos between the Archangels Michael and Gabriel (photo Dumbarton Oaks, Washington, D.C.)
10. Manasija, monastery church, nave, soffit of arch above tympanum of west door. The Hand of God between Solomon and David (from V. Petković, *La peinture serbe du Moyen Âge*, II. PL. CCIV)
11. Trebizond, church of St. Sophia, north porch, lunette, detail. Jacob's Vision of the Ladder and Jacob Wrestling with the Angel (courtesy The Russell Trust)
12. Ohrid, church of St. Clement, narthex, north bay, west section. Jacob's Vision of the Ladder and Jacob Wrestling with the Angel (courtesy Macedonian Institute for the Protection of Historical Monuments, Skoplje)
13. Lesnovo, monastery church. Jacob Wrestling with the Angel
14. Lesnovo, monastery church. Moses and the Burning Bush
15. Mount Athos, Vatopedi 602 (Octateuch), fol. 345v. The Bearing of the Ark of the Covenant (courtesy Princeton-Athos Expedition)
16. Mount Sinai, monastery of St. Catherine, chapel (courtesy Michigan-Princeton-Alexandria Expedition to Mount Sinai)
17. Gračanica, monastery church, bema, north wall. The Tabernacle of Moses
18. Istanbul, Fethiye Djami (church of St. Mary Pammakaristos), south façade, west end, arched niche. The Three Priests before the Altar, and the "Closed Door" (fragment) (photo Dumbarton Oaks, Washington, D.C.)
19. Ohrid, church of St. Clement, narthex, south bay, east section. The "Closed Door" (courtesy Gordana Babić)

PLANS AND SECTIONS AT END OF BOOK

1. General plan of the Kariye Djami
2. Plan of the outer and inner narthexes
3. Section of outer narthex, Bays 1–6, looking east
4. Section of outer narthex, Bays 1–6, looking west
5. Section of outer narthex, Bays 6 and 7, looking north
6. Section of outer narthex, Bays 6 and 7, looking south
7. Section of inner narthex, Bays 1–4, and of outer narthex, Bay 7, looking east
8. Section of inner narthex, Bays 1–4, and of outer narthex, Bay 7, looking west
9. Plan of the parecclesion, upper zone
10. Plan of the parecclesion, lower zone
11. Section of the parecclesion, looking south
12. Section of the parecclesion, looking north

xvi

Abbreviations

ActaSS	*Acta Sanctorum*
AJA	*American Journal of Archaeology*
ArtB	*Art Bulletin*
Bonn	*Corpus Scriptorum Historiae Byzantinae*, ed. B. G. Niebuhr et al. (Bonn, 1828–97)
BZ	*Byzantinische Zeitschrift*
CA	*Cahiers archéologiques*
DACL	*Dictionnaire d'archéologie chrétienne et de liturgie*, eds. F. Cabrol and H. Leclercq (Paris, 1907–53)
DOP	*Dumbarton Oaks Papers*
GBA	*Gazette des Beaux-Arts*
JOeBG	*Jahrbuch der Oesterreichischen Byzantinischen Gesellschaft* (since 1969: *JOeB, Jahrbuch der Oesterreichischen Byzantinistik*)
MemPontAcc	*Memorie della Pontificia Accademia romana di archeologia*
MonPiot	*Fondation Eugène Piot, Monuments et Mémoires*, publiés par l'Académie des Inscriptions et Belles-Lettres
OCP	*Orientalia Christiana Periodica*
PG	*Patrologiae cursus completus, Series Graeca*, ed. J.-P. Migne
PL	*Patrologiae cursus completus, Series Latina*, ed. J.-P. Migne
RA	*Revue archéologique*
RAC	*Rivista di archeologia cristiana*
RE	*Paulys Real-Encyclopädie der classischen Altertumswissenschaft*, eds. G. Wissowa and others
REB	*Revue des études byzantines*
REG	*Revue des études grecques*
RHR	*Revue de l'histoire des religions*
ROC	*Revue de l'Orient chrétien*
Teubner	*Bibliotheca Scriptorum Graecorum et Romanorum Teubneriana* (Leipzig)
VS	*Vizantijskij Sbornik*
VV	*Vizantijskij Vremennik*
ZRVI	*Zbornik Radova Vizantološkog Instituta*

The Artistic Climate in Byzantium During the Palaeologan Period

ANDRÉ GRABAR

This text was written in 1965.
A. GRABAR

The Artistic Climate in Byzantium
During the Palaeologan Period

THE ARCHITECTURE of the church of the Chora and more particularly the mosaics and mural paintings that decorate it form an ensemble which is generally regarded as a masterpiece of Byzantine art. In my opinion this ensemble is unquestionably an original creation, many features of which are not found anywhere else. But whatever its degree of originality—which the disappearance of so many contemporary monuments prevents us from precisely determining—the Chora naturally shares in the inescapable condition of all works of art in having numberless connections with its historical milieu. Some of these connections can probably no longer be discerned, given the scarcity of works that have been preserved. Others, however, are unmistakable, and in the studies of this volume dealing with the mosaics and frescoes of this church the writers refer to numerous related works in order better to define the art of the Chora. This monument is thus seen to take its place in various series of similar works, at a certain stage of artistic evolution.

Naturally these studies have their point of departure in the Chora itself; therefore the works belonging to the same environment are considered only in so far as they resemble its decoration.

My own study will take the opposite course. It proposes to lead the reader, as it were, to the doors of the Chora without taking him into it. To reach the Chora, it seeks to begin further back in time and space, and also to give an idea of the artistic climate which created the art of this church. Thus, before studying the art of the Chora itself, the reader is invited to scan its horizon and to familiarize himself with the Byzantine art of the Palaeologi amid which the Chora came to birth.

Social Milieu

FOR CENTURIES the art that we call Byzantine was practiced in the vast territory belonging to the Eastern Empire. From the seventh century and with the advance of the Muslim Arabs, this territory had steadily diminished, with a concomitant reduction in the extent of Byzantine art, whose fate was inseparably linked with that of the Empire. But this trend ceased when new Christian kingdoms began to be established on the soil of the Empire—Christian Bulgaria in the ninth century, Latin and Serb kingdoms in the twelfth and thirteenth centuries. Politically these countries were not dependent upon Byzantium, but Byzantine art continued to be practiced in them. Still other countries, situated beyond the frontiers of the Empire but converted by Byzantine missionaries—Russia, for example, and Georgia—adopted the same art. In short, from the year 1000, but especially from the twelfth century onward, and including the entire Palaeologan period, Byzantine art expanded over areas far greater than the Greek Empire then governed from Constantinople. In all the provinces wrested from the Empire and in all the countries converted by the Byzantine missionary movement, Byzantine art reigned unchallenged as it did within what was left of the Empire, and nothing better testifies to the prestige it enjoyed among Byzantium's neighbors and to the closeness of its connection with the Orthodox religion. Then too, as is well known, the enemies of the Empire, the very peoples who opposed it on the battlefield, continued to regard Constantinople as the spiritual capital of the world of which they considered themselves a part, and they admitted, tacitly or not, that the church of Constantinople enjoyed a primacy over the other Orthodox churches. Under these conditions it was only natural that religious art, as we know it in the para-Byzantine countries, everywhere followed the example of the religious art of the Empire, small and politically weak though the Empire had become. This trend, of course, did not exclude various manifestations of local taste and regional practices; but for centuries there was a general readiness, throughout the Orthodox countries, to keep informed about the latest Byzantine works and to imitate them. So it came about that, many centuries after their respective conversions and despite the existence everywhere of regional schools at this period, these countries welcomed and imitated the innovations of Palaeologan art when they were brought to their knowledge.

In other words, although the Byzantine Empire under the Palaeologi was a small and weak state, nevertheless the art that was practiced in it crossed its frontiers and spread to a far larger territory, which can be quite accurately defined. It includes, apart from the Empire proper with its two great cities of Constantinople and Salonika, the province of Morea in the southern Peloponnesus, which had close political connections with Constantinople and was governed by Palaeologi and by descendants of other great Constantinopolitan families. The same art flourished in the neighboring countries, Bulgaria and Serbia, which emulated Byzantium. The princes and bishops who ruled there during the Palaeologan period sedulously followed Byzantine fashions and, even if they departed from them for a time, seized every opportunity to receive a new lesson from the Byzantine art of the epoch. The princes, some of whom must have been more powerful than the impoverished basileis of Constantinople, had means of commanding the services of the best artists from the workshops of Constantinople or Salonika; and it is for this reason that the works of art of the thirteenth and fourteenth centuries in their countries rank among the most beautiful and most typical productions of Palaeologan art. The Empire of Trebizond was also readily reached by echoes of the new Constantinopolitan fashions. On the other hand, in some purely Greek provinces Palaeologan art is little represented or altogether absent. Thus in Attica and in Boeotia, which were then in the hands of the Catalans, Byzantine churches of the thirteenth and fourteenth centuries are extremely modest. Here the most important monuments belong to the eleventh century, before the Crusades. To be sure, Epirus was in Greek hands, but the princes who reigned there were hostile to the Palaeologi of Constantinople. So the fashionable art of the capital rarely reached Arta and the other cities of the province, and what was practiced there was often a provincial art.

Thus the geographical map of Palaeologan art has its special characteristics and is not the same as the map of the Byzantine art that immediately preceded it. Socially too, the situation is new. Before the time of the Latin Empire of Constantinople, under the Comneni and their predecessors, the finest monuments in the capital and the provinces were founded and endowed by the emperors and the high dignitaries of the State and the Church. During the final period, at the time of Metochites' restoration of the Chora, all religious [foundations—usually monastic churches—were instituted by representatives of the most illustrious and powerful of the noble families. These families were the repositories of wealth and power, it was they who gave Byzantium her emperors and high officials, and indeed her bishops, writers, and humanists. Few in number, they were all related to one another and liked to commemorate the fact when the occasion arose (for example, in portraits). Art under the Palaeologi was cultivated within the confines of these families and hence flourished wherever this high Byzantine aristocracy carried it. But it was essentially an art which this aristocracy liked to enjoy close to its residences, that is, principally in Constantinople, or in Salonika, or wherever else one of its representatives, whether as emperor, provincial governor, or bishop, was called upon to live, or where he undertook to build a monastery (with the thought of retiring there or of resting there after his death). It has been well and often said that the Byzantine State under the Palaeologi retained nothing of the earlier Empire but the name.

It is to certain countries of Eastern Europe, countries in which the moral authority of the emperor of Byzantium and of the Orthodox Church of Constantinople still prevailed, that the elements of the high culture cultivated by the great families of the capital of the Empire were transplanted; whereas Italy asked Byzantium only for teachers, for technicians, with whose instruction she would do as she pleased. From the fourteenth century on Italian humanism had little in common with the humanism centered at the residences of the high Byzantine aristocracy.

Among the particular features of Byzantine humanism was one which it obviously could not share with similar tendencies in other countries. To cultivate the literature of antiquity was, in Byzantium, to continue or to revive the high culture of the ancients, who expressed themselves in the same language and hence were direct ancestors. For a long time the subjects of the emperor of Constantinople did not recognize their Greekness. But they were led to do so by those from whom they wished to distinguish themselves, the new nations that pressed in on them from every side, invading or threatening the Empire—Latins, Slavs, and Turks. The Byzantines ended by recognizing their Greek nationality, and this came about precisely at the period that coincides with the beginnings of the reign of the Palaeologi. The Byzantine was Greek, and the Empire a preeminently Greek state. Hence the traditional admiration for antiquity inevitably took on a national and patriotic tone; the high quality of classic literature and its long existence became a matter of pride for the Greeks, as well as a weapon in the hands of the defenders of the Greek Empire of Byzantium. The spokesmen for both groups were the same—the men who formed the high society of Constantinople.

Religion

SINCE THE Orthodox Church served as the vehicle for Byzantine art of the end of the Middle Ages, which spread as far as the Orthodox countries extended, religious life proper, as practiced in Byzantium, determined more than one characteristic of that art. I am thinking especially of the form of piety that was then current among the Byzantines, particularly among the leisure classes of Constantinople and the provinces, and that commissioned the execution of religious architectural monuments and paintings: a piety conservative and traditionalistic in character. It has its principal expression in assiduous attendance at church services and in scrupulous observance of the consecrated rites. The faithful are attached to these public prayers, know the prayers and chants by heart, participate in the sacraments, give alms and offerings to their favorite sanctuaries. Their dream is to make their offering in the form of an act of foundation, and to contribute, if not indeed a large or small monastery or church, at least a chapel abutting a church, an inconostasis, an icon, mural paintings, and most frequently some funerary disposition for the donor family. It is customary to consider any act of religious foundation to have very great merit in the eyes of God, and the large number of offerings of this type, though they are often modest, bears eloquent witness to the fact.

Palaeologan art in particular includes a large number of sanctuaries or parts of sanctuaries, of funerary monuments, of mural decorations, and of objects of piety which have this votive origin. With the name of the donor we often find his portrait and—looking more closely—some indications of personal taste or of a preference in personal devotion. Under the Palaeologi conditions were scarcely favorable for large-scale artistic enterprises requiring much time to execute; whereas monuments of moderate size and reasonable cost, which could be executed fairly rapidly, remained feasible and in fact were produced in great numbers. It is principally small monasteries that were built and decorated by the pious Byzantine donors of the period. The Church was all-powerful in such circles, and it is to the austere programs of the monks that the art was made to conform by these aristocrats who paid for it. The great majority of works in the Palaeologan period, and certainly all those of high artistic value, were produced for the benefit of monks. However, neither an elegant and even refined painting style nor echoes of classical models were excluded, especially during the earliest period of Palaeologan rule. For the donors, belonging to the Byzantine nobility, could admire the classical writers and everything that stemmed from antiquity without either renouncing the Orthodox religion or deviating from it in the slightest. This society seems to have been unaware of the possible conflict between Orthodox piety and humanistic studies, the practices of Christian piety always remaining the determining factor in the conduct of its members. It is in consequence of this state of things that almost all Byzantine works under the Palaeologi are functionally religious, even though they show many traces of the taste for the classic.

Another correspondence between Palaeologan art and the forms of religiosity dominant in this society appears in the fact that under the Palaeologi art became more closely connected with offices celebrated in the churches. Never before had artists shown so great a desire to reflect the various aspects of the cult, or to explain their mystical essence, or to create iconographic counterparts to liturgical hymns.

Nothing, however, better reveals the close connection between religious life and artistic activity under the Palaeologi than a comparison between the evolution of art from the middle of the thirteenth to the end of the fourteenth century and the manifestations of religious thought during the same period. As I said above, Byzantine religious life continued under the Palaeologi just as it had before, without dissidences or new heresies but also without revolutionary innovations in Orthodox thought. But historians of ideas note a certain intellectual ferment in Byzantium under the first Palaeologi, that is, toward the end of the thirteenth century and in the first half of the fourteenth. This ferment subsides after 1350 and does not recur. In the field of art, and especially in religious painting, we note a similar break, which coincides chronologically with the other. It is tempting to relate these two series of facts, and a comparison between them appears to justify the connection: the two phases in the evolution of Palaeologan art may well reflect two sets of tendencies that manifested themselves among Byzantine religious thinkers at this period, the one appearing earlier, the other later.

The earlier tendencies were best voiced by Barlaam the Calabrian, who, probably inspired by the West whence he came, opened a road that, had Greek Orthodoxy followed it, would have readapted the Church to the problems of the period. More than one of the opinions he expressed could have inspired or explained the new tendencies manifest in the religious painting of his time. Barlaam and his friends cited the authority of Aristotle to justify and encourage study of the physical world, of all that is registered by the senses. The tendency in the art of the time to observe nature more closely, and especially to take a stronger interest than before in the countless aspects of sensible reality, may well be related to these doctrines of Barlaam and his friends.

This is true for a first period probably beginning before the return of the emperors to Constantinople in 1261, and continuing down to the forties of the fourteenth century, during which a certain liberalism or relaxation in Byzantium was favorable to more or less new initiatives in every field. The same state of mind manifested itself in the affirmations of Barlaam the Calabrian, who proposed the study of the material world as distinct from theology, and in the attempts of the painters of the period to give an integral place in their art to a larger number of elements drawn from the reality around them. Though this tendency did not produce a genuinely realistic current, it was manifested here and there in many paintings inspired from life. Just as classical studies, traditional though they were in Byzantium, became more effective through progress in critical methods, so artists learned to draw greater profit from their imitations of antique models. This is strikingly apparent when we look at the beautiful mural paintings of the second half of the thirteenth century. Each of these works has its own particular character, which is never the case, to the same degree, with earlier paintings, and this trait tends to disappear by the second third of the fourteenth century. This element of individuality is rarely expressed in striking innovations, but appears rather in the manner in which the artist interprets tradition and the concrete model he imitates. It is here that the more critical method allows either recourse to unusual models (as at Mileševo, where certain Salonikan mosaics, five centuries old, supply the inspiration) and their very "modern" interpretation revealing the artist's personality on the one hand, or, on the other, an assimilation of the classical tradition complete enough to open the way to imitation of reality. This is what we find at Sopočani, which offers the most classic ensemble of Byzantine paintings both in spirit and in form, and at the same time the one most advanced in the depiction of the human body, of drapery, of objects, and of architectures. It is through classical models that the painter here learns to represent fullness of faces, accurate foreshortening, volume of draperies, weight of stones and columns. Realism is here learned not by departing from antique models but by studying them. For this to come about required that the artist cease to see in the works of the past only motifs to be imitated and, instead, grasp the spirit that created them and the inner structure that conditions their art.

In considering such accomplished works, we realize the range of the experiments that the Byzantine artists, as individuals, were beginning to make under the earlier Palaeologi. We see them foreshadowing the discoveries of Cavallini and Giotto, and at the same time those of the

7

Italian painters of the fifteenth century who will revive the great style of classical painting—always, however, basing their experimentation both on antique models and on the Byzantine painting of the period, that is, presenting simultaneously what, in Italy, will appear in different contexts and at different times.

These variously exploratory works all belong to the early Palaeologan period; and already before its end their originality tends to lessen. The change is neither violent nor sudden. The painters progressively give up broadening the field of their experiments in imitating reality by resorting to classical methods or otherwise, and, though they preserve most of the symbolical and other themes introduced during the preceding decades, they markedly return to the traditionalistic method: the artist follows the example set by his predecessors, whose works, of whatever age, are models, that is, motifs to be imitated. This return to the traditional method in all likelihood corresponds—and chronologically coincides almost exactly—with the victory of the Hesychasts, who, from 1340 and particularly after 1350, dominate the Byzantine Church. Their triumph subjects Byzantium, for the last century of its existence, to the influence of the monks and of the monastic spirit, hostile to critical studies, to the secular sciences, and to antique culture as well as to all the innovations that are beginning to revolutionize the Latin West. I should add—and here, too, the correspondence with the history of ideas must be emphasized—that the paintings of this second chronological stage testify both to an obvious retreat of individualistic and innovating initiatives and to a return to the aesthetic ideals typical of Byzantine tradition. The cold and even hard elegance of works of this type, the seriousness and immobility of these images, are called upon to parallel the doctrine of Gregory Palamas, which is also deeply anchored in the Byzantine past and which supposes that religious images translate an intelligible reality and that, through these conventional figurations, the spiritual eyes of the believer can contemplate God and trace the ineffable course of the history of salvation.

Under these circumstances it would be wrong to exaggerate either the realistic trend of Byzantine art under the early Palaeologi or the possibility of a more active influence of the innovating thought of Barlaam and his group on the religious painters who were their contemporaries. The realism of the former did not go very far, and before inspiring the painters, the influence of more liberal thinkers should have produced the beginnings of a natural science in Byzantium. This, as we know, did not develop. But what is legitimate to regard as a probable echo of this first intellectual current, or at least as a counterpart to it, is the individual contribution of each painter to the work he was commissioned to do. Of all the works of Byzantine art that have come down to us, it is in the paintings of the second half of the thirteenth century and the beginning of the fourteenth that we always find the greatest degree of individuality.

As for the second stage, which culminates about 1350 in the victory of Barlaam's opponents, the Hesychasts, with Gregory Palamas at their head, its role in the evolution of the art of the time is at least as probable. The Hesychasts brought about the triumph of monastic rigorism, of hostility toward everything that appeared to derive from the Roman Church, including investigation of the sensible world, by reaffirming the traditional Byzantine conviction that God could be known "directly," that is, through a life of piety in the bosom of the Church and through the sacraments that lead every believer to a mystic communion with Christ. In the language of art these ideas could be translated by figurations emphasizing the "reality" of the divine presence of Christ in liturgy, in knowledge, and, more generally, in every evocation of the first parousia; if art could contribute to the work of salvation pursued by the Church, it was by reminding the faithful that the Incarnation had opened the way to the "deification" of every man. A program of this kind, which would conform to the Byzantine traditions of the early Middle Ages, obviously cut religious art off from real life and prevented it from renewing itself by means of individual initiative. Now, what we find around 1350, and sometimes earlier, are artistic creations of precisely this type, and the paintings of the Chora basically foreshadow their flowering. The modest innovations of the preceding period are not relinquished, but no new ones are made. These innovations are merely added to earlier models, and painters imitate them in the same way as they imitate those earlier models. They are, as it were, canonized in their turn; thus Byzantine art finally will find itself at a dead end.

Everything considered, the surviving sources are too few to enable us to draw definite conclusions from a comparison between the paintings of the Palaeologan period and the intellectual aspects of Byzantine religious life. However, through the evidence at our disposal we discern that painting under the early Palaeologi results in achievements that differ from those of the later period in a way comparable to that in which the ideas of a Barlaam are opposed to those of a Palamas.

Classical Studies

HOWEVER, another aspect of intellectual activity in Byzantium under the Palaeologi must be mentioned in connection with the art then practiced: the classical studies that were inspired by a profound admiration for antiquity. These classical and humanistic studies will be discussed in the chapters devoted to Metochites and the intellectual and religious life of Byzantium at the period of the restoration of the Chora. The reader will find that the taste for the products of antiquity was very much alive in Constantinople under the Palaeologi and that, at the period with which we are concerned, humanists were active among the high Byzantine aristocracy. Some of the humanists belonged to it, as did Metochites; others were technicians—specialists in ancient literature and pedagogues, who, whether laymen or monks, were listened to and were supported by the great of this world. When we refer to this very lively interest in antiquity among the Byzantines we must, then, think of a quite definite social milieu, which, though very much restricted in the number of those who belonged to it, was extremely influential, since the administration of the Byzantine State, and of its wealth, was in the hands of its members. The admiration which this milieu professed for the classical heritage was certainly not very original for Byzantium, for the ancient writers had been studied and frequently imitated in Constantinople at all periods, and more especially from the ninth century on. However, this attitude, which was only normal among people whose language went back to that of the ancient Hellenes, attained a new importance after the trials of the thirteenth century, trials which recurred in the fourteenth. Consciousness of the great Greek past transmitted by the Greek writers of antiquity enabled the Byzantines to stand more firmly against the new, threatening populations who were crowding in upon what was left of the old Greek Empire. To the redoubtable strength of these populations, the cultivated society of Constantinople responded by declaring itself the heir to the oldest and the highest of literary cultures. At the time when, as I have already remarked, the Greek sense of nationality was born, the testimony of classical literature became a means of "self-determination" for the Byzantines of the ruling class in the face of the Franks, the Italians, the Catalans, the Slavs, the Turks.

But to what degree does this humanism, which promotes the study and imitation of the ancient authors, historians and poets, scholars and astronomers, extend its curiosity and its admiration to art, architecture, and works of painting and sculpture? The question is by no means idle, even if it may not admit of an answer in simple and reasonably clear terms. In architecture, for example, nothing reveals any influence of the building or decorative arts of the Greeks of antiquity. This absence of any attempt to imitate antique monuments is, in any case, not peculiar to the Byzantine Middle Ages. Since monumental art is closely connected with the function of the edifice and the material available, there is no return to the models of classical architecture except under unusually favorable circumstances, as in the West from the time of the Renaissance on.

The Byzantine churches of the Palaeologan period, like those which preceded them, were untouched by any tendency to imitate antiquity. I will pass over the sculpture of the period, which has been too little studied (and which, in any case, is very limited in scope), and confine my attention to its painting: mosaics, frescoes, manuscript illuminations, paintings on wood. These paintings derive from others that preceded them and are in no way revolutionary; but among the features that are new in relation to works of the immediate past, a practiced eye easily perceives that the Palaeologan painters are frequently reviving motifs and procedures that come to them from antique painting. Here they go far beyond anything that has been done before to bring about a new flowering of antique art, not only in intention but also in accomplishment.

These revivals postulate a taste for antique art which parallels that of the Humanists in their imitations of ancient writers. But, just as Byzantine literary works do, the paintings of the Palaeologan period include a large number of imitations of antique models, occasionally of high quality, and yet reveal the superficial nature of these contacts with antique productions. As far as literature is concerned, one notes that it is the vocabulary and style of the ancients which the Byzantines both seek to imitate and are most successful in imitating, and that, in the range of literary styles, it is the flowery and elaborate or even the precious discourse that is the object of the most concentrated effort of imitation. This style is extended to the epistolary art, to scientific treatises, and to sermons—an indication of a certain misunderstanding of literary genres and a tendency to confuse the aesthetic values of antiquity with the artifices of rhetoric. These findings are completely applicable to Palaeologan painting, in which borrowings from antique models are very numerous (drawings of the human figure and of its movements and attitudes, draperies, landscapes and representation of space, various pictorial motifs), and yet the art of these paintings has essentially nothing in common with that of their models. In fact, this art is no less medieval than that which the Byzantines practiced in the previous centuries, and indeed certain Greek paintings of the tenth century (for example, the illuminations of the Psalter Paris. gr. 139) come closer to the original works of antiquity. It is to models of this type especially that Palaeologan painting owes one of its most characteristic general effects—that of the pictorial, of movement, of a certain affected grace. This arises from the fact that, even when the subject demands immobility, the figures enveloped in their draperies suggest a more or less violent movement which has just ceased or is just about to begin. This suggested movement is not always justified by the subject, as it is in antique art and in the art of the Renaissance. The furniture and the architecture which surround the figures hollow out a certain spatial depth for them, but we very soon become aware of the artifices of this procedure when we see that the suggested space is not continuous, as it is in antique art or in the Renaissance art that rediscovers it. In addition, the buildings, the massive furniture, the costumes, even the structure of the human body, strike us as having a certain inconsistency: aside from the pictorial and dynamic effect mentioned above, if we consider only a particular detail or part, references to reality seem to be established normally (a wall of a certain measurable thickness, a normal projection of a piece of furniture, a series of folds such as one does see); but if we look at the ensemble, these references disappear (the wall suggests no partition that we can recall; the piece of furniture cannot, as a mass, insert itself into a given space as happens in reality; the garment to which the series of folds belongs has neither the form nor the position of any known drapery of garments). Here again is an inconsistency that appears neither in antique art nor in the art of the Renaissance. One could multiply these observations, which would all lead to the same conclusion: borrowings from the repertory of antique paintings are numerous, and the number of these borrowings only increases the further one goes in the study of Palaeologan art. But in the majority of cases these transplants from antiquity into the paintings produced in the Palaeologan period do not result in an abandonment of the medieval structure of painting but serve only to enrich these works by superimposing upon the antique schemas a network of motifs comparable to stylistic figures in literature.

These observations, however, do not suffice to define the position of Palaeologan painting in respect to antique art. On the one hand, as we saw, this painting is not homogeneous, and does not always and everywhere have the same reaction to the teaching of antiquity. On the other hand, almost all the paintings that have come down to us from this period are religious and this obliges us to consider the following special problem: Did not the teaching of antique art receive a particular interpretation by reason of the Christian programs of the painters, an interpretation that could tend both to limit and intentionally to modify its application?

The second alternative can be considered only imperfectly, given the almost complete absence (at least among works that have been preserved) of secular paintings of the Palaeologan period. However, none of those that have come down to us—the illuminations of the Chronicle of John Skylitzes, of the Romance of Alexander, of the Life of Barlaam and Joasaph, of medical treatises— are closer to, or more completely integrated into, the aesthetics of antiquity than are the religious works. Indeed, one has the clear impression that these secular paintings of the Palaeologan period show less unity than the religious paintings, and that the examples that have come down to us follow different models, created at different times and in different artistic milieus. Some of these paintings, such as the illustrations for the Romance of Alexander, at S. Giorgio dei Greci, Venice, are more clearly reminiscent of the antique than others; on the other hand, there are some in which admiration for antique art does not appear at all, as in the famous illuminations of the Chronicle of Skylitzes, at Madrid. Hence, without being categorical, I should be inclined to say that in the domain of Palaeologan painting echoes of this admiration are to be found mainly, and almost exclusively, in religious painting, be it in manuscript illustrations, in icons, or in mural decoration of churches.

Surprising as it may at first appear, this observation is nevertheless not inconsistent with what we know of Byzantine religious literature of the same period—at any rate, in the sense that imitations of the antique appear in that literature if not exclusively at least chiefly in sermons, in lives and panegyrics of saints, and in other writings in the domain of religion and ritual. It is here above all that custom compels the writer to exhibit a certain familiarity with philology, to employ choice terms and a complicated and distinguished style—an art which was learned from the study of classical authors. This literature provides the real counterpart to the religious paintings with antique motifs that we find in the Palaeologan period, at the Chora and elsewhere; in both cases there is a similarly precious style as well as a stock of thought and feeling that is completely medieval despite the numerous borrowings from antiquity.

I will make one further remark in this connection. The models of the Byzantine humanists included the works of the fourth-century Fathers, and these Christian writers did indeed still employ a language and style very close to classic literature. Yet the fact remains that the antiquity which humanists like Metochites called upon was for the most part Christianized antiquity, which was closer to them both in its spirit and in its subjects than pagan antiquity and which, moreover, was more accessible, for the works of the Christian Fathers were far better known, being constantly copied, throughout the centuries, for general use, while those of the pagan writers, being older and heterodox, were within the reach of only a few. This last point is even truer of paintings. How often did men of the thirteenth and fourteenth centuries in Byzantium have the opportunity to see an antique painting of pagan times and of pagan content? It is not principally through Christian paintings, which originated in the times of the Fathers and which normally conveyed a quantity of antique forms and motifs, that the Palaeologan painters were able to enter into contact with the tradition of antique art? These matters will be treated in detail further on, in my investigation of the direct sources of the Palaeologan painters. But I may say at this point that the imitation of the antique was not a contribution introducing an explosive element into Byzantine painting of this period. Handed down with the body of earlier but perfectly orthodox and Greek painting, it was an integral part of the "tradition" and hence was acceptable to the most conservative. Thus the monuments themselves impose the following conclusion: in Palaeologan painting the classic factor in no way served a rationalistic or liberal cause, as it did in the contemporary art of Italy, where the discovery of antiquity and the progressive integration of its creations into the new art proceeded in step with an assimilation of antique science and its methods.

Sources of Palaeologan Art

THE ART practiced in Byzantium at the period of the Chora mosaics and frescoes had behind it a tradition of more than a thousand years, and those who practiced it were conscious of this antiquity and proud of it. They endeavored to prolong the tradition and only rarely, and unconsciously, would break with it. This very ancient tradition was therefore a characteristic of Palaeologan art, and perhaps its determining trait.

In practice, this means that an architectural monument or painting produced in the Palaeologan period, such as the Chora, comprised numerous elements—techniques and treatment, iconographic themes, and even details of various figurations—which had been originally established many centuries before and often in various places and at various times. To be sure, this was the case everywhere in the Middle Ages, but nowhere else was the period covered by an uninterrupted artistic activity so long as in Byzantium, and nowhere else was there so strong and so steady an adherence to the models inherited from the past. Hence, at the time of the Palaeologi, no other art existed that could carry with it so many ancient echoes of a past which extended over a thousand years.

Among the arts of the thirteenth and fourteenth centuries, only Palaeologan art continued an aesthetic of the end of antiquity, stocked with numerous motifs and technical procedures crystallized in the century of Constantine. It was the only art of its time that was in a position to combine in its works elements that went as far back as the end of antiquity with others that came to it from models of the tenth, eleventh, and twelfth centuries—these combinations being made possible by the continuity in the practice of the arts at Constantinople. Time had less effect than elsewhere on an art whose practice had never been interrupted for an appreciably long period and which had remained in the service of the same society and—the fact is essential—retained almost the same social function through the ages, a function that gave it little connection with what is most subject to the fluctuations of history, that is, with daily reality. This art was essentially a religious art, and a religious art that dared attempt to represent the irrational; and where it extended to the domain of the secular, it still let itself be channeled by preconceived ideas and by theories that concealed reality and its incessant changes: whether dealing with familiar objects or contemporary events, it preferred to hold to established concepts and use typological formulas in place of direct reflections of reality.

Thus it is apparent why and how Byzantine art of the last centuries of the Middle Ages could remain more faithful to a great number of ancient traditions than could contemporary art in Western Europe, or in Armenia, or even in Muslim countries. This certainly does not mean, however, that the Byzantine artists of the Palaeologan period were only contemptible copyists of more or less ancient models. On the contrary, they had their own taste and their own way of expressing themselves; but the margin in which they were allowed to affirm their own artistic temperament was not very wide. It perhaps requires a certain knowledge of medieval art to understand what part of a Palaeologan work belongs to it alone.

First, there is initiative in the choice of models to follow. When we consider the long and uninterrupted, or almost uninterrupted, practice of artistic activities in Byzantium, we realize the importance of this initiative, for, the longer the period covered by the practice of an art, the more numerous are the possible and different models it can offer.

In this respect the study of the works of the Palaeologan period is highly instructive. In fact, we see them now looking back to models of the fifth or sixth century, now reviving motifs or themes known to us from works of the Macedonian "renaissance" of the tenth century, or again basing themselves on immediate antecedents—creations of the twelfth century. No period of Byzantine history practiced an art so eclectic in its choice of models; and this is a primary trait to be noted in the general characterization of Palaeologan art.

Is it not possible to go further and to discover, in the interpretation of earlier models, some reflections of what, as regards themes and forms, seemed to correspond most directly to the taste and the aspirations of Byzantine society under the Palaeologi? Without attempting to give an exhaustive answer, I will note some trends that I consider characteristic. First of all, there is a taste—very typical of the period—for going into detail, for multiplying examples, for stating everything, for combining several different elements into a whole. This sort of verbosity resulted in the erection of architectural ensembles composed of numerous distinct units with different functions, or in the juxtaposition of long cycles of images that elsewhere appeared separately and were less extensive.

The period of Byzantine history that preceded the Palaeologan flowering had given preference to sober, severe works, to laconism in everything. Hence, in noting the opposite tendency in the works of the Palaeologan period, the first art critics perceptive enough to comment on it—Feodor Shmit or Josef Strzygowski, for example—advanced the hypothesis that the Greek artists of the fourteenth century were influenced by distant Syrian models. For it is, in fact, in certain Syrian or Greco-Oriental works of the end of antiquity that two features typical of Palaeologan works are found: the frequent influence of the Apocrypha, and a garrulous narrative imagery that delights in lingering over details. These associations were valid in the sense that the Palaeologan works did in fact have certain analogies with the Syrian monuments of the sixth and seventh centuries. But since a large number of Palaeologan works have become known, it is no longer possible to suppose, in each instance, the influence of an illustrated Syrian manuscript, always hypothetical; nevertheless it remains true and significant that Palaeologan art made extensive use of models known to us in certain manuscript paintings of the sixth and seventh centuries which might have been Syrian but which certainly, in Byzantine territory, were for the most part Greek. The art of the time of Justinian had a fondness for narrative images and detailed cycles, and it illustrated the Apocrypha. The artists of the Palaeologan period could find their models there. This holds true for more than one category of works typical of Palaeologan art— architectural decoration, systems of church decoration, and many iconographic subjects.

To continue our examination of the element of originality in the revivals of ancient models in the thirteenth and fourteenth centuries: the Palaeologan artists drew from a source which, to them, was very ancient—the art of the great Justinian. But in many cases they must have known only the echoes of it that were produced in the period of the renaissance of the tenth and eleventh centuries, and these intermediaries left an unmistakable imprint on Palaeologan art. One should perhaps say that at the end of the Middle Ages artists would have found it very difficult to assimilate models of the end of antiquity, had not the versions of the tenth and eleventh centuries been available. This appears to be confirmed by Gothic paintings that attempted, without intermediaries of the earlier Middle Ages, to interpret the models of late antiquity: the filiation is hardly recognizable. In Byzantium, on the other hand, thanks to the springboard of the Macedonian renaissance, Palaeologan art succeeded in creating new versions of models from the Justinianic period, without changing these models beyond recognition, and once again making them serve in the framework of the Byzantine aesthetic. Byzantine works of the time of the Macedonian renaissance must have been those which principally instructed Palaeologan artists in the art of the early Byzantine period. Disastrous as they were, the hundred and fifty years of iconoclasm had spared a sufficient number of works created before this crisis to make it possible for artists to imitate some of their elements as soon as the persecution of images was halted. But the three centuries and more separating this renaissance itself from the Palaeologan period could not but further decrease the number of original works of pre-iconoclastic art, thus reducing the artists of the thirteenth and fourteenth centuries to following the versions made during the Macedonian renaissance.

Finally, in choosing models to follow, these artists of the Palaeologan period by no means excluded the creations of the two centuries that immediately preceded theirs. Some Palaeologan paintings simply take over motifs typical of the eleventh century. On the other hand, the works of the twelfth century, and especially certain monuments of its second half, directly foreshadow the exploration in the areas of content and form that will determine the character of Palaeologan art. In many respects it is at this time that the Byzantine artistic experiment begins which will have its full development a century later. Between the two periods there is the half-century of the Latin domination of Constantinople (1204–61), and since very little is known about Byzantine activity in the capital during this time, it has been supposed that the work of the artists stopped completely. But this is an *a priori* hypothesis, for an equally complete absence of major Comnenian works in Constantinople has never led to any doubt as to the continuity of artistic work in the capital. To be sure, in Constantinople itself there were fewer imperial or princely foundations; but others exist, no less elaborate, created by foreign sovereigns, who customarily took the basileus of Byzantium as their example. In any case, nothing prevents our supposing that what was begun under the Comneni may have been continued and developed after them, before the advent of the Palaeologi as well as during their reign.

In so far as sources from the twelfth century, or even the eleventh, are concerned, all classes of monuments of that period, being relatively recent, could have reached the Palaeologan artists. But, for earlier periods, only mosaics—always rare—retained enough freshness, at a distance of three centuries and more, to inspire an artist; while it was book illumination that became almost the only agent by which ancient models were transmitted. Palaeologan art is precisely an example of such transmissions and of the influence that the peculiarities of the art of the miniature exercised on monumental art. In all its painting techniques, including mosaic, Palaeologan art adopted features that, in terms of their Macedonian renaissance sources, belonged more particularly to miniature. So it happens that the works of the Palaeologans, even when monumental, often resemble enlarged book illustrations.

What is true of the figurative arts is equally true of architecture. Here too the Palaeologan period was in the presence of a millenary tradition, which it carried on to the extent of its needs and of its economic and technical resources. The architecture of the period was as attentive as the figurative arts to earlier tradition, of which it was only a partially renewed version. As in the case of the figurative arts, the Palaeologan architect sought wherever he could to reproduce the models furnished him by earlier monuments, the most recent as well as the more ancient. Here again, this did not prevent him from setting perhaps involuntarily the mark of his taste, and of the taste of his time, on the work he created. He chose his model from among many that were equally possible, and adapted it to the needs of the edifice he was building. Of course, in architecture the program imposed on him by the founder and the means at his disposal exerted greater influence than in the case of the painter or sculptor. However, between one case and another, the differences in scale and in richness of decoration are not very great, and it is above all the interior arrangement of churches, the grouping of chapels and porticoes around the nave, which give Palaeologan churches an individual accent. Such an accent is certainly more perceptible in this period than earlier.

*   *
*

Palaeologan art is always regarded as a part of Byzantine art in general—and rightly so. It is, in fact, the Byzantine art of the end of the Middle Ages. But there is no reason for not also considering it in the framework of the Mediterranean and European arts of the same period. This point of view, which is not often adopted but is perfectly legitimate, has the advantage of better bringing out a side of Palaeologan art which relates it to these other contemporary arts.

15

When we see the Byzantine artists increasingly ready to study the monuments of the past (from antiquity to the high Middle Ages) and rapidly enriching themselves by contact with these works; when we see them so happily combining these returns to antique examples with the observation of nature around them, we are only noting in Byzantium tendencies that—to different degrees and with different methods and results—were manifesting themselves at the time in all the neighboring countries. There is certainly no question of reducing all these other more or less contemporary experiments to identical formulas; but the general direction of the artists' researches was obviously the same. For Byzantium this was true more especially in the thirteenth century, original artistic exploration practically ceasing in the century that followed.

At this point it is not superfluous to recall that everywhere the artists of the end of the Middle Ages tended to return to the path of the art that imitates nature—or rather the appearance of the material world. This was in fact a return, after a thousand years of a more or less abstract and symbolic art, to what had been achieved earlier—in the classical period, in the time of the Hellenistic kingdoms and the Roman Empire. The curve of the decline of this art, of its forms and techniques, about the third century of our era, is balanced by the countercurve of the renewal of the art of nature imitation at the end of the Middle Ages. Palaeologan art is the Byzantine branch of this stage—one of the most precocious branches at its beginnings, thanks to the contribution, greater here than elsewhere, of antique models; but it was to be prevented from bearing as notable fruits as did the West in respect to the end sought, that is, the imitation of nature.

Nevertheless, it is in the Byzantine art of the Palaeologans—and already from the end of the twelfth century—that we see the earliest attempts and the first most notable technical achievements in what was to be the greatest preoccupation of thirteenth-century art everywhere in the Mediterranean countries and in Europe, that is, the representation of emotion: the emotions of the artist interpreting a theme, and—in the images he creates—the emotions of those whom he is called upon to represent. It is these emotional values that distinguish Palaeologan work, and the work of the late Middle Ages in general, from the achievements realized in its time by Greco-Roman antiquity.

Theodore Metochites, the Chora, and the Intellectual Trends of His Time

IHOR ŠEVČENKO

This study, like several others appearing in the present volume, grew out of a lecture given at the Dumbarton Oaks Symposium of 1960. In preparing it for publication, the last time in early 1968, I kept the lecture form and size—thus additions to the main text and reworkings in it amount to no more than a quarter of the whole. On the other hand, the apparatus—footnotes, appendices, and the amount of Greek in both—grew to sizable proportions. This dichotomy between the main text and apparatus should be of convenience to both the general reader and the specialist in fourteenth-century cultural history. The text is mainly for the former; the apparatus, mainly for the latter; and Appendix I, with a free translation of *Logos* 15, is for both.

To make the study largely self-contained, most of the manuscript sources are quoted *in extenso*. Repeating passages of *Logos* 15 at the bottom of the page obviates turning back and forth to Appendix I. Frequent references to my *Etudes* of 1962 by page alone are an exception to the rule; this exception, however, has helped to trim the footnotes. These do not claim bibliographical completeness beyond the beginning of 1968.

I wish to express my thanks to Mrs. Alice-Mary Talbot for her assistance in preparing the manuscript of this study for print.

The main text was first published, in French without footnotes and appendices in *Art et société à Byzance sous les Paléologues*, Actes du Colloque organisé par l'Association internationale des études byzantines à Venise en Septembre 1968 (Bibliothèque de l'Institut hellénique d'études byzantines et post-byzantines de Venise, No. 4; Venice, 1971), pp. 13–39.

I. ŠEVČENKO

Theodore Metochites, the Chora, and the Intellectual Trends of His Time

· I ·

ANTIQUE literary and scientific culture was endemic in Byzantium, and the Byzantines were too familiar with it to react to antiquity as violently as did the West, which had almost forgotten it for centuries. What we call Byzantine renaissances are just intensifications of the elite's contacts with antiquity—which were never lost—rather than rediscoveries of ancient culture. The renaissance of the early Palaeologi was one such intensification of an uninterrupted tradition.

That some sixty years of Latin intrusion in Constantinople between the Fourth Crusade and the arrival of the Palaeologi there in 1261 did not interrupt this tradition, can be shown merely by mentioning the names of the most prominent teachers of the thirteenth and fourteenth centuries. As a young boy, Nicephorus Blemmydes (1197–ca. 1272), the most erudite man in the Nicaean Empire, may have improved his oratory by listening to Nicetas Choniates (d. 1212–13), who had emigrated to Nicaea after the catastrophe of 1204; from 1213 on, Blemmydes certainly was learning logic from another émigré, the "consul of philosophers" Demetrios Karykes.[1] In the Nicaean Empire, Blemmydes was the teacher of George Akropolites (1217–82), professor and statesman.[2] Back in the city, Akropolites taught Gregory of Cyprus (1241–90), professor turned patriarch;[3] Gregory of Cyprus taught Nicephorus Choumnos (ca. 1260–1327)[4] and was a model of eloquence for our Theodore Metochites (1270–1332).[5] In the exact sciences Metochites was the teacher of Nicephorus Gregoras (ca. 1291/6–1360), an encyclopedist and himself a professor.[6] In sum, an uninterrupted series of teacher-pupil relationships, extending through the middle of the fourteenth century, links the period before the Fourth Crusade with the Palaeologan revival.

If this revival presents some puzzles, it is not because of the scarcity of sources, for not much of the writing of the time seems to have been lost. Authors of the late thirteenth and early

---

1 Blemmydes started his rhetorical studies in Nicaea about 1209, see *Curriculum vitae et Carmina*, ed. A. Heisenberg, Teubner (1896), pp. 2, 10, 55.7–8; Choniates pronounced speeches in that city until at least 1210, perhaps until his death in 1212/13. For Blemmydes' work with Karykes in Smyrna, see ibid., pp. xii, 55.11–19.

2 George Akropolites, *Hist.*, ed. A. Heisenberg, in *Georgii Acropolitae Opera*, Teubner (1903), I, pp. 50.3–6, 106.9–11; Blemmydes, *Curriculum vitae*, ibid., p. xvii (Akropolites' work with Blemmydes started in 1238).

3 Gregory of Cyprus, *Autobiography*, ed. W. Lameere, in *La tradition manuscrite de la correspondance de Grégoire de Chypre* (Brussels and Rome, 1937), p. 185.5–20. Gregory's pupil Pachymeres in turn taught the mendicant poet of Andronicus II's and III's time, Manuel Philes.

4 Gregory of Cyprus, Letter 57, ed. S. Eustratiades, in

'Εκκλησιαστικὸς Φάρος, 2 (1908), p. 202; Nicephorus Choumnos, Πρὸς τοὺς δυσχεραίνοντας . . . , ed. J.-Fr. Boissonade, in *Anecdota Graeca e Codicibus Regiis*, III (Paris, 1831; reprint, Hildesheim, 1962), p. 367. Cf. J. Verpeaux, *Nicéphore Choumnos, homme d'état et humaniste byzantin (ca. 1250/1255–1327)* (Paris, 1959), pp. 29–31; I. Ševčenko, *Etudes sur la polémique entre Théodore Métochite et Nicéphore Choumnos* (Brussels, 1962) (hereafter referred to as *Etudes*), p. 25 and n. 3.

5 *Etudes*, p. 41 and n. 4.

6 Nicephorus Gregoras, *Hist.*, VIII.5, Bonn (1829), I, p. 309.4–8; VIII.7, ibid., p. 322.4–6; Theodore Metochites (hereafter, when his works are cited, referred to as TM), Poem 4, Paris. gr. 1776, fols. 64r–65r; cf. R. Guilland, "Les poésies inédites de Théodore Métochite," *Byzantion*, 3 (1926), pp. 270–71.

fourteenth centuries fared better in this respect than their predecessors, since only one major debacle, the catastrophe of 1453, separates their time from the period when Westerners began to collect Greek manuscripts on a grand scale. Juxtapose Nicephorus Choumnos' literary heritage with that of the learned rhetorician of the twelfth century, Nicephorus Basilakes. Both authors arranged for the publication of their collected works;[7] in addition, both have left us lists with the titles of their writings. All the titles mentioned by Choumnos are extant, while the majority of those mentioned by Basilakes is lost.[8] What goes for Choumnos goes for Metochites as well. Of his works we lack only his correspondence, and the fault is ours: the two manuscripts which contained his letters perished in the Escurial Library during the fire of 1671.[9]

Not only members of high society like Choumnos and Metochites, but minor people as well, succeeded in preserving their works for posterity. We even wish that some of these works had perished, like Michael Gabras' correspondence, bulky but pathologically empty of content.[10] Thus it is not the dearth of material but its abundance, its intractability, and the fact that much of it is unpublished that still stand in the way of a clear picture of the Palaeologan revival.

As in China, so in Byzantium emperors attached a great deal of importance to the education of their civil servants. This was as true in the fourth century as it was in the thirteenth and fourteenth.[11] John III Vatatzes and after him Michael VIII saw to it that their future officials received proper—which meant literary—training.[12] Thus the elite among court officials and prelates set a high premium on literary culture, production, and patronage. Familiarity with the classics and a facile pen could bring more than the applause of the connoisseur—literary or scholarly success could open the way to high dignities in the state bureaucracy or the ecclesiastical hierarchy. A young litterateur could fancy that he was carrying a high official's insignia in his bag full of notes on a difficult author.

But not everybody could end at the top. If you failed, you gravitated around those who succeeded: you joined the ranks of impoverished intellectuals who preyed on the literary interests

---

7 For Choumnos, see *Etudes*, p. 119; for Basilakes, E. Miller, "Préface d'un auteur byzantin," *Annuaire de l'Association pour l'encouragement des études grecques en France*, 7 (1873), pp. 137, 152. For a critical edition of the Preface, cf. now A. Garzya, "Il *Prologo* di Niceforo Basilace," *Annali della Facoltà di Lettere e Filosofia della Università di Macerata*, 1 (1968), pp. 259–71.

8 Choumnos: Πρὸς τοὺς δυσχεραίνοντας, pp. 377–78; Basilakes: Miller, "Préface," pp. 144–45, 155–57. More than half of the surviving works of Basilakes have been transmitted anonymously or under a wrong name. See the good analysis in A. Garzya, ed., *Niceforo Basilace: Encomio di Adriano Comneno* (Naples, 1965), pp. 11–23, and in idem, "Intorno al prologo di Niceforo Basilace," *JOeBG*, 18 (1968), pp. 57–71, esp. pp. 69–71 (list of works); for the late date of the *Prologue*, cf. idem, "Un lettré du milieu du XIIᵉ siècle: Nicéphore Basilakès," *Revue des études sud-est européennes*, 8 (1970), p. 616.

9 See my *Etudes*, p. 9, n. 3. For Metochites' Letter to monk Senacherim, see Appendix II below. The following short letter, requesting the gift of a book or books (from the books' author?), is found in Uppsaliensis gr. 28, fol. 169r: Τοῦ μεγάλου λογοθέτου: Νέμεις, ὥς φασι, τὰς βίβλους τοῖς φίλοις, κατ' ἀμφότερα προσέχων τὸν νοῦν καὶ διαιρῶν καὶ κρίνων καὶ τῇ νομῇ χρώμενος· καὶ λόγων καὶ τύχης κράτος. δι' ἀμφότερα γοῦν ἡμῖν, ἢ δι' ἕτερον πάντως καὶ ὁπότερον κρίνοις ἄν, νέμοις ἄν· εἰ δὴ μή, καὶ ὡς φίλοις, καὶ σαυτοῦ καὶ τῶν λόγων.

The context in which the letter appears (works by Maximus Planudes, Manuel Moschopoulos, Thomas Magister, Nicephorus Gregoras, George Lakapenos, Andronicus Zarides, Manuel Philes) points to the first half of the fourteenth century as its date; on account of the letter's bibliophile contents, the "Great Logothete" who wrote it was in all probability either our

Metochites or Constantine Akropolites (see n. 18 below). At present, I cannot decide between these two most likely authors, as the letter is too short for stylistic analysis. I did not find the letter in Constantine Akropolites' epistolary collection, preserved in Ambrosianus gr. H 81 sup., fols. 270r–333v. Still, Akropolites seems to be the more likely candidate, since he did compose numerous short and witty letters, while Metochites lacked both brevity and wit. For the best description of Uppsaliensis gr. 28, see S. Lindstam, *Georgii Lacapeni Epistulae X Priores cum Epimerismis Editae* (Uppsala, 1910), pp. liv–lx.

10 M. Treu, "Der Philosoph Joseph," *BZ*, 8 (1899), pp. 50–52; idem, *BZ*, 4 (1895), pp. 4–5.

11 For the fourth century, see *Codex Theodosianus*, XIV.1.1 (Constantius, May 15, 367); in general, see A. M. Andreades, "Le recrutement des fonctionnaires et les universités dans l'empire byzantin," reprinted in his *Oeuvres*, I (Athens, 1938), pp. 545–62 (this somewhat disappointing article covers the period from the eighth to the twelfth centuries only). For comparing Byzantine practices with Confucianism or Mandarinism, see H.-G. Beck, *Theodoros Metochites, die Krise des byzantinischen Weltbildes im 14. Jahrhundert* (Munich, 1952), p. 51, and G. Mathew, *Byzantine Aesthetics* (London, 1963), p. 53.

12 For Vatatzes, see Theodore II Lascaris, *Laudation* of George Akropolites, in Nic. Blemmydes, *Curriculum vitae*, ed. Heisenberg, p. xvii, n. 2 (George Akropolites and four other pupils); for Michael VIII, see George Pachymeres, *Hist.*, VI.25–26, Bonn (1835), I, pp. 495.14–496.2 (special training for Constantine Akropolites, George's son, and Theodore Muzalon); cf. Gregory of Cyprus, *Laudation* of Michael VIII, *PG*, 142, col. 381B–D (revival of learning).

or the snobbery of the rich.[13] You could beg for government grants, write petitions, eulogies or occasional poetry, an epitaph to be placed in a church over a dignitary's tomb,[14] a dirge, a wedding song. If all else failed, you could teach.[15] But if you did obtain a place at the patron's table, or a sinecure in a monastery, you could become a scholar, hunt for manuscripts, edit an ancient author, prepare an anthology of useful sayings, sacred and profane, collect proverbs, write a commentary on a scientific text, or publish an encyclopedia. I have just alluded to some of the activities of Maximus Planudes, Barlaam of Calabria, Isaac Argyros, and Joseph the Philosopher.

The social position of a Byzantine litterateur did not tell the whole story of his literary output. The character of this output also depended on the genre to which it belonged, the poetic form which it affected,[16] its secular or sacred contents, and the level of the language in which it was couched. Various combinations were possible here: an imperial prince could write a romance of chivalry in the popular language and politic verse;[17] a high lay official could devote most of his leisure to the composition of Saints' lives in pure Attic style;[18] and a scholarly editor of the classics could adorn his laudation of a Father of the Church with numerous scriptural quotations.[19]

The highest prestige in literary society came to those who could claim familiarity with the classics and abstruse scientific matters and discuss them in a precious style.[20] In the 1280's a princess reproached Gregory of Cyprus, the patriarch of Constantinople, for having written to her in a "priestly fashion." In his reply the piqued prelate explained that his style was at least

---

13 I. Ševčenko, "Alexios Makrembolites and His 'Dialogue between the Rich and the Poor,'" *ZRVI*, 65, No. 6 (1960), pp. 187–88 and nn. 2–5.

14 The epitaph of the Great Constable Michael Tornikes preserved in the *parecclesion* of the Chora church is a good example. For Tornikes, cf. G. Schmalzbauer, "Die Tornikioi in der Palaiologenzeit," *JOeBG*, 18 (1969), pp. 115–35; cf. esp. no. 22, pp. 131–32. For the text, see Vol. 1 of this work, pp. 276–77. I attribute this epitaph to Manuel Philes, who produced verses for special occasions, including versified inscriptions in churches, by the hundred. Cf. the following parallels between the epitaph of Tornikes (= T) and poems (mostly epitaphs) bearing Philes' name:

a) T 2–4: ἐξελέγξει . . . . ὥσπερ μίμους, βέλτιστε, πιθήκους λέων; see *Poem* to Andronicus III, ed. M. Gedeon, Μανουὴλ τοῦ Φιλῆ ἱστορικὰ ποιήματα, in Ἐκκλησιαστικὴ Ἀλήθεια, 3 (1882–83), p. 219: ὅτι μὴ πίθηκος εὐθὺς ὁ βρυχητίας λέων . . . . ἐγίνου.

b) T 19: ἥλιε καὶ γῆ καὶ τελευταῖοι κρότοι; see *Epitaph* on Asanina, ed. Gedeon, p. 249: ἥλιε καὶ γῆ καὶ μεταπτώσεις τύχης; *Poem* to Protostrator Glabas, ed. E. Miller, *Manuelis Philae Carmina*, II (Paris, 1857), p. 107: ἥλιε καὶ γῆ καὶ σχολὴ καὶ βιβλία; *Epitaph* on paracoemomenus Tornikes, ed. Gedeon, p. 658: Κομνηνοφυής, ὦ τελευταίων κρότων; *Epitaph* on Sophianos, ed. Ae. Martini, *Manuelis Philae Carmina Inedita*, in *Atti della R. Accademia di Archeologia Lettere e Belle Arti*, 20 (suppl.) (Naples, 1900), p. 122 (= *Poem* 84, 19): καὶ τἆλλα (βαβαὶ τῶν τελευταίων κρότων).

c) T 20: πενθεῖ δὲ μικροῦ πᾶν τὸ Ῥωμαίων γένος; see *Epitaph* on Asanina, ed. Gedeon, p. 249: βροντῶσά τις ἦν εἰς τὸ Ῥωμαίων γένος.

d) T uses the word Ἐδέμ in the last line. In Philes' published epitaphs, this word occurs twelve times: in seven out of the twelve times it falls in the last line; in the remaining five instances, it is placed in the last line but one or the last but two.

15 Maximus Planudes, Thomas Magister, Theodore Hyrtakenos, Nicephorus Gregoras, Alexios Makrembolites under the two Andronici, and John Chortasmenos under Manuel II were teachers. Even Manuel Philes found the time to be διδάσκαλος μεγάλων μαθημάτων between writing his petitions, cf. *Poem* Τῷ πρωτοβεστιαρίῳ, ed. Gedeon, p. 216.

16 Planudes could turn out good elegiacs, iambics, and lowly "politic" fifteen-syllable verses indiscriminately. His politic verse, however, is somewhat unusual, since he wrote it in classical rather than in semipopular language. See Sp. Lampros, Ἐπιγράμματα Μαξίμου Πλανούδη, in Νέος Ἑλληνομνήμων,

13 (1916), pp. 414–21.

17 Prince: Andronicus Palaeologus (A. Th. Papadopulos, *Versuch einer Genealogie der Palaiologen, 1259–1453* [Munich, 1938; reprint, Amsterdam, 1962], No. 7), first cousin of Andronicus II; romance: *Love Story of Callimachus and Chrysorrhoe*, written between 1310 and 1340; see M. Pichard, tr. and ed., *Le roman de Callimaque et de Chrysorrhoé* (Paris, 1956), pp. xv–xxviii. —The reading of Manuel Philes' poem to our Andronicus, which gives the contents of a romance written by the latter, convinced me that Andronicus did write a *Callimachus and Chrysorrhoe*; the question may be only whether the text we possess (transmitted in one late manuscript) is precisely the same as that composed by the prince. B. Knös, "Qui est l'auteur du roman de Callimaque et Chrysorrhoè," Ἑλληνικά, 17 (1962), pp. 274–95, is of little help, since he cannot make up his mind, either on the author's person, or on the kind of language in which the romance was composed, see esp. p. 295. For a cautious, but on the whole positive, attitude towards Andronicus' authorship, see H. Hunger, "Un roman byzantin et son atmosphère: Callimaque et Chrysorrhoè," *Travaux et Mémoires*, 3 (Centre de recherche d'histoire et civilisation byzantines; Paris, 1968), esp. pp. 421–22, and H.-G. Beck in *BZ*, 62 (1969), p. 76 (why should theories [about Andronicus' authorship] not be right?).

18 Lay official: Grand Logothete Constantine Akropolites. On Akropolites as a hagiographer, see H.-G. Beck, *Kirche und theologische Literatur im byzantinischen Reich* (Munich, 1959), pp. 698–99, and D. M. Nicol, "Constantine Akropolites: A Prosopographical Note," *DOP*, 19 (1965), pp. 249–56, esp. pp. 254–56. M. Treu, "Ein Kritiker des Timarion," *BZ*, 1 (1892), pp. 363–64, found Akropolites' classical language to be more correct and natural than that of any other Byzantine author known to him. Akropolites objected to the twelfth-century dialogue "Timarion" not only on account of its contents, but also because, he said, the author's Atticism was that of a Tartar arriving in Constantinople and attempting to study Greek.

19 Thomas (Theodulos) Magister, *Laudation of Gregory of Nazianzus*, PG, 145, cols. 215–348; cf. Verpeaux, *Choumnos* (as in n. 4 above), p. 119, and my remarks on this page of Verpeaux in *Speculum*, 35 (1960), pp. 492–93.

20 See, as examples, Nicephorus Gregoras' letter to Pepagomenos (R. Guilland, ed. and tr., *Correspondance de Nicéphore Grégoras* [Paris, 1927], No. 48), discussing a passage in *Encomium Romae* by Aelius Aristides, and Gregoras' dialogue *Florentios*, ed. A. Jahn, *Neue Jahrbücher für Philologie und Pädagogik*, Suppl. 10,4 (1844). See also my *Études*, pp. 95–97.

clear, but to show his abilities he answered in a manner so involved that even if the princess could understand him, a modern editor could not.[21]

Sophisticated officials, learned parasites circling around them, classicistic fashion mixed with Christian dogma in imitation of the Cappadocian Fathers, the doting over precious style, all of this is familiar in all periods of Byzantine history. Yet some features of this literary society appear to be peculiar to the Palaeologan revival, perhaps simply because we know this society, or could know it if we cared, better than that of the so-called Macedonian and even the Comnenian renaissance.

First of all, to judge by the correspondence and the occasional poetry of the time, it was a small society of a small state, where everybody knew everybody, wrote to everybody, and was related by marriage to everybody, had begged everybody for gifts or taught everybody's children. As on other occasions in history, even such a small milieu was able to produce an impressive revival.

Second, this was a society in which, along with the inevitable oratorical windbags, technical scholars played a prominent role. We owe the preservation of antique authors like Iamblichus and Nonnos of Panopolis to their diligence;[22] their work was first rate, even by our standards.[23] By our definition these technical scholars were philologists, but for them philology meant love of everything written in the remote past. This included technical, geographical, mathematical, and astronomical writings. The compendia of the four sciences of the *Quadrivium* made in the thirteenth century by a Blemmydes or a Pachymeres no longer satisfied more inquisitive minds. The mathematicians Euclid and Diophantos were commented; Ptolemy's *Geography* was rediscovered, his *Tetrabiblos* consulted; his *Almagest* and *Harmonics* were studied; his commentator Theon was copied and parts of the commentary which were considered lost were written anew.[24]

---

21 The princess was the niece of Michael VIII, Theodora Raoulaina Palaeologina (Papadopulos, *Genealogie*, No. 34), an author in her own right; she exchanged letters on books—and books themselves—with Maximus Planudes and Nicephorus Choumnos, as well as with Gregory of Cyprus. Text of Gregory's reply in S. Kugeas, "Zur Geschichte der Münchener Thukydideshandschrift Augustanus F," *BZ*, 16 (1907), pp. 598–600. For the passage on p. 599,17–29 to make sense, its punctuation has to be changed in 8 places: proof that the editor has had difficulty understanding it.

22 For Iamblichus, see my *Etudes*, pp. 80, n. 3, and 87; our manuscript tradition of Nonnos is based on Laurentianus 32.16, which represents an edition by Planudes. If it is true that Planudes edited the model of the Arethas manuscript Mosquensis gr. 315 (441, Vladimir), the only witness for most of Arethas' works, then he saved an important Byzantine from oblivion. See C. Wendel, "Planudea," *BZ*, 40 (1940), pp. 418–26; idem, in *RE*, 20,2 (Stuttgart, 1950), col. 2222, Nos. 44–51; col. 2230, No. 38. For a list of early Palaeologan manuscripts which are the oldest or the best witnesses for their respective authors, see H. Hunger, "Von Wissenschaft und Kunst der frühen Palaiologenzeit," *JOeBG*, 8 (1959), pp. 123–55, esp. pp. 124–25. Cf. also, for this and the following paragraph, the concise but excellent article by R. Browning, "Recentiores Non Deteriores," *University of London, Institute of Classical Studies, Bulletin*, 7 (1960), pp. 11–21, who surveys the evidence for the use of old, including uncial, exemplars of classical authors in editions made by Planudes and other scholars of his time.

23 In some cases it was too good. For some time, modern scholars felt that the two Leptinean Declamations attributed to Aelius Aristides were not by him but by a third- or fourth-century author. Only in 1942 did it become apparent that the author of these Declamations was Thomas (Theodulos) Magister, one of the technicians of the first half of the fourteenth century. See F. W. Lenz, "On the Authorship of the Leptinean Declamations Attributed to Aristides," *American Journal of*

Philology, 63 (1942), pp. 154–73; idem ed., *Fünf Reden Thomas Magisters* (Leiden, 1963), esp. pp. x–xv.

24 Euclid and Diophantos: commentaries by Planudes, who also asked Manuel Bryennios for a copy of Diophantos in order to collate it with his own. See Wendel, "Planudea," *BZ*, 40 (1940), pp. 415–17; *RE*, 20,2 (1950), cols. 2227, No. 35, and 2228, No. 36; M. Treu ed., *Maximi Monachi Planudis Epistulae* (Breslau, 1890; reprint, Amsterdam, 1960), Ep. 33,7–8. Ptolemy's *Geography* was rediscovered by Planudes in Vaticanus gr. 177; see *RE*, ibid., col. 2228, No. 37. For the study of the *Almagest*, see TM, Στοιχείωσις ἐπὶ τῇ ἀστρονομικῇ ἐπιστήμῃ (*Introduction to Astronomy*), e.g. in Vaticanus gr. 1365, passim; Marcianus gr. 312 (N.C. 710) is a copy of the *Almagest* annotated by Gregoras; see J. L. Heiberg ed., *Claudii Ptolemaei Opera*, II, Teubner (1907), pp. xx–xxi, and my "Some Autographs of Nicephorus Gregoras," *ZRVI*, 67, No. 8,2 (1964) = *Mélanges Georges Ostrogorsky*, II, p. 446 and n. 41. For Ptolemy's *Harmonics*, see I. Düring, "Die Harmonielehre des Klaudios Ptolemaios," *Göteborgs Högskolas arsskrift*, 36, 1 (1930), pp. lxxviii–xc (studies by Manuel Bryennios, Metochites, Gregoras and his students, Barlaam, Isaac Argyros), and Laurentianus S. Marco 356, fol. 279v. *Tetrabiblos*: see my *Etudes*, p. 115, n. 3. Out of eighteen known manuscripts of Theon's *Commentary*, eight belong surely and two probably to the fourteenth century. One of them, Vaticanus gr. 1087, was in the hands of Nicephorus Gregoras; see A. Rome, ed., *Commentaires de Pappus*, I (Rome, 1931) = *Studi e Testi*, 54, p. XXI; my *Etudes*, pp. 113, n. 5, and 280; ibid., *Addenda* to p. 282, n. 3, and my "Some Autographs," p. 446. Marcianus gr. 325 (N.C. 518) was Gregoras' copy of Theon's *Handy Tables*; see my *Etudes*, pp. 137, n. 6, and 260, n. 1, and "Some Autographs," p. 447. For Theon's "lost" commentary to Book 3 of the *Almagest* (in fact it is preserved in Laurentianus 28.18, a *codex unicus*) a substitution was provided by Nicolaus Kabasilas (born ca. 1320), ed. in the *editio princeps* of the *Almagest* (Basel, 1538), pp. 131–94 (for a detailed description of this edition, cf. Rome, p. v).

Third, this was a society whose members loved books, professed an insatiable thirst for knowledge, and showed it in their actions. Imperial princesses copied ancient authors in their own hand or paid for precious bindings;[25] scholars hunted for good and old copies of texts, perhaps written in uncial script, and discussed the techniques of producing a new manuscript and of acquiring parchment for it.[26] They tenaciously followed the fate of a book which they had lent and which had not been returned. They were disturbed by the state of the libraries in which they worked.[27] Young men begged the initiated to teach them astronomy, that sublime science, the knowledge of which Andronicus II thought should be restricted to a chosen few.[28]

One of the puzzles of this revival is that it acquired momentum—at least in literature and science—not during the reign of Michael VIII, soon after the reconquest of the city in 1261, but more than twenty years later, under Andronicus II, who ascended the throne in December of 1282. However, by the eighties and nineties of the thirteenth century, the period of feverish antiquarianism was in full swing. Thus it coincided with the boyhood and young adult years of Theodore Metochites, prime minister and man of letters under Andronicus II.[29] Seen in this perspective, Metochites' erudition, which dazzled many of his contemporaries and in our time made a Wilamowitz-Moellendorff give up the attempt to identify some of his references,[30] becomes less of a mystery. It was made possible by the zealous preparatory activity of the

25 Theodora Raoulaina Palaeologina, who possessed a library of her own and provided her literary friends with books, copied Vaticanus gr. 1899, an important manuscript of Aelius Aristides; see Kugeas, "Zur Geschichte . . . (as in n. 21 above)," pp. 594–95; Treu, *Planudis Epistulae*, pp. 245–47; Lampros, Ἐπιγράμματα Μαξίμου Πλανούδη, pp. 414–21. Empress Theodora, wife of Michael VIII, was praised by Theodore Metochites for βίβλων ἐπιμελὴς περικόσμησις; see his *Logos* 9, Vindobonensis ph. gr. 95, fol. 184v. The "queen of the whole East" who restored and dedicated a Gospel to the Chora may have been Andronicus' half-sister, Mary the Despoina of the Mongols; see P. A. Underwood in *DOP*, 12 (1958), p. 287, n. 50, and P. N. Papageorgiou in *BZ*, 3 (1894), pp. 325–29; see also, most recently, H. Belting, *Das illuminierte Buch in der spätbyzantinischen Gesellschaft* [Abh. der Heidelberger Akad. der Wiss., Philos.-hist. Klasse, Jahrgang 1970, 1. Abh.] (1970), esp. pp. 46–47. In 1291–92, Constantine Akropolites, then still Logothete of the Treasury, copied the Hierosol. S. Sepulchri 40 (rhetorical pieces) in his own hand; ed. Heisenberg, II, Teubner, p. xxiv.

26 Blemmydes, p. 36.8–25 (hunting for books in Salonika, Mt. Athos, and Larissa); Kugeas, pp. 596–602; Treu, *Planudis Epistulae*, Epp. 33.7–10, 35 (Planudes to Bryennios); Epp. 95.19–35, 100, 115.35–37 (to Melchisedek Akropolites); Epp. 78.37–41, 86.94–98, 106.36–45, 109.10–18 (to Alexios Philanthropenos). See also Laurent. S. Marco 356, fols. 290v–291r (the anonymous author asks for an astronomical work [Ptolemy], in order to copy it): δώσεις δὲ πῶς; εἰ τὴν τὰς τῶν σφαιρικῶν σωμάτων κινήσεις καὶ τῶν πλανωμένων καὶ ἀπλανῶν διευκρινοῦσαν βίβλον πέμψεις ἡμῖν, ὡς ἂν σημειωσάμενοι τὰ σελίδια [columns of tables?] καὶ ὡς ἐνὸν συνοπτικώτατα ἐγχαράξαντες πλαξὶ καρδίας πρότερον ἢ χάρτῃ, ἔπειτα ἀποστείλωμεν.

27 Treu, *Planudis Epistulae*, Ep. 67.58–102 (Planudes to George Muzalon). Cf. C. Wendel, "Planudes als Bücherfreund," *Zentralblatt für Bibliothekswesen*, 58 (1941), pp. 77–87; and A. Turyn, *Dated Greek Manuscripts of the Thirteenth and Fourteenth Centuries in the Libraries of Italy* (Chicago, 1972), Vol. I, p. 80.

28 See my *Etudes*, p. 87, n. 3, and Laurent. S. Marco 356, fol. 280v, where the anonymous author asks Aktouarios to teach him the "pinnacle of sciences," that is, astronomy: δοίη δὲ [i.e., ὁ θεός] καὶ τοῦ κορυφαίου μετασχεῖν με μαθήματος παρὰ τῆς σῆς σοφίας, ὡς ἐφικτόν. Cf. young Gregoras' plea to Metochites, *Hist.*, VIII.7, Bonn (1829), I, pp. 322.19–327.5. On Metochites' reluctance to teach Gregoras astronomy, see n. 133 below.

29 For bibliography on Metochites down to 1960, see my *Etudes*, passim, esp. p. 3, n. 1; to the list of works quoted there, add J. Strzygowski, "Das Epithalamion des Paläologen Andronikos II," *BZ*, 10 (1901), esp. p. 567; Sp. Lampros, Αἱ μονῳδίαι Ἀλεξίου τοῦ Λαμπηνοῦ, in Νέος Ἑλληνομνήμων, 11 (1914), esp. pp. 373–75; N. P. Kondakov, *Očerki i zametki po istorii srednevekovago iskusstva i kul'tury* (Prague, 1929), p. 282 (discusses Metochites' headgear in the Chora mosaic); D. C. Hesseling, "Byzantijnse weelde, na vervlogen velvaart," *Hermeneus*, 10 (1938), pp. 81–84; idem, "Een Konstitutioneel Keizerschap," *Hermeneus*, 11 (1939), pp. 89–93; D. D. Kotsakes, Ἡ ἀστρονομία καὶ ἡ ἀστρολογία κατὰ τοὺς βυζαντινοὺς χρόνους, in Ἐπετηρὶς Ἑταιρείας Βυζαντινῶν Σπουδῶν, 24 (1954), esp. pp. 212–13, 225; Hunger, "Von Wissenschaft und Kunst" (as in n. 22 above), pp. 137–39, 147–48, 151–55; M. Gigante, "Il saggio critico di Teodoro Metochites su Demostene e Aristide," *La parola del passato*, 20 (1965), pp. 51–92, passim; idem, "Teodoro Metochites critico letterario," *Rivista di studi bizantini e neoellenici*, N.S., 2–3 (XII–XIV) (1965–66), pp. 211–12; idem, "Per l'interpretazione di Teodoro Metochites quale umanista bizantino," *Rivista di studi bizantini e neoellenici*, N.S., 4 (XIV) (1967), pp. 11–25; idem, "Il ciclo delle poesie inedite di Teodoro Metochites a se stesso o sull' instabilità della vita," *Byzantinische Forschungen*, 2 = Polychordia, Festschrift Franz Dölger, 2 (Amsterdam, 1967), pp. 204–24; idem, ed., *Teodoro Metochites, saggio critico su Demostene e Aristide* (Milan and Varese, 1969) (essentially it is "Il saggio" with the addition of valuable indices); article "Metochites, Theodoros," in Θρησκευτικὴ καὶ Ἠθικὴ Ἐγκυκλοπαιδεία, 8 (1966), cols. 1098–1101; E. Fenster, *Laudes Constantinopolitanae* (Miscellanea Byzantina Monacensia, 9, ed. H.-G. Beck, Munich, 1968), pp. 183–84, 196–209; S. Runciman, *The Last Byzantine Renaissance* (Cambridge, 1971), passim, esp. pp. 63–65; R. Guilland, "Les logothètes. Etudes sur l'administration de l'Empire byzantin," *REB*, 29 (1971), esp. pp. 110–13.

30 *Aristoteles und Athen*, I (Berlin, 1893), p. 293, n. 8: "I do not know these men," i.e., Phoebias and Chaeremon, mentioned by Metochites in *Miscellanea* (Theodori Metochitae Miscellanea Philosophica et Historica, ed. Ch. G. Müller and Th. Kiessling [Leipzig, 1821; reprint, Amsterdam, 1966], p. 668), "and have nothing to say about them. But surely Theodore did not invent them." See also "Lesefrüchte, XCVIII," *Hermes*, 40 (1905), pp. 129–30: four fragments transmitted by Metochites are genuine, if not literal, reminiscences from Pindar, and were culled from some ancient writer of *Moralia*: "der ist zu suchen."

generation of technical scholars flourishing in the last two decades of the thirteenth century. For instance, we shall see in some detail how Metochites' learning was influenced by one of these professional scholars, Maximus Planudes.[31]

· II ·

Contemporaries have left three portraits of Metochites. Flatterers and petitioners drew him as a just, liberal, warmhearted, and affable statesman, a second Nestor or Hermes in mellifluous eloquence, a second Ptolemy in astronomy, a reincarnation of Plato, in short, Philosophy personified.[32] The features of their portrait are as regular and empty as those of Metochites' picture in the narthex of the Chora. Metochites' friend and disciple Gregoras drew his picture with loving care, but objected to his patron's unorthodox style.[33] Most modern scholars have used Gregoras for their model.[34] Finally, Metochites' enemies caricatured him as a verbose, pompous, incomprehensible bore, or a gifted and learned man indeed, but marked by two vices: first, boastful self-love and infatuation with his own intelligence; second, extreme avarice. His vainglory was so great, one of them said, that he despised and destroyed everybody, save for himself and his kin.[35]

Superimposed, these three portraits show only two overlapping features: that Metochites was

31 For a well-drawn general picture of the Palaeologan revival, see Hunger, "Von Wissenschaft und Kunst" (as in n. 22 above). For Nicaean roots of the Palaeologan revival, cf. A. Tuillier, "Recherches sur les origines de la Renaissance byzantine au XIIIᵉ siècle," *Bulletin de l'Association Guillaume Budé* (1955, no. 3), pp. 71–76.

It is difficult to evaluate Gregory of Cyprus' passages which extol Michael VIII for having brought about the revival of learning and letters in Constantinople just after 1261. Granted, there must have been something to this ἀναβίωσις λόγων; we should not exaggerate it, however, nor should we believe in the absolute rule of ἀνεπιστημοσύνη, as Gregory puts it, prior to 1261, since: (1) the Nicaean period (during which Gregory himself received some of his training) was anything but bleak and surely boasted more than the lonely literary figure of George Akropolites—the latter was singled out by Gregory probably because he was in the audience while Gregory was delivering his panegyric; (2) the fruits of the Palaeologan revival began to appear only in the reign of Andronicus II. For the passages, cf. Gregory of Cyprus, Encomion of Michael VIII, ed. Boissonade, *Anecdota Graeca* (as in n. 4 above), I (1829), pp. 352–54.

32 See Manuel Moschopoulos, *Letter* II to Metochites, in *Speculum*, 27 (1952), p. 142, line 33: διὰ τῆς εὐγενεστάτης σου ψυχῆς καὶ συμπαθεστάτης; Thomas Magister, Πρὸς τόν . . . . Ἰσαάκ . . . . περὶ τοῦ εἰς Βυζάντιον ἀνάπλου, ed. M. Treu, "Die Gesandtschaftsreise des Rhetors Theodulos Magistros," *Jahrbücher für klassische Philologie*, Suppl. 27 (1902), p. 10: οὐκ αἴρων ὑψοῦ τὴν γνώμην . . . . ἀλλ' ἐπιεικείας ὡς οὐκ οἶδ' εἴ τις φροντίζων; idem, *Letter* to Metochites, PG, 145, col. 421B: καὶ μηδὲν δεηθεῖσι πολλάκις ἔδωκας, καὶ δεηθέντων μειζόνων ἠξίωσας; idem, *Speech* to Metochites, PG, 145, col. 388A: γλῶτταν ἡδίω μέλιτος ἴσχεις ὑπὲρ τὸν Ὁμήρου Νέστορα; idem, *Letter* to Metochites, PG, 145, col. 405A: Ἑρμοῦ λογίου τύπος . . . . καὶ ὢν καὶ καλούμενος; cf. col. 405D (both allusions to Aelius Aristides, *Or.* 46, ed. W. Dindorf, *Aristides* [reprint, Hildesheim, 1964], II, p. 398); Theodore Hyrtakenos, Letter to Metochites, No. 18, ed. F. J. G. la Porte-du Theil, *Notices et extraits des manuscrits de la Bibliothèque Nationale*, 5 (1798), p. 737: ὦ καὶ τοῦ Πυλίου Νέστορος μελιχρότερε; Manuel Philes, *Poem* to Metochites, ed. E. Miller, *Manuelis Philae Carmina*, I (Paris, 1855), p. 315: Ἑρμῆ βραβευτὰ τῆς ὑπὲρ γῆν Ἀτθίδος (i.e., Metochites and his daughter Irene?); cf. idem, *Dirge* on Metochites' son-in-law John Palaeologus (poem surely commissioned by Metochites and his daughter Irene, John's widow), ed. Martini (as in note 14 above), p. 139.29, where John is referred to as ὡς γὰρ ἀφ'

Ἑρμοῦ τὴν Ἀθηνᾶν λαμβάνων, i.e., marrying Metochites' daughter; idem, ed. Martini, p. 139.23–27: ⟨John⟩ συνεζύγη | τῇ τοῦ μεγάλου φιλτάτῃ λογοθέτου | . . . . | τοῦ καινοφανοῦς πανταχοῦ γῆς ἀστέρος, | ὃν ἡ φύσις τέθεικεν ο ὐ ρ α ν ο δ ρ ό μ ο ν; Gregoras, *Dirge* on Metochites, *Hist.*, X.2, Bonn (1829), I, pp. 479.23–480.3: μετεμψύχωσιν . . . . ἐπ' ἐκείνῳ γενέσθαι, καὶ πάντων ὁμοῦ τὰς ψυχάς, Ὁμήρου καὶ Πλάτωνος καὶ Πτολεμαίου . . . . ἐν ἑνὶ τούτῳ σώματι συνδραμεῖν καὶ διατρίβειν . . . . ἐν βίῳ, lifted, in part literally, from Gregoras' *Letter* to Metochites, No. 48, ed. St. Bezdeki, in *Ephemeris Dacoromana*, 2 (1924), pp. 271.31–272.7, = No. 14, Guilland, *Correspondance de . . . Grégoras* (as in n. 20 above), p. 65.16–30; Gregoras, the same *Letter*, ed. Bezdeki, p. 271.24–28, = Guilland, p. 65.6–13: εἴ τίς σε τέχνην προσείποι τεχνῶν καὶ ἐπιστήμην ἐπιστημῶν καὶ γνῶσιν τῶν ὄντων ἧ ὄντα ἐστί [these are the three definitions of Philosophy taught at school], σφόδρα ἂν βάλοι κατὰ σκοπόν . . . . κινδυνεύω . . . . νομίζειν . . . . τὴν σὴν πρὸς ἡμᾶς ἐπιφάνειαν ἐπιδημίαν εἰς ἀνθρώπους εἶναι σοφίας ἁπάσης, ψυχὴν καὶ σῶμα προσειληφυίας; cf. Gregoras, another *Letter* to Metochites, No. 47, ed. Bezdeki, p. 269.7–10: if Metochites were known in antiquity, his glory would transcend that of Pythagoras and Plato. Finally, if Michael Gabras' *Letter* τινὶ τῶν δυνατῶν (Marcianus gr. 446, fols. 62r–63v) was originally addressed to Metochites, then Metochites' soul was described as the seat of the Muses (fol. 62r): ὢ σὺ Μουσῶν ὡς ἀληθῶς χωρίον ἔχων τὴν ψυχήν. See Fenster, *Laudes* (as in n. 29 above), p. 332.

33 *Hist.*, I, VII.11, Bonn, pp. 271.2–273.4. On style, ibid., p. 272.6–14; see my *Etudes*, pp. 35–36. The epithet βιβλιοθήκη . . . . ἔμψυχος, which Gregoras applied to Metochites (ibid., p. 272.3–4), appears in an earlier Byzantine text, a short anonymous Life of Isidore of Pelusium: βιβλιοθήκη τις δεικνύμενος ἔμψυχος, ed. M. Smith in Εὐχαριστήριον . . . Α. Σ. Ἀλιβισάτου (Athens, 1958), p. 436.

34 See, above all, Ch. Diehl, *Etudes byzantines* (Paris, 1905), esp. pp. 397–406.

35 Cf. the two lampoons by Nicephorus Choumnos discussed in my *Etudes*, passim (summary on pp. 21–33) and the unpublished *Enseignemens ou ordenances pour un seigneur qui a guerres et grans gouvernemens a faire* (e.g. MS. Brussels, Bibliothèque Royale, No. 11042), by Andronicus II's son, Theodore Palaeologus, Marquis of Montferrat. On this text and its author, see p. 30 and n. 83 below. In the *Enseignemens*, fol. 83r a, it is said of Metochites that he *despisoit et anichiloit tous, fors li et cilz que de li estoient nés.*

a learned man; that his style was difficult. As I should like to go beyond this, I shall draw a Metochites of my own. Here and there, the attempt will be conjectural, but on the whole it will be verifiable, as it will rest on the results of new research done in the past fifteen years.

Theodore Metochites was born in Constantinople in the year 1270[36] into a cultivated household. His father was George Metochites, an ardent pro-unionist, an associate of the Patriarch John Bekkos, and an ambassador of Michael VIII to the Papal curia.[37] Metochites' parents believed in starting their child's education early and they supervised it themselves.[38] He must have spent a comfortable, if studious, early childhood—at least until 1283, when the violent anti-unionist reaction that followed Michael VIII's death sent his parents into banishment in Asia Minor, and their son with them.[39] Metochites' education was interrupted by this catastrophe, but he continued studying by himself, and in any case the interruption did not last long. At the age of thirteen he was enrolled in a school where he went through the *Trivium* and *Quadrivium*.[40]

For others, study might be a matter of routine; for him, it was a matter of survival. Son of disgraced parents, he could neither look to them for help nor ever hope—or so he thought—for imperial favor.[41] Left to his own resources, he banked on his natural intellectual gifts and decided to become a scholar.

When Metochites finished school, he continued to study on his own; he steeped himself in the classics, especially the rhetoricians.[42] Not yet twenty years of age, he tried his own hand at literature, composing exercises on Greek history and several eulogies of the Saints. At the same time, this precocious mind read ancient philosophers and the sacred books, and studied theology [43] —but of the orthodox variety, of course, for he was a prudent young man and had no desire to follow the example of his stubborn father.

A turning point in Metochites' life occurred in 1290, when he was slightly over twenty years of age.[44] The Emperor Andronicus II had recently come to Asia Minor on a tour of inspection and visited Nicaea.[45] It was perhaps there that the young man, already noted for his learning, was brought to Andronicus' attention. The Emperor took a fancy to Metochites, especially

---

36 *Etudes*, pp. 129–34, 269–71. There I stated that the date of 1269 could also be entertained, although it was difficult to square with the chronological framework offered by Pachymeres, and with other information coming from Metochites himself; ibid., esp. p. 129 and n. 6. I gave too much credence to the note in Vindobonensis hist. gr. 99, fol. 35v, offering March 1296 as the birth date of the future Andronicus III. This in turn would date the marriage of his parents, Michael IX and Rita, which occurred on a January 16, to January 1295; the embassy of the 25-year-old Metochites to Cyprus and Armenia to 1294; and, consequently, his birth to 1269. However, in the *Etudes*, I overlooked two pieces of evidence: (1) the explicit passage of the short Chronicle published by B. T. Gorjanov, *VV*, N.S., 2 (27) (1949), esp. p. 282, lines 34–35, and republished by R.-J. Loenertz, *OCP*, 29 (1963), esp. pp. 333 and 348 (No. 11)—there, the birth of Andronicus III is dated to March 25, 1297, not 1296; (2) a passage in the letter of Frederick III of Sicily to Jacob II of Aragon, dated April 3, 1296, where Frederick still assumed that the eldest son (*primogenitus*) of Emperor Andronicus II (i.e., Michael IX) was a bachelor; C. Marinescu, "Tentatives de mariage de deux fils d'Andronic II Paléologue avec des princesses latines," *Revue historique du Sud-Est européen*, 1 (1924), p. 143. Had Michael IX's marriage occurred in January of 1295, Frederick would have known it by April of the next year. Hence, the marriage of Michael was celebrated on January 16, 1296, Metochites went on his embassy in 1295, and his birth is to be put in 1270.

37 *Etudes*, pp. 130–35, 270.

38 TM, *Poem* 1, vv. 343–44, 347–49, ed. M. Treu, *Dichtungen des Gross-Logotheten Theodoros Metochites* (Potsdam, 1895): εὖτε γὰρ εἴλαχον ἐλθέμεν εἰν φάει βιότοιο, | ἐξαῦτις σχεδὸν οἵ με φύσαντες λουγίοις δῶκαν | . . . . | πὰρ γονέων μάν, ὥς κε προσθέμαν εἰν λόγοισιν, | εὖ φερόμαν.

39 *Etudes*, pp. 134, 271.

40 TM, *Poem* 1, vv. 356–80: Metochites first studied γραμματικάν (v. 360), δρόμος γλώττης . . . . κατὰ ῥήτρας [vv. 364–65], λογικά [v. 374]; then, ἰδμοσύνας μαθαμάτων . . . . πισσύρεων, οἷς ἁ φιλοσουφία τετμήαται [vv. 378–79].

41 TM, *Poem* 1, vv. 429–31: cf. *Etudes*, pp. 132–33.

42 TM, *Poem* 1, vv. 389–401: τοὐνθεῦτ' ἐξαποέρσας ἐμαυτὸν ἀκροάσιος | ὄσσε τε νοῦν τ' ἐδόμαν ἀπάσῃ σχολᾷ πρότερ' ἀνδρῶν | κείνων πανσούφων πονέειν συντάγματ' ἐπιών | . . . . | . . . . καὶ τό γε μάλιστ' εἰν διαφυᾷ | λέξιος καὶ δρουμήμασι φωνᾶς ἀσκήσει τε.

43 TM, *Poem* 1, vv. 403–19: ἐκδόσιάς τ' ἐπιτυχέος φωνᾶς ἔνεικά τινας | κρέσσονα δόξαν ἐμοὶ τῆς ἡλικίης φεροίσας, | χ' ὡς δράματι προτέροις θ' Ἑλλήνων πρήγμασί τισιν | ἱστοριῶν ἀνὰ κεῖθεν ἀτ' εἴθιστ' ἐκ παλαιῶν | ἀέθλευσ' ἀπολέξας . . . . | . . . . | καὶ τισιν εὐφαμίαις σέβας ἐμπιπλὰς θεοῖο | προσπούλοισιν, ἄων κε μέ τις κινέεσκε χρειώ. | . . . . | σὺν δ' ἄρα καὶ φιλοσουφίας οὓς ἔχομες θησαυρούς | . . . . | πᾶσα δ' ἔην ἀτὰρ ἀνάγκα καὶ ἱρῶν βίβλων | ἀπτόμενον πονέειν . . . . | ἰδμοσύναν τ' ἐκτώμαν ἄφυκτον θειοσεβίης.

44 TM, *Poem* 1, v. 421: αὐτὰρ ἐείκοσιν εἴτεα γινάμενος κάτι γε πρός.

45 *Etudes*, p. 139.

after having heard him pronounce a eulogy of the city of Nicaea,[46] and took him into his service, in spite of the fact that Metochites' father was still a state prisoner.[47] The impossible had happened. Metochites felt that hard work had been rewarded, erudition and literary talent appreciated; and for the rest of his life he maintained that culture was man's only durable and inalienable acquisition, since it provided him with the most secure shelter in the storms of life.[48]

From that time on, Metochites' advancement was rapid. After less than a year of service in the Emperor's retinue (which meant traveling with him through Asia Minor), the young man was granted the court title Logothete of the Herds and, with it, membership in the senatorial class.[49] Later on, when Metochites reminisced on this rapid rise, he noted with satisfaction that his dignity had come to him free of charge.[50] When his turn came to distribute dignities, he was less generous.

In the early nineties Metochites was sent out on several minor embassies.[51] He must have done well, for when he was only twenty-five years old he was entrusted with a more important task. In 1295 he was the junior member of a two-man delegation which went to Cyprus and then to Cilician Armenia; its task was to bring back a bride for the Emperor's son and co-ruler, Michael IX. This embassy was a vast undertaking; seven ships were needed to transport the envoys and their retinue. The ambassadors left Cyprus empty-handed, since its Catholic Lusignan ruler insisted on awaiting Rome's *placet* for the marriage. From Cyprus they proceeded to the Armenian King Het'um II, who offered a choice between his two sisters. Michael IX married the elder one, Rita, in January of 1296.[52] Metochites was rewarded with a new court title, Logothete of the Emperor's Private Estates.[53]

Marital diplomacy seems to have become Metochites' special province for a time. In 1299, he arranged the marriage between the Serbian King Stephen Milutin and the small daughter of Andronicus II, Simonis. The marriage contract itself was only the last stage in long negotiations involving territorial questions, rectification of frontiers, and exchanges of fugitives and hostages.[54]

46 TM, *Poem* 1, vv. 437–46: οὑμὸς γὰρ ὅδ' ἄναξ . . . . | . . . . | καλέεταί μ' ἐς ἑωυτοῦ φιλοκαλίᾳ κινηθείς, | . . . . | κατ' ἄρ' κλεῖος ἐμοὶ σοφίης, Metochites reports with his customary modesty. For a somewhat conjectural assertion that the Νικαεύς was pronounced in the presence of Andronicus II, see *Etudes*, p. 137. On this laudation in general, see in the last place, Fenster, *Laudes* (as in n. 29 above), pp. 183–84.

47 TM, *Poem* 1, vv. 431–32, 447–48, 549.

48 TM, Ἠθικὸς ἢ περὶ παιδείας, Vindobon. ph. gr. 95 (*Logos* 10), fol. 199r: παιδεία τοίνυν ἐν τούτῳ καὶ πρῶτον, καὶ τὰ τῆς σοφίας ἀγαθά, παραμένει τῶν κατὰ τὸν βίον ἁπάντων πιστῶς εἰς ἅπασαν τῷ κτησαμένῳ ζωήν. καὶ οὐκ ἔστιν, οὔκ, ἀφαιρεῖσθαι μήτε τὸν ἀπὸ ταύτης πλοῦτον ἐχθρόν, ὅτι μὴ πέφυκε [for it is by nature impossible?], μήτε τὴν ἀπὸ ταύτης δόξαν, ὅ,τι μὴ κρείττω γένοιτο [i.e., except by showing his superiority in culture?]. τῷ ὄντι γὰρ πρὸς ταύτην ὥσπερ εἰς ἄσυλόν τι τέμενος ἠυτομοληκότα τινὰ καὶ καταστάντα, ἔξεστιν ἐπ' ἀσφαλοῦς ἑστήξειν, καὶ μηκέτι καθάπαξ ἔπειτα μὴ δεδιέναι, μήτε χρόνων ἐπιβουλὴν καὶ ἀνωμαλίαν, μήτε τυράννου βασκανίαν τε καὶ πλεονεξίαν, μητ' ἄλλην ἅπασαν ἐχθρῶν ἐπήρειαν, ἀλλὰ πάντ' ἂν μᾶλλον ἄνω καὶ κάτω γίγνοιτο καὶ μεταχωροίη καὶ τρέποιτο, ἢ νοῦς ὁτῳοῦν ἀφαιρεθείη σώφρων καὶ λογισμὸς ἔντεχνος, καὶ ἣν ἐπιστήμη καὶ παιδεία τοῖς θιασώταις καὶ σπουδασταῖς φέρουσα ἐνῴκισεν εὐδαιμονίαν καὶ τρυφήν. Cf. ibid., fol. 199v: παιδείας δὲ θησαυροὺς καὶ κλέος οὐδεὶς μήποτ' ἴσχυσεν οὔτ' ἐνεδρεύσας, καὶ εἰ μάλιστα φθόνῳ τήκοιτο, οὔτ' ἐπιδήλως ἐπιθέμενος, ἀφελέσθαι τοῦ κτησαμένου· μένει δ' οἷον συμφυὲς κάλλος καὶ ἀναπάλειπτον, οὔτ' ὄμμασι βασκάνοις οὔτε χερσὶ τεμνόμενον. καὶ ταύτην, οἶμαί, τις λέγων μόνην παρασκευὴν ἀκαταγώνιστον πρὸς πᾶσαν

δυσμένειαν καὶ ἀνεπιχείρητον, οὐκ ἂν ἴσως ἁμάρτῃ [read: ἁμάρτοι] λέγων. About a century after Metochites, John Chortasmenos expressed his belief in the absolute value of that inalienable acquisition we call knowledge. See Vindobon. suppl. gr. 75, fol. 212v, and H. Hunger, "Johannes Chortasmenos, ein byzantinischer Intellektueller der späten Palaiologenzeit," *Wiener Studien*, 70 (1957), p. 163.

49 TM, *Poem* 1, vv. 450–64; cf. *Etudes*, pp. 272–74.

50 *Poem* 1, v. 457: πρίν τι ἐνεῖκαι πραττόμενόν γ' ἄλλαγμ' ὤνιον.

51 TM, *Poem* 1, vv. 468–70: καί τ' εἰν πρεσβείῃσιν, ἄων μάλα μέμβλετ' ἄνακτι | ἐκλόγιμον πολέων ἀπο [i.e., selected from among many] πεμψάμενός με βασιλεὺς | αὐτὸς ἁμαρτέμεν οὐκ ἄρ' ἔδοξε.

52 See n. 36 above and TM, *Poem* 1, vv. 475–514; J. Verpeaux, "Notes chronologiques sur les livres II et III . . . de Georges Pachymère," *REB*, 17 (1959), esp. pp. 170–73 (Verpeaux wrongly proposed January 1295); also Pia Schmid, *Die diplomatischen Beziehungen zwischen Konstantinopel und Kairo zu Beginn des 14. Jahrhunderts* (typewritten thesis, Munich, 1956), p. 147, nn. 673 and 674.

53 TM, *Poem* 1, vv. 515–21, esp. vv. 515–18: αὐτὰρ ἔπειτα διὰ πάντεσσιν ἀεὶ προυχώρευν | δόξῃ τ' ἐργασίῃσι πολυτιμάτοις ὄλβῳ τε οὐνόμασί τ' ἐκ βασιλέως ἀπ' ἐκ τῶν εἰς τὰ [i.e., from one to another] μείζον' ἀεὶ 'πικλήδην νούμιμα βασιλήια. Cf. my *Etudes*, p. 272.

54 TM, *Poem* 1, vv. 560–73: idem, *Logos* 8, Πρεσβευτικός, ed. K. N. Sathas, Μεσαιωνικὴ Βιβλιοθήκη, I (Venice, 1872), pp. 154–93 passim; cf. M. Laskaris, *Vizantiske princeze u srednevekovnoj Srbiji* (Belgrade, 1926), pp. 59–66; Schmid, p. 143, n. 662; *Etudes*, p. 140.

To settle the problems connected with the wedding, Metochites made, in all, five journeys to Serbia.[55]

His ambassadorial career ended with the Serbian marriage. Andronicus II now preferred to keep him closer to home, although occasionally he did send him on missions within the Empire.[56] The most important and delicate of these occurred in 1303, when Yolanda-Irene of Montferrat, Andronicus II's Italian wife, departed for Salonika. She was given administrative powers there, but she could not be trusted: the Emperor needed his own man in her entourage to keep an eye on her. He sent Metochites as her Prime Minister.[57] This post turned out to be an apprenticeship, for less than two years later the Emperor summoned him back to the capital and made him Prime Minister of the whole Empire. This second great turning point in Metochites' career occurred in 1305–06. Nicephorus Choumnos, Metochites' predecessor as Prime Minister, was pushed into the background by the appointment [58]—a slight that gave rise to the long enmity between the two men and ended only with their deaths.

No function in the Empire was more important than that which Metochites was to perform from that date until the end of his political career. He was the mediator between the Emperor and his subjects, a grand vizier.[59] Simultaneously with his new position Metochites received yet another court title, that of Logothete of the Treasury.[60] Soon afterwards, he gave his daughter in marriage to John Palaeologus, the Emperor's nephew—a coup which made him almost equal to his eclipsed rival, Choumnos. Now he, too, was related to the imperial house.[61]

In the years that followed, Metochites read petitions,[62] listened to flatteries, relished praise of his style and his prodigiously swift pen,[63] granted or refused favors, granted or denied to

55 TM, *Poem* 1, v. 578: πεντάκι κεῖσε γὰρ οὕνεκα τῶνδ' ἐγὼν πρεσβεύω; this is repeated in vv. 708–09.

56 TM, *Poem* 1, vv. 709–17, esp. vv. 709–13: ἔπειτα | τήλοθ' ἀτάρ με χώρας ἐεῖο βασιλεὺς πέμπειν | αἱρέετ' οὐκέτι · ἐν δ' ἄρα οἴκοθι πολλὸν χρῆτο, | πώρρω τ' ἐν σφετέροις ἅ μάλα μέμβλοιτ' ἔργα οἱ | πέμπετ' ἐφετμὰς ἑκάστοτ' ἔμοιγε διδούς . . . .

57 *Etudes*, pp. 275–79.

58 *Etudes*, pp. 149–51.

59 *Etudes*, p. 6, n. 4, to be modified in the light of R.-J. Loenertz, "Le chancelier impérial à Byzance," *OCP*, 26 (1960), pp. 275–300.

60 TM, *Poem* 1, vv. 764–65: αὐτίκα μέν γ' ἐμὲ τιμᾷ βασιλεὺς ἔξοχ' ἄλλῳ | οὐνόματι μάλ' ὑπειρόχῳ, πάρος ἤεπερ ἦεν. Cf. *Etudes*, pp. 272–73.

61 On the marriage of Irene, see, e.g., TM, *Poem* 1, vv. 766–75; Papadopulos, *Genealogie* (as in n. 17 above), No. 38; *Etudes*, pp. 149–50. If I understand *Poem* 1, v. 790 correctly, Andronicus II gave two daughters of his nephews (or nieces) to two sons of Metochites in marriage: τῶν [i.e., ὧν "of whom"] δέ τε δύο θυγατράσιν ἀδελφιδῶν μῖξε. The most likely candidates for wives of these two sons of Metochites are to be looked for among the granddaughters of (*a*) Theodore Palaeologus and the daughter of Libadarios (Papadopulos, No. 43); (*b*) Irene Palaeologina and John III Asan (Papadopulos, No. 44); and (*c*) Mary of the Mongols and Abaga (Papadopulos, No. 54; cf. No. 55, where an Asan marries Mary's daughter). Such marriage connections could explain the presence of the Asan monograms on the garments of the deceased depicted on frescoes in the tombs at the Chora (see P.A. Underwood, Vol. 1 of this work, pp. 284–86, and idem, in *DOP*, 13 [1959], pp. 219, 225). Perhaps even the presence of the mosaic of Mary of the Mongols in the inner narthex of the Chora can be explained as an act of familial piety, cf. P.A. Underwood, "The Deisis Mosaic in the Kahrie Cami at Istanbul," *Late Classical and Mediaeval Studies in Honor of A.M. Friend, Jr.*, ed. K. Weitzmann (Princeton, 1955), pp. 258–60; idem, *DOP*, 9 and 10 (1955–56), p. 295, and 12 (1958), pp. 286–87.

62 See, as an example, the letter of Gregory, Archbishop of Bulgaria, to a Great Logothete (surely Metochites), ed. Lampros in Νέος Ἑλληνομνήμων, 14, 2–4 (1920), pp. 344–45: would the

Logothete again intercede with the Emperor on behalf of a nun [abbess of a small nunnery?] who lost her landed property (γηδίου), which had fed her and other old women (γραΐδίων)? The affair seems to have been delicate, since the nun was out of favor; therefore, the Logothete was reminded of the Christian duty to love one's enemies.

63 Examples: a) *Letter* of Patriarch John Glykys to a Logothete of the Treasury (Metochites), Laurentianus 57.24, fol. 126v: . . . . ἀγγελίας ἐφ' ἡμᾶς ἡκούσης νῦν μὲν λόγων εὖ πεποιημένων, καινῶν ἀεὶ τὴν ὥραν οὐχ ἧττον δὲ καὶ ῥώμην, καὶ ἔτι γε μὴν τὸ τάχος τε καὶ τὸν τόνον ἐπὶ πλεῖστον ἥκοντα, καὶ ὡς οὐκ ἔστι συνορᾶν δι' ὅσου κλέπτοντος τοῦ τάχους τὸ μέτρον, νῦν δὲ γνώμης εὖ βεβουλευμένης καὶ τῶν κοινῶν ἀεί τι ὡς γοῦν ἔξεστιν ὀρθούσης, ἢ τινός γε μὲν ἑτέρου τῶν ἐπαινεῖν πειθόντων πεπραγμένου καὶ πείσοντος, †ὃν σὺ πολλῶν†, εὖ μάλα ὡς ἐν κοινῷ τινι θεάτρῳ τῷ μεγάλῳ συνεδρίῳ νύκτα καὶ ἡμέραν πολιτευόμενος καὶ χρηματίζων, τὰς ἁπάντων ἔχεις ἤδη γλώσσας ἐπὶ σαυτὸν καὶ τὸ σὸν θαῦμα κινήσας. It is not quite certain that the letter dates from Glykys' days as Patriarch (1315–19), but it is probable, since he was already old at the time of writing; see references to his "dissolving and ragged" body on fol. 127r.

b) Nicephorus Gregoras' *Letter* to Joseph the Philosopher (date: after 1323), Guilland, *Correspondance de . . . Grégoras* (as in n. 20 above), pp. 59.31–61.4, and Treu, in *BZ*, 8 (1899), p. 58.3–7: καὶ γὰρ καὶ ἀεὶ (read: εἰ; H. Grégoire, in *Byzantion*, 3 [1926], p. 474) σχολαστικός τις ὢν ὁ ἀνήρ [i.e., Metochites] τοσαῦτα καὶ τοιαῦτ' ἐδημιούργει, ὁποῖα καὶ ὅσα καὶ λέγων καὶ γράφων διατελεῖ τὸν πάντα αἰῶνα, καὶ οὕτω θαῦμα ἂν ἦν· νῦν δὲ τοσούτοις καὶ τοσοῦτο φλεγμαίνουσι θορύβοις περιαντλούμενος καὶ ὑπὲρ θαῦμα τίθησι τὸ θαῦμα. Gregoras repeated the same compliment verbatim in his *Letter* to Metochites, No. 47, ed. Bezdeki (as in n. 32 above), p. 270.35–38.

c) Thomas Magister, *Letter* to Metochites, *PG*, 145, cols. 404C–410D, esp. 405C: μαρτυροῦσι μὲν οὖν οἷς λέγω καὶ πόλεις καὶ ἔθνη καὶ δῆμος ἅπας ὑπὸ σοῦ σωζόμενος . . . . μαρτυρεῖ δὲ καὶ ἃ καθ' ἑκάστην ὡς εἰπεῖν τίκτεις βιβλία, θαύματος πρόσω καὶ τοῖς τε οὖσι τοῖς τε ἐπιγιγνομένοις παισὶ ῥητόρων.

delegations the right of audience before the Emperor,[64] and dealt with foreign governments.[65] Above all he sold dignities, land grants,[66] and sinecures. But amidst the activities of public affairs, he never lost his love of letters. He got rich by day, he studied and wrote by night.[67] He composed essays on human nature, ancient authors, and history; he wrote a long disquisition on culture, and a eulogy of Constantinople.[68] These were elevated subjects. He also wrote poetic epitaphs—on the death of the Empress Irene (d. 1317), of the co-Emperor Michael IX (d. 1320).[69] These were routine subjects, usually entrusted to hired hacks around the capital. The hacks, however, wrote in Byzantine dodecasyllables, and everybody could understand them; Metochites wrote in inept hexameters replete with Doric and Aeolic forms of his own concoction, and only a few people, both in his time and today, could fathom his verse.[70]

As it was never too late to learn, at the age of forty-three Metochites, encouraged by the Emperor,[71] took up astronomy. He unearthed a scholar, Michael Bryennios, whose knowledge of astronomy went back to someone coming from "Persia." [72] He set Bryennios up in his house, and by 1316–17, after three years of study and writing, produced a bulky introduction to astronomy in two books, full of mostly genuine but sometimes dubious learning.[73]

About 1316 Metochites turned to the restoration of the Chora.[74] As an imperial monastery,

64 See Thomas Magister, in Treu, "Die Gesandtschaftsreise" (as in n. 32 above), p. 10: Metochites was so well disposed toward the delegation headed by Magister, ὥσθ᾽ ἕνεκ᾽ αὐτοῦ τάχιστ᾽ ἂν ἦμεν ἔξω πραγμάτων· [unfortunately] πολλῆς .... ἀσχολίας οὔσης ἐν μέσῳ οὐκ ἐξεγένεθ᾽ ἡμᾶς αὐτίκα πρὸς βασιλέως ἐλθεῖν ἀκοάς.

65 Metochites' letter to Charles IV the Fair of France (date: early 1327), in which he called himself *ex misericordia et gratia domini sui excellentissimi imperatoris Graecorum magnus Logotheta;* ed. H. Omont, "Projet de réunion des églises grecque et latine sous Charles le Bel en 1327," *Bibliothèque de l'Ecole des Chartes,* 53 (1892), pp. 254–57. The letter was in response to a missive that Metochites himself had received from Charles. That he, rather than Andronicus II, was the addressee is a measure of the importance the French court attached to the person of the Byzantine Prime Minister. In putting out unionist feelers, Andronicus II and his minister wanted to neutralize the idea of the crusade, revived under Charles IV. See T. Käppeli, "Benedetto di Asinago da Como (d. 1339)," *Archivum Fratrum Praedicatorum,* 11 (1941), p. 85.

66 See Theodore Hyrtakenos, *Letter* to Metochites, No. 20, ed. La Porte-du Theil, (as in note 32 above), p. 739: now is the time for Theodore Hyrtakenos to obtain the promised plot of land from the Emperor, ὁπόθ᾽ ὁ μέγας ἐν λογισταῖς [i.e., the Great Logothete Metochites] οὐ περὶ τὰς ἐν θαλάμοις νύμφας ...., ἀλλ᾽ ἐν Νύμφαις τῷ χωρίῳ [where?] πλέθροις τε καὶ ὅροις γεωργικοῖς .... καὶ προνοιῶν ἐπισκέψεσι, καὶ οἰκονομιῶν ἀρχοντικῶν ἐπιδόσεσι καὶ παραδόσεσι, ὁ τῆς ἱερεῦς [sic; read ἱερᾶς?] γεωδαισίαις καθηγεμών.

67 Gregoras, *Hist.,* VII.11, Bonn, I, pp. 272.17–273.3.

68 *Miscellanea,* Chs. 5, 30, 32, 33, 35, 41, 49, 50, 52, 54, 55, 59, 60, 62–64, 68, 69, 88–91, 95, 120 (human nature); 14–19, 71 (ancient authors); 92, 93, 99–111, 113–15 (history); *Logos* 10 (cf. *Etudes,* p. 141 and n. 2); *Logos* 11, Βυζάντιος ἢ περὶ τῆς βασιλίδος μεγαλοπόλεως, Vindobon. ph. gr. 95, fols. 233v–302v. For a good analysis of the Βυζάντιος in the light of other writings belonging to the same genre, see Fenster, *Laudes* (as in note 29 above), pp. 196–209. On pp. 207 and 331, n. 3, Fenster considers the Βυζάντιος "with some assurance" as a work of Metochites' youth. This seems to be too early a dating. In *Etudes,* p. 141, I implied that Theodore Metochites' praise of Constantinople (= *Logos* 11) was roughly contemporary with *Logos* 10, if somewhat later than it; as for *Logos* 10, I ascribed it to the time when Theodore Metochites was married, had children, and when his political career was already in full bloom, and I still hold to this view. I must, however, mention a difficulty in dating the Βυζάντιος, of which I became aware since writing the *Etudes:* On fol. 298v, this work contains a purportedly Demos-

thenic bon-mot with a "Marxist" tinge which, says Theodore Metochites, he had already quoted in another writing of his: Δημοσθένης αὐτὸς ἔπειθ᾽ ὕστερον [i.e., after Euripides] ...., ὡς ἄρα καὶ πρότερον ἐν ἄλλοις ἡμῖν εἴρηται, ὁποῖά ποτ᾽ ἂν ᾖ, φησί, τοῖς ἀνθρώποις τὰ πράγματα, τοιαῦτα καὶ τὰ φρονήματα γίγνεται. To my knowledge, this saying occurs again only in *Logos* 17, fol. 359v (Gigante, "Il saggio (as in n. 29 above), pp. 14.11–13, p. 81, without indication of source): Δημοσθένης φησὶν ὁποῖά ποτ᾽ ἂν ᾖ τισι τὰ πράγματα, τοιαῦτα καὶ τὰ φρονήματα γίγνεσθαι. This is embarrassing, since *Logos* 17 is surely later than 1330; see, e.g., *Etudes,* p. 143. Putting the Βυζάντιος after 1330/31 seems out of the question; we must therefore assume one of two things: either the Demosthenic bon-mot occurs in some other (relatively early) writing by Metochites as well and has escaped my attention there, or the Βυζάντιος underwent late redactional changes before being written down in Vindobon. ph. gr. 95.

69 TM, *Poem* 7, Ἐπιτάφιοι εἰς τὴν Αὔγουσταν Εἰρήνην τὴν σύζυγον τοῦ θειοτάτου βασιλέως Ἀνδρονίκου τοῦ Παλαιολόγου, e.g., Paris. gr. 1776, fols. 99v–108v (best manuscript); TM, *Poem* 8, Ἐπιτάφιοι εἰς τὸν νέον ἄνακτα Μιχαὴλ τὸν Παλαιολόγον υἱὸν τοῦ θειοτάτου βασιλέως Ἀνδρονίκου τοῦ Παλαιολόγου, Paris. gr. 1776, fols. 108v–119r; cf. Guilland, "Les poésies" (as in n. 6 above), pp. 281–87.

70 While discussing Paris. gr. 1776, Charles Benoît Hase (1780–1864), Keeper of Greek Manuscripts at the Bibliothèque Nationale, delivered himself of the following remark: *fuit autem hic Theodorus Metochita poëta supra quam dici potest ineptus.* Cf. Paris. suppl. gr. 710, p. 401; cf. also E. Miller in *Journal des Savants* (April, 1874), pp. 278–79, and Hesseling, "Byzantijnse weelde ..." (as in n. 29 above), p. 83. The latest, and somewhat panegyric, study on Metochites' poetry is Gigante, "Il ciclo" (as in n. 29 above).

71 TM, *Poem* 1, vv. 651–58; cf. my *Etudes,* pp. 87, n. 3, 128, 167.

72 TM, *Poem* 1, vv. 630–45; cf. my *Etudes,* p. 115, n. 6. This someone from Persia may have been George Chioniades, who did go to Persia before 1301 in order to learn astronomy there. See N. A. Oikonomides in Ἀρχεῖον Πόντου, 20 (1955), pp. 43–44. Metochites tells us that Andronicus II urged him to learn from Bryennios, even though the latter was an obscure individual and socially Metochites' inferior: *Poem* 1, vv. 665–67: σὺ δ᾽ ἂν ἀέξαις | μαθών, μὴ δ᾽ ἀλέγιζ᾽, εἰ πουλὺ γ᾽ ἥττονος ἀνδρός | σεῖο τιμᾶν τε λόγους τε κἀφανοῦς μαθεῖν χρειώ.

73 TM, *Poem* 1, vv. 671–74; cf. my *Etudes,* pp. 42–44; 92, n. 4; 105, n. 3; 109–17, esp. p. 115; 129; 280–86.

74 For the date, see Appendix III, pp. 90–91.

the Chora was under the protection and administration of the imperial house. This did not amount to much, for, although the monastery functioned, it was in a dilapidated state.[75] The Emperor himself had suggested that Metochites should undertake the direction of its restoration.[76] Metochites went to work, assisted by a young man, Nicephorus Gregoras.[77] Both the demolishing and the reconstruction proceeded rapidly, and in early Lent of 1321 Metochites could attend services in the splendidly decorated church of the monastery.[78]

About the time of Easter of 1321, Metochites was granted the highest court dignity of his career, that of Great Logothete.[79] Not content with this dignity alone, he saw to it that from now on the title would be upgraded in the court hierarchy, so that he could rank four places above his rival Choumnos, who, according to the old system, would have been his immediate neighbor at court ceremonies.[80] But Metochites could not enjoy his victory in peace. Just before this, the troubles had begun which would last until the end of his life. First, a civil war had broken out between Andronicus II and his grandson, Andronicus III. Metochites' loyalties were clear, for his fortunes were linked with those of the old Emperor; but his sons tergiversated.[81] The first phase of the civil war ended in a draw, but the truce was uneasy. Then, in the old Emperor's camp, old and new hatreds flared up against the Prime Minister. About 1325 Choumnos, beaten in politics, started a literary attack. In three pamphlets he accused an anonymous adversary of being a repetitious and obscure writer and a bad astronomer to boot. Metochites replied in kind, deriding the excessive clarity of Choumnos' style and his ignorance of elementary science.[82]

---

75 For the Chora as a βασιλικὴ μονή, cf. the ingenious deduction in Wendel, "Planudea," *BZ*, 40 (1940), p. 407. Originally, a βασιλικὴ μονή was a monastery protected by an emperor and exempt from interference by any other secular authority. See P. de Meester, *De Monachico Statu Iuxta Disciplinam Byzantinam* (Rome, 1942), p. 104; J. von Zhishman, *Das Stifterrecht . . . in der morgenländischen Kirche* (Vienna, 1888), p. 19. By the early fifteenth century, an imperial monastery was treated by the *despotes* Andronicus II (1408–23) as his private possession, inherited from his grandfather, John V. See F. Dölger, *Aus den Schatzkammern des Heiligen Berges* (Munich, 1948), No. 30, pp. 84–86 (esp. line 6: ὡς γονικὴ ἡμετέρα ἡ μονὴ αὕτη); also pp. 72, 79. For the Chora's sorry state before the restoration, see, e.g., *Poem* 1, vv. 1004–05: ταύταν ὁ πάντ' ἀγαθ' εἶν ῥοᾷ παρασύρων χροῦνος | πάρ τ' ὀλίγου φθορᾷ πέμπετο; and the ironical remark of Patriarch Athanasius I, *Letter* 11 (to the Emperor Andronicus II), Vat. gr. 2219, fol. 6v: ἡ δὲ ἐμὲ δεχομένη κέλλα [at the time of writing Athanasius resided in the Chora], εἰ ἦν δυνατὸν χωρεῖν ἐν αὐτῇ τὸν ὑπ' ἀνέμου κινούμενον μύλωνα, οἱ μοναχοὶ τῆς Χώρας πολὺν ἐκέρδαινον ἄλευρον. According to Mrs. Alice-Mary Talbot, who is preparing an edition of Athanasius' letters, *Letter* 11 dates from about 1305. See, furthermore, Athanasius' *Letter* 23 (Vat. gr. 2219, fol. 12r), dating most probably from late spring 1305; in this letter, Athanasius proposes that a number of prelates assemble at the Chora on a Sunday, before going to the Imperial Palace at Blachernae. Conclusion: the Chora, dilapidated as it was, was habitable and in use by 1305. (V. Laurent, *Les Regestes des Actes du Patriarcat de Constantinople*, vol. I, fasc. IV [1971] pp. 415 and 427–28 [= Nos. 1621 and 1624], dates Athanasius' *Letter* 11 to the summer of 1304/5, and *Letter* 23 to the winter of 1305/6).

76 TM, *Poem* 1, vv. 994–95: ἀτάρ μ' ἵκετο νοῦον, | οἷον ἄρ' αὐτὸς [i.e., Andronicus II] καὶ τόδε μ' ἔργον ἀνά τ' ἥγειρεν . . . . ; vv. 1005–07: ἀεὶ δ' ἦρα βασιλεὺς | τήνδε [i.e., Chora] μάλ' ἀνστῆσαι πρό τ' ἀγαγεῖν, ἢ πάρος ἦεν, | καί μ' ἴφι ἀνὰ τόδ' ἔργον ἀείρει καὐτὸν ἐρῶντα. Even before the work of restoration was undertaken, Metochites had been a benefactor of the monastery: TM, *Poem* 2, ed. Treu, *Dichtungen*, vv. 28–29: πόθεον δ' ἐπὶ μέζον ἀείρειν ἐξῆς, | τὰ πόνεον πρό τ' ἐγ ὼ ν ἐς ἄμεινον ἀεὶ τὴν μουνήν.

77 Gregoras, *Hist.*, XXII.2, Bonn, II, pp. 1045.22–1046.2; text of the passage in Appendix III below, p. 90.

78 Speed of work: TM, *Poem* 1, v. 1019: κάββαλον ὧχ'; vv. 1020–21: αἶψα δὲ καινὴν | στῆσ'; v. 1025: στῆσα . . . . καρπαλίμως, ὡς κεν νῦν ὁρᾶται. The interior decoration of the Chora had been "recently" completed by the first week of Lent 1321; see Gregoras, *Hist.*, VIII.5, Bonn, I, p. 303.11–18.

79 *Etudes*, p. 19, n. 1.

80 *Etudes*, pp. 157–61, 168; J. Verpeaux, *Pseudo-Kodinos, Traité des Offices* (Paris, 1966), pp. 28–29.

81 In 1321, Demetrius and Nicephorus Metochites betrayed Andronicus II's and their father's plans, directed against Andronicus III, to the latter and put themselves at his disposal; cf. Cantacuzenus, *Hist.*, I.13, Bonn (1828), I, p. 63.4–10. In 1326, Michael Lascaris Metochites was attested as governor of Melnik; Cantacuzenus, *Hist.* I.43, Bonn, I, p. 210.1. However, by early 1328 Andronicus II seems to have relieved Michael of this post, for at that time we find a Nicephorus Basilikos as the top man of Melnik, either loyal to the old Emperor or obeying neither of the warring Andronici, depending on whether we follow Gregoras, *Hist.*, IX.5, Bonn, I, pp. 413.22–414.15 or Cantacuzenus, *Hist.*, I.55, Bonn, I, p. 285.3–5. Th.N. Vlachos, *Die Geschichte der byzantinischen Stadt Melenikon* (Salonika, 1969), p. 52, is of little use for our purpose. Demetrius Angelus Metochites' position was quite tolerable under Andronicus III, at least in the beginning months of the new regime: a document dating probably from October 1328 (and not later than October 1331) refers to Demetrius as the recently appointed governor of Serres and οἰκεῖος of the young Emperor; see A. Guillou, *Les archives de Saint-Jean-Prodrome sur le mont Ménécée* (Paris, 1955), No. 23, lines 13–15. This would indicate that Demetrius had not been too vigorously opposed to Andronicus III in the later stages of the civil war. In fact, by early 1328 the people who occupied Strumica, the town where Demetrius had been governor in 1326 (but was he still governor there as late as 1328?), while refusing to open the city's gates to Andronicus III, declared themselves neutral and said that they would sit out the war between the young Emperor and his grandfather: this is to be inferred from Cantacuzenus, *Hist.*, I.56, Bonn, I, p. 285.17–19.

82 See my *Etudes*, passim, esp. pp. 21–33, 144, 162 and n. 5, 188–265.

One of Andronicus II's sons, Theodore, Marquis of Montferrat,[83] who commuted between Italy and Byzantium in the hope of succeeding to the throne of Constantinople, also had no love for Metochites. As he was a professional soldier, he could not understand why, during the civil war, Andronicus had relied on his Prime Minister, who, he justly maintained, did not understand the first thing about military matters, rather than upon the Marquis himself.[84] Even before the civil war, Metochites' power over the the Emperor was such that, between Metochites and the Marquis, Andronicus sided with the Minister rather than with his own son.[85] The Marquis, frustrated, played an equivocal part in the civil war.[86] In 1326, while still in Constantinople, he attacked Metochites obliquely in writing. In 1330, back home in Montferrat, he did it openly, attributing Andronicus' fall and the calamities of the Empire to the Emperor's "evil genius." [87]

On top of that, in 1326 Metochites' son-in-law, John Palaeologus, attempted a rebellion against Andronicus II, his uncle. This time again, Metochites' own sons flirted with the rebel.[88] The embarrassing situation was soon terminated by John's death, but Metochites was somewhat compromised. In 1327, with the civil war between the Andronici in its third and final stage, he foresaw the outcome. He feared a popular rebellion and he trembled for his possessions. In his dreams, he saw a thief stealing the key to the room where he kept his treasures.[89]

Finally, early in 1328 a plot was formed to have Metochites deposed. A delegation of dignitaries from Constantinople, where Andronicus II and his Prime Minister were entrenched, came to Andronicus III and offered to deliver the capital to him on the condition that he would condemn Metochites to perpetual disgrace.[90] This was a euphemism for blinding, perhaps execution. Andronicus III refused to be bound by promises, for he expected soon to take the capital by force, and so he did. The fall of the city, in the night of May 23–24, 1328,[91] terminated Metochites' political career: he was exiled to Didymoteichos in Thrace, where he remained until 1330.[92]

Now he was a man of leisure. As a matter of fact he could say, with Aeschylus' Prometheus, that he had more leisure than he craved.[93] He was in disgrace—a fallen Prime Minister of a fallen

---

83 On Theodore Palaeologus, Marquis of Montferrat, and his *Enseignemens*, in which he attacked Metochites, see *Etudes*, pp. 6, n. 4; 150–51; 163–66, with bibliography, to which add D. Zakythinos, " 'Ο Μαρκίων τοῦ Μομφερράτου Θεόδωρος Α' Παλαιολόγος καὶ ὁ βασιλεὺς τῆς Γαλλίας Φίλιππος ὁ Σ'," in 'Επετηρὶς 'Εταιρείας Βυζαντινῶν Σπουδῶν, 11 (1935), pp. 16–28, and, most recently, A. E. Laiou, "A Byzantine Prince Latinized: Theodore Paleologus, Marquis of Montferrat," *Byzantion*, 38 (1968), pp. 368–410.

84 *Enseignemens*, fol. 85r: *il* [i.e., Andronicus II] *ne me vouloit croire en nulle manière, ne fier soy en mon conseil, mais croioit en toutes chosez le conseil de celi gouverneur* [i.e., Metochites] *et y adjoustoit foy, especialment en fait de guerre et en hanter armez, en quoy il ne se cognoissoit de riens, car il n'avoit oncques usé ès dites choses.*

85 *Enseignemens*, fol. 83r: Out of the purest of motives, Theodore warned his imperial father that he would alienate his relatives, his grandees, and his subjects on account of Metochites, who was not able to suffer his equal, but behaved according to the proverb *chien en cuisine son pareil ne désire*. All this was in vain. *Mais ledit monseigneur mon père ne creoit pas pour mes prières, ce que je le monstroie apertement, mais se mouvoit ausi comme à ire contre moy, et racontoit tout à celi gouverneur* [i.e., Metochites].

86 *Enseignemens*, fol. 85r–85v: *Mais puisque je veoie et comprenoie apertement que toute la gent de celi empire estoit mal ordenée contre dit monseigneur et père* [i.e., Andronicus II] *pour l'occasion du devant dit gouverneur* [i.e., Metochites], *et que il ne faisoient point leur faiz par raison ne per manière ou par l'usage des armes ne de guerre . . . , si ne veil pas . . . moy meller en nulle manière . . . , mais traîtai en telle manière . . . , que puisque*

ladite guerre [i.e., the civil war] *ot pris fin . . . , je eschapai de touz lez dis perils, et que je fu loé de mes II devant dis seigneurs* [i.e., both Andronicus II and Andronicus III], *et que à la bonne volenté d'iceulz . . . je repairai à ma dite Marquiseté de Montferrant.* Gregoras, IX.1, Bonn, I, p. 396.2–21 is more explicit and calls Theodore the spy of Andronicus III at the court of Andronicus II.

87 *Etudes*, pp. 164–65.

88 Apprised of John's rebellion, both Demetrius Angelus Metochites, governor of Strumica, and Michael Lascaris Metochites, governor of Melnik, wrote ambiguous letters to their sister and their brother-in-law in which they reminded them of past friendship and of family bonds. This incriminating correspondence was intercepted, passed on to Andronicus III, and forwarded by him to Theodore Metochites; Cantacuzenus, I.43, Bonn, I, pp. 209.23–211.15.

89 Gregoras, *Hist.*, IX.5, Bonn, I, pp. 412.4–413.2.

90 *Etudes*, p. 166 and n. 3.

91 On the date of the city's fall, cf. now Loenertz in *OCP*, 30 (1964), esp. pp. 39 and 43.

92 Gregoras, *Hist.*, IX.7, Bonn, I, p. 428.20–21. On the date of 1330, see my *Etudes*, p. 8, n. 2.

93 The opening sentence of *Logos* 17 (dating from 1330/31, see *Etudes*, p. 143) runs as follows: ἔτυχον μέν, σχολῆς ἐμοὶ παρούσης πλείονος ἢ θέλω, κατ' Αἰσχύλον ἐρεῖν [*Prom. Vinct.*, v. 818], ἐν χερσὶν ἔχων βιβλί' ἄττα τῶν Δημοσθένους, cf. TM, 'Επιστασία καὶ κρίσις τῆς τῶν δύο ῥητόρων εὐδοκιμήσεως τοῦ τε Δημοσθένους καὶ 'Αριστείδου, Vindobon. ph. gr. 95, fol. 356r; cf. now Gigante, "Il saggio" (as in n. 29 above) p. 74.

Emperor whose right-hand man he had been for over twenty years—a man of sixty, painfully sick and obsessed with the thought of approaching death.[94]

In one sense his life had been a failure. He had wanted to be rich. For years he had been receiving grants, either for himself or for his monastery, from the Emperor. For years he had been using his power to get his cut whenever an administrative dignity was conferred upon a petitioner, often without regard to that petitioner's competence. As the new official would pass the expense on by exploiting the peasants and other "good people" in the region allotted to him,[95] it was said that Metochites' wealth was made of the blood and tears of the poor.[96] He still proudly recalled his possessions in gold and silver, his vineyards, his herds of cattle, of sheep, of camels, his houses, and his palatial mansion with its marble floors, its large courtyard, its fountains, and its gardens.[97] He had been excessively devoted to his children's material welfare,[98] but here too he had failed. Now his children, accustomed to comforts, would have to suffer poverty.[99] From his daughter's marriage to the Emperor's nephew, he had expected not only happiness for her and his grandchildren, but also advantages for himself in his old age. But his son-in-law John Palaeologus had died. Thus, early in 1327 Metochites was saddled with the additional responsibility of caring for his grandchildren.[100] For some time before his son-in-law's death, plans had been maturing in his mind to retire voluntarily from the affairs of the world.[101] He wanted to retire to the Chora,[102] which he had restored.

---

94 *Etudes*, p. 143, n. 2; TM, Πρὸς τοὺς μοναχοὺς τῆς Χώρας ἐπὶ τῇ τελευτῇ τοῦ πρώτου καθηγουμένου αὐτῶν Λουκᾶ, μονῳδία τε ἐπ᾽ αὐτῷ καὶ προτροπὴ αὐτοῖς εἰς τὴν ἐπιμέλειαν τοῦ καλοῦ (*Logos* 15), Vindobon. ph. gr. 95, fol. 333r (below, App. I, p. **9**.11-13); TM, *Poem* 9 (date: 1327), Paris. gr. 1776, fols. 115v-116r: τοὔνεκ᾽ ἐγὼν ἐφάμην ἀΐδηλα πέρατ᾽ ἔμεν᾽ ἀεὶ | πᾶσι βίου· ὅσα 9᾽ ἤματα λεῖπτ᾽ ἔμοιγε ζωῆς, | τοῖσιν ἔπειτ᾽ ἐμέ γ᾽ ἀνάγκη διαμπερὲς ἀεὶ | μάλ᾽ ἀχνύμενον ἑλκέμεν ἔμπης βίοτον αἰνόν [this on account of John Palaeologus' death] | . . . . | αἴ9᾽ ὄφελ᾽ εἴη μῆκος ὀλίγον ὅπερ μοι λεῖπται | λοιπὸν ἔτι βιότοιο, τὸ δ᾽ ἄν μοι κέρδιον εἴη.

95 *Enseignemens*, fol. 82v a-b: il [i.e., Metochites] *ne faisoit a nul riens sanz grant louier ou grant treü, non pas en examinant ne en considérant en aucune manière la faculté des personnes, fors tant seulement a ceulz qui li donnoient louier et treüs. Si que par celi treü cil qui li donnoient prenoient les offices de li, et ne vouloient pas perdre ce que il donnoient, et s'estudioient gaingnier pour leur treü tant comme il pouvoient, et prenoient sanz raison et sanz riens regarder, ne honneur ne amour ne conscience vers dieu, mais roboient la peccune des bons hommez et des laboureurs de terre. Et pour ce aussi comme touz se mouvoient a ire et a haine contre celi gouverneur* [i.e., Metochites]. In Theodore's eyes, venality of offices and the general exploitation of peasantry that followed from it were among the chief causes of Byzantium's plight in his day.

96 Gregoras, *Hist.*, IX.6, Bonn, I, pp. 425.23-426.9, esp. 426. 1-2: τῶν μεμψιμοίρων λεγόντων τά τε ἄλλα καὶ ὡς πενήτων ἦν αἵματά τε καὶ δάκρυα τὰ τοιαῦτα χρήματα [i.e., Metochites' wealth].

97 TM, *Poem* 1, vv. 875-77: the Emperor's gifts to Metochites consisted εἴν κτεάτεσσί τε, εἴν χρυσῷ εἴν ἀργύρῳ τε, | εἴν πολυαρί9μοισί τε βουτοῖς παντοίοισι. *Poem* 19, Εἰς ἑαυτὸν ἔτι μετὰ τὴν τροπὴν τῆς κατ᾽ αὐτὸν τύχης, Paris. gr. 1776, fols. 225v-235r; partial edition by R. Guilland, "Le palais de Théodore Métochite," *REG*, 35 (1922), pp. 82-95, esp. lines 215, 222, 212-14 (where one should read ἑωνημέν᾽ ἐμοί "bought by me" [i.e., houses], instead of ἐὰν ἐμὲν ἐμοί; we know nothing of Metochites as collector of "antiquités soigneusement entretenues," postulated by Guilland, ibid., p. 93), and pp. 180-99. On marble floors in Metochites' house, see Gregoras, *Hist.*, IX.13, Bonn, I, p. 459.19-20.

98 *Logos* 10, fol. 219r-219v: ταῦτά με δὴ νυκτός τε καὶ με9᾽ ἡμέραν ἀεί πως γρηγορεῖν ἀναγκάζει τε καὶ καταπείθει, πάντ᾽ οἶμαι τρόπον βίοτον σφίσι [i.e., my children] ποριζόμενον ὅντινα ἔξεστιν, οὐ νῦν δὴ μόνον, ἀλλ᾽ ἄρ᾽ ἀσφαλῆ καὶ με9ύστερον

ἐμοῦ τελευτῶντος . . . . ταῖς γε μὴν παρ9ένοις αὐταῖς οὐκ ἄλλως ἢ 9ησαυρῶν πολυταλάντων ἔξεστι τινὰ κηδη καλλίῳ καὶ σεμνότερα πρίασ9αι, καὶ δὴ τοῦτ᾽ ἀεὶ πρόεισιν οὐκ οἶδ᾽ ὅπως μετὰ τοῦ χρόνου, καὶ πλείω κατατι9έναι καὶ φέρειν ἀνάγκην ἡμεῖς ἔχομεν ἢ κα9᾽ ὅσα ἀπημπολήμε9α ταῖς τῶν ἡμετέρων αὐτοὶ παίδων μητράσιν. Cf. TM, *Poem* 15 (date: after 1328), Paris. gr. 1776, fol. 195v: ἀμφὶ τέκνων φρούντισα παιδείης τ᾽ ἀγα9ῶν ἢ ᾽ἔασι ψυχᾶς ἀ9ανάτοιο | σὺν δὲ 9᾽ ἃ σώματος εὐπραγίης 9᾽ ἅμα δὴ βιότοιο, | τίπτ᾽ ἐρέω, διὰ 9᾽ ἤματα πάντα διά τε νύκτας | τηκόμενος κέαρ τῶνδ᾽ ἀδινάων, μεριμνάων δὴ | πῶς ἄρα τι σφίσι βέλτιον ἅμαδις ἀμφί γ᾽ ἕκαστα | γίγνοι9᾽ ἀγα9ά.

99 *Logos* 15, fol. 330v (below, App. I, **2**.8-10): Metochites deplores not only his own ruin, but also φιλτάτων καὶ τέκνων—καὶ προσκείσ9ω, μηδ᾽ ὀλίγων τούτων—ἐρραστωνευμένην ἀγωγὴν τέως κα9άπαξ οἴχεσ9αι καὶ μεταβαλεῖν εἰς πᾶν αὐτό9εν ταλαιπωρίας καὶ πᾶν ἐργῶδες.

100 TM, *Poem* 9, fol. 113r (date: 1327): τοῖος ἔην ἐμὸς οὔνεκά σευ [i.e., John Palaeologus] νόος ἠδ᾽ ἐλπορὴ | πάρος, ἀτὰρ τάδ᾽ ἄπαντ᾽ οἴχονται ἠύτ᾽ ὄνειρος· σύ τε νέκυς κέεσ᾽ ἄπνους, σύν τε τά 9᾽ ἡμέτερά τε. | τά τε σὰ λεῖπτ᾽ ἐμοὶ τέκεα πολύπουν᾽ ἄχ9ε᾽ ἅμα | οἷσι μάλα νύ τ᾽ ἐπείγουσά μ᾽ ἱκάνει ῥὰ χρειὼ | ἀμφιμέλειν διαμπερὲς ὅττι ποτέ σφιν ἔστ᾽ εὖ. Cf. fol. 126v: . . . . ἠδέ τε τάδε φίλτατα σεῖο | σύν 9᾽ ἅμαδις τέκεα λει9έντ᾽ ἐπὶ γήραος οὐδῷ | νυνί γ᾽ ἐμοὶ πᾶσ᾽ ἀναγκαίη διδόοντα φρόντιν [*sic* accent] | ἀμφ᾽ ἄρ᾽ ἔχειν σφίσιν ἄτροπον.

101 *Poem* 9, fol. 113r-113v: John's death thwarted Metochites' plans: κἄν ἄρα τίποτ᾽ ἐγὼν νόεον ψυχᾶς ἀμφ᾽ ἕνεκά μοι | βέλτιον, ὄφρα γενοίμην πρηγμάτεως ἀπάτερθεν | ἠδὲ 9᾽ ὑλήεντος βυ9οῦ τύρβης τε πόνων τε | . . . . | λιμένος ἀμφ᾽ ἄρα εὐδίοοντος ἀσείστου, | τὰ δέ τε πάντα σύ γ᾽ ἄμπαλιν ἐξ ἄρ᾽ ἔωσας ἐμεῖο.

102 TM, *Poem* 2, vv. 393-94, 427-29: αἴ9᾽ ὄφελον συναύλια κοινὰ | ἄμμιν ἔχειν, ἀνέρες μάκαρες Χώραν οἰκεῦντες and τοὔνεκα δὴ καί κεν μάλα ἤραμ᾽ ἐγὼν ἀπάνευθεν | ἐκ βιότοιο γεγὼς τύχης τε πάσης τὶ μὲν ἐσ9λῆς, | τὶ δὲ χερείοισιν ὑμῖν [i.e., the monks of the Chora] ὁμέστιος ἔμμεν᾽ αἰέν. Cf. *Logos* 15 (date: after 1328), fol. 334r (App. I, **11**.8-10): by your death, Metochites apostrophizes the Chora's abbot Lucas, ὦ πόσης ἐλπίδος, πόσης ἡδονῆς ἐπιδόξου μοι καὶ τρυφῆς κάλλιστ᾽ ἐν βελτίστοις τῆς σῆς ξυντυχίας, καὶ ἴσως τοῦ λοιποῦ ξυμβιώσεως, ῆς ἐκ μακροῦ πό9ος ἐμέ–καὶ αὐτὸς ἤδεις—εἶχεν, ἐμὲ νῦν ἀφείλου. Metochites entertained the idea of entering the Chora even before his present plight,

Everything was well prepared. To provide the Chora with ample sources of revenue, Metochites bought some fertile lands and vineyards not far from the city. He also assigned some of his previously held property to the monastery.[103] But the chief contribution came from the Emperor himself: as a special favor, greater than that ever given either to Metochites or to any other official under similar circumstances, Andronicus II issued chrysobulls granting landed property to the Chora both in the vicinity of the capital and in more distant regions.[104] The newly established monastery became a vast enterprise with a public hospital, a public kitchen, and an administrative apparatus to collect revenue from its lands.[105] The monastic community was large; monks were invited to the new foundation from many places, including Asia Minor.[106] These monks, who owed Metochites so much, would pray for the remission of his sins, and Christ would listen to the litanies sung by uncorrupted beings on behalf of a man stained with the mire of this world.[107] He was a sinner indeed: in his long climb to the summit of power, he had received blows and had in turn dealt many, either in the bright daylight or under the cover of darkness. He had been overweening toward some, fearful of involvement in an open struggle with others. To some, he had been an unjust helper; to others, an unjust enemy.[108]

But Metochites did not leave the work of expiation for his sins to the monks alone. He liked to attend day and night services in person; and he may even have sung along with the *psaltai* whom he had carefully recruited for the monastery.[109] In moments of stress—and there were many after 1321, when the civil war broke out—Metochites could find a haven and solace in the Chora.[110] Contemplation of the great *Deesis* mosaic in the inner narthex would set his mind at rest and

---

ibid., fols. 332v–333r (App. I, **8**.11–15): καὶ οὐχ ἧττον ἢ πρὶν ἐν τῷ νῦν ἐργώδει . . . . καὶ πολυκύμονι χρόνῳ . . . . εἶχεν . . . . ἐλπίς . . . . ὡς ἄρα γενοίμην αὐτὸς παρὰ τῇ μονῇ, καὶ τὸ λοιπὸν ἐμοὶ τῆς ζωῆς . . . . τῇδ' οὐκ ἀηδῶς ἄν βιωσοίμην.

103 TM, *Poem* 1, vv. 1264–72: τάων [i.e., the Chora's sources of revenue] δὴ τὰ μὲν ὤνητ' ἀπ' ἄρ ἐμεῖο πλεῖστα· | γῇ τ' ἀρόσιμος ὅπη ἄρα εἰν χώροισι πουλλοῖς | πυροφόρος πάνυ πουλύγονος τόσση καὶ τόσση, | ἀπειρέσια μήκεα εὖ μάλ' ἔχοντα φουρᾶς· | ἀμπελώνων τ' αὖ εὐγαιοτάτων ἀμύθητον | χρῆμ' ἀνὰ τῆσδε πέριξ μεγάλης πτόλιος ἐσθλόν, | τοὺς μὲν ἐγὼ κατεφύτευσα τοῦδ' ἄστεος ἄγχι. | καὶ τὰ μέν, | ὡς γ' ἔφην, ἔασιν ὠνήσιμ' ἐμεῖο, | τὰ δέ τ' αὐτόθεν ἐκ τῶν μοι πρό τ' ἐόντων φουρά.

104 TM, *Poem* 1, vv. 1283–93: τάδε τ' ἄναξ χάριν αὐτὸς ἐμὴν νέμε τῇ μονᾷ, μέζω | ἢ μὰν ἐμοίγε πασάων ἄλλων, ἃς δότο πολλὰς | ἄλλας ἐπ' ἄλλησι συνεχεῖς δῆτ' ἔξοχα πολλῶν, | οἳ σὺν ἐμοὶ πρό τ' ἐμεῦ θεράποντες ἐοῖο ἄριστοι· | δῶκε βασιλεὺς πρός τε θήκατο τῇ μονᾷ πολλοὺς | εἰν κτεάτεσσι πορισμούς, ἄγχι τε τούς γε πλεῦνας, | καί τέ γ' ἐνίους πόρρω, θησαυρίσματ' ἐπαρκῆ | δι' ἄρα πάντ' αἰῶνα βέβαια, δοῦμά γ' ἄσειστον | ἔμπεδον αἰέν, ἅτ' εἴθισται βασιλεῦσι ποιεῖν, | κρατύνας ἢ μάλ' ἐπιδοὺς θεσπιά τ' ἀκράδαντα.

105 Newness of the establishment: in *Logos* 15, fol. 331r (App. I, **3**.15), Metochites referred to the Chora's monastic community as νεόδμητον ἐποικοδόμησιν. The passage on fol. 335r (App. I, **14**.16–17) implies that monks had been in "training" for a relatively short time: καὶ πολλῶν ἐτῶν ἠσκημένους ἄμεινον. Public kitchen and hospital: ibid., fol. 336r (App. I, **17**.1–6): τὸ πρὸς τοὺς ἐπιδεεῖς ἔτ' ἔξω· . . . . τῆς ἀναγκαστῆς αὐτῆς τροφῆς . . . . κατ' ἔθος ἐκ τῶν ἐνόντων μεταδοτικόν . . . . μηδὲν ἧττον ἢ πρὶν ἐν τῷ νῦν . . . . καιρῷ· τὸ πρὸς τοὺς κάμνοντας ἐν νόσοις συμπαθές, καὶ πρὸς ἐπικουρίαν ἧντιν' ἔξεστιν ἕτοιμον διὰ τῆς ἐνούσης, εὖ μάλ' ὡς ἴστε, παρασκευῆς καὶ χρονίας ἤδη μάλιστ' . . . . ἐμέλησεν ἐμοὶ καὶ μηδὲν μᾶλλον τοῖς ἐντὸς . . . . ἢ καὶ τοῖς ἔξωθεν. There was a special superintendent who took care of the sick, ibid. (App. I, **17**.11–12): καὶ μελέτω μὲν τούτου πλεῖστον τῷ ταύτης ἐπιτρόπῳ καὶ ἐπιμελητῇ τῆς διακονίας.

Administration of monastic properties: ibid., fol. 336v (App. I, **18**.10–15); cf. n. 128 below.

106 TM, *Poem* 1, vv. 1212–13: μουναστὰς ἀτὰρ ἄλλοθεν ἄλλους νύ τ' ἀπολέξας | ξύν τ' ἀγήοχ' ἀριστίνδην. We even know the name of one of the monks from Asia Minor whom Metochites summoned to enter the new community: it was Makarios, who had left his home on account of Turkish incursions. Makarios, however, declined Metochites' invitation, for he yearned for more stringent forms of ascetic life. See Philotheos of Selymbria, Λόγος εἰς τὸν ὅσιον πατέρα ἡμῶν Μακάριον, ed. A. Papadopoulos-Kerameus, in Μαυρογορδάτειος Βιβλιοθήκη ('Ο ἐν Κωνσταντινουπόλει Ἑλληνικὸς Φιλολογικὸς Σύλλογος), Suppl. to Vol. 17 (Constantinople, 1886), esp. pp. 49–50.

107 TM, *Poem* 2, vv. 531–34: χ' ὕμμες ἱλήκοιτ' αὐτὸν [i.e., Christ] ἐμοί, Χώρας μονασταὶ | μάκαρες, ὑπὲρ ἐμεῖο λιτεύμενοι· ὡς γ' ἴσως | ὄφλετε, ὅττι κεν αὐτὸς ἐγὼ μάλα πουλλ' ἀμφ' ὑμῖν | προφρονέως κ' ἐμόγησα.

108 TM, *Poem* 2, vv. 411–22: Metochites should have joined the monks of the Chora, rather than πουλλοῖς ξυμφύραντ' ἄρα βορβόροισιν | . . . . | δυσχερέ' ἀνήνυτον ἁμαρτάνοντα διαμπάξ, | ἄσπετα μάλ' ἀέθλοντα, βαλλόμενον βάλλοντα | ἀμφαδὸν ὑπό τε νυκτιλόχοις κακοβουλίῃσι, | . . . . | τοῖς μὲν ἄρα βριάοντα, τοῖς δ' ἄρ ἐπιτρομάοντα | μάρνασθ' ἀνὰ φύλοπιν λευγαλέαν ἐπίδηλον, | τοῖς μὲν ἄδικον ἐπίκουρον, | ἀτὰρ ἄδικον ἄλλοις | ἐχθρόν.

109 See *Logos* 15, fol. 333r (App. I, **9**.14–17): καὶ τοίνυν ἐμεμνήμην ἡμερῶν ἀρχαίων . . . . ἐν αἷς ποτ' ἐγὼ τῷ βελτίστῳ ποιμένι [i.e., Lucas] συμπαρῆν ἐπὶ τοῦ ἱεροῦ, καὶ τοῦ καλοῦ χοροῦ συντελὴς ἦν, καὶ θιασώτης ἐν τοῖς πρὸς θεὸν ὕμνοις, ἡμέρας τε καὶ μεθ' ἡμέραν, νυκτὸς ἔστιν ὅτε καὶ πάννυχος ἔστιν ὅτε, καὶ συναδολεσχῶν τὰ θεῖα καὶ τοῖς τοῦ Χριστοῦ μυστηρίοις ἐνθεάζων. On singers, see *Poem* 1, vv. 1229–30: Metochites recruited οὕς νύ τ' ἄρ ἔθισται, | πρός τε μάλ' ἔμμεν' ὑμνῳδοὺς ἀπολέκτους χρεία.

110 See TM, *Poem* 2, vv. 154–57, addressing the Virgin: ἀτὰρ πουλλάκι συμφοράμασι μεγάλοις αὐτὸς | κατ' ἄρ βαπτόμενός γ' ἐμὸν ἧτορ, ἔπειτ' αὐτίκα | ὦκα μάλ' ἧια ἠύτε λιμένα ἔς γε τὴν σὰν | Χώραν, ἀχωρήτοιο θεοῖο πάναγνε χώρα.

relieve both his fears of imminent ruin and his sense of guilt.[111] In his own eyes the restoration of the Chora justified some of his rapaciousness. Poverty, he said, reduced the usefulness of men engaged in public life: what pauper could erect public or private buildings for use or for show? What pauper could be a benefactor of monks, either because he followed God's commandments or on account of his own refinement, noble character, and love of beauty?[112]

About 1326 he began to think seriously of retiring to the monastery.[113] However, he procrastinated too long. In May of 1328 came the fall, the pillage of his house, confiscation of all his possessions, and banishment to Didymoteichos.[114] But if he were ever allowed to return to Constantinople, he could still hope to enter the monastery. First of all, canon law provided that the founder of a monastery who had become destitute through no fault of his own had the right to demand support from his foundation.[115] Moreover, Metochites had an ally in the Chora, namely Lucas, a friend of long standing whom he had picked from among many candidates to be the first abbot of the restored monastery.[116] Lucas had the best credentials: he had grown up in the monastic communities of Asia Minor,[117] a milieu in which Metochites had spent his boyhood, which he had greatly esteemed and had remembered fondly in after years.[118] He was a bit on the simple side, for his speech was plain, but he was a good organizer and recruiter of monks.[119] He knew of Metochites' plans to retire to the monastery and could be counted on to receive Metochites with open arms whenever he would be released from exile. In the meantime, Lucas would steer the monastery, now deprived of Metochites' protection,[120] through difficult times.

---

111 Ibid., vv. 165–74: . . . . λῦτο δ' ἔνϑεν ἄρ ἄλγε' ἐμεῖο, | . . . . | ὡς μόνον ἀμφ' εἰκὼ μερόπεσσιν ὁμοίην Χριστοῦ | ὄσσε φέρον, ὅς κεν ὀπώποι· πρὸς δὲ | ματρὸς ἐοῖο πάρ' ἔγγιον [sic Paris. gr. 1776, fol. 40r; see n. 249 below] αὐτῷ λιτεούσης. | οὔκ ἂν ἔγωγε μυϑήσασϑ' οἷός τ' εἴην, ὡς κεν | αὐτόϑ' ἀγανὸν ἐμὸν κέαρ ἀλλάττοιτ' εὐηνὲς [i.q. εὐήνιον?] ἀμφὶ γάλην' ὁράων [cf. Euripides, Orestes, v. 279] καταπαῦόν τ' ἀλεγεινά, | ὄσσα δέ τ' ἄχϑεα κατ' ἄρ ἤγχεν ἐμεῖο ψυχάν.

112 Miscellanea, Ch. 84, esp. pp. 553–54: an impecunious person πρὸς τίνας ἂν χρείας τοῦ γένους καὶ τῆς πατρίδος ταχὺς ἀπαντῆσαι βοηϑὸς καὶ χορηγὸς εὐγενής τε καὶ ἐλευϑέριος, δεῆσαν; . . . . τίνας οἰκοδομὰς δημοσίας καὶ τίνας κατασκευὰς ἢ κατ' ἀνάγκην ἢ κατ' ἐπίδειξιν; τίνας ἰδίας αὖϑις ὡσαύτως λαμπρὰς λαμπρῶς ἀνιστὰς ἐπιχειρήσας ἀνύτειν . . . . οἷός τ' ἂν εἴη; τίσιν ἀνϑρώποις ἀνακειμένοις ϑεῷ καὶ λατρευταῖς ϑεοῦ, καὶ μόνῳ ζῆν ἑλομένοις ϑεῷ φιλάνϑρωπος ὀφϑείη, τὰ μὲν κατ' ἐντολὴν ϑείαν, τὰ δὲ τῆς ἀρετῆς αἰδοῖ καὶ φύσεως ἀστειότητι, καὶ τοιούτοις ἐμπρέψαι μάλα μὲν ἔργοις τιμίοις . . . . πρὸς ἃ πολλοὺς μὲν ἐλευϑέριοι καὶ φιλόκαλοι τρόποι πολλάκις ἐνάγουσι. Grand seigneur that he was, Metochites often expressed his scorn for the uneducated and for the lower classes. In Logos 10, he dismissed the "great mass," living like beasts and making no use of reason, fol. 191r: φημὶ δ' ὢν τις καὶ λόγος ἐστὶ βραχύς [i.e., the mediocrities belittling literature]. τῶν γὰρ δὴ πλειόνων τουτωνὶ τί ἂν τις καὶ μεμνῆτο, οἳ ϑρεμμάτων δίκην ἐπ' αἰσϑήσει μόνῃ τὸν ἅπαντα βίοτον ἐξανύτουσι; In the Miscellanea, Ch. 96, pp. 606 and 615, he made a case against democracy: Evil prevails in life; it follows that in an egalitarian system bad people would come out on top, while those who are superior would be silenced or even would lose their wealth and lives. The licentious mob is unbearable. All democracies are sickly, even if they are ruled by laws. The reason for this? Equality among people, whereas people are unequal by nature. Numerous examples could be quoted in support of this, both from ancient and from contemporary history: Genoa is rich, famous, boasts a powerful navy and military successes; yet, factions are sapping its strength from within.

113 Cf. nn. 101 and 102.

114 Gregoras, Hist., IX.6, Bonn, I, p. 425.11–23, and IX.7, ibid., p. 428.20–21.

115 S. Troicki, "Ktitorsko pravo u Vizantiji i u Nemanjičkoj Srbiji," Glas Srpske Kraljevske Akademije, 168 (1935), p. 120.

116 Logos 15, fol. 330r (App. I, 1.8): πόλλ' ἔτη, says Metochites, καὶ γὰρ ἤδη τοῦ ἀνδρὸς [i.e., Lucas] πεπειραμένος; fol. 331r (App. I, 4.7–8): ἀνὴρ οὕτω βέλτιστος ἐμοί. . . . καὶ συνήϑης χρόνιος, καὶ φιλῶν διαφερόντως; fol. 333r (App. I, 8.16–17): ἀνδρὶ φίλῳ [i.e., Lucas] . . . . πολλὴν πίστιν εὐνοίας—χρόνος ἐξ ὅτου μακρός—ἐμοὶ παρασχόντι; for choice of Lucas, fol. 333v (App. I, 11.1–2): καί μοι πρὸς τὸν ἐκκάοντα τῇ μονῇ πόϑον ἐν καιρῷ πολλῶν ἐκλόγιμος δειχϑεὶς καὶ καϑ' ὅσον ἄρα τις ἐστιν ἱκανόχρεος αὐτῇ τῇ μονῇ καὶ τῷ πόϑῳ; for Lucas as first abbot, fol. 330r (App. I, title): . . . . ἐπὶ τῇ τελευτῇ τοῦ πρώτου καϑηγουμένου.

117 Logos 15, fol. 333v (App. I, 10.3–11): Lucas was πολὺ μάλιστ' ἐκ μακροῦ βέλτιστα συνησκεμένος τῇ πείρα ταύτῃ [i.e., monastic discipline] καὶ τῶν καλλίστων ἐπιστήμη καὶ ἐκδοχῇ πάνυ τοι ϑαυμαστῶν ἀνδρῶν . . . . οὓς Ἰωνία τε καὶ Ἀσία πλείστους ἤνεγκέ τε καὶ ἔϑρεψε; καὶ κατ' ἐκείνους ἄρα τοὺς τόπους εἶχεν [i.e., "there were;" one of Metochites' rare vulgarisms], ὡς ἴσασιν ἅπαντες, πλεῖστά τε καὶ κομιδῇ περιφανέστατ', ἤπερ ἀλλοθί πη, μοναχικὰ συστήματα . . . . οἷς ἐννεάσας ἀνὴρ κἀκ πρώτης ἡλικίας καὶ παιδικῆς ἔτι πολλῶν ἐτῶν συνασκηϑείς, ... ἕξιν . . . . ἄσειστον . . . . ἐπὶ τούτοις ἐβεβαιώσατο. It was in Asia Minor that Lucas must have learned the ornate and meticulous fashion of conducting religious services: combine the passage just quoted with fol. 331v (App. I, 5.11–17): ὢ τῆς ἐν εὐχαῖς . . . . ἀγωγῆς ἀσχόλου . . . . ὢ τῆς ἐν ὑμνωδίαις . . . . καὶ πρὸς ϑεὸν ἐντυχίαις ἅμα παντὶ τῷ κοσμίῳ πάσης ἱκανώσεως καὶ ἀκριβείας· καὶ τῶν ἐν δευτέρῳ δοκούντων ἐνίοις καὶ ἥττονος λόγου.

118 Études, p. 270 with nn. 2 and 3.

119 Logos 15, fol. 331r–331v (App. I, 4.9–22): ὢ τῆς ἀκόμψου σοι [i.e., Lucas] γλώττης . . . . ὢ . . . . ὁμιλίας λόγων ἁπλῶς καὶ φωνῆς . . . . καὶ λέγοντι μὲν ἁπλοϊκῶς [i.e., Lucas] τὰ μάλιστ' ἐπεοικότα καϑάπαξ . . . . τοὺς ὑπὸ σὲ πείϑεσϑαι . . . . On recruiting, see fol. 332r (App. I, 6.9): τοῖς ὑπ' αὐτοῦ νεολέκτοις; and fol. 333v (App. I, 10.13): αὐτὸς ἠκρίβωσατο τὴν ἐπιλογήν.

120 Logos 15, fol. 330v (App. I, 3.5–7): χειμὼν τ' ἔξωϑεν καταιγίζει κατὰ τὸ παραστὰν τοῦ καιροῦ, ἐμοὶ δ' ἔχει τὰ πράγμαϑ' ὡς ἔχει, καὶ τὴν ἐμὴν ἐπικουρίαν ἀφήρησϑε, ἥτις ποτ' ἄρ' ἦν ἂν ἡ ἐμὴ τοῖς ἐμοῖς ὑμῖν ἐπικουρία. Cf. fol. 338r (App. I, 22.1–2), where Metochites deplores the difficulties that befell the Chora διὰ τὴν ἀντίπραξιν ὅπως ἄρα τοῦ καιροῦ, καὶ τοῦ καϑηγεμόνος ἐρημίαν, καὶ ἴσως καὶ τῆς

But while Metochites was in exile, Lucas died.[121] The blow could not have been heavier. What would become of the Chora? A banished man, Metochites could not make use of his prerogatives as a founder and had no decisive voice in the election of Lucas's successor.[122] The monastic community was of recent date and had not yet acquired that *esprit de corps* which comes only with tradition.[123] Would it remain unharmed with Metochites away and Lucas dead? Would the workers employed in the monastery or the monks entrusted with administrative tasks abstain from stealing its property? Would quarrels among the monks be avoided? Above all, would the Chora's vast properties, expecially those situated far from the capital, withstand the attacks of land-hungry supporters of the new regime?[124] Finally, what would become of the Chora's rich library and of Metochites' own works deposited there?

Seized by anxiety, he wrote a long letter[125] to the monks of the Chora, exhorting them to maintain peace and unanimity and to continue Lucas's policies.[126] The letter, seemingly dictated to an amanuensis, was compulsively repetitious; this time, the tiresome traits of Metochites' style were intensified by old age, unhappiness of exile, and emotional shock. The monks of the Chora must have been learned indeed to comprehend the letter's untidy periods, made up of synonymous phrases, strung one after another, and of mixed metaphors sprinkled with rare or unattested words. But even this amorphous flow carried some hard practical advice. In this time of trial, the monastery should continue its charitable activities; alms should be distributed,

---

ἡμετέρας ἐπικουρίας. Cf. fol. 334v (App. I, **12**.18–21): [Metochites is powerless] ὦ τί ποτ' ἂν ἐγὼ χρησαίμην νῦν οὕτως ἐργώδει τῇ τύχῃ καὶ χαλεποῖς τοῖς πράγμασιν, ἐνταῦθ' ὑπερόριος πόρρωθι ξυλλαχὼν ὑμῖν, καὶ μὴ κατ' ἔφεσιν ὅ,τι ποτ' ἔχων ὑμῖν δρᾶν; ἀλλὰ μὴν καὶ εἰ παρὼν ἔτυχον ἂν ὑμῖν, τί ποτ' ἂν ἔδρων, ὁπότε τὸ πρᾶγμα πάντοθεν δυσχερὲς ὁρῶσιν;
121 Metochites learned about Lucas' death, *Logos* 15, fol. 330r (App. I, **1**.5–6): ὡς δ' ἀμέλει νῦν τὴν τελευτὴν ἐπυθόμην τοῦ καλλίστου πάντα τὴν κατὰ θεὸν πολιτείαν ὑμῖν ἡγεμόνος, τί ποτ' ἐρῶ; Lucas died while Metochites was in exile, fol. 331r (App. I, **4**.6–7): ἀνὴρ ἐκεῖνος ἐκδημήσας–ὑπερορίῳ νῦν ἔμοιγε–καὶ τελευτήσας τὸν παρόντα βίον. Lucas died an old man, fol. 335r (App. I, **15**.1): τιμήσατε τὸν μακαρίτην ἐκεῖνον πρεσβύτην πατέρα.
122 This can be deduced from a passage in *Logos* 15, fol. 335r (App. I, **14**.6–17), where Metochites speaks of Lucas's successor. Either the successor will be a monk from the Chora (such is Metochites' wish; he hopes that the monks wish it as well), *or he will be an outsider*. If the former is the case, then things will run as usual; if the latter, the monks should prove by their good behavior how easy the new abbot's functions will be. On the various ways of electing abbots in Byzantine monasteries (usual method: vote by the community; frequent exclusion of outsiders, *exokouritai*), see R. Janin, "Le Monachisme byzantin au moyen-âge: Commende et typica (Xᵉ–XIVᵉ siècle)," *REB*, 22 (1964), esp. pp. 25–28.
123 *Logos* 15, fol. 330v (App. I, **3**.3–5): νεοταγεῖς γὰρ ὑμεῖς καὶ οὐκέτι πω τὰ καθ' ὑμᾶς εὐπαγῆ· ἔσωθί τε μήποτ' οὐ χρόνια καθάπαξ τῷ καθεστῶτι, μηδ' ἀκράδαντα καὶ θάρρος ἔχοντα καὶ πίστιν τῇ συνεχείᾳ τῆς καθιδρύσεως καὶ συμπήξεως.
124 *Logos* 15, fol. 337r–337v (App. I, **20**.7–13): πολὺ δὲ μάλιστ' ἢ κατ' αὐτὰ μέλει [i.e., is of concern to Metochites] τοῦ μηδένας ἐξ ὑμῶν, τὴν αὐτῶν [i.e., monastic property] ἐπισκοπὴν καὶ διοίκησιν πιστευθέντας, σκαιωρεῖσθαι σφίσιν ἴδια τὰ κοινὰ καὶ δυσνοϊκῶς ἀνδραποδίζεσθαι σὺν δόλῳ καὶ λωποδυτεῖν καὶ ὑπευθύνους εἶναι τοιαύταις αἰσχίσταις κακουργίαις καὶ κλοπαῖς· περὶ ὧν, ἐμοὶ δοκεῖν, κἂν ἐπί τινων τοῦ πολλοῦ λεώ, καὶ δημοτῶν τινων ἀποχειροβιώτων ἀνδρῶν, κἀκ παντὸς τρόπου προθεμένων πορίζεσθαι .... αἰσχύνοιτό τις; cf. fol. 337r (App. I, **19**.3–4), warning against ἔνιοι τῶν φαύλων ἐπιτρόπων, ἐν τοῖς τοιούτοις κακοὶ κακῶς χρησάμενοι τῇ διοικήσει καὶ νοσφισάμενοι τὰ κοινά. On

avoiding quarrels, cf. fol. 335v (App. I, **15**.8–12): ἀπέστω πᾶσα δύσχρηστος ἔρις ὑμῶν .... ἀπέστω φθόνος, ἀπέστω φιλαρχία, κακοῦργον ἦθος ἀπέστω .... καὶ ὅσα τῆς πονηρᾶς ἕξεως .... ἀπέστω καὶ κακοσχόλου, καὶ θόρυβον καὶ σάλον ἐμποιούσης τῷ συστήματι. ὁμοφροσύνη πρὸ πάντων ἤτω πᾶσι πᾶσα. On danger to the monastery's more distant possessions, cf. fol. 336v (App. I, **18**.10–15): καὶ τοίνυν τηρητέον μὲν καὶ προσεκτέον εὖ μάλ' ἀσχολουμένους τὸν νοῦν, ὡς ἂν ἄρ' εἰκὸς τόδε καὶ ἀνεμέσητον, ἄττα κατὰ τὴν μονὴν τεθησαύρισται καὶ περὶ τὴν μονὴν ἔγγιον, καὶ σπουδαστέον ἀθθῶν, τὴν ἐντεῦθεν ἐπιεικῶς συντέλειαν. προσεκτέον δὲ πρός γ' ὑμῖν καὶ ἄττα ἐκτός, καὶ πολὺ μάλιστ' ἐνταῦθα προσεκτέον τὸν νοῦν, πλείονά τε γὰρ καὶ πολλῆς ἐπιμελείας δεόμενα, διὰ τὴν πλείον' ἴσως ἐνοχλοῦσαν ἐν σφίσι τῶν ἐπ' ἐρημίας ἐπανισταμένων ἐπήρειαν.
125 This letter (*Logos* 15, from which I abundantly quoted in previous notes), is entitled Πρὸς τοὺς μοναχοὺς τῆς Χώρας ἐπὶ τῇ τελευτῇ τοῦ πρώτου καθηγουμένου αὐτῶν Λουκᾶ· μονῳδία τε ἐπ' αὐτῷ καὶ προτροπὴ αὐτοῖς εἰς τὴν ἐπιμέλειαν τοῦ καλοῦ, and is published below, as Appendix I. For contents, but not for style, which is lucid, concise, and elegant in one case and illiterate in the other, good contemporary parallels to Metochites' Letter are: (1) the *Speech on the Restoration of the Church of the Resurrection* (addressed to monks, since the "Church" was really a monastery) by Constantine Akropolites, ed. H. Delehaye, "Constantini Acropolitae Hagiographi Byzantini Epistularum Manipulus," *Analecta Bollandiana*, 51 (1933), pp. 279–84, and (2) Patriarch Athanasius I's letters contained in Vat. gr. 2219: To an abbot elected by his own monastery (fols. 176v–178r); To a monastery on Mount Athos which had requested an abbot from among members of its community (fols. 178r–181v); and To the monks of the Lavra of St. Athanasius who had requested an abbot (fols. 249r–252r).
126 Unanimity: *Logos* 15, fol. 334v (App. I, **13**.6–8): πρῶτον μὲν τὸν τῆς εἰρήνης καὶ ὁμονοίας ὑμῖν σύνδεσμον μὴ λύσαντες, καὶ ὡς ἐν ἄρα σῶμα συμφυὲς καὶ ἡρμοσμένον εὖ μάλα τὸν εἰωθότα τέως τρόπον, τὴν καλὴν ἀγωγὴν τηροῦντες, καὶ κινούμενοι. ... Cf. fol. 335v (App. I, **16**.1–4): τὸ κοινωνικὸν διὰ πάντων ὡσαύτως ἤτω .... τὸ φιλόκοινον καὶ φιλάλληλον, καὶ τοῖς ταπεινοῖς ἐπικύπτον τε καὶ συμπῖπτον. On continuity of policies, see fol. 335r (App. I, **13**.16–18): καὶ τηροῖθ' ὡσαύτως ἀλώβητα τἀνδρός, μηδὲν ἧττον ὡς ἄρα πρίν, τἀπιτάγματα. καὶ οὐκ οἶδ' ὅ,τι ποτ' ἂν ἄμεινον ὑμῖν εἴη τοῦδε τὸν ἀεὶ χρόνον.

hospital services, for which it was well equipped, dispensed, and hardships countered by hard work.[127] Experienced and energetic men should be chosen to administer the Chora's landed properties and to ward off covetous hands, which were stretching toward its outlying possessions.[128]

The point which caused him most concern, Metochites put at the end of the epistle: it had to do with the monastery's library. Nothing would make him more unhappy than to learn that the collection he had deposited at the Chora had suffered from neglect, that books had been damaged by worms, had decayed, or had been taken away. The monks owed it to their benefactor that the Chora's books should be preserved with utmost care.[129]

But would these pious exhortations be effective? The collection was of interest mainly to lay scholars; its scope transcended the needs and interests of the monks, although some of them might have found it useful on occasion.[130] To make doubly sure, he wrote another missive, dealing exclusively with the books. This was in the form of a poem addressed to Nicephorus Gregoras.[131] Metochites had taken a great interest in this able young man more than twenty years his junior. He had initiated him into astronomy, settled him in the Chora soon after the restoration, and made him preceptor to two of his children.[132] In the poem he applied a mixture of moral pressure and flattery. He reminded Gregoras of his past favors, made him successor to his astronomical fame, and even intimated that the Chora had been restored so that Gregoras might have congenial surroundings in which to pursue his studies [133]—Christ and the Virgin

127 *Logos* 15, fol. 336r (App. I, **17**.1–7): Metochites recommended τὸ πρὸς τοὺς ἐπιδεεῖς ἔτ' ἔξω καὶ πολλοὺς καὶ τῆς ἀναγκαστῆς αὐτῆς τροφῆς καὶ τῶν ἀπαραιτήτων τῇ φύσει δασμῶν κατ' ἔθος ἐκ τῶν ἐνόντων μεταδοτικὸν καὶ φίλοικτον τῇ χρείᾳ, καὶ μηδὲν ἧττον ἢ πρίν, ἐν τῷ νῦν ὑμῖν τῆς δυσκολίας καιρῷ· τὸ πρὸς τοὺς κάμνοντας . . . . συμπα-θές, καὶ πρὸς ἐπικουρίαν ἥντιν' ἔξεστιν ἕτοιμον διὰ τῆς ἐνούσης, εὖ μάλ' ὡς ἴστε, παρασκευῆς καὶ χρονίας ἤδη μάλιστ' ἐξ ἀρχῆς προθέσεως, καὶ ἧς μάλιστ' ἐμέλησεν ἐμοί· καὶ μηδὲν μᾶλλον τοῖς ἐντὸς καὶ συμβιοῦσί τε καὶ συντρόφοις, ἢ καὶ τοῖς ἔξωθεν οἱστισινοῦν, ὅποι ἄρα παρείκοι. For exhortation to hard work, see, fol. 338r (App. I, **22**.1–4): εἰ δὲ καὶ νῦν ὑμῖν τὸ τῆς χρήσεως ἐργωδέστερον, ξυμβὰν διὰ τὴν ἀντίπραξιν ὅπως ἄρα τοῦ καιροῦ . . . . ὑμῖν, ἐπείγεσθαι καὶ π ο ν ε ῖ ν ἐ σ τ ι π λ έ ο ν, καὶ ὅσον ἐν καιρῷ τῆς χρείας, καὶ ἡ τῶν πραγμάτων ἀνάγκη πράττεται. καὶ δὴ πονεῖτε μάλισθ' οὕτω κρίνοντες ἢ δέοι ἂν καὶ πλεονεκτεῖτε τοῖς καμάτοις.

128 *Logos* 15, fol. 336v (App. I, **18**.15–20): καὶ διανεμητέον τοὺς περὶ τούτων [i.e., monastic properties, especially the outlying ones] πόνους καὶ τὴν φροντίδα πεπειραμένοις ἀνδράσι καὶ τὸ πιστὸν τῆς λειτουργίας ἐντεῦθεν ἔχουσιν· ἅμα μὲν πρὸς τὸ γιγνόμενον ἅπαν καὶ τὴν ἄσχολον καὶ τεχνικὴν ἕξιν τῆς ἐργασίας καὶ πάντ' εὐδιοίκητον ἀνύτειν· ἅμα δὲ καὶ πρὸς τὸ κρατερῶς καὶ μὴ ἀνειμένως μηδ' ἀσθενῶς ἀποδίδεσθαι καὶ συνίστασθαι καὶ συναεθλεύειν πρὸς τοὺς ἐπιτιθεμένους ἑκάστοτε μετὰ τοῦ καιροῦ, καὶ δύνασθαί πως οἰκονομεῖν τε καὶ φέρειν γεννικῶς τὰ ξυμπίπτοντα. Cf. fol. 337r (App. I, **20**.1–7): καὶ τοίνυν ὡς οὐκ ἀδόκητον ὃ νῦν ἐλέγομεν, φυλάτ-τεσθαι καὶ κατασφαλίσασθαι τὴν τῶν ὑμετέρων ἐπισκοπὴν καὶ διοίκησιν τοῖς μεταχειρίζειν ἀποτεταγμένοις ταῦτ' ἐξ ὑμῶν· ὡς ἐμοὶ μὲν καὶ τοῦ μηδὲν ὑποσυλᾶσθαι καὶ παραιρεῖσθαι τῶν ἐπιβαλλόντων καὶ διαφερόντων ὑμῖν . . . . πολὺ μέλει—ἢ τί γὰρ οὔ;—καὶ τὸ πρὸς τοὺς ἐπηρεαστὰς ἀνθίστασθαι, καὶ μὴ ὀλιγώρως ἐκκεῖσθαι τὰ ὑμέτερα συγχωρεῖν τῇ κατὰ σφᾶς αὐτοὺς βίᾳ καὶ ταῖς ἁρπαγαῖς, καὶ ὥστε χειμάρρου δίκην ταῖς αὐτῶν ἐπιδρομαῖς παρασύρεσθαι.

129 *Logos* 15, fol. 339r (App. I, **24**.5–12): ὡς ἐμοί γ' ἂν ἀλγεινότατον εἴη, καὶ οὐκ οἶδ' εἴ τινος ἧττον ἄλλου τῶν ἐμοὶ δυσχερῶν, καὶ μέσης ἁπτόμενον δριμύτατα γένοιτ' ἄν, οἶμαι, τῆς καρδίας, εἰ ἄρα πυθοίμην ἄλλως περὶ τούτων, ἢ ὡς ἐπιτέλλω καὶ βούλομαι, καί τιν' αὐτῶν [i.e., the books] ἀμέλει σεσυλημένα πυθοίμην, καὶ τὴν μονὴν ἐρημωθεῖσαν αὐτῶν καὶ χηρεύουσάν, τινα δὲ καὶ ἀτημελήτως ἔχοντα, θριπηδέστατα

130 *Logos* 15, fol. 338v (App. I, **23**.3–9): τὸν μὲν ἐγὼ φθάσας πλοῦτον [i.e., the collection] ἐνεθέμην τῇ μονῇ . . . . καὶ ἴσως οὐ χρειωδέστατον τῇ μονῇ μόνον, ἀλλὰ καὶ ὑπὲρ τὴν ὑμῶν χρείαν λυσιτελέστατον, καὶ περισπούδαστον καὶ ποθεινὸν εὖ μάλα τοι τοῖς περὶ λόγους ἔχουσι· καὶ παρὰ τῇ μονῇ τάχ' ἂν ἐστιν οἷς καὶ ἔστιν ὅτε, μᾶλλον δ' ἀεὶ τόδ' ἐστὶ καὶ πολλοῖς ἄλλοις ἐκτός.

131 *Poem* 4, fols. 59v–69r: Εἰς τὸν σοφὸν Νικηφόρον τὸν Γρηγορᾶν ὑποθῆκαι, καὶ περὶ τῶν οἰκείων συνταγμάτων. Summary and extracts by Guilland, "Les poésies" (as in n. 6 above), pp. 269–80. The poem was written from exile, see Gregoras, *Hist.*, VIII.5, Bonn, I, p. 309.8–11: Metochites διάδοχον τῆς αὐτοῦ σοφίας ἐπεποιήκει με. δείκνυσι δὲ τοῦτο σαφέστερον ἔν τε ταῖς πρὸς ἐμὲ τούτου ἐπιστολαῖς [these are lost], ἔν τε τοῖς ἔπεσιν [i.e., *Poem* 4], ἃ πεποίηκεν ὕστερον ἐ ν τ ῇ ἐ ξ ο ρ ί ᾳ α ὐ τ ο ῦ.

132 Astronomy: see Gregoras, *Hist.*, VIII.7, Bonn, I, p. 322.4–6 and p. 327.5–9; TM, *Poem* 4, fol. 64v, reproduced in Guilland, "Les poésies," p. 271 (in Guilland's line 179, read ἀμφ' ἵμερόν τ'). Stay at the Chora: Gregoras, *Hist.*, VIII.5, Bonn, I, pp. 308.24–309.2. Preceptorship: ibid., p. 309.15–19; cf. R. Guilland, *Essai sur Nicéphore Grégoras: l'homme et l'oeuvre* (Paris, 1926), pp. 7–8.

133 Past favors: *Poem* 4, fol. 67r–67v: ὅττι κεν ὄφλεις τάδ' [i.e., the preservation of Metochites' writings] ἆρ ἐμοιγε-πουλλὸν | οὕνεκα, καὐτὸς ἐρέεις σύ, ἠδέ τε πάντες ὅσοισιν | ἡμέες ἐσμὲν ἀρίγνωτοι, ἔασι δέ γε συχνοὶ | οἵ . . . . ἴσασι μάλ' ἀτμητα | τὰ σὰ δι' ἄρα συνάρσαντ' ἀφορμῇσι πολλαῖς· | τῶν ἕνεκ' ὄφλων, ὡς γ' ἐφάμην, χάριν ἄτροπόν μοι, | μνῆστιν ἐμεῖο σὺ μήποτε λίποις. Initiation into astronomy and succession to astronomical fame: ibid., fol. 64r: αὐτὰρ ἔπειτα πονοίης ἀμφί τ' αὖ τεττάρων | βιβλίων μαθηματικῶν εὐμαθίαν, ὧν κεν | μάλ' ἔρασαι, τῶν δ' αὖ μάλιστ' ἀστρουνομίης | πουλυτίμοιο

Mary would forgive him for this new dedication of a building which he had dedicated to each of them in turn. From exile, Metochites appointed Gregoras guardian of his whole literary output—"the dividends of our wisdom"—and of the Chora's library and entreated him to preserve these treasures, and especially his own astronomical work, for the benefit of future generations.[134]

The two years of exile were the worst of Metochites' life. He was treated harshly and insulted. His illness required a special diet, and the wine, fish, pulse, and vegetables of Didymoteichos were abominable. The *vin du pays* turned sour in no time, fruits in general were scarce, and figs were simply not to be found.[135] But after two years in Didymoteichos [136] he was allowed to return to Constantinople and to settle in the Chora. When he looked out from his window and saw the nearby spot where his mansion had stood before May 1328, he was overcome by grief.[137] But at least the Chora remained untouched. The popular ire had stopped short of it, although for a moment it, too, had been seriously threatened by the rabble.[138]

He also found that his missives sent from Didymoteichos had produced the desired effect: the Chora's library had been preserved. This large public library included almost complete collections of sacred and secular authors and, among the latter, works of philosophers and poets. He was prouder of it than of any other gift he had given to the monastery.[139]

μεγαλωνύμου, τὴν ἄρ ἐμεῖο | ἐκδεξάμενος, ἂν σουφοῖσι γένου [*sic* accent] περίφαμος. Cf. fol. 65r: πάντ᾽ ἐμέθεν διδάχαο ᾽πιτυχῶς εὖ μάλ᾽ ἀνύσας. Cf. fol. 64v (passage published in Guilland, "Les poésies," p. 271), where Metochites asserted that he had "eagerly" and "generously" expounded the tenets of astronomy to his pupil Gregoras: ἐσσυμένως γὰρ ἐγὼν ἀπηγεόμην and κτήσαο . . . . πάντα . . . . ἄ φ θ ο ν ᾽ ἐμεῖο. Gregoras, however, intimated that at first Metochites had been reluctant to teach him astronomy, *Hist.*, VIII.7, Bonn, I, p. 322.6–10, esp. p. 322.7–8: ο ὐ δ ᾽ αὐτῆς δὴ τῆς ἀστρονομίας ἄ φ θ ό ν ω ς μεταδιδόναι ἐβούλετο. Metochites wrote his *Poem* 4 to Gregoras after 1328; intervening years, the teacher's point of view, and exile may have dimmed his recollections. Chora restored for Gregoras, and Gregoras, in a strange pun, called "Chora" (container) of Metochites' literary heritage: *Poem* 4, fols. 68v–69r, passage reproduced in Guilland, "Les poésies," pp. 277–78 (in line 340, read γένε᾽ and τεκέεσσ᾽; in line 341, read ὥς κ᾽ ἐν; in line 349, read δέχνοιο; in line 359, read πρόφρονι νῷ; in line 360, read ἐρίηρος).

134 *Poem* 4, fol. 65r, reproduced in Guilland, "Les poésies," p. 272 (in Guilland's line 208, read παρτίθεμ᾽ αὐτός; in line 209, read βίβλι᾽ ἅπερ; in line 210, read ἔραμ᾽; in line 212, read μογοστόκοιο᾽ and ἔμοιγε; in line 215, read ἄμαδις; in line 216, read παρασύρητ᾽ ἄν; in line 218, read ὑστατίοισιν ἔτεσσιν). Cf. *Poem* 4, fol. 67v (Guilland, "Les poésies," p. 275; in line 298, read σύν μοι; in line 299, read ποήματ᾽; in line 300, read χρούνοις; in line 303, read σύνταγμ᾽); fol. 67r (Guilland, "Les poésies," p. 274), followed by these lines: καί σ᾽ ἐπιτάρροθον ἠδέ τ᾽ ἐ π ί τ ρ ο π ο ν ἀμφ᾽ ἄρα σφιν | παρτίθεμαι μελεδωνόν τ᾽ αὖ ἀπὸ λοιγὸν ἐέργειν | σφείων [i.e., Metochites' literary works]; fol. 68r–68v (Guilland, "Les poésies," p. 276; in line 333, read ἔραμ᾽ ὧν σοι δῆτ᾽ ἐπιτέλλω; in line 335, read παρμείνειε), especially: σοὶ γὰρ ἐ π ι τ ρ ό π ῳ τάδε παρτίθεμ᾽ ἀσφαλίσασθαι; see, finally, fols. 68v–69r (Guilland, "Les poésies," p. 277) for entrusting the Chora's whole collection to Gregoras, and the expression ἐκτόκια σοφίης ἀμεδαπῆς. In his later life, Gregoras may have had Metochites' *Poem* 4 and its repeated use of the term ἐπίτροπος in mind when he claimed (*Hist.*, XXII.2, Bonn, II, p. 1046.3–6) that Metochites had entrusted him with the supervision (ἐπιτροπήν) of the "better and more necessary" parts of the Chora (i.e., its library?) and that thus in a sense (τρόπον τινά) he made him his successor (διάδοχος).

135 Illness and harsh treatment by ruffians at Didymoteichos: Gregoras, *Hist.*, IX.8, Bonn, I, p. 431.9–14. Bad wine and food: see Metochites' letter to the monk Methodius Senacherim (resident of Stagira?) in which he discussed the body and the smoothness of wines. Summary of the letter in *Speculum*, 27 (1952), p. 155, n. 76 *a*; text, from Vaticanus Urbinas gr. 151, fols. 378r–379v, published below, Appendix II, pp. 86–89. If Metochites suffered considerably in exile, it was because his palate had been accustomed to the wines, fish, and vegetables of Constantinople, which were relished (τρυφῶμεν) by Byzantine gourmets (οἱ τῇ γαστρὶ χαριζόμενοι); see George Akropolites' letter to John Tornikes ed. Heisenberg, *Georgii Acropolitae Opera*, Teubner (1903), II, pp. 68.35–69.3: ἢ καὶ τὰ πολυειδῆ τῶν ἰχθύων ἔθνη ὡς οὐδὲν ἡγῇ . . . . καὶ τὰς διαφόρους ὀπώρας καὶ τὰς ἀνθοσμίας [i.e., bouquet] τῶν οἴνων . . . . ὧν ἡ Κωνσταντίνου μετέσχεν ὑπερπλησμίως;

136 *Études*, p. 8, n. 2.

137 Gregoras, *Hist.*, IX.13, Bonn, I, pp. 458.23–459.3; 459.13–18. Metochites was especially distressed by the removal of the (marble?) floor tiles from his palace. The floor was made a gift to the ruler of "western Scythians" [Tartars?], and Gregoras considered this to have been an unprecedented event; ibid., p. 459.18–24. However, a somewhat later parallel may be adduced: the Turks of Umūr-Paşa valued the floor tiles of a church so highly that they removed them in batches and carried them away on their ships; Irène Mélikoff-Sayar, tr. and ed., *Le Destān d'Umūr Pacha* (Bibliothèque byzantine: Documents, 2; [Paris, 1954], p. 87, v. 1151).

138 See my "Observations" (as in n. 129 above), pp. 285–86. See also TM, *Logos* 15, fol. 330v (App. I, **2.**8–16), on the dangers which threatened the Chora in 1328: καὶ προσκείσθω . . . . καὶ τοῦτο δ᾽ ἀμέλει κατ᾽ ὀφθαλμοὺς ὡσανεὶ καθορᾶν ἐν κινδύνῳ καὶ φθορᾶς ἐν χρῷ γεγονός· τὸ καθ᾽ ὑμᾶς φημι σαφῶς οὑτωσὶ καὶ τὴν μονήν.

139 TM, *Logos* 15, fol. 339r (App. I, **24.**3–5): . . . . καὶ οὐχ ἱερὰ μόνον, ἀλλὰ καὶ τῆς ἔξω περιττῆς σοφίας, καὶ οὐδ᾽ ὑμῖν [i.e., the monks] ἔστιν οἷστισιν ἴσως ἄρα περιφρονητῆς καὶ ἀχρείου—καὶ πολλοῖς ἄλλοις χρειωδέστατ᾽ αἰεί. Cf. *Poem* 4, fol. 69r, reproduced in Guilland, "Les poésies" (as in n. 6 above), p. 277, vv. 352–56; cf. *Poem* 1, vv. 1145–52: . . . . ταμεῖον ἔτ᾽ αὐτὴν [i.e., the Chora] . . . . | παντοίων θέμαι ἠδὲ πολυαρίθμων βίβλων, | ἠμὲν ὅσαι τῆς ἡμετέρης σοφίης ἔασι . . . . | . . . . | ἠδ᾽ ἐθ᾽ ὅσαι τῆς θύραθεν Ἑλλήνων σοφίης | χ᾽ αὗται πουλλαὶ κ α ὶ σ χ ε δ ὸ ν ἅ ς τ᾽ ἐ γ ν ώ κ α μ ε ν, οἵ γε | ἀμφὶ λόγους σπουδὴν ἔχομεν; cf. vv. 1166–68. On the public character of the library, see vv. 1160–61 (φιλανθρώπευμα πάγκοινόν γ᾽ ἐκκείμενον ἔς τ᾽ ἄρα πάντας βρουτούς), 1166–68 (ἐκκέεται χρῆσις πάγκοινος), 1177 (βίβλους κοινὸν ἀν᾽ ἅπασιν ἀγαθόν); cf. Maximus Planudes' Ep. 67 (to Theodore Muzalon), lines 56–57, ed. Treu, . . . *Planudis Epistulae*, p. 83: μαρτύριον ἡ καθ᾽ ἡμᾶς ἡδὲ μονὴ τὴν βασιλικὴν βιβλιοθήκην τοῖς φιλομαθέσι προτείνουσα· αὕτη μὲν γὰρ ἐπ᾽ ἐλάχιστα ταῖς ἐν αὐτῇ χρῆται

Of course, Metochites overstated his case when he claimed to have founded the collection. The imperial monastery of the Chora had already possessed an imperial library, and some forty years earlier the learned Maximus Planudes attempted to take care of it, but at his time the condition of the books was no better than the condition of the monastery itself.[140] Thus Metochites could take credit for establishing the largest and the best of all the monastic libraries of the capital.[141] His own works were among the choicest items of the collection, for the good Gregoras did justify the hopes which Metochites had placed in him. In these volumes, written on parchment, the titles of sections imitated the ancient lettering of Constantine Porphyrogennitos' time.[142] The volumes themselves were authenticated by monograms for "logothete," for "Theodoros," and for "Metochites," inscribed on the first and the last pages (Figs. A, B), the same monograms which he had placed on the cornice of the main dome in the church of the monastery (Figs. C a–d).[143] Thus, when he looked at these de luxe volumes, Metochites could think that his life had not quite been a failure.

The two years of his stay in the Chora were bleak: he wrote a few poems deploring his fate, a rhetorical piece, perhaps a life of a saint;[144] he worried about his sons, imprisoned by the government;[145] he suffered further from illness. He died on the thirteenth of March of 1332 as the monk Theoleptos, probably assuming the monastic garb on his deathbed; he was buried in the monastery he had restored.[146]

· III ·

Metochites' writings—his Commentaries on Aristotle, his Miscellaneous Essays, his Introduction to Astronomy, his Orations, and his Poems—amount to almost nineteen hundred folios.[147] Sources, models, and authorities can be detected in this bulky output. Metochites

---

βίβλοις, τοῖς δ' ἄλλοις κοινὸν ἀνέῳγε πρυτανεῖον καὶ ἄφθονον. This "monastery of ours" is the Chora; see Wendel, "Planudea," *BZ*, 40 (1940), p. 407. On the pride which Metochites took in the library, see *Logos* 15, fol. 338v (App. I, **23**.9–13): καὶ οὐκ οἶδα τί ποτ' ἂν ἄμεινον εἴη τῆς ἐμῆς προνοίας τῇ μονῇ καὶ συντελείας φιλανθρώπευμα, καὶ βιωφελέστατον ἐν παντὶ κατ' ἀνθρώπους . . . . ἢ τὸ χρῆμα τοῦτο καὶ ἡ πολυέραστος αὕτη τὸν ἀεὶ χρόνον οὐσία, καὶ μὴ δαπανώμενος, κἂν εἰ μάλιστ' ἐκφέροιτο, καὶ πρὸς πολλούς, θησαυρός.

140 Bindings were decaying, the librarian gave no account of his activity, the lending service kept no adequate records, and books were disappearing or deteriorating in vast numbers. See Wendel, "Planudes als Bücherfreund" (as in n. 27 above), p. 82; and Planudes' Ep. p. 67 (to Theodore Muzalon), lines 54–114, ed. Treu, . . . *Planudis Epistulae*, pp. 83–85.

141 In *Logos* 15, fol. 338v (App. I, **23**.2–6), Metochites thus admonished the monks: ὅπως φυλάσσοιτέ μοι τὰ ταμιεῖα τοῦ καλλίστου πλούτου, τῶν πολυτιμήτων βίβλων, ἐν ἀσφαλεῖ . . . . τὸν μὲν ἐγὼ φθάσας πλοῦτον ἐνεθέμην τῇ μονῇ προνοήσας, πλεῖστον ἀμέλει, καὶ οὐκ οἶδ' εἰ καὶ ἄλλη ποι τοσοῦτον· ἔφην δ' ἄν, εἰ μὴ νεμεσητά γ' ἴσως ἦν καὶ φορτικὸν ἔδοξεν ἄν, εἰ καὶ παρὰ ταῖς ἄλλαις αὐτόθι πάσαις μοναῖς τοσοῦτον ἅμα τῷ τοιοῦτον εἶναι. Realizing Metochites' ambitions, his contemporaries must have enriched the Chora's library by their donations. We know of one, perhaps even of two, such gestures. To repay Metochites for past favors and in order to elicit new ones from him, Dionysios, Metropolitan of Mitylene, offered the Chora a volume of *Ascetica* and had Manuel Philes write a dedicatory poem on that occasion, see Ἐκ προσώπου τοῦ μητροπολίτου Μιτυλήνης Θεοδοσίου [read: Διονυσίου] τῷ μεγάλῳ λογοθέτῃ διὰ βιβλίον, ὃ προσήνεξε τῇ αὐτοῦ μονῇ τῆς Χώρας, ed. Gedeon, pp. 658–59. A δέσποινα Maria Comnene Palaeologina, styled ἡ τῆς Ἑῴας βασιλίς, commissioned a poet to write a dedication in a now missing eleventh-century (?) Gospel, which she had found badly damaged, "in this foreign land;" she had provided it with a luxury binding and offered it to the Virgin of the Chora

(text of the poem in *BZ*, 3 [1894], pp. 326–27). The noble lady may have been Mary, Despoina of the Mongols (Papadopulos, *Genealogie*, No. 54), an older contemporary of Metochites and a patroness of the Chora, and the poet who wrote the dedication may have been Manuel Philes. See the astute reasoning by C. Mango and P. A. Underwood in *DOP*, 12 (1958), p. 287, n. 50, and the fact that the poem's closing line speaks of τῆς Ἐδὲμ κατοικίαν, a turn of phrase of which Philes was very fond; see end of n. 14 above.

142 This is true of the uncials in Vat. gr. 1365 and Paris. gr. 1776. The lettering of Vindobon. ph. gr. 95 and Paris. gr. 2003 imitates the elegant Constantinopolitan "pearlscript" of the eleventh century; see H. Hunger, *Studien zur griechischen Paläographie* (Vienna, 1954), pp. 30–31 and PL. X.

143 Paris. gr. 2003, fols. 7r and 278r (*Miscellanea*, written in Metochites' time; see Figs. A and B below); Marcianus gr. 239 (N.C. 911), fols. 1r and 557r (Commentaries on Aristotle; variant: γενικοῦ; the manuscript exhibits the signature of Bessarion [fol. 1r]; it was copied from an "authenticated" manuscript, whose monograms it took over); Vindobon. ph. gr. 8, sixteenth century, fol. 4v (*Miscellanea*; the whole manuscript, monograms and all, goes back to Paris. gr. 2003). For Metochites' monograms carved in bosses on the dome cornice of the nave of the Chora, see Underwood in *DOP*, 12 (1958), p. 270, and Fig. C a–d below.

144 Some (which?) of the *Poems* 14–20, cf. Guilland, "Les poésies," pp. 298–301; *Logoi* 17 and 18, cf. *Etudes*, p. 143.

145 Gregoras, *Hist.*, X.2, Bonn, I, p. 474.15–18. In view of the information gathered in n. 81 above, it would be surprising if Demetrius Angelus were among the arrested sons of Metochites.

146 See my *Etudes*, p. 8, n. 2, and, now, Loenertz in *OCP*, 30 (1964), pp. 40 and 51; he advocates the date of March 14 or "13 at night."

147 More exactly, to 1881 folios, sum total of folios in Parisini graeci 1886 (318 fols.), 1935 (294 fols.), 2003 (278 fols.), 1776 (240 fols.), Vindobon. ph. gr. 95 (373 fols.), and Vat. gr. 1365 (378 fols.).

knew much more than the rank and file writer, who, in poetry, would be satisfied with two books of the Iliad, Hesiod, some Pindar, three tragedies each of Sophocles and Euripides, some Theocritus;[148] and in prose, with Aelius Aristides, an oration or two by Demosthenes, and Gregory of Nazianzus' Eulogy of St. Basil. Metochites knew all of Gregory, especially his poetry;[149] he read and reread Thucydides[150] and especially Plutarch.[151] In addition to Plutarch, he discussed Philo and Dio of Prusa and mentioned some eighty other authors, many of whom he had actually read. He was reticent about some others, like Iamblichus and Proclus, whom he plagiarized.[152] Being a sophisticated author, he often quoted by allusion and paraphrase.[153] Being a hasty writer, he sometimes misunderstood his sources, even if they were as familiar to him as Lucian or Plutarch;[154] or he mistook for Plato what was not by that author, when he copied a Platonic quotation from Iamblichus;[155] or he quoted Archilochus, but thought he was quoting a

148 See A. Dain, "A propos de l'étude des poètes anciens à Byzance," *Studi in onore di Ugo Enrico Paoli* (Florence, 1956), pp. 195–201, esp. 198–99; Dain discusses both the Moschopulean *Sylloge* and the lampoon written by Metochites' contemporary John (?) Katrares against the monk Neophytos Prodromenos. To expose Neophytos' ignorance, Katrares quoted authors whom his enemy scorned or of whom he was ignorant. The list consists of Euripides, Aeschylus, Sophocles, Aristophanes, Hesiod, *Gnomic Sayings* by Ps.-Menander, Pindar, and Homer. Neophytos did learn Theocritus, Katrares granted him this much, but it was because he had been a shepherd a short time before; he also knew the *Gnomic Sayings* by Theognis, relevant to the plight of a pauper like himself (see Theognis, *Eleg.*, 1, vv. 175–78). Irony aside, Katrares gave the list of poets whom a second-rate bookman was likely to have read in school. Note that the mediocre Γνῶμαι of Ps.-Menander are given a place of honor between Hesiod and Pindar. See I. Dujčev, "Proučvanija vŭrxu bŭlgarskoto srednovekovie: XVIII. Bŭlgarski dumy vŭv vizantijski stixove ot XIV vek," *Sbornik na bŭlgarskata Akademija na Naukite*, 41 (1949), esp. p. 140, lines 127–48.

149 Metochites was interested in Gregory and his work, witness his *Logos 6*, a *Eulogy* of Gregory, in Vindobon. ph. gr. 95, fols. 97r–145v, and his *Poem 6*, On Three Hierarchs, Paris. gr. 1776, fols. 81v–99v; since Gregory's versified autobiography is in a form unparalleled in Greek literature (R. Keydell, "Die literar-historische Stellung der Gedichte Gregors von Nazianz," *Atti dell' VIII Congresso Internazionale di Studi Bizantini* [= *Studi bizantini e neoellenici*, 7; Rome, 1953], pp. 134–43, esp. 140), it is fair to say that Gregory's autobiographical poems, several of them written in incorrect hexameters, must have influenced Metochites' choice of hexameter for his own autobiographical writings. Both Gregory's *De rebus suis*, PG, 37, cols. 969–1017, and Metochites' *Poem 1* are ostensibly hymns to Christ; the title of Gregory's poem (Περὶ τῶν καθ' ἑαυτόν) inspired one part of the title of Metochites' *Poem 1* (περὶ τῶν καθ' αὑτόν). Moreover, Metochites' poetry does show textual coincidences with that of Gregory, and these coincidences go beyond common borrowings from Homeric diction. Four examples: (1) Compare Gregory's *De rebus suis*, line 1, PG, 37, col. 969A, Χριστὲ ἄναξ, with TM, *Poem 1*, v. 70, Χριστὲ ἄναξ; (2) Gregory, ibid., line 65, PG, 37, col. 975A, Σηρῶν καλὰ νήματα, also *Ad Hellenium*, lines 21–22, PG, 37, col. 1453A, and Gregory's epigram in *Anthol. Pal.*, VIII, 105.4, Σηρῶν . . . . νήματα λεπταλέα, with TM, *Poem 1*, v. 1080, Σηρῶν νήματα πολύστροφα; (3) Gregory, *De rebus suis*, line 42, PG, 37, col. 973A, ἀμφαγαπῶντες, with TM, *Poem 1*, v. 93, ἀμφαγαπάζοντα (both authors have a predilection for prefixing verbs with ἀμφί); (4) Gregory, *Nicobuli patris ad filium*, line 152, PG, 37, col. 1532A, Θεὸν ὑψιμέδοντα, with TM, *Poem 1*, vv. 1–2, πᾶϊ Θεοῖο ὑψιμέδων. Here again Metochites helps us modify the prevalent view that Gregory's verses did not influence Greek poetry of subsequent times (so Keydell, p. 142); in addition to Metochites, his younger contemporary Michael-Macarius Chrysokephalos, from 1336 on Metropolitan of Philadelphia, imitated Gregory's hexameters, in the colophon

to Marcianus gr. 83 (N.C. 512), a manuscript of Gregory's poems, which Michael had copied himself. For this metric colophon, dated July 2, 1327, see M. I. Manousakas, Μακαρίου Φιλαδελφείας τοῦ Χρυσοκεφάλου ἀνέκδοτα χρονικὰ σημειώματα (1344–1346) εἰς δύο αὐτογράφους Μαρκιανοὺς κώδικας, in Θησαυρίσματα τοῦ Ἑλληνικοῦ Ἰνστιτούτου Βυζαντινῶν καὶ Μεταβυζαντινῶν Σπουδῶν, 4 (1967), pp. 7–19, esp. pp. 8–9; cf. ibid., p. 224, n. 1 (corrections to the text on p. 9). Other Byzantine poets (including such a near-contemporary of Metochites as Nicephorus Blemmydes) did imitate Gregory, but, in contradistinction to our author, they drew upon the rhythmical prose of Gregory's sermons rather than upon his poetry. See I. Sajdak, *De Gregorio Nazianzeno Poetarum Christianorum Fonte* (Kraków, 1917), esp. pp. 59–69 (the book does not mention Metochites or Chrysokephalos). For a possible dependence of Metochites on a Planudean edition of Gregory's poems, see n. 175 below.

150 See *Etudes*, p. 58 and nn. 3–5, and B. Hemmerdinger, *Essai sur l'histoire du texte de Thucydide* (Paris, 1955), pp. 43–46 (very conjectural; to be read with caution).

151 See pp. 41–42 and nn. 154 and 170 below.

152 See *Miscellanea*, Chs. 15, 18, and 71, and the index of authors, ibid., pp. 836–38; on Iamblichus and Proclus, see my *Etudes*, pp. 77–87, 105 and n. 3.

153 In *Logos 6*, Εἰς τὸν ἅγιον Γρηγόριον τὸν Θεολόγον, fol. 140r, Gregory is the only person to share the epithet "theologian" with μαθητήν . . . . τὴν τοῦ υἱοῦ θεολογίαν βροντήσαντα, i.e., John the Evangelist. A less refined writer would simply have said υἱὸν βροντῆς, which was the routine translation of the Hebrew meaning of the name John.

154 Compare (1) *Logos 17*, fol. 36ov (Gigante, "Il saggio" (as in n. 29 above), Ch. 17.6–15, pp. 82–83): ὁ δ' αὐτός [i.e., Philip of Macedon] καί τινων τῶν αὐτοῦ μετὰ τὴν ἐν Χαιρωνείᾳ νίκην αὐτοῦ . . . . ὑβριζόντων τοῖς πράγμασι καὶ καταμωκωμένων Δημοσθένην . . . . καὶ κόρδακος ἐν χρήσει προφερόντων καὶ βωμολοχούντων τὰ τῶν ψηφισμάτων προοίμια, Δημοσθένης Δημοσθένους Παιανιεύς—ὁ δὲ μάλιστ' ἐπιτίμα σφίσι, κατὰ νοῦν ὑπερβαλλόντως ἑαυτοῦ γινόμενος καὶ . . . . δειμαίνων, ὅπως ἐπὶ μιᾶς ἡμέρας ἀνὴρ τοῖς αὐτοῦ πολιτεύμασι καὶ ψηφίσμασιν ἐπέστησε τόν τε περὶ τῆς ἀρχῆς αὐτῷ καὶ τὸν περὶ ψυχῆς κίνδυνον with Plutarch's *Demosthenes*, 20, where it is Philip himself who becomes inebriated and sings the beginning of Demosthenes' decree; (2) *Logos 17*, fol. 36ov (Gigante, "Il saggio," Ch. 18.1–3, p. 83): ἀλλ' ἄρα δὴ καὶ Παρμενίων αὐτός, ὁ τὰ μάλιστα τῶν ὑπ' αὐτῷ δὴ στρατηγούντων, παραπλήσια τὸν ἄνδρα, καίπερ ἔχθιστον κρίνων, θαυμάζων, τὴν αὐτοῦ μακαρίζει πατρίδα τῆς εὐποτμίας αὐτοῦ with Lucian's *Demosthenis Encomium*, 33, where Parmenion *scoffs* at Demosthenes; (3) *Logos 17*, fol. 36ov (Gigante, "Il saggio," Ch. 18.8–15, p. 83), where a paraphrase of a saying in *Demosth. enc.*, 34, is put into the mouth of Parmenion, while the original attributes it to Philip. Metochites must have hastily read ἐγὼ δέ, ὁ Παρμενίων ἔφη instead of ἐγὼ δέ, ὦ Παρμενίων, ἔφη at the beginning of Lucian's *Demosth. enc.*, 34.

155 See my *Etudes*, pp. 79–81.

A. Fol. 7 r, at end of Table of Contents

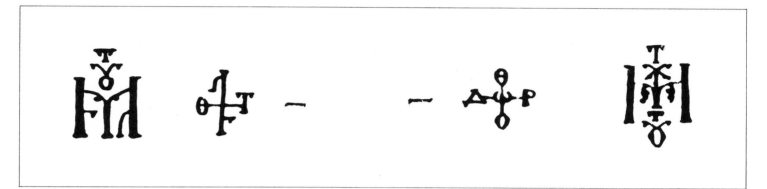

B. Fol. 278 r, at end of Text

Paris gr. 2003 (Metochites, *Miscellanea*), Monograms of title and name of Author

a. East
Θεόδωρος

b. West
Μετοχίτης

c. South
λογοθέτης

d. North
κ(αὶ) κτήτωρ

C *a-d*. Kariye Djami, Nave. Cornice at base of dome. Monograms at four
cardinal points giving name and title of Metochites

proverb.[156] Being an intelligent man, he was able to make up a spurious quotation of Sappho from what he had read about her in Aelius Aristides.[157]

Like his contemporaries, Metochites obeyed the rules of genres, especially when he was young, and put on a different garb for different literary occasions. The plan of his first eulogy of the Emperor Andronicus II comes straight from the theoretician of rhetoric, Menander.[158] In his highly oratorical praise of Gregory of Nazianzus, he extolled the secular studies of the Saint and irately asserted the importance of secular wisdom; he refused to go into the details of such an obvious matter.[159] But in a religious poem, while he conceded to the monks of the Chora that secular wisdom was of some use, he said that it was so mostly because it enabled the Christians to know their enemies and thus to fight them more effectively.[160] In his philosophical essays, he hesitated to say which life was preferable, the contemplative or the active.[161] But in a religious poem again, he had no doubts that the contemplative life was superior.[162]

To Metochites, scholarly and even practical achievement was not possible without prior consultation of the ancient historians.[163] The soil of natural genius could bear fruit only if it was enriched by ancient writings.[164] Commerce with works about antiquity kept one spellbound and created an insatiable desire for more historical knowledge—a spell and a desire which had to be experienced to be understood.[165] All this modern scholars call humanism, without defining what they mean by this term.[166] But occasionally Metochites quenched his thirst for antiquity in less

156 See *Logos* 6, Εἰς τὸν ἅγιον Γρηγόριον τὸν Θεολόγον, fols. 136v-137r: καὶ τήν . . . . καλῶς μεμαγμένην, κατὰ τὴν παροιμίαν, μάζαν. Compare Archilochus, fr. 2; Metochites could have read this line of Archilochus in Athenaeus, *Deipnosoph.* I.30f, in Synesius, *Ep.* 130 (p. 717, ed. Hercher), and in *Suda* (Suidas) s.vv. ὑπνομαχῶ and Ἰσμαρικὸς οἶνος.

157 See my "A New Fragment of Sappho?" *The Annals of the Ukrainian Academy of Arts and Sciences in the U.S.*, 1 (1951), pp. 150-52.

158 *Logos* 5, Βασιλικὸς πρῶτος, Vindobon. ph. gr. 95, fols. 81r-96v; cf. Menander, Περὶ ἐπιδεικτικῶν, ed. L. Spengel, *Rhetores Graeci*, III, Teubner (1856), pp. 368-77. On βασιλικὸς λόγος, see, e.g., T. C. Burgess, "Epideictic Literature," *Chicago University Studies in Classical Philology*, 3 (1902), esp. pp. 113-42.

159 *Logos* 6, Εἰς τὸν ἅγιον Γρηγόριον τὸν Θεολόγον, Vindobon. ph. gr. 95, fol. 101r-101v: τῆς μέντοι παιδείας αὐτῆς, καὶ τῆς τῶν ἔξωθεν λόγων χρείας ἕν γε τοῖς ἡμετέροις καὶ θείοις, ἔδοξεν [i.e., to Gregory] ἀντιποιητέον εἶναι καὶ σπουδαστέον ὡς ἔνι μάλιστα. . . . τὸ δ' ὅπως ἄρα καὶ ὅτου χάριν καὶ τίνα τρόπον, καὶ ὅσον τὸ ἀπὸ τούτων χρήσιμον, τίς οὕτως ἂν εἴη παντάπασι καταγέλαστος ἄνθρωπος καὶ δυστυχής, καὶ ὄντως πόρρω καὶ λόγου καὶ νοῦ παντός, ὥστε καὶ ἐπεξιέναι νῦν καὶ διδάσκειν πειρᾶσθαι; . . . . καὶ τί χρὴ λοιπὸν εἰς ἀπόδειξιν ἔτ' ἄλλο προφέρειν ἢ προσεπιφέρειν καὶ πράγματ' ἔχειν καὶ ἀγωνίζεσθαι, ὡς ὅτι τοῦτο πολὺ βέλτιστον καὶ λυσιτελέστατον;

160 *Poem* 1, vv. 1168-75. Acquaintance with secular wisdom was also useful to Christians, Metochites added in the same passage, because by comparing it to Divine wisdom [i.e., theology], they could realize the superiority of the latter.

161 *Miscellanea*, Ch. 75, pp. 497-504, esp. the final verdict on p. 504: καὶ οὐκ οἶδ' ὁποῖ τὸ πλεῖον νέμειν ἐστίν, ἢ τῷ περὶ τὴν ἀγαθοεργίαν ἑτοιμοτέρῳ βίῳ, ἢ ᾧ τὸ σύγγνωμον ἑτοιμότερον, ἐν οἷς ἡ φύσις εὐόλισθος [since the errors of conduct committed by a man engaged in active life are more excusable than those committed by monks]. In *Logos* 10, fol. 213r-213v, Metochites considered complete withdrawal from active life as abolition of politics. Yet, politics was a very important part (καλλίστου μέρους) of philosophy; understood as the art of the possible, it was capable of leading one to great achievements.

162 *Poem* 2, vv. 432-35 (Metochites yearns to join the community of the Chora; were this possible, he would purchase this privilege with all his earthly possessions): οὐ μόνον, ὅττι κε

φέρτερον ἀντ' ἄρα πάντων ἐσθλῶν | θεοσεβίη καί τ' ἀρετῆς ἔργα σπουδαῖα, | ἀλλ' ὅτι καί τι γλυκερὸν ἀπράγμων ἄφροντις βίοτος.

163 *Miscellanea*, Ch. 111, "On Uses of History for Creative Writers," pp. 734-50; see esp. p. 735: no achievement is possible in the field of learning without acquaintance with ancient historians and ancient history. Pp. 739-40: the ancients were interested in history not only for the sake of pure knowledge, but also for practical reasons. P. 745: examples culled from history are universally useful, in matters both military and political—whether in intercourse with rulers, in political discussion, or on embassies. In the course of his own active life, sometimes studded with achievements, sometimes fraught with dangers, Metochites derived practical advantages from his knowledge of history. Pp. 748-50: knowledge of history expands our existence both in space and in time.

164 The metaphor Metochites uses is that of irrigation: *Miscellanea*, ibid., p. 735: οὐδὲ δύναιτ' ἂν μόνος τις ἑαυτῷ χρῆσθαι, καὶ τῆς οἴκοθεν εὐγενείας αὐτοῦ, κἂν εἰ ἄκρος τὴν φύσιν, πάντ' ἀγχίνους. . . . δεῖ γὰρ καὶ τῆς ἐκ τῶν παλαιῶν ἀ ρ δ ε ί α ς εἰς συμμαχίαν.

165 *Logos* 10, fol. 206v: ἡ δὲ περὶ τὴν ἱστορίαν ὅλως ῥοπή, καὶ πραγμάτων μετρίως ἐποπτεῦσαι παλαιῶν ἀφηγήσεις, οὕτως ἀκάματον ὡς ἀληθῶς ἔρων [ἔρον manuscript] ἐνέσταζε τῇ ψυχῇ καὶ τοσοῦτο δηγματῶδες ἀεὶ νύττον θέλγηθρον, ὡς οὐκ ἄλλο τί ποτ' οὐδέν· οὐδ' ἔστι καθάπαξ ἀναμαθεῖν, ὅστις ἄρα μὴ πεπείραται παθών. οὐ γὰρ ἔστιν ὅπως ἄν τις κόρος καὶ μέτρον ὁτιοῦν γένοιτο τῇ περὶ ταῦτα φιλοπραγμοσύνῃ . . . . , ἀλλ' ἀεί ποτέ τι προσλαμβάνων ὁ σπουδάζων . . . . ζητεῖ . . . . ἀνορύττων, ἅττα δὴ πάλαι πρότερον χρόνων καὶ πραγμάτων ἄλλαις ἐπιδρομαῖς συγκέχωσται.

166 There is some justification in thinking of humanism in connection with Metochites, for there are some new stirrings in his writings, and on one occasion I myself call him "pre-humanistic" (see p. 51 below). For all that, I believe that lately we have been too lavish in using the word "humanism" when writing about the Palaeologan revival. August Heisenberg had a point when he wrote some forty years ago: "Humanismus ist vielleicht doch ein zu stolzes Wort für das, was jetzt von Theodoros Metochites und Nikephoros Gregoras gepflegt wurde, denn diese . . . ausgezeichneten . . . und . . . gelehrten Männer strebten nicht nach einer neuen Menschlichkeit"; see "Das Problem der Renaissance in Byzanz," *Historische Zeitschrift*, 133 (1925), esp. p. 410. Among the modern views of the problem,

remote, namely Byzantine, sources: he based a development on the deeper religious meaning of the seemingly obscene Hermae in Athens on ten lines from a poem by Gregory of Nazianzus;[167] borrowed a story of the rebuilding of Tralles after the disastrous earthquake which razed that city in Augustus' time, from the Byzantine historian Agathias;[168] and quoted a saying about Aeschines from Photius.[169]

Metochites' humanism—meaning here knowledge of antiquity—and his learning in general owed much to the activity of one of the Byzantines of the preceding generation, Maximus Planudes (d. ca. 1305), who was connected with the library of the Chora about a quarter of a century before Metochites took it over. By Metochites' own admission, the main source of his historical knowledge and many of his quotations was "the most learned Plutarch."[170] This

---

Pertusi's scepticism concerning the existence of 14th-century Byzantine humanism (there was intensification of knowledge of antiquity, but no renaissance, "perchè non ci fu problema") deserves preference over the enthusiasm of Gigante. Oppose A. Pertusi, *Leonzio Pilato fra Petrarca e Boccaccio* (Venice and Rome, 1964), Ch. VII: "Cultura bizantina e primo umanesimo italiano," pp. 475–520, esp. 503 and n. 3; 516–19, esp. 517, nn. 2 and 3, to Gigante, "Per l'interpretazione" (as in n. 29 above) and to J. Verpeaux, "Byzance et l'humanisme (position du problème)," *Bulletin de l'Association Guillaume Budé*, (1952, no. 3), pp. 25–38. Cf. also the cautious formulation in Fenster, *Laudes* (as in n. 29 above), p. 193. For further literature on Western humanism and Byzantium, cf. W. O. Schmitt, "Lateinische Literatur in Byzanz," *JOeBG*, 17 (1968), p. 129, n. 8.— The undeniable contribution of Byzantine scholars to the technical aspects of Western humanism is another matter. Cf., e.g., K. M. Setton, "The Byzantine Background to the Italian Renaissance," *Proceedings of the American Philosophical Society*, 100 (1956), pp. 1–76.

167 In *Logos* 3 on the Archangel Michael, Metochites compared the material representations of angels with the Hermae in Athens: when angels were described as winged, for instance, this was only a symbolic reminder of their immaterial nature; the case was very much like that of the Hermae in Athens, which symbolically alluded to mysteries and delivered a double message: one to the initiated, another to the profane. See Vindobon. ph. gr. 95, fol. 41v: εἰ δέ τις . . . . μὴ τοῖς ὁρωμένοις καθάπαξ ἁλίσκοιτο, δι' αὐτοῦ [i.e., the visible symbol] προχωρήσει πρὸς τὸ δηλούμενον καὶ ἀνακαλύψει τἀπόρρητον καὶ κρυπτόμενον, ὃν τρόπον εἶχον οἱ πρὸς ταῖς ὁδοῖς Ἀθήνησιν Ἑρμαῖ πάλαι, καὶ τοῖς πολλοῖς ἐν παρόδῳ προκείμενοι, καὶ τοῖς γ' ἐξεταστικοῖς καὶ τῶν μυστηρίων ἐπόπταις καὶ πολυπράγμοσιν· οὗτος ὁ λόγος τῶν ὑλικῶν ἐκτυπωμάτων ἐπὶ τὴν ἄϋλον φύσιν καὶ ἀσχημάτιστον. All this embroidering goes back, I submit, to Gregory of Nazianzus' Poem to Nemesius, lines 130–40, *PG*, 37, col. 1561A, especially to lines 134–36: if pagan religious writings do have a hidden meaning, which is ὑφειμένος εἴδει μάχλῳ, σεμνότερος, πινυτοῖσιν ὁρώμενος, ἀμφιπρόσωπος, Ἑρμᾶς δίγλυφος, οἷα πρόσω τὸ μέν, ἄλλο δ' ὄπισθεν, then you must realize that Christian Scriptures, too, have two kinds of meaning (διπλοῦς λόγος).

168 The story is that of Chaeremon, the "farmer" of Siderous near Tralles. After the earthquake of 27 B.C., Chaeremon traveled to Spain, where Augustus was campaigning, and obtained his help in rebuilding and recolonizing the city. Agathias, *Hist.*, II, 17 (ed. R. Keydell [Berlin, 1967], pp. 62.23–64.3), seems to be the only preserved witness for this episode; thus he is the most likely source for Metochites, who retells the story—with embellishments—when he comes to speak about Andronicus II's recolonizing Tralles about 1280. He finds Andronicus' merits to be greater than those of Augustus, since he helped the city spontaneously, while Augustus had to be prompted by a petitioner. See *Logos* 5, Vindobon. ph. gr. 95 [= V], fol. 88r–88v: καὶ νῦν ἡ περιφανὴς πόλις αἱ Τράλλεις [τράλεις V] ἔστηκε διὰ σέ, προσκτησαμένη καὶ τοῦτο πάντως εἰς εὐκλείας περιουσίαν, ὅτι νῦν ἔστηκε διὰ σέ· καὶ τοῦτο πλέον ἴσως εἰς δόξαν τῇ πόλει, ἢ τὸ πάλαι περὶ αὐτὴν παραπλήσιον ἐκείνων τῶν χρόνων, ὅτ' ἐπὶ τοῦ μεγάλου Καίσαρος

Αὐγούστου σεισμοῦ τυραννίδι καταχωσθεῖσα καὶ τοιαύτης ἀωρίας καὶ συμφορᾶς παρανάλωμα γενομένη παρ' αὐτὸ τῆς τύχης τὸ ἀκμαιότατον, ὑπ' αὐτοῦ δὴ σεβαστοῦ Καίσαρος οὗπερ εἴρηται νέ ἀνίσταται μάλ' αὖθις ῥᾷστα. καὶ μὴν λόγος οὑτοσὶ φθάνει γ' ἐκεῖθεν ὡς ἡμᾶς ἥκων· ἄνδρα τῶν τιν' ἐποίκων αὐτῆς, τῶν πολλῶν ἕνα καὶ καθάπαξ ἄσημον καὶ ταπεινῇ τύχῃ χρώμενον—Χαιρήμων ὄνομα τάνδρί—τοῦτον [fol. 88v] οὖν φασι τὸν Χαιρήμονα, δεινὰ πράττουσαν τὴν πατρίδα ὁρῶντα, φρονῆσαί τι μέγα καὶ ὑπὲρ αὐτὸν ὄντως, καὶ διὰ τοσούτου πρὸς ὃν εἴρηται τάχιστ' αὐτοκράτορα γενόμενον δηλῶσαί τε Τράλλεις [τράλεις V] τὴν πόλιν κειμένην καὶ παρακαλέσαι πρὸς τὴν φιλανθρωπίαν τῆς πόλεως· ὥστ' ἴσως καὶ προαρπάζει Χαιρήμων τὸ κλέος οὑτοσί, πῶς ἂν ἐρεῖ τις, ἢ τό γε δεύτερον δικαίως ἂν μερίζοιτο καὶ ξυλλαγχάνοι Καίσαρι. καὶ οὐδέν γε τοσοῦτον ἐκεῖθεν ἄρα τῇ πόλει, ἥ γε μὴ μόνον ἤρκεσεν—ὥστε τὸ φιλότιμον αὐτὸ τοῦ Καίσαρος ἀνεγεῖραι—τὸ τῆς συμφορᾶς ἀδόκητον ἀθρόον καὶ τὸ τοῦ πάθους ἐλεεινὸν οὕτως, καὶ ταῦτα παρ' αὐτὴν ὡς ἔφην τὴν ἀκμὴν τῆς τύχης, ἀλλ' ἔπειτ' αὐτῇ γε καὶ τῆς τοῦ Χαιρήμονος ἐδέησε γνώμης εἰς τὴν πικρὰν τύχην καὶ μεγαλοψυχίας· κἂν εἰ μή γε θερμότερος ἦν αὐτῇ Χαιρήμων πολίτης, πάλαι πρότερον ἴσως ἡ μεγαλώνυμος πόλις αἱ Τράλλεις [τράλεις V] πάντως ἂν ᾤχετο καθάπαξ. ἀλλὰ σοί γε, βασιλεῦ, οὐδὲν ἀλλ' ἢ γνώμη διαρκὴς οἴκοθεν ἀπέχρησε μόνη πρὸς τοσοῦτον φιλότιμον ἔργον, ὅθεν σοι καὶ τὸ καλὸν ἀμιγὲς καὶ οὐδείς σοι τοῦδε μερίτης, οὐ Χαιρήμων, οὐχ ὁστισοῦν, καὶ τῇ πόλει μείζων ὁ κόσμος ἐκ τοῦδε καὶ προσθήκη καλλίστη τοῖς παλαιοῖς διηγήμασιν. οὕτω μὲν οὖν τοσοῦτ' ἔργον ἐν κατεπράχθη τηνικαῦτα τῶν χρόνων ἐκείνη σχολάζοντί σοι, πάρεργον ὁδοῦ, φασί, τοῦ σκοποῦ τῆς σῆς ἐκδημίας, κράτιστε βασιλεῦ. On Agathias' passage and, *pace* Metochites' epithet "farmer," on Chaeremon's important social status, see T. R. S. Broughton, "Some Non-Colonial Coloni of Augustus," *Transactions and Proceedings of the American Philological Association*, 66 (1935), esp. pp. 20–22; on Andronicus II's "refounding" Tralles-Andronicopolis and the date of this short-lived enterprise, see my *Etudes*, p. 137, n. 6.

169 *Etudes*, p. 255 (*Logos* 14, apparatus to **29.**1–13).

170 Πολυμαθέστατος Πλούταρχος: *Miscellanea*, Ch. 3, p. 23. Why should one search for information in numerous pre-Plutarchian sources, Metochites asked, if you could find everything easily accessible (ἐκ τοῦ προχείρου) in Plutarch himself? See *Miscellanea*, Ch. 71, pp. 473–74. Some examples, culled mostly from *Logos* 10, quoted by folio, will show that Metochites practiced what he preached. For fol. 204v, καὶ περιέπλει [i.e., Pericles] γε ἑκατὸν [i.e., ναυσί] μεθύστερον ἔπειτα τὴν Πελοπόννησον, cf. *Pericles*, 19: ἐθαυμάσθη [i.e., Pericles] περιπλεύσας Πελοπόννησον. . . . ἑκατὸν τριήρεσιν, cf. also *Pericles*, 34. For fols. 204v–205r, Λύσανδρος . . . . κρεωδότης ἦν Ἀγησιλάου, καὶ μετ' ὀλίγον αὖθις ἐν Ἁλιάρτῳ, καθάπερεὶ πελταστής τις ἢ ὁπλίτης Λάκων εἰς ἔπιπτεν, cf. *Agesilaus*, 8: αὐτοῦ [i.e., Lysander] καθάψασθαι βουλόμενος Ἀγησίλαος ἀπέδειξε κρεοδαίτην, and *Lysandri et Sullae comp.*, 4: Λύσανδρος δὲ πελταστοῦ . . . . δίκην ἀκλεῶς παραναλώσας ἑαυτόν. For fol. 206r, Δημάδης μὲν οὖν ἔλεγε, πυθομένοις Ἀθηναίων Ἀλέξανδρον ἐν Σούσοις τελευτῆσαι καὶ ταραττομένοις, μὴ πείθεσθαι· πάλαι γὰρ ἂν ὄζειν τὴν οἰκουμένην νεκροῦ, ὡς τὸ ἐκείνου σῶμα τῆς οἰκουμένης σχεδὸν ὄν, καὶ ταύτην ἀναγκαῖον συμπάσχειν ὁτιοῦν αὐτῷ πεπονθότι,

reliance on Plutarch, much more extensive than that shown by any Byzantine of Michael VIII's time, would hardly have been possible without the editions which Planudes undertook in the 1290's. When Planudes was working on his first edition of Plutarch's collected works, he was a resident of the Chora. About the year 1300, he moved on to the monastery τοῦ ᾿Ακαταλήπτου,[171] but he did not take all his books with him. We know, for instance, that the master copy of Plutarch's second edition [172] was left somewhere else, in my opinion in the Chora.[173] In the Preface to his *Introduction to Astronomy*, Metochites quoted several authors whom he had studied while learning that science.[174] We are impressed until we realize that he has given us much of the table of contents of a late antique introductory collection called ῾Ο μικρὸς ἀστρονομούμενος. Again, a manuscript of this collection, the present Vaticanus gr. 202, was in the possession of Maximus Planudes when he was residing in the Chora, and it remained in the Chora's library even after Planudes had left.[175] Autograph scholarly notes compiled by Metochites' pupil Nicephorus Gregoras, who, among other things, was the Chora's librarian, depend greatly on the collection of excerpts made by Planudes.[176] Gregoras may have found a copy of that collection in the Chora.[177]

A product of the Palaeologan revival, Metochites was not only a man of culture but also a technician. He considered himself to be the successor and brotherly spirit of the great astronomers Hipparchus, Ptolemy, and Theon.[178] How good was he as a technician? For intelligence and understanding Ptolemy, he deserves an excellent mark; for scientific honesty, a less excellent

cf. *Phocion*, 22.3: ᾿Αθηναίοις ᾿Ασκληπιάδου τοῦ ῾Ιππάρχου τεθνάναι προσαγγείλαντος ᾿Αλέξανδρον, ὁ μὲν Δημάδης ἐκέλευε μὴ προσέχειν· πάλαι γὰρ ἂν ὅλην ὄζειν νεκροῦ τὴν οἰκουμένην (for *Poem* 1, vv. 846–48, cf. *Phocion*, 1 and *Praecepta ger. reipubl.*, 6 [p. 803A] = Demades' fr. 17, ed. V. de Falco, *Collana di Studi Greci*, 25 [2nd ed., Naples, 1954]). For fol. 223v, πλησίστιοι, φασί, φέρονται (cf. *Miscellanea*, Ch. 115, p. 777), cf. *Cato Maior*, 2: πλησίστιος ἐπὶ τὸν πόλεμον φερόμενος. For fol. 223v, κέχηνεν ἄελπτον πρὸς δέλεαρ, φησὶν ἡ ποίησις, θύννος βολαῖος ὡς στροβούμενος, cf. *De sera numinis vind.*, 10 (p. 554F): θύννος βολαῖος πέλαγος ὡς διαστροβεῖ, repeated in *Lucullus*, 1. For fol. 227r, καὶ Διογένης μὲν ὁ Κύων παριὼν ᾿Αθήνησιν οὕτω, καὶ μειράκιόν τι τῶν εὐγενῶν ἰδὼν ἐν καπηλείῳ, ἐπειδὴ καταιδεσάμενον ἐκεῖνον προῆλθεν ἔσω κρυπτόμενος, 'ἀλλὰ σύ γε', ἔφησεν, 'οὐχ ὁρᾷς ὡς ἔτι μᾶλλον ἔσω τοῦ δεινοῦ γίγνη καὶ τῆς αἰσχύνης, ἣν δοκεῖς φεύγειν'; cf. *Quomodo quis*, 11 (p. 82CD): χάριεν γὰρ τὸ τοῦ Διογένους πρός τινα νεανίσκον ὀφθέντα μὲν ἐν καπηλείῳ, καταφυγόντα δ' εἰς τὸ καπηλεῖον, 'ὅσῳ' γὰρ εἶπεν 'ἐνδοτέρω φεύγεις, μᾶλλον ἐν τῷ καπηλείῳ γίγνη'. Finally, for Metochites' *Preface* to the Commentaries on Aristotle, ed. H. J. Drossaart Lulofs, *Aristotelis De Somno et Vigilia liber* (Leiden, 1943), p. 11, lines 19–20, τὸ τῆς ἑρμηνείας . . . . δυσθήρατον καθάπαξ καὶ δύσληπτον, cf. *Quomodo adol. poetas aud. deb.*, 2 (p. 17E): ἀλήθεια . . . . εὖ μάλα δυσθήρατός ἐστι καὶ δύσληπτος. Cf. in general *Miscellanea*, Ch. 115, pp. 775–92; the historical data of this chapter derive from Plutarch's lives of Alcibiades, Demetrius, and Eumenes.

171 Wendel, "Planudea" (as in n. 24 above), pp. 406–10. For bibliography on Planudes, see, in addition to works cited in nn. 171–76 here, Pertusi, *Leonzio Pilato*, p. 502, n. 4, M. Gigante, "La cultura latina a Bisanzio nel secolo XIII," *La Parola del Passato*, 17 (1962), pp. 39–49, and Schmitt, "Lateinische Literatur . . . .," pp. 127–47, passim (Pertusi and Schmitt as in n. 166 above). On Planudes' death ca. 1305, cf. A. Dondaine, "Contra Graecos: premiers écrits polémiques des Dominicains d'Orient," *Archivum Fratrum Praedicatorum*, 21 (1951), pp. 320–446, esp. 421–22.

172 On Planudes' editions of Plutarch, see A. Diller, "Codices Planudei," *BZ*, 37 (1937), p. 296; Wendel, "Planudea," (as in note 24 above), pp. 410–14; idem, "Planudes als Bücherfreund" (as in note 27 above); idem, *RE*, 20, 2 (1950), col. 2223, No.

32; A. Diller, "Pletho and Plutarch," *Scriptorium*, 8 (1954), pp. 123–27.

173 Wendel, "Planudes als Bücherfreund," p. 86; idem, *RE*, 20, 2 col. 2225.28–33. John Chortasmenos, a bibliophile who flourished ca. 1400, annotated Paris. gr. 1671, the master copy of this second Planudean edition, on fols. 12r and 18r–20r of its second part. Chortasmenos may have found this manuscript in the Chora, for he seems to have been connected with the Chora's library: he put ownership remarks into at least two manuscripts, Vat. gr. 1365 and Seragliensis gr. 85, stating that they belonged to the Chora; see my *Etudes*, pp. 43, n. 1, and 281.

174 Passage in Sathas (as in n. 54 above), p. πη'.

175 Wendel, "Planudea," p. 417, and idem, "Planudes als Bücherfreund," p. 85. Metochites may owe a debt to Planudes even for his unusual reliance on Gregory of Nazianzus' classicizing hexameters. Between 1283 and 1299—perhaps while he was a resident of the Chora—Planudes published an Anthology (the present Laurentianus 32.16) which included most of Gregory's poetry. For the best description of this manuscript, in part written by Planudes himself, see C. Gallavotti, "Planudea," *Bollettino del Comitato per la preparazione della Edizione Nazionale dei Classici Greci e Latini*, N.S., 7 (1959), pp. 25–50, esp. 37–48.

176 The manuscript is Palatinus gr. 129. On its being an autograph of Gregoras, see, e.g., my *Etudes*, p. 61, n. 5, and my "Some Autographs," (as in note 24 above), esp. p. 449 and n. 50. On Planudes' Συναγωγή in Gregoras' manuscript, see A. Biedl, *Zur Textgeschichte des Laertios Diogenes: Das grosse Exzerpt Φ* (Vatican City, 1955) = *Studi e Testi*, 184, p. 84.

177 Until recently, we knew of only a few volumes belonging to the Chora library, for we had to rely on notes or colophons alone, see K. and S. Lake, *Dated Minuscule Manuscripts to the Year 1200*, X (1939), Ms. 401 = PL. 755–757, and *Etudes*, pp. 43, n. 1, 281. Now that the handwritings of Metochites and Gregoras have been identified, the number of attributions has grown and there is hope for further progress in the future. For the autograph remarks of Metochites, see *Etudes*, pp. 58, n. 5, 282, n. 3, and PL. II, IV, VII. For Gregoras' autographs, see *Etudes*, pp. 280, 282 and n. 3 and the addendum to this note in the list of corrigenda; p. 284; and PL. V, VI; see also my "Some Autographs," Figs. 1–8.

178 *Logos* 14, **30**.5–9, in *Etudes*, p. 255.

one. This Logothete of the Treasury kept his astronomical accounts in a strange way. One chapter of his *Introduction to Astronomy* contains a catalogue of the fixed stars. Metochites explained at length that owing to the precession of the equinoxes, a slow apparent movement of the sphere of the fixed stars, their position in longitude changes at a rate of one degree per hundred years. As his catalogue was based on Ptolemy, who lived about twelve hundred years before him, he was going to bring the positions of the stars up to date. When we turn to the catalogue itself, we find that he did nothing of the sort. His tables reproduce Ptolemy exactly. If Metochites, or his secretary, had kept his promise, the difference for each star would have amounted to about twelve degrees, using the Ptolemaic system. In reality it amounted to more and the discrepancy could have been ascertained just by using the astrolabe.[179]

Late antique and Byzantine astronomers were aware that Plato and Aristotle differed in their cosmology from Ptolemy.[180] Plato assumed seven "revolutions" and Ptolemy eight spheres, for the latter took into account the precession of the equinoxes. The two philosophers also differed from Ptolemy on the order of the planets. Still, for most learned Byzantines, Plato and Aristotle could not be wrong; for Metochites, neither could Ptolemy.

Metochites solved the problem of the eight spheres in a cavalier fashion. He repeatedly quoted the passage of Plato's *Epinomis* where the seven movements are mentioned, but he changed the word "seven," *hepta*, into "venerable," *septas*, and added the word "eight" afterwards.[181] As for the order of the planets, he kept the Ptolemaic system; explained, quite rightly, "This is the opinion that prevails among most astronomers"; but added—although he should have known better—"and Plato and Aristotle agree with it." [182] In both instances the agreement was produced in favor of Ptolemy, on whom, Metochites said, nobody in his senses should try to improve.[183]

However, we must give Metochites his due. He assures us that he read Ptolemy more than twice, and we should believe him. He transposed the tables of Theon to a new starting point which coincided with the first year of Andronicus II's reign, a feat which must have increased his favor with the Emperor.[184] He did launch a fashion and he endowed astronomy with social prestige. Armed with his exclusive knowledge, able to predict eclipses, he could deride his enemy Choumnos, who thought that the sphere of the fixed stars moved, if at all, one degree per year— to an informed Byzantine this was ten thousand percent wrong—and who suggested that the cause of the slowness of this movement was, of all things, the braking effect of the waters which, according to Genesis, were above the firmament.[185]

· IV ·

If we limit ourselves to his sources, models, and authorities, Metochites dissolves into another, if unusually learned, Byzantine of the Palaeologan revival. But when the sources are peeled off, a

179 See my *Etudes*, p. 92, n. 4, for a discussion of Metochites' catalogue of fixed stars. In one of the best manuscripts of the *Introduction to Astronomy*, Vat. gr. 1365, a Byzantine reader added the words "in his [i.e., Ptolemy's] times" (fol. 231v, lower margin) and "according to assumptions prevalent in the times of Ptolemy" (fol. 233v, margin) next to the tables and discussion of the angular distances of Venus and Mercury from the Sun. That reader was aware that the tables and data had not been made to agree with the new starting point in calculations of 1283, which Metochites had introduced, but were taken over, without change, from Ptolemy's *Almagest* or from Theon of Alexandria's *Handy Tables*.

180 *Etudes*, p. 95 and n. 1.

181 See *Etudes*, pp. 97–99, where the passage from *Introduction to Astronomy*, I, 5 (Vat. gr. 1365, fol. 20r) is quoted *in extenso*.

182 *Introduction to Astronomy*, I, 16 (Vat. gr. 1365, fol. 34r); for quotation of this passage, see my *Etudes*, p. 97, n. 1.

183 *Miscellanea*, Ch. 13, p. 102: Πτολεμαῖος . . . . χώραν ἑξῆς οὐ παρῆκεν οὐδενὶ τῶν ἁπάντων φέρειν . . . . πλέον περὶ . . . . ἀστρονομίαν, οὔκουν γε ὅστις μὴ μαίνεται. As for Plato, he was interested in astronomy but was not very proficient in it; ibid., p. 103.

184 Date of the new *epochē*: Oct. 6, 1283; see my *Etudes*, pp. 112–13.

185 *Etudes*, p. 94, n. 2, where the passage on the braking waters above the firmament is reproduced from Patmiacus gr. 127, fol. 5r–5v.

hundred folios analyzed away, another hundred accounted for by repetitions and self-quotations, the core of Metochites still remains. This core holds out two temptations: first, to claim for Metochites an independent mind and, second, to give to his texts a psychological explanation. So rarely are Byzantinists even presented with such temptations that I shall yield to both of them.

Originality was praised by Metochites' contemporaries, since the concept of originality, too, was familiar to the Byzantines—on paper; this praise, however, is not to be taken very seriously. Planudes told Manuel Bryennios, Metochites' teacher in astronomy, that a philosopher should not follow the path of the crowd, and that to behave independently, like the seven planets, was better than merely to describe the planets' movements. However, the purpose of all this was only to say, "Do not be like everybody else, and do lend me a copy of the mathematician Diophantos."[186] Choumnos refused to consider Plato and Aristotle as oracles, and he proceeded to refute their cosmological and physical views. But he thumbed his nose at these philosophers from behind the wall of scriptural passages.[187]

Metochites was self-conscious about the originality of his own work. What topic could be found which had not been treated by writers of antiquity or of the Christian past?[188] They had said everything in advance. Metochites' generation had come too late and was left with nothing original to offer.[189] When he mentioned rules of rhetorical composition, it was not only to show that he knew them, but also to observe that he felt uncomfortable in their harness.[190] In spite of

---

186 Treu, . . . *Planudis Epistulae* (as in n. 24 above), *Ep.* 33, esp. lines 17–23 and 33–37. Sense of the simile: the apparent movement of the few planets is opposed to that of the sphere of the many fixed stars.

187 See Choumnos' *Letter* 39 to Metochites, ed. Boissonade, in *Anecdota Nova* (Paris, 1844; reprint, Hildesheim, 1962), pp. 48–50; analysis of the letter in *Etudes*, pp. 13–14. For invoking the Bible against Aristotle, see Choumnos' unpublished treatise, "It Is Not Impossible . . . That Water Be Assigned a Place . . . above the Firmament," e.g. in Patmiacus gr. 127, fols. 71r–81v; for analysis of the treatise, see Verpeaux, *Choumnos* (as in n. 4 above), pp. 138–40; for a quotation from it, see my *Etudes*, p. 94, n. 2.

188 *Miscellanea*, Ch.1, pp. 13–18, entitled, in part, ὅτι οὐκ ἔστι νῦν λέγειν; *Logos* 10, fol. 201r: εἰσὶ γάρ, ὄντως εἰσί, πάλαι λόγοι περὶ πάντων ἐσκευασμένοι τοῖς ἀνδράσιν [i.e., the ancients] ἡμῶν ἕνεκεν εἰς ἕτοιμον χρῆσιν; *Logos* 10, fols. 201v–202r: ἀλλ' ἔμοιγε δοκῶ κάλλιστα ἂν οὕτως ἔχειν τὸν λόγον. . . . εἴ τις τοῖς πρὸ ἡμῶν ἐκείνοις σοφοῖς καὶ θεσπεσίοις ἀνδράσι δι' ὧν καταλελοίπασιν ἡμῖν ἐν ταῖς βίβλοις συγγίγνοιτο λόγων. . . . ποῦ γὰρ ἄν τις ἄλλοις συγγένοιτο κρείττοσι; . . . . ἢ περὶ τίνος ἄρα καὶ ζητήσας οὐχ εὑρήσεις αὐτίκα αὐτόθεν πάλαι τοῖς ἀνδράσι ἀνευρημένα δόγματα καὶ λόγους ἠσφαλισμένους καὶ τὸ πιστὸν ἔχοντας; ἐπεὶ καὶ περὶ πάντων ἀκριβέστατα προεῖπον καὶ προύθεντο νόμους καὶ κλήρους αὐτάρκεις, ἀπολαύειν ἀπόνως τοῖς ἐξῆς ἡμῖν καὶ οὐδὲν οὔτ' ἀνεπίγνωστον οὔτ' ἄρρητον παρεῖται, ἀλλ' ἅπασιν εἴαται, πᾶσιν ἀνεπληρώθη. . . . βέλτιόν ἐστι τῷ ὄντι, κατὰ τὸν παλαιὸν εἰρημένον λόγον [i.e., *Diog. Laertius*, VII, 2: the words of the oracle to Zeno], συγχρωτίζεσθαι τούτοις καὶ νεκροῖς ἢ τοῖς ζῶσι νεκροῖς [i.e., Metochites' contemporaries] καὶ μηδ' ὅτι ζῶσιν ἐπαίουσι.

189 *Miscellanea*, as in the preceding note; *Logos* 10, fol. 195v: καὶ οὐκ οἶδ' ὅ,τι δεῖ πλείω περὶ τούτων [i.e., instability of life] λέγειν, ὅπουγε μηδέν ἐστιν ἀμέλει καινὸν ὃ μή πω πρότερον ἐνίοις εἴρηται, οὐδ' ὁ πολυπραγμονέστατος καὶ περιεργότατος ἔχει τι πλέον ἀνύσαι καὶ προενεγκεῖν, κἂν ὅ,τι μάλιστα βούλοιτο, ὃ μὴ δὴ πρότερον συννενόηται. On this point, see also Beck, *Metochites* (as in n. 11 above), p. 51.

190 Examples of allusions to rules:
a) Example from an early work, the *Eulogy* of Gregory of

Nazianzus: Metochites reached the point where one was supposed to mention the parents of the person eulogized; he wished this rule had not existed; if he followed it, the impression might arise that he was referring to Gregory's parents merely out of deference to the rules; in fact, he would have spoken of Gregory's parents, rule or no rule, for they were important to the subject. See *Logos* 6, fol. 98r–98v: μέλλοντι δέ μοι λοιπὸν ἤδη, πρὸς τὴν ἀρχὴν τῶν ἐγκωμίων καθισταμένῳ, τῶν τοῦ μεγάλου [i.e., Gregory] μεμνῆσθαι πατέρων, λογισμὸς οὗτος ἔπεισι καί μοι σφόδρα ἦν βουλομένῳ μὴ νόμον εἶναι τὸν ἐπιτάττοντα περὶ τούτων ἐνταῦθα, ὡς ἂν μὴ δοκοίην ἀμέλει πρὸς τὴν τῶν λόγων τέχνην ἀφοσιούμενος καὶ δουλεύων τῇ περὶ τῶν τοιούτων ἀνάγκη—ἅτε μὴ ἄλλως ἐξὸν ἢ νενομισμένα, κατὰ τὴν παροιμίαν, βαδίζειν . . . . ἐνθάδε προεπιχειρεῖν καὶ τρίβειν. Having reached the end of his work, Metochites found it difficult to apply the rule of σύγκρισις, *de rigueur* in eulogies, to his hero. See *Logos* 6, fol. 142v: ἔγωγε τοίνυν ἐνταῦθα παραβάλλειν βουλόμενος καὶ παρατιθέναι τοῖς αὐτοῦ τὰ τῶν ἄλλων καὶ νόμους ἀποπληροῦν ἐγκωμίων, τούτους ἄρα δὴ δοκοῦντας πάλαι τεθεῖσθαι καλῶς, οὐκ οἶδα τί ποτ' ἂν χρησαίμην.

b) Example from a late work, Preface to the *Life* of St. John the Younger (written after 1330): Metochites refused to obey rules prevailing in secular writings, such as those requiring the preliminary mention of the hero's country of origin and his ancestry, for in John's case there was nothing of importance to be said on the subject. John's case offered a chance for doing the very opposite of what the rules prescribed: the very fact that John issued from lowly peasant stock and was born in an obscure village near Didymoteichos contributed to the glory of this pearl, formed in a humble oyster shell. See *Vita S. Iohannis Iunioris*, ed. H. Delehaye and P. Peeters in *Acta SS Novembris*, IV (Brussels, 1925), p. 680A–D.

To profess disregard for the ἔξωθεν ἐγκωμίων νόμοι, the Profane Laws of Eulogy, to quote them just the same, and to follow them after all—all this Metochites probably copied from St. Basil, St. Gregory of Nyssa, and St. Gregory of Nazianzus, whose practice is wittily described by H. Delehaye, *Les passions des martyrs et les genres littéraires* (Brussels, 1921), pp. 191–95; however, the twist—John's lowly origins made his achievements the more resplendent—seems to have been Metochites' own.

his protests, he did obey the rules, but he gave them a twist. His tormented style, although based on that of the Second Sophistics, is the result of his desire to be different.

Except for Ptolemy, Metochites examined venerable authorities with a critical eye, and the eye was his own, not the watchful eye of the Church. Ancient writers and philosophers did not live up to their promises. It would have been better if Hermogenes' *On the Method of Perfect Eloquence* and Aristotle's *Metaphysics* had perished. Both authors aroused the reader's expectations and then let him down.[191] Plato and Aristotle had not solved all the philosophical problems.[192] In one respect, philosophers were no different from the rest of humanity: they contradicted each other and themselves;[193] they also wanted to appear as more than they were: when Aristotle had no clear solution to a philosophical issue, he purposely affected an obscure style, and thus tried to conceal his difficulties from the confused reader.[194] Even the great Pythagoras committed a hoax when he tried to impress the world with his doctrine of metempsychosis.[195] On the other hand, the much maligned Epicurus' teachings were not altogether unreasonable, since all men strove after pleasure and the enjoyment of more sublimated pleasures was admissible and lawful; Pyrrhonism, too, had some point, since the only really dependable truths were those offered by Divine Revelation.[196]

Most worrisome of all, the philosophers' precepts concerning society could not be applied in real life. These men proved the point themselves by withdrawing from practical politics and abstaining from following their own rules.[197] Plato maintained that philosophy alone sufficed to run the state; unfortunately, this was not so; these were only beautiful and dignified words, not susceptible of realization.[198] All the model emperors and commanders dreamed up by philosophers just were not to be seen among living men. People whose laws had been successfully applied in society were not philosophers but doers: for instance, Numa Pompilius, that founder of Rome's greatness and predecessor of the Byzantine emperors; Cyrus; or Hanno the Cartha-

191 TM, *Miscellanea*, Ch. 21, esp. pp. 155–57 (Hermogenes and Aristotle); Ch. 3, pp. 28–29; 31 (Aristotle alone).

192 *Miscellanea*, Ch. 10, esp. pp. 75–77.

193 *Miscellanea*, Ch. 54, esp. pp. 309–10: ἥψασθ' ἡ νόσος αὕτη καὶ τῶν τὴν ἀλήθειαν τῶν ὄντων κατὰ φιλοσοφίαν σπουδὴν ἐχόντων .... καὶ πλείσταις οὐ πρὸς ἀλλήλους μόνον .... ἐναντιώσεσι .... ἐνέχονται καὶ τοῖς σκώπτουσιν ἀφορμὰς ὥστε κατατρέχειν .... τῆς φιλοσοφίας παρέχονται, ἀλλὰ καὶ πρὸς ἑαυτούς .... ἐναντιολογίαις περιπίπτουσιν. Cf. Ch. 3, esp. p. 24: ὧν [i.e., philosophical problems] πολλή τις ἐξέτασις τοῖς ἐλλογίμοις, καὶ ἄλλως ἄλλοι περὶ αὐτῶν καὶ τἀναντί' ἔδοξαν; p. 25: βούλεται μὲν γὰρ ὁ ἀνὴρ [i.e., Aristotle] πάντας αἰτιᾶσθαι τοὺς πρὸ αὐτοῦ; p. 26: καὶ τοῦτο δῆλον, ὅτε μὴ περὶ πάνθ' ἅ προτίθεται ὁ αὐτός ἐστιν [i.e., Aristotle]; p. 34: οὕτω δὴ τοῖς τἀναντία βουλομένοις περὶ ψυχῆς ἀφορμαὶ τοῦ 'Αριστοτέλους δίδονται; Ch. 61, esp. p. 376: καὶ τοῦθ' ὁρᾶν ἔστιν.... ἐπὶ τῶν φιλοσοφησάντων .... μὴ μόνον ἀλλήλοις.... διατεινομένων τἀναντιώτατα.... ἀλλ' ἔστιν οὗ καὶ ἑαυτοῖς καὶ περιπίπτοντων οἷς ἐν ἄλλοις φθάσαντες εἰρήκεσαν. Cf. Ch. 80, esp. p. 525 (on philosophers' divergent views on politics).

194 *Miscellanea*, Ch. 3, pp. 23–34. On this and similar accusations which Metochites leveled at Aristotle, see B. Tatakis, "Aristote critiqué par Théodore Métochites," *Mélanges offerts a Octave et Melpo Merlier*, II (Athens, 1956), pp. 439–45.

195 *Miscellanea*, Ch. 52, esp. p. 298.

196 a) Epicurus: *Logos* 10, fol. 207v: striving for pleasure is a general phenomenon; hence 'Επίκουρος .... καὶ συχνοὶ τῶν ἐλλογίμων παλαιῶν ἀνδρῶν στασιῶται τῆς αἱρέσεως, ἡδονὴν τὸ πᾶν ἐν βίῳ τέλος καὶ τῆς ἀνθρωπίνης ὁρμῆς καὶ γνώμης νομίσαντες, ἔδοξαν οὐ πάνυ τοι φορτικῶς οὐδ' ἀηδῶς ἀποφήνασθαι; cf. fol. 208v: εἴπερ οὐ καθάπαξ φλαῦρόν τι καὶ εὐδιάβλητον τὸ τῆς ἡδονῆς τοῦτο χρῆμα, ὡς οὐκ ἔγωγε οἶμαι, ἀλλ' ἔστιν ὅτε καὶ οὔ, καὶ ἐφ' οἷστισι δέδοται καὶ

νενόμισται; cf. fol. 209v: ἡδονὴν δέ, ὡς ἔοικεν, οὐ πᾶσαν, οὐδὲ παντάπασιν, ὀστρακιστέον, οὐδ' ἀποκηρυκτέον ἀνθρώπων, ἀλλὰ πλείστην μὲν ἴσως [i.e., that of the flesh], τὴν δὲ [i.e., that of the mind] οὔ. b) Pyrrhonism: *Miscellanea*, Ch. 61, esp. pp. 370–71: μήποτε προσμαρτυρία .... ἐπὶ τοῖς 'Εφεκτικοῖς κληθεῖσι τῶν κατὰ φιλοσοφίαν .... καὶ τοίνυν οὐδ' ἐξοστρακιστέον ἐξ 'Ελλήνων τελείως τὸ δόγμα, οὐδ' ἀπορριπτέον ἀνεπιστρόφως. Cf. p. 375: μόνα δὲ τὰ πάσης ἐπέκεινα σοφίας ἐκ θεοῦ πάντως εἰλημμένα περὶ αὐτοῦ θεοῦ. ... περιγίγνεται τῷ κράτει τῆς ἀληθείας τίμια. ... δόγματα.

197 *Miscellanea*, Chs. 80 and 81; pp. 524–37, esp. p. 526: philosophical writings on politics are λόγοι δ' οὖν ἄλλως καὶ πρὸς τὸν σκοπὸν ἀνήνυτοι· καὶ οὐδένες. ... τῶν εἰπόντων οὔτ' ἐχρήσαντ' ἄρα τοῖς λόγους αὐτῶν, οὔτε μήποτε χρήσαιντο, ὅτι μηδ' οἷόν τε, ἀλλ' ἔξω τῆς ἀνθρωπίνης ἀγωγῆς καθάπαξ φέρονται καὶ ἃ μὴ πέφυκεν εὐκολίᾳ γλώττης ἀναζωγραφοῦσι καὶ ὑποτίθενται; cf. p. 533: philosophers πάντως ἑαυτοὺς ἀνικάνους πρὸς τὴν χρῆσιν τῆς πολιτικῆς φιλοσοφίας καὶ ἀγωγῆς. ... προδεικνύντες ἔφευγον τὰ πράγματα, τοὺς ἐλέγχους ἐπὶ τῇ χρήσει φεύγοντες.

198 *Logos* 10, fol. 212r–212v: ἐπεὶ καὶ Πλάτωνι, καὶ εἴ τινί ποτ' ἄλλῳ τῶν παλαιῶν ἐκείνων ἀνδρῶν καὶ πανσόφων, περὶ φιλοσοφίας μάλιστα ἠγώνισται, ὡς μόνον ἐν πολιτικοῖς αὔταρκες πράγμασι .... καὶ μόνον ἐφάμιλλόν ἐστι βασιλείᾳ πρὸς ὄντως οἰκονομίαν ἡρμοσμένην ἀνθρώπων, καὶ διὰ μόνου τούτου, συνελόντος ἐρεῖν, ἅπαντ' ἂν ὀρθοῖντο τοῦ βίου πράγματα. ... οὐ πεισόμεθα μὲν πάντως ἐπιχειροῦντι καὶ βουλομένῳ .... γνωσόμεθα δὲ ὅμως καὶ συγγνωσόμεθα .... οἷς διὰ παντὸς ἐσχόλασε τοῦ βίου συνηγοροῦντι. Cf. fol. 212v: ἀλλὰ ταῦτα [i.e., Plato's views on the importance of philosophy in |politics] μὲν ἔστιν .... λόγοι μόνον, μὴ .... πεῖραν ἐν τοῖς πράγμασι δόντες· καὶ κάλλιστα μὲν εἴρηνται καὶ πάνυ τοι σεμνῶς, φύσιν δ' ὅμως οὐκ ἔχει τινὰ τελευτῆσαί τε καὶ πραχθῆναι.

ginian. Metochites the man of letters may have admired Plato's precepts; but Metochites the Prime Minister felt more comfortable among the fellow-administrators of the past. When he turned to books for answers to his everyday problems, he found that they gave none; no wonder that he showed his disappointment.[199]

The Byzantine rule in Asia Minor collapsed under Metochites' own eyes. He became Prime Minister at a time when the Catalans, brought to Byzantium to help in the struggle with the Turks, were themselves pillaging its western provinces.[200] In his own words, twice or three times during his tenure of office he feared the utter destruction of his state and hoped to die before witnessing what the near future seemed to hold in store for the Empire.[201] Such a man would no longer subscribe to the belief to which Byzantine intellectuals had clung for centuries: a belief in their empire, universal and co-eternal with the world, and in their civilization, unique and superior to all others.

Metochites was the first among the writers of the fourteenth and fifteenth centuries to see Byzantium not as a final state in the scheme of world history but as just one of the empires obeying the universal law of creation and destruction.[202] With the men of letters of his generation, Metochites was still proud of Byzantine civilization, which included ancient Greek culture, for to him, as to thirteenth-century writers of the Nicaean Empire, the Byzantines were of the same race as the ancient Greeks.[203] Doubts as to the superiority of Byzantine civilization began to occur several decades after his death. But Metochites did not see this civilization as unique. If the Greek past was known down to its smallest details, this was due to the accident of literary transmission and showed only how important literature was. It was conceivable that memorable achievements of some foreign peoples, which might have equaled or surpassed those of the Greeks, had been recorded by their own historians, but that the Byzantines were ignorant of these records—as ignorant as the foreign peoples themselves were of the Hellenic past, omitted by their writers from works composed in their native tongues.[204] Metochites' views on world history were relativistic.

---

199 *Miscellanea*, Ch. 81, esp. p. 532: philosophers τὸν κατ' αὐτοὺς καὶ πολιτικὸν καὶ βασιλικὸν καὶ ἡγεμονικὸν [i.e., ἄνδρα] ἔξω τοῦ γιγνομένου παντὸς [i.e., realm of possibility] κατ' ἀνθρώπους δεικνύουσι, καὶ οὐχ οἷον ἐν ἀνθρώποις ὁρᾶσθαι. On Numa Pompilius, Cyrus, and Hanno, see Ch. 80, esp. pp. 529–30; as for the laws excogitated by Plato and Aristotle, no nation, whether Hellenic or barbaric, whether in their own time or later on, found any use for them; cf. p. 531.

200 About 1305: see my *Etudes*, pp. 149–51.

201 *Miscellanea*, Ch. 28, esp. pp. 191–92: ξυμβέβηκε γὰρ τὰ Ῥωμαίων πράγματα κομιδῆ νοσῆσαι καὶ δυσχερέσι τύχαις πάντοθεν τῶν ἐκ γειτόνων ἀνθρώπων. . . . ἐν κλύδωσι μεγάλοις γενέσθαι τοῖς νέοις τούτοις καθ' ἡμᾶς χρόνοις. . . . ὥστε καὶ μικροῦ πρὸς τοῖς ἐσχάτοις γενέσθαι δὶς ποῦ καὶ τρίς, ἢ καὶ πλεῖν ἔτι. Cf. p. 193: καὶ πολλάκις ἔγωγ' ἐμαυτῷ ξύνοιδα τῶν τελευταίων ἐν χρῷ κινδύνων γενέσθαι ἐντεῦθεν . . . . τῇ . . . . τῶν κοινῶν ἐπιστασία . . . . τῷ δεσπότῃ [i.e., Andronicus II] συμμετέχων. Cf. Ch. 38, esp. pp. 242–43: σωφρονούντων ἂν εἴη . . . . ἀνθρώπων . . . . ἐπαίειν . . . . ἐξ οἵων οἷοι γεγόναμεν· ἀλγεῖν δ' ὅμως καὶ δεδιέναι . . . . τοῖς φθάσασι τοὺς ἐσχάτους κινδύνους ἀνάγκη πᾶσα . . . . καὶ τῶν νῦν πραγμάτων γιγόμενος καὶ κλέπτων ἐμαυτὸν τῆς περὶ ἐμὲ πολλάκις ἀσχολίας, πάσης ἐλπίδος αὐτόθεν ἀποχωρῶ, καὶ θανάτου μάλιστ' ἐρῶ τέως, πρὶν ἢ κατιδεῖν ἃ κατιδεῖν ἀνάγκην εἶναι πᾶσαν οἶμαι τοὺς ἐπ' ὀλίγου ἐν τοῖς ζῶσιν ἀρκέσοντας.

202 On this and other points related to the Byzantine conceptions of history, see my "The Decline of Byzantium as Seen through the Eyes of Its Intellectuals," *DOP*, 15 (1961), pp. 179–86.

203 See *Miscellanea*, Ch. 93, p. 595: The Hellenes wrote down their deeds for posterity, παραπέμποντες τῷ χρόνῳ καὶ ἡμῖν, οἳ καὶ τοῦ γένους ἐσμὲν καὶ τῆς γλώττης αὐτοῖς κοινωνοὶ καὶ διάδοχοι; cf. Ch. 115, esp. p. 792: δεῆσαν . . . . ἐνίων μνησθῆναι πρὸς τὸν λόγον ὑποδειγμάτων [culled from ancient Greek historians] . . . . ἐμνήσθημεν· καὶ ἴσως γε δικαιότερον, τῶν ἐκ τῆς αὐτῆς ἡμῖν γλώττης ἱστορίᾳ παραπεμπομένων εἰς ἡμᾶς καὶ ταύτοῦ γένους. Accordingly, on occasion Metochites called the Byzantines "Hellenes" rather than "Romans"; see *Logos* 7, Vindobon. ph. gr. 95, fol. 150v: Andronicus II did all in his power ὑπὲρ τῆς τῶν σῶν Ἑλλήνων σωτηρίας; cf. *Poem* 1, v. 937: the rulers of Epirus τάδ' ἐφ' ἡμέας ἔδρασαν ὁμοφύλους Ἕλληνας. By claiming continuity between ancient Greece and his own time, Metochites both joined a strain in late-Byzantine intellectual history—attested in thirteenth-century Nicaea, a city where he spent some time in his youth—and anticipated widespread modern-Greek attitudes. See, for the Byzantine period, S. Runciman, "Byzantine and Hellene in the Fourteenth Century," Τόμος Κωνσταντίνου Ἁρμενοπούλου (Salonika, 1952), pp. 27–31 (recommended more for its data than for its conclusions); P. K. Chrestou, Αἱ περιπέτειαι τῶν ἐθνικῶν ὀνομάτων τῶν Ἑλλήνων (Salonika, 1960), pp. 46–49; and A. E. Bakalopoulos, Ἱστορία τοῦ Νέου Ἑλληνισμοῦ, I (Salonika, 1961), pp. 67–77 (especially valuable for the usage of Nicaean writers, who employed the terms γένος and διάδοχοι); see further the English recasting of the same book, *Origins of the Greek Nation* (1970), pp. 36–43.

204 *Logos* 10, fol. 204v: Ἕλληνές τε . . . . πλεῖστα συνεγράψαντο τῶν ἄλλων, καὶ περὶ αὐτῶν [αὑτῶν manuscript]

Metochites even had his noble barbarians. Their portrait was drawn without Christian frills and with conscious reference to antique sources. The models for the portrait were the Tartars of the Golden Horde. In Metochites' parlance, they were called Scythians, for he assumed that the Mongols and Qypčaqs were the ancient Scythians' direct descendants. Up to Metochites' time, the Scythians provided the only exception to the universal law of creation and destruction, for no external force had subdued them yet, not Darius, not even Alexander the Great. True, they were nomads dwelling in tents of felt cloth and their life was uncivilized. But this naturally simple existence could perhaps explain the strength of their populous empire. It was unencumbered by the burden of civilization, and this simplicity had its advantages. The Scythians, free of the legalistic paraphernalia usual among civilized peoples, were more just than the latter. Homer attested to it, and Metochites could confirm that the Scythians of his day—that is to say, the Tartars—had maintained these ancestral virtues.[205]

Byzantine scholars were interested in the chronology of the authors they studied, but their picture of antiquity was a two-dimensional canvas: in it, Pythagoras stood next to Socrates, Aristophanes next to Lucian, and Demosthenes was paired off with an orator of the Second Sophistics. On occasion, Metochites showed a sense of historical perspective. Thus, he felt that he and his generation had certain advantages over Socrates, who had not had at his disposal the treasures on which it could freely draw. In Socrates' time, philosophy had not yet differentiated into its diverse branches, nor had it coped with many problems concerning Nature. As a harmoniously constructed system, it dated only from the Hellenistic and Roman periods.[206]

In 1330, Metochites wrote a comparison between Demosthenes and Aelius Aristides.[207] The genre was not new, nor was the topic. It had its bibliography—Lucian, Plutarch, Dionysius of Halicarnassus, Sopatros, Hermogenes; Metochites used or knew all of it.[208] But the main point, he claimed, was his own, and it was this: Demosthenes lived in a free democratic community. He was a man of action and his eloquence had to take political reality into account—it was not a rhetorical exercise, but a vital involvement. A man standing in front of the people had no time for blunders or verbosity. Aristides, on the other hand, lived in an absolute monarchy; the times

---

δὴ μάλιστα πλεῖστα ἢ περὶ τῶν ἄλλων· καὶ τοίνυν ἅπαντα τὰ αὐτῶν ἴσμεν παμπλήρη, καὶ μείζω καὶ μείω. Cf. fol. 205r: καὶ ταῦτα δὴ πάντα καὶ μνήμης ἠξιοῦντο πλείστης καὶ συγγραφόντων· . . . . πόσοι δὲ τὰς αὐτὰς ἢ καὶ μείζους . . . . ἐπεδείξαντο πράξεις, ἃ δὴ μηδενὸς ἢ βραχέος ἀξιωθέντα τυχὸν ἔνια λόγου . . . . λέλυνται παντάπασιν, οἶμαι, λήθης ἐντελοῦς ὀλέθρῳ. On fol. 205r-205v Metochites singled out "many Italian cities" of his own time (he must have meant Genoa and Venice): they displayed considerable land and sea power, and were in almost every respect similar to the Greek cities of the past. Yet, they were not considered especially glorious, for they lacked the pen of a Thucydides or a Theopompus ready to record their accomplishments. See, for similar considerations, *Miscellanea*, Ch. 93, pp. 591–96, esp. pp. 595–96: ἴσως δ' ἂν καὶ παρ' ἄλλοις τῶν ἐθνῶν εἴη . . . . τὰ κατ' αὐτοὺς ἑκάστους τιμῆς ἐν συγγραφαῖς οἰκείαις καὶ μνήμης ἀξιούμενα . . . . καὶ ὥσπερ . . . . τὰ κατ' ἐκείνους ἡμῖν ἀγνοεῖται, ὅτι μὴ τοῖς Ἑλληνικοῖς ξυγγραφεῦσι περὶ ἐκείνων ἐμέλησεν, οὕτως ἂν ἴσως κἀκείνοις τὰ περὶ ἡμῶν ἀγνοῆται, ὅτι μὴ τοῖς κατ' ἐκείνους ξυγγραφεῦσι περὶ τὰ ἡμέτερα πονεῖν ἐμέλησεν. On this point, see Beck, *Metochites* (as in n. 11 above), p. 93.

205 *Miscellanea*, Ch. 110, pp. 723–34.

206 *Logos* 10, fol. 203r: ἄλλως τε μὴν ποῦ τηνικαῦτα Σωκράτης τοσούτους εὕρατο θησαυροὺς ὁπόσους νῦν ἡμεῖς ἔχομεν, τῶν ἀπ' ἐκείνου τοσούτων χρόνων μεγίστην τὴν προσθήκην ἐμποιησάντων . . . . ; οὔτε φιλοσοφίας οὐδέπω

καὶ τότε . . . . ἠκριβωμένης . . . . οὐδέ . . . . πρὸς τὴν τῶν ὄντων ἅπασαν καὶ τῆς φύσεως ἑτερότητα ἐπιχειρούσης, μηδ' εἰς μυρίους ὅσους ὀχετούς . . . . κατατετμημένης . . . . οὐδέπω τῆς τέχνης . . . . πεπηγμένης οὐδ' ὅρους ἐντελεῖς . . . . καὶ συνθήματα δεξαμένης καὶ τεταγμένης. Cf. fol. 203v: ἔπειθ' ἑξῆς εἴπετο πραγμάτων Ἑλληνικῶν καὶ Ῥωμαϊκῶν ὄγκος τοσοῦτος, ὑφ' ὧν, ὥσπερ ἐστὶ φύσις, ἐξαπτομένη προδήλως σοφία συμπαρέθει . . . . τοῖς καιροῖς αὐτοῖς ἐπιδιδοῦσι . . . . συμπαρεκτεινομένη καὶ προκόπτουσα.

207 *Logos* 17, Vindobon. ph. gr. 95, fols. 356r–363v, 354r–354v, 364r; the text is now available in Gigante, "Il saggio," pp. 74–92, and in the same author's *Teodoro Metochites, saggio critico* (both as in note 29 above). However, I cite from "Il saggio." See also my *Etudes*, pp. 143 and 179–80.

208 For the use of Pseudo-Lucian's (or Lucian's: on this point, see T. Sinko, who defends the Encomium's authenticity in "Nowa forma enkomion u Lucjana z Samosat," *Eos, Organ Polskiego Towarzystwa Filologicznego*, 44,2 [Wrocław, 1950], pp. 3–14) *Demosthenis encomium* in *Logos* 17, see the apparatus in Gigante, "Il saggio," *ad* Chs. 11.2, 17.1, 18.8, 21.10 (to which one should add *Dem. enc.* 14 *ad* 23.11 and 34.14); for Dionysius of Halicarnassus, Gigante, *ad* 15.11; for Plutarch and Pseudo-Plutarch, Gigante, *ad* 6.1, 8.16, 10.11, 17.1; for Hermogenes, Gigante, *ad* Chs. 10.11, 28.11, 28.14; it is most likely that Metochites read Sopatros' *Prolegomena* to Aristides; in any case, he quotes the name of this late-fourth century (?) theoretician of rhetoric in his *Logos* 14, **12**.7, see *Etudes*, p. 235.

allowed him to abandon all quest for offices and to devote himself to his purely rhetorical and epideictic studies.[209] Curiously, to Metochites this meant that Aristides enjoyed more freedom of speech: as he was not submitted to pressures coming from his audience, he could follow his inspiration. His volubility and elegance in treating subjects of the remote past were admirable. But if he had been a contemporary of the events he treated, and stood in front of a real council, he would either have had to change his ways or he would have been removed from political life. Demosthenes had to adapt himself to political reality, talk concisely, and talk sense;[210] in this one respect Metochites gave preference to Demosthenes.[211] As for Aristides, he could just talk and talk and talk. But when it came to recommending models of eloquence for students of his time, Metochites had to prefer Aristides, for these students lived under the same kind of regime, namely monarchy; consequently, they needed the same kind of oratory: epideictic above all, and free-flowing—that is, verbose.[212] Some of Metochites' conclusions are modern,[213] some strange; but they were drawn by an intelligent man who thought for himself.

He also was a self-centered, anxious, and sensitive man who constantly spoke about himself. His preoccupation with himself led him to twist the rules of the genre and break the canons of mimesis. It is camouflaged as reflections on human nature and it accounts for much that is unusual in his writings. The Dirge for his son-in-law turns into a long reproach: by dying, the deceased upset Metochites' plans for his family's future;[214] a Speech on culture becomes an oblique attack on his literary enemies.[215] His Essay on the saying "live in obscurity" (λάθε βιώσας) was inspired by Plutarch's piece on the same subject, but while Plutarch attacked Epicurus, Metochites talked about himself. He proved that the saying might apply to lowly people, but the cultured and wealthy would remain in the public eye, for they could neither avoid involvement in the affairs of this world nor withstand the temptations of fame.[216] When Metochites defended Philo's harsh style and Synesius' disregard for the atticizing rules of lexicography, he defended himself.[217] When he was irritated by mediocrities, who were envious of outstanding person-

209 The main passage is *Logos* 17, fol. 358r (Gigante, "Il saggio," Ch. 8.10–25, pp. 77–78); see also fol. 359v (Gigante, Ch. 15.6–8, p. 81); fol. 36or (Gigante, Ch. 31.1–5, p. 90). See, finally, the summary of *Logos* 17, Ch. 8, in Gigante, p. 61.

210 *Logos* 17, fol. 358r–358v (Gigante, "Il saggio," Ch. 9.1–12, p. 78); fol. 359v (Gigante, Ch. 14.1–7, p. 80); fol. 361r (Gigante, Ch. 20.1–13, p. 84).

211 *Logos* 17, fol. 354v (Gigante, "Il saggio," Ch. 34.7–11, p. 91).

212 *Logos* 17, fol. 364r (Gigante, "Il saggio," Chs. 34.18–35.6, p. 92).—That Metochites did not advocate constitutional monarchy for his time was shown by Hesseling, "Een Konstitutioneel . . ." (as in n. 29 above).

213 W. Schmid observed in his *Der Atticismus in seinen Hauptvertretern*, II (Stuttgart, 1889), pp. 15–16, that while old rhetoric never lost the inner relationship with its subject matter, the eloquence of an Aristides lacked the firm ground of reality; it was at its best when it treated subjects lying half a millennium away and pondered issues which had been decided long ago. See also L. Méridier, *L'influence de la seconde sophistique sur l'œuvre de Grégoire de Nysse* (Paris, 1906), p. 9.

214 *Poem* 9, fols. 112v–113r; now the fortunes of Metochites' own children, too, would take a turn for the worse: τίσιν ἄρα ξυνέλαχον ἄθλιος πρήγμασι δεινοῖς,| καί θ' ὁράων νέκυν οὐ πρό τε θανεῖν ἐλπίδ' εἶχον | ἠδέ τ' ἔραον, οἵων βέλτιον ἔμμεν ἔμοιγε | οὕνεκά τε ψυχᾶς ἡμετέρας ἅ τε νούμιμ' ἔασιν, | . . . . | οὕνεκα τ' αὖ τεκέων, ὄφρα κε πέλωνται | ὑστατίοισιν ἔτεσι τεθνειῶτος ἐμοῖο | . . . . εὐδαίμονα διὰ σέο πραπίδεσσί τε κεδναῖς | . . . . | . . . . ἀτὰρ τάδ' ἅπαντ' οἴχονται ἠΰτ' ὄνειρος. Cf. fol. 126v, quoted in n. 100 above.

215 *Logos* 10, fols. 213v–217v, esp. fol. 216r–216v: ὃ καί πολλάκις ξυνορῶν ἐν ἐμαυτῷ, κατεθαύμασα, καί λελύπημαι

τὴν κοινὴν ἁμαρτίαν σοφίας, ὥσπερ τἆλλ' ἅπαντα, καί τύχην, καί ὅπως ἀεί βάλλομεν ἕκαστος ἀλλήλους ἐκ τάφανοῦς σπουδῇ καί προθυμίᾳ πάσῃ, καί καταστρέφομεν, τὸ κράτος ἑαυτοῖς μόνον ἅπαντες κατακληροῦν ἀγῶνα προτιθέμενοι· τά ἡμέτερα λοιπόν αὐτῶν ὡς, οἶμαι, ἔχει καί αὐτά παραπλήσ', οὐχ ὁρῶμεν ἕκαστος. καί νοσοῦμεν μέν τά οἰκεῖα, νοσοῦμεν δέ τἀλλότρια πλεῖν ἤ ἔχει, κρίνοντες ἀμφότερα, τῇ μέν φιλαιτοῦντες, τῇ δέ βασκαίνοντες . . . . 'πάντ' ἔχει', φάσκοντες, 'εὖ' τά καί τά ὅμως εἰ προσῆν, ἀναίτιον παντάπασι τοὔργον [i.e., our enemy's literary work] ἂν ἦν· καί παρεντίθεμεν ἴσως, ἃ μή προσόντα μεγίστην . . . . δείκνυσι τὴν ζημίαν.

216 *Miscellanea*, Ch. 72, pp. 481–84. That Plutarch was the source for Metochites' information on Epicurus, is also apparent from *Miscellanea*, Ch. 71, esp. pp. 468–71 (Plutarch rejects Epicurus' view on God, but makes use of the sound parts of his doctrine). However, Metochites (and his milieu) drew upon some *florilegium* for the quotation, going back to the Epicurean school, on the human race living in a "city without walls" with respect to Death (= H. Usener, *Epicurea* [Leipzig, 1887], fr. 339, p. 228; A. Körte, "Metrodori Epicurei fragmenta," *Jahrbücher für classische Philologie*, Suppl. 17 [1890], fr. 51, p. 562). This quotation occurs in *Miscellanea*, Ch. 27, p. 179; in *Poem* 20, Paris. gr. 1776, fol. 238r–238v; and in the collection of excerpts by Nicephorus Gregoras, the Heidelbergensis Palatinus gr. 129, fol. 23r, lines 9–11. *Pace* Gigante, "Per l'interpretazione" (as in note 29 above), pp. 21–25, the use of this Epicurean metaphor does not suffice to establish Metochites as a humanist, nor does it constitute proof of "the excellence of his literary taste." Cf. nn. 166 above and 229 below.

217 See *Miscellanea*, Ch. 16, *On Philo*, esp. p. 123: οὐ γάρ παντάπασιν ἔξω οὐδ' ἀνοίκειον τοῦ σεμνοῦ τε καί ἀξιωματικοῦ τό τραχύ τῆς φωνῆς, ὡς ἡ τέχνη βούλεται καί νομίζει;

alities' different behavior, by "outstanding personalities" he meant himself.[218] When he found in self-love, which included the love of one's family, the explanation for acquisitiveness, regardless of public opinion, he was explaining himself.[219]

When, to while away the days of his forced retirement at the Chora, the old man Metochites reread himself in his deluxe volumes, he was struck by passages that applied to his own plight. One of these passages dealt with people embroiled in political affairs and went on to explain that many noble and otherwise moderate men were engulfed by this kind of life, against both their better judgment and their natural inclinations. They were swept along, yielding to their rulers, to bonds of love towards their own children, or to ambition. On the margin next to this passage, Metochites wrote in the bold and still clear hand of a *grand seigneur*: "I, the author, am speaking the truth, God be my witness. This is the way I lived myself." Another passage described how men who had known wealth, power, and prosperity would suddenly fall upon evil days. Nothing in this world was permanent; everything was apt to turn into its very opposite. On the margin, Metochites added: "This I, too, experienced a short time after having written these lines." Finally, a third passage asked what assurance there was that a healthy man would not be stricken by illness, and a wealthy one would not experience utter destitution. To it, Metochites appended this gloss: "I, too, experienced what I had foretold."[220]

The main preoccupation of his earlier years, however, was the dichotomy in his own existence. He wanted to be a scholar, he became a politician. He abandoned literature in midstream [221] but

---

cf. Ch. 18, *On Synesius*, esp. pp. 137–39: ἀλλὰ καὶ ᾿Αττικῆς δή τινος καλλιεπείας . . . . βραχὺ τῷ ἀνδρὶ μέλει . . . . καίτοιγε μὴ τοῖς ὀνόμασι χρώμενος ὅμως οὕτω, ἀλλ' ἐξιὼν ἔστιν ὅτε . . . . τῆς κοινῆς ἕξεως καὶ γνωρίμου . . . . καὶ εἰς ἀνόδευτ' ἀδεῶς ἄγων . . . . χαίρει . . . . ὡς ἄρα τις αὐτοκράτωρ . . . . καὶ ἑαυτῷ θαρρεῖ καινίζων τῇ χρήσει . . . . καὶ μὴ τῶν εἰκότων ἐκπίπτων διὰ τὸ περὶ ταύτην ἄκρον τὴν τέχνην. There follows an apology *pro domo sua*: ἐπεὶ μηδὲ συγγνωστὸν πάντως τὸ ξενίζων . . . . , ἢν μὴ μετ' ἀσφαλείας καὶ τῶν τῆς τέχνης νομίμων ὁρῷτο· ἢν δ' ἄρ' οὕτως εὐθαρσής τις εἴη καὶ χρώμενος ἔξω τῆς τῶν πολλῶν ἀγωγῆς ἀκλόνητος, ἴσως καὶ θαυμάζειν μᾶλλόν ἐστιν ἄξιος, ὡς ἄρα καὶ Συνέσιος ὄντως αὐτός. For less admiring judgments of Byzantine and modern critics on Metochites' own style, see *Études*, pp. 35–41.

218 *Logos* 10, fol. 216r: the mediocrities ἃ γὰρ δὴ καὶ σφᾶς ᾠήθησαν κατειργάσθαι, μόγις μὲν ἴσως, ἀλλ' ὅμως καὶ τοῖς ἄλλοις κατατίθενται καὶ ξυγχωροῦσιν· ἃ δὴ μή, βασκαίνουσιν ὡς ἔπειθ' οἷόν τέ ἐστι τοῖς ἀρίστοις, καὶ τῆς φύσεως αὐτῆς κατεξανίστανται καὶ κατηγοροῦσιν, ὡς οὐκ ἐξὸν ὅλως, καὶ περιτρέπειν παντὶ σθένει χρῆναι νομίζουσι, καὶ καταμετρεῖν εἰς ἑαυτοὺς ὅρους ἃ τ' ἔξεστι ἅ τε μή, καὶ τὸ μὲν κατ' αὐτοὺς δοκεῖν σπουδάζουσι παντέλειον, ἢν δέ τι καὶ πλέον ἀκούωσι, τοῦτο μὴ σωφρονεῖν.

219 *Logos* 10, fol. 190r–190v (self-love affects all men): ἅπαντες γὰρ ἑαυτοὺς φιλοῦσιν εἰς ὅσον ἂν ἥκῃ καὶ δύναιντο πλεῖστον, καὶ τοσοῦτον–ἴσως ἀνεύθυνον, ὡς νομίζεται–ὥστε καὶ πάντα διὰ τοῦτο μόνον ῥαδίως τολμᾶν· καὶ βούλοιντ' ἂν τὰ πάντα σφίσι πρὸς τὸ βέλτιστον ἐσκευάσθαι, καί, τὸ δεύτερον ἔτι, μάλισθ' οὕτως ἐσκευάσθαι δοκεῖν. Cf. *Miscellanea*, Ch. 118, esp. p. 808: τὸ δ' αἴτιον ἴσως φιλαυτία· ὅλοι γὰρ ἐκείνων εἰσὶ τῶν . . . . ἐπεράστων κἀκείνοις, ὡς εἰπεῖν, οὐσίωνται . . . . καὶ τὸ φιλεῖν ἑαυτὸν ἀμέλει καὶ τὰ καίρια καὶ βέλτισθ' ἑαυτῷ, καὶ οἷς συνουσίωται, πάντων ἄτρεπτον καὶ ἀνεπίστροφον τῶν ἔξω· καὶ κόρον οὐδεὶς ἑαυτοῦ λαμβάνει καὶ τῶν αὐτοῦ καὶ κατὰ φύσιν οἰκείων. See ibid., Ch. 76, esp. p. 505, for explaining attachment to one's own children by self-love. Metochites' pupil Gregoras, too, was conscious of the self and praised ambition, φιλοτιμία, which he called "the soul of the soul." See his *Life of John of Heraclea*, in V. Laurent, "La vie de Jean, métropolite d'Héraclée du Pont, par Nicéphore Grégoras," ᾿Αρχεῖον Πόντου, 6 (1934), pp. 19, 29, lines 1–10, esp. lines 4–5;

Gregoras, *Letter* to Metochites, ed. Bezdeki (as in n. 32 above), p. 272.31–35, = No. 14, Guilland, *Correspondance de . . Grégoras* (as in n. 20 above), p. 69.6–12.

220 See the *Miscellanea* in Paris gr. 2003 (a deluxe volume in Metochites' collected works; see *Études*, p. 282 and n. 3), fol. 115r–115v, commenting upon Ch. 62, esp. pp. 382–83: ἀληθεύω θεοῦ ἐφορῶντος ἔγωγ' ὁ ξυγγράφων· οὕτω δὴ βεβίωκα (for the meaning ξυγγράφων = "author," see George Akropolites, *Hist.*, ed. Heisenberg, p. 164.17: κἀμὲ αὐτὸν τὸν ξυγγράφοντα; Akropolites speaks of himself as author of the work in which these words are found); cf. ibid., fol. 52r, commenting upon Ch. 28, esp. p. 187: πεπείραμαι καὶ ἐγὼ τούτου μετὰ βραχὺ τοῦ ταῦτα γράψαι; cf. ibid., fol. 49r, commenting upon Ch. 27, esp. p. 178: ὡς δὴ καὶ αὐτὸς ἔγωγ' ὧν προύλεγον οὕτω, πεπείραμαι. For reproduction of these three autograph remarks by Metochites, see my *Études*, PL. II and VII. For another possible autograph remark by him, see *Études*, n. 3 and PL. IV. I now believe that the corrections introduced into the text of Metochites' *Poems* in Paris. gr. 1776 are by the author himself. Some or all of the marginal remarks of Paris. gr. 2003 reappear in the margins of a number of secondary manuscripts of the *Miscellanea*, such as Coislinianus 165, fol. 137r–137v; Estensis gr. 228 (α.o. 4.17), quire 7, fol. 4v; quire 15, fol. 18v; Vindobon. ph. gr. 8, fols. 52v, 115r–115v; Metochion Panagiou Taphou 628 (*olim* 1167), fol. 114r; in these manuscripts, the marginal remarks are by the hand of the main scribe, an indication that the manuscripts themselves go back to Paris. gr. 2003. Finally, Cizensis 64 (25), the basis of the Müller-Kiesling edition of the *Miscellanea*, seems to have incorporated the ὡς δὴ καὶ αὐτός, etc. marginal remark into the main text; see *Miscellanea*, p. 178.

221 See *Logos* 10, fols. 217v–218r: ὄφελον μὲν μήποθ' οὕτω διατεθῆναι, ἀπετράπην δ' ὅμως τῶν λόγων, ἐν ἄλλοις ὡς ἂν τῳ δόξαι πράγμασι· . . . . οὗ δὴ χάριν ἄρ' ἔγωγε καὶ μέσην αὐτὴν δέδηγμαι τὴν καρδίαν, καὶ μεμνημένος οὐκ ἔχω φέρειν, ὅπως ἐν αὐτῷ μέσῳ πλῷ τῆς σοφίας καὶ ἴσως οὔρια πλέον, ἀθρόον οὐκ οἶδ' ὅπως πρύμναν ἐκρουσάμην καὶ τρέχων ἄλλην, ἄλλην μεταβέβηκα . . . . καὶ προσταλαιπωρῶ . . . . ζητῶν ἄρα ἐκείνων τὸν ἔρωτα— μὴ γὰρ οὕτω δὴ μανείην ὡς παντάπασιν ἀφεῖσθαι τῶν καλῶν παιδικῶν—ἐμὸς δ' ὅμως ὅστις ἂν καὶ γενοίμην . . . . ἀνάγκη πάντως ἀπαραιτήτῳ συνὼν ἑκάστοτε . . . . πρὸς κῦμα διαμιλλᾶσθαι καὶ χειμῶνα φροντίδων ἄλλοτ' ἄλλων . . . . τῷ ὄντι γὰρ πολλή τις ἔοικεν ἀνωμαλία καὶ ζάλη κατέχειν

hoped to keep it up along with his political activities and the care of his family. He thought he could do both with equal energy; he discovered that he had been wrong.[222] But he could no longer withdraw from practical life; to do so would have been cowardly and contrary to his sense of self-esteem. He was too involved, enslaved by marriage and tied down by the time-consuming care for the future of his children.[223] He did not control life, he was controlled by it. Enemies lurked everywhere. Everything in human life was unstable, an unpredictable dice game. Our actions, views, and thoughts teemed with inconsistencies and contradictions. Instability was a recurrent motif in Metochites' writings, and it reflected the stresses to which both he and Byzantium were exposed throughout his lifetime.[224] In an awkward metaphor, he likened practical life and its labyrinthine meanderings to a moody, vicious, and indomitable beast, which one had to muzzle before turning to the study of letters.[225] We are all caught in an enormous net, he said—again speaking of himself—and tossed about in it without hope of escape.[226]

There was, however, one chance: one could achieve immortality on earth. Survival among men came above all through literary endeavors; however, immortality might also be acquired through the practice of some visual art—that of a sculptor, painter, or architect. Phidias, Poly-

---

τῶν ἐλλογίμων καὶ πεπαιδευμένων ἐκείνους ἀνδρῶν, ὅσοι, τοὺς λόγους λειποτακτήσαντες, φέροντες ἑαυτοὺς ἐνεχείρισαν κοσμικαῖς οἶμαί τισι μικρολογίαις καὶ θορύβοις καὶ πράγμασιν.

222 See *Logos* 10, fol. 219r: πεπείραμαι δὲ καὶ αὐτὸς καὶ κατανενόηκα τοῦθ', ὥσπερ δὴ καὶ ἄλλως τις, σφόδρα· καὶ πάνυ μὲν ἠβουλόμην πανδέξιός τις εἶναι καὶ ἀμφότερα [i.e., politics and literature] ὡς ἀληθῶς ἐξαρκεῖν καὶ πρὸς οὐδέτερον ἐνδεῖν . . . . καὶ μὴν ὤμην γε οὕτω πρότερον ἐξεῖναι, καὶ οὕτω δὴ σαφῶς μετετιθέμην ἄρα καὶ προσηπτόμην πολιτικῶν δή τινων τούτων . . . . καὶ ἀναγκαίας ἐνταῦθα λοιπὸν κτήσεως καὶ συνδιαγωγῆς φιλτάτων . . . . ὡς οὐκ ἀφεξόμενος . . . . τῆς πρότερον ἐν λόγοις καὶ παιδείᾳ σπουδῆς . . . .· νυνὶ δ' ἀμέλει κινδυνεύω μαθεῖν . . . . ὡς πάντα μᾶλλον ἢ ἀμφότερα ταῦτα ἔξεστι σπουδάζειν ὁντιναοῦν. Cf. fol. 219v: οὐ γὰρ δὴ μόνον, ὥς φασιν, ο ὐ κ ἔ ξ ε σ τ ι τ ο ῖ ς ἐ ν λ ύ π α ι ς γ ε ω μ ε τ ρ ε ῖ ν (see D. K. Karathanasis, *Sprichwörter und sprichwörtliche Redensarten . . . in den rhetorischen Schriften . . . des XII. Jahrhunderts* [Speyer, 1936], No. 111), ἀλλ' οὐδὲ φιλοσοφεῖν ὅλως οὐδ' ἐπιχειρεῖν λόγοις, ὧν οὐκ ἄλλως ἐστὶν ἐπικαίρως ἅπτεσθαι, ἢ παρασκευῇ ψυχῆς ἀκμαζούσῃ καὶ διανοίας ἀσείστῳ φρονήματι, ἀπηλλαγμένης συγχύσεως πάσης καὶ νόσου κακοσχόλου. Metochites' dilemma was not unique, either in Byzantine or in later times. For Byzantium, see the regrets which the Grand Heteriarch Manuel Straboromanos uttered in his *Speech* to Emperor Alexius I, ed. P. Gautier, in *REB*, 23 (1965), pp. 186.29–187.2: ἐγὼ δὲ ἐβουλόμην παρὰ μέρος διδόναι πολιτείᾳ καὶ λόγοις, ἀνάγκῃ καὶ πόθῳ τὸν βίον συμμερισάμενος . . . . καί με περιέπτησαν ἐλπίδες εὐθὺς μάλα πολλαί . . . . αἱ δὲ ἄρα ἦσαν, ὡς καὶ πάλαι τις εἶπε, γρηγοροῦντος ἐνύπνια.

223 See *Miscellanea*, Ch. 72, esp. p. 484: πολὺ γ' ἀηδέστατον τὸ δι' ἀτυχίαν λειποτακτεῖν τὰ πράγματα [i.e., practical and political life] δοκεῖν, οὐ δι' εὐγένειάν τινα γνώμης καὶ μεγαλοφροσύνην. For distracting effects of the care of one's children, see *Logos* 10, fol. 219r: τὰ γὰρ δὴ θήλεα καὶ ὁ νεογνῆς μοι παῖς οὗτος ἄρρην παντάπασί με κατέσχεν ἤδη καὶ πάντων ἀπέστησεν ἄρα καὶ ἀπήγαγε βίᾳ τῶν ἄλλων. Cf. fol. 218v: ταῦτα γὰρ οὔτ' ἀποθέσθαι τοῦ λοιποῦ ἔξεστιν, ὅτῳ δὴ ξυμβέβηκε . . . . βίοτον ὄντινα ἄρα ἐλέοσθαι καὶ ξυνοικίαν καὶ διαδοχήν τινα παίδων . . . . οὔθ' ὅλως συμβατικῶς ἔχει τοῖς ἐλλογίμοις πρὸς τὸν ἐξ ἀρχῆς σκοπόν, ἀλλ' ἀεὶ ζημίαν ἐμποιοῦσι τῷ νῷ πλείστην, καὶ τ ο ῦ μ ε γ ί σ τ ο υ κ τ ή μ α τ ο ς ἀ φ α ί ρ ε σ ι ν, τ ο ῦ κ α ι ρ ο ῦ; cf. *Poem* 2, vv. 379, 382–86: αἴθ' ὄφελόν τ' ἀγονός τ' ἄζυξ τελέθειν μακάριος | . . . ὥς κεν μόνος ἠδέ τε κοῦφος | ἄ δ ε τ ο ς αὐτόθεν εἶχον ἐμαυτῷ χρῆσθ' ἄτερθεν | πουλλῶν σκώλων παρ' ὅσος ἀριθμὸς τεκέεσσι· | τάδε γάρ εἰσι π ε δ ή μ α τ' ἄτροπον ἀμφιμέλειν σφιν | τούς γε τεκόντας ἐπείγοντα καὶ μὴ

σφίσιν αὐτοῖς, | ὥς γ' ἐράουσιν, ἐλεύθερ' ἐῶντα μούνοις ζώειν. See, furthermore, *Miscellanea*, Ch. 76, esp. p. 507, on the slavery of marriage, and Ch. 48, esp. p. 280, on the troubles which an outwardly successful man often has with his family. These remarks are couched in impersonal terms, but I take them to be autobiographical.

224 (a) Instability: *Logos* 10, fol. 195v: ὅτι μὲν δὴ τὰ πάνθ' ἡμῖν κατὰ τὸν βίοτον τόνδε ῥεῖ, καὶ οὐδὲν πιστὸν παντάπασιν οὐδὲ μόνιμον οὔθ' ἵσταται; cf. fol. 224v: καὶ πάνθ' ὡς ἀληθῶς τὰ κατ' ἀνθρώπους . . . . ὥσπερ ἐν ἀτεκμάρτοις πεττείαις μεταχωρεῖ καὶ μετακυβεύεται· ἀμείβει γὰρ ὁ μέν τις εὐπραγίαν εἰς τοὐναντίον, ὁ δὲ θάτερον εἰς εὐπραγίαν. Cf. *Miscellanea*, Ch. 60, esp. p. 365: καίτοι αὐτὰ γὰρ ἀεὶ τἀνθρώπινα πολύνοσα καὶ μυρίᾳ μεταβάλλοντα τροπῇ; cf. Ch. 67, esp. pp. 413–14: τὸ γὰρ ἀβέβαιον κατὰ φύσιν ἐν τοῖς ὑπὸ γένεσιν καὶ ῥέουσιν ἀεὶ τοῖσδε πράγμασι . . . . ζητοῦν μεταβάλλειν ἐξ ἀνάγκης . . . . εἰς τἀναντία τρέπεται; cf. Ch. 87, esp. pp. 571–72; Ch. 110, p. 725: καὶ ἀεὶ ταῦτ' ἐναλλὰξ ἔρχεται ταῖς τοῦ χρόνου καὶ τῆς τύχης πεττείαις καὶ οὐδὲν μόνιμον ἐν ἀνθρώποις οὐδ' ἄτρεπτον; see, finally, the whole Ch. 115, pp. 775–92, on the instability of human affairs, with examples drawn from the lives of Alcibiades, Demetrius Poliorcetes, Eumenes; the source of factual information was again Plutarch, see n. 170 above. (b) Contradictions and inconsistency in human actions, opinions, and thoughts: *Logos* 10, fols. 196v–197r: καὶ πάσης ἀνωμαλίας τε καὶ ἀναντιότητος καὶ ἀοριστίας ἅ τε πράττομεν πλήρη καὶ ἃ νοοῦμεν, οὐχ ἥκιστα δὴ καὶ λέγομεν; cf. fol. 215r: καὶ οὐδεμία παρ' ἀνθρώποις οὐκ ἔστι περὶ ὁτουοῦν συμφωνία οὐδὲ θέλησις οὐδὲ κρίσις ἄρα κοινή, ἀλλ' ἃ τοῖσδ' ἀρέσκει καὶ πρόσκεινται καὶ προσέχουσιν εὖ μάλα, τοῖς δὲ οὔ . . . . καίτοι τί λέγω; ἃ νῦν νομίζομεν, ἔπειτ' ὀλίγου ὕστερον οὔ, οὔθ' ἡμῖν αὐτοῖς αὖθις ξυνδοκεῖ. Cf. *Miscellanea*, Ch. 54, pp. 305–11.

225 *Logos* 10, fol. 220r: καὶ τόν γε δὴ συνετὸν ὄντως καὶ σώφρονα ταύτης [i.e., of culture and letters] ἐραστήν . . . . δεῖ . . . . τῆς ἐν βιοτικοῖς σπουδάσμασι . . . . περιπλανήσεως . . . . ἀποσχέσθαι . . . . καὶ μηθ' ὅλως ἀποχωρεῖν ταύτης [i.e., culture again] . . . . μηθ' ὥσπερ δ υ σ μ ε τ α χ ε ι ρ ί σ τ ῳ τ ι ν ὶ καὶ π ο λ υ τ ρ ό π ῳ καὶ κ α κ ο ύ ρ γ ῳ κ α ὶ β ι α ί ῳ θ η ρ ί ῳ σ υ μ π λ ε κ ό μ ε ν ο ν, κ α τ α τ ι - θ α σ σ ε ῦ σ α ι λ ο ι π ὸ ν . . . . δ ο κ ε ῖ ν ῥ ᾷ σ τ α κ α ὶ κ η μ α γ ω γ ῆ σ α ι [cf. my *Etudes*, p. 38, n. 1 bis], ὡς ἐξεῖναι οἱ [i.e., the friend of culture] τάχα καὶ πρὸς ἄλλοις ἔχειν . . . . ἄττα δὴ πλείστης σπουδῆς καὶ ἀσχολίας ἁπάσης δεῖται.

226 *Logos* 10, fol. 221v: καὶ ὥσπερ ἐν πανθήρῳ τινὶ σαγήνῃ κοινῇ πάντες συνδεδέμεθά τε καὶ καταγχόμεθα καὶ περιστρεφόμεθ', ἄλλοτ' ἄλλως ἄττοντες, καὶ πάντ' ἄφυκτα.

gnotus, and "Zeuxippus"—Zeuxis—were antique examples that came to mind; in Byzantine times, there was "our Eulalios," [227] the famous painter and mosaicist. Here again, Metochites was original, un-Byzantine, and pre-humanistic: first, because he conceived of immortality in secular terms; secondly, because he adduced the Christian Eulalios [228] side by side with secular and antique *exempla*,[229] thirdly, because he valued representational arts *au pair* with letters.

Human nature, he said, continuing his inquiry into secular immortality, desired unending fame, even though death did prevent us from witnessing it. In striving for glory after death, we tasted here and now the pleasures of a future in which we would have no part.[230] Therefore, Metochites wanted to make sure that his works would be preserved and would last for all time to come.[231]

· V ·

We know by now that Metochites was conscious of the problem of originality, that he was preoccupied with himself, and that occasionally he departed from the norm. However, the Chora's iconographical program, original in some points, is on the whole conservative. It would

227 *Logos* 10, fol. 211v: εἰσὶ μὲν οἳ φασιν ἀθάνατον μόνον ὑπὸ παιδείας γίνεσθαι τὸν σπουδαῖον· λείπεται γὰρ τἀνδρί, φασί, μνήμη πολυμήκης ἑξῆς καὶ κλέος ἀείζωον ὑφ' ὧν ἔλιπε λόγων. τοῦτο μὲν οὐ τοῦ σοφοῦ [i.e., a man of letters] μόνον ἔοικεν εἶναι, ἀλλ' ἀμέλει καὶ ἄλλων ἐπ' ἄλλοις, καὶ μικροῖς τε καὶ μείζοσι· καὶ Φειδίου καὶ Πολυγνώτου καὶ καθ' ἡμᾶς Εὐλαλίου, Ζευξίππου τε καὶ Λυσίππου, εἶθ [εἶθ manuscript]' οὗτινος βούλει, οἳ δόκιμοι γεγόνασιν ἐν τέχναις αἷστισιν ἄρα, καὶ ὧν ἔργα χειρῶν παραμένειν ἔχει. καὶ τὸν μὲν οἱ λόγοι, τοὺς δὲ γραφαὶ καὶ ἀγάλματα, τοὺς δ' ἄλλα μηχανήματα, τοὺς δὲ οἰκοδομαί τινες καὶ νεώρια, τοὺς δ' ἄλλο τίποτ' ἄλλους παραπέμπουσι καὶ διδάσκουσι, τὸν ὅμοιον τρόπον, ὡς φασιν, οὐ θνήσκοντα. Cf. fol. 212r: ἐζητοῦμεν γάρ, νῦν εἶναι, ... εἰ μόνον . . . . οἱ λόγοι τὸν δημιουργὸν ἔπειτ' ἀθανάτῳ μνήμῃ παραπέμπουσι . . . . · καὶ καθεωρῶμεν ὡς οὐδὲν ἧττον οὐκ ἐπιλήστους οὐδὲ θνητοὺς διὰ τὴν μνήμην ταύτην οὐδὲ τἆλλα τοὺς ἄλλους πατέρας ὧν εἰσιν ἐῶσι. For mention of Phidias and Zeuxis, see Photius, *Homily* 10, §5, ed. B. Laourdas, Φωτίου Ὁμιλίαι, in Ἑλληνικά, Παράρτημα, 12 (1959), p. 102.8–9; cf. C. A. Mango, tr. and ed., *The Homilies of Photius, Patriarch of Constantinople*, [Dumbarton Oaks Studies, 3] (1958), p. 187 (Photius found the art of these men of antiquity inferior to that of the mosaicist of the ninth-century church of Our Lady of the Pharos); for (laudatory) mention of Phidias and Lysippus, "famous even now," see Constantine Manasses' *Ecphrasis* of a wall mosaic in the Great Palace, ed. L. Sternbach, in "Beiträge zur Kunstgeschichte," *Jahreshefte des Österreichischen Archäologischen Institutes in Wien*, 5 (1902), Beiblatt, col. 75.22–23.

228 With his new *testimonium* on Eulalios, Metochites joins the three authors previously known to have mentioned the artist (Theodore Prodromos, Nicholas Mesarites, and Nicephorus Kallistos Xanthopoulos—the last was a friend of Metochites, see *Poem* 12, Paris. gr. 1776, fols. 162r–170v). For the texts, see, e.g., N. A. Bees, "Kunstgeschichtliche Untersuchungen über die Eulalios-Frage und den Mosaikschmuck der Apostelkirche zu Konstantinopel," *Repertorium für Kunstwissenschaft*, 39 (1916), pp. 97–117, 231–51; 40 (1917), pp. 59–77, 185; A. Heisenberg, "Die Zeit des byzantinischen Malers Eulalios," *Philologische Wochenschrift*, 41 (1921), cols. 1024–32; N. Malickij, "Remarques sur la date des mosaïques de l'église des Saints-Apôtres," *Byzantion*, 3 (1926), pp. 123–51; G. Downey, "Nikolaos Mesarites, Description of the Church of the Holy Apostles at Constantinople," *Transactions of the American Philosophical Society*, N.S., 47 (1957), pp. 857–924, esp. pp. 860, 883, 910. Unfortunately, Metochites' *testimonium* helps little with the one vexed point of the *Eulalios-Frage*, namely the artist's date. The texts, especially that of Prodromos published e.g. by Maiuri (see the subsequent note) indicate to my satisfaction that Eulalios' *floruit* is to be put into the twelfth century. Did Meto-

chites learn Eulalios' name in connection with the work done in the twelfth-century Chora under the auspices of his famous predecessor Isaac the Sebastocrator?

229 Theodore Prodromos did mention both Eulalios and Praxiteles, but he kept the Christian and the pagan in two different contexts: one was that of a semijocular begging poem written in vulgar speech; the other, that of an encomium composed in higher style; see, for the begging poem, e.g. A. Maiuri, "Una nuova poesia di Teodoro Prodromo in greco volgare," *BZ*, 23 (1914–19), pp. 397–407, esp. pp. 399–400 (lines 42–48) and 404 (where the meaning, *pace* Maiuri, is "even the great Eulalios would not have been able to paint a portrait of Prodromos equal to the model itself"); for the encomium, E. Miller, "Poëmes historiques de Théodore Prodrome," *RA*, N.S., 25 (1873), p. 346 (esp. line 186: Praxiteles); idem, *Recueil des historiens des Croisades: Historiens grecs*, II (Paris, 1881), p. 745 (esp. line 599: Apelles). Both passages are conveniently quoted in Heisenberg, "Die Zeit," p. 1029. For another mention of Praxiteles and Apelles by Prodromos, in which their vast superiority to modern painters is implied, see K. Welz, *Analecta byzantina. Carmina inedita Theodori Prodromi et Stephani Physopalamitae* (Leipzig, 1910), pp. 15–16 (= lines 9–10 and 13; I owe this last example to the courtesy of Mr. Henry Maguire). Thus Prodromos, a run-of-the-mill learned Byzantine of the twelfth century, kept his contexts straight; in Metochites' juxtaposition of Eulalios with Phidias, the frames of reference were mixed in a pre-Renaissance fashion; a run-of-the-mill Renaissance humanist would have omitted the medieval artist's name altogether.

230 *Poem* 4, fol. 68r: τίς δέ κε, δυνάμενός γ' ἀτελεύτητον κλέος εὑρεῖν, | οὐ πρόθυμος μάλ' ἐπείγετ' ἀνὰ τόδε πουλὺ ἐράων, | κἂν εἰ μηδὲν ἄξιοι τῆς ἔρατ' αὐτὸς δόξης, | τυχὼν ἤτε θανὼν πάρος, ἤτ' ἀπόδημος ἄοπτος | τηλόθ' ἐὼν ἀδόκητός θ' οὐράαν οὐράασθαί τε; | . . . . | ἀλλ' ἄρ' ὅμως τοῖος πέλετ' ἀνδρόμεος νόος, αἰέν | ἶφι ὀριγνόμενος δόξης, κ' εἰ μηδὲν ἄξει | τῶν κε τιμώντων· τοῦ θ' ἕνεκα καὶ τ' αὖ μετὰ μοῦρον | εἴραμεν ἔμμεν ἀγακλέες περίφαμοι βρουτοί | ταρπόμενοι φαντάσμασι νῦν ἀμφί γε τὸ 'πιόν, | ὅττ' οὐ λεύσομεν οὐκ ἀκούομεν ἤύτε πάρος | ἢ γενόμεθ' ἀνούσιοι τελέθοντες ἄοπτοι.

231 *Poem* 4, fol. 65r: καί σοι [i.e., Nicephorus Gregoras] παρτίθεμ' αὐτός, ἃ συντέταχ' ἄλλυδις ἄλλα | βιβλί', ἅπερ γ' οἶσθ' ἡμέτερ', ἃ μοι φίλτατα πάντων· | ἄττ' ἔραμ' ἄσυλά μοι μενέειν ἀνὰ πάντ' αἰῶ, | τάων δὴ πολύ γ' ἀμφιμέμηλα, φίλων ἅτε τέκνων· | ἄττα μογοστόκοισ' ὠδῖσι γένοντ' ἄρ' ἔμοιγε, | ἄφθιτά τ' εἴραμαι βιόειν ἀζήμιά τ' αἰέν. See Guilland, "Les poésies" (as in n. 6 above), p. 272. Immortality among men was Metochites' paramount goal; it seemed less important to him what kind of immortality would be his: if immortality through success would be denied to him, he could claim immortality through reverses; *Logos* 15, fol. 332r (App. I, 6.16–20).

have been astonishing had it been otherwise. For Metochites, there was one sphere in which not only originality, but even involvement was to be avoided: this was theology.

Time and again, Metochites admonished himself not to raise theological problems deliberately and not to go into details.[232] This was dangerous, especially now, he said in two works—one of his early, another of his mature, period—when there is nothing easier for the mob than to attack prominent and cultivated people under the pretext of unmasking heresy.[233] He knew well the strength of those vipers: one could be tainted for life with their insinuations.[234] Thus it was more prudent to avoid discussing religious matters and to worship the unattainable in silence.[235]

Metochites followed his own advice. He would insert short professions of Chalcedonian dogma in his writings, whether they dealt with secular or sacred matters;[236] in passing, he would made requisite statements on the procession of the Holy Ghost from the Father alone and leave it at that;[237] he would assert with passion that scientific astronomy presented no danger to orthodoxy.[238] He would as passionately condemn astrology—which he practiced[239]—for it was harmful to religious dogma.[240] Above all, this sophisticate would strive for simplicity and for

232 Reasonable (σαόφρονες) people worship God, wisely following the commands of the mysteries. They do not delve into them (μὴ διζεύμενοί πως); those who do are foolish and prepare their own downfall (μητιόοντες σφίσιν ὄλεθρον); see *Poem* 1, vv. 58–61, 67. Maximus Planudes, too, shunned involvement in theological matters; see *Ep.* 113, to Alexius Philanthropenos, lines 41–43, ed. Treu, ... *Planudis Epistulae* (as in n. 24 above), p. 154: νῦν μὲν φυσικός ἐστι [i.e., Melchisedek Akropolites] .... νῦν δὲ θεολογικός, ἅπερ ἐγὼ μάλιστα πάντων δέδοικα καὶ οὐκ ἔστιν ὅτε τούτῳ πρόσειμι πλὴν ⟨ὑπ'⟩ add. Ziegler⟩ ἀνάγκης. See *RE*, 20, 2 (1950), col. 2205, nos. 10–18.

233 The early work is *Logos* 3, On the Archangel Michael, esp. fol. 34v. There Metochites explained the procession of the Holy Ghost from the Father alone, and continued: καὶ ταῦτα μὲν εἰς τοσοῦτο· οὐδὲ γὰρ ἴσως ὑπὲρ ταῦτα δέον ἡμῖν ἐκτείνεσθαι, ἀλλὰ ταῖς ἁπλαῖς τῆς θεολογίας ἱστάναι τὸν νοῦν θέσεσιν· ὅτι μήτ' ἄλλοτ' ἦν ἀσφαλές, μήτ' ἐν τοῖς νῦν μάλιστα καιροῖς, περαιτέρω προϊέναι καὶ διερευνᾶσθαι τὰ περὶ θεοῦ. ἐξὸν δὲ οὕτω ἁπλῶς εὐσεβεῖν καὶ ῥᾶστα καλῶς τε καὶ ἀσφαλῶς ἔχειν, φεύγοντα τὸ δυσχερὲς τῆς ζητήσεως, ἄνοια πάντως ἂν εἴη μεγίστη, κινδύνων ἀλόγως τοσούτων κατατολμᾶν καὶ λόγον ὑπέχειν τοῖς πλείοσιν. The work of mature years is *Logos* 10, esp. fol. 194r: ἡμῖν δέ, οἷς μεγίστη ζημία .... ἑνὸς ὄντος τἀληθοῦς περὶ θεοῦ, ὥσπερ ἄρα καὶ περὶ παντὸς ἄλλου πράγματος, ἁμαρτεῖν κατὰ βραχύ, ... τί τὸ κινοῦν, τίς ἀνάγκη καθ' οὕτω μεγίστου τινὸς κινδύνου κύβον ῥίπτειν καὶ ὠθεῖσθαι; καὶ μάλιστα νῦν ἀμέλει, τούτων τῶν καιρῶν, ἡνίχ' ὡς οὐδὲν ἄλλο τι τῶν ἁπάντων τοῖς πλείοσι πρόχειρον ἐπὶ γλώσσαις ἐπενεγκεῖν ἔγκλημα, δόγματος ἀλλοτριότητα καὶ κακοδοξίαν, ῥᾶον ἢ σκῶμμά τι τῶν οὐδενὸς λόγου.

234 *Logos* 10, fol. 194v: ἡμεῖς δὲ νῦν ὅμως τοσοῦτο κατὰ τῶν ἀστείων ἐνίοτε καὶ ἐνίων τὸ τῶν βδελ[λ]υρῶν τούτων ἀνδρῶν καὶ φθορέων .... κράτος ὁρῶμεν, ὥστε .... κατὰ τῶν ζῴων τὰ ἰόβολα κρύφα καὶ δολίως ἐπιφυομένους παντάπασιν ἐξολλῦναι. ἦν γάρ τι πού παραφθέγξωνταί καὶ προστρίψωνταί τι τοιοῦτον ὡτωοῦν ἔγκλημα, παραχρῆμα κατήγνυσται, καὶ οὕτως ἐνέδυ κατὰ τοῦ ἀνδρὸς καὶ ἥψατο δευσοποιὸν τὸ αἰτίαμα, ὡς θᾶττον ἄν, κατὰ τὴν παροιμίαν, ἐξεῖναι κεράμῳ [sic ms. e corr.] τὴν θάλασσαν ἀντλῆσαι (cf. *Corpus Paroemiographorum Graecorum*, ed. E. L. Leutsch and F. G. Schneidewin, I [Göttingen, 1839], 446, App. IV, 58), ἢ τοῦ παντὸς ἐκεῖνον λοιπὸν βίου τοὐνειδος ἀπολῦσαι καὶ ἀποτρίψασθαι.

235 *Logos* 10, fol. 195r: ταῦτ' ἄρα, ἐγώ φημι, παντὸς μᾶλλον εὐλαβητέον τὴν περὶ τῶν θείων πολυπραγμοσύνην, οὐ μόνον πολιτικώτερον οὕτω πρὸς τὴν ἐφεδρεύουσαν βασκανίαν, ὡς εἴρηται, κεχρημένος, ἀλλ' ὅτι καὶ τῷ παντὶ βέλτιον ὡς ἀληθῶς καὶ λυσιτελέστερον σιγῇ τιμᾶν τὰ ἀνέφικτα καὶ τὸν ἐκ τοῦ μὴ τυχεῖν ἐπιχειροῦντα κίνδυνον δεδιέναι καὶ φεύγειν.

236 *Poem* 1, vv. 68–87; *Logos* 10, fols. 192r–193r.

237 *Logos* 3, fol. 34v: τὸ πνεῦμα .... ἐκ τοῦ πατρὸς ἐκπορεύεται; *Logos* 6, fol. 121r: τὸ πνεῦμα δὲ τὸ ἅγιον ἐκπορευόμενον ἐκ τοῦ πατρός. These declarations on the Single Procession of the Holy Ghost were indispensable for political survival, but they were embarrassing for human reasons, hence their brevity. The human reasons were that Metochites' father composed a long (and, but for some excerpts, still unpublished) treatise on the *Double* Procession of the Holy Ghost, Vat. gr. 1716, fols. 1r–77v; see C. Giannelli and P. Canart, *Codices Vaticani Graeci: Codices 1684–1744* (Bybliothecae Apostolicae Vaticanae Codices Manu Scripti Recensiti; Rome, 1961), p. 83.

238 *Introduction to Astronomy*, I, 5, Vat. gr. 1365, fol. 21r (= Vat. gr. 182, fol. 18r–18v): τοῦτο μέν γε καὶ ἀκίνδυνον παντάπασι καὶ ἀζήμιον τῇ καθ' ἡμᾶς χριστιανικῇ θεοσεβείᾳ καὶ πίστει, τὸ περὶ τῶν κινήσεων, τῶν ὁμαλῶν τε καὶ ἀνομάλων, καὶ τῶν πρὸς ἀλλήλους σχηματισμῶν ἡλίου τε καὶ σελήνης καὶ τῶν πέντε πλανωμένων, ἔτι δὲ καὶ ἀπλανῶν ἀστέρων ἀκριβῶς ἐπίστασθαι .... τί γὰρ ἐν τούτοις τὸ προξενοῦν ζημίαν τῇ πίστει; Astronomy is just another science; it studies with precision that which the crowd observes in a crude fashion, when, for instance, it speaks of the full or new moon (which it calls ἀπόχυσις and γέννα, respectively); these crude observations are innocent; why should the precise ones be reprehensible? Gregoras went a step further; in a Platonizing passage, he praised scientific astronomy as a "ladder" leading to the understanding of the Divine: see *Life of John of Heraclea* in Laurent, "La vie de Jean" (as in n. 219 above), p. 60, lines 8–10: ἀλλ' ἡ τῶν οὐρανίων ἐποπτεία μέγα τι καὶ σεμνότατον πρᾶγμα διαπεφύκει καὶ προσεχὴς τῆς θεολογίας κλῖμαξ. See, for further passages, ibid., p. 60, n. 5.

239 See Gregoras, *Hist.*, VIII.5, Bonn, I, pp. 303.11–312.15, esp. 305.17–19: early in 1321, upset by a portent (the neighing of a horse on the fresco of St. George in the Blachernae palace), Metochites and Andronicus consulted prophetic books and computed a horoscope (θεμάτιον ἐξέθεντο). Manuel Philes seems to have alluded to Metochites' astrological practices in a poem celebrating Andronicus III's successful coup of May 1328: with the young Emperor's victory, gone, he said, were the haughty dignitaries and the "oracular ambiguity which hinted at the ⟨propitious⟩ times on the basis of astral terms [or: calculations]": μαντικὴ λοξότης, αἰνισσομένη τοὺς καιροὺς ἐπὶ ῥητοῖς ἀστρῴοις. Philes claimed to have suffered under Metochites' regime. For the text of the poem, see Gedeon (as in n. 14 above), pp. 219–20; see ibid., p. 655, for Gedeon's plausible conjecture that Philes had Metochites in mind.

240 *Introduction to Astronomy*, I, 5, Vat. gr. 1365, fol. 21v (Vat. gr. 182, fols. 18v–19r): ἀλλ' ἴσως ἐνίους ταράττει θάτερον τῆς ἀστρολογικῆς μέρος, ὃ περὶ τὸ προγνωστικὸν καταγίνεται, καὶ τὰς κινήσεις .... τῶν ἀστέρων .... καὶ τοὺς πρὸς ἀλλήλους σχηματισμοὺς αἴτιά πως εἶναι τῶν γιγνομένων

disengagement.[241] In his verbose discussion of the various subdivisions of contemplative philosophy, the passage on theology is the shortest of all: for the ancient Greeks, theology had presented problems; for Christians, it presented none, for they had the Revelation and had only to follow the Scriptures.[242] Some twenty years earlier, Metochites had asserted that the works of St. Basil and of Gregory of Nazianzus were sufficient as a defense against those who attacked one's faith. And—he added, quoting St. Paul—everyone should say about the two Fathers, "This is my defense to those who would examine me."[243]

Those who would examine Theodore Metochites were his enemies, who all knew who his father was. George Metochites was a relic of the discredited policy of the previous reign, a supporter of the union with the Roman Church—a *latinophrōn*—who refused to recant. For over forty years he had clung to his opinions and suffered for them, first in a fortress on an island in the Bay of Nicomedia, then in a more comfortable confinement near the Blachernae palace.[244] In all these years his son, whether climbing the slope of power, walking along its ridge, or dabbling in astrology on the side, had to watch his step, for his enemies watched him, too. Why play with fire? All deeper involvement in theological matters had to be avoided and replaced by professions of not only complete, but even banal, religious conformity; salvation lay in safety.[245] Thus to expect traces of bold experimentation in the program of the Chora is to expect the unlikely. For Metochites as I know him, the Chora had to be *recherché* but conservative. For the rest, the best masters of the capital would attend to details.

For Metochites, the Chora had to be these things: It had to be among the best monasteries in the world,[246] for he was ambitious and could afford the best. In wealth, he was considered second

---

ἀπάντων σπουδάζει δεικνύναι . . . . τοῦτό γε μὴν προδήλως πάνυ τοι καὶ ἀναντιρρήτως λυμαίνεται τῇ πίστει καὶ τῇ καθ' ἡμᾶς χριστιανικῇ θεοσεβείᾳ, καὶ αὐτὸς ἐγὼ καὶ φρονεῖν οὕτως ἐμαυτὸν πείθω πάνυ τοι καρτερῶς καὶ ἀτρέπτως . . . . καὶ κηρύττειν πρὸς πάντας ἀξιῶ, τὴν ἀσφάλειαν ἐμαυτῷ τῶν δογμάτων τῆς ἀληθείας καὶ τῆς πίστεως παριστάνων . . . . καὶ καταμεμφόμενος εὖ μάλα καὶ καταγελῶν, ὅστις ἄλλος [*leg.* ἄλλως?] καὶ φρονεῖ καὶ λέγει. Astrology leads to fatalism and dissolution of moral standards. Moreover, Ptolemy, who, to be sure, did deal with astrology, warned in the Preface to his *Tetrabiblos* that while astronomy was an exact science, astrology was not. Cf. *Introduction to Astronomy*, I, 5, Vat. gr. 1365, fol. 23r (Vat. gr. 182, fol. 20r): ὅσοι δὲ τὰς ἐκ τῆς τῶν ἀστέρων κινήσεων αἰτίας καὶ τὸ ἐντεῦθεν προγνωστικὸν φιλονεικοῦσι καὶ βιάζονται, ... ληρεῖν μοι δοκοῦσι . . . . οὗτοί γε μὴν καὶ λυμαίνονται τοῖς εὐσεβέσι δόγμασι . . . . καὶ σφόδρ' ἔγωγε τοὺς τοιούτους ἀποστρέφομαι καὶ ἀποτροπιάζομαι καὶ τοὺς ἄλλους οὕτω φρονεῖν ἀξιῶ.

241 *Logos* 10, fol. 193r: τῷ ὄντι γὰρ καὶ ἄριστον εἶναι καὶ ἀσφαλέστατον ἁπλοϊκῶς τε καθόλου καὶ ἐλευθέρως ἐν ὀλιγότητι γνώμης εὐσεβεῖν καὶ μηδὲν πλέον τοῦ προχείρου διατρίβειν πειρᾶσθαι, μηδὲ περαιτέρω ἢ κατὰ τοὺς πολλοὺς τε καὶ ἀγροικοτέρους φιλοσοφεῖν· ὡς ἔγωγε, ὅστις—ἐξὸν οὕτως ἀκινδύνως θεοσεβεῖν—ἔπειθ' ἑκών γε αὐτοῦ πράγματα αἱρεῖται καὶ ἀπόρρητα καὶ καινότερα περὶ τῶν θείων ἐπιχειρεῖ σοφίζεσθαι καὶ ἰχνηλατεῖν, μὴ πρὸς ἡντιναοῦν ἀνάγκην, μὴ πρὸς ἡντιναοῦν ὄνησιν—τοῦτον ἂν εἶναι φαίην δυστυχῆ σφόδρα καὶ ἀνούστατον.

242 *Introduction to Astronomy*, I, 2, Vat. gr. 1365, fol. 15r–15v (Vat. gr. 182, fol. 12r–12v): τεττάρων δὴ τούτων ὄντων τῶν τοῦ θεωρητικοῦ εἰδῶν· τὸ μὲν θεολογικὸν τοῖς πάλαι τῶν Ἑλλήνων φιλοσόφοις ἐκ τῶν οἴκοθεν αὐτοῖς λογισμῶν σπουδασθὲν καὶ μὴ ἐκ προλήψεων καὶ θέσεων ἔστιν οἷς ἀλλοτριοτάτων καὶ παντάπασιν ἀπεξενωμένων τῶν δικαίων τῆς θείας φύσεως, εὐέλεγκτόν ἐστι κατ' αὐτοὺς καὶ δῆλον ἀτευκτόν . . . . τοῖς γε . . . . νοῦν ἔχουσι τοῦ προτεθειμένου σκοποῦ· ἡμῖν δὲ τοῖς ἀπ' αὐτοῦ τοῦ θεοῦ καὶ θείων

ἀνδρῶν δι' αὐτοῦ καὶ τῆς ἐξ αὐτοῦ φωταυγείας . . . . μυσταγωγηθέντων . . . . διδαχθεῖσι καὶ διαδεξαμένοις τὰς περὶ τῶν θείων ἀσφαλεῖς καθόλου πρώτας ἀρχάς. . . . καὶ προλήψεις, οὐ μόνον ἔστιν ἐκεῖθεν ἔπειθ' οὕτω ῥᾳδίως τε ἅμα καὶ ἁπλανῶς ἐπιτυγχάνειν τῆς θεολογικῆς σοφίας καὶ θεωρίας, ἀλλὰ καὶ ἀκινδύνως εὖ μάλα. . . . τοιγαροῦν ἡμῖν τοῖς ἀπὸ τοῦ Χριστοῦ . . . . ἀσφαλές ἐστι τὸ θεολογικόν. The *Introduction to Astronomy* was written about 1317. See my *Etudes*, p. 129.

243 *Logos* 6, fol. 144v: τίς γὰρ οὐκ ἂν εὖ φρονῶν οἶμαι μετὰ τούτων [i.e., Basil and Gregory] ἕλοιτο συντάττεσθαι . . . . καὶ οὐ πιστεῦσαι τῇ μεγάλῃ τῶν ἀνδρῶν σοφίᾳ, πρὸς πᾶσαν μάχην τῶν ἐναντίων καὶ πολεμούντων καὶ κακουργούντων ἔξωθεν καὶ κατεπιχειρούντων τῆς ἐκκλησίας αὐτοὺς ἀρκεῖν μόνους ἀξιῶν, καὶ τὰ κατ' αὐτοὺς εἰς ἀπολογίαν ἀντιφέρειν παντὶ δύσνῳ καὶ κακοήθει. . . . καὶ τοῦτ' ἂν εἰκότως τῶν ἀποστολικῶν ῥημάτων φάναι πάντα τινά. . . . · ἡ ἐμὴ ἀπολογία τοῖς ἐμὲ ἀνακρίνουσιν αὕτη ἐστίν [I Cor. 9:3]. *Logos* 6 is prior to 1294/95. See my *Etudes*, p. 139.

244 See *Etudes*, pp. 130–35, with bibliography, to which two encyclopedia articles may be added: M. Buchberger, *Lexikon für Theologie und Kirche*, 4 (Freiburg im Breisgau, 1960), cols. 703–04 (by V. Laurent), and Θρησκευτικὴ καὶ Ἠθικὴ Ἐγκυκλοπαιδεία, 8 (Athens, 1966), cols. 1097–98 (by J. Patinot).

245 The two word clusters that give flavor to Metochites' declarations on faith are ἀσφαλής, ἀσφάλεια, "safe," "safety," and κίνδυνος, ἀκίνδυνος, "danger," "safe." These words appear eleven times (five and six times, respectively) in texts quoted in nn. 234, 236, 239, 241–43 above.

246 Constantinople, Metochites believed, had more and better monasteries than any other city in the world; Chora was to be among the best in Constantinople, hence in the whole world: see *Poem* 2, vv. 254–56 and 265–69: αὐτὸς ἐγὼν περικαλλέα τήνδ' ἄρα μουνάν | πολλὸν ἀμείνω πολλῶν στῆσ' ἐπὶ τῆσδε πόλιος, | . . . . ἃ ταμεῖον ἀρίτιμον πέλεθ' . . . . | . . . . | ἀμυδὶς ἅπαν ἔχον καὶ πρός γ' ἅπασιν ἑτέροισι | μουνὰς ἀριθμῷ πλείονας, ἢ παρ' ἑκάστοις ἄλλοις | ἀνθρώποισιν ὁμοῦ πολίεσσί τε πάσαις . . . . | . . . . κάλλει τε φερίστας ἀπασάων

only to the Emperor himself. He became the new founder both because he wished to please the Emperor and because he emulated other founders of his own and past generations, to whom he was bound by marriage or by the stronger bonds of enmity—the Dowager-Empress Theodora, Princess Theodora Palaeologina, Michael Dukas Tarchaniotes Glabas, and, of course, Nicephorus Choumnos.[247]

Secondly, the Chora had to have the best monastic library in the capital, for next to himself and his offspring he liked books more than anything else.[248] When in his poems he spoke of the interior decoration of the Chora, he enwrapped the reader in a mild golden glow radiating from the mosaics. Behind this haze almost no contours are discernible: it required an accidental checking of the printed text of one of his poems against the manuscript to find out that he did refer to the great *Deesis* mosaic after all.[249] But when Metochites came to speak of the Chora's books, he was on his own ground.[250]

For Metochites the Christian, the Chora had to perform the services which any *ktētor* expected from his foundation: to provide him with a haven in the difficult moments of his career and with a permanent refuge in his old age.[251] The monastery and the lands donated to it had to be his investment in eternal life.[252] But in the scheme of Metochites the egocentric, the Chora's main function was to satisfy his craving for secular immortality. He drove the point home over and over again. The Emperor thought that restoring the Chora would bring eternal glory to his minister.[253] Both the Chora and its library, on which Metochites spent a great deal of money and

---

ἄλλων. Consequently, Metochites continued, ἱδρυσάμην τήνδε | τὴν μονάν, ὦ πάναγνε βασίλει', ... | . . . . | σεῦ τέμενος τόδ' ἀπ' ἐξαίρετον ἢ μάλ' ἀληθῶς | παντὸς ὁρατοῦ κόσμου [here: world] πασάων τε πόλιων.

247 Theodora (d. 1303), mother of Andronicus II, endowed and enlarged the early tenth-century monastery of Lips (Feneri Isa Camii); Princess Theodora (d. 1300, see Papadopulos, *Genealogie*, no. 34, and n. 21 above) refounded the sixth-century (?) monastery of St. Andrew in Crisi (Hocamustafapaşa Camii). These two imperial ladies were grandmothers of Metochites' son-in-law. Michael Dukas Tarchaniotes Glabas: the precise date of his death is unknown; I assume that he died between 1306 and 1308, for he is referred to as alive in Pachymeres, *Hist.*, V.28, Bonn (1835), II, p. 445.13–17 (time: 1306) and as τὸν τοῦ θεοῦ ἄνθρωπον ἐκεῖνον, which I take to mean "that late man of God," by the same author in another passage, *Hist.*, III.30, Bonn, II, p. 271.16–19. Pachymeres wrote about 1308. See a similar guess by C. A. Mango and E. J. W. Hawkins, in *DOP*, 18 (1964), p. 330: Glabas died "ca. 1310, even a little earlier." Glabas refounded, and his widow had enlarged, the monastery of the Virgin Pammakaristos (Fethiye Camii). Glabas' connection with Metochites through marriage can be deduced from a passage in the latter's *Logos* 8, describing the embassy Metochites undertook to the court of the Serbian king Stephen Milutin in 1299. On his way to the Serbians, Metochites stayed with the Emperor's top man in Salonika, who "as you know" was "my close relative by marriage." About 1299, the Emperor's top general in Salonika was Glabas. He is attested in that city as late as 1303. See Sathas, Μεσαιωνικὴ Βιβλιοθήκη, I (1872), p. 168.23–25, and p. ρλβ', n. 2; Pachymeres, *Hist.*, III.30, Bonn, II, pp. 272.1–7. On Glabas see, e.g., G. I. Theocharides, Μιχαὴλ Δούκας Γλαβᾶς Ταρχανειώτης, in Ἀριστοτέλειον Πανεπιστήμιον Θεσσαλονίκης, Ἐπιστημονικὴ Ἐπετηρίς . . . Φιλοσοφικῆς Σχολῆς, 7 (1956), pp. 183–206 (with older literature), esp. 200–202; and D. I. Polemis, *The Doukai: A Contribution to Byzantine Prosopography* (London, 1968), p. 121, No. 89. Choumnos (d. 1327) restored the eleventh-century (?) monastery of the Virgin Γοργοεπήκοος; Choumnos' daughter, Irene, restored and endowed the monastery of Christ Φιλάνθρωπος. For a similar list of imperial and private founders, or rather restorers, of monasteries in the capital about 1300, see V. Laurent, "Une Fondation monastique de Nicéphore Choumnos," *REB*, 12 (1954), p. 32, nn. 1 and 2.

248 *Logos* 10, fol. 210v: ὡς οὐδὲν τίποτ' ἄλλο γένοιτ' ἂν καθ' ἀνθρώπους ἥδιον ὅταν τις ἑαυτοῦ γενόμενος ὅλος καὶ ἐν ταῖς βίβλοις καὶ σοφίᾳ νεύσεως καὶ τρυφῆς καὶ συνουσίας . . . . ἔπειθ' οὕτω . . . . ὥσπερ ἀφ' ὑψηλῆς τινος σκοπιᾶς ἀπόλυτον ἐπόπτην ἀφήσει πρὸς ξύμπαντα τὸν κόσμον . . . . τὸν νοῦν καὶ περισκοποῖτο. For Metochites' views on the size and quality of the Chora's library, see n. 141 above.

249 In *Poem* 1, vv. 165–69, Metochites says: "The travails of my heart dissolved into nothing as soon as I looked at the joyful grace of the ⟨Chora⟩ Church; as soon as I rested my eyes on the image of Christ resembling human beings, an image from which such grace descended, and which inspired such an ineffable admiration in the onlooker." For the Greek, see n. 111 above. The printed text then continues, vv. 169–70: πρὸς δὲ | μητρὸς ἑοῖο παρ' ἄλλον αὐτῷ λιτεούσης, where παρ' ἄλλον makes little sense. In Paris. gr. 1776, fol. 40r, however, I read "παρ' ἔγγιον," "nearby," and the passage becomes clear: "moreover, ⟨when I looked at the image⟩ of His Mother, ⟨who stood⟩ nearby in an attitude of prayer." As "nearby" means close to the image of Christ, the reference is to the large Deesis in the east wall of the inner narthex of the Chora. Ἔγγιον does occur elsewhere in Metochites; see *Logos* 15, fol. 336v (App. I, **18.**12): περὶ τὴν μονὴν ἔγγιον.

250 See pp. 35–37 and nn. 129–30, 141 above.

251 In *Logos* 15, fols. 332v–333r (App. I, **8.**12–15) Metochites expressed his hope of spending his last days in the monastery: ἔπειτά με . . . . εἶχεν . . . . ἐλπίς . . . . ὡς ἄρα θεοῦ βουλομένου . . . . γενοίμην αὐτὸς παρὰ τῇ μονῇ, καὶ τὸ λοιπὸν ἐμοὶ τῆς ζωῆς, ὅ,τί ποτ' ἂν εἴη, τῇδ' οὐκ ἀηδῶς ἂν βιωσοίμην.

252 *Logos* 15, fol. 330v (App. I, **2.**17–19): the Chora is κέρδος καὶ πλοῦτος of Metochites' soul, and πρὸς τὴν μέλλουσαν ἀπέραντον εὐζωΐαν οὐ παρασκευὴ μᾶλλον, ἢ καὶ ἀσφαλὲς ἐχέγγυον [security] καὶ χρηστῆς ἐλπίδος ὑπόθεσις [I take it to mean here ὑποθήκη, "deposit"]; *Poem* 1, vv. 1274–78, ed. Treu, *Dichtungen* (as in n. 38 above): ἄφθιτον ἀλαθέως τόδ' [i.e., lands donated to the monastery] ὄνειαρ αἰέν, ἀεὶ μένον, ἀμφιπεμπόμενον πάντ' αἰῶ | ἀμφοτέροισιν, ἐμοί τ' ἠδ' αὖ τεκέεσσι φίλοισι, | διαρκέστατος . . . . | κλῆρος . . . . , μυρίον ἐσθλόν.

253 *Poem* 1, vv. 1010–11: In Andronicus II's opinion, rebuilding the Chora would result in ψυχᾶς ἐμᾶς [i.e., of Metochites] μέγ' ὄνειαρ καί τε κλεῖος | ἄφθιτον αἰὲν ἅπαντα διαμπερὲς ἀνὰ χροῦνον.

effort, would perpetuate his memory among later generations.[254] Several of his achievements might assure him of immortality, he said—alluding to his astronomical treatise—but among all his works, the Chora constituted his chief claim to it:[255] a claim not so much to the eternal life in which the righteous contemplate God—for when he spoke of the Christian beyond, Metochites usually saw there the threat of eternal punishment—as to the glory of a mortal, remembered by unending generations of other mortals.[256]

Metochites made good this claim, at least in Byzantium, for his wisdom was acclaimed, his authority invoked, and some of his works read and used by learned Byzantines until the very end of the Empire. "Now wisdom has perished," exclaimed Gregoras in an epigram in which he mourned his teacher's death. Philotheos of Selymbria called Metochites a "leader and teacher of future generations on account of the literary works which he left" to posterity. During the Palamite controversy, both the anti-Palamite Gregoras and the pro-Palamite Patriarch Philotheos Kokkinos quoted the deceased Metochites on behalf of their causes: the former asserted that Metochites had been horrified by what he learned about the incipient heresy; the latter maintained that Metochites had been greatly impressed with young Palamas' intelligence and his knowledge of Aristotle. Isaac Argyros probably knew and John Chortasmenos certainly read Metochites' *Introduction to Astronomy;* George Gemistos Plethon considered Metochites to have been the best of Ptolemy's commentators; and Gennadios Scholarios used Metochites' commentaries on Aristotle for his own commentaries on this author. Finally, it is possible that George Karbones, a fourteenth-century author of a *Laudation* of Constantinople, was influenced by Metochites' *Logos* 11, Βυζάντιος.[257]

However, the "mortals" by whom Metochites hoped to be remembered—and admired—include us as well. Without forgetting his faults, we, too, should grant him some of our admiration. To have given us the Chora he had to be a man of wealth, taste, and intelligence. He did not have to be a perfect gentleman.

---

254 The Chora: *Poem* 2, vv. 222–25, 231–34: τὴν μὲν [i.e., the Chora] ἐγὼν ἵδρυσα ὄνειαρ ψυχᾶς ἐμεῖο, | . . . . | . . . . σύν τ' ἀναλώμασι σύν τε καμάτοις πουλλοῖς· | . . . . | πρὸς δ' ἔτι κόσμεον ἐμοὶ νῦν ἀνά ϑ' ὕστατ' αἰῶ | μνήμαν ἐν ὀψιγόνοισιν ἐμεῖο πολυτίμητον, κάρτ' ἐρατεινὴν δι' ἅπασι μερόπεσσι βρουτοῖς, for all men are ambitious: ἦ μάλα φιλότιμοι γὰρ ἅπαντες ἔασ' ἄνϑρωποι. The Chora's library: *Logos* 15, fol. 338v (App. I, **23.**17–21): when Metochites thought of the book collection he had built up at the Chora, he felt uplifted: καὶ τέρπομαι, πῶς οἴεσϑε [he wrote to the monks] πρὸς τὸ μέλλον ἀφορῶν καὶ ὅσος ἀνϑρώποις ἐστὶ βίος καὶ ζωῆς μήκη καὶ μονῆς [i.e., duration] τῷ κόσμῳ, ὡς οὐ μή ποτ' ἂν ἐμέ τε καὶ ὑμᾶς ἐπιλείψαι μάλιστ' ἀγαϑὴ καὶ τύχη καὶ μνήμη καὶ κλέος τοῦ παγκοίνου τοῦδε κατ' ἀνϑρώπους χρησίμου καὶ καλοῦ, καὶ τῶν ἐναποκειμένων παρ' ὑμῖν κειμηλίων.

255 *Poem* 2, vv. 198–203, 209–13: Χώρα . . . . ὦ κτῆμ' ἐμὸν ἄδιον ἢ πάντ' ἄλλα, | ὅσσα κατὰ βίον ἡμέτερα κάρϑ'

ἱμερόεντα, | ἅττ' ἂρ ἔοργα ἠδ' ὅσοις ξυνέλαχον ἐσϑλοῖς· | καί γ' ἑκάτερϑεν ἐμοὶ τάδ' ἔασι, τάων καί τ' ἐλπὶς | οὕνεκ' ἐμεῖο μναμοσύναν τάχα κεν ἔμμεν ὀψιγόνοισιν ἀνϑρώποισιν.

256 See *Poem* 2, vv. 210–13: ἐξ ἂρ ἐγὼ τῶν, οὐλίγα δ' οἶδ' ἔασι τάδ' [i.e., my other achievements] ἐμεῖο, | λείπομ' ἑκάστων, ἅττα ποτ' ἐντί, πὰρ τόδε ἔργον | ἡμέτερόν [i.e., the restoration of the Chora] κεν μνῆστιν ἐμεῦ λείφϑ' ἐσσομένοισι βρουτοῖσι μερόπεσσι μετούπισϑεν ϑανόντος.

257 See S. G. Mercati, "Sulle poesie di Niceforo Gregora," and "Nota all' epigramma di Niceforo Gregora in morte del Metochita," *Bessarione*, 22 (1918), pp. 97, 237–38; Philotheos of Selymbria, Λόγος εἰς Μακάριον (as in n. 106 above), p. 50; Gregoras, *Hist.*, XIX.1, Bonn, II, p. 919.5–15; Philotheos Kokkinos, *Vita Palamae*, PG, 151, cols. 559D–560A; my *Etudes*, pp. 112–14; and Fenster, *Laudes* (as in n. 29 above), pp. 204, 327–35.

Appendix I

METOCHITES' LETTER TO THE MONKS OF THE CHORA (LOGOS 15)*

A word on the translation of the Letter. Any translator of Metochites into English labors under a double handicap: the English language's aversion to hot air and the notorious obscurity of Metochites' prose.[1] Faced, in Greek, with a stylistic theory that puts a premium on elegant variation and an author who would rather make the same point in three different ways—all of them narrow misses—than in one, the translator into English has the choice between giving the bare meaning, that is, rendering, say, "those suffering in illnesses" by "sick" (and I did so in 17,3–4), or being as convoluted as the original, in order to convey its flavor. On the whole, I followed the second course; hence such phrases as "some of them were organized along the principle of dwelling in common, living and settling together in large numbers" (10,7–8), instead of "some of them were coenobitic monks."

In coping with Metochites' obscure passages, I have often resorted to paraphrase; on occasion, the paraphrase has turned into interpretation, and interpretation has sometimes been a stab in the dark (e.g., 6,11–12). In one passage (5,17–18) I gave up the attempt of providing any rendering at all.

The following system of signs has been adopted in this Appendix:

CONSPECTUS SIGLORUM

TEXTUS

⟨ ⟩   uncis additiones a me probatas
†   crucibus corruptelas et locos obscuros denotavi

APPARATUS

V   Codex Vindobonensis philologicus graecus 95
V^1, V^2 . . . codicis V manus prima, secunda . . .
V^x manus codicis V de qua mihi nihil certi constat
$V^{mg, sv}$ codex V in margine, supra versum
( )   uncis rotundis amplectuntur solutiones compendiorum codicis
[ ]   uncis quadratis amplectuntur litterae evanidae quae certe suppleri possunt
⟦ ⟧   his uncis amplectuntur litterae erasae
. .   singula pro litteris ponuntur puncta quae nec legi nec suppleri certe possunt
F   Fontes et loci paralleli
Ad compendia TM; *Etudes;* Treu, *Dichtungen;* Leutsch-Schneidewin elucidanda, cf. notas 6, 4, 38, 234 supra, ad textum praesentis lucubrationis pertinentes.

---

*The letter is from Vindobonensis ph. gr. 95, fols. 330r–339r. See above, p. 34, n. 125. For the description of the Vindobonensis, its orthography, and the principles adopted in editing its texts—and followed in the present edition—the reader is referred to my *Etudes*, pp. 177–85 (on p. 179 read *Logos* 16 [Πρός τινα φίλον] instead of *Logos* 15 [Πρὸς τοὺς μοναχοὺς τῆς Χώρας]);

see also the expert description of the Vindobonensis in H. Hunger, *Katalog der griechischen Handschriften der Österreichischen Nationalbibliothek*, Part 1 (*Museion*, N.S., IV,1; Vienna, 1961), pp. 202–04.
   1 See *Etudes*, pp. 35–41, esp. p. 40, n. 2; and pp. 24–25, 28 above.

ΠΡΟΣ ΤΟΥΣ ΜΟΝΑΧΟΥΣ ΤΗΣ ΧΩΡΑΣ ΕΠΙ ΤΗΙ ΤΕΛΕΥΤΗΙ
ΤΟΥ ΠΡΩΤΟΥ ΚΑΘΗΓΟΥΜΕΝΟΥ ΑΥΤΩΝ ΛΟΥΚΑ· ΜΟΝΩΙΔΙΑ ΤΕ
ΕΠ' ΑΥΤΩΙ ΚΑΙ ΠΡΟΤΡΟΠΗ ΑΥΤΟΙΣ ΕΙΣ ΤΗΝ ΕΠΙΜΕΛΕΙΑΝ
ΤΟΥ ΚΑΛΟΥ

1. [fol. 330r] Ἐμοὶ παντὸς μᾶλλον, ἄνδρες φίλοι, λατρευταὶ τοῦ θεοῦ, τὰ καθ' ὑμᾶς εὖ ἔχειν καὶ ἀεὶ μὲν πρότερον, νυνὶ δὲ μάλιστα, περισπούδαστον, τοῖσδε ξυγκεκυρηκότι τοῖς πράγμασιν, οὐκ οἶδ' ὡς εἴ τῳ ἄλλῳ, τί ποτ' ἂν ἄλλο· καὶ τόδε δή τί μοι λείπεται ζώπυρον ἐλπίδος χρηστῆς ἐπὶ τοσούτοις ἄρα τοῖς ἀλγεινοῖς καὶ παραμυθίας ὁπῃοῦν ἀφορμή, νῦν τε τῷ βίῳ, ὅσον ἄρα
5 λοιπὸν εἴη, καὶ μεθύστερον. ὡς δ' ἀμέλει νῦν τὴν τελευτὴν ἐπυθόμην τοῦ καλλίστου πάντα τὴν κατὰ θεὸν πολιτείαν ὑμῖν ἡγεμόνος, τί ποτ' ἐρῶ; τί ποτε πέπονθα; μέσην αὐτὴν δέδηγμαι τὴν καρδίαν, κλύδωνι παντάπασιν ἀπογνώσεως πάσης ἀγαθῆς ἐλπίδος, αὐτίκα αὐτόθεν, ὅσαι ἡμέραι τε καὶ νύκτες, ταράττομαι καὶ ναυαγῶ. πόλλ' ἔτη καὶ γὰρ ἤδη τοῦ ἀνδρὸς πεπειραμένος, οὐ μόνον τῆς πρὸς ἐμὲ γνησίας καὶ μεγάλης εὐνοίας, καὶ τοῦ πιστοῦ τῆς ἑταιρίας λιμένος, καὶ
10 τῶν ἀδολωτάτων ἠθῶν καὶ τῆς ἀποιήτου γνώμης—ἃ μὴ πολλῶν ἐστιν ἐν τοῖς νῦν καιροῖς μηδ' ἔστιν εὐπόριστα ξυλλαχεῖν—ἀλλὰ καὶ πρὸς τὴν ἀρχικὴν καθ' ὑμᾶς πρυμνῆτιν ἐπιστασίαν δοκιμῆς καὶ ἱκανώσεως, ἅπαν τὸ γιγνόμενον, τῇ μοναχικῇ συνοικίᾳ καὶ τῷ βίῳ, τὰς πλείστας ἐπ' αὐτῷ καὶ μεγίστας εἶχον ἐλπίδας, ἦ μὴν καλῶς ὑμῖν ἔχειν καὶ τῇ μονῇ τὰ πράγματα τὸν ἐγχωροῦντα τρόπον ἀεί, περιόντος τῷ βίῳ τοῦ ἀνδρὸς καὶ παρ' ὑμῖν ὄντος, κἂν ὅπως ἄρ' ἐγὼ
15 φεροίμην τῷ πολυστρόφῳ καὶ πάντ' ἀπίστῳ καὶ πολυπλάνῳ τῷδε βίῳ, κἂν εἰ φθάσας τελευτήσαιμι τὴν ζωὴν ἐν τῇ παρούσῃ δυσχρηστίᾳ τοῦ βίου καὶ δυσχερείᾳ καὶ πράγμασιν ἐργώδεσιν, εἰ δή τῳ καὶ ἄλλῳ ποτέ.

2. Καὶ τοίνυν ὡς ἀωρίᾳ τοσαύτῃ τῶν ἐμῶν τῶνδ' ἐλπίδων ἀνὴρ οἴχεται, λιπὼν ὑμᾶς ἐν σάλῳ τοσούτῳ, δέος ἂν εἰκότως ἐμὲ νῦν ἔχοι περὶ τῇ μονῇ καὶ ὑμῖν· τὸ δ' οἴκτιστον καὶ μέγιστον καὶ τελευταῖον, μὴ ἄρα πως ἐν ἐσχάτοις ἐσχάτων κακοῖς καὶ πανωλείᾳ τὰ κατ' ἐμὲ πράγματα, καὶ ἤδη παντάπασιν ὄλλυται μετ' ἤχου τοὐμόν, ἔοικε, μνημόσυνον, ὡς ἱεροί φασι
5 λόγοι. καὶ τοῦτο προσημαίνονταί μοι κρίματ', ἐντεῦθεν μεταστάντος ἐν τῷ νῦν εἶναι τἀνδρὸς δηλαδή, καὶ ψῆφοι θεοῦ σὺν δίκῃ ὡς ἔμοιγε προσήκειν καὶ χρῆναι ταῖς τοσαύταις ἁμαρτίαις ἐμαῖς· ὥστε μὴ μόνον τὰ κατὰ τὸν βίοτον τόνδ' ἅπαντά μοι τετράφθαι, καὶ πᾶσαν εὐετηρίαν καὶ [fol. 330v] πολυδοξίαν καὶ πλοῦτον ἔρρειν ἀθρόον, καὶ φιλτάτων καὶ τέκνων—καὶ προσκείσθω μηδ' ὀλίγων τούτων—ἐρραστωνευμένην ἀγωγὴν τέως καθάπαξ οἴχεσθαι καὶ μεταβαλεῖν
10 εἰς πᾶν αὐτόθεν ταλαιπωρίας καὶ πᾶν ἐργῶδες, κἀμὲ τῇδε νῦν ὑπερόριον κάμνειν ἐν τοσούτοις— τά τε ἄλλα καὶ νόσοις χαλεπαῖς—παλαίοντα, ἀλλὰ καὶ ὃ πρὸ πάντων ἦν ἐμοὶ καὶ ἀντὶ πάντων λέλειπτο καὶ ἤρκει βιοῦν ἔτι πω γεννικῶς καὶ ὡς φιλοσόφοις ἐπέοικεν, ὀλιγωρίᾳ κραταιᾷ τῶν οἰχομένων, ἃ μὴ δή ποτε βέβηκεν ὁτῳοῦν μηδὲ τὸ πιστὸν ἔχει—καὶ πάντων ἀβελτερώτατος, ὃς ἂν ἄλλως δοκοίη καὶ ὁτιοῦν μέγα φρονεῖν αὐτοῖς ἀξιοίη καὶ πεποιθέναι—καὶ τοῦτο δ' ἀμέλει κατ'
15 ὀφθαλμοὺς ὡσανεὶ καθορᾶν ἐν κινδύνῳ καὶ φθορᾶς ἐν χρῷ γεγονός· τὸ καθ' ὑμᾶς φημὶ σαφῶς οὑτωσὶ καὶ τὴν μονήν. ὃ δῆτα καὶ νῦν καὶ τὸν ἐπιόντ' ἀνθρώποις χρόνον πάντων ἄξιον ἐμοί,

FONTES ET LOCI PARALLELI

2,4 ὄλλυται μετ' ἤχου et μνημόσυνον : cf. Ps. 9:7

VARIAE LECTIONES

1,8 πεπειραμένος V² e corr. : -μαι V? 2,1 ὑμᾶς V¹ e corr. : ἡμᾶς V 2 ἔχοι V¹ e corr. : ἔχει V 5 εἶναι V

TO THE MONKS OF THE CHORA, ON THE OCCASION OF THE DEATH OF THEIR FIRST ABBOT LUCAS; LAMENT OVER HIM AND EXHORTATION TO THEM TO PURSUE THE GOOD WITH DILIGENCE

1. [fol. 330r] Friends and worshippers of God, it was always my ardent desire in the past that you should fare well; but just now, when I have met with the present adverse circumstances, I believe I wish it more than anybody else has ever desired anything. This indeed is the ray of good hope that remains to me amidst so many painful experiences; this is my consolation, both for the remaining part of my life here on earth and for what is to follow. However, when I learned about the demise of the most excellent leader in your life according to God—what shall I say about my feelings?—the news pierced me through the heart. By day and by night I am tossed about and overwhelmed by this sudden storm of hopelessness and despond. For many a year have I known the qualities of that man from experience; not only have I enjoyed his genuine and great benevolence towards me, not only have I been sheltered in the safe haven of his friendship, not only have I relied on his guileless character and his forthright mind—all of which is not shared by many or frequently met with nowadays—but also I have had the proof of how well he was leading and governing you and how eminently adapted he was to living in a monastic community. Hence, I cherished the highest and fondest hopes that both your own and the monastery's affairs would be in the best possible state for as long as that man lived and stayed among you; it would matter little how I myself fared in the midst of this changing, untrustworthy, and meandering life, and whether I should precede him in death, in the present annoying difficulties of existence and in circumstances as painful to me as they ever have been to another man.

2. Now that that man is gone at so unpropitious a time for the fulfillment of those hopes of mine, and now that he has left you in such great perplexity, it is quite natural that I should be seized by fear for the monastery and for yourselves. However, what is most lamentable—the last straw—is the thought that my own affairs are in utter ruin and in a state of complete dissolution and that "my memorial has been" utterly "destroyed with a noise," as the Holy Writ has it. That such a lot justly befits me and that such is my destiny on account of the magnitude of my sins is clearly indicated by the just verdicts of God and by His judgment, since that man has now left this world. As a result, all my material life has undergone a complete change; my prosperity, [fol. 330v] my fame, and my riches have disappeared all at once; the hitherto carefree existence of my children—and, may I add, there are quite a few of them—has been suddenly shattered and turned into a life of difficulties and misery; and I myself am suffering here in exile and struggling with so many hardships—among them a serious illness. To top it all, that very thing which I cherished above all else, which had remained to me a substitute for everything and which alone enabled me to lead a life which was still noble and worthy of a philosopher, a life of utter disregard for that which is transitory, unstable, and unreliable—and whoever may believe differently and lay great store in such vanities and put his trust in them is a silly man indeed—even that very thing I now behold, with my own eyes, as it were, in danger and on the brink of destruction; in plain talk, I am referring to yourselves and to the monastery. This monastery has meant more than anything in the world to me; it is so now and will be in the time to come. It was a work

59

φιλοκαλίας εὐγενοῦς ἔργον καὶ νοῦ καρπὸς σώφρονος, καὶ ψυχῆς ἀσάλευτον ἀληθῶς κέρδος καὶ
πλοῦτος, καὶ πρὸς τὴν μέλλουσαν ἀπέραντον εὐζωΐαν οὐ παρασκευὴ μᾶλλον, ἢ καὶ ἀσφαλὲς
ἐχέγγυον καὶ χρηστῆς ἐλπίδος ὑπόθεσις, καὶ ὥστε μόνον ἀποχρῆναι τὸν ἐμὸν λογισμὸν κα-
20 θιστᾶν ἐν ῥᾴονι διαθέσει καὶ πάντων ὑπέρτερον, εὐδιεινᾶ καὶ κοῦφον, εὖ μάλ' ἀνύτοντα.

3. Ὡς δέ μοι τόδε τὸ δέος οὐ πόρρω λόγου φέρει, μάλιστα δὲ καιρὸν ἔχει—καίτοι βουλοίμην
κομιδῇ μὴ οὕτως ἔχειν, ἀλλ' ἀστοχεῖν γνώμης αὐτός, ναί, δέσποτα Σῶτερ, ναί, δέσποτ' ἀλε-
ξίκακε—ὡς δ' ἄρ' ὅμως, ᾗπερ ἔφην, ἔχει—νεοταγεῖς γὰρ ὑμεῖς καὶ οὐκέτι πω τὰ καθ' ὑμᾶς εὐπαγῆ·
ἔσωθί τε μήποτ' οὐ χρόνια καθάπαξ τῷ καθεστῶτι, μηδ' ἀκράδαντα, καὶ θάρρος ἔχοντα καὶ
5 πίστιν τῇ συνεχείᾳ τῆς καθιδρύσεως καὶ συμπήξεως, χειμών τ' ἔξωθεν καταιγίζει κατὰ τὸ
παραστὰν τοῦ καιροῦ, ἐμοὶ δ' ἔχει τὰ πράγμαθ' ὡς ἔχει, καὶ τὴν ἐμὴν ἐπικουρίαν ἀφῄρησθε,
ἥτις ποτ' ἄρ' ἦν ἂν ἡ ἐμὴ τοῖς ἐμοῖς ὑμῖν ἐπικουρία. καὶ πρός γ' ἔτι λοιπὸν ἤδη προσαφῄρησθε
καὶ τὸν καλὸν ὑμῖν ἐπιστάτην τῆς συντάξεως καὶ ἄριστον, καὶ τελεώτατον τεχνίτην τῇ καθ' ὑμᾶς
σπουδῇ, καὶ ἀρχηγὸν αὐτὸν τῆς καθ' ὑμᾶς δημιουργίας καὶ κοινωνίας καὶ συμβιώσεως, καὶ
10 πάντ' αἰδοῖον ὑμῖν, καὶ μάλισθ' ὑμῶν ἐφ' ὅσον οἷόν τ' ἐστὶν ἐπιμελῆ, καὶ φροντιστὴν ἄτροπον
ἐν παντὶ τοῦ καιροῦ, κοινῇ τε καὶ ἰδίᾳ, καὶ καμάτων ἁπάντων εὖ μάλ' ἀήττητον. καὶ τοίνυν
ἀθρόον, οὕτω δῆτ' ἔχοντες, ἀφῃρημένοι τοῖς νῦν ὑμεῖς καιροῖς, ὃν εἴχετε σοφὸν ἀρχιτέκτονα τῆς
κατὰ θεὸν οἰκοδομῆς καὶ θεμέλιον ἀποστολικὸν ὑποθέμενον, καὶ τῆς [fol. 331r] πήξεως καὶ τῆς
εὐαρμοστίας ὑμῖν ἐπόπτην ἐνεργὸν ἀεὶ καὶ ἄγρυπνον, περιδεῆ κομιδῇ νῦν ἐμὲ περὶ ὑμῖν ἔχετε,
15 μὴ παντάπασι παρασυρῆτε τὸν καλὸν θεμέλιον καὶ τὴν νεόδμητον ἐποικοδόμησιν τῷ χειμῶνι
καὶ ταῖς ἐνοχλήσεσι τοῦ καιροῦ. καὶ πολὺς ἐντεῦθεν ὁ τάραχος ἐμοί, καὶ λογισμοὶ πανωλείας,
ὡς ἔφην, ἐμὲ τρύχουσι, καὶ οὐκ ἔχω τίς γένωμαι τῇ τελευτῇ τοῦ ἀνδρός, οὗ ζῶντος ἐν εὐελπιστίας
τέως ὥρμουν λιμένι, γαλήνης ὑμῖν τὸ μέρος ἀπολαύων ποθεινῆς καὶ πάντων εὐκταιοτάτης.

4. Καὶ τοῦτο μέν, ὡς ἀληθῶς, ὃ πλεῖν ἢ κατ' ἄλλ' ἐπιεικῶς ἐπείγει καὶ μάλιστα τὴν ἐμὴν
κατάγχει καρδίαν, καὶ βαπτίζει βυθοῖς ἀθυμίας εἰς ἐσχάτην μικροῦ τὴν ἀπόγνωσιν. καὶ τί γὰρ
οὐκ ἔμελλον, ὅς γε πάντων ὑμᾶς τε καὶ τὰ καθ' ὑμᾶς εὖ ἔχειν, ᾗπερ ἔφην, ἐν πρώτοις τοῦτ' ἦγον,
καὶ πρότερον, εὖ πράττων καὶ οὔρια πολὺ μάλιστα κατὰ τὸν βίον φερόμενος, καὶ νῦν δή, τοῖς
5 κατ' ἐμὲ τοῖσδε πράγμασιν, οἷς συνέλαχον κομιδῇ πονηρῶς. ἀλλὰ μὴν καὶ τόδ' ἀμέλει ὁπόσον
ἂν ἔπειτ' εἰς ἀνίας βαρυτάτης ἀφορμὴν ἐμοί, ἀνὴρ ἐκεῖνος ἐκδημήσας—ὑπερορίῳ νῦν ἔμοιγε—
καὶ τελευτήσας τὸν παρόντα βίον, ἀνὴρ οὕτω βέλτιστος ἐμοὶ καὶ τὰ μέγιστα καὶ καιριώτατα
χρήσιμος καὶ βιωφελέστατος, καὶ συνήθης χρόνιος, καὶ φιλῶν διαφερόντως, καὶ παραπλησίως
φιλούμενος. ὢ τῆς ἀποιήτου σοι, κάλλιστε Λουκᾶ, γνώμης καὶ πάσης διπλόης ἐκτός· ὢ τῆς
10 ἀκόμψου σοι γλώττης καὶ πάσης ἀλλοτρίας εὐτραπελίας καὶ πάσης πρὸς χάριν ἡδυεπείας, καὶ
οὐ μᾶλλον τοῖς ταπεινοτέροις καὶ ἥττονος τάξεως, ἢ τοῖς ὑψηλοτέροις καὶ ὑπερέχουσιν, οἷς
δὴ καὶ νόμιμον ἤδη τὸ χαρίζεσθαι γίγνεται τοῖς, οὐκ οἶδ' ὁπότερον ἂν φαίην, οἰκονομικώτερον,
ἤ, τἀληθέστερον ἐρεῖν, ἀνελευθέρως καὶ ἀφιλοσόφως βιοῦσιν. ὢ τῆς γαληνοτάτης ψυχῆς καὶ
πάντων ἀκύμονος καὶ πάσης ἐπηρείας ὑπερτέρας καὶ ἀζημίου, καὶ παντὸς ἔξωθεν πράγματος
15 ταράττοντος καὶ τὸν θυμὸν ἐκκάοντος· ὢ τοῦ πάντα σεμνοῦ προσχήματος, αὐτόθεν ἰδεῖν, καὶ

F 3,12 τῆς—13 ἀποστολικόν : cf. Eph. 2:20-21   17 ὡς ἔφην : cf. 2,3
  4,3 ᾗπερ ἔφην : cf. 1,1

3,6 τ(ὴν) ἐμ(ὴν) ἐπικουρίαν V¹ˢᵛ : τῆς ἐμῆς -ρίας V   18 τέως Vˣˢᵛ
4,4 τοῖς V¹ e corr. : τῆς V

of noble love for things good and beautiful, the fruit of a prudent mind, and assured a truly secure profit and wealth for the soul; it was not so much a preparation as a safe pledge for a happy life without end and an investment in future good hopes. The thought of this monastery was alone capable of putting my mind into a more easy disposition, lifting it above all preoccupations, making it feel unburdened and peaceful, and enabling it to function well.

3. That this fear of mine is not unfounded; rather, that it is most appropriate at this time—I wish it were not so at all and my opinion off the mark, yes, Oh Lord and Savior, yes, Oh Lord shielding us all from evil—that, nevertheless, facts are as I have told them to be—for you have been only recently established and things have not settled with you as yet: inside, I fear, you have not had enough time to achieve stability and coherence, or that self-confidence and trust which continuity brings to a tightly built establishment; outside, a storm is raging at the present moment; and, my affairs being what they are, you have been deprived of my assistance, whatever this assistance of mine may have been for you, my people. In addition to all this, you have been deprived of the good chief of your community, the most accomplished craftsman in the shaping of your goals and himself a leader of your adventure in common living. You revered that man; he, in turn, took care of you to the utmost of his ability, devoted his unswerving attention to you at all times, both in public and in private, and was undaunted by any task. Suddenly, at the present time and in your present circumstances, you were bereft of the man who had been the wise architect of that creation set up according to God's wishes, who had laid the apostolic cornerstone and [fol. 331r] who was the vigorous and ever watchful overseer of your unity and your adjustment to each other; now, therefore, you have made me anxious about yourselves and fearful that that worthy cornerstone and that newly erected building of yours might be violently swept away by the storm and the tribulations of the time. Hence my great agitation and, to say it again, my gnawing apprehensions of utter destruction. I am beside myself on account of the death of that man who, as long as he lived, kept me at anchor in the haven of good hope and gave me a share in the enjoyment of that very peace for which you long so much and pray more than for anything else.

4. This, truth to tell, is what weighs on my heart most heavily and mightily stifles it; it submerges me in deep despond, so that I have reached the very limit of despair. No wonder I feel this way: as I already have said, I have considered your welfare to be my chief concern both in the past, when I was faring well and was sailing through life under a favorable wind, and now, in the midst of those affairs of mine which have become my bitterly sorry lot. In addition, how much cause for the deepest discontent that man provided me with by departing from among us and leaving this life—and by doing that now, while I am in exile. This man was an excellent person for my purposes; I could rely upon him in the most important and crucial moments of life; he was a friend of long standing; he loved me exceedingly and was in turn requited with similar love. How straightforward was your mind, my best Lucas, and how free of all ambiguity; how unadorned your speech and how free of all contrived elegance and those sweetish utterances that only aim to please. You were no more this way with people of a humbler and lower station in life than with the high and mighty; the latter, by long custom, have come to expect flattery from men who—how should I put it—lead lives of tactful compromise, or more truthfully, of servitude unworthy of a philosopher. How serene and utterly calm was your soul, above the reach of any insult, immune to it, and beyond any external stimulus that might cause disturbance or kindle the emotions; how easy was it to discern the decorous monastic garb you were wearing;

61

προβλήματος, καὶ διὰ πάντων παραπλησίως ὁμιλίας λόγων ἁπλῶς καὶ φωνῆς, βαδίσματος, στάσεως, ἕδρας, τῶν ἄλλων πάντων πραγμάτων, μάλισθ᾽ ὡς ἄρα καιρὸν ἔχει τούτων ἕκαστον ἀμέλει κατὰ μοναχοὺς βιοῦσι καὶ κατὰ μοναχοὺς ἄρχουσι καὶ ἡγεμόσι τοιοῦδε συντάγματος. ὡς ἄρα καὶ διὰ πάντων τούτων αὐτόθεν ὁρωμένῳ σοι παιδεύεσθαι τοὺς ἑκάστοθ᾽ ὁρῶντας

20 ἐξεῖναι καὶ βελτιοῦσθαι πρὸς τὸ καίριον ἀμηγέπη τῆς χρήσεως· καὶ λέγοντι μὲν ἁπλοϊκῶς τὰ μάλιστ᾽ ἐπε[fol. 331v]οικότα καθάπαξ, ἐπιτυχέστατα τῷ σεμνῷ βίῳ τῷδε, τοὺς ὑπὸ σὲ πείθεσθαι καὶ τυποῦσθαι πάντας τοὺς τοῦ καλοῦ χαρακτῆρας, καὶ σιωπῶντι δὲ τῷ καθ᾽ ἕκαστα πεφυκότι καὶ ἡρμοσμένῳ τῆς χρήσεως οὐδὲν ἧττον πείθεσθαι καὶ τυποῦσθαι πρὸς τἄμεινον αἰεί.

5. Ὦ τῆς ἱεροτελεστίαις καὶ τῇ θεουργῷ σπονδείᾳ καὶ τῷ φρικτῷ τῆς ἀναιμάκτου θυσίας μυστηρίῳ—τί τις ἐρεῖ; —διαθέσεως σῆς ἔνδοθεν τῇ ψυχῇ, θειασμοῦ παντὸς ἔμπλεῳ καὶ βακχείας ἱερᾶς, καὶ πᾶν ἀνθρώπινον ὑπερβαινούσης τε καὶ ὑπερφρονούσης, ἢ κοσμίας τε καὶ πανσέμνου διοικήσεως, πάνθ᾽ ἕκαστ᾽ ἀνύτειν τιμίως τε καὶ ξὺν ⟨αἰδοῖ⟩ πλείστῃ τὸ γιγνόμενον ἅπαν τῆς

5 χρείας· ὡς μάλ᾽ αὐτόθεν αὐτίκα μὴ μόνον τοὺς συντελεῖς ἄλλους τῆς ἱερᾶς ἁγιστείας καὶ συνδια- σώτας λειτουργοὺς τῆς παναγνου θυσίας ἑαυτῶν κομιδῇ γίγνεσθαι, ἤ, κρεῖττον ἴσως ἐρεῖν, ἑαυτῶν ἐξίστασθαι, καὶ τῶν κατ᾽ ἔθος ἀνθρώποις ἀποχωρεῖν, ὡς εἰπεῖν, καὶ παραβάλλεσθαι πλεῖν ἢ κατὰ φύσιν, ἀλλὰ καὶ τοὺς ἔξωθεν ἐποπτεύοντας θάμβους οἵου παμπλείστου καὶ ἅμα ἡδονῆς ἀρρήτου καὶ γλυκυθυμίας πίμπλασθαι, καὶ προσέχειν εὖ μάλα τὸν νοῦν, ὡς ἄρα τι

10 γιγνόμενον ἐπιεικῶς τῶν κατ᾽ ἀνθρώπους θειότατον καὶ σεβασμιώτατον καὶ μάλα τοι καταναγ- κάζον τὴν εἰς θεὸν ἐπιστροφήν τε καὶ ἐπιμέλειαν ἑαυτῶν καί τινος ἀμείνονος ἕξεως· ὦ τῆς ἐν εὐχαῖς ἀκλινοῦς τοῦ νοῦ προσεδρείας καὶ ἀγωγῆς ἀσχόλου, καὶ τάξεως ἑνοειδοῦς καὶ ἀμερίστου καὶ παντάπασιν ἀπολύτου πάντων καὶ ἀτυρβάστου πρὸς τὴν πρόθεσιν ἀνύτειν, ὡς ἂν ἐκτὸς τοῦ μοχθηροῦ τοῦδε καὶ γαιώδους συνδυασμοῦ καὶ τῶν ἀφύκτων δεσμῶν τῆς σαρκός· ὦ τῆς

15 ἐν ὑμνῳδίαις καὶ χαριστηρίοις καὶ ἱλαστηρίοις καὶ ἱκετηρίοις κρότοις τε καὶ πρὸς θεὸν ἐντυχίαις ἅμα παντὶ τῷ κοσμίῳ πάσης ἱκανώσεως καὶ ἀκριβείας· καὶ τῶν ἐν δευτέρῳ δοκούντων ἐνίοις καὶ ἥττονος λόγου, καὶ ἴσως οὐδ᾽ ἀπαραιτήτων ὀλιγωρεῖσθαι, †τῆς συνεχείας τῶν ἄλλων, ἢ κα- θάπαξ ἐν ἀσχολίᾳ καὶ οὐκ ἀζήμιος, ἀλλὰ πολὺ μάλιστ᾽ ἄτροπος ὀφείλεται †, κἀνταῦθα φεύγοντας ἄλλῃ φέρειν, μή ποτ᾽ ἀνεύθυνον εἴη τοῖς σώφροσιν.

6. Ἔγωγέ τοι, νῦν ἐπελθὸν ἐμῇ μνήμῃ περὶ τούτων ἐρεῖν, ὦ τίς γένωμαι; πῶς ἐνέγκω τὸ πάθος; παραχρῆμα λοιπὸν ἐντεῦθεν συγκέχυμαι τοὺς λογισμούς, καὶ μὴν ἐκτόπως ἔτι διπλῇ μερίζομαι· τὶ μέν, τοῖς φανταστικοῖς τῶν πραγμάτων πίναξιν ἐμπίπτων καὶ κατοπτριζόμενος καὶ ὡσπερεὶ συνών, μάλισθ᾽ ὅλος ἔχομαι τῇδε θαυμαστῶς ὅπως, καὶ [fol. 332r] τιν᾽ ἄρρητον

5 καὶ ξένην συνδιατίθεμαι κοινωνίαν καὶ κρᾶσιν σεβασμοῦ μετὰ τερπωλῆς· τὶ δέ, τῆς τῶν πραγ- μάτων ἐρημίας ὄντως γιγνόμενος καὶ γιγνόμενος ἔπειτ᾽ ἐπ᾽ ἐμαυτοῦ κατὰ τὸ παραστὰν ἀθρῶν, αὐτόθεν στενοῦμαι τὸ ζῆν, μικροῦ τὸ ζωτικὸν ἐκλείπων πνεῦμα, καὶ κατ᾽ ὀλίγον λυόμενος τὴν συνέχειαν καὶ τὸν σύνδεσμον αὐτὸν τοῦ εἶναι. ὦ πῶς ποτ᾽ οἴχεται νῦν εἶναι τὰ πάνσεμνα καὶ λυσιτελέστατα τἀνδρὸς ἐκείνου τῇ συναυλίᾳ, τοῖς ὑπ᾽ αὐτοῦ νεολέκτοις, τοῖς προβεβηκόσιν

10 ἡλικίᾳ, ὁμοῦ γέ τοι πᾶσι τοῖς τυπουμένοις ὑπ᾽ αὐτοῦ, τὸ γιγνόμενον ἑκάστῳ καὶ προσῆκον ἰδίᾳ σὺν λόγῳ καὶ κοινῇ πρὸς συμφυΐαν τῷ καλῷ, ⟨καὶ⟩, ὡς ἄρ᾽ ἑνοειδῶς δέοι ἄν, ἀρτιοῦσθαι τῇ κοινῇ χρήσει καὶ πάνθ᾽ ἡρμοσμένως ἐφάμιλλα παραβάλλεσθαι. ὦ πῶς ποτ᾽, ἐκλελοιπότος,

---

F 6,9/10 νεολέκτοις, τοῖς προβεβηκόσιν ἡλικίᾳ : cf. litteras Athanasii Patriarchae ad monachos M. Laurae, προβεβηκόσι τε πᾶσιν καὶ νέοις, Vat. gr. 2219, fol. 249v.

5,1 ἱεροτελεστίαις V² e corr. : -ας V?   7 παραβά[λλε]σθαι V   17 τῆς—18 ὀφείλεται] non perspicio
6,1 ἐμῇ V¹ˢᵛ : ἐμοί V   4 ὅλος V¹ˢᵛ : ὅλως V   5 κρᾶσιν V   6 ἐπ᾽ V¹ˢᵛ : ἐν V   ἀθρῶν V   11 supplevi : κα[λῶ] . . . ὡς V   12 ἐκλελ[οι]πότος V

how uniformly simple was your discourse and how even your tone of voice, whenever you spoke. Your gait, your stance, the way you were sitting, all other things—all of it was most befitting and appropriate to a monk, a leader of monks and the head of such an important community. Thus, the very moment they saw you, the witnesses were edified and could progress, owing to all these qualities of yours, toward an appropriate code of behavior. Whenever you spoke, in a simple and most seemly [fol. 331v] fashion, befitting the seriousness of the monastic way of life, your subordinates could be persuaded and their minds molded after all the patterns of the Good; whenever you were silent, they were no less persuaded and molded for the Better, thanks to your appropriate behavior, befitting all occasions.

5. How wondrous, during the solemnization of Sacred Rites and Divine Liturgical Service and the performance of the awe-inspiring Mystery of the Bloodless Sacrifice, was the inner state of your soul, filled to the brim with inspiration and with Holy Bacchic frenzy, transcending and scorning all human condition; or, should one not rather say, how orderly and decorous was your ministration, how capable of accomplishing everything required by the usage with dignity and the greatest reverence. Hence not only did other participants in the Holy Service and the concelebrants of the most Revered Sacrifice right away take hold of themselves; or, to say it perhaps more appropriately, not only did they leap outside of themselves, leave, as it were, the sphere of customary human concerns, and venture beyond human nature, but also the onlookers outside the altar were filled both with most intense awe and with ineffable joy and sweetness of mind; they turned their attention to the Service as to an event most Divine and worthy of worship among men, which was forcing them to turn towards God, to take care of their own spiritual well-being, and to adopt some finer attitudes in their lives. How unswervingly did your mind persevere in prayers; how constant was your observance of them; how single-minded, and undivided, was your disposition, completely detached from anything else and calmly directed towards its purpose, as if you were outside of this burdensome and earthly union, and free from the inescapable bonds of the flesh. How great was your orderliness, combined with self-sufficiency and precision, in hymns and songs addressing God, whether in those expressing thanks, those propitiatory, or those imploring Him for assistance; for to neglect things which some people consider as secondary and of lesser importance and as perhaps not indispensable† τῆς συνεχείας —ὀφείλεται† to leave this matter and to turn elsewhere, might bring blame upon the prudent.

6. Now that my memory has moved me to talk about these things, what shall become of me? How shall I bear the suffering? At present, my thoughts have become confused and I am strangely split in two. On the one hand, looking into the tablets of imagination, beholding myself there as if in a mirror, and being present, as it were, at the events, I remain entirely there in some wondrous fashion, and [fol. 332r] experience an ineffable and strange communion, and mixture of reverence and joy. On the other hand, as I realize that, in fact, I am removed from affairs, as I later waken and contemplate things as they are, I am instantly almost stifled to death, I am at my last gasp, as it were, and the very continuity and bonds of existence are slowly being loosened in me. Alas, gone is now the decorous and most advantageous influence of that man Lucas upon the monastic community, upon the novices he had chosen himself, upon those more advanced in age, in sum, gone is, for all those who were being molded by him, what was best, most fitting and reasonable for each of them, both as individuals and as members of the community, for achieving union with the Good, for achieving unity and perfection in the course of common living, and for establishing the most fitting model for comparison and competition. Alas, now that

63

ὥσπερ ἐν χοροῦ καὶ μέλους συντάγματι, τοῦ κορυφαίου, τοῦ λοιποῦ κίνδυνος ὕποπτος καὶ πάντ᾽
ἄνω καὶ κάτω δέος ἐσεῖσθαι· ὢ τίς ἐβάσκηνε δαίμων ἔφεδρος ἀεὶ καὶ ληστεύων, οὐκ ἀναίδην
15 μᾶλλον, ἢ κρύφα τε καὶ σὺν δόλῳ, καὶ σκαιωρούμενος, ἀκάμας καὶ ἄϋπνος τὸν ἀεὶ χρόνον, τὴν
προκοπὴν τῶν βελτίστων καὶ λωποδυτῶν· ὢ πόσον μάλισθ᾽ ἡ τῶν ἐμῶν ἁμαρτάδων κραταί-
ωσις ἴσχυσε, καὶ τἀνομήματα τῶν ἐπιταγμάτων θεοῦ, ὑφ᾽ ὧν, ἔοικε, πάντα κατερείπεται τἀμὰ
πράγματα καὶ πάγκοινα τῇ φθορᾷ χωρεῖ, καὶ περιφανῆ με ταῖς συμφοραῖς ποιεῖται, νῦν τε
εἶναι καὶ τοῖς μεθύστερον ἴσως ἀνθρώποις, οὐδ᾽ ὅ,τί ποτ᾽ ἄρ᾽ εὐελπιστίας ἐμοὶ λείπει καὶ μνήμης
20 ἐπὶ χρηστοῖς ἐμπύρευμα· καὶ ὃ γὰρ ἐμοὶ παντὸς μᾶλλον ποθεινόν τε καὶ τίμιον, καὶ μόνον ἐπὶ
ξυμφορᾷ τοσαύτῃ τῶν ἀλγεινῶν ἤρκει, φέρον ἥντινα δὴ ῥᾳστώνην καὶ πνεῦμά πως οὔριον καὶ
κοῦφον τῇ πάντ᾽ ἐμῇ ταλαιπώρῳ ψυχῇ, τὸ δὲ καὶ αὐτό, τραπὲν καὶ νοσῆσαν, ἐν σάλῳ λοιπὸν
ἤδη προδήλῳ νῦν.

7. Καὶ προσθήκη μοι σὺ γίγνῃ τῶν ἄλλων μείζων, ὦ βέλτιστ᾽ ἀνδρῶν καὶ φίλτατε, καὶ
κ ο λ ο φ ὼ ν τῆς παροιμίας, ἐπαύξων ταῖς ἀποφράσι τύχαις τὰς πικρὰς ψήφους, καὶ μάλιστ᾽ ἐπιση-
μαίνων αὐτὸς τοῖς φθάσασι δεινοῖς καὶ κράτος ἐργωδέστατον ἀπαντᾶν σφίσι διδούς· καὶ ὃν σὺ
διὰ παντός σοι τοῦ ζῆν διαφερόντως ἤρας εὖ εἶναι πάντα πράγματα, καὶ ψυχὴν καὶ σῶμα—καὶ
5 διὰ παντὸς ἠπείγου ταῖς εὐχαῖς, καὶ πλεῖστον πονεῖν ἠξίους ἐμοί, καὶ πρὸς πάντα κάματον
ὅπως ἄρ᾽ ὁπῃοῦν ἔξεστιν, οὐκ ἂν μήποτ᾽ ἀποτρέπεσθαι, νῦν ἔλαθες ἤδη—μεταλλάξας τὸ ζῆν
ἐπὶ πᾶσι πράγμασιν ἐμοὶ δυσχερέσι καὶ χαλεποῖς, εἰ δή ποτέ [fol. 332v] τινι καὶ ἄλλῳ τῶν
ἁπάντων—τελευτῶν αὐτὸς ἐμὲ λοιπὸν τῷ βαρυτάτῳ κινδύνῳ περιβαλών, καὶ ὥστε παλαίειν
ἀφορήτοις ὀδύναις καὶ λογισμῶν τρικυμίαις, ἄκων μὲν καί, οἶδα, μάλ᾽ ἀηδῶς, ἀλλ᾽ ὅμως αἴτιος
10 ἐμοὶ γεγονώς. καὶ ζημιοῖς μὲν τὴν φίλην σοι μονὴν καὶ ἀντὶ πάντων σοι τιμωμένην, καὶ εἰς ἣν
ἅπαν σοι τὸ κατὰ φύσιν οἷόν τε ὂν καθάπαξ ἐξεχεῖτο τῇ ψυχῇ, καὶ τὰ σὰ φίλτατα, τοὺς σοὺς
μοναστάς, οὓς ἀμέλει τοσούτους ὠδίνησας κατὰ θεὸν καὶ χρόνιος ἤδη κάλλιστα καλλίστους
ἐθρέψω, τὴν σὴν φιλτάτην καὶ καλλίστην ἐπιστασίαν, ἔτι πω μάλιστ᾽ ἐπίχρειον σφίσι· ζημιοῖς δ᾽
ἐμὲ τὴν σὴν ἐπέραστόν μοι πάνυ τοι πλεῖστον, καὶ οὐκ οἶδ᾽ ὡς εἴ τί ποτ᾽ ἄλλο, ζωήν, καί, νῦν γε
15 μάλιστ᾽, ἐπὶ τῶν κατ᾽ ἐμὲ τῶνδε πραγμάτων, καὶ τὴν σὴν ἐν εὐχῇ μοι μεγίστην καὶ πόθοις
μεγίστοις ὑπὲρ ἄλλ᾽ ὁτιοῦν ἅπαν καὶ ἴσως ἐν ἐλπίσι πρόσοψιν καὶ ξυντυχίαν. ὃ καὶ μόνον ἐν
φαντασίαις ἐμαυτῷ χαριζόμενος, ὡς ἄρ᾽ εἰώθασι τὰ κατὰ βούλησιν καὶ πόθον ἄνθρωποι ῥᾷσθ᾽
ἑαυτοῖς χαρίζεσθαι καὶ δοκεῖν, ῥᾷον εὖ μάλ᾽ εἶχον ἐντεῦθεν, καὶ κούφως ἀνωρθούμην ταῖς ἐλπίσι,
καὶ κατέπαυον τὰ λυποῦντα, καί πως ἐν γαλήνῃ τῶνδ᾽ ἀποχωρῶν, φιλοσοφώτερον ταύτῃ πως
20 ἠξίουν βιοῦν.

8. Μαρτύρομαι τὸν ἀόρατον αὐτὸν ἐπόπτην ἁπάντων θεόν, καὶ τῶν ἐν ἀδύτοις καὶ μυχοῖς
καρδίας αὐτῶν, ὡς οὐ τηνάλλως οὑτοσί μοι νῦν ὁ λόγος εἴρηται, λόγος ἄλλως οὕτως ἐκχυθείς·
ἀλλὰ μάλιστα μὲν ἐμὲ καὶ ἀεὶ πρότερον, εὐθηνούμενον κατὰ τὸν βίον καὶ πολυδόξως ἀνύτοντα,
καὶ νῦν ἔτι, πλεῖστον—ὡς ἄρ᾽ εἰπὼν ἔφθην ἀρχόμενος τοῦ νυνὶ λόγου—φλέγων ἐκτόπως εἶχέ
5 τε καὶ ἔχει περὶ τὴν μονὴν πόθος τε καὶ σπουδή, ὑπερβαλλόντως ἐξηρτημένης μοι τῇδε τῆς

F **7,**2 κολοφών : cf. Leutsch-Schneidewin, I, 336; II, 119, 482
8,4 εἰπὼν ἔφθην : cf. **1,**1/2

6,14 ὦ Vˣ e corr. : εἰ V
7,18 κούφ(ως) V¹ˢᵛ : κοῦφος V
8,2 τηνάλλως V   οὑτοσί V¹ˢᵛ : οὑτωσί V

the conductor has left the body of a lyric choir, as it were, danger must be envisaged and fears entertained that everything will be upside down. What evil spirit has cast his envy upon us, forever lurking and plundering and stealing away the progress of the best, not as much in the open as on the sly and surreptitiously, by mischievous devices, without ever relenting, or ever closing an eye? By how much has the strength of my sins and of my transgressions of God's command-ments prevailed; sins and transgressions which, as it appears, caused the ruin of all my affairs and made them all together take the turn down the road of destruction. They make me stand out in my misery, both among my contemporaries and perhaps among the future generations; my sins leave me no good hope or hidden spark of expectation of being remembered for my good deeds; in fact, that very thing for which I had longed more, which I had valued more than anything else and which alone was to me a sufficient remedy against suffering in such a great calamity—since it brought me some solace and blew some favorable and light breeze upon my unhappy soul—even this very thing, changed and affected by ills, is now in an obvious state of instability.

7. You, Lucas, the best and most beloved of men, have become the largest increment in all my tribulations, and the proverbial last straw; you added to the burden of the bitter decrees of unhappy fate; above all, you sealed my past calamities and thereby increased their intensity well-nigh to the point where they no longer can be withstood. And myself, the man whom, throughout your life, you ardently wished to fare well in all respects, both in soul and in body—and you were always eagerly praying for it and deemed it worthwhile to toil hard on my behalf and never to turn away from any effort whatever, however spent; now, however, you seem not to have realized that by your death, by departing from this life while my affairs were as difficult and in as unpleasant a state as any experienced [fol. 332v] by anybody at any time, you exposed me to the most serious danger, and caused me—if reluctantly, I know, and unwillingly—to struggle with unbearable suffering and be exposed to stormy broodings. On the one hand, you have deprived your beloved monastery—which you cherished more than anything else on earth and toward which flowed all the natural capacity of your soul—and your own children, the monks—whom you have brought forth in such large numbers in the name of God and have been raising in the best manner and with the best results for so many years—of your most friendly and best guidance, of which they were still in great need. On the other hand, you have deprived me of your life, a thing most beloved by me, more than anything I could name; especially now, in the present state of my affairs, you have deprived me of your sight and company, for which I had greatly prayed and greatly longed, perhaps more than for anything else for which I had hoped. When I as much as granted to myself this eventuality in my imagination, as people are wont to grant to themselves, in their minds, things which they desire and long for, I was relieved right away, my burden was lightened, my hopes permitted me to arise, I soothed my sufferings, and as, in some sense, I peacefully receded from reality around me, I could claim that in such a fashion I was living in a more philosophical manner.

8. I invoke the testimony of God, the invisible observer of all things, even of those hidden in the impenetrable recesses of people's hearts, that the words which I have just uttered here are not in vain and that these words have not been just poured out for no purpose. As I said previously, at the beginning of this present essay, throughout my earlier days, when my life was thriving and full of splendid accomplishments, no less than now, I was and continue to be seized by burning longing and interest for the monastery; my heart is attached to it; it draws, as it were,

65

καρδίας καὶ ὡσανεὶ ζωηφόρον ἐντεῦθεν πνεούσης, καὶ θαλπομένης αὔραις ἀτεχνῶς εὐενδότοις ἔνδον, καὶ δροσοφόροις κατὰ παντὸς τοῦ λυποῦντος. καὶ τὸ περιλειφθῆναί μοι τὴν μονὴν ἐν ἀγαθοῖς, ὡς ἄρ' εἶχε τέως καὶ ἀεὶ πρόσω ἤει, καὶ τοῦ χρόνου καθάπαξ ἀθῷον καὶ ἀλώβητον καὶ πάσης ἐπηρείας, κομιδῇ πάντων εὐκταιότατον καὶ πάντων ἐμοὶ τιμώμενον· καὶ τόδ' εἶναι
10 μάλιστ' ἐπεπείσμην ἀσφαλέστατα μετὰ τῆς ἐπιστασίας τοῦ πεῖραν ἄσειστον ἐν τούτοις δεδωκότος ἡγεμόνος Λουκᾶ, καὶ οὐχ ἧττον ἢ πρὶν ἐν τῷ νῦν ἐργώδει καὶ δυσαντήτῳ μοι καὶ πολυκύμονι χρόνῳ. ἔπειτά με πάσης ἀφῃρημένον πρὶν δοκούσης εὐπραγίας καὶ ἀφειμένον αὐτὸν οἶμαι τοῖς λογισμοῖς [fol. 333r] ἐπὶ τούτοις εἶχεν ἅμα πόθος τε καὶ ἐλπίς, ἴσως μὲν ἀπατηλὴ καὶ ψευδής, ἴσως δ' οὔ, εἶχε δ' ὅμως, ὡς ἄρα θεοῦ βουλομένου καὶ κινοῦντος γενοίμην αὐτὸς
15 παρὰ τῇ μονῇ, καὶ τὸ λοιπὸν ἐμοὶ τῆς ζωῆς, ὅ,τί ποτ' ἂν εἴη, τῇδ' οὐκ ἀηδῶς ἂν βιωσοίμην· καὶ μάλιστ' οὐκ ἀηδῶς, συνὼν τἀνδρὶ τῷδε, ἀνδρὶ φίλῳ τε καὶ κατὰ θεὸν πατρί, καὶ ἅμα πολλὴν πίστιν εὐνοίας—χρόνος ἐξ ὅτου μακρός—ἐμοὶ παρασχόντι, καὶ πίστιν ἀρίστης ἡγεμονίας ἀναμφίλεκτον πολυετῆ τῇ μονῇ, καὶ ταῦτα τὴν ἀρχὴν συνισταμένῃ καὶ χωρούσῃ πρὸς οὐσίαν τέως καὶ πῆξιν, ᾗ δὴ καὶ μάλιστ' ἐργωδέστερον εὖ χρήσασθαι καὶ κατὰ πρόθεσιν ἀνῦσαι, ἢ
20 καὶ ὁπῃοῦν ἀνεκτῶς ἐσκευασμένῃ καὶ συνεστώσῃ χρήσασθαι.

9. Καί πως ταῦτ' ἔχων ἐν νῷ καὶ κατ' ἐλπίδα κούφως, ᾗπερ ἔφην, ἤνυτον, κἀνταῦθα τρίβων ἀλγεινῶς ἔτι πω· καὶ τῇ φανταστικῇ ῥᾷστ' εὐδρομίᾳ καὶ τάχει καὶ τῷ κατὰ πάντων καὶ ὄντων καὶ δοκούντων δυσχερεστάτων καὶ δυσανύστων κράτει τε καὶ ἐξουσίᾳ καὶ παντὸς ἀδείᾳ προσκόμματος ταχὺς ἀνύτων, ἐν μέσοις ἦν αὐτόθι καὶ συνῆν τῷ καλῷ συντάγματι, καὶ συνῆν τῷ
5 καλῷ πατρί· καὶ συνδιέφερον μέν, ὅ,τί ποτ' ἄρα τὸ γιγνόμενον ἐμοί, τὰ καθ' ὑμᾶς εὖ εἶναι καὶ πράττειν ὡς βέλτιστα, συνδιετιθέμην δ' ἐγὼ πρὸς τἄμεινον ἑκάστοτ', ἀνιών, οὐ μᾶλλον τῶν ἀνιόντων καὶ τῶν ἐκ τοῦ χρόνου δυσχερῶν καὶ τῆς πικρᾶς τύχης, ἢ τοῦ κατάγχοντος βάρους, τῶν ἐμῶν κατὰ τὸν βίον ἀνομημάτων, ἃ πλεῖσθ' ὅσα δυστυχὴς ἐγὼ καὶ ἀβέλτερος ὡμαδὸν ἐπεσώρευσα, παντάπασιν ὀλιγωρίᾳ τῶν ἐπιταγμάτων τοῦ θεοῦ βιώσας, καὶ τῆς ἐπειγούσης
10 ὑπερβαλλόντως τὴν ψυχὴν ἀχθηδόνος ἐντεῦθεν ἀναφέρων, καὶ οὔρια τοῦ λοιποῦ πνεύματι γαλήνης ταῖς ἐλπίσιν ἀγόμενος, εὐπλοῶν πρὸς τέλους λιμένα μὴ πάνυ τοι πόρρω κατὰ φύσιν ἑκάστοτ' ἀνθρώποις ἅπασι, καὶ τῷ κατ' ἐμὲ λοιπὸν ἤδη γήρᾳ μάλιστα, καὶ ὅσον οὐκ ἤδη τάχιστ' ἐκ γειτόνων τῷ κοινῷ πέρατι, τῷ θανάτῳ· κἀντεῦθεν καὶ τοῖς παρελθοῦσιν ἀνεχώρουν ἐπανιών, καὶ τοίνυν ἐμεμνήμην ἡμερῶν ἀρχαίων, καὶ μῆνας ἡμερῶν ἐπόθουν τῶν ἔμπροσθεν,
15 ἐν αἷς ποτ' ἐγὼ τῷ βελτίστῳ ποιμένι συμπαρῆν ἐπὶ τοῦ ἱεροῦ, καὶ τοῦ καλοῦ χοροῦ συντελὴς ἦν, καὶ θιασώτης ἐν τοῖς πρὸς θεὸν ὕμνοις, ἡμέρας τε καὶ μεθ' ἡμέραν, νυκτὸς ἔστιν ὅτε καὶ πάννυχος ἔστιν ὅτε, καὶ συναδολεσχῶν τὰ θεῖα καὶ τοῖς τοῦ Χριστοῦ μυστηρίοις ἐνθεάζων, καὶ ταῖς ἑορτασίμοις τοῦ κοινοῦ δεσπότου τῶν ἡμερῶν [fol. 333v] εὖ μάλ' ἀγαλλόμενος, καὶ φαιδρύνων καὶ τέρπων τὴν ψυχὴν ἡδονὴν ὄντως ἐξειπεῖν μήποτ' οὐ ῥᾳδίαν, ἁγνοτάτην καὶ πρὸς
20 θεὸν καὶ θεοῦ λατρείαν ἄγουσαν, καὶ κηλοῦσαν εὐαφῶς πάνυ τοι τὸ συνεζευγμένον τῆς ψυχῆς ἄλογον, μᾶλλον δὲ λογικοῖς πρέπουσαν εὖ μάλα, καὶ πρέπουσαν κατὰ φύσιν ἐν τοῖς ἱεροῖς καὶ θείοις οἰκείαν οὕτω, καὶ ἅμα σύγκρατον σέβας καὶ χάρμα, πλεῖστον οἷον εὐάγωγον, ἄρρητον.

F 9,1 ᾗπερ ἔφην : cf. 7,18   14 μῆνας ἡμερῶν : cf. Gen. 29:14; Num. 11:20 et 21; IV Reg. 15:13; Ju. 3:10; Job 3:6 et 29:2

8,18 καί²] καὶ V
9,3 δυσχερεστάτω V : add. -ν V²ᵃᵛ   5 ὑμᾶς scripsi : ἡμᾶς V   13 ἐγγειτόνων V, cf. TM, *Logos* 14, **35**,23, *Etudes*, p. 263 in apparatu

66

some life-giving air from there and is inwardly soothed by breezes of perfect mildness which bring it refreshing dew against any sorrow. And it is my most prayed for and cherished wish that the monastery should continue to fare well, as was the case in the past when it was continually progressing, and that it be unaffected by the damage of time or by any other threat. I was convinced that this would be the case, if it were under the leadership of Abbot Lucas, who had proven himself beyond any doubt in this respect; and that no less than in the past it would be so now, in these, for me, difficult, turbulent, and menacing times. Furthermore, when I was deprived of all my former apparent prosperity and was subdued in my mind, [fol. 233r] I had a longing and hope concerning that matter—a hope perhaps treacherous and false, perhaps not, but in any case a gripping hope—that, God willing and helping, I myself would come to the monastery and would live there not unhappily, for whatever time might be allotted to the remainder of my life. Of course, I would be living not unhappily, since I would enjoy the company of that man, a friend and a father according to God; a person who had convinced me of his benevolence long ago, and the monastery of the highest quality of his leadership throughout the many years of his tenure. This was so, although at first this monastery was being set up, was taking shape and acquiring consistency—and it is more difficult to administer and accomplish things according to one's plans in such circumstances than it is to administer them when a monastery has been more or less set up and functioning.

9. And since, as I previously said, I kept these things in mind and cherished such hopes, I was able to carry on with some ease, even though I continued to lead a painful existence here. I was quickly able, with great speed and ease, to transport myself on the swift wings of imagination, and, by dint of the strength, power, and immunity it gives one against all real and imaginary difficulties, challenging tasks, and obstacles, I was instantly in the midst of monks, lived in the good community, and was together with the good father. I was lending a helping hand, as much as I could, so that you would thrive and fare as well as possible. In turn, I was affected by the community in my gradual progress for the better; I was overcoming not so much the vexations and difficulties due to the present time and to my bitter fate, as the stifling burden of the sins committed throughout my life—unhappy and miserable being that I am, I have heaped a multitude of them upon my shoulders, since I have lived in utter disregard of God's commandments; furthermore, I was recovering from the heaviness which for that reason so strongly weighed upon my soul; henceforth, my hopes having put me on the wings of a peaceful and favorable breeze, I was approaching the port of final destination; by nature this port is close to all men at all times; it is especially close by in my old age, which very soon will be bordering on that limit common to all, namely death. I was also able to remove myself from here by returning to the events of the past; I remembered the old days and was longing for those months of days gone by, when I was present in the altar space along with the best of shepherds; when I was a member of the good choir and of the religious community singing hymns to God—I did it during both day and evening, sometimes at night, and sometimes throughout the whole night; when I was discussing things divine with the monks and was inspired by Christ's mysteries; and when, on the days of the feasts of the Lord of us all [fol. 333v] I was filled with joy and was cheering and gladdening my soul with a pleasure indeed difficult to describe; it is most chaste, and leads towards God and His worship; it gently charms the irrational part linked to our soul; or rather it befits rational beings quite well and does so by dint of what is natural and peculiar to matters sacred and divine, and by dint of a mixture of reverence and of plentiful, peaceful,

καὶ ταῦθ᾽ ἕκαστα πάντως ὑπὸ τῷ καλῷ τελετάρχῃ καὶ τεχνίτῃ πάντων ἐπιλέκτῳ καὶ τῆς εἰθι-
σμένης ἐν τούτοις ἐς τἀκριβέστατον ἀγωγῆς, καὶ νομίμῳ τῇ κατὰ μοναχοὺς πανσέμνῳ τε καὶ
25 παναρμονίῳ τοῦ πολιτεύματος ἁγιστείᾳ τε καὶ ἱερᾷ συντάξει.

10. Καὶ τίς γὰρ οὕτω τὰ θεῖα πεπαιδευμένος ἐνεργός τε καθ᾽ αὑτὸν ἰδίᾳ καὶ κοινῇ τύπος
καὶ νομοθέτης ἡγεῖσθαι πολλῶν, ἅτ᾽, οἶμαι, κατὰ φύσιν οἰκειότατ᾽ ἔχων ἔοικεν αὐτὸς τῇ χρήσει—
καὶ ἴσμεν, ὅσοι καὶ ἴσμεν τὸν ἄνδρα καὶ πεπειράμεθα—καὶ πολὺ μάλιστ᾽ ἐκ μακροῦ βέλτιστα
συνησκημένος τῇ πείρᾳ ταύτῃ καὶ τῶν καλλίστων ἐπιστήμῃ καὶ ἐκδοχῇ πάνυ τοι θαυμαστῶν
5 ἀνδρῶν καὶ ἄκρων ἐν τούτοις, οὓς Ἰωνία τε καὶ Ἀσία πλείστους ἤνεγκέ τε καὶ ἔθρεψε; καὶ κατ᾽
ἐκείνους ἄρα τοὺς τόπους εἶχεν, ὡς ἴσασιν ἅπαντες, πλεῖστά τε καὶ κομιδῇ περιφανέστατ᾽, ἤπερ
ἄλλοθί πῃ, μοναχικὰ συστήματα, τοῦτο μὲν ἐν κοινωνικαῖς συνοικίαις καὶ συμβιώσεσι καὶ συναυ-
λίαις πολυαρίθμοις, τοῦτο δ᾽ ἐν ἡσυχίοις καὶ ἀμίκτοις ἐρημίαις καὶ ἀναχωρήσεσιν· οἷς ἐννεάσας
ἀνὴρ κἀκ πρώτης ἡλικίας καὶ παιδικῆς ἔτι πολλῶν ἐτῶν συνασκηθείς, καὶ τὸ κατὰ φύσιν μά-
10 λιστ᾽ οἴκοθεν οἰκεῖον ἔχων τῷ βίῳ καὶ στοιχειώδη τινὰ κρᾶσιν, ὡς εἰπεῖν, ἕξιν ἐντεῦθεν ἄσειστον,
εὖ μάλ᾽ ἀραρυῖαν, ἐπὶ τούτοις ἐβεβαιώσατο. καὶ ἦν γὰρ ἐνταῦθα πᾶς ὁ νοῦς αὐτῷ καὶ
πάνθ᾽ ὁμοῦ τὰ πράγματα καὶ πρὸς οὐδὲν μήποτ᾽ ἄλλ᾽ ὁτιοῦν οὔ—καὶ εἰ δή τις ἄλλος ὁτῳοῦν
ἄλλῳ, μᾶλλον δέ, εἰ δή τις ἄλλος ἐν τούτῳ· καὶ αὐτὸς ἠκριβώσατο τὴν ἐπιλογὴν καὶ τὸ δοκι-
μασθὲν ἅπαν καὶ τὰ νόμιμα τῆς πάντα καλλίστης αἱρέσεως, καὶ τὴν τέχνην εὖ μάλα καθ᾽ αὑτὸν
15 χρῆσθαι καὶ παιδεύειν ἑτέρους.

11. Καί μοι πρὸς τὸν ἐκκάοντα τῇ μονῇ πόθον ἐν καιρῷ πολλῶν ἐκλόγιμος δειχθεὶς καὶ
καθ᾽ ὅσον οἷόν τ᾽ ἐστὶν ἱκανόχρειος αὐτῇ τῇ μονῇ καὶ τῷ πόθῳ, τῇ πείρᾳ πόλλ᾽ ἔτη συνεχῶς
ἀφ᾽ οὗ μέχρι δεῦρο καὶ ἐς νῦν, καὶ πλείστας ἀγαθὰς ἐλπίδας ἐναποθέμενος καὶ εἰς φλόγα λαμ-
πρὰν ἀναρριπίσας τοῖς ἐμοῖς [fol. 334r] λογισμοῖς, ὥστ᾽ ἀμέλει καὶ νῦν εἶναι τῷ βίῳ περιόντος,
5 καὶ τελευτήσαντος ἴσως ἐμοῦ φθάντος τὴν ζωήν—ἀδόκητά μοι λοιπὸν ἤδη κατέσβεσε πάσας—ὢ
τί ποτ᾽ ἐρῶ;—καὶ ὁ πάντα γαληνὸς καὶ πρᾷος καὶ πᾶσιν ἡδύς, καὶ πάντων ἐμοὶ πλεῖστον ἡδύς,
λαθὼν ἄρα νῦν ἔπειτ᾽ ἔμοιγε πικρότατον κομιδῇ καὶ δύσχρηστον κατακιρνᾷ πόμ᾽ ἀηδίας καὶ
ἀθρόον τῇ τελευτῇ. ὢ πόσης ἐλπίδος, πόσης ἡδονῆς ἐπιδόξου μοι καὶ τρυφῆς κάλλιστ᾽ ἐν βελ-
τίστοις τῆς σῆς ξυντυχίας, καὶ ἴσως τοῦ λοιποῦ ξυμβιώσεως, ἧς ἐκ μακροῦ πόθος ἐμέ—καὶ
10 αὐτὸς ᾔδεις—εἶχεν, ἐμὲ νῦν ἀφείλου· ὢ μηδενὶ μὲν πλὴν ἢ σεαυτῷ καὶ ταῖς σαῖς ἴσως ἑτοιμασίαις
καὶ τῇ μεταστάσει τῶν τῇδε καὶ παρασκευῇ μὴ κατὰ καιρὸν τελευτήσας τὰ παρόντα καὶ τὴν
ζωήν· μηδενὶ δὲ τοῦθ᾽ οὕτως ὡς ἐμοί, τῷ πάντων σοι φιλτάτῳ, καὶ τῇ πολυεράστῳ σοὶ μονῇ,
καὶ ἧς ὅλος ἀπλήστως εἶχες συνεῖναι καὶ περιεῖχου, καὶ τὴν κατ᾽ αὐτὴν βελτίωσιν καὶ προα-
γωγὴν ἐς τἄμεινον ἀεὶ πάντα τρόπον ἐπόνεις ἀκάμας, καὶ δῇτ᾽ εὖ μάλ᾽ ἀνύτων ὅσαι ἡμέραι
15 συνεχῶς ἑξῆς ἐπιεικῶς ἔχαιρες, καὶ ὡς οὔποτ᾽ ἂν ὁστισοῦν ἄλλος φιλτάτων εὐετηρίᾳ καὶ τύχης
ἀγαθῆς ὑπερβολαῖς.

12. Καὶ νῦν ὢ πῶς ποτε ταύτην ἔλιπες ἐρήμην, καὶ τοὺς αὐτῆς τροφίμους, τὰ σὰ φίλτατ᾽,
ἀθλίως ὀρφανικά, πολλοῖς γόοις καὶ δυσελπιστίᾳ τοῦ μέλλοντος συνόντα καὶ τειρόμενα, καὶ σέ,

F **10**,11 εὖ—ἀραρυῖαν : cf., e.g., Hom., H 339 et 438

10,8 ἡσύχοις V : add. -ῐ- Vˣ
11,2 ἱκανόχρειος V¹ e corr. : -ειον τ V?   3 ἀφοῦ V   10 πλήν Vˣ e corr. : πλεῖν V   11 μή add. V¹ˢᵛ   13 ὅλος
V¹ˢᵛ : ὅλως V
12,1 ὢ πῶς Vˣ e corr. : V quid?

and ineffable delight. And all that was happening under the full guidance of Lucas, that good leader in Divine Mysteries and the chosen master craftsman of all things, but especially of the traditional and most strict observance in these matters; and was following the customary, most majestic and harmonious rites and holy services of the monastic community.

10. Indeed, who was as educated in matters divine as Lucas was, as vigorous in their private pursuit, and as much of a model and legislator in leading the many? It was so, in my view, inasmuch as he seemed most naturally attuned to this kind of exercise—and those among us who have known the man and have had an opportunity of dealing with him know it very well. Furthermore, he had been excellently trained in this undertaking very long ago, having drawn upon the knowledge and tradition coming from the best and most admirable men, outstanding in this field, large numbers of whom came from and grew up in Ionia and Asia. It is a matter of general knowledge that numerous monastic establishments, as outstanding as those found anywhere else, existed in those regions; some of them were organized along the principle of dwelling in common, living and settling together in large numbers; others, along that of quiet and isolated eremitic and anachoretic existence. Our man passed his youth in this milieu and, from the tender age of childhood, spent long years of training there; he was endowed with a natural bent of his own for this kind of life and with, so to speak, an elemental affinity for it; such were the foundations on which he was able to secure for himself an unshakable and systematic outlook. All his mind and all his actions were concentrated on these matters: he never paid attention to anything else—he spent on this as much as anybody has spent on anything, or rather, as much as anybody has spent on this; and he himself had thoroughly mastered all the processes of selection, the novitiate[?], the rules pertaining to this most worthy calling, and the art of applying those rules to oneself and to the education of others.

11. Selected from among many, he was shown to me at a proper time, when the love for the monastery was burning inside me, as a most useful man, both for the monastery and for that love of mine; this on account of the many years of his experience, extending without interruption until that very moment. He instilled many good hopes into my mind and fanned them into a bright flame, [fol. 334r] so that if now he were still alive and perchance my life had already come to its end—unexpectedly, he has now extinguished all those hopes—Oh what should I say? and that always calm and mild man, sweet towards all, and more dear to me than any other, that very man surprised me when, by his death, he mixed for me a most bitter, intractable, nauseating, and instant potion. Oh how great was the hope of which you now have bereft me, how great the anticipation of the pleasure and the most exquisite enjoyment of your company—and perhaps even of spending the rest of my life with you; this was the hope and the anticipation which, as you yourself knew well, I had been cherishing for a long time. The end which you put both to the present [?] and to your own life was untimely for everyone, except perhaps for yourself, well prepared as you were to move on away from this world; and for no one was your death more untimely than for me, your best friend, and for the monastery which you loved so much; you were always thirsting to live in it; you were exceedingly attached to it; you toiled continuously and in every imaginable manner to bring about its improvement and promote its progress; you were succeeding in this endeavor every single day, and then you rejoiced in it, mildly, but more than some other man would rejoice seeing his children thriving and enjoying the overflow of good fortune.

12. And now how could you have left it deserted, and abandoned its nurslings, your children, in dire orphanhood? They wail and are consumed by despair of the future; they long for you,

τὸν κατὰ θεὸν ὠδινήσαντα καὶ καλῶς τε καὶ εὐαγώγως τρέφοντα, μάλα τοι ποθοῦντα καὶ
περιαθροῦντ᾽ ἂν ἴσως ἰδέσθαι πάντη δεινῶς οἰκτρότατα, καὶ ὡς ἂν ἀπιστοῦντα, τῷ μὴ βού-
5 λεσθαι μηδὲ προσδοκᾶν, τὴν σὴν ἐκδημίαν καὶ στέρησιν; καθάπερ ἀμέλει τὸ ἀπογεγαλακτι-
σμένον τὴν μητέρα ποθεῖ, συμβὰν ὅπως ἄρα γενομένη ἀπόδημον τῶν οἴκοι, καὶ πλανᾶται διὰ
πάντων ὁρῶν κατὰ ταύτης ζήτησιν, καταρραινόμενον παρειὰς καὶ πᾶν τὸ σῶμα δάκρυσι, καὶ
γοερὸν ὀλολύζον, καὶ πολὺν αὐτόθεν τὸν οἶκτον τῶν ὁρώντων ἐφελκόμενον. ὢ τί ποτ᾽ ἂν
αὐτοῖς ἀρκέσοι πρὸς τὸ παραστὰν τῆς δυσχερείας, ὥστε ῥᾶον σφᾶς ὁπηοῦν θέσθαι, μετὰ τὴν
10 πεῖραν καὶ πίστιν τῆς συμφορᾶς, ἐν τοῖς πράγμασιν; ὢ τίς ἀντὶ σοῦ τε καὶ κατὰ σέ, ἤ, μᾶλλον
τό γε μετριώτερον ἴσως ἐρεῖ, ὅ,τι ἐγγυτάτω κατὰ σέ, τὴν σὴν ἀντιλήψεται σφίσι τάξιν;
μάλιστα μέν γε καὶ εἰ κατὰ σέ τις ἂν εἴη—τὸ δὲ καθάπαξ δυσχερέστατον, καὶ τίς ποτ᾽ ἂν ἀξιό-
χρεως τοῦδ᾽ ἐγγυητὴς εἴη κἂν τῇ νῦν πρός γ᾽ ἔτ᾽ αὐ[fol. 334v]τοῦ καιροῦ δυσκολίᾳ καὶ τῷ
σάλῳ καὶ τῇ δυσέργῳ πάνυ τοι χρήσει;—εἰ δ᾽ οὖν τις ἂν καὶ εἴη, ἀλλὰ τό γ᾽ ἔθιμον ἀνθρώποις
15 καὶ πείρᾳ μακρᾷ δοκιμασθέν τε καὶ κάλλισθ᾽ ἡρμοσμένον, ἐπιεικῶς πλεῖστον ἕλκει τε καὶ ἔχει·
καὶ ἀφηρημένον καὶ ἀποτμηθὲν καὶ γενόμενον ἐκ μέσου, πῶς ἂν εἴποι τις ὅσον ἐστὶν ἀλγεινόν,
καὶ πόσον τινὰ τὸν αὐτοῦ πόθον καὶ τὴν ζήτησιν καὶ τὴν εὔνοιαν τοὺς πεπειραμένους πράττεται; ὢ τί ποτ᾽ ἂν ἐν τοιούτοις νῦν ἐγὼ γενοίμην· ὢ τί ποτ᾽ ἂν ἐγὼ χρησαίμην νῦν οὕτως
ἐργώδει τῇ τύχῃ καὶ χαλεποῖς τοῖς πράγμασιν, ἐνταῦθ᾽ ὑπερόριος πόρρωθι ξυλλαχὼν ὑμῖν, καὶ
20 μὴ κατ᾽ ἔφεσιν ὅ,τι ποτ᾽ ἔχων ὑμῖν δρᾶν; ἀλλὰ μὴν καὶ εἰ παρὼν ἔτυχον ἂν ὑμῖν, τί ποτ᾽ ἂν
ἔδρων, ὁπότε τὸ πρᾶγμα πάντοθεν δυσχερὲς ὁρῶσιν;

13. Ἀλλ᾽ ἄρ᾽ ὑμεῖς, ἄνδρες φίλοι καὶ καλῶς ὑπ᾽ ἐκείνου πεπαιδευμένοι, μὴ καταμελεῖν μὲν
τεθνηκότος πατρὸς μηδὲ τῆς ὁσίας ἐκείνῳ καὶ τῶν νομίμων καὶ προσηκόντων ὑμῖν τε καὶ τῷ
πατρί, μηδ᾽ ὡς ἂν ἀνεπαισθήτως ἄγειν τῆς τοσαύτης ἐκείνου ζημίας· αὐτοὶ δ᾽ ὅπως μὴ καθάπαξ
ὅμως ἀπογνοίητε τῶν καλῶν ἔτι πω, μηδὲ τῶν εἰκότων μάλιστ᾽ αὖ ὑμῖν, ἀλλὰ καθ᾽ ὅσον ἔστιν,
5 ἀντὶ πάντων ὑμῖν αὐτοῖς ὑμεῖς αὐτοὶ γένοισθε, ἀντὶ τοῦ μεταστάντος πατρός, ἀντὶ τοῦ μακρὰν
ὄντος νῦν ἐμοῦ, ἀνθ᾽ ὑμῶν αὐτῶν. γένοισθε δ᾽ ὁμοῦ ταῦτα καὶ μάλ᾽ ἐπαινεῖν ἀξίως· πρῶτον μὲν
τὸν τῆς εἰρήνης καὶ ὁμονοίας ὑμῖν σύνδεσμον μὴ λύσαντες, καὶ ὡς ἓν ἄρα σῶμα συμφυὲς καὶ
ἡρμοσμένον εὖ μάλα τὸν εἰωθότα τέως τρόπον, τὴν καλὴν ἀγωγὴν τηροῦντες, καὶ κινούμενοι
ὡς ἂν εἰ καὶ μιᾷ τελειοποιῷ ψυχῇ καὶ ζωτικῇ τῷ κατ᾽ ἐκεῖνον τύπῳ καὶ τοῖς δεδομένοις τῷ βίῳ
10 νομίμοις, καὶ ὡς ἂν χθές που καὶ τρίτην ἡμέραν, ὡς πρὸς παρόνθ᾽ ὁρῶντες ἔπειτ᾽ αὖ τὸν ἄνδρα—
καὶ γὰρ καὶ νῦν αὖ ὑμῖν πάρεστι, καὶ μέσος ἔτι πω θεοῦ καὶ ὑμῶν, μάλιστ᾽ ἐμοὶ δοκεῖν, ἀνὴρ
ἵσταται, πρεσβεύων λιπαρῶς ὡς μάλα τοι τρανότατα καὶ προσάγων ὑμᾶς, τὴν καλὴν αὐτοῦ
μάνδραν καὶ ποίμνην, ἀζήμιον εὐχρήστοις αὐτοῦ νομαῖς, ὅσα καὶ γινώσκων τὰ αὐτοῦ, πάντας
ὑμᾶς, καὶ ὑφ᾽ ὑμῶν αὐτὸς γινωσκόμενος, κατ᾽ ἔθος τὸν νοῦν προσεχόντων τοῖς ἐπιτάγμασι τῆς
15 πρὶν ἐπιστασίας ἐκείνου, καὶ μήτινα παθόντων λήθην, ὡς μήποτ᾽ ὄφελον εἴη τοῦθ᾽ [fol. 335r]
ὑμῖν· καὶ γινώσκοιτ᾽ ἐκεῖνος ἄτροπος καθάπαξ τὸν εἰθισμένον τρόπον ὑμῖν, καὶ τηροῖθ᾽ ὡσαύτως ἀλώβητα τἀνδρός, μηδὲν ἧττον ὡς ἄρα πρίν, τἀπιτάγματα. καὶ οὐκ οἶδ᾽ ὅ,τί ποτ᾽ ἂν
ἄμεινον ὑμῖν εἴη τοῦδε τὸν ἀεὶ χρόνον· καὶ αὐτοὶ πάντως ἴστε, κἀγὼ δ᾽ οὐχ ἧττον, καὶ πάντες
ὅσοις τοι τὰ καθ᾽ ὑμᾶς ξυμβέβηκεν εἰδέναι καὶ πεῖραν ἀμηγέπη τινὰ κἀκείνου καὶ ὑμῶν σχεῖν.

12,10 πίστιν] non satis perspicio, cf. TM, *Logos* 13, **20**,16, *Etudes*, p. 213; an πύστιν legendum?
13,19 ἀμηγέπη V

the one who has begotten them according to God and was bringing them up so well in a spirit of docility. They look about and everywhere wretchedly, perhaps expecting to see you; they as much as disbelieve both your departure and their bereavement, since both are contrary to their wishes, and so unexpected: in the same fashion a freshly weaned child longs for its mother, who perchance has had to leave the house; it wanders about and looks everywhere in search for her; it profusely drenches its cheeks and all its body with tears and cries miserably; and thus arouses instant compassion in the onlookers. What will be the remedy for their present calamity, so that they might more easily adapt to practical life, after having experienced and accepted [?] the mournful event? Who like you, or perhaps, to speak with more moderation, who as much like you as possible, will take your place among them in your stead? Even if there were somebody like you—a difficult thing to achieve indeed; moreover, who could be a reliable guarantor for effecting this, especially again in the present [fol. 334v] difficult and unstable times and in a situation so difficult to handle?—even if there were some such man, still, people are fairly strongly attracted and held by things to which they have been accustomed or which, by dint of long experience, have proven themselves and turned out to be perfectly suitable. When such things are taken away or cut off, and disappear from the midst of us, they cause an inestimable amount of pain; it is difficult to express the intensity of the longing, of the search, and of the love which they elicit from those familiar with them. What should become of me in such circumstances? How should I handle my present difficult fate, my distasteful existence, banished that I am here far from you and unable to do a single thing that I might wish to do for you? However, if even by chance I were present among you, what would I be able to do? All those who have eyes see that the situation is difficult, no matter how one looks at it.

13. As for you, my friends so well educated by him, do not neglect your deceased father; do not fail to perform the funeral rites and other customary devotions which befit you as well as him; do not show indifference in the face of such a great loss as his departure; on the other hand, do not utterly despair lest what is good, and worthy of you, might not come back again; but rather rely, as much as you can, upon yourselves in place of everything: of the deceased father; of me, far away that I am from you; and of yourselves. You should become all these things at once, and this will be worthy of praise. First of all, do not dissolve the bond of peace and concord; observe the virtuous way of life, as one body as naturally united and closely knit as you have been accustomed to be in the past; be moved, as if by one perfecting and vivifying soul, by his example and by the rules which have been given to guide you in your monastic life; and look towards him as if he still were present, as if it were yesterday, or the day before yesterday—indeed he is present among you even now, and, so it seems to me, he is still standing as intermediary between God and yourselves, interceding on your behalf earnestly and in a most audible voice, and leading you, his good sheep and flock, safe from harm, to his luscious grazing grounds; he does it, because he recognizes what is his, namely, all of you; you, too, recognize him, since you continue the habit of observing the commandments which date from the time of his rule over you; nor do you forget them, a thing which must never happen [fol. 335r] to you; continue to recognize him, without change, in the same accustomed fashion. Observe the commandments of that man in their entirety no less than you used to observe them in the past. I do not know of anything that could be better for you than this for all time to come; you yourselves know it no less than I and than all those who happen to know about you, and have had some experience with both you and him.

14. Βέλτιστος δ' ἂν ὡς ἀληθῶς, ἐγώ μοι δοκῶ, κἀκεῖνος ἔσοιτο καὶ πολὺ δρῶν ὡς ἂν συνοί-
σειν αὐτῷ τε καὶ ὑμῖν, ὅς, ἔπειτ' αὐτὸς ἔσοιτο—πάντως δ' ἔσοιτο καὶ οὐκ ἔστιν ἄλλως—ἐπὶ
τῆς ἐκείνου διαδοχῆς καὶ ποιμαντικῆς ὑμῖν, εἰ κατ' ἐκεῖνον ὑμῖν χρῷτο καὶ τοὺς ἐκείνου τύπους
τῆς ἀγωγῆς καὶ πάντα πράγμαθ', ὡς ἄρ' ἐκείνου πεπείρασθε. ἢ τί γὰρ ἂν ἄμεινον ἔπειτ' ἐκεῖνος
5 ἔχοι χρῆσθαι καὶ προσωτέρω καὶ πρὸς ἐπίδοσιν φέρον; καί μοι τοῦτ' εὐκταῖον ἰδεῖν πάνυ τοι
καὶ ἀεὶ καθορᾶν, καὶ ἀεὶ καθορᾶσθαι τῇ τε μονῇ καὶ ὑμῖν. καὶ τοίνυν ἐπεὶ τὸν ἡγησόμενον ὅπως
ποτ' ἄρα πᾶσα ἀνάγκη δοθῆναι μετ' οὐ πολὺ τῇ μονῇ, καὶ τοῦτον ἢ πάντως ἐξ ὑμῶν ὄντινα
δὴ καὶ τῆς ὑμῶν συναυλίας καὶ συντρόφου βιοτῆς—ὡς εἴθε τοῦθ' οὕτως εἴη κατ' ἐμὸν πόθον
καὶ ἴσως ὑμῶν, οἶμαι—ἢ καί τιν' ἄλλοθεν νέον ὑμῖν ἐπίδημον—εἰ μὲν ἐξ ὑμῶν ὁ παρ' ὑμῖν αὐτὸς
10 ἡγησόμενος, ἔξεστιν αὐτόθεν ἀμέλει χρῆσθαι κατ' ἔθος καὶ οἷς αὐτὸς ἔστεργε καὶ καλῶς ἔχειν τὸ
γιγνόμενον ἅπαν ἠξίου, καὶ οὐδὲν ὅ,τι μὴ χρηστὸν ὑμῖν παρεῖναι—καὶ οὐδεὶς γὰρ ἄλλως τῶν
παρ' ὑμῖν, ὅσα γ' ἐμὲ εἰδέναι, κοὔτι πλέον ἐξεῖναι κρίνων ᾤετο—καὶ οἷς ὡσαύτως ὑμεῖς πάντες
ἐστέργετε καὶ ἠξιοῦτ' εὖ μάλα κοινῇ· εἰ δ' ἐκλόγιμος ἴσως ὅθεν ἄρ' ἄλλος ἄλλοθεν—ὡς εἴη γε
οὗτος, ὅστις ἂν ἔσοιτο, κατὰ θεὸν ἐκλόγιμος—φθάσαντες ὑμεῖς δείξατε τῇ συνασκήσει κατ'
15 ἔθος τῶν καλῶν, ὡς ὀλίγος αὐτῷ πόνος ἔσοιτο τῇ πρὸς τὰ βέλτισθ' ἡγεμονίᾳ, πρὸς ἄνδρας
εὖ μάλ' ἠγμένους καὶ γεγυμνασμένους τὸν κατὰ θεὸν βίοτον καὶ πολλῶν ἐτῶν ἠσκημένους
ἄμεινον.

15. Τιμήσατε τὸν μακαρίτην ἐκεῖνον πρεσβύτην πατέρα· τιμήσατε νῦν μάλισθ', ὃν ἐτιμᾶτε
κομιδῇ περιόντα καὶ διαφερόντως ἐποθεῖτε, ποθοῦντα καὶ αὐτὸν διαφερόντως ὑμᾶς, καὶ ὑπὲρ
ἄλλο πᾶν περισπούδαστον ἀνθρώποις καὶ τιμῆς ἀξιούμενον τὰ καθ' ὑμᾶς τιμῶντα, καὶ ὑμῶν
ἀκορέστως ἐξεχόμενον καὶ τὴν καρδίαν ὅλην ἐκχεόμενον ὑμῖν· τιμήσαθ' ὑμᾶς αὐτούς, ἐν ἀρίστοις
5 ἀνύτοντας τέως τὸν βίον καὶ νομίμοις ἐν ἀρίστοις καὶ μὴ μετα[fol. 335v]βάλλοντας τοῖς καιροῖς μηδὲ τρεπομένους ἐπιστασίας ἐρημίᾳ τῶν βελτίστων καὶ προσηκόντων ἀποδείξαντες· καὶ
μάλισθ' ἑαυτῶν καὶ τῆς κατ' ἐξουσίαν ὑμῖν ψήφου τἀγαθόν, οὐ τῆς ἡγεμονικῆς ἀνάγκης καὶ
βίας, ἀποδείξαντες. ἀπέστω πᾶσα δύσχρηστος ἔρις ὑμῶν, ἔρις δέ γε καὶ ἅμιλλα τῇ βελτιώσει
μάλιστ' ἔστω κατὰ πρόθεσιν ὑμῖν· ἀπέστω φθόνος, ἀπέστω φιλαρχία, κακοῦργον ἦθος ἀπέστω,
10 διαβεβλήσθω πᾶν ἄτακτον καὶ φαῦλον καὶ δύσεργον ὑμῖν· καὶ ὅσα τῆς πονηρᾶς ἕξεως ἁπάσης
ἀπέστω καὶ κακοσχόλου, καὶ θόρυβον καὶ σάλον ἐμποιούσης τῷ συστήματι. ὁμοφροσύνη πρὸ
πάντων ἤτω πᾶσι πᾶσα περὶ τῶν ἱερῶν τὴν ἐπιμέλειαν, περὶ τὰς εὐχάς, περὶ τοὺς ὕμνους τοῦ
θεοῦ καὶ τὴν λατρείαν, ὡς εἴθισθε· ὁ κόσμος, ὃς ἄρα καὶ πρίν, ὁ περὶ τὸν νεὼν καὶ τὰ κάλλιστ'
εὐαγῆ καὶ σεμνὰ πάντα συνθήματα, ὡς δὲ περὶ τὸ ἱερὸν ἄδυτον καὶ τὴν πάναγνον τράπεζαν,
15 καὶ τὰς μυστικὰς ἀναιμάκτους τελετὰς καὶ σπονδείας, καὶ τὸ μέγα θῦμα καὶ θεοῦ καλλιέρημα.
πρὸς δέ, τὸ παρ' ἑκάστων ξυγκεχωρηκὸς ἑκάστῳ πρὸς τὸ καθ' αὑτὸν ἑκάστῳ καὶ οἰκεῖον καὶ
δεδομένον τῆς λειτουργίας· κόσμος ἅπας τῷ καθεστῶτι τῶν νομίμων ἐν τάξει· κόσμος ᾗ δέοι ἂν
ἐν κρότοις καὶ διατόροις ἄσμασι καὶ νενόμισται· κόσμος ἐν σιωπῇ καὶ γαληναῖς ἀνθομολογήσεσι.

14,3 ὑμῖν¹ V¹ e corr. : ὑμῶν V   5 φέρον V¹ˢᵛ : φέρειν V   10 καί² add. V¹ˢᵛ
15,5 νομίμ(οις) V¹ˢᵛ : νομίμους V   13 malim εἴθισται, cf. TM, *Poema* 1, v. 1292, ed. Treu, *Dichtungen*

14. In my opinion, that man will be truly excellent and will act to his and your own advantage who, once he enters upon Lucas' succession, and is your shepherd—there surely will be such a man and it cannot be otherwise—if that man deals with you as Lucas did, uses his methods as a model, and in all things follows your experience of the deceased. What other course would be better for Lucas' successor, and lead to further improvement? I ardently wish that I might see this happen and, from then on, see it continuing to happen; and it is the monastery's and your own wish that you should be always following this course. Since the monastery will of necessity receive its future abbot before long; since, furthermore, this abbot will be either one coming from among you and from among your community who had been brought up living with you—it is my desire, and perhaps yours as well, that it might happen this way—or he will be a new man coming to you from some outside place—now, then, if your future abbot comes from among you, it will right away be possible to follow the customary ways, those with which Lucas had been content and found satisfactory to the highest degree, and you will be having nothing but what is beneficial to you—to the best of my knowledge, none from among you thought otherwise; none assumed that further improvement could possibly be achieved—and the ways with which all of you had been likewise content and which you found greatly satisfactory by common agreement; if, on the other hand, the one chosen should be from some other place—may this elect person, whoever he is, be chosen according to God's wish—then you should take the first step and show to him, by practicing together with him the good actions to which you have been accustomed, that he will be able to lead you towards excellence with little effort, dealing as he will be with men who have been well directed, well exercised in the life according to God, and trained better than another community would have been even after a long number of years.

15. Show honor to your old father of blessed memory; show honor especially now to the man whom you honored and greatly loved when he was still alive; the man who, in turn, greatly loved you and valued everything that concerned you more highly than anything that men may value and desire; the man who experienced an insatiable attachment to you and who poured out his whole heart for your sake; show honor to yourselves by proving two things, that in the past you were leading the best of lives and obeying the best of laws and that you have not changed [fol. 335v] with the times and that the absence of a leader has not turned you away from what is best and most appropriate; and above all, by showing that the Good in you results from your own decisions, arrived at by your own free will, and not from coercion and force imposed by your superior. May all obstreperous contentiousness be absent from among you; may the only contention and competition present in your minds be over who will show most improvement. May envy be absent, and lust for power, and evil-working malice; you should reject all that is disorderly, evil, and apt to get out of hand; you should banish all evil and malicious attitudes, which introduce confusion and turmoil into the community. Above all, may there be complete harmony among all of you concerning the care of things sacred, concerning prayers, concerning hymns to God and the worship of Him in the manner to which you have been accustomed. May there also be orderliness, such as used to prevail in the past, concerning the church itself and all the most beautiful, revered, and holy covenants [?], as well as concerning the holy altar space, the most revered altar table, the mystic bloodless rites and liturgical services, and the Great Offering and Sacrifice acceptable to God. Furthermore, may each one of you yield to any other what is that brother's particular and given assignment; may there be absolute order in the regular observance of the customary rules; customary and appropriate order in praises of God and in loud songs; order in silence and in the calm of mutual confessions.

16. Τὸ κοινωνικὸν διὰ πάντων ὡσαύτως ἤτω καὶ εὐξύμβλητον ἀλλήλοις· τὸ αἰδοῖον εὖ μάλα καὶ τίμιον τῶν ἀπὸ τῆς δευτέρας καὶ ἥττονος τάξεως τοῖς προέχουσι καὶ βαθμοῦ κρείττονος, ἢ γήρᾳ, ἢ συνέσει, ἢ τῆς ἱερατείας ἀξίᾳ· καὶ αὖ τῶνδε μηδὲν ἧττον τὸ φιλόκοινον καὶ φιλάλληλον, καὶ τοῖς ταπεινοῖς ἐπικύπτον τε καὶ συμπίπτον εἰς ἑνοποιὸν τοῦ συντάγματος σύνδεσμον
5 πρὸς τοὺς ἰδιωτεύοντας καὶ τὴν γνώμην ὀλίγους, καὶ δεομένους ἐπικουρίας τῶν τελειοτέρων τε καὶ κρειττόνων, καὶ ὀφειλόντων, ὡς ἰσχυροτέρων, τὰ τῶν ἀσθενεστέρων, κατὰ τὴν ἐντολήν, βαστάζειν· τὸ ὑπεῖκον καὶ ἀφιλόνεικον πρὸς τοὺς ἐπὶ τῶν διοικήσεων, καὶ πάσης βασκάνου μεμψιμοιρίας καὶ ἀκαιρίας καὶ μικρογνώμονος καὶ ἀνελευθέρου λογοποιίας ἀλλότριον· τῶν δὲ καὶ αὐτῶν τὸ καθάπαξ ἐπιμελὲς καὶ πάντα τρόπον ἄνοσον καὶ εὐγενὲς τῇ διοικήσει· τὸ πρὸς
10 τοὺς ἐπὶ τῆς χρείας καὶ τῆς τῶν ἀναγκαίων διακόνους ὑπηρεσίας καὶ ὑποβεβηκότας ὑπουργοὺς ἄτυφον τῶν ὑπερεχόντων καὶ ἀνολίγωρον, καὶ ὥστε καθάπαξ μηδένα τῶν μικροτέρων σκανδαλίσθαι, κατὰ τὸν [fol. 336r] εὐαγγελικὸν λόγον καὶ τὸ φιλάνθρωπον ἐπίταγμα—φεύγοντας τὸ παραλειπόμενον ἀσύμφορον καὶ τὴν τοῦ κατακρίματος διὰ τὴν περιφρόνησιν ταύτην δυσχέρειαν, καὶ κάλλιστα δὴ πεπεισμένους ὅσον ἐστὶν ἀποτρόπαιον θεῷ τὸ κατοφρυῶσθαι τῶν
15 ἡττόνων καὶ κατεξανίστασθαι καὶ μέγα φρονεῖν ἐπ᾽ αὐτοῖς· τῶν δὲ καὶ αὐτῶν τὸ φίλεργόν τε καὶ ἐπίμονον τῇ χρήσει, καὶ πρὸς τὸ πεφυκὸς τῶν πόνων, καὶ πᾶν τὸ γιγνόμενον ἐνδελεχές.

17. Τὸ πρὸς τοὺς ἐπιδεεῖς ἔτ᾽ ἔξω καὶ πολλοὺς ἀμέλει καὶ τῆς ἀναγκαστῆς αὐτῆς τροφῆς καὶ τῶν ἀπαραιτήτων τῇ φύσει δασμῶν κατ᾽ ἔθος ἐκ τῶν ἐνόντων μεταδοτικὸν καὶ φίλοικτον τῇ χρείᾳ, καὶ μηδὲν ἧττον ἢ πρὶν ἐν τῷ νῦν ὑμῖν τῆς δυσκολίας καιρῷ· τὸ πρὸς τοὺς κάμνοντας ἐν νόσοις συμπαθές, καὶ πρὸς ἐπικουρίαν ἥντιν᾽ ἔξεστιν ἕτοιμον διὰ τῆς ἐνούσης, εὖ μάλ᾽ ὡς ἴστε,
5 παρασκευῆς καὶ χρονίας ἤδη μάλιστ᾽ ἐξ ἀρχῆς προθέσεως, καὶ ἧς μάλιστ᾽ ἐμέλησεν ἐμοί· καὶ μηδὲν μᾶλλον τοῖς ἐντὸς καὶ συμβιοῦσί τε καὶ συντρόφοις, ἢ καὶ τοῖς ἔξωθεν οἱστισινοῦν. ὅποι ἄρα παρείκοι καὶ οἷόν τ᾽ ἐστίν, ἐκτείνειν τὴν συμμαχίαν τῇ κοινῇ φύσει κατὰ τῆς ἐνοχλούσης ἐπαναστάσεως καὶ ἐπηρείας, καὶ προσέχειν τῇ τῶν ἀσθενούντων ἐπισκέψει καὶ προσέχειν τῷ ταύτην οἰκείαν ποιουμένῳ καὶ εἰς ἑαυτὸν λογιζομένῳ μετὰ τῶν ἄλλων τῆς φιλανθρωπίας ἐπιταγ-
10 μάτων Χριστῷ· καὶ πᾶσα πρόφασις ἐνταῦθα καὶ πᾶσα τυραννοῦσ᾽ ἀνάγκη καὶ νῦν μάλισθ᾽ ὑμῖν ἀπέστω, καὶ εἰ δή τι ἄλλο, καὶ τοῦτο ὑμῖν ἐπιεικῶς ἔστω προὔργου· καὶ μελέτω μὲν τούτου πλεῖστον τῷ ταύτης ἐπιτρόπῳ καὶ ἐπιμελητῇ τῆς διακονίας, μελέτω δὲ πᾶσι κοινῇ. καὶ καθάπαξ μελέτω πᾶσιν ὑμῖν τοῦ τε καθ᾽ ἑαυτὸν ἑκάστῳ προσήκοντος εἰς ἀνδραγαθίαν, ἣν ἀμέλει τοῦ βίου καὶ τῆς καθ᾽ ὑμᾶς αἱρέσεώς τε καὶ ἐπαγγελίας καὶ ἔνστασις πράττεται, καὶ τοῦ κοινῇ δὲ
15 προσήκοντος οὐχ ἧττον μελέτω· ὡς οὐδὲν μᾶλλον ἕκαστος ἑαυτῷ, ἢ τῷ κοινῷ πάντες συντάγματι, ζῆν εἵλεσθε καὶ συνήρμοσθε, καὶ μέλειν ἀλλήλων καὶ τοῦ κοινῇ συνοίσοντος καὶ κοσμίου, τὸ σύνθημα καὶ ἡ πρόθεσις ὑμῖν, καὶ προθεσμία τὸν ἅπαντα κατὰ τὴν μονὴν βίον καὶ τὸν τῆς ζωῆς ὅρον ὑμῖν. μελέτω δὲ τῶνδε δὴ πάντων, καὶ ὃς ἐπὶ ῥητοῖς νῦν ὑμῖν ἐπίλεκτος ὥρισται

F   **16**,6 ὀφειλόντων—7 βαστάζειν : cf. Rom. 15:1   11 μηδένα—13 ἀσύμφορον : cf. Matt. 18:1-6   16 πόνων—ἐνδελεχές : cf. Plut., *Marius*, 6.2

16,4 εἰς] [[(καὶ)]] εἰς V   15 ἐπ᾽ αὐτοῖς] malim ἐφ᾽ αὐτοῖς
17,13-14 τοῦ βίου—14 ἔνστασις πράττεται] τοῦ βίου—ἐνστάσεως πράττεται V, cf. **22**,3/4, ἡ τῶν πραγμάτων ἀνάγκη πράττεται; sed fortasse τοῦ βίου ⟨πρόθεσις⟩—ἐνστάσεως πράττεται aut τοῦ βίου—ἐνστάσεως πράττετε legendum, cf. TM, *Logos* 13, **15**,7, *Études*, p. 205 in apparatu   17 τ(όν)² add. V¹ˢᵛ

16. May the spirit of community and of mutual conciliation equally prevail among all of you; may those of second and lesser rank show reverence and respect toward those enjoying prominence and higher standing, either on account of their advanced age, their wisdom, or their priestly dignity. In turn, the latter, too, should be no less eager in showing their love for the community and for their neighbors; they should descend toward the humble and strengthen the bond that unites the community by drawing close to the simple monks and to those who, being poor in spirit, need help from their more accomplished betters, obliged by God's command to carry the burden of the weaker on account of their own greater strength. You should obey those who have been given administrative tasks, and you should not seek to quarrel with them; in dealing with them, be free from all envy, querulousness, impropriety, and narrow-minded and mean gossip-mongering. As for the latter, they should be utterly devoted to fulfilling their tasks in a sound and noble fashion. Those in positions of prominence should abstain from giving themselves airs and showing contempt toward attendants performing needed and necessary tasks, and toward menial help; thus, no one among those of lower station will be scandalized, the [fol. 336r] word of the Gospel and the Commandment of the Lover of Men will be followed, and prominent monks will avoid both disadvantages ensuing from the neglect ⟨of that word⟩ and difficulties ensuing from condemnation for such a contempt; they will keep well in mind how sternly God averts his face from those who browbeat lesser people, tread upon them, and think too highly of themselves. In turn, lesser people should be assiduous, persistent in the fulfilment of their tasks, and persevering, to the highest degree, in whatever may be the nature of their labors.

17. Show the customary liberality and compassion toward the needy outsiders—numerous, to be sure—by using the monastery's resources and distributing to them the necessary food, that ineluctable tribute which we have to pay to Nature; this practice should continue no less vigorously now, in these times of hardship for all of you, than it did in the past. Show compassion toward the sick and be ready to extend all possible help to them through means which, as you well know, have been available in the monastery for that purpose for a long time, from the very beginning, and with which I was very much concerned. This assistance should extend both to those who are inside the monastery, live together with you, and are sharing your way of life and to outsiders, whoever they may be. Wherever possible, assist Nature, to whose laws we are all subject, in her battle against ⟨sickness'⟩ annoying insurrection and abuse; attend to the visiting of the sick and thereby attend to Christ, who makes visiting them His own concern and applies it to Himself, along with His other Commands concerning love of our fellow man. Abstain altogether from all excuses and references to overwhelming necessity, especially nowadays; in all fairness, you should attend to the sick as much as to anything else. The superintendent in charge of this service is the person who should be most concerned with all this, but all of you should be concerned with it as well. In general, all of you should be concerned with what is proper for each one of you individually in leading you to the practice of manly virtue, which is clearly required from you by your way of life, your choice, and the profession you have made; however, you should be no less concerned with observing what is proper for all of you together; this because all of you resolved, and have been brought together, to live not as much each for himself as for the sake of the whole community. Your covenant and purpose is concern for each other and for what is useful and decorous for the whole community; and the appointed time for observing this is the whole time of your stay in the monastery, until the end of your lives. All these things, too, should be the concern of the person who has been conditionally chosen as the caretaker and administrator

καθόλου τῇ κοινῇ φροντίδι τῶν καθ᾽ ὑμᾶς καὶ διοικήσει, μέχρι καὶ τῆς ἐπιλογῆς καὶ τῶν ἀρχαι-
20 ρεσιῶν καὶ τῶν ψήφων τοῦ κατ᾽ ἔθος ὑμῖν καθάπαξ ἡγησομένου· καὶ τῶνδ᾽ αὐτῷ μελέτω
παντάπασιν ἠπειγμένως τε καὶ ἀγρύπνως, ὡς ἂν τάδ᾽ ἅπαντα πιστευθέντι, καὶ μὴν ἑκόντι γε
ὄντι καταθεμένῳ πρὸς τὴν λειτουργίαν, καὶ πρὸς τὸ βάρος ἑαυτὸν ὑπο[fol. 336v]θεμένῳ τῆς
χρείας, καὶ ὡς ἂν αὐτῷ περὶ τούτων ἁπάντων θεῷ λόγον ἀποδώσοντι.

18. Πρὸς δὲ τούτοις ἔτι καὶ αὐτῷ τε καὶ πᾶσιν ὑμῖν μελέτω—καὶ γὰρ ἔτι πω μετὰ τῆς τοῦ
σώματος χρείας βιοῦσιν ὑμῖν καὶ τῶνδε δεῖ, καὶ ἄφυκτά πως καθάπαξ τῇδ᾽ ὑμῖν ἐστι—καὶ τῶν
τῆς ζωῆς ἀφορμῶν καὶ ὁπόσ᾽ ἐμοὶ φθάσαντ᾽ ἀποχρώντως, οἶμαι, καὶ πρός γ᾽ ἴσως ἔτι, πρὸς τὴν
σωματικὴν ταύτην ὑμῖν ἀπαραίτητον εἴσπραξιν καὶ αὐτάρκειαν ἐσκεύασται καὶ ἀποτετάχαται
5 προσοδήματα. καὶ οἶδα μὲν ἔγωγε, ὡς ἄρα πολὺ μάλιστ᾽ ἐνταῦθα τὸ ἀντίξουν ὑμῖν διὰ τὴν
ἀντίπνοιαν ἐμοὶ τῶν πραγμάτων καὶ τοῦ καιροῦ, ἀλλὰ καὶ ὅμως ⟨οὐκ⟩ ἀποδειλιατέον ἐστὶν
ὑμῖν καὶ πονητέον ἐνταῦθα καὶ ἐπιμελητέον καὶ πάντα κάματον ἀνθαιρετέον καθ᾽ ὅσον οἷόν τέ
ἐστι καὶ ταῖς ψυχαῖς ὑμῖν ἀκίνδυνον. ὡς οὐκ ἔστιν ἄλλως χρῆσθαι παντὶ δῆλον· καὶ βέλτιον
ὑμῖν οὕτως ἔσται, ἢ καταναρκήσασι καὶ μὴ πονοῦσι πλεῖστον ὅσον ἐν τούτοις, ἀλλ᾽ ἀτημε-
10 λήτως ἔχουσι πρὸς τὴν ἐπήρειαν τοῦ καιροῦ. καὶ τοίνυν τηρητέον μὲν καὶ προσεκτέον εὖ μάλ᾽
ἀσχολουμένους τὸν νοῦν, ὡς ἂν ἄρ᾽ εἰκὸς τόδε καὶ ἀνεμέσητον, ἄττα κατὰ τὴν μονὴν τεθησαύρισται καὶ περὶ τὴν μονὴν ἔγγιον, καὶ σπουδαστέον ἀθῷον τὴν ἐντεῦθεν ἐπιεικῶς συντέλειαν.
προσεκτέον δὲ πρός γ᾽ ὑμῖν καὶ ἄττα ἐκτός, καὶ πολὺ μάλιστ᾽ ἐνταῦθα προσεκτέον τὸν νοῦν,
πλείονά τε γὰρ καὶ πολλῆς ἐπιμελείας δεόμενα, διὰ τὴν πλείον᾽ ἴσως ἐνοχλοῦσαν ἐν σφίσι τῶν
15 ἐπ᾽ ἐρημίας ἐπανισταμένων ἐπήρειαν. καὶ διανεμητέον τοὺς περὶ τούτων πόνους καὶ τὴν φροντίδα πεπειραμένοις ἀνδράσι καὶ τὸ πιστὸν τῆς λειτουργίας ἐντεῦθεν ἔχουσιν· ἅμα μὲν πρὸς τὸ
γιγνόμενον ἅπαν καὶ τὴν ἄσχολον καὶ τεχνικὴν ἕξιν τῆς ἐργασίας καὶ πάντ᾽ εὐδιοίκητον ἀνύτειν.
ἅμα δὲ καὶ πρὸς τὸ κρατερῶς καὶ μὴ ἀνειμένως μηδ᾽ ἀσθενῶς ἀποδύεσθαι καὶ συνίστασθαι καὶ
συναεθλεύειν πρὸς τοὺς ἐπιτιθεμένους ἑκάστοτε μετὰ τοῦ καιροῦ, καὶ δύνασθαί πως οἰκονομεῖν
20 τε καὶ φέρειν γεννικῶς τὰ ξυμπίπτοντα πάντ᾽ ἐργώδη, καὶ μὴ τῶν προσηκόντων ἑκάστοις
ὀλιγωρεῖν ἀμηγέπη· καὶ ἅμα—τρίτον ἐρεῖν, ὃ καὶ ἴσως ἐρεῖν αἰσχύνοιτ᾽ ἄν τις καὶ ἴσως ὅλως
ἀμφιγνοεῖν αἰσχύνοιτο—πρὸς τὸ τοῦ ἤθους καὶ τῶν τρόπων εἰλικρινὲς καὶ πάσης προσπαθείας
ἑαυτοῖς καὶ ἰδιοκτησίας καὶ καπηλείας ἀνώτερον.

19. Ὃ παντάπασι μὲν ὡς ἀληθῶς ἀποτρόπαιον καὶ ἀπευκταιότατον, ὥστε καὶ μόνον ἐρεῖν,
ὡς ἔφην, ὥστε καὶ μόνον ἐν νῷ θέσθαι, καὶ μοναχικῆς μεγαλοφροσύνης καὶ ἐλευθερίας ἀλλοτρι-
ώτατον· ὑπο[fol. 337r]πτον δὲ πεποιήκασιν ἔνιοι τῶν φαύλων ἐπιτρόπων, ἐν τοῖς τοιούτοις
κακοὶ κακῶς χρησάμενοι τῇ διοικήσει καὶ νοσφισάμενοι τὰ κοινά, μᾶλλον δ᾽ ἱεροσυλήσαντες,
5 ἀληθέστατ᾽ ἐρεῖν, τἀναθήματα τῷ θεῷ. καὶ πόρρωθεν τῶν χρόνων καὶ τὴν ἀρχὴν ἐκ μακροῦ
Ἀνανίας τε καὶ ἡ τοῖς τρόποις, οὐ τῷ γάμῳ μόνον, κοινωνὸς αὐτῷ Σάπφειρα· καὶ ἡλικιῶτις γὰρ
ἐστιν ἡ νόσος αὕτη τῇ Χριστοῦ διδασκαλίᾳ καὶ τῇ κοινωνικῇ ταύτῃ συνδιαιτήσει τῶν ἐπιλέ-
κτων ἀνθρώπων τοῖς θείοις δόγμασι, τὴν πρώτην εὐθὺς ἀρχομένου τοῦ κηρύγματος· οἳ δὴ μὴ
πρὸς οὐδεμίαν ἀνάγκην παραβαλλόμενοι, ἢ βίαν καὶ δεσμὸν ὄντιν᾽ ἄρα, ἢ δέος ἄφυκτον, ἀλλ᾽
10 ἑκόντες ὄντες ζηλοῦν ἑλόμενοι γνώμης καὶ κρίσεως αὐτεξουσιότητι τὰ βέλτιστα, καὶ τὰ οἰκεῖα,
πραττομένου μηδενός, εἰς μέσον φέρειν ἀξιώσαντες τῷ Χριστῷ καὶ τῇ ὑπ᾽ αὐτὸν ἀδελφότητι,

F   19,6 Ἀνανίας—19 δραττόμενον : cf. Acta Ap. 5:1–11

17,19 (καί)³ add. V¹ˢᵛ
18,6 addendum putavi, nisi forte auctor praepositioni ἀπο- vim negativam tribuerit   8 ὑμῖν Vˣ e corr. : -ῶν V   11
τόδε V¹ˢᵛ : τῶδε V   καί add. V²ᵐᵍ
19,6 ἀνανίας V   12 κτὴν κτῆσιν V   17 ἀνομοῦντ(ας) V¹ˢᵛ : -τες V   ἀσεβοῦντ(ες) V²ˢᵛ : -τας V   18 αὐτ(ῆς)
V¹ˢᵛ : αὐτοῖς V

of your communal affairs, until the choice and election by ballot [?] of the one who, according to tradition, will be your regular abbot. The acting abbot should take care of all these things with vigor and vigilance, because they have been entrusted to him, because he has consented of his own free will to undertake this task and sustain [fol. 336v] the burden of this activity, and because he will render account to God for all of it.

18. In addition to all this, both the acting abbot and all of you should show concern for the sources of livelihood and revenue which I previously set aside and endowed to satisfy, comfortably, perhaps even more than comfortably, the indispensable requirements of your bodies and to make you self-sufficient; living as you are for the time being in need of your bodies, you need these things as well, and cannot dispense with them altogether as long as you are here on earth. I know very well that you are experiencing many setbacks precisely in these matters, my affairs having taken a bad turn and times being unpropitious; however, you must not lose courage in the face of all this, but rather work hard, be diligent, and choose to exert yourselves as much as possible without endangering your souls. It should be obvious to anyone that there is no other way; and, if you act thus, you will be better off than if you remain numb, fail to devote all your efforts to this, and are negligent in the face of present adversity. Therefore, you should—within the limits of what is proper and irreproachable—preserve and diligently attend to those assets which are located in the monastery proper and in its close vicinity, and you should see to it that the revenues coming from these two sources should remain reasonably unharmed. Moreover, you should pay attention—particular attention—to the monastery's outlying possessions, these possessions being both more numerous and in need of greater care; the latter is true, since they may be possibly exposed to more annoying abuse by people threatening them in the outlying places. These tasks and cares should be entrusted to experienced men, people who, by their very experience, would inspire confidence in their services. They should be experienced enough, first, to fulfill their tasks to the best of their ability, with assiduity, technical competence, and administrative skill; secondly, to strip for action and vigorously, rather than feebly and carelessly, engage and struggle against anyone who at any time might attack the monastery, to handle wisely and to bear nobly all the difficulties that may befall them, and not to fail to do some justice to what each given circumstance may require; thirdly—some people might be embarrassed to say it at all, embarrassed even to have doubts on this account—to be of pure character and upright ways, and above all selfish passion, desire of personal gain, and venality.

19. These, as I mentioned before, are utterly objectionable and abominable things indeed merely to be spoken of or thought—and as alien as anything is to the magnanimity and liberality behooving the monastic profession. However, some of the unworthy stewards made such suspicions [fol. 337r] justified, since, bad people that they were, they acted dishonestly in administering affairs of this kind, and misappropriated common property, or rather, truth to tell, sacrilegiously plundered that which had been offered to God. To be sure, Ananias and Sapphira, who shared his vices as well as his bed, lived long ago and at the early beginnings ⟨of our Faith⟩; for this illness is contemporaneous with the teaching of Christ itself and with the intercourse among those men chosen by God's decree who formed a community when the Christian message was at its very beginnings. Ananias and Sapphira were exposed to no pressure of necessity or force or constraint or terror from which there was no escape; when they chose the Best, they did it of their own free will and with their sovereign mind and judgment; they decided, without anyone demanding it, to bring their possessions openly to the fore and offer them to Christ and to the brotherhood

καὶ τὴν κτῆσιν τοῦδ' ἕνεκα πριαμένοις ἀποδόμενοι, τὸ τίμημα τοῖς ἀποστόλοις προσάγοντες—
οἳ δ' ἔπειτα, φαῦλοι φαύλως καὶ δυστυχεῖς ἄνθρωποι καὶ πάντων ὡς ἀληθῶς ἀνούστατοι καὶ
ἀθλιώτατοι, τὰ οἰκεῖα καὶ ὧν ἦσαν αὐτοὶ δεσπόται ν ο σ φ ι σ ά μ ε ν ο ι καὶ ὑφελόμενοι κρύφα,
15 καὶ λαθεῖν πειρώμενοι, καὶ λαθεῖν δόξαντες, καὶ Χριστὸν ἀπατηλῶς κλέψαι καὶ τοὺς αὐτοῦ
θεράποντας τὴν ψῆφον τοῦ καλοῦ καὶ τῆς ἀρετῆς τὴν τελείωσιν, ἔλαθον μᾶλλον ἑαυτοὺς τοῖς
ἐσχάτοις περιβαλόντες δεινοῖς, ὡς ἀνομοῦντας διακενῆς, καὶ τὰ μέγιστ' ἀσεβοῦντες εἰς τὸ παντ-
έφορον αὐτὸ τοῦ θεοῦ καὶ διὰ πάντων χωροῦν, κἂν τοῖς μυχοῖς αὐτῆς τῆς καρδίας, καὶ πάντων
δραττόμενον.

20. Καὶ τοίνυν ὡς οὐκ ἀδόκητον ὃ νῦν ἐλέγομεν, φυλάττεσθαι καὶ κατασφαλίσασθαι τὴν
τῶν ὑμετέρων ἐπισκοπὴν καὶ διοίκησιν τοῖς μεταχειρίζειν ἀποτεταγμένοις ταῦτ' ἐξ ὑμῶν· ὡς
ἐμοὶ μὲν καὶ τοῦ μηδὲν ὑποσυλᾶσθαι καὶ παραιρεῖσθαι τῶν ἐπιβαλλόντων καὶ διαφερόντων
ὑμῖν, καὶ πᾶν τὸ καθ' ὑμᾶς τῆς γιγνομένης τυγχάνον ἐπιμελείας ἀμείωτόν τε καὶ ἀθῷον ἥκειν
5 τῇ μονῇ, πολὺ μέλει—ἢ τί γὰρ οὔ;—καὶ τὸ πρὸς τοὺς ἐπηρεαστὰς ἀνθίστασθαι, καὶ μὴ ὀλιγώρως ἐκκεῖσθαι τὰ ὑμέτερα συγχωρεῖν τῇ κατὰ σφᾶς αὐτοὺς βίᾳ καὶ ταῖς ἁρπαγαῖς, καὶ ὥστε
χειμάρρου δίκην ταῖς αὐτῶν ἐπιδρομαῖς παρασύρεσθαι, καὶ τοῦδ' αὐτοῦ μέλει. πολὺ δὲ μάλιστ'
ἢ κατ' αὐτὰ μέλει τοῦ μηδένας ἐξ ὑμῶν, τὴν αὐτῶν ἐπισκοπὴν καὶ διοίκησιν πιστευθέντας,
σκαιωρεῖσθαι σφίσιν ἴδια τὰ κοινὰ καὶ δυσνοϊκῶς [fol. 337v] ἀνδραποδίζεσθαι σὺν δόλῳ καὶ
10 λωποδυτεῖν καὶ ὑπευθύνους εἶναι τοιαύταις αἰσχίσταις κακουργίαις καὶ κλοπαῖς. περὶ ὧν, ἐμοὶ
δοκεῖν, κἂν ἐπί τινων τοῦ πολλοῦ λεώ, καὶ δημοτῶν τινων ἀποχειροβιώτων ἀνδρῶν, κἀκ παντὸς τρόπου προθεμένων πορίζεσθαι, μᾶλλον δὲ καὶ τελωνικῶς ἀναίδην ζώντων καί, κατὰ τοὺς
κόρακας, οἷς ἂν ἑκάστοτε ξυλλάχωσιν εἰς κατάβρωσιν ἐπιχαινόντων, αἰσχύνοιτό τις καὶ κομιδῇ
μυσάττοιτο, εἰ πιστευθέντες ἄττα δὴ καὶ προνοεῖν ἂν ἐπιτεταγμένοι, οἳ δ' ἔπειτα τούτοις
15 διαλυμαίνοιντο, καὶ τοιούτοις ἔργοις ἐνέχοιντο, καὶ σφέτερ' αὐτῶν, ἐπιβούλως χρώμενοι, κακοὶ
κακῶς ἐντεῦθεν καταπράττοιντο κέρδη. μή μοι γένοιτο περὶ ὑμῶν τινὸς τοιοῦτόν τι κάκιστον
καὶ σφόδρ' ἀηδίας καὶ ἀσχημοσύνης ἐσχάτης αἰσθέσθαι, ἢ τινῶν κακηγορούντων πυθέσθαι,
ἐπιχαιρεκάκῳ μὲν ἴσως προθέσει καὶ τρόπῳ δυσνοϊκῷ καὶ κακοσχόλῳ, πυθέσθαι δ' ὅμως ἐπα-
ληθευόντων ἐφ' ὑμᾶς αὐτούς. ἐπεὶ καὶ λανθάνειν οὐκ ἔστι καθάπαξ οὕτω δὴ χρωμένους τούς
20 γε τοιούτους, καὶ περὶ ταῦτα δεινοὺς ἐκτόπως καὶ φιλοσκώμμονας· εἰ δὲ καὶ λανθάνοιεν—ὃ
πολλοῦ δέοι ἄν, ἢ παντὸς μᾶλλον ἀδύνατον, οἶμαι, οὐδ' ἂν εἴ τις, ὡς ἔπος εἰπεῖν, τὸν παροιμι-
ώδη Γ ύ γ ο υ δ α κ τ ύ λ ι ο ν περιελίξοιτο—ἀλλ' οὐκ ἂν πάντως λάθοιεν τὸν ἐπὶ πάντων ἐπόπτην
ἀόρατον αὐτὸν θεόν, οὐδ' ἀποδράσαιεν τὴν φθάνουσαν ἅπαντας, καὶ τοὺς ταχυτάτους αὐτοὺς
δοκοῦντας, δίκην θεοῦ καὶ λόγους πραττομένην ἑκάστων τῶν κατ' ἀνθρώπους, καὶ βίου παν-
25 τός, καὶ πάσης διοικήσεως. καὶ τοίνυν ἵνα μὴ ἀπατῷντο σοφιζόμενοι τὰ μὴ πεφυκότα, μᾶλλον
δ' ἀμαθαίνοιεν ὡς ἀληθῶς ἄττα μὴ ἐχρῆν καθάπαξ καὶ ἄττα πᾶσι δῆλα, τηρούντων δὴ τὸ
προσῆκον κατ' αὐτοὺς τῇ προαιρέσει τοῦ βίου, τηρούντων δ' ἑαυτούς, ὅσα γε εἰκὸς ἐπὶ τῆς
θεϊκῆς ἐποπτείας, ἧς ἀμέλει πάντ' ἐπίπροσθεν χωρεῖ καὶ φέρεται, καὶ οὐδὲν μή ποτ' οὔ.

F **19**,16 ἀρετῆς τὴν τελείωσιν : cf. Arist., *Phys.*, 246a13
20,22 Γύγου δακτύλιον : cf. Leutsch-Schneidewin, I, 232; II, 20–21, 353 et alibi   22 πάντων ἐπόπτην—23 θεόν : cf. Esth. 5:1; III Mach. 2:21

20,4 (καὶ) ἄθωον V   8 πιστευθέντ(ας) V¹ˢᵛ : -το(ς) V   14 μισάττοιτο V   19 χρωμέν(ους) V²ˢᵛ : χρωμένοις V
28 καὶ² V

which had gathered around Him; for this purpose, they sold their property to buyers to bring the proceeds of this sale to the Apostles—and then this very couple of evil, wretched, and, in truth, most mindless and miserable of people unworthily appropriated to themselves what belonged to them, since they themselves were the owners, withholding some of it surreptitiously and trying to remain undetected; they appeared to have succeeded in keeping their secret and in fraudulently obtaining from Christ and his disciples the reward of good action and the attainment of virtue [?]; in fact, they failed to realize that they involved themselves in more dire danger, since they had broken the law needlessly, and that they were guilty of the greatest impiety against God, that all-seeing eye, which penetrates everywhere, even to the innermost recesses of our hearts, and encompasses everything in its sight.

20. Accordingly, those from among you who have been assigned to handling such things should provide safeguards for and keep a watchful eye on the correct supervision and administration of your property, as if what I had just said were likely to happen. For I am highly concerned —why should it be otherwise—that nothing of what belongs to you or is your property should be secretly taken away and removed, and that all that is yours should be treated with all possible care and should come to the monastery undiminished and unharmed; furthermore, I am concerned that you should oppose threats to the monastery's possessions and that you should not be so negligent as to permit your properties to be exposed to the violence and plunder of those who threaten them, and so eventually to be dissipated, like a torrent, through their encroachments. However, I am most concerned that no one from among you who is entrusted with the supervision and administration of common property should scheme to appropriate it to himself and use [fol. 337v] malevolent deceit in order to gain control over it, plunder it, and be found guilty of such abominable wickedness and thefts. It seems to me, concerning this point, that even if those involved belonged to the lowest strata and were men of people living by the labor of their own hands and striving after gain regardless of the means employed, in short, living without restraint in a mercenary fashion, like ravens who, with gaping beaks, want to devour whatever falls to their lot—even then one would be embarrassed and overcome with utter disgust if, entrusted with some things and told to take care of them, these people would instead damage them, be involved in other similar doings, and would treacherously strive, those wretches, to obtain from all this an advantage for themselves. May I never observe such a most evil, utterly disgusting and disgraceful thing in any of you; may I never learn about it from some slanderers who, motivated perhaps by joy at a neighbor's misfortune or by their own malevolent and mischievous ways, nevertheless would be telling the truth about you. For if one does such things, one cannot hide from such people, highly proficient and full of malicious wit in such matters as they are; even should one be able to conceal what one has done, which is hardly possible—or rather, in my opinion, utterly impossible, even if someone should, so to speak, turn the proverbial ring of Gyges—even then one would not be able to escape the invisible beholder of all things, God Himself, or run away from God's justice, which outruns all, even those who appear to themselves to be the swiftest, and which demands an account for all the actions of men, for their whole lives, and for all they administer. In order that such people may not delude themselves and indulge in sophistries about things which are just not so, or rather, so that they may not show their complete ignorance of what they should have known well and what is obvious to everyone, they should preserve what is proper for the kind of life which they have chosen, and should, furthermore, preserve themselves—a plausible course under the scrutiny of God, in front of whom everything is moving and happening and whom nothing escapes.

21. Καὶ ὑμεῖς δὲ κοινῇ τηρεῖν πᾶν τὸ εἰκὸς ἐν τούτοις, εὐθεῖ συνειδότι στοιχοῦντες, καὶ τὴν ἐπιλογὴν ἐν καιρῷ πάντα τρόπον ποιούμενοι, καὶ πᾶσαν προσπάθειαν ἀποποιούμενοι καὶ μικρογνωμοσύνην τε καὶ μικρολογίαν· καὶ θεὸν τὸν ἐπόπτην ὡσαύτως πρὸ ὀφθαλμῶν ἔχειν, καὶ τὴν ἔφεδρον ἀεὶ πάντων δίκην, καὶ πάσης οὐχ ἥκιστ᾽ ὀλιγωρίας καὶ κακουργίας. καὶ οὐ
5 λέγω νῦν τοῦθ᾽ ὑμῖν πρὸς τὴν ἐπήρειαν καὶ δυσκολίαν τοῦ καιροῦ—καὶ τοῦτο μὲν νῦν ὑμῖν ὅσον, καὶ τὸ πρᾶγμα [fol. 338r] μάλιστ᾽ ἐπίχρειον νῦν ἐπεῖγον (ἢ πῶς γὰρ οὔ;) κἂν ὁπόσῃ φροντίδων ἀκμῇ καὶ ἐπιμελείας τὰ καθ᾽ ὑμᾶς, ἀκριβῶς ἴστε πάντως—ἀλλ᾽ ἄρ᾽ ἔγωγε κατὰ παντὸς ἀμέλει καθάπαξ τοῦ χρόνου τάδε φημί, ὅπως ποτ᾽ ἂν ἔχοι, κἂν εἰ εὖ ὑμῖν καὶ ὡς ἑτέρως φέροιτο. κατὰ παντὸς γὰρ ὑμῖν τοῦ χρόνου καὶ πραγμάτων κατὰ πάντων καθάπαξ ἡ τοῦ βίου πρόθεσις,
10 καὶ οὐ νῦν ἑκάστοτε μᾶλλον, οὐδ᾽ ἧττον, ἢ καὶ ὁτὲ πάσης τῆς ζωῆς, οὐδ᾽ ἄλλως χθὲς καὶ πρὸ τρίτης ἢ νῦν, οὐδ᾽ ἄλλως ἢ νῦν τῇ ὑστεραίᾳ καὶ μετέπειθ᾽ ἑξῆς· οὐδ᾽ ἔξωθεν ἐν εὐκολίᾳ βιοῦσιν ἄλλως, ἄλλως δὲ βιοῦσιν ἄλλως· οὐδὲ πρὸς ἅπασαν δυσχέρειαν καὶ ἀντίπραξιν καὶ δυσχρηστίαν ὁπηοῦν ἐναλλάττειν. τὰ καθ᾽ ὑμᾶς συνθήματα καὶ αἱ πρὸς θεὸν παρρησίᾳ τὴν πρώτην ὁμολογίαι, ἀλλ᾽ ἴστε μὲν ὑμεῖς, οἷα, ἴσασι δ᾽ ἅπαντες σχεδὸν ἄνθρωποι, καὶ ὅσοι τὰ καθ᾽ ὑμᾶς ὅλως
15 ἴσασι· καὶ τῶνδ᾽ ὑμᾶς ἀεὶ μεμνῆσθαι κἂν παντὶ τῷ παραστάντι τοῦ καιροῦ, καὶ μεμνημένους ὡς εἰκὸς ἐφ᾽ ὅσον οἷόν τέ ἐστιν ἀεὶ παραβάλλεσθαι καὶ τηρεῖν, καὶ μὴ προδιδόναι μηδ᾽ ἐλλείπειν τὴν τάξιν, ἐφ᾽ ἧς ὑμεῖς ὑμᾶς αὐτοὺς ἐπὶ καλοῦ προεστήσασθε τοῦ σχήματος καὶ συντάγματος.

22. Εἰ δὲ καὶ νῦν ὑμῖν τὸ τῆς χρήσεως ἐργωδέστερον, ξυμβὰν διὰ τὴν ἀντίπραξιν ὅπως ἄρα τοῦ καιροῦ, καὶ τὴν τοῦ καθηγεμόνος ἐρημίαν, καὶ ἴσως καὶ τῆς ἡμετέρας ἐπικουρίας ὑμῖν, ἐπείγεσθαι καὶ πονεῖν ἔστι πλέον, καὶ ὅσον ἐν καιρῷ τῆς χρείας, καὶ ἡ τῶν πραγμάτων ἀνάγκη πράττεται. καὶ δὴ πονεῖτε μάλισθ᾽ οὕτω κρίνοντες ᾗ δέοι ἂν καὶ πλεονεκτεῖτε τοῖς καμάτοις,
5 περίεργον ἔχειν ἀπαιτούμενοι τὴν ἐπιμέλειαν, καὶ μηδὲν μήποτε μεθιέμενοι τῶν εἰκότων καὶ τοῦ γιγνομένου τῆς χρήσεως· ἀγαπῴην ἂν ἔγωγ᾽ εὖ μάλα, καὶ τοῦτο μάλιστ᾽ ἐπαινετῶς ὑμῖν. ταῦτ᾽ ἄρα καὶ ὅπως πλεῖστον ὅσον οἷόν τ᾽ ἐστὶν ὑμεῖς τῶν πόνων ἐνταῦθα καὶ τῆς σπουδῆς συνεισάγοιτε, καὶ γίγνοισθε μὲν ἐπιμελεῖς τοῦ καθ᾽ αὑτὸν ἕκαστος προσήκοντος, γίγνοισθε δ᾽ ἔτι πάντες ὁμοῦ τοῦ κοινῇ τῇ μονῇ συνοίσοντος· καὶ τοῦτο ἔν τε τοῖς θειοτέροις καὶ τῷ κατὰ
10 θεὸν βίῳ καὶ πολιτεύματι, ἔν τε τοῖς κατὰ τὴν σωματικὴν αὐτὴν χρείαν, καὶ ἅττα πᾶσα ἀνάγκη καὶ οὐκ ἔστιν ἄλλως συνίστασθαι καὶ ζῆν, καὶ πρὸς τὴν πρώτην ὑψηλὴν ἀνύτειν ἀπροσκόπως πρόθεσιν. καὶ τοῦτο, μηδὲν μᾶλλον, μηδὲν ἧττον, ἐν τοῖς ἔνδον καὶ οἴκοι τῇ μονῇ, ἢ καὶ τοῖς ἔξωθι, πάντα τὸν ἐνόντα τρόπον ὅπως ἀζήμιον ἔσται, οὐ μᾶλλον τοῖς προσοδήμασι καὶ ταῖς [fol. 338v] χρείαις, ἢ τῷ κατὰ θεὸν ὑμῶν ἐπαγγέλματι.

23. Ἀλλ᾽ ἐπειδὴ ταῦτα μετρίως ἔμοιγ᾽ εἴρηται, φέρε καὶ τόδε προστίθημι, καὶ γὰρ οὐκ ἂν μοι παραδραμεῖν ἀνεκτόν· ὅπως φυλάσσοιτέ μοι τὰ ταμιεῖα τοῦ καλλίστου πλούτου, τῶν πολυτιμήτων βίβλων, ἐν ἀσφαλεῖ καὶ ἄσυλα, πάσης ἐπηρείας ἀνώτερά τε καὶ κρείττω. τὸν μὲν ἐγὼ φθάσας πλοῦτον ἐνεθέμην τῇ μονῇ προνοήσας, πλεῖστον ἀμέλει καὶ οὐκ οἶδ᾽ εἰ καὶ ἄλλη
5 ποι τοσοῦτον· ἔφην δ᾽ ἄν, εἰ μὴ νεμεσητά γ᾽ ἴσως ἦν καὶ φορτικὸν ἔδοξεν ἄν, εἰ καὶ παρὰ ταῖς ἄλλαις αὐτόθι πάσαις μοναῖς τοσοῦτον, ἅμα τῷ τοιοῦτον εἶναι· καὶ ἴσως οὐ χρειωδέστατον τῇ μονῇ μόνον, ἀλλὰ καὶ ὑπὲρ τὴν ὑμῶν χρείαν λυσιτελέστατον, καὶ περισπούδαστον καὶ ποθεινὸν

F   **21**,3 θεὸν τὸν ἐπόπτην : cf. **20**,22/23

21,1 καὶ¹ V   4 οὐχήκιστ᾽ V
22,6 inter χρήσεως et ἀγαπῴην excidit fortasse aliquid
23,1 μετρί(ως) V   3 βιβλ[[ί]]ων V

21. You, too, as members of the community, should observe what is decorous in such things and keep your consciences clear; attend to the elections ⟨of administrative officers?⟩ always at appropriate times, shun all passionate involvement, narrow-mindedness, and cattiness; you too should keep God, the beholder of all things, before your own eyes—God and His justice sitting in judgment in all matters, especially those involving negligence and wickedness. And I am not saying this with reference to the abuse and difficulties with which you have to cope at present— for you know very precisely yourselves how big these difficulties are, what the most necessary and pressing thing [fol. 338r] at the present moment is (how would it be otherwise?), and that your affairs require the utmost attention and diligence; what I am saying applies altogether to any point in time and to any situation, no matter how you might fare then, well or badly. For the way of life which you have chosen is for all time and all circumstances, and to be enforced no more or no less right now than at any other point in your lives; nor should it be different yesterday or the day before from what it is now, or tomorrow, or some later day; or different when you live outwardly comfortable lives and different again when the conditions of your lives change; nor must you change in the face of any difficulty, adverse action, or disadvantage. You yourselves know what covenants and what outspoken professions you have made before God at the very outset; and almost all men know about that, too, as many as know about you at all; these covenants and professions you must keep in your mind at all times, and while doing so, as far as is reasonably possible, you must keep them before your own eyes and observe them; you must not betray or desert the army wherein you have put yourselves in the forward ranks, that is, in the good monastic formation and order.

22. If your life is now beset with difficulties, this having happened somehow because times are adverse, because you are bereft of your abbot, and perhaps because I am no longer able to assist you, then you must exert yourselves and work harder, as much as the events force this upon you. Work hard, using your own judgment as to what is indicated, and eagerly assume more and more onerous tasks, since you are required to act with particular diligence and to perform unrelentingly what is appropriate and best—I should be greatly pleased if it were so, and this would be most praiseworthy of you [?]. For that reason, assign to yourselves as much work and effort as possible; each of you should excel both in fulfilling your individual obligations and in doing what is beneficial to the monastery as a whole. This should apply both to religious matters and your life and conduct according to God, and to matters referring to bodily needs, being in the realm of necessity and without which body and soul cannot be kept together, without which one is not able to go on living or to pursue freely the high and foremost purpose. Moreover, this should apply in precisely the same degree to what is within the precincts of the monastery and to its outlying possessions, so that not only the revenue and the [fol. 338v] needs of the monastery, but your very profession to live according to God would suffer no harm whatsoever.

23. Since I have said enough on this topic, let me add this point, which I cannot bear to omit: keep, for my sake, the storehouses of the best wealth, namely the priceless books, in safety, unharmed, and above and beyond any abuse. I prudently placed this wealth in the monastery; it is indeed enormous and I do not know whether it is equaled by that of any other place; if it were not for the risk of incurring God's wrath and appearing vulgar, I would have said that I did not know whether there was such a wealth of books, both in quantity and in quality, in all the city's monasteries taken together. This collection is absolutely indispensable—and perhaps not only to the monastery itself, since its usefulness may transcend your own needs—much desired and

εὖ μάλα τοι τοῖς περὶ λόγους ἔχουσι· καὶ παρὰ τῇ μονῇ τάχ' ἂν ἔστιν οἷς καὶ ἔστιν ὅτε, μᾶλλον
δ' ἀεὶ τόδ' ἐστὶ καὶ πολλοῖς ἄλλοις ἐκτός. καὶ οὐκ οἶδα τί ποτ' ἂν ἄμεινον εἴη τῆς ἐμῆς προνοίας
10 τῇ μονῇ καὶ συντελείας φιλανθρώπευμα, καὶ βιωφελέστατον ἐν παντὶ κατ' ἀνθρώπους, ἢ
φιλοτίμημα ταύτῃ καὶ περίδοξον ἅμα τῷ σεμνῷ καὶ κοσμίῳ καθ' ὑμᾶς, ἢ τὸ χρῆμα τοῦτο καὶ ἡ
πολυέραστος αὕτη τὸν ἀεὶ χρόνον οὐσία, καὶ ὁ μὴ δαπανώμενος, κἂν εἰ μάλιστ' ἐκφέροιτο, καὶ
πρὸς πολλούς, θησαυρός. ἔγωγέ τοι τῇ παρασκευῇ ταύτῃ καὶ ταμειουχίᾳ καθ' ὑμᾶς μάλιστ' ἐν
ἐμαυτοῦ χαίρω μεμνημένος· μέμνημαι δ' ὁσημέραι, καὶ οὐκ οἶδ' ὅτε μή, κἂν παντὶ τῷ παριστα-
15 μένῳ τοῦ καιροῦ καὶ πᾶσι κατ' ἐμὲ πράγμασι. καὶ πάντοτ' ἀναψυχῆς μοι κατὰ πάσης ἀνίας
τόδ' ἀφορμή, μεμνημένῳ καὶ λαμβάνοντ' εἰς νοῦν, οἷον τόδ' εὐγενὲς ἔργον εἰς τὸν βίον εἴργασμαι
καὶ φορὰν κατ' ἀνθρώπους εἰσήνεγκα, καί μοι πολλοῦ τιμᾶται, καὶ ἥδιστ' ἐκτόπως. καὶ τέρπο-
μαι, πῶς οἴεσθε, πρὸς τὸ μέλλον ἀφορῶν καὶ ὅσος ἀνθρώποις ἐστὶ βίος καὶ ζωῆς μήκη καὶ μονῆς
τῷ κόσμῳ, ὡς οὐ μή ποτ' ἂν ἐμέ τε καὶ ὑμᾶς ἐπιλείψαι μάλιστ' ἀγαθὴ καὶ τύχη καὶ μνήμη καὶ
20 κλέος τοῦ παγκοίνου τοῦδε κατ' ἀνθρώπους χρησίμου καὶ καλοῦ, καὶ τῶν ἐναποκειμένων παρ'
ὑμῖν κειμηλίων τῷ βίῳ, καὶ τῆς οὐ μᾶλλον ἀναγκαστῆς ἢ καὶ ἡδίστης καὶ ἀκενώτου μὲν οὖν
ἀνθρώποις χρήσεως καὶ μετουσίας τῶνδε ῥᾷστ' εὐπορίστως, ὧν ἄρ' ἑκάστων ἅπαντι δεῖ· δεῖ
δὲ καὶ ἀεὶ δεήσει κατὰ τὸν βίον τε καὶ κατ' ἀνθρώπους, καὶ οὔποτε μᾶλλον ἢ καὶ ἧττον, ἢ
πρότερον ἐκείνοις ὧν ἡ μεγάλη φήμη καὶ δόξα καὶ τὸ κράτος ἐν λόγοις, ἢ τοῖς κἂν τῷ νῦν εἶναι
25 τῶν καλῶν ἐρασταῖς οἷστισινοῦν, ἢ μετέπειθ' ἑξῆς. μόνα γὰρ ταῦτα τὸν ἀεὶ χρόνον ἐν βροτοῖς
ἀγήρω παιδικά, ταὐτὰ μένοντα [fol. 339r] καὶ οὐ παραρρέοντα τοῖς ἀεὶ φιλοκάλοις.

24. Ταύτῃ τοι καὶ μελέτω πάνυ τοι περὶ τούτων ὑμῖν, καὶ φυλαττέσθων ἀμείωτα τὰ κάλλιστα ταῦτα χρήμαθ' ὑμῖν καὶ θησαυρίσματα, καὶ περισπούδαστα κομιδῇ τὸν ἅπαντ' ἀνθρώποις αἰῶνα· καὶ χρειωδέσταθ' ὑμῖν τε πάντως οἴκαδε—καὶ οὐχ ἱερὰ μόνον, ἀλλὰ καὶ τῆς ἔξω
περιττῆς σοφίας, καὶ οὐδ' ὑμῖν ἔστιν οἷστισιν ἴσως ἄρα περιφρονητῆς καὶ ἀχρείου—καὶ πολλοῖς
5 ἄλλοις χρειωδέστατ' αἰεί· κἂν ἐπιμελείᾳ πάσῃ φυλαττέσθων ἀλώβητα. ὡς ἐμοί γ' ἂν ἀλγεινότατον εἴη, καὶ οὐκ οἶδ' εἴ τινος ἧττον ἄλλου τῶν ἐμοὶ δυσχερῶν, καὶ μέσης ἁπτόμενον δριμύτατα γένοιτ' ἄν, οἶμαι, τῆς καρδίας, εἰ ἄρα πυθοίμην ἄλλως περὶ τούτων, ἢ ὡς ἐπιτέλλω
καὶ βούλομαι, καί τιν' αὐτῶν ἀμέλει σεσυλημένα πυθοίμην, καὶ τὴν μονὴν ἐρημωθεῖσαν αὐτῶν
καὶ χηρεύουσαν, τινὰ δὲ καὶ ἀτημελήτως ἔχοντα, θριπηδέστατα καὶ εὐρωτιῶντα καὶ φθορᾶς
10 ἐγγύς· ὡς οὐκ ὄφελον μή τί ποτε τούτων εἴη, μήτε πυθοίμην τοῦτ' αὐτός, καὶ ὑμῶν πολὺ τῆς
φροντίδος καὶ φυλακῆς ἐν τούτοις διδόντων κατ' ἔφεσιν ἐμὴν καὶ μάλισθ' ὡς ἀληθῶς ὀφειλήν,
ἣν οὐκ ἂν εἰκότως ἀποφευκτέα ὑμῖν ἐστιν, ἐν δευτέρῳ θεμένοις.

25. Ἐγὼ μὲν οὖν ἄττα δὴ ξυννενόηκα βέλτισθ' ὑμῖν, διὰ βραχέων ὑπέμνησα, τὰ δίκαι'
ἐμαυτῷ καὶ ὑμῖν ἴσως ποιῶν· θεὸς δ' αὐτὸς δοίη, καὶ γένοιτ' ἄν, ὅ,τί ποτε κἀμοί τε καὶ ὑμῖν
συνοῖσον.

23,19 ἀγαθῇ V
24,2 ταυτα V   3 καὶ¹ V   τε add. V²ˢᵛ   οὐχ' ἱερά V   6 ἧττον add. Vˣˢᵛ (an auctor manu propria?)   τῶν Vˣˢᵛ (an
auctor manu propria?) : ὧν V   9 καὶ¹ V   θριπηδέστατα i.q. θριπήδεστα; de forma, cf. Liddell-Scott-Jones ad locum   12
ἀποφευκτέα V²ˢᵛ : -έον V

greatly longed for as it is by all men of letters. Some members of the monastic community, too, might find it useful on occasion; however, this would be true at all times of the large number of outsiders. I would be hard put to say what act of philanthropy resulting from my prudent contribution to the monastery was ever of greater effectiveness or general use to men, or which act of pride brought more glory to the monastery and more respectability and decorum to all of you, than the gift of these objects to you, of this property which will be coveted for all times to come, of this treasure inexhaustible even if distributed lavishly, and among the many. Whenever I recall this provision of mine and this trust which you administer, I inwardly rejoice; I recall it every day, and constantly think of it: constantly, that is, at every moment and in all circumstances. This is to me a source of lasting relief in all distress, to recall and revolve in my mind that I have done such a noble deed for the benefit of the world and that I have made such a contribution to mankind; I value it all very highly and it gives me exceeding pleasure. And I rejoice, you may be sure of it, looking toward the future, and to whatever length of time has been allotted to men to live and to stay on this earth, since I know that both you and I will forever enjoy good fate, memory, and glory on account of this good and useful deed of ours for the benefit of all men, on account of the treasures deposited with you for the whole world, and on account of the fact that men will be able to use these no less sweet than indispensable and inexhaustible treasures, and partake of them without any difficulty, each according to his need. This need does and shall exist among men; it remains the same, whether we think of people of the past, who owe their fame, glory, and power to letters, or of some of our contemporaries, passionately pursuing the Good, or finally, of those who shall come after us. For among mortals works of letters are the only objects of love that stay forever young; to lovers of the Good, they always remain the same [fol. 339r] and do not slip away with time.

24. For that reason, take good care of the collection; preserve these exquisite objects and treasures undiminished, as they will be much desired by men for all time to come; they are indispensable both to you, for home use—and not only the sacred books, but also those of the exterior and superfluous wisdom, which even some from among you might not disdain or find useless—and to many other readers, forever; preserve them with utmost diligence. It would cause me a great deal of suffering, probably as much as any other of my vexations, and would be, I fear, a blow going straight to the middle of my heart, should I learn that my wishes and commands concerning the collection are being disregarded, that some of the books have been looted, and that the monastery has been bereft of them and remains without them, while other books are being neglected, eaten by worms, or all but decayed. May this never happen and may I myself never learn such a thing; you will give much thought and watchful care to this, because you will respect my desires, but most of all, to speak the truth, because you owe it to me and because it would be unseemly for you to escape this obligation by relegating it to second place.

25. I have briefly suggested some things upon which I have reflected and which I consider to be best for you; I owed it to myself, and perhaps to you as well. May God Himself grant whatever might bring most good both to you and to me, Amen.

WORD INDEX

This list includes the following: (1) words, word forms, and meanings not attested in dictionaries by Liddell-Scott-Jones (or its *Supplement* of 1968), Demetrakos, and Lampe (such entries are preceded by an asterisk *); (2) words attested, in the same meaning, only in other writings by Metochites (the only exception to this rule is προσόδημα).

Unless otherwise indicated, references are to paragraph and line of *Logos* 15.

* ἀρτιόομαι, *to be perfected; to be made complete*, **6**,11; Lampe, s.v. ἀρτιόω, gives the meaning "make sound, heal."

* δυσνοϊκός, *malevolent*, **20**,18.

δυσνοϊκῶς, *malevolently*, **20**,9; TM, *Miscellanea*, p. 419,13; *idem, Logos* 14, **27**,18 (*Etudes*, p. 253).

* ἐρραστωνευμένος, *free of cares*, **2**,9.

* ἔσωθι, *inside*, **3**,4.

* εὐπορίστως, *so as to be easily obtained*, **23**,22; cf. εὐπόριστα, **1**,11.

* ἱκανόχρειος, *satisfactory, useful*, **11**,2.

ἱκάνωσις, *sufficiency, fitness*, **1**,12, **5**,16; TM, *Miscellanea*, p. 685, last line. For ἱκάνωσις in the sense "attribution of sufficient quantity," see the fiscal treatise, ed. F. Dölger, *Beiträge zur Geschichte der byzantinischen Finanzverwaltung* . . . = *Byzantinisches Archiv*, 9 (1928), pp. 115, 117–18, 122–23.

* νεοταγής, *recently established*, **3**,3.

* πόρρωθι, *far away*, **12**,19.

προσόδημα, *revenue*, **18**,5, **22**,13; TM, *Miscellanea*, p. 512,7, cf. *Etudes*, p. 38, n. 1; Athanasius I, Patriarch of Constantinople, *Letter to the Clergy of St. Sophia*, Vat. gr. 2219, fols. 219v, 220r.

* πρυμνῆτις, adj. fem., *steering, directing*, **1**,11.

* σκαιωρέομαι, *devise mischievously*, **6**,15, **20**,9; Liddell-Scott-Jones and Demetrakos have only σκαιωρέω.

* ταμειουχία, *stewardship, trust*, **23**,13.

* τελωνικῶς, *in the manner of a tax-farmer, in a mercenary fashion, oppressively*, **20**,12.

Appendix II

METOCHITES' LETTER TO MONK SENACHERIM*

ΤΟΥ ΣΟΦΩΤΑΤΟΥ ΚΑΙ ΛΟΓΙΩΤΑΤΟΥ ΜΕΓΑΛΟΥ ΛΟΓΟΘΕΤΟΥ ΤΟΥ ΜΕΤΟΧΙΤΟΥ ΤΩΙ ΜΟΝΑΧΩΙ ΚΥΡΩΙ ΜΕΘΟΔΙΩΙ ΤΩΙ ΣΕΝΑΧΗΡΕΙΜ

1. [fol. 378r] Εὖγέ σοι, ὦ βέλτιστε ἀνδρῶν, πρὸς θεοῦ γένοιτο τῆς εὐποιΐας, εὖγέ σοι· κεκόμισται γὰρ ἀζήμιος ὢν οὐχ ἅπαξ, ἀλλὰ καὶ δὶς ἤδη πεπόμφεις οἶνον, ἐπίχρειος ὅδε πολὺ μάλισθ᾽ ἡμῖν οὕτω νοσοῦσι καὶ κάμνουσιν ἐνθάδε· οὐχ ὅτιπερ ἐκτόπως ὁ ἐκ Σταγείρων αὐτόθεν πηγάζων πάντῃ τε καὶ πᾶσιν οἶνος ἥδιστος χρήσασθαι καὶ βέλτιστος ἅπασαν ἕξιν οἴνῳ προ-
5 σήκουσαν, εἰ δή τις καὶ τῶν ἄλλος ἄλλοθεν ἐπαινετῶν, καὶ ἐν φήμῃ πομπεύων, ἀλλ᾽ ὅτι καὶ παντάπασιν ἐνθένδ᾽ ἡμῖν δυσχερῶς καὶ πάνυ τοι πονήρως ἡ τοῦ οἴνου χρῆσις ἔχει. μετὰ γὰρ μῆνα Μάϊον ἐπιστάντα πάντες οἰνῶναι ἐνθάδε καὶ οἰνοκάπηλοι, προσκείσθω δ᾽ ἴσως καὶ οἰνο- πόται, κακοδαίμονες, ἀπορίᾳ ξυνόντες καὶ ἀηδῶς ἔχοντες κομιδῇ, ὡς ἂν οἱ μὲν ἔχειν παρέχειν καὶ ἐπαρκεῖν, οἱ δ᾽ ἔχειν ἔπειτα χρῆσθαι. ἅπας γὰρ ἐγχώριος οἶνος ἐκεῖθεν αὐτίκα νοσεῖ καὶ
10 δυσχρηστίᾳ πάνυ τοι κακοπραγεῖ καὶ ζημιοῦται τὴν οὐσίαν καὶ ὑπεύθυνος ἀποδείκνυται καὶ ἔκτροπος καὶ ὀξίνης καὶ πᾶσιν ἀνθρώποις μή τινα δὴ καιρόν, μάλιστα δὲ νοσοῦσιν, ἔχων, ὅτι μὴ τοῖς ἐκ μακροῦ φαύλοις εἰθισμένοις καὶ οἴνῳ παντί, κἂν ὅπως ποτ᾽ ἔχῃ, οἴνῳ δ᾽ οὖν, [*rasura* of 10 letters] ὅλως χαίρουσιν, ὡς ἄρ᾽ οἱ πολλοὶ τῶν ἐνταῦθα κατὰ χώραν πεφύκασι, θαῦμα ὡς ἀληθῶς ὁρώμενοι, δυστυχεῖς οὕτως ἄνθρωποι. ταῦτ᾽ ἄρα καὶ ὅσοι τὴν φύσιν ἀστεῖοι καὶ
15 τῶν πολλῶν ἄμεινον πράττουσι, καὶ οὐ καθ᾽ ἡμᾶς νῦν ἐνθάδε, καὶ ῥᾷσθ᾽ ὁπῃοῦν ἔχουσι χρῆσθαι, μάλισθ᾽ οἵδε διαφερόντως περὶ τούτων ἐπιμελὲς τίθενται καὶ ἄλλοθέν πως, ὅθεν καὶ ὅπως ἂν ἐξείη, τὴν τοῦ οἴνου σφίσι χρῆσιν ἐπίδημον διοικοῦσι καὶ ὑπερορίως ἱκανοῦνται, προνοοῦντες [fol. 378v] τὴν ἀπαραίτητον χρείαν.

2. Ἀτὰρ ἐμοὶ τόδ᾽ ὅσῳ δυσχερέστατον, οὕτως ἐνθάδε πράττοντι καὶ διατρίβειν ἀνάγκην ἔχοντι καὶ οὕτω παλαίοντι πονήρως ἐργώδει νόσῳ, παντί που δῆλον, καὶ ῥᾴδιον συλλογίσα- σθαι, ὅπως σοι μάλιστα καιρὸν ἡμῖν ἔχει τὸ δῶρον, ὁ οἶνος, ἐν τῷδε τοῦ ἔτους ἀποσταλείς, μάλιστ᾽ ἐπιπόθητον καὶ ἀπαραίτητον ἡμῖν τὸ χρῆμα, εἰ ἄρ᾽ ὁτιοῦν δὴ τὰ καθ᾽ ἡμᾶς ἀρκέσαι
5 δεῖ τῇ ζωῇ. οὕτω δ᾽ ἡμεῖς εὐγνώμονές σοι τῇ χάριτι καὶ οὕτω θαρρεῖν ἐοίκαμεν ἀμέλει τῇ σῇ καλοκἀγαθίᾳ, ὥστε καὶ παρρησίᾳ αἰτεῖν καὶ ἀπαιτεῖν, ὡς εἰπεῖν, τῆς σῆς φιλικῆς τελειότητος καὶ γνώμης ἀθῴου καθάπαξ ἀξιοῦμεν τὴν ἐν τούτῳ χάριν, καὶ σοι μέλειν περὶ τούτου κομιδῇ γε ἡμῖν ἀπορουμένοις καὶ μηδ᾽ ὁτιοῦν πρὸς ἡμῶν ποιουμένοις, ἀλλὰ παντάπασιν ἀποτρεπο- μένοις τὴν ἐνταῦθα κατὰ χώραν τοῦ οἴνου χρῆσιν. καὶ τοσοῦτόν γε, προσεπαύξοντες ἔτι σοί τε
10 τὰ τῆς εὐποιΐας καὶ ἡμῖν τὰ τῆς ὀφειλῆς ἐπὶ τῇ χάριτι, προστίθεμεν, ὅπως πέμποιθ᾽ ἡμῖν ὁ οἶνος ὃς ἂν καὶ πέμποιτο, μὴ δὴ πολὺ μάλιστ᾽ ἀκμαῖος τὴν φύσιν καὶ κραταιός, ὁποῖοι δὴ μάλιστ᾽ αὐτόθεν οἱ πλείους ἀναπηγάζουσι καὶ μάλισθ᾽ οἱ καὶ πρόωροι γίγνονται τοῦ καθάπαξ νενομι- σμένου τὸ ἔτος καιροῦ τῆς οἰνώδους πεπάνσεως καὶ τελεσφόρου κατ᾽ αὐτὸν ἄρα μῆν᾽ Αὔγουστον· οἱ δὲ καὶ πάνυ τοι τῆς ἕξεως πεφύκασιν, οἶσθα καὶ αὐτός, βριαροὶ καὶ ἡβῶντες τὴν κατὰ φύσιν

---

* From Vaticanus Urbinas gr. 151, fols. 378r–379v. See above, p. 36, n. 135. For the English rendering, cf. my remarks at the beginning of Appendix I above.

LETTER OF THE MOST WISE AND LEARNED GREAT LOGOTHETE METOCHITES TO SIR METHODIUS SENACHERIM THE MONK

1. [fol. 378r] May God repay you, the best of men, for your benefaction, may God repay you for it. Indeed, the wine, of which it is not the first but the second shipment, has arrived undamaged. It is of utmost usefulness to me in my illness and suffering here: not only because the wine originating in Stagira over there is extraordinarily sweet to drink and outstanding in all the qualities appropriate to any first-rate and renowned wine coming from any region whatsoever, but also because it is extremely difficult and bothersome for me to drink local wine at all. In fact, come May, everybody here becomes a wine trader and wine merchant—and, may I add, a wine drinker as well; these wretched people suffer a constant shortage and are unwilling, indeed, either to offer wine in sufficient amounts, or to have a spare quantity for later use. The reason for it is that from that date on all local wine deteriorates right away, becomes undrinkable and its substance is subject to damage; it turns bad, tastes sour, and is of no avail to anybody, let alone a sick person, unless one has been accustomed to bad wines for a long time and enjoys any wine of any quality as long as it is wine, and most of the local inhabitants are made just that way. A wondrous sight to see, these unhappy people. Hence those who are urbane by nature and live in better circumstances than the many—not the way I am here at present—and can afford it without difficulty—those people show particular care in these matters and assure for themselves the use of imported wine by all means at their disposal; to satisfy their [fol. 378v] indispensable need, they get it from outside.

2. It should be clear to anybody how difficult all this is for me in my present condition and on account of my forced sojourn here, moreover on account of my painful struggle with my burdensome illness; it is also easy to realize that your gift, namely the wine which you sent at this time of the year, was most timely indeed; if anything around me here should be of any assistance in my survival, this thing is the one which I feel to be most indispensable and which I miss the most. I am so grateful to you for this kindness and so encouraged by your noble gesture that I make bold to request, nay demand, so to speak, that favor from your friendly perfection and your pure mind: please take care of this matter, since I am completely at a loss, cannot adjust to, but am turning away altogether from, the drinking of the local wine. I shall only add, thus enlarging the extent of your beneficence and that of my own indebtedness on account of your favor, that whatever wine you might send us should not be at its full strength—such are for the most part the wines which grow over there, especially those which are made ⟨from grapes gathered⟩ before the prescribed season each year, namely the very month of August, and have not gone through the process of maturation which brings wine to its perfection. You know yourself what the characteristics of such wines are. They are strong and at the height of their natural warmth,

15 θέρμην καὶ στίλβοντες, ὥσπερ ἐκσπινθηρίζοντες, καὶ παχύτεροι τὸ σῶμα καὶ πλεῖστον ὑπέ-
ρυθροι καὶ βαρεῖς καὶ σφοδροὶ τοῖς σώμασι ἐμπίπτοντες, πρὸς τῆς νόσου μάλισθ᾽ οἵδε γίγνονται
καὶ ἀνιῶσι προσεπιδιδόντες τῇ συμφορᾷ. σοὶ μέντοι, βέλτιστε, μέλειν ὅπως ἡμῖν καίρι᾽ ἕξει
καθάπαξ τὰ τῆς σῆς χάριτος καὶ τὸ μάλιστ᾽ ἐπίχρειον δῶρον ὁ οἶνος, οὐκ ἄμετρος καὶ δυσέν-
τευκτος χρῆσθαι τὴν ἕξιν [fol. 379r] αὐτὴν τοῦ θερμοῦ, καὶ πρὸς τὸ ἐρυθρὸν μὲν ὁπηοῦν, οὐ
20 πολὺ δ᾽ ἄκρατος κεχρωσμένος, καὶ λεῖός τε καὶ εὐαγώγως ἐγχεόμενος καὶ κοῦφος, μὴ παχύς,
ἀλλ᾽ ἀβαρὴς τὸ σῶμα καὶ διάλεπτος, οἵους οἶσθα, καὶ αὐτὸς ἔγωγ᾽ οἶδα, κατὰ χώραν αὐτόθεν
ἀναδιδόσθαι πολλούς· οὕτω μὲν οὖν πᾶσαν ἡμῖν τὴν ἐνταῦθα δυσχρηστίαν ἰάσῃ τοῦ τόπου
καὶ πολὺ μάλιστ᾽ ἐπικουρήσαις ἡμῖν κατὰ τῆς νόσου.

3. Ὡς οὐδὲν ἄρ᾽ ἡμῖν ἐντεῦθεν ἥδιστον οὐδὲ χρήσιμον, οὐ νοσοῦσιν, οὐχ ὑγιαίνουσιν, οὐ
πόσιν, οὐ βρῶσιν, καὶ μάλισθ᾽ ὁπότε κατὰ τὴν χριστιανικὴν ἀγωγὴν ἀπόκρεῳ τῇ τροφῇ
γιγνόμεθα καὶ πᾶσα ἀνάγκη τοῖς ὄψοις χρῆσθαι, τοῖς ἐκ θαλάττης ἢ ποταμῶν ἢ ὅλως ὑδάτων·
ἥ τε γὰρ θάλαττα τοῖς ἐνθάδ᾽ οἰκοῦσιν οἶσθα ὡς πορρωτάτω, καὶ τὰ ἐκ τῶν ποταμῶν τῶν
5 τῇδε θηρώμενα οὐκ οἶδα μὲν εἰ καὶ τοῖς ἄλλοις, πάντως δ᾽ οὐκ ἂν ἄλλως οἶμαι, ἔμοιγ᾽ οὖν ἐκτόπως
ἀχρεῖα καὶ ἀηδῆ καὶ οὐδὲν νόστιμον προσφέρειν ἔχοντα. καὶ λείπεται μόνα τοῖς ἐν τῷδε τοῦ
καιροῦ [manuscript: τοῦ καιρῶ] τῆς χρείας ὄσπρια καὶ ὅσα ἐκ κηπευμάτων λαχανώδη· νὴ τὴν
φιλίαν, οὐδὲ ταῦτα κατὰ καιρὸν ὄντα τὴν ἕξιν οὐδ᾽ εὐφυῶς οὐδ᾽ ὅσα οὐδ᾽ ὁπότε δέοι ἂν ῥᾴδια
πορίσασθαι, ἄλλως τε δὲ καὶ τοῖς ἐν νόσοις κατ᾽ ἐμὲ πολυζήμια καὶ δεινῶς τάδε λυμαινόμενα.

4. Ἀλλὰ μὴν καὶ τὰ ἐκ δένδρων ὡραῖα καὶ προσηνῆ μὲν καὶ ἥδιστα κατὰ φύσιν, ἀτὰρ δὴ καὶ
ταῖς νόσοις ἄττα ἐπίχρεια καὶ λυσιτελῆ, ὀλίγα τε ἐνθάδε καὶ οὐ τελεσφόρα τὸ γιγνόμενον ἅπαν
κατὰ φύσιν τῆς ἕξεως ὄντα· τινὰ δὲ καὶ παντάπασιν ἀσύμβατα τῇ χώρᾳ καὶ καθάπαξ ἐκλέλοιπε.
σῦκα μέν γ᾽ ἐνταῦθα μή ποτ᾽ ἔσται πορίσασθαι, οὐ μᾶλλόν γε ἢ ἐν Ἰνδοῖς χιόνα, φασίν, οὐδ᾽
5 ἔστιν ἀνιὸν ἐκ τῆς γῆς ἐνθάδε ἢ ταύτην ὁπηοῦν ἐπικοσμοῦν καὶ ἐπίσκεπόν τε καὶ σκιάζον φυτὸν
ἡ συκῆ, οὐ μᾶλλον ἢ κατὰ Σκύθας, καὶ ὅσοι [fol. 379v] κατὰ τὰ βορειότερα πρόσοικοι, τὸ
δένδρον ὁ φοῖνιξ.

5. Καὶ τάδε σοι πλεῖν ἢ κατ᾽ ἐπιστολὴν ἴσως τήνδ᾽ εἴρηται, μὴ πάνυ τοι δ᾽ ἔξω τοῦ καιροῦ,
οἶμαι· εὖ γὰρ δῆλον ὡς ἄρ᾽ ἐν ὁποίοις ἐμοί, νῦν γε εἶναι, τρίβοντι καὶ χαλεπῶς οὕτω πειρωμένῳ
παρὰ πᾶν τὸ πρότερον ἔθος, αὐτὸς εὐγενὴς ἑώρασαι καὶ πολὺ χρήσιμος, ἐν τῷδε δὴ μάλιστα
τῷ τῆς χρείας ἐπὶ πλεῖστον ἥκοντι τῆς κατὰ τὸν οἶνον ἀπαραιτήτου χρήσεως.

they glitter as if they were sparkling; their body is at its full; for the most part they are reddish in color and their effect on the human body is heavy and strong; such wines are apt to contribute to illness and have an irritating effect by aggravating the suffering. Take care then, the best of men, that that favor of yours and that most useful gift, namely wine, reach us at the proper time; it should not be excessive and difficult to imbibe with respect [fol. 379r] to its warmth, it should be rose rather than deeply red, it should be smooth and easy to pour in and light and thin rather than full-bodied and heavy; you know—as, by the way, I know myself—that many such wines are grown in the country around Stagira. If you do this, you will remove all difficulties in this matter with which the place here has saddled me, and you will have helped me very much to combat my illness.

3. The fact is that nothing pleasant or useful comes to me from here, either in illness or in health, either when it comes to drinks or to comestibles. This is especially true whenever, following the Christian way of life, I abstain from meat and am obliged to turn to a fish diet: to sea fish, to river fish, or in general to aquatic food. As you know, local inhabitants are very far removed from the sea and whatever is caught in the local rivers is utterly useless, unpleasant, and tasteless to me—I do not know for sure whether it seems so to others as well, although I suspect that it cannot be otherwise. What remains alone in the fasting season is pulse and vegetables grown in gardens. By friendship, these things, too, are of no avail, either by their state or by their quality, nor are they easily available: neither in quantities nor at times desired. Moreover, this kind of food brings serious harm to people affected by an illness like mine.

4. On top of that, tree fruits of the season, mild and rather sweet by nature, some of them wholesome and useful in case of illness, are scarce here and never come to the fullness of their natural potentialities, while some of the fruits do not agree with the soil here and have entirely disappeared. For instance, it will never be possible to get figs here; they are as rare as, to use a proverb, snow is in India. A plant called "fig tree" just does not grow from the ground here nor does it adorn, shelter, or cast shadow upon it, no more than the date palm can be found among the Scythians and [fol. 379v] their neighbors living further to the north.

5. I have told you perhaps more than the present letter required, but I trust that what has been said was not out of place. For it is clear how difficult my present circumstances are, how hard my present experience is, and how different from all my former way of life; and you showed yourself both as a noble and useful person, when I was precisely in most urgent need to have the indispensable use of wine.[1]

---

1 Two centuries before Metochites, another intellectual made similar complaints in similar circumstances and from a nearby region. Nicephorus Basilakes (on him, see p. 20, above) fell ill in his exile—or self-imposed exile—at Philippopolis (Plovdiv); from there, he penned a letter to his pupils, in which he gave vent to his disgust with the miserable quality of the prunes, pears, melons, and grapes of the region. Wine was simply undrinkable. Surprisingly enough, Basilakes reserved his special scorn for the retsina wine, "destroyer of heads and eyes." Texts in A. Garzya, "Quattro epistole inedite di Niceforo Basilace," *BZ*, 56 (1963), esp. pp. 232–33.

Appendix III

WHEN DID WORK ON THE CHORA'S RESTORATION BEGIN?*

AT THE AGE of sixty Gregoras recalled that he had been of great assistance to Metochites throughout the period of the Chora's restoration: his assistantship started at the very moment when Metochites took over the monastery: πολλὰ [this is Boivin's conjecture; πολλούς MSS] δὲ καὶ τῷ τὴν μονὴν εὐθὺς ἀναδεξαμένῳ καὶ ἐγκαινίζοντι φιλοτίμῳ γνώμῃ καὶ χειρὶ σοφωτάτῳ ἐκείνῳ ἀνδρὶ συνηράμην, ἐς ὅσα τε χρείας ἐκείνῳ καὶ ἡμῖν ἔδει καὶ ὅσα τὸ τοῦ φίλτρου δυνάμενον ἡμῖν ὑπηγόρευε.[1] Gregoras had to be already a resident of Constantinople in order to be able to help Metochites with the work at the Chora. We know that he came to the capital from Heracleia on the Pontus as a young man. Assuming that Gregoras is correct in stating that he served Metochites from the very moment when the latter took over the monastery, the *terminus non ante quem* for the beginning of the restoration work at the Chora is the date of Gregoras' arrival in the capital. This *terminus* may even be put about a year after the arrival: we should give the young man from the provinces some time for social ascent, before he could enter into the good graces of Metochites, by then the highest official of the Empire.

Thus the problem would be easily solved if we knew the date of Gregoras' arrival in Constantinople with precision: unfortunately, we do not know it. Two modern authors give the year 1315 or 1316 as that date.[2] However, it is based merely on the passage of Gregoras where we learn that at the age of between twenty and twenty-one he was a frequent visitor of John Glykys (Patriarch from April 1315 on) and discussed literary subjects with him.[3] All this means no more than that Gregoras already was in Constantinople at the age of twenty; it does not necessarily mean that he arrived there at that age. Grecu, to whom we owe the latest study on the chronology of Gregoras' life, saw the difficulty.[4]

We cannot even establish the precise date of Gregoras' discussions with Glykys, for we do not know the date of his birth. Guilland puts it at about 1295, Laurent, at about 1296,[5] but both authors deduce it from the passage which I just mentioned: Gregoras' narrative concerning his literary discussions with Glykys.

Gregoras himself gave contradictory information about his age. At one point of his *History* he inserted the remark that he was twenty-seven between two passages, both datable into the year 1321.[6] This would mean that he was born in 1294.

A difficulty arises here, however. In Book XXII.2 of the *History*, he said that "today" (τήμερον) he was sixty.[7] The events described in this passage were those of 1351. If he did refer to these events when saying "today," then he implied that he had been born in 1291.[8]

---

* See above, p. 28, n. 74.

1 Gregoras, *Hist.*, XXII.2, Bonn (1830), II, pp. 1045.22–1046.2.

2 R. Guilland, *Essai sur Nicéphore Grégoras: L'homme et l'oeuvre* (Paris, 1926), p. 6; V. Laurent, "La vie de Jean, métropolite d'Héraclée du Pont, par Nicéphore Grégoras," Ἀρχεῖον Πόντου, 6 (1934), p. 21, to be combined with the same author's "La personnalité de Jean d'Héraclée (1250–1328), oncle et précepteur de Nicéphore Grégoras," Ἑλληνικά, 3 (1930), p. 307.

3 Gregoras, *Hist.*, VII.11, Bonn (1829), I, pp. 270–71; the expression σχολαῖς λογικαῖς, on p. 270.22, does not necessarily

mean that Gregoras had gone to Glykys' school and that these discussions had to precede April of 1315.

4 V. Grecu, "Das Geburtsjahr des byzantinischen Geschichtsschreibers Nikephoros Gregoras," *Académie Roumaine: Bulletin de la section historique*, 27 (1946), pp. 1 and 6 of the offprint.

5 Guilland, *Essai*, p. 4; Laurent, "La vie de Jean," p. 14, and "La personnalité," p. 311.

6 *Hist.*, VIII.8, Bonn, I, p. 328.6, a remark occurring between I, p. 319 and I, pp. 352–53.

7 *Hist.*, XXII.2, Bonn, II, p. 1045.20.

8 This is the view of Grecu, "Das Geburtsjahr," p. 3.

But if he referred to the moment of his writing Book XXII.2 (as I believe he did), then he may have said that he had been born in 1292 or later.[9]

Thus, depending on our choice of the date of Gregoras' birth, his presence in Constantinople would fall not later than 1311, 1312, or 1314/15. I prefer the last of these dates, for it is based on the most explicit passages of Gregoras.[10] Moreover, I assume that Gregoras came to know Metochites about 1315. Gregoras' contacts with Glykys I attribute to the mediation of his uncle John, Bishop of Heracleia on the Pontus, in whose company, I imagine, Gregoras first came to the capital. John was present in Constantinople in 1315, since he signed a patriarchal document in this year.[11] Closer contacts between the Bishop John of Heracleia and John Glykys must have started when the latter became patriarch (April 1315). Glykys may have introduced John of Heracleia's nephew Gregoras to his old friend Metochites sometime in 1315/16. In conclusion, I believe that the work of restoration at the Chora started about 1316, although I am not able to offer a conclusive proof for this dating. In any case, it should not have started before 1312.

9 In 1292, assuming that Guilland, *Essai*, p. 42, is right in dating the composition of Gregoras' Book XXII.2 into August–September 1352; Guilland seems to base his dating on Gregoras, *Hist.*, XXVII.15, Bonn (1855), III, p. 136.

10 *Hist.*, VIII.8, Bonn, I, p. 328.6, and VII.11, ibid., pp. 270–71.
11 Fr. Miklosich and J. Müller, *Acta et Diplomata Graeca Medii Aevi Sacra et Profana*, I (Vienna, 1860), p. 5.

Spiritual Trends in Byzantium in the Late Thirteenth and Early Fourteenth Centuries

JOHN MEYENDORFF

This study was first published in *Art et société à Byzance sous les Paléologues*, Actes du Colloque organisé par l'Association internationale des études byzantines à Venise en Septembre 1968 (Bibliothèque de l'Institut hellénique d'études byzantines et post-byzantines de Venise, No. 4; Venice, 1971), pp. 53–71.

J. MEYENDORFF

Spiritual Trends in Byzantium in the Late Thirteenth and Early Fourteenth Centuries

SINCE Byzantine art of the Palaeologan period was, in its main preserved monuments, a religious and ecclesiastical art, it is obvious that the contemporary spiritual and theological trends in Byzantium could have had some impact on the artistic developments of the time. Spirituality and art were the expressions of the same religious conscience, of the same Byzantine "mind." It is, therefore, quite proper to ask ourselves what elements in the field of Byzantine literature, philosophy, or spirituality corresponded to the new trends that appeared in the middle of the thirteenth century in the field of art and also to the interruption of some of these trends in the middle of the fourteenth century.

It has already been noted that the Byzantine civilization throughout its history had to face an almost permanent inner struggle. On the one hand, community of language, tradition of learning, and philosophical interest led many Byzantine scholars to devote their lives to the study of Greek antiquity. On the other hand, these classical studies always found fervent critics in Byzantium who considered ancient Greek literature and philosophy the products of paganism and, therefore, dangerous to Christians. This second group, predominantly monastic, could always find quotations in favor of its point of view in the Fathers of the fourth and fifth centuries who fought the remnants of pagan Neoplatonism and considered the very word ἕλλην to be synonymous with "pagan." Opposition between these two types of mind appeared, explicitly or implicitly, in the struggle between Photians and Ignatians in the ninth century. In the eleventh century the famous philosopher Michael Psellos had to face troubles and was opposed by Xiphilinos and Cerularius. His contemporary, Symeon the New Theologian, violently attacked in his *Hymns* every kind of secular philosophical interest. Finally, John Italos, a disciple of Psellos, was condemned, during a famous trial held under Alexius Comnenus, for being a follower of the ancient Greek philosophers. These two groups were still alive in Byzantine society in the late thirteenth century: both were even going through a period of significant revival. The Byzantine lovers of Greek antiquity counted among themselves a few prominent personalities, and Byzantine monasticism was entering into a period of spiritual revival with the growth of the Hesychast movement. All this gave an extraordinary richness to the intellectual life of the time.

The historian of Byzantine literature and the historian of Byzantine art are obviously both very much concerned with the role played by the traditions of antiquity in their respective fields. It may even be assumed that they both touch here one of the essential problems of Byzantine civilization, and there is no doubt of the fact that they can help each other very much in the understanding of the legacy of Byzantium. This is particularly true for the period we are studying here, since a certain revival of the spirit of antiquity is precisely one of the essential features of the so-called "Palaeologan renaissance."

In this connection it should be pointed out, however, that during the first decades following the recovery of Constantinople by Michael VIII, no outward tension between humanists and monks, between the lovers of antiquity and the Christian ascetics, is noticeable, although the memory of past struggles could not of course have disappeared. The late thirteenth and early fourteenth centuries were periods of outward peace between the two trends of thought, which coexisted and even seemed to enrich each other to a certain extent. In both camps there was a majority for adopting a common stand on the major issues of the day, and for opposing at the same time the unionist policy of Michael VIII and the extremism of the Arsenite zealots, who were fighting the official church.

This peace between the Byzantine intellectuals and the monastic party coincides chronologically with the restoration of the monastery of the Chora by Theodore Metochites. It is illustrated by later documents, such as the *Encomion* of Gregory Palamas by his disciple the Patriarch Philotheos Kokkinos, who emphasizes that the Hesychast theologian was, in his younger days, a disciple of both Metochites and the austere ascetic Athanasius I.[1] And Palamas himself, writing in about 1356 against Nicephorus Gregoras, a disciple of Metochites, proudly recalls his studies with the great humanist and reminds the reader that Metochites once publicly praised his knowledge of Aristotle: "If Aristotle himself were present, he said, he would praise [Palamas]."[2] It is, therefore, clear that a man like Metochites was not anathema to the Byzantine monks and that they even held him up as a model to some of his disciples. On the other hand, an ecclesiastical personality such as Theoleptus, Metropolitan of Philadelphia, prominent leader of Byzantine Hesychasm, could be at the same time a spiritual teacher of Gregory Palamas [3] and a close friend of the Choumnoi family, whose younger generation was in the forefront of the anti-Palamite camp in the thirteen-forties. It was only in 1337–38, in the early correspondence between Gregory Palamas and Barlaam the Calabrian, that the conflict arose again between monks and humanists, and became almost immediately one of great violence.

Without attempting to grasp all the implications of the problem, I will try to present here the leading figures in the spiritual and ascetic revival of the first years of the Palaeologan period and try to discover the reasons why the tradition they represented finally came into conflict with contemporary Byzantine humanism.

Historians of the nineteenth and early twentieth centuries usually represented the controversies of the fourteenth century as having resulted from the emergence in Byzantium of a new "movement" or school of spirituality, called "Hesychasm" or "Palamism." This emergence was linked with the name of Gregory of Sinai, whose *Life*, written by Callistos, Patriarch of Constantinople, was published in 1896 by I. Pomialovskii.[4] In reality, the customary panegyrical style of Callistos conspicuously overemphasizes the role of Gregory and implies that before his arrival on Mount Athos the tradition of "pure prayer" was all but lost on the Holy Mountain and even in the entire Byzantine world, and that it was restored by Gregory. This *Life* was the main source for all those who affirmed that Hesychasm, being a specifically Sinaitic form of spirituality,

---

1 *PG*, 151, cols. 559D–560A. The *Encomion* was most probably composed in connection with the canonization of Palamas in 1368.

2 *Against Gregoras*, I, Paris. Coislinianus 100, fol. 236r, quoted in J. Meyendorff, *Introduction à l'étude de Grégoire Palamas*

(Paris, 1959), p. 47, n. 1. Philotheos recalls the incident in his *Encomion, loc. cit.*

3 Philotheos, *Encomion, PG*, 151, col. 561A; cf. Meyendorff, *Introduction*, pp. 49–50.

4 In *Zapiski istoriko-filologicheskago fakul'teta Imperatorskago S. Peterburzhskago Universiteta*, 35 (1896), pp. 1–64.

was unknown in Byzantium before the fourteenth century. A more comprehensive study of contemporary sources, however, gives a quite different picture of Byzantine spiritual life in the Palaeologan period. First of all, "Hesychasm," as a tradition, is acknowledged nowadays as going back to the origins of Christian monasticism.[5] By Hesychasm we do not mean necessarily the psychosomatic method of prayer, attacked by Barlaam, but the spiritual school which teaches that God reveals himself to man in an immediate communion when man refers to him constantly, in pure "monological" prayer, called the "prayer of the mind" (νοερὰ προσευχή) or the "prayer of the heart," consisting in the permanent presence of the *name* of God in the heart of man. In various forms and formulations, the tradition of the "Jesus prayer" is present throughout the entire history of Eastern Christian monasticism, and its revival in the late-Byzantine period was a movement back to tradition, not an innovation.

On the other hand, we should ask ourselves what the specific features of the late-Byzantine Hesychasm were as compared with the tradition to which it undoubtedly did belong, and what its impact was on the contemporary civilization of Byzantium. As a starting point we shall take the list given by Gregory Palamas of the great authorities acknowledged by the monks, in about 1340, as being their spiritual leaders. These authorities, according to Palamas, supported the same kind of spirituality that Barlaam was attacking, including the psychosomatic method of prayer. Along with a few secondary figures, of whom we know almost nothing, the list refers to the great names Symeon the New Theologian, Nicephorus the Hesychast, Theoleptus of Philadelphia, and Athanasius I, Patriarch of Constantinople.[6] None of these figures has anything to do with Mount Sinai. Symeon, the great mystic of the eleventh century, lived in Constantinople long before the Palaeologan period, and Nicephorus, a contemporary of Michael VIII, is an authority on the psychosomatic method of prayer. The other two happen to be eminent personalities of the late thirteenth and early fourteenth centuries, the period which interests us most here. Both were early contemporaries of Gregory Palamas, who says of them that they transmitted the Hesychast tradition to him personally "through their own mouth."

Until recently, Theoleptus, Metropolitan of Philadelphia, was known primarily as the author of a short treatise on prayer included in the *Philocalia*, the famous collection of spiritual writings made by Nicodemus Hagiorites and published in the late eighteenth century.[7] However, recent research on his unpublished writings has shown him to be a rather prolific writer and has attracted attention to his activities in the ecclesiastical affairs of the time.[8] An opponent of the Union of Lyons, Theoleptus showed himself also an active bishop and a very decided adversary of the Arsenite schism, and he was influential enough to venture open disagreement with several patriarchs on points of ecclesiastical policy and discipline. All this shows us that Byzantine Hesychasm of that time was far from being the teaching of an esoteric, ascetic, and subjectivist

5 Cf. I. Hausherr, "L'Hésychasme, étude de spiritualité," *OCP*, 22 (1956), pp. 5–40, 247–85.

6 *Triades pour la défense des saints hésychastes*, I.2.§12, ed. J. Meyendorff (Spicilegium Sacrum Lovaniense, Etudes et documents, 30; Louvain, 1959), p. 99. In another passage, Palamas speaks of himself as a close disciple of Theoleptus (*Triades*, II.2.§3, ibid., p. 323). Philotheos states that this acquaintance with Theoleptus decided Palamas' monastic vocation.

7 Like all the other spiritual writings published in the *Philocalia*, this treatise of Theoleptus was reprinted in *PG*, 143, cols. 381–404.

8 Cf. J. Gouillard, "Théolepte, métropolite de Philadelphie," *Dictionnaire de théologie catholique*, XV,1 (Paris, 1946), cols. 339–41; S. Salaville, "Formes ou méthodes de prière d'après un Byzantin du XIVe siècle," *Echos d'Orient*, 39 (1940), pp. 1–25; idem, "La vie monastique grecque au début du XIVe siècle d'après un discours inédit de Théolepte de Philadelphie," *Etudes byzantines*, II (1944), pp. 119–25; idem, "Une lettre et un discours inédits de Théolepte de Philadelphie," *REB*, 5 (1947), pp. 101–15; idem, "Deux documents inédits sur les dissensions religieuses byzantines entre 1275 et 1310," ibid., pp. 116–36; idem, "Un directeur spirituel à Byzance au début du XIVe siècle: Théolepte de Philadelphie," *Mélanges Joseph de Ghellinck*, II (Gembloux, 1951), pp. 877–87; V. Laurent, "Une princesse byzantine au cloître: Irène-Eulogie Choumnos Paléologine," *Echos d'Orient*, 29 (1930), pp. 29–60; idem, "Les crises religieuses à Byzance: Le schisme antiarsénite du métropolite de Philadelphie Théolepte," *REB*, 18 (1960), pp. 45–54.

sect, interested only in the personal spiritual progress of the individual, but was a movement of religious revival, very much involved in the visible and social life of the church. The position of Theoleptus, especially in his writings against the Arsenites, is that true communion with God—whether individual or collective—is possible only within the visible framework of the sacramental life of the church. In many ways, his beliefs appear to foreshadow the sacramental realism and mysticism of Palamas and Nicholas Cabasilas, which were based upon the belief that God is present in the church neither symbolically nor subjectively but in all reality, and that Christian spirituality, like every other Christian religious act, must reflect this objective Presence. What is important to note is that Byzantine Hesychasm of the Palaeologan period clearly appears to have largely overcome the spiritualistic, Platonic, and Messalian tendencies which had existed in Eastern monasticism since the fourth century.

The figure of the Patriarch Athanasius I, also quoted by Palamas as a leader of Hesychasm, is even more typical in this respect. Athanasius twice occupied the Patriarchal See of Constantinople (1289–93, 1303–09). We may note, *en passant*, that he chose the monastery of the Chora as one of his favorite residences: he held regular services there [9] and asked Andronicus II to build a mill nearby so that the monks of the monastery could supply him regularly with wheat.[10] It was also at the Chora that he once convened the bishops before a collective visit to the neighboring palace of Blachernae.[11] All this almost immediately preceded the restoration of the Chora by Metochites in the years before 1320.

During both his patriarchates, Athanasius revealed himself to be one of the most drastic reformers of ecclesiastical life and order since the time of John Chrysostom.[12] His enemies accused him of illiteracy and fanaticism, and his biographer, Theoktistos, acknowledges that the Patriarch "studied little of general sciences" (ὀλίγα τῶν ἐγκυκλίων ἐκμελετήσας).[13] The language of his letters is, indeed, simple and without any pretence to literary perfection. Athanasius was the very type of the austere Byzantine monk, for whom the Kingdom of Heaven was the only real value in life. As soon as he became Patriarch, he directed a frontal attack on everything contrary to Christian ethics and church canons, expelling metropolitans from the capital and obliging them to reside in their own dioceses, forcing the clergy of Hagia Sophia to fulfill their duties regularly, criticizing openly the behavior of the Byzantine court and even of the Emperor's children, stating clearly his opinion in state affairs, such as the question of the Catalan "Big Company." However, Athanasius' main concern was in the social field: he attacked violently everyone—bishop, monk, or layman—who enriched himself at the expense of the poor, and he made every effort to help those in need, using for this purpose the income of the church. He gave his support to the secularization of certain church property by the Emperor and made every attempt to control the wealth of the monasteries.[14]

9 Theoktistos Studites, Life of Athanasius, ed. H. Delehaye, in *Mélanges d'archéologie et d'histoire*, 17 (1897), p. 72.

10 Letter to the Emperor, Vaticanus gr. 2219, fol. 6v. The correspondence of Patriarch Athanasius with Andronicus II will appear in a critical edition by Alice-Mary Talbot.

11 Letter to the Bishops, *PG*, 142, col. 513. Athanasius used to reside in the Chora regularly for periods of 8 or 10 days (Letter to the Emperor, Vaticanus gr. 2219, fol. 8r).

12 His personality is known to us mainly through his vast correspondence, almost entirely unpublished but partially analyzed by R. Guilland ("La correspondance inédite d'Athanase, patriarche de Constantinople [1289–1293; 1304–1310]," *Mélanges Charles Diehl*, I [Paris, 1930], pp. 121–40) and N. Banescu ("Le Patriarche Athanase Ier et Andronic II Paléologue —État religieux, politique et social de l'Empire," Académie

Roumaine, *Bulletin de la section historique*, 23 [1942], pp. 29–56). Two Lives of Athanasius have also been preserved: one by Theoktistos Studites (cf. A. Ehrhard, *Überlieferung und Bestand des hagiographischen und homiletischen Literatur der griechischen Kirche*, III,2,1/2 [= *Texte und Untersuchungen zur Geschichte der altchristlichen Literatur*, 52,2,1/2 [Berlin, 1952], p. 991), published in excerpts by H. Delehaye (ed. cit.) and in its full text by A. Papadopoulos-Kerameus (*Zapiski istoriko-filologicheskago fakul'teta Imperatorskago S. Peterburzhskago Universiteta*, 76 [1905], pp. 1–51); and another by Joseph Calothetos (ed. Athanasios, in Θρᾳκικά, 13 [1940], pp. 59–107).

13 Ed. Papadopoulos-Kerameus, p. 26; τοῦ λόγου τὰ δεύτερα φέρων, ibid., p. 63. Cf. also Nicephorus Gregoras, *Hist.*, VI.5, Bonn (1829), I, p. 180.

14 Cf. Meyendorff, *Introduction*, pp. 35–39.

These activities of Athanasius illustrate the new authority acquired by the church during the Palaeologan period, a moral authority that grew with the political decay of the state, as George Ostrogorsky has rightly noted.[15] The Hesychast patriarchs of the fourteenth century—Athanasius, Callistos, Philotheos—were the main architects of this new power acquired by the Patriarchate of Constantinople, which enabled the church often to pursue a policy independent from that of the Emperor, particularly in the matter of relations with the West, and to be the main instrument of the persistence of Byzantine influence in Slavic countries. At this point we may, however, ask ourselves whether Athanasius' monastic austerity, his lack of interest in humanistic studies, and his social concern for the poor were elements favorable to the development of the main artistic trends of the time. Of course, Athanasius was a tradition-minded Byzantine, and his devotion to the holy images was undoubtedly strong. In his unpublished correspondence there are at least three letters which give an idea of his attitude toward these subjects. In one of them he formally thanks Andronicus II for his donation of a chalice to the Church of the Holy Apostles.[16] In another letter, also addressed to the Emperor, he violently attacks a state diginitary for having destroyed (πατάξαι λαζευτηρίῳ) a figure of Christ—probably a mosaic—in one of the famous churches of Constantinople (ἕνα τῶν περικλύτων ναῶν); the Patriarch protests against this destruction of the artistic treasures in the capital, for Byzantium, according to him, has already suffered enough from the barbarians—presumably the Latins—and should not be despoiled also by the Byzantines themselves.[17] Athanasius, therefore, was far from being an iconoclast. However, in a third letter, also addressed to Andronicus II, he speaks with some reluctance on the subject of the decoration of churches. He begins by praising those who decorate them but immediately stresses the *moral* value of any Christian sacrifice: "In the other [worldly] affairs, it is not the same to be rich and to be poor, but when you offer something to God, the more you are zealous, the more you are rich." [18] And he goes on to explain to the Emperor that this zeal can express itself in any act of worship and not necessarily in the decorating of churches. Andronicus himself never ceases, according to the Patriarch, to adorn the tabernacle—not the tabernacle built by human hands, but the one that was established by God himself, which can be decorated only with spiritual works; thus he supplants all those emperors, his predecessors, who decorated the churches with precious stones and various ornaments.[19] This letter of Athanasius would seem to be almost a condemnation of the rich ornamentation of the churches; it ends with an appeal to Andronicus to care more about the good behavior of those who use the churches than about the outward splendor of the sacred buildings. Such feelings—and also perhaps some measures taken by the austere Patriarch that were even more drastic—possibly explain the accusation of iconoclasm brought against him by his enemies.[20]

We know that Athanasius himself established four temples in Constantinople, of which two were monastic churches, like the Chora.[21] Although nothing of them is left we can assume that Athanasius was consistent with the austere attitude he expressed in his letter to Andronicus II,

15 *History of the Byzantine State*, tr. Joan Hussey (Oxford, 1956; rev. ed., Rutgers U. Press with illus.: New Brunswick, N.J., 1957), p. 486.

16 Vaticanus gr. 2219, fols. 72v–73r.

17 Vat. gr. 2219, fols. 71v–72v.

18 Ἐν ἄλλοις μὲν τὴν διαφορὰν τοῦ πλουτεῖν καὶ τοῦ πένεσθαι, ἐν δέ γε τοῖς πρὸς τὸ θεῖον, τὸν προθυμότερον πλουσιώτερον, Vat. gr. 2219, fol. 45.

19 Vat. gr. 2219, fol. 45v.

20 Calothetos, Life, ed. Athanasios, pp. 102–03; Theoktistos, Life, ed. Papadopoulos-Kerameus, pp. 37–38.

21 Theoktistos, Life, ed. Delehaye, p. 74; Calothetos, Life, ed. Athanasios, p. 95. Cf. R. Janin, *La géographie ecclésiastique de l'Empire byzantin*, I: *Le siège de Constantinople et le Patriarcat oecuménique*, Vol. III, *Les églises et les monastères* (Paris, 1953), pp. 14–15, 497, 518. The monastery of Christ, near the Xerolophos, where Athanasius retired and where he was buried, remained as one of the main centers of the Hesychast movement during the 14th century.

and did not decorate his buildings in the same magnificent fashion Metochites used at the Chora. Wealthy dignitaries and humanists, and not the Hesychast ascetics, had the necessary means, the necessary interest, and the necessary taste to become the promoters of what is called the "Palaeologan renaissance."

From examining the figures of Theoleptus and Athanasius, to whom Palamas refers explicitly as the main leaders of the Hesychast movement, we have gained some idea of the main trends of spirituality among the Byzantine monks of that time: sacramental realism, with a correlative interest in the affairs and structure of the visible historical church, individual perfection being unthinkable unless belonging to the visible society where the sacraments are performed; and austere puritanism, reflecting the eremitic origins of the movement, its lack of interest in material wealth, and its ascetic approach to life. Traditionally, the followers of this monastic trend were opposed to all attempts at reviving the ideas of pagan antiquity in the Byzantine world. However, as we have already seen, in the late thirteenth and early fourteenth centuries there were no signs of open friction between monks and humanists.

What, then, was the real nature of the conflict between Barlaam the Calabrian and Gregory Palamas, who began their great struggle in about 1337 and almost immediately focused their discussion on the meaning of ancient Greek philosophy and of pagan antiquity in general?

The mission of Barlaam, a Greek monk from southern Italy, who came to Constantinople in about 1330, searching in the Eastern world for the true fatherland of Aristotle and Plato, was to draw to a logical and daring conclusion certain presuppositions which many Byzantine humanists shared privately or implicitly. Since the writings of the ancient Greek philosophers are worthy of being [transcribed] and read, since schools and universities teach the ἐγκύκλιος παίδευσις extensively, since, therefore, ideas of classical antiquity are part of the all-human inheritance of wisdom, why not apply these ideas to theology and to the whole sphere of religion? Is it right to anathematize all the ideas of Plato, whom Michael Psellos has acknowledged as the greatest of all philosophers?

It has been thought and said that Barlaam came to Byzantium as an agent of papal policy and that he was a follower of Western scholasticism. Indeed, he was nothing of the sort. If he brought something fresh with him from Italy, it was a new spirit of fearless passion for antiquity, the spirit of the Italian Renaissance.

"Renaissance" is a word that has been used and abused in connection with Byzantine civilization. We are now accustomed to speak of the "Macedonian renaissance" of the ninth and tenth centuries and of the "Palaeologan renaissance" of the late thirteenth. And it is true that a new interest in antiquity was apparent during these periods, but this interest was not by any means sufficient to break the essential principles of medieval civilization, as the Italian Quattrocento was later to do. The Byzantines never *discovered* Plato and Aristotle: their conservative society never forgot that the late-Neoplatonic philosophers, such as Proclus or Porphyrius, were the last enemies of Christianity, that they were attacked by the Church Fathers of the fourth and fifth centuries, and that Theodosius' and Justinian's legislation suppressed the pagan universities, where pagan philosophy was taught as the final word of human knowledge. The Latin West, when it discovered Aristotle in the twelfth century and later when it revived the humanistic ideals of antiquity, was really converted to a new wisdom, whose pagan connotation was practically unnoticed or ignored. For the Byzantines, Greek antiquity was a part of their own past, expressed in their own language: they could not be *converted* to it. The rejection of paganism and the adoption of Christianity had been a slow and painful process throughout the fourth, the fifth, and even the sixth centuries. The struggle had left vivid memories and deep scars which excluded, in the following periods, any sudden return to the wisdom of ancient Greece.

This is true at least of Byzantine society taken as a whole. A few individuals appeared from time to time who had some feeling of nostalgia for the ancient "Hellas," but they could never break through the walls of the Christian, medieval, theocratic fortress of Byzantine civilization. The result of this situation was an obvious lack of creative vigor and organic outburst in what is called "Byzantine humanism." Artificially imitating the language of Plato or Demosthenes, ordering very costly copies of their writings, repeating their cosmological and methodological ideas, Byzantine intellectuals were, at the same time, fervent followers of the unchangeable rites of the church, under which these same ancient writers were anathematized, and occasionally were not reluctant to write very classical and orthodox theological treatises, which had no direct connection with their humanistic interests. These different and contradictory elements of Byzantine culture, put side by side as in an encyclopedia without any real synthesis, could not give birth to a cultural revolution similar to the Italian Renaissance. The Byzantine "renaissance" provoked slight changes in taste and in outlook, but the medieval patterns of mind were never really abandoned.

The mission of Barlaam the Calabrian was to break the fragile equilibrium on which Byzantine civilization was based, by drawing religious and theological conclusions from the premises admitted by many humanists and thus provoking the reaction of the church. For example, Barlaam was not afraid to proclaim, in letters addressed to Palamas, that a definite similarity existed between the writings of Pseudo-Dionysius the Areopagite and of the late Neoplatonists [22] and that therefore the ancient philosophers, in spite of their paganism, could be considered as "enlightened by God" because they "understood that God was inaccessible." [23] This double conclusion—"the philosophers are enlightened" and "God is inaccessible"—is the very basis of Barlaam's thought and of his conception of God-man relationships. The possibility of "enlightenment" of non-Christians meant practically that there was no essential difference between those who were in Christ, in the church, and shared in the redemptive grace, and those who achieved a high wisdom outside the Christian revelation. The idea of the "inaccessibility of God" corresponded in Barlaam's mind to an Aristotelian theory of knowledge, according to which the senses are the unique instrument leading to every "gnosis," including that of God; but, since God is an immaterial spirit and since our senses are unable to reach him, no knowledge of his being is possible at all. No apodictic reasoning is possible in theology. God remains ultimately out of human reach. The enlightenment of wise men, both in and outside the Christian church, is simply an act of God's omnipotence, and it does not imply any real communion between God and man.

This conception was altogether foreign to the tradition of the Eastern Fathers, who always insisted that real deification ("theosis") was accessible to man, and accessible precisely in Christ through his saving and redemptive act, and not outside the realm of redemption. It definitely went beyond the traditional Byzantine attitude toward the relationship between theology and ancient philosophy and practically promoted the idea of an autonomous realm of thought, where human knowledge could develop itself without the transforming power of grace and without any

---

22 *Barlaam Calabro: Epistole greche, i primordi episodici e dottrinari delle lotte esicaste*, ed. G. Schirò (Palermo, 1954), Ep. III, p. 298.
23 Ibid., Ep. I, p. 262.

religious sanction. On these points, Barlaam was certainly a Westerner and already a man of the Renaissance. On the other hand, his Platonic conception of the universe included a spiritualistic anthropology, according to which the ultimate aim of prayer and religion was a dematerialization of the human spirit and its liberation from the bonds of the flesh; this position led him to attack the Hesychast method of prayer, inasmuch as this method assumed the participation in the prayer of both soul and body.

The writings of Barlaam forced many Byzantine humanists to make a decisive choice, since they brought to a logical conclusion some of the ideas that, until this time, had somehow artificially coexisted with the rigid Byzantine orthodoxy. A striking example of this evolution may be brought in here. It relates to a minor point but happens to be singularly relevant to the Mariological iconography of the Chora, where the feast and the liturgy of the Presentation of the Virgin in the Temple play quite a special role. Nicephorus Gregoras, a pupil of Metochites, who in his younger days may have had something to do with the decoration of the Chora monastery, became in the second half of the fourteenth century the last leader of anti-Palamism in Byzantium. And we learn from his own *History* that, when he was imprisoned in the Chora for his opposition to the official church, he refused to take part in the celebration of the feast of the Presentation of the Virgin in the Temple. He speaks of the feast with scorn as being celebrated only by his "jailers." [24] This passage by Gregoras seems to imply that the Mariological iconography of the Chora was related to a very special celebration of the Presentation in the monastery, but it also shows what an evolution was going on in the minds of Byzantine humanists between the time when Metochites decorated the Chora and the later years of Gregoras. Another document specifies the reason for Gregoras' opposition to the feast: a prelate of the time, Philotheos of Selymbria, anathematizes Gregoras because he does not believe "that the Mother of God did really enter the Holy of Holies, since the Great Priest alone [in the Old Testament] used to enter it once a year." [25] The attitude of Gregoras was, therefore, that of a historical critic reluctant to admit, even as a religious symbol, any reality or legend not based on scientific experience. It is obvious that humanists of his kind were led, in connection with the controversies between Barlaam and Palamas, to break the medieval patterns which were still accepted in the time when Metochites decorated the Chora.

This evolution could not but provoke a violent protest from many ecclesiastics. It was very fortunate, then, that the Byzantine church found as her spokesman an eminent theologian, capable of fighting Barlaamism without falling into reactionary obscurantism and able to defend the only essential position of traditional Byzantine Christianity: that God, although unknown and inaccessible in his essence, is present and active in the world, in the whole of creation; that Christians, through sacramental communion, can be united with him and be really "deified," by making divine their own lives and by belonging to Christ's Body. This was the essential idea of Palamas' opposition to Barlaam and his followers. And it is worth noting here that he also wrote a whole treatise on the Presentation of the Virgin in the Temple and that one of his preserved sermons deals with the topic; according to his biographer, the Patriarch Philotheos, Palamas, in writing the treatise, had in view "those who dared to despise the mysteries of the

---

24 *Hist.*, XXIV.3, Bonn (1855), III, p. 3.

25 F. Miklosich and J. Müller, *Acta et Diplomata Graeca Medii Aevi Sacra et Profana*, I (Vienna, 1860), p. 490. The document looks like a paragraph of the Synodicon. It has no date, but it is signed by Philotheos, Metropolitan of Selymbria, who may have submitted it to the Synod as a projected addition to the anathemas against Barlaam and Akindynos. This would explain its presence among the *Acta* of the Patriarchate.

feast." [26] There is no doubt that ideas similar to those of Gregoras were known to Palamas when he wrote the treatise. There is not, however, the slightest attempt in his work to defend as such the historicity of the Virgin's life in the Temple, but only to stress its typological value, as an example of progressive purification and spiritual preparation for the Incarnation.

It is not possible here to deal extensively with all the issues involved in the controversy between Barlaam and Gregory Palamas. Therefore, I will mention only one doctrinal issue, which touches the very essence of the problem and at the same time is directly relevant to the problem of religious art: I mean the question of religious symbols.

One of the first arguments used by Barlaam against the Hesychasts was that God is an intelligible Essence and that no material vision of him is possible, except through symbols. This argument was directed mainly against Hesychast mystical experiences—their claim to see the "uncreated light" of Mount Tabor with their material eyes—but it was just as valid in other issues. Barlaam considered the light which appeared during Christ's Transfiguration as "a sensible light, visible through the air simply to induce wonder" in the disciples; if some of the Fathers called this light "deity," it was only because it was a symbol of deity.[27] The only possible way in which our body, our senses, and our material eyes can see God is by "imagining" him (τὸ φανταστικόν) [28] through material symbols. Akindynos and Nicephorus Gregoras, the later leaders of Byzantine anti-Palamism, although they differed from Barlaam on some doctrinal issues, held exactly the same ideas on the role of symbols, *as the only means for us to approach God.* For example, Akindynos likes to refer to the Old Testament visions in order to prove that every vision of God necessarily goes through a material symbol, accessible to our senses. The angels themselves can be seen only through symbols, because they are immaterial. The same idea is repeated by Nicephorus Gregoras: "We have a universal dogma of the church, revealed by our God and Savior, Jesus Christ, through his disciples: it is absolutely impossible to see God without the mediation of material symbols and types." [29] This symbolism of the anti-Palamitic theologians corresponds exactly to their Aristotelian approach to gnosiology and their refusal to accept the idea of a supersensual and supernatural—although not necessarily immaterial—way of knowing God.

It was not the first time in the history of Byzantium that the role of symbolism in religion had been at issue. The famous Canon 82 of the Trullan Council (692) had already specified that "types and symbols" were no longer the true objects of Christian worship and Christian experience: "Embracing, therefore, the ancient types and shadows as symbols of the truth," said the Canon, ". . . we prefer grace and truth, receiving it as the fulfillment of the Law." The Canon goes on to forbid the representation of Christ in the form of a lamb and prescribes that his representation be in true human form, "that we may recall to our memory his conversation in the flesh, his passion and salutary death, and his redemption which was brought for the whole world."

Although this 82nd Canon deals with only one specific iconographic pattern, which goes back to primitive Christianity, it uses an argument of general value: Christians do not need symbols when they have the reality itself. This is especially true of Old Testament symbols whose only

---

26 Philotheos, *Encomion*, PG, 151, col. 581C. The treatise was published among Palamas' homilies by S. K. Oikonomos, Τοῦ ἐν ἁγίοις πατρὸς ἡμῶν Γρηγορίου ἀρχιεπισκόπου Θεσσαλονίκης τοῦ Παλαμᾶ ὁμιλίαι ΚΒ' (Athens, 1861), pp. 131–80.

27 Quoted by Palamas in *Triades*, III.1.§11, ed. Meyendorff, p. 576.

28 Ep. IV, ed. Schirò, p. 315.

29 These and other similar texts of Akindynos and Gregoras are quoted in Meyendorff, *Introduction*, pp. 260–61.

meaning consists in pointing to New Testament realities. Is this principle on which the Canon is founded not applicable to any symbolic iconography, such as that of the parecclesion of the Chora?

The statement of the Council is, on the other hand, most probably connected with certain general tendencies in both the philosophical thought and the pictorial art of its own time. Thus, André Grabar has traced back to the sixth and seventh centuries some specific iconographical symbols, representing the Intelligible, and has connected them with the works of Pseudo-Dionysius and Maximus the Confessor.[30] And indeed recent studies on the Platonism of the Areopagite stress very clearly the central role played by symbolism in his conception of the relations between God and man: it is through symbols that God, invisible and unapproachable, reveals himself, and the sacrament of the Eucharist itself becomes a symbol of an intelligible union with an Intelligible God.[31] It was, therefore, only natural for Barlaam to present his own philosophy merely as a commentary on the unknown author, unanimously considered by Barlaam's contemporaries as "the great Dionysius," convert of St. Paul in Athens, who is mentioned in the Book of Acts.

Of course, Gregory Palamas also recognized the authority of Dionysius—and we know that this authority was highly regarded in the contemporary West as well—but the very fact that the Dionysian corpus was susceptible of various interpretations is proof that the central problems of a Christian Neoplatonism were not entirely solved by its author. Palamas, for his part, interpreted Dionysius in the tradition of St. Maximus the Confessor, applying to him a Christocentric corrective and practically eliminating all symbolism in conceiving of the relations between God and man. His very idea of "deification" implied not a symbolical but a real union—in Christ first, in a hypostatic sense, and then in all Christians by an act of God's grace. This act of grace, according to Palamas, gives to every Christian a new way of approaching God, a new power which is neither "sensual" nor "immaterial" but which implies that the whole man—body and soul—is transformed and thus becomes able to contemplate God in a new way. "How can we still have symbols again, again mirrors, again enigmas? How can a face-to-face vision become again an object of hope? If [the Kingdom of Heaven] is made again of symbols, of mirrors, and of enigmas, it means that our hopes were deceived, that we were outwitted by fallacies: hoping to *acquire* Divinity through the promise, we are not even allowed to see the Divinity, but only a sensible light, a nature absolutely foreign to Divinity." [32]

Admitting the traditional symbolical interpretation of the Old Testament theophanies, Palamas affirms that with the coming on earth of the Logos, after his Incarnation, an immediate vision and communion became accessible to man. "When the intellect becomes supra-celestial, as if it were the companion of [Christ], who ascended for our salvation above the heavens, when it is there united with God . . . and contemplates supernatural and mysterious visions, full of a sublime knowledge . . . , then it contemplates, not sacred symbols, not even the variety of Holy Scriptures, but it is embellished by the Beauty which is the source of all beauty, and it is illumined by the light of God." [33]

It is possible to find a great number of Palamite texts of the same kind, and they all tend to affirm the reality of God's presence through the Incarnation. "Before the Incarnation of the

30 A. Grabar, "La représentation de l'Intelligible dans l'art byzantin du moyen-âge," in *Actes du VIe Congrès International d'Etudes Byzantines*, II (Paris, 1951), pp. 127–43.

31 R. Roques, *L'univers dionysien: Structure hiérarchique du monde selon le Pseudo-Denys* (Paris, 1954), pp. 267–72.
32 *Triades*, III.1.§11, ed. Meyendorff, p. 579.
33 *Triades*, I.3.§5, ed. Meyendorff, p. 117.

Word of God," he proclaims, "the Kingdom of Heaven was far from us, as the heaven is distant from the earth (Ps. 103:11), but when the King of Heaven came to abide in us, when he agreed to be united with us, then the Kingdom of Heaven became near to us." [34] And, of course, "the body of Christ is really the body of God, not a symbol," as Palamas states in his treatises against Akindynos.[35]

It is therefore not difficult to measure the distance which separates Palamas from the Platonism of Dionysius the Areopagite. His doctrine was in the spirit of the Quinisext Council: the reality of the Incarnation, the truth of the deified flesh of Christ and of his Saints was at the center.

After the period of peaceful coexistence and the sudden violence of the controversy with Barlaam and his followers, the Hesychast tendency definitely won the battle in Byzantium at the Councils of 1347 and 1351. As I tried to show in the beginning, when speaking of the leading teachers of fourteenth-century Hesychasm, it was a triumph neither of an esoteric sect nor of systematic obscurantism, but of ecclesiastical zealots, of social reformers preaching poverty, and of religious maximalists denying to any non-Christian system of thought the chance to compete, in the minds of Christians, with Christ's revelation. Former Athonite monks, Isidoros, Callistos, Philotheos, occupied the patriarchal throne. The ascetic spirit, which Athanasius I had tried to promote, prevailed in the church. In this respect, the last will of Patriarch Isidoros, who died in 1350, is a symptomatic document. The personal property of this ecumenical patriarch consisted of one encolpion, a few clothes, and a small amount of oil and wine. All this was to be divided among the clerics, the sisters of a monastery—described as very poor—and the monks who lived with Isidoros in the patriarchate; and the two latter beneficiaries were themselves to give to "my brothers, the poor"—this is the expression of the Patriarch—a part of what they received.[36] This concern for the poor is also expressed in other parts of the will. The same concern is apparent in many of the activities of Patriarch Philotheos [37] and is very clearly proclaimed in the sermons of Gregory Palamas in Salonika. And if, on the other hand, we consider the whole Hesychast tradition as it developed in the Eastern church, penetrating Russia and the Balkan countries, this same ascetic and moralistic attitude, this same disdain for richly decorated churches, appears as a constant element of Hesychast spirituality.[38] Joined with the antisymbolical theological position of the Palamite school of thought, all this was certainly not very conducive to the development of a conception of art that called for not only iconographic symbolism but also rich donations for purely aesthetic purposes. We may notice here that, like Patriarch Athanasius I some forty years earlier, Palamas was accused of iconoclastic acts by his adversaries: he was supposedly an enemy "of the holy images, of the sacred vessels and of other adornments of Christianity" (τῶν ἁγίων εἰκόνων καὶ ἱερῶν σκευῶν καὶ τῆς ἄλλης χριστιανικῆς εὐταξίας).[39] More precisely, he was said to have profaned icons in the monastery of the Peribleptos in Constantinople.[40]

---

34 *Capita physica*, 56, *PG*, 151, col. 1161C.
35 VII.15, Paris. Coislinianus 98, fols. 195v–96r.
36 Miklosich and Müller, *Acta*, I, pp. 287–94.
37 Cf. Meyendorff, *Introduction*, p. 38.
38 In the Slavic lands, and more especially in Moscovite Russia, the repercussions of the Hesychast victory of 1351 were minimal on the level of theological speculation. There was no need there to fight against "Barlaamitic" humanism. Hesychast literature, reviving religious zeal and spirituality, as well as the pan-Orthodox social and political ideology of the monks who took control of the patriarchate of Constantinople (Patriarchs Callistos, Philotheos, and their Russian agents and friends)

contributed to the remarkable and genuinely original religious art, whose main representatives, in the late 14th century, were Theophanes the Greek and his disciple Andrei Rublev. On this development, see N. K. Goleizovsky, "Isikhazm i russkaia zhivopis' XIV–XV vv.," *VV*, 29 (1968), pp. 196–210, and G. M. Prokhorov, "Isikhazm i obshchestvennaia mysl' v Vostochnoi Evrope v XIV v.," *Akademia Nauk SSSR, Institut russkoi literatury, Otdel drevne-russkoi literatury, Trudy*, 23 (1968), pp. 86–108.
39 *Antipalamite Tome of 1347*, *PG*, 150, col. 884B.
40 Ibid., col. 882B; cf. also Gregoras, *Hist.*, XXIV.2, Bonn (1830), II, p. 1146.

Nowhere do we find, in the Hesychast literature of the time, any open criticism of the artistic style that prevailed in the early Palaeologan epoch, but it seems reasonable to suggest that the triumph of the Hesychasts, in the middle of the fourteenth century, did coincide with a change of taste in Byzantine society and did break the inner cultural impetus which was behind the thirteenth century.

This relatively easy victory did not altogether eliminate Byzantine humanism,[41] neither did it produce a real revolution in the field of art, but it showed again that there was in Byzantium no real ground for a true "renaissance." The interest in classical antiquity never extended beyond a rather closed circle of scholars and dignitaries, who may have led, for some time, the cultural progress of their generation but who were never able or willing to oppose an integrated and consistent "Weltanschauung" against the medieval patterns of mind. Byzantine society produced not a Petrarch, a Dante, or a Giotto, but rather a number of learned and skeptical encyclopedists, who could infuse new elements into existing traditions but not revolutionize their times or the minds of their contemporaries.[42] As long as these new humanistic elements were coexisting peacefully with tradition, the results could be very remarkable: and the Kariye Djami is an example, in the field of art, of what this degree of new humanistic blood could produce in the field.

But as soon as Byzantine humanism entered into conflict with the traditional patterns—and the conflict recurred throughout the career of Barlaam the Calabrian—its real weakness immediately became apparent, especially when it was confronted with an integrated, consistent, and balanced spirituality. This very consistency of Palamite thought explains its victory and its final and solid grasp on the masses of Eastern Christians.

On the doctrinal level, the controversy between Barlaam and Palamas was already an encounter between, on the one hand, the spirit of the Renaissance, the ideal of a humanity autonomous from God and thus establishing its life on earth by its own means, according to its own rules, and, more precisely, according to the eternal achievements of ancient Hellenism—and, on the other hand, the Christian doctrine of man deified, "a man made God because God became man," accepting, in his entire life and activity, the presence, the judgment, and the collaboration of God. It was well beyond the capabilities of the Byzantine humanists to promote consistently the first of these positions; they were actually far from the really revolutionary spirit which was in that very time reshaping the Western European world. The triumph of their adversaries was therefore inevitable.

This triumph, undoubtedly, had the negative aspect of arresting a development. But, we can still ask ourselves, Would this development have led very far? Was it in the power of the old Byzantine civilization to start a new page in the cultural history of humanity? And did not rather the victory of Hesychasm play an essentially positive role on a somehow different level by preserving consistently a few eternal values which helped the Eastern Christians to face the already unavoidable dark ages of their history?

41 See particularly D. M. Nicol, "The Byzantine Church and Hellenic Learning in the Fourteenth Century," *Studies in Church History*, V, ed. G. J. Cuming (Leiden, 1969), pp. 23–56.

42 The pedantic *jeux d'esprit* of the Byzantine intellectuals of the late 13th century are well described in J. Verpeaux,

Nicéphore Choumnos, homme d'état et humaniste byzantin (ca. 1250/1255–1327) (Paris, 1959), and especially in I. Ševčenko, *Etudes sur la polémique entre Théodore Métochite et Nicéphore Choumnos* (Brussels, 1962).

The Style of the Kariye Djami and its Place in the Development of Palaeologan Art

OTTO DEMUS

The following chapter was written in 1960. Nobody, least of all the author (who was the first to deliver his manuscript), thought then that so long a time would elapse before it would see the light of day. In the meantime, a good many books and papers, some of great importance, have been published on the subject of Palaeologan painting, which thus has become one of the most actively explored domains of the history of Byzantine art. A succession of other pressing obligations made it impossible, however, for the author to rewrite his contribution or even to incorporate in it the results of recent work. However, at the end of the chapter is a short list of the more important publications which have come out during the last few years and are not quoted in the text. While he believes that the broad lines of his study are still correct, the author is only too painfully aware that there are numerous details which will invite criticism.

O. DEMUS

The Style of the Kariye Djami and its Place
in the Development of Palaeologan Art

The Style of the Decoration of the Kariye

1. MOSAIC AND FRESCO

It will be shown in the accompanying studies that the mosaics and the frescoes of the Kariye Djami—excepting those of the tombs—must be regarded as more or less contemporary parts of a homogeneous program. Certain features common to both, certain idiosyncrasies and tricks of design, modeling, and coloring—like the giving of hook-shaped tips to garments, an oddity which looks almost like the personal signature of an individual designer;[1] the drawing of feet with heavy black shadows attached to them (Vol. 2, PL. 234, 241, 260; Vol. 3, PL. 355, 460), as if they were clad in sandals, with the necessary strings omitted; and several others, not to speak of common types of faces, architectures, and (rarely) ornamental motifs—point even to a close interrelation of the various workshops active in the church. In some cases, the mosaicists seem to have borrowed from fresco painters—if not from those of the parecclesion, at least from some of their predecessors: certain mosaic faces, especially those of a scale somewhat larger than that of the faces contained in scenic representations—faces of saints, for instance, show highlights in the shape of three to five parallel commas (PL. 18, 289), a "technique" which certainly originated in fresco (or icon painting) and not in mosaic. Another technique borrowed from fresco (or miniature painting?) is that of modeling through seemingly (in the fresco: actually) superimposed layers of three or even four shades. As a rule, however, mosaic and fresco employed fundamentally different means and effects. The mosaicists naturally produced their effects rather by employing color differentiations, the fresco painters more by contrasts and gradations of tone, so that the entire color scheme of the frescoes tends somewhat toward the monochrome. This gives to the frescoes on the one hand a certain monotony, on the other, perhaps, a greater homogeneity. The fresco painter could never compete with the many-hued brilliance of the mosaics; nor did he have occasion to use the mosaicists' technical refinements, such as the checkerboard pattern of minute tesserae, the alternating lines of variegated shades, the interlocked "tongues" of different colors—painterly techniques almost, akin to those of late nineteenth-century pointillism. He used, in their stead, the comparatively straightforward technique of superimposed layers, the lighter ones laid over the darker in sharply defined patterns and the highlights added last. Contemplating the role of the two techniques in the period of the Kariye, one cannot fail to realize that the subtle and complicated art of mosaic was, in a way, at the end

---

1 The hook-shaped ending is also found in the miniatures of Codex Sinaiticus 152, of 1346 (Evangelists, e.g., fol. 389v, our Fig. 48).

of its possibilities—was, actually, becoming outmoded, to be replaced by the simpler and less costly technique of fresco, which seems to have answered better the needs of the time.

Apart from the discrepancies inherent in the respective technical characters and historical situations of the two branches of Byzantine monumental painting, there are other, more subtle differences among the various parts of the Kariye decoration. The fact that this decoration was carried out according to one general concept does not necessarily mean that the various parts were made at exactly the same time. It is, on the contrary, quite logical to assume that there was a certain sequence in the actual making of the mosaics and the frescoes, the mosaics of the nave having been completed first, those of the narthexes second, and the frescoes of the parecclesion third. The plausibility of this suggested sequence is actually borne out by a comparison of figures of related iconographic character and function. The templon icon of the Virgin, forming part of the decoration of the nave (PL. 329), shows a figure of statuesque dignity, full of a deeply moving, quiet expression. The modeling of the calm and tender face is evenly rounded, almost sculptural in effect. Compared with this figure, that of a standing Virgin on the east wall of the outer narthex (PL. 316) seems considerably flatter, with a less continuous, less suggestive modeling, more mannered as regards the drapery, and somewhat empty as regards the very refined face. Finally, the fresco Virgin in the bema of the parecclesion (PL. 486) is more agitated than the others and still flatter in the modeling, with an emphasis on broken and zigzag lines, splintered, almost abstract shapes, and jagged highlights.

It will be seen later on that this change from a rounded, continuous modeling and a curvilinear design to flat schemes produced by straight lines and abstract shapes is a typical change seemingly telescoping the development of Palaeologan painting within the space of a few years. The intensive work in the Kariye created, apparently, something like hothouse conditions, which speeded up the development of a style which in any case must have been in a critical phase at the time of the decoration.

2. THE CANONS OF THE PALAEOLOGAN STYLE

The Palaeologan style has been appraised in widely different manners according to the various standpoints of the authors who have dealt with early fourteenth-century painting. Some scholars consider it as the beginning of a new art, others as the end of an old one; some call it neo-Hellenistic [2] and see in it the continuation of a movement that began as early as the twelfth century, others believe that it was a recent and rapid growth, the outcome of one of the great revolutions in the realm of Byzantine art.[3] Discrepancies similar to those in the various conceptions of the Palaeologan style in general exist also with regard to the mosaics and frescoes of the Kariye in particular. Quite apart from the widely differing evaluations of the works themselves, as copies of earlier cycles on the one hand [4] or as highly personal and entirely independent creations on the other, their style has been variously labeled "classicist"[5] or "academic," "baroque" or "mannerist";[6] scholars have sometimes stressed their dramatic, sometimes their intimate character; sometimes their realism, sometimes their decorative qualities. The

2 P. Muratoff, *La peinture byzantine*, tr. J. Chuzeville (Paris, 1928), pp. 117 ff., 127 ff., 146 ff.

3 G. A. Soteriou, "Die byzantinische Malerei des XIV. Jahrh. in Griechenland," Ἑλληνικά, 1 (1928), p. 100.

4 F. Shmit, Kakhriè-Džami (=*Izvestija Russkogo Arxeologičeskogo Instituta v Konstantinopolě*, 11), I (Sofia, 1906), passim, esp. pp. 156 ff.

5 M. Alpatov, "Die Fresken der Kachrie Djami in Konstantinopel," *Münchner Jahrbuch der bildenden Kunst*, 6 (1929), pp. 345 ff.

6 F. Shmit, "La 'renaissance' de la peinture byzantine au XIVᵉ siècle," *RA*, 4th series, Vol. 20 (July–Dec. 1912), pp. 127 ff.

mosaics—there has not yet been much discussion of the frescoes—have by some authorities been counted among the characteristic examples of the "Macedonian" school, by others among those of the "Cretan."[7] The explanation of this curious lack of conformity in the assessment of the Palaeologan style in general and that of the Kariye in particular is to be found in the complexity of this art.

Palaeologan art transcends in every possible way the canons of the hieratic art of medieval Byzantium, from which it stems, and those of Hellenistic art, to which it is connected by one of the many revivals of the Greek past which were such an important element in Byzantine life and art. At first glance it seems, indeed, as if Palaeologan art had no acknowledged canons whatsoever; as if the painters of this period had simply preferred the abnormal to the normal, the distorted to the regular, the chaotic to the harmonious. On closer scrutiny, however, one discovers the existence of a canon of taste no less well defined than that of the art of European Mannerism as against the art of the Renaissance.[8]

A careful analysis of the mosaics and frescoes of the Kariye will show, it is hoped, that this canon was also valid for them.

3. THE FIGURE STYLE OF THE KARIYE

A. Heads and Faces

The wide range of possibilities within the framework of this canon can be seen, to begin with, in the faces of the mosaic and fresco figures; they represent a great number of types, from Hellenistic elegance to grotesque oddity. Some of the warrior saints are thoroughly typical of the first category: they even recall works like the mosaics of Daphni[9] or the frescoes of Nerezi.[10] Their vigor and their gracefulness are reminiscent of the best products of the Comnenian revival. There are, however, other figures in which Greek "beauty" has turned into a somewhat empty prettiness: most angels and all the maidens who accompany the youthful Virgin (PL. 123, 134) show stereotyped faces, composed of minute features, which are rather doll-like and insipid.

In another variety of "beautiful" heads, the traditional types are interpreted in a hard and smooth manner, the egg-shaped faces with their large, overmodeled features being treated somewhat like ivory carvings (PL. 501). The suggestive force of this modeling is so strong that, for instance, the hair and beard of Christ Chalkites in the Deesis appear to be only an outer layer of the hard, smooth substance of which the face seems to consist. Similar smooth and hard forms are to be found among the angels of the parecclesion dome and the angels and apostles of the Last Judgment (PL. 376). These types of faces, harking back to Hellenistic models, are not the only ones to adhere to old traditions. The portraits too follow earlier prototypes, but their models were of an entirely different kind. They are to be sought among the purely linear, flat designs of the Comnenian period, like the portraits of John II and Irene in the Hagia Sophia.[11] It is an odd but incontestable fact that the portrait faces of Isaac Comnenus (PL. 37 a), Melane (PL.

7 In regard to the use of these terms see O. Demus, "Die Entstehung des Paläologenstils in der Malerei," *Berichte zum XI. Internationalen Byzantinisten-Kongress, München, 1958,* IV,2 (Munich, 1958), pp. 8 ff.

8 Ibid., pp. 12 ff.

9 Compare E. Diez and O. Demus, *Byzantine Mosaics in Greece: Hosios Lucas and Daphni* (Cambridge, Mass., 1931),

Figs. 56, 57 (Joel, Micah), with the Kariye's St. Sabas Stratelates (PL. 500).

10 O. Bihalji-Merin, *Fresken und Ikonen: Mittelalterliche Kunst in Serbien und Makedonien* (Munich, 1958), PL. 21.

11 Th. Whittemore, *The Mosaics of Haghia Sophia at Istanbul: Third Preliminary Report, The Imperial Portraits of the South Gallery* (Oxford, 1942), PL. 26, 31.

37 b), and Theodore Metochites (PL. 28) are the most traditional and the least "realistic" of all the faces represented in the mosaics and frescoes of the Kariye. Their designs are purely conceptual: they show hardly any plastic modeling and not the smallest trace of personal characterization. The force of fashion was apparently so strong that it admitted of hardly any differentiation of the masks, except for variations in the form of hair, beard, and eyebrows, variations which were themselves dictated by fashion. Thus, the main difference between the portraits of Isaac and Metochites lies in the fact that the latter is presented with orientalizing features and a hat of contemporary fashion, while the Comnenian scheme of the posthumous portrait of Isaac has not been modified by that taste. All the types mentioned so far may be classed as traditional—Hellenistic or aulic. There are, however, others which could be called specifically Palaeologan. These are all distinguished by the fact that some parts of the faces seem to have been overemphasized or deformed compared with "Hellenistic" types. Some heads are topped by very high "toupees" so that they look much larger and higher than normal (PL. 298, 304); in other cases the occiput is jutting out like a monstrous excrescence (PL. 322); bulbous foreheads stand in curious contrast to receding chins (PL. 323, beardless figure in center); noses are either too long, too thick, or too short, cut away in obtuse angles, recalling some faces in the paintings of El Greco (PL. 209). The characteristics of old age, of youth, of illness are exaggerated: old men are represented as Methuselahs, youths as children. With all this, the attempts of the painters or mosaicists at rendering psychological moods, at lending specific expression to the faces of figures involved, actively or passively, in some critical situation, do not seem to have come off: the expression, for instance, of the Virgin in the scene of Joseph Taking Leave (PL. 149), or that of Joseph's son in the same mosaic (PL. 150), can hardly be interpreted in any specific way. Other faces show a similar unspecified "concern" or an expression of seeming distrust, with the eyes half averted or looking at their objects obliquely; this expression (if it is an expression) of uneasiness and suspicion, mingled with a certain veiled appeal to the beholder, may, indeed, be called the characteristic psychic habitus of painted figures in Palaeologan art, just as the "archaic smile" was the typical "expression" in Greek and early Gothic sculpture.

In a very few cases we find a realistic approach to expression or psychological characterization: blindness, for instance, is not rendered through the emptiness of the glance alone; the cast and the expression of the face itself suggest it in an astonishingly convincing way (PL. 263). Another impressive example of realism is the deeply lined, sorrowful face of the widow beseeching Christ to resuscitate her son (PL. 362). But in almost all these cases expression is being produced not so much by distorting or, at least, adjusting otherwise normal features but by selecting and representing an expressive type, a "habitus," suggesting, for instance, sorrow through haggard, deeply furrowed faces, joy through youthful, rounded ones.

In addition to choosing an adequate type, the mosaic and fresco masters had yet another means of fitting the faces of their figures to the required contexts: they varied the carriage, the position of the heads with regard to the vertical and the horizontal axes to a much greater degree than this had ever been done before; thus they exploited the different effects produced by a raised or by a lowered head and combined these attitudes with raised or lowered glances, sometimes joining them crosswise, that is, by depicting, for instance, a lowered head with eyes looking upward. The oddest effects of this kind are to be found in The Torments of the Damned, where there are heads in all possible and impossible attitudes, including one upside down (PL. 401). As regards the turning of heads round the vertical axis, the most frequent projections are still the three-quarter view and the full face; but the profile, rather rare in pre-Palaeologan times, is appearing much more frequently than ever before, although confined, as usual, to secondary figures in narrative scenes.[12] The fact that the profile is used more often does not, however, mean that the artists succeeded any better in the designing of it. In most cases the profile view was rendered by cutting away the averted side of a face in three-quarter view (PL. 101, 144, 178); in others, the pursed lips and the chin are jutting out very strongly, giving to the faces a snout-like appearance. In such "profiles" even the modeling goes entirely wrong: dark red lines cut up the faces in an almost absurd way, so that the result looks thoroughly inhuman (PL. 169).

Among the strangest products of the designers' tendency to break through the old established rules of monumental painting are the mosaicists' attempts at representing faces in "lost profile." Most of the few examples, all rather grotesque, are in the southern part of the outer narthex (PL. 179, 187, 193); nothing of the kind is to be found in the fresco cycle. The completely misunderstood form in which these "lost profiles" are represented seems to argue for their having been copied from rather distant models.

B. Hands

There is a certain difference between the treatment of hands in the mosaics and that in the frescoes. In the narthexes and especially in the nave, in the templon icons, the hands are designed and modeled as a rule in an organic way, curvilinear, pliable, and expressive (PL. 320). In the frescoes, on the other hand, (and in some mosaics) they are often devoid of innervation, looking like forks, the prongs widely and sharply separated from each other (PL. 351). This is especially noticeable where the backs of the hands are seen. One odd projection of the fist is found in both mosaics and frescoes: in some instances it looks as if the designer had forgotten to separate the fingers or at least to indicate the knuckles; but what he really aimed at was something akin to the lost profile of the face, a kind of lost profile of the fist (PL. 295, 481).

C. Feet

As characteristic of the Palaeologan style as the fork-like hands are certain ways of designing feet. Feet of two such types are to be found in the Kariye side by side: very slender, almost "Gothic" shod feet, which are the rule in frontal figures, especially single saints in quiet attitudes (PL. 294, 295, 304, 306 b); and, secondly, curiously misshapen bare feet, which look somewhat like flatirons (PL. 215, 254, 256). This variety of the club foot occurs most frequently in profile or three-quarter figures taking part in narrative scenes; it is high, broad, tumescent, the toes drawn in; the thin legs are stuck into the feet, as it were, without ankles or other articulation.

D. Proportion and Anatomy

The figures in both frescoes and mosaics are, with few exceptions, very tall and slender. Their rather small heads make them appear even more so. This is especially marked in some single figures, e.g., the Church Fathers and the warrior saints, not to mention the angels and the forefathers of Christ and the Virgin in the domes. These latter figures were lengthened (and rendered especially long-legged) partly in order to counteract perspective foreshortening, as was the rule already in middle-Byzantine monumental art.[13] Seated and enthroned figures, on the other hand, like the Enthroned Christ of the *ktetor*'s image or the Apostles of the Last Judgment

---

12 O. Demus, *Byzantine Mosaic Decoration: Aspects of Monumental Art in Byzantium* (London, 1948), p. 8.
13 Ibid., pp. 30 ff.

(PL. 27, 376), have long upper bodies and comparatively short legs. These are the general rules that govern the proportions of the figures in the Kariye, quite in contrast to a great number of Palaeologan manuscripts, the figures of which tend to be short and squat, with large heads.[14] There is, however, one image in the Kariye the proportions of which are quite different from those of the rest, namely the Christ Chalkites in the Deesis (PL. 36), which has a long upper body and legs so extremely short that it looks downright disproportionate. If this effect was caused by the desire of the artist to counteract the perspective foreshortening of the upper half of the huge figure by making it very long (and the legs relatively short), the device was certainly not successful, mainly because the figure can be viewed not only from directly opposite and underneath, where the appearance is actually almost normal, but also obliquely, with an almost grotesque result; the more so since the figure has extremely broad, bottle-shaped hips, which make it look somewhat feminine. The broadness of the hips is, as a matter of fact, not confined to this figure; it is almost the rule for toga-clad walking or bending figures in near-profile. Christ in the miracle scenes of the mosaics; Moses, Jacob, and the Levites in the frescoes; and many other figures (PL. 438, 444, 455) are not narrowed at the waist; the back contour is bulging out rather than showing a waistline. This line gives to the figures a rather comic resemblance to fishes or performing seals, a resemblance which is heightened in the frescoes by the shiny, "wet" effect of the modeling (PL. 455), and in some standing figures by the fact that the garments are drawn tightly together around the knees (PL. 97, 156).

Curiously enough, female figures are hardly affected by this "fashionable" deformation. Babies are usually stocky, healthy creatures; children too are rather sturdy, almost Herculean (PL. 214). One of the Magi is fashioned like a child (PL. 173); so are the naked "souls" in the Last Judgment. One might speak of a certain "puttifying" tendency (PL. 386). The naked souls show little enough understanding of functional anatomy; still less is to be found in the nude figures in The Torments of the Damned (PL. 398). The most unrealistic and inorganic figures are, however, those of the evil spirits in the Last Judgment, who are leading the souls to Hell (PL. 389). They are sketched in with a few white strokes only, scribbles that look almost like consciously funny caricatures.

E. Movement

From the few nudes one gains the impression that the designers were somewhat at a loss when dealing with the human body "in the raw." They needed garments and draperies in order to convey structure, attitudes, movement, and actions. They certainly did not conceive of figures in motion by imagining them as nudes and clothing them in garments afterwards, so to speak, as was the rule in Classical and Renaissance art. The fully draped figure was for these mosaicists and fresco painters a homogeneous entity. Only by means of the draped figure could they express what they had to express. Speed and intensity of movement, expressiveness of postures and attitudes appear to be much heightened in comparison with earlier painting. One might even speak of a certain functional realism if it were not for the fact that all the movements and attitudes are typified, even theatrical. The effect can be heroic, as in the figures of the Angel slaying the Assyrians (PL. 464) and of Christ liberating Adam and Eve from Hades (PL. 343); energetic, as in the rushing movement of Joachim in the Blessing of the Priests (PL. 110); psychologically

---

14 E.g., the miniatures of Paris, Bibliothèque Nationale gr. 54; see H. Omont, *Miniatures des plus anciens manuscrits grecs* *de la Bibliothèque Nationale du VIe au XIVe siècle* (Paris, 1929), PL. XC–XCVI.

intense, as in the figures of Adam and Eve in the Anastasis (PL. 342), of the Widow pleading for her son (PL. 361), and of Joseph and his sons with the Virgin in the scenes illustrated in Plates 143 and 148. Compared with those in earlier paintings the movements of all these figures seem to be intensified or accelerated. In order to enhance this effect, the artists distorted at times the anatomy of the figures. The miracle-working Christ, for instance, is represented in near-profile as far as the body is concerned, while the face is rendered in a three-quarter view, and fitted with an extremely long neck, in fact a sort of "horse neck," in order to bring the head as much forward as possible and to suggest with this the direction in which the "emanation of will power" is functioning (PL. 273, 279). For the same reason arms and hands are lengthened (PL. 273).

Some of the movements depicted are highly complex, like that of Joseph as he turns in his stride to look back at the Virgin in the scene of Joseph Taking the Virgin to His House (PL. 144), or of Joseph's son in the scene of Joseph Taking Leave of the Virgin (PL. 150), or of Christ in the scene of the Woman with the Issue of Blood (PL. 269); all these movements could be described in similar words but are entirely different from one another in the actual representation. Not in every case has the artist succeeded: some figures, like that of Joseph (PL. 144), look grotesquely wrong. A few secondary figures are presented in back view, seated (Mothers Mourning Their Children, Multiplication of Loaves, PL. 195, 239) or standing (Herod Inquiring of the Priests and Scribes, PL. 177): the latter are quite frequent in the Herod cycle, where there is also the greatest number of profile figures (PL. 192, 193). The "tour-de-force" character of these figures is clearly apparent in the scene of Herod Inquiring of the Priests and Scribes (PL. 177): Herod himself is seen almost from the back, with his face in profile; the guard standing behind his throne is also represented in back view, with lost profile, but is turning away from Herod. It is quite clear that the designer was not able to arrange the two back views in a rational spatial relationship but was so taken with this new possibility of projection that he did not mind getting lost in the tangle of directions. It will be seen later on that this and other compositions of the Herod cycle do not go back to earlier models but were made up by the designer of the mosaics himself, who snatched this opportunity for introducing the most modern and most recherché figure schemes. This approach, and the manner in which traditional attitudes are being deformed in order to make them more intense, more expressive, and more histrionic, is highly characteristic of the phase in the development of Byzantine art which the mosaics and frescoes of the Kariye illustrate.

F. Costume and Drapery

The "fashionable" and the artificial elements naturally come to the foreground in the treatment of dress—much more, by the way, in the mosaics than in the frescoes. Many recent fashions are to be found—for instance, in the costume of the donor Metochites (PL. 28) and in that of the saint wearing a mantle with empty sleeves (PL. 311). What is even more remarkable is that contemporary fashions invade also narrative representations: Cyrenius, in the Enrollment for Taxation (PL. 160), wears a headgear similar to that of Metochites; and some of the women, for instance one of the temple maidens in the Presentation of the Virgin (PL. 123), show the contemporary fashion of wearing the cloak drawn over the head and tied in a knot above the forehead.[15] Curious details are the colored shawls worn by some of the Old Testament personages

15 A similar fashion is depicted in the one original mosaic of the façade and in the scenes of the Moses cycle in the narthex of San Marco, Venice. See S. Bettini, *Mosaici antichi di San Marco a Venezia* (Bergamo [1944]), PL. XC, LXXXIX.

in the parecclesion (e.g., the last of the figures accompanying King Solomon before the Ark in PL. 459); others (the first figure in the same group) are distinguished by a stripe across the chest; clavi of a shape that is to be met with in early Christian and in Macedonian works also make their appearance (last figure with Solomon, mentioned above, PL. 459; one of the Levites carrying the Ark, PL. 455). The most fantastic elements occur again in the Herod cycle, especially headdresses, helmets, pieces of armor, etc. (PL. 184, 190).

Most of the figures, however, are clad in traditional "classical" garb. But even these garments are often arranged in an unusual, and sometimes in a fantastic, way. The toga is very often "turned up" at the bottom seam, the turned part looking like a scarf slung around the legs (PL. 138, 166, 364); in other figures the toga is worn as a kind of double cape, with ample zigzag folds at the back (PL. 460). The hook-shaped tips of hanging folds and ends have already been mentioned as well as the empty sleeves of mantles. An especially odd feature is hands and arms wrapped in garments and appearing like amputated stumps: one of the most eccentric examples is the left arm of Eve in the Anastasis (PL. 347).

Flying folds and ends are frequently shaped as shells open in front, sometimes with contours in zigzag and hooked tips (PL. 219). These devices, truly Palaeologan features, contrast oddly with genuinely classical features like the arched, flying veils that frame some heads like huge haloes (PL. 104). Especially richly varied are the antique costumes of the ancestors of Christ in the southern dome of the inner narthex (PL. 46 ff.). The thirty-nine figures show hardly any repetition in motif or syntax, and hardly any of these figures are presented as a symmetrical design. Everywhere we meet with unexpected accents, complications, and odd configurations of folds. Taken all in all, the mosaic decoration of the dome can be regarded as the supreme test of the designer's imaginative force.

G. Modeling

The extremely complicated design of the garments is realized neither through form-delineating lines nor through continuous modeling. Properly speaking, there are no purely linear elements at all, excepting seams and contours; all specific surface differentiation consists of broken and splintery forms, sometimes so elongated as to appear almost as lines, in other cases polygonal. There are few curves—they are more frequent in the mosaics than in the frescoes; most of the "strokes" are straight or angular, and they are usually pointed; groups of tongue-shaped splinters form interlocking combs, bundles of near-lines produce a plissé effect, "rays" issuing from white patches suggest "exploding" lights. The resulting shapes are often very bizarre, but they are never boring. Folds are never "rolls" stuck onto general shapes that existed without them; they are part of the whole, facets of richly differentiated bodies. The relief of the figures is achieved not so much by continuous modeling as by the bold juxtaposition of different, sometimes complementary, colors and tones: in both mosaics and frescoes we encounter the means and effects of optical illusionism. Only the heads are modeled in a seemingly continuous way, but even there the neighboring tones and colors are set down side by side without proper grading, except in the very large heads, where grading and blending of colors are achieved through checkered or tongue-shaped interpenetrations (PL. 40, 41).

The relief of the figures is heightened by a certain way of lighting, which in many instances goes so far as to present one side of the figure in light colors liberally splashed with white while the other is merged in half or total shadow, so that the figure can be said to be lit from one side

(PL. 57, center). In the majority of the cases, however, the light seems to fall on the figures from the front, lighting up the middle axis and vanishing into half-shadows at the contours. The light along the central axis of the figures is almost always broken up into abstract parts, which, however, fit together like pieces of a puzzle so as to produce a distinct, if discontinuous, strip of light. This gives to the figures a gleaming appearance, which on the one hand enhances the effect of roundness and on the other makes the figures less heavy, less material. In certain cases these figures assume a kind of vitreous quality, which goes very well with the actual substance of the mosaics and which endows the frescoes with a certain transparency (PL. 109, 119, 369, 438, 451).

In the faces, white lights appear as a series of commas on forehead or cheek—a technique that has been called "Cretan" and that appears in both mosaics and frescoes together with modeling practices that have been dubbed "Macedonian;" both kinds of modeling seem to have had their origin in Constantinopolitan art.

It is, perhaps, not astonishing that in this art in which illusionistic practices play such an important part there should also be proper cast shadows, as, for instance, in the large bust of Christ above the door from the outer to the inner narthex, where there is an oblique shadow cast by chin and beard onto the neck (PL. 18).

Generally speaking, the mosaicists of the Kariye went further in the direction of illusionism than the fresco painters of the parecclesion: there is a kind of "openness" in their handling of forms, a certain sketchiness in their technique, which might appear as ruggedness, were it not for the small scale of the works concerned. As a matter of fact this sketchiness is to be found in the small-scale mosaics only; in the large figures (especially in the Deesis, PL. 36), we find rather a certain slickness and smoothness, produced by the all too regular texture of the small tesserae. The frescoes of the parecclesion stand midway between these two extremes: the technique is free enough to show the brushwork, but the strokes, patches, and dots have regular, one might even say conventional, forms. Some of the shapes and lights seem to suggest the greatest rapidity of execution, though they were actually produced in a rather careful technique—an indication that what was wanted was not real sketchiness but only the appearance of it,[16] a "stylized" sketchiness, so to speak. The best parallels and, indeed, the models for all these illusionistic practices can be found not in Comnenian but in Macedonian and late-antique painting.

H. Spatial Projection of Figures

It was in Palaeologan art for the first time that human bodies were presented from viewpoints other than "normal." In the Kariye, there are figures (or parts of figures) that are seen as if from above, and others that are seen as if from below. The angle of projection is sometimes very steep, as in the pendentives of the parecclesion, where the feet and legs of the Hymnographers are seen as if from above and projected onto the footstools (PL. 426, 429, 430, 433). The dome provides a mild example of the reverse projection: the dalmatic of one of the angels is so projected that it can be seen into from below (PL. 422). Much more impressive examples can be found among the mosaic figures—for example a saint in court costume (PL. 311) and some ancestors of Christ and the Virgin (Joseph, Issachar, PL. 62, 60; Mishael, Daniel, PL. 80), figures whose garments are designed so strongly *di sotto in sù* that the lower hems are presented as ellipses and the garments themselves as tubes open at the bottom. This approach would seem to be something quite

---

16 See Fr. Gerke, "Das Problem des 'Vollendeten' und die Unmöglichkeit des 'Unvollendeten' in der byzantinischen Kunst," *Das Unvollendete als künstlerische Form*, A Symposium, J. A. Schmoll gen. Eisenwerth, ed. (Bern and Munich, 1959), pp. 13 ff.

singular in an art that knew perspective only in the Greek sense of corrections, of preventive distortions,[17] an art for which space existed only outside the picture (as real space, intervening between the picture and the beholder), never "behind" the picture plane. However, the anomaly is not as great as it seems. The figures subject to these novel practices of projection, apart from the fact that they are few, are without exception *single* figures, never figures in scenic compositions. These single figures can be regarded as "existing" in the same space as the beholder, like statues, without being shut off from this real space by an imaginary picture plane. Furthermore, these odd projections do not concern the entire figures but only parts of them. The figure of Joseph (PL. 62), for instance, is given in absolutely normal projection as regards the main part of the body; it is only the lower hem of the garment that is designed *di sotto in sù*. The same is true of the other figures "seen from below" and, conversely, of the Hymnographers, whose legs and feet are "seen from above" while the upper parts of their bodies are rendered in normal, orthogonal projection. This discrepancy of projection in one and the same figure creates such great stresses that some of the figures appear to be actually disjointed at the hips, especially seated figures like the Hymnographer shown in Plate 429, so that it is difficult to imagine how body and thighs fit together.

4. REPRESENTATION OF ARCHITECTURE

The elements of architectural representation in the mosaics and frescoes of the Kariye are treated, without exception, as "exteriors," that is, as though seen from outside, although the motifs themselves, baldachins, apses, niches, etc., are derived from interiors, including furniture. Thus, we do not find those box-shaped rooms which are so often to be met with in late antique and in Italian Duecento art. In the Kariye, as in earlier Byzantine painting, the fact that a scene is to be imagined as taking place in an interior is indicated by curtains or hangings draped or stretched over or between individual architectural elements.

These individual elements differ essentially, in some respects, from those occurring in earlier Byzantine works: compared with the latter, they have more substance, a certain materialness, and a certain spatial quality. The simplest elements are walls and upright blocks, the latter often perforated by slits, windows, or doors. They are frequently roofed over and thus are characterized as towers or houses. The more complicated of these "houses" send out oblique wings, or terraces; balconies on consoles or columns are attached to some; others are provided with stairs, baldachins, apses, niches, or domes. Some of the structures are quite absurdly complicated —architectural fantasies the only "real" thing about which is their material character (PL. 93).

In addition to these "houses" we find sprawling and spreading configurations or scaffoldings composed of walls, columns, and shapeless architraves (PL. 109); airy baldachins and porches standing by themselves and leading nowhere (PL. 119, 126). The greatest number of structures have the shape of niches of one form or another, rectangular or semicircular. Some of them contain slits in otherwise massive blocks (PL. 135, 177), others have open doors (PL. 138); they all show that the designers were thoroughly, and helplessly, obsessed with the problem of enclosed space in its contrast with open space. Quite remarkable in this respect is the inability of the designers to correlate the exteriors of these structures with what little is visible of their

---

17 Cf. Demus, *Byzantine Mosaic Decoration*, pp. 30 ff. and 90, n. 1; on the classical use of "eurhythmic" corrections see E. Panofsky, "The History of the Theory of Human Proportions as a Reflection of the History of Styles," reprinted in his *Meaning in the Visual Arts* (Garden City, N.Y., 1955), pp. 62 ff.

interiors. One of the most striking examples of this inability concerns the exedra in the mosaic depicting the Virgin Receiving the Skein of Purple Wool (PL. 130). This exedra is really meant to form a kind of monumental back to the curved throne-bench of the three priests. But the curve of the bench is much flatter than that of the exedra—it looks as if the bench had slipped out of the exedra or as if the exedra were made of a springy substance and had contracted, detaching itself from the bench. In any case, this incompatibility of the two parts shows that in Byzantine architectural representation interiors were not considered "inhabitable" by human figures. The figures were taken out of these narrow enclosures and placed in a more comfortable spatial ambient in front of the empty shells. The incompatibility of interiors and exteriors is not the only one inherent in the architectural representations of the Kariye: another is the seemingly complete lack of coordination in the projection of two or more architectural units in the same composition. There are pictures in which all these units may be seen from below, others in which all may be seen from above; but in most compositions the high and the low viewpoints are employed side by side, so that of two adjacent structures one may be shown *di sotto in sù*, the other *di sopra*. The Virgin Receiving the Skein of Purple Wool is again a case in point: the exedra on the left is seen from above, the "slotted" structure on the right from below. Rational optics cannot have provided the reason for this diversity, in the form either of perspective or of eurythmy in the classical sense, since both kinds of projection appear at the same height or distance from the eye of the beholder; they are even to be found immediately adjoining, as in the composition of Joseph Reproaching the Virgin (PL. 151). One might even say that the mixing of the two projections in one composition was the rule, and consistency (in the modern sense) the exception. As a matter of fact, the choice of viewpoint was not a representational but a purely compositional matter.

This matter is, of course, intimately connected with the general function of the architectural elements in the Kariye mosaics and frescoes.[18] Compared with earlier representations, those of the Kariye are thronged with architectural motifs. There are compositions (e.g., PL. 148) in which every figure has its own architectural background, as it were, which not only provides emphasis and relief but also gives resonance to the movements and to the gestures of the figures. The simplest motif is a sheltering niche; this concept can be widened, as in the scene of the First Seven Steps of the Virgin (PL. 104), where the two adults, St. Anne and the maid, are placed below two tower-like structures, which jut out on either side, while the Virgin is enfolded in the niche created by the receding walls. The normal architectural accompaniment of a "dialogue" consists of two separate structures rising like canopies above the two main figures and turned toward each other obliquely, in three-quarter views that parallel the three-quarter profiles of the figures. The two motifs are often connected by a low wall—see, for example, the Enrollment for Taxation (PL. 159). The principle of parallelism of figures and architectural motifs is in most cases carefully observed: the structures in the Birth of the Virgin, for instance, echo exactly the near-profile of St. Anne and the almost frontal attitude of Joachim (PL. 98). Where there is only one dominant direction of movement, as in the Flight into Egypt (PL. 182), Christ Taken to Jerusalem for Passover (PL. 206), or Herod Ordering the Massacre of the Innocents (PL. 184), the pictures contain only one architectural motif, or one cluster of motifs; in such scenes the motif is the source or the goal of the movement.

18 Cf. V. N. Lazarev, *Istorija vizantijskoj živopisi*, I (Moscow, 1947), pp. 214 ff.; Alpatov, "Die Fresken der Kachrie Djami," pp. 345 ff.

The particular shape of any given motif is conditioned by a number of factors, from the iconographical to the purely compositional. Naturally, the palace of Herod would have to look somewhat different from the house of Joseph, although this kind of differentiation is not as consistent as might be expected. One of the most interesting factors is the one which is connected with the mechanism and the psychological motivation of an action, a happening. There are "active" and there are "passive" motifs, expansive and shrinking ones, some which are connected with the source and others, with the goal of a movement. One could not, for instance, exchange the two architectural motifs in the Virgin Receiving the Skein of Purple Wool (PL. 131): the slotted tower on the right accompanies quite clearly the direction of the movement, while the exedra on the left serves as a terminus, in front of which the cortège of the maidens comes to a halt.

However, the architectural motifs of the Kariye are not only accents and punctuation marks of the compositions; they have, in addition, a specifically spatial function. Every one of the units creates around itself an aura of spatial tension; it is as if the thin and vague spatial atmosphere which pervades the compositions had been condensed in each motif. The designers did all they could to link these isolated spatial "nuclei" with each other, to bridge the gaps between them: they connected them by means of walls, thus creating a stage with limited spatial implications. Since the walls run in most cases parallel to the picture plane, the resulting "platform" is a "relief stage," and, since the depth of the architectural motifs is not very great, this relief stage is rather shallow. The shallowness fits the figure compositions, because they too develop mainly parallel to the picture plane. The depth of the stage cannot always be measured accurately, because the base of the walls is quite often not indicated at all, the walls and terrain melting into each other (PL. 109, 274).

5. LANDSCAPE

The combinations of stage floor, terrain, and architectural as well as landscape "backdrop" follow in the Kariye neither purely rational and representational nor purely decorative principles. The bottom zone of the terrain consists quite frequently of a dark green strip of varying breadth, often divided into two "layers" of slightly varied color. This strip, which is also to be found in mosaics of the Macedonian period,[19] represented originally the floor of the "stage." In the Kariye, however, its function is somewhat ambiguous: in some instances, especially in the well-ordered compositions of the lunettes and in some of the arches, including those of the parecclesion (PL. 159, 406), it actually fills this role, while in other scenes, for example, those of the Herod cycle and the Infancy of Christ, most figures are represented as standing not on or within the green strip but above it, in a much more realistically characterized "terrain" (PL. 184, 206). In other cases the bottom strip has been reduced to a merely decorative band, but seldom has it been suppressed completely. It seems to have lost most of its original representational function and to have become a unifying factor in the overall scheme of the decoration.

The next layer consists of gray, yellow, or brown "terrain," often divided up by ridges and folds that sometimes serve as floor lines for the figures. This "terrain" melts quite frequently into the architectural motifs and into the third horizontal layer, the mountains of the background. Rounded hills are most frequent in the Herod cycle, while in most other compositions the

19 E.g., in the door lunette of the narthex and the portraits of Church Fathers of the nave of St. Sophia in Istanbul.

mountains are topped with outcrops of sharp, flinty rock, frequently designed as overhangs or combined to form fantastic "architectures"—bridges, gateways, or caves (PL. 217). The outcrops exhibit a certain materialness and a certain thickness, although they are reminiscent of papier-mâché stage props rather than of stone. Similarly broken forms are used in depicting the banks of rivers and lakes (PL. 217). All these elements, together with trees and shrubs, are frequently combined to form what is meant to be a coherent landscape. This coherence is, however, a purely additive one; the sum total of the constituent elements never really amounts to a continuous landscape. The scenery is built up in very much the same way as the architectural stage, hills and rocks taking the place of buildings. Here too we are confronted by a general spatial atmosphere in which some specific spatial motifs are embedded: it is chaos on the point of crystallization, space *in statu nascendi*, sometimes dynamic and turbulent, sometimes pedantic; almost always impressive and hardly ever quite convincing.

6. COMPOSITION

Architecture and landscape are the most important means for joining together the elements of composition, for welding them into a whole. This whole can be either a framed, self-contained "picture"; a scenic unit that is part of a larger combination; an entire portion of the wall or the vaulting system, containing several scenic or figural units; or, finally, the entire decoration of one or both narthexes and of the parecclesion. Thus, there is a complete hierarchy of "wholes," from the smallest to the most comprehensive; and only in the smallest unit does the single scene coincide with the compositional whole.

The simple units are to be found mainly in the lunettes, the arches, and the pendentives. Their nuclei are, as a rule, one or two groups of figures, arranged in antithetic opposition, in certain cases in the form of continuous friezes, and, in a few instances, as allover patterns without any prevalent direction of movement. These basic elements were invented by the designers themselves in only a small minority of the Kariye compositions; in most cases they were part of the artistic heritage of Byzantium, a heritage that was both manifold and homogeneous and that was transmitted from one generation to the next by model books of various kinds.[20]

The idea of Feodor Shmit, who believed that the mosaics of the Kariye had been copied from an earlier fresco cycle in the church itself, has long been abandoned.[21] There is still, however, the question of what exactly the model books used by the designers of the Kariye contained—single figures and groups of figures only or also entire compositions. That the latter must have been included in addition to the former is proved by the identity of entire compositions in cycles as far removed from each other in time and space as, for example, the mosaics of the church at Daphni [22] and those of the Kariye itself. In both cycles the Annunciation to St. Anne (in Kariye, PL. 93), for instance, not only contains the same figural elements—these elements are, in addition, shown in identical relation to each other and to the whole, although the scene fills the left half of a lunette in Daphni as against the right half in the Kariye. The similarity of the two compositions (and of other pairs) is too specific to be explained by the existence of literary "hermeneias"; nor can it be the effect of a direct relationship of prototype and copy; it can be understood only if one assumes the existence of model books which contained

20 For discussions of the role of model books see O. Demus, *The Mosaics of Norman Sicily* (London, 1949), pp. 137 ff.; E. Kitzinger, *The Mosaics of Monreale* (Palermo, 1960), p. 84.

21 *Kakhrie-džami*, pp. 156 ff.
22 Diez and Demus, *Byzantine Mosaics in Greece*, Fig. 109.

entire compositional schemes and which were extremely long-lived, being copied again and again and modernized in the process to a certain degree only, that is, with regard to the single motifs but not to the compositional schemes themselves.

These schemes, together with the traditional motifs, furnished to the designers of the Kariye the raw material, which had to be brought up to date, edited, and rearranged. According to the formats to be filled, some compositions would have to be condensed, others diluted: it is as if the schemes were elastic, to be compressed or stretched at will. If, for instance, the spatial relationship of the figures in the Raising of the Daughter of Jairus (PL. 363)—Jairus appears rather far back, behind his house—has lost something of its clarity by the lateral compression of the composition, the effect of stretching a composition beyond its normal limits is at times even more disturbing. Some pictorial schemes, like those of the Presentation of the Virgin in the Temple and Christ Healing the Leper (PL. 119, 247) are drawn out so much that they have completely lost their coherence, in spite of the insertion of architectural motifs—a twofold porch meant to motivate the change of direction in the cortège of the maidens in the first case, a wall with rectangular niches in the second case. In many instances it seemed expedient to fill one frame with two scenes or, at least, with two or more phases of the narrative joined together (PL. 148, 152), some of these combinations having been firmly established for centuries, others newly invented. Other scenes, again, were divided to fill two or more compartments. Most of these adjustments had been used in earlier periods too, but never before had the flexibility and elasticity of Byzantine compositional schemes been so heavily taxed as they were in the mosaics and the frescoes of the Kariye. These far-reaching alterations were, in fact, made possible only by the lavish use of "stage props." Pillar-like corner motifs provide inner frames, tower-like structures serve as caesurae, extended walls prevent the falling apart of over-stretched pictorial schemes, and hills are often the only means of supplying some sort of cohesion to scenes that lack a firm compositional structure. This is to an especially high degree the case in those mosaics for which there existed no adequate compositional models, namely some of the scenes of the Herod cycle ([103]–[110]). This cycle, for special reasons connected with the distribution of the program, was spun out so as to fill no fewer than eight lunettes—including the Return of the Holy Family from Egypt, even nine. At least one of these, the second of the compositions representing the Massacre of the Innocents [108] (the first [107] is combined with the representation of Herod sending out soldiers), was newly invented by the designer himself. The lack of a specific model manifests itself not only in the rather daring and "modernistic," if awkward, poses and movements of the figures themselves, all of which are seen in profile or back views, but also in the loose, so-to-speak spineless compositions—if the pattern of scattered figures and rounded hill contours can be called a composition at all. The lines of the hills are indeed the only visible tendons in an otherwise amorphous surface; certain groups are framed by them, and some figures are partly cut off by their contours and, consequently, pushed back into a second plane.

If a "composition" like this is at all representative of the tendencies of the period, these tendencies must have gone a long way toward the dissolving of all firm bonds that had kept compositions together in earlier Byzantine art. The disintegration, it is true, hardly ever went as far as it does in The Massacre of the Innocents, but the trend can be seen in almost all images. Equilibrium, for instance, does not seem to have had the importance in the Kariye that it possessed in earlier periods. To name one example only, the lunette showing the donor kneeling before the Enthroned Christ (PL. 26) appears definitely one-sided if it is compared with the compositionally analogous dedicatory mosaic of Leo the Wise in the narthex of the Hagia Sophia.[23] In the latter the enthroned All-Ruler is represented in strict frontality, while in the Kariye he is turned somewhat to the left, thus occupying more space in the left half of the lunette than in the right, with the effect that the figure of the donor seems to be squeezed into the left corner and a large empty space is created on the right of the throne. If this means any-thing at all—and it is hardly believable that this lack of balance should have occurred by mere chance—then equilibrium must have ceased to be what it was before, namely one of the most important compositional principles, and have been supplanted by asymmetry, instability, and unrest.

As a matter of fact, the principles which had governed surface composition before would have been of little use to the designers of the Kariye, who had to deal with areas extremely dif-ficult to fill. The complicated architectural forms of the narthexes and the parecclesion forbade simple solutions like those employed in Macedonia, for instance, where compositions were often arranged in friezes—the easiest format for accommodating a narrative cycle. The domical vaults of the Kariye are neither cupolas, which would lend themselves to being decorated with a continuous frieze, nor cross-groined vaults, which would take four triangularly arranged "pic-tures," but domed squares with awkward squinches. The latter had to be filled with subsidiary scenes or motifs, mostly in a smaller scale; with landscape elements; or with specific corner motifs, perhaps derived, as Professor Grabar has suggested,[24] from early Byzantine prototypes, as in the case of the peacocks, other birds, or vegetal forms in the vaults that illustrate the child-hood of the Virgin. In this way the corners were got rid of; but the remaining surfaces of the vaults were still difficult enough to fill. Unfortunately, three of the nine vaults of the two nar-thexes have lost all or the greatest part of their mosaics, so that only six still show (or permit the reconstruction of) the original arrangement. Two of these, namely the vaults of the sixth and seventh bays, which are badly preserved, seem to have contained annular, continuous friezes of as many as six scenes. Of the other vaults four are well preserved; each shows a dif-ferent solution. The vault containing the representations of John the Baptist Bearing Witness of Christ (II) and of The Temptation (PL. 216) seems, at first glance, to have been treated as a dome rising above a circular base, complete with center medallion and inscriptions arranged in circular curves around it. The figures too, and the stage on which they stand, appear to be arranged in a continuous circle. On closer inspection, however, it can be seen that they belong to two separate compositions, one filling the north, the other the south half of the vault. The landscape shows two caesuras in the transverse (west-east) axis, so that there are really two separate landscape stages. The one in the scene of St. John's testimony is built up high at the ends so as to enfold the scene and to separate it from the other one, while at the same time it follows the curve of the vault by its very structure. The opposite half of the vault is less homogeneous—and quite legitimately so, since it contains four successive phases of The Temptation of Christ. However, these four scenes are connected with each other by a more or less continuous background.

An entirely different scheme was adopted for the large vault of the entrance bay of the outer narthex; each of the two themes represented—The Miracle at Cana and The Multiplication of Loaves (PL. 228)—is divided into two scenes, with Christ as the main figure in each. Each of

23 Th. Whittemore, *The Mosaics of St. Sophia at Istanbul: Preliminary Report on the First Year's Work, 1931–1932* (Paris, 1933).

24 A. Grabar, "La décoration des coupoles à Karye Camii et les peintures italiennes du Dugento," *JOeBG*, 6 (1957), pp. 111 ff.

the four scenes is so arranged as to have its center of gravity in one of the four corners. Thus the compositional scheme of the vault is ruled by the diagonal axes, not by the transverse axes as the preceding vault is.

The second bay of the inner narthex, containing representations of the Virgin Blessed by the Priests and the Virgin Caressed by Her Parents (PL. 108), is arranged somewhat like the vault containing the Temptation; the caesuras, however, are not in the tranverse but in the longitudinal (north-south) axis. In addition, the arrangement is not circular but consists of two scenes treated as independent compositions confronting each other as if they were placed on opposite walls. One of the architectural motifs, namely the house to the right of Joachim and Anne, has been badly distorted, with the intention to make it cover almost a quarter of the vault's surface. The curious piece of architecture that forms the stage of the scene opposite is even more drawn out and distorted—a straggling, spiky sort of scaffolding, discordant in the extreme. The only thing that welds these two compositions together is the artifice of radially arranging four sharply cut forms, which converge toward the center and seem about to grip the central medallion as in a vise.

Similarly discordant is the composition in the vault of the entrance bay of the inner narthex (PL. 119), which has only one scene, drawn out to encircle the whole circumference of the vault. The main motif—the Holy of Holies, the Virgin, and the High Priest—had to be in the main (west-east) axis, prefacing, as it were, the entrance into the nave; in addition, it had to be large enough to function as a crowning motif for the door lunette. Thus, the apex of the baldachin reaches as far as the center of the vault and, consequently, leaves no room for a central medallion. The architectural motif opposite the baldachin, in the shape of a double doorway, was introduced mainly to provide a turning point for the procession of maidens.

In all these examples, the mosaicist stretched, compressed, or disjointed and recast the inherited compositions in an often very disharmonious shape, all in order to fit them to the special conditions, to make them conform to the special functions allotted to them in the overall composition of the whole. The awkward solutions arrived at show that the task was a new one and was, consequently, approached in an experimental spirit. In the mosaics, the chief means for this reshaping and reconditioning of traditional compositional schemes were elements of scenery—architectural and landscape motifs. In the fresco representation of the Last Judgment (PL. 368) their place was taken, quite logically, by cloud motifs. The choirs of Hierarchs, Hosioi, Holy Women, Martyrs, Apostles, and Prophets are gathered into "cloud continents" bounded by ragged contours and detaching themselves as irregular, light shapes from the dark blue ground; the oddness of these cloud islands is emphasized by the contrast with the smooth circular forms of the Scroll of Heaven and the mandorla of the Supreme Judge: the whole is reminiscent of a collage in which tattered patches of torn paper are used alongside carefully cut out shapes.

The overall composition of the vault containing this subject is even freer than the composition of the mosaics: the forms seem to float in the basin of the vault, the "sky"; the pendentives are coloristically differentiated extensions of the main expanse of the dome; the lunettes on either side of it are also treated as annexes of the great composition. Thus, the pendentive figure of Abraham, with Lazarus in his bosom (PL. 394), really belongs to, and is thematically and coloristically a continuation of the composition of the northern lunette, the representation of Paradise (PL. 404); the architectural articulation (the frame) which divides the lunette from the dome and the pendentive is not "taken seriously." A similar relation between pendentive and lunette can be seen on the south side, the location of the Torments of the Damned (PL. 398, 453), with the difference that the lunette is not cut off from the dome. As a matter of fact, the whole decoration of this bay would fall apart if it were not for the subtle coloristic balance and, above all, for the two circular shapes (the Scroll of Heaven and the mandorla) placed in the central axis and thus made part of a string of medallions that mark the zenith of the entire vaulting system of the chapel, from the western arch right through to the mandorla of the Anastasis in the apse (PL. 338). There, in the conch, the movement comes to an end, in the white figure of Christ, held in suspension, as it were, between the sharp pink shapes of the two sarcophagi and the beetling crags rent asunder by the *descensus;* and between the straining forms of Adam and Eve, one dark red, the other blue (PL. 341). The Anastasis is the perfect terminus of all formal movement within the entire chapel, the goal where all the unrest ends. Thus, the single units of the fresco decoration must be seen as parts of a highly organized whole. All the disharmonies of composition, the sprawling architectures—one pointing this, the other that way; one seen from above, the other, in the same picture, from below—all this makes sense if the whole is considered. One realizes that the single picture, at least in the parecclesion, is not meant to be seen by itself, as an isolated entity; that it is meant to be part of a whole, in thought, shape, and color, and that the tension of forms, the array of rugged and conflicting shapes that almost explode the single pictures provide just the forces to bind all those single items together and fuse them into a new whole, an entity of a higher order. This is why the compositions are not saturated, why there is always some "surplus" of movement, of direction; the disharmony of the single form or "picture" provides the impetus for linking it up with the neighboring or the opposing entities.

This impetus is so strong that it transcends the frames, which are, in any case, rather meager in the parecclesion, and disregards architectural articulations. Thus, it would be quite wrong to look at the frescoes of the parecclesion as an "architectural decoration" with a careful and correct emphasizing of functional lines, joints, and surfaces, as was the case in early-Byzantine art. There is nothing functional about these paintings in the sense of a subservience to the logic of architecture. The walls and vaults provide hardly more than the necessary supports for a work of painting that exists, so to speak, all by itself, in a space of its own creation. This space is not a homogeneous space; it is rather an agglomeration, a sequence of spaces, which should be read discursively, not seen and appreciated with one glance. This is the essential difference between western post-Renaissance decorations, which are to be seen as optically homogeneous systems, and the painted interior of the Kariye's parecclesion, in which the multiplicity of spatial accents forces the beholder into a discursive, dynamic perception.

The mosaic decoration of the narthexes is, in this respect, less radical, one might say less modern, in the sense of the new "antifunctional" tendencies of Palaeologan art. Apart from the greater surface that is given over to them, ornamental motifs have in the mosaics a much more important function than in the frescoes. The string of medallions, for instance, which marks the zenith of the parecclesion and which becomes amalgamated with the figural composition by featuring busts, haloes, mandorlas, and the Scroll of Heaven, appears in the inner narthex as a series of geometrical disks or wheel-shaped designs, filled with conventional patterns only. These different attitudes of the mosaicists and the fresco painters toward ornament are, of course, based to a certain extent on tendencies inherent in the two techniques: mosaic tends more to decorative configurations of abstract shapes than does fresco. But not all frescoes are poor and not all mosaics rich in ornament; for instance, the mosaics that decorate the sepulchral chapel of Michael Glabas on the south side of the Fethiye Djami [25] show hardly any ornament at all. This decoration orginated at about the same time as that of the Kariye narthexes; but it shows the growing antagonism of Palaeologan art toward ornament much more clearly than that of the Kariye. It may have also contributed to making the frescoes of the Kariye's parecclesion—which, as has been said above, comprise the last stage in the decoration of the church and hence are slightly later than the mosaics of the narthexes—somewhat more austere than the latter.

This comparative austerity is not the only "modern" or "progressive" feature of the Kariye frescoes; the painters seem to have been much more sure of themselves and their new means than the mosaicists. It has been pointed out above how little the latter were able to invent new iconographic or compositional schemes, how dismally they failed, for instance, in the case of The Massacre of the Innocents (PL. 184, 190). There is also an odd lack of coordination between homologous parts of the decor. For example, figures of saints belonging to the same category (e.g., the martyrs in the arches of the outer narthex) are represented in varying sizes and at different heights: some are standing on the lower margin of the arch (e.g., the saint left of the entrance door from the outer to the inner narthex, PL. 304), others (e.g., the symmetrically corresponding figure, PL. 305) higher up; some of the dark green strips of "ground" on which these figures stand are broad, others narrow. One gets the impression that the designer could not have cared less about the regularity or irregularity of his layout. There is a kind of uncertainty about it all which seems to indicate that the designers were not really familiar any more with a complicated decorative system. As a matter of fact, this kind of system was on the point of breaking up, partly because of the introduction of features that could not very well be brought into accordance with the rest; one of these novel features is the discrepancy of size in adjacent parts of the decoration. The most outstanding example of this in the Kariye is the so-called Deesis, the commemorative panel for Melane the Nun and Isaac Comnenus (PL. 36). The main figure of the panel, Christ Chalkites, is over four meters high and thus almost five times as large as the figures in the immediately adjoining pendentives; the latter look even smaller because of their greater distance from the eye of the beholder. Middle-Byzantine mosaic decoration had known a great contrast of scale in only one case, namely that of the Pantocrator medallion in the main dome of a church, or the bust of the Pantocrator in the conch of the apse. But this representation was the most distant of all figures; it was, furthermore, secluded in the zenith medallion of the cupola or the semidome of the apse; and it was, finally, not a full figure but only a bust and thus somewhat *hors concours* as regards the other parts of the decoration. The lower limits of the Christ Chalkites of the Kariye, in contrast, are placed below the eye level of the beholder, and thus the figure seems frighteningly large. For the same reason, the "preventive distortions" of the figure do not work in the sense of middle-Byzantine "perspective" but only create an impression of awkward "wrongness."

There is another inadequacy about this figure connected with its immense size and its nearness: the checkerboard pattern of the modeling technique, made necessary by the large size and the limited number of tones at the disposition of the mosaicist, does not blend at this short distance as it would were the figure high up at the zenith of a dome.

Corresponding difficulties had to be met with at the other end of the scale, when it came to the rendering of very small forms. As there are certain limits to the possible smallness of the tesserae, the modeling of features below a certain scale is apt to be difficult—such features will,

[25] P. A. Underwood, "Notes on the Work of the Byzantine Institute in Istanbul: 1957–1959," *DOP*, 14 (1960), pp. 215 ff.

at least, look somewhat sketchy. This is, indeed, the case with the faces of the Virgin as a child and of the maidens of her escort (PL. 103, at full size, 119 ff.). The smallness of the tesserae used in these faces had yet another untoward consequence: since the little cubes stick out less far from the setting bed than the larger ones, the mosaic surface of the heads is actually somewhat concave.

None of these difficulties and limitations existed for the fresco painter; he could choose his format and his technique freely and was altogether much more independent of his technique. It is evident, then, that in a period which admitted of greater contrasts in scale in its decorations than was the earlier practice, and which, generally speaking, called for a greater flexibility in technique and form, fresco painters had better chances than mosaicists. About the work of the latter there is something strained, something artificial; they suggest highly specialized virtuosi who, in spite of all their training and cunning, cannot quite bring it off. Compared with the mosaics, the frescoes seem not more harmonious—this being a quality not in demand in that period—but more spontaneous, more legitimate. Fresco appears to have been the more adequate medium in which to realize the ideals of the somewhat overripe phase to which the decoration of the Kariye belongs. One might even say that the leading artists (or artist) were primarily fresco painters by training and not mosaicists.

At this late period, the decorating of an ecclesiastic building, and especially that of a narthex, was no longer regarded as a sacred undertaking but rather as an artistic performance. The monk had been replaced by the professional artist, who saw no reason to refrain from trying out experimental solutions and who sought more after artistic effects than after the values of timeless grandeur. At the same time, the attitudes of the figures and the expressions of the faces suggest the birth of a new type of religious feeling, a more humane, a more "lay" sentiment, still coupled with, and veiled by, a certain self-consciousness, even a certain diffidence, which make the direct appeal to the beholder even more touching. This is what makes the mosaics and the frescoes of the Kariye so deeply stirring, so impressive esthetically, and, at the same time, so problematic if they are regarded in the perspective of the sacred art of earlier periods. They are something new, the products of a deep crisis, of a revolution greater than that of the iconoclastic controversy, greater than any other revolution in the development of Byzantine art. This revolution did not begin at the time of the decoration of the Kariye, in the second decade of the fourteenth century, but a long time before. An attempt will be made, in the next section, to trace the course of this revolution from its very beginning and to determine the place the mosaicists and the painters of the Kariye occupied in the process.

Origin and Development of the Style of the Kariye[26]

1. THE TWELFTH CENTURY

The date at which this greatest revolution in the field of Byzantine painting began is still a matter of dispute. It has been argued by a group of scholars [27] that the new style came into being

26 In preparing this essay I have made use, to a certain extent, of my own paper, "Die Entstehung des Paläologenstils in der Malerei," with bibliography. See also Lazarev, *Istorija*, I, pp. 157 ff., and Sv. Radojčić, "Die Entstehung der Malerei der Paläologischen Renaissance," *JOeBG*, 7 (1958), pp. 105 ff.

27 M. Alpatov [Alpatoff], "Eine Reise nach Konstantinopel, Nicäa und Trapezunt, 2," *Repertorium für Kunstwissenschaft*, 49 (1928), pp. 63 ff.; Lazarev, *Istorija*, I, p. 163 and passim; idem, "Duccio and Thirteenth-Century Greek Ikons," *The Burlington Magazine*, 59 (1931), pp. 154 ff.; idem, "Novyj pamjatnik konstantinopol'skoj miniatjury XIII veka," *VV*, N.S., 5 (1952), pp. 178 ff.

only one or two decades after the return of the Palaeologi to Constantinople, while other art historians [28] believe some of the essential characteristics of the style to have emerged soon after the middle of the twelfth century, in the mannerist phase of Comnenian art.

The differences between these two extreme schools of thought concern more than mere chronology; they touch on fundamental problems of the history of Byzantine art. According to the second of these two views, the development of Byzantine painting went through three great phases—the *trois âges d'or* of early Byzantinology: the first tinged by the afterglow of late Hellenism, the second representing the sternly ascetic and formalistic medieval phase, the third signifying the baroque hypertrophy of this art. This is, naturally, a highly artificial scheme, within which it is hardly possible to do justice to any development, let alone the very complex development of Byzantine painting, with its many renascences and oscillating movements.

Entirely disregarded in this schematic picture is the late-Comnenian style, a style which has lately been described by several authors as a clearly definable and very important phase in the development of Byzantine painting.[29] The style differs from the classicist style of the eleventh century by its expressiveness, its agitated linearism, and the dynamic movement of the figures. This very linearism and the integrated rhythm of the flat compositions distinguish the late-Comnenian from the Palaeologan style, on the other hand, and make the late-Comnenian in this way a movement *sui generis*. Its most striking characteristic is, indeed, the prominent part played by line. Multiple, streamlined, rhythmical, and agitated lines are employed to produce the effect of transient movement in low relief. Rippling undulations, gliding curves, and dynamic complications become an end in themselves; arabesques of white lines articulate and often contort the faces of figures, who seem in a perpetual hurry and agitation, rushing about, gesticulating, and grimacing, their movements echoed by trees and hill contours, which have been aptly described as their magnified silhouettes.[30] Single pictures are not only bound to each other by the overflow of movement so as to form chains of consecutive scenes but are also part of highly organized larger wholes, filling even entire walls. Very small and very large formats are to be found in the same decoration and produce odd contrasts of scale, while the blending, subdued colors make for homogeneity. The technique ranges from meticulous dryness to a certain sketchiness (the latter to be found especially in small-scale paintings and mosaics), a sketchiness that goes very well with the swift rhythm of line and movement.

The monuments of this high-speed linear mannerism of the later twelfth century can be found throughout the whole Byzantine world, from Sicily to Cyprus and from Macedonia to Russia. The immense extension of this area makes it certain that the movement spread from a great center outward; Constantinople has been rightly suggested as the birthplace of the style. There remains, however, the fact that a certain region of the empire seems to have been especially susceptible to the more extreme forms of the style, namely Macedonia. It is there that we find the wildest exaggerations of linear play, the most complicated entanglements, and convolutions that are at times downright absurd (Fig. 1).[31] Moreover, a certain tendency toward linear movement can be seen in Macedonian paintings that greatly precede in date the general sway of the

28 Muratoff, *La peinture byzantine*, pp. 129 ff.

29 V. Lazarev, "The Mosaics of Cefalù," *ArtB*, 17 (1935), pp. 184 ff.; idem, *Istorija*, I, pp. 121 ff.; idem, *Freski Staroj Ladogi* (Moscow, 1960), passim; Demus, *Norman Sicily*, pp. 369 ff.; A. Xyngopoulos, *Thessalonique et la peinture macédonienne* (Athens, 1955), pp. 15 ff.; Kitzinger, *Monreale*, pp. 69 ff.

30 Kitzinger, *Monreale*, p. 87.

31 See especially the frescoes of Kurbinovo, dated 1191 (M. Rajković, "Les fresques de Kurbinovo et leur auteur" [in Serbian with French résumé], *ZRVI*, 44, No. 3 [1955], pp. 207 ff.; Bihalji-Merin, *Fresken und Ikonen*, PL. 15), and of Hagioi Anargyroi in Kastoria (S. Pelekanides, Καστορία [Salonika, 1953], PL. 1–42, esp. 7, 8).

style. For instance, the fresco of the Ascension, in St. Sophia in Ohrid (Fig. 2),[32] which originated perhaps a century before the bulk of the other examples of this linear mannerism, exhibits, so to speak, a prenatal variety of the style, whereas nothing of the kind is to be found at that date in the capital. In addition, the style survived in Macedonia well into the second half of the thirteenth century, in frescoes and illuminated manuscripts.[33] Thus, Macedonia seems to have been, if not the cradle, at least the main "habitat" of the more extreme varieties of late-Comnenian mannerism.

The provincial Macedonian monuments show what became of this style when it was left to itself. Complication was heaped upon complication; there seems to have been no way out of the labyrinth of linear contortions, very much as was the case with an interesting parallel of this cul-de-sac development, namely the so-called zigzag style of German and Austrian late Romanesque. The change—one might almost say the liberation—had to come from outside the charmed circle; and it is quite possible that the antidote was already developing in Constantinople immediately before the capital fell to the Latins in 1204. Although there are no monuments of this period in Constantinople itself, it is possible to draw conclusions from certain forms that made their appearance in the provinces about the turn of the century. Some of these forms appear in works which, in the main, still follow the late-Comnenian canon of linear mannerism: at Staraya Ladoga, for instance, we find that the lines begin to be supplanted by abstract shapes, light-colored broken and spiky surface configurations that stand out from a dark ground.[34] The forms assume a metallic quality, a hardness and precision which make them quite different from the yielding, streamlined curves of linear mannerism.

2. THE BEGINNINGS OF THE MONUMENTAL STYLE

The new style—which, to distinguish it from the late-Comnenian style, might be called the style of the Angeli period (1185-1204)—found its first clearly definable realization in those parts of the fresco decoration of Vladimir cathedral in Russia (Last Judgment, Fig. 3) which, according to Professor Lazarev, were painted by Constantinopolitan masters.[35] The style is characterized not only by the new kind of modeling described above, with splashes of light sending out centrifugal or parallel, comblike rays in abstract designs of great vigor, but also by a new simplicity of outline, a quiet beauty of the faces, and a certain grandeur of composition, which, though far from being rigid, is certainly more static than was the rule in the preceding decades. Thoroughly new though it is, the style seems, to a certain extent, a return to tendencies that were characteristic of the tenth and eleventh centuries.

The further evolution of the new monumental style belongs to the thirteenth century. It seems to have been an almost universal movement, except in provincial backwaters like western Macedonia—a movement that embraced not only fresco but also icon painting: the icon of the

32 Sv. Radojčić and D. Talbot Rice, *Yugoslavia: Mediaeval Frescoes* (UNESCO World Art Series, 4 [Greenwich, Conn.], New York Graphic Society, 1955), p. 16, PL. I–VIII; G. Millet and A. Frolow, *La peinture du Moyen Âge en Yougoslavie (Serbie, Macédoine et Monténégro)*, I (Paris, 1954), PL. 1–10; Bihalji-Merin, *Fresken und Iconen*, PL. 1, 3–12; P. Miljković-Pepek, "Matériaux sur l'art macédonien du moyen âge: Les fresques du sanctuaire de Sainte-Sophie d'Ochrid" (in Serbian with French résumé), *Recueil des travaux (1955-1956)* (Publications du Musée Archéologique—Skopje), I (1956), pp. 37ff.

33 D. Koco and P. Miljković-Pepek, *Manastir* (Skoplje,

1958); O. Demus, "Studien zur byzantinischen Buchmalerei des 13. Jahrhunderts," *JOeBG*, 9 (1960), pp. 77 ff.

34 Lazarev, *Freski Staroj Ladogi*, PL. 19–32, 37, 40, 44, 46.

35 Lazarev, *Istorija*, I, pp. 123 f.; II (Moscow, 1948), PL. 188–94; bibliography on p. 322, n. 61, of Vol. I. The style of the frescoes of Vladimir has been recognized as representing a new phase by Kitzinger, *Monreale*, p. 78. On the division of hands see Lazarev [Lasareff], "La méthode de collaboration des maîtres byzantins et russes," *Classica et Mediaevalia*, 17 (1956), pp. 75 ff.

Virgin Orant in the Tretiakov Gallery in Moscow,[36] to quote only one example, shows quite clearly the two main qualities of the style, monumental grandeur and abstract hardness (Fig. 4).

The style reached its first climax in a few decorations which date from the first and second decades of the thirteenth century. Two of these decorations are to be found in Serbia: one, of around 1220, a fragment only, in Žiča;[37] the other, of 1208–09, an entire cycle, which has lost most of its original surface, in the church of the Virgin, Studenica.[38] There is documentary evidence that the leading painter of Žiča came from Constantinople.[39] In both cycles, scenes and figures are fewer and larger than in the decorations of the preceding period. There is a lot of empty space, which imparts to the compositions a kind of airy grandeur. Line is used as contour and as a means of articulation—it has ceased to be an end in itself. Instead of the wild, ascetic, and even distorted faces of late-Comnenian painting [40] we find now summarily modeled features with open, normal, almost benign expressions (Fig. 5). The modeling is done with a certain reserve; the large forms show a measured overall relief without any individual feature coming to the foreground.

It was this dignified and neutral style, a kind of "classicism" with normal, average forms and with a certain grandeur, which became the basis of the new development. The first phase of this development lasted until after the middle of the thirteenth century. While preserving those qualities which imparted to them their grandeur as surface patterns, including the jagged highlights, the figures were gradually acquiring a new, statuesque quality; their ampleness ceased to be a matter of flat expanse only and began to involve volume and bodily weight.

The key monument of this phase is the fresco decoration of the church of the Ascension at Mileševo, of the 1230's (Fig. 6).[41] In relation to what came afterwards, this monument, and, indeed, the entire stylistic phase, might be called preclassical. There is a quiet dignity of form and content, from the lapidary pattern of the chrysography to the monumental simplicity of the grand compositions; from the powerful faces to the solemn magnificence of the entire decoration.

Although the frescoes of Mileševo are a work of royal patronage, they are not free from certain provincialisms: some of the drawing is rather summary, some of the modeling crude; and the entire color scheme as well as the technique makes it quite clear that the wall paintings were meant as ersatz for mosaics, complete with a tesserae network painted onto the yellow (representing golden) ground. Thus, the paintings seem to reflect an art of mosaic, a greater, a metropolitan art. They seem to; but we do not know whether this "metropolitan" art, seemingly postulated by the decoration of Mileševo and other works, did really exist. We must at least reckon with the possibility that this style of decoration was evolved in the diaspora, on the basis of memories of a movement that was initiated before 1204 in the capital. On the other hand, there might have existed a secondary center, which, if not the source, could have been the focal point for the radiation of the style. This center was certainly not the residence of the Serbian court, because the paintings that most closely resemble the frescoes of Mileševo, paintings that must belong to the same school if not to the same hand, have been found not in Serbia but in the little village

36 *Istorija Russkogo Iskusstva*, ed. I. E. Grabar, I (Akademija Nauk SSSR, Institut Istorii Iskusstv; Moscow, 1953), p. 490, with illustrations.
37 Millet and Frolow, *Peinture*, I, PL. 53, 55.
38 Ibid., PL. 32–42; Demus, "Die Entstehung," p. 26.
39 Sv. Radojčić, *Majstori starog srpskog slikarstva* (Belgrade, 1955), pp. 5, 13.

40 E.g., Vatopedi, fragment showing the heads of Sts. Peter and Paul, of 1197–98; see G. Millet, *Monuments de l'Athos* (Paris, 1927), PL. 98,1.
41 Millet and Frolow, *Peinture* I, PL. 63–83; Radojčić and Talbot Rice, *Yugoslavia*, PL. XII–XIV; the recently cleaned cycle in the church of the Apostles in the Patriarchate of Peć, approximately contemporary, still awaits publication.

church of Oropos in Boeotia.[42] As it is not likely that the Serbian kral called in a painter from Boeotia, or that the village elders of Oropos invited a painter from Serbia, there must have been a common source; and the claim of Salonika to have been this common source or, at least, the radiation center of this style should not be dismissed too lightly.[43]

The style of Mileševo already shows some of the features listed above as characteristic traits of the style of the Kariye. The odd-shaped feet (the "flatiron" type) make their appearance, as do certain types of faces. These features, and the overmodeling of certain details, the gain in volume, and the occurrence of huge figures in the lower zone of the decoration side by side with much smaller ones [44]—these are, indeed, traits which point forward to the Palaeologan style, without, however, making the decoration of Mileševo a Palaeologan monument. In some respects, as a matter of fact, the painters of Mileševo showed themselves rather conservative, especially with regard to architectural and landscape elements, which are on the whole rather scarce in this statuesque art and lack, when they occur, specific spatial qualities.

Little more than a decade later these qualities are present, as a matter of course, in cycles which in other respects are less "modern" than the frescoes of Mileševo. One of the painters of Morača,[45] for instance, working soon after 1252 in a style that still employed late-Comnenian figure schemes, composed his architectural motifs of heavy and solid blocks. The same kind of situation occurs in even the most conservative of the at least four or five "manners" that can be found in the decoration of the key monument of the third quarter of the century, the church of the Holy Trinity at Sopoćani [46]—a monument that will have to be dealt with at some length because it illustrates, as no other fresco decoration of the period does, the emergence of the new style. The entire pictorial history of the thirteenth century seems to be telescoped in this truly regal ensemble. The earliest parts of it are even more linear, more "Comnenian" than the frescoes of Morača, although they must be somewhat later. However, the exact dates of the various parts of the decoration of Sopoćani are still in dispute. Not even the representation of the Death of Queen Anna (Dandolo), the mother of Sopoćani's founder, King Uroš I,[47] is securely dated, because we do not know for certain when this event took place, except that it must have been some time between 1250 and 1280. This is no more helpful than the lead given by the reign of the founder himself, from 1243 to 1276. However, even a more exact dating of the Death of Queen Anna would not help very much, since this scene is painted in a style entirely different from that of the other paintings in the church; the phenomenon that portraiture—and the scene is composed of portraits—follows an evolution of its own, entirely different from that of religious painting, has already been met with in the Kariye mosaics. Another piece of evidence, based on the supposed identity of three figures of the apse procession, seems to put that part of the decoration at a date after 1263.[48] To add to the confusion, another fresco, in the southwest corner of the nave, which contains the image of the founder, his predecessors, and his two sons,[49]

42 M. Chatzidakis, Βυζαντινὲς τοιχογραφίες στὸν Ὠρωπό, in Δελτίον τῆς Χριστιανικῆς Ἀρχαιολογικῆς Ἑταιρείας, 4th series, 1 (1959), pp. 87 ff.

43 Xyngopoulos, *Thessalonique*, passim.

44 This last feature is also to be found in Oropos (Chatzidakis, Βυζαντινὲς τοιχογραφίες, PL. 33, 38).

45 Millet and Frolow, *Peinture*, I, PL. 82; A. Skovran-Vukčević, "Les fresques du XIIIᵉ siècle au monastère de Morača" (in Serbian with French résumé), ZRVI, 59, No. 5 (1958), pp. 149 ff., esp. Fig. 5, upper half. For other monuments connected with the style of Morača, see V. J. Djurić, "Un atelier de

peinture dans la Serbie du XIIIᵉ siècle," *Starinar*, N.S., 12 (1961), pp. 63 ff.

46 Millet and Frolow, *Peinture*, II (Paris, 1957), PL. 1–48; Radojčić and Talbot Rice, *Yugoslavia*, PL. XV–XIX; for further bibliography see Demus, "Die Entstehung," p. 23.

47 Millet and Frolow, *Peinture*, II, PL. 47; D. Winfield, "Four Historical Compositions from the Medieval Kingdom of Serbia," *Byzantinoslavica*, 19 (1958), pp. 251 ff., esp. p. 277.

48 Winfield, "Four Historical Compositions," p. 277, n. 9, quotes an attempt by S. Mandić to identify one of the figures as Sabas II.

49 Millet and Frolow, *Peinture*, II, PL. 45, 46.

shows pentimenti which make it unsafe to rely too firmly on the dates indicated by it—the later sixties or the early seventies.

Among the earliest frescoes of the decoration are, in any case, those of the narthex,[50] which may have been completed at an early date in order to provide a fitting ambience for the sepulcher of Queen Anna; at the same time, or even a few years earlier, must have originated the now lost paintings of the dome of the nave, which carried an inscription the most interesting part of which, with the date, is missing.[51] The stylistically most archaic of the existing figures of the nave are the prophets and patriarchs in the upper reaches of the piers and arches (Fig. 7), which show a linear treatment of the drapery that is quite Comnenian in character, certainly more antiquated than the style of Mileševo. A more "local" style than that of Mileševo is also to be seen in two of the Evangelists of the pendentives, who wear garments with tightly folded, undulating hems in the old "Macedonian" manner (Fig. 8); the architectural framework of these figures, however, is more up to date than anything in Mileševo or Morača. The other two Evangelists are much more modern, in both attitude and modeling, and the architectural settings anticipate mature Palaeologan motifs, with loggias, balconies, etc., all giving the impression of having volume (Fig. 9).

3. THE CLASSICAL PHASE

But even these two "modern" Evangelists appear conservative if they are compared with the Christological scenes of the nave. These latter are much bolder as regards volume and spatial qualities, but their most impressive characteristics are their compositional grandeur, their luminous colorism, and their classical humanism. There is nothing in earlier painting to compare, for instance, with the grand composition of the Dormition, which fills almost the entire west wall (Fig. 10). The familiar iconographic scheme has been instilled with a new life; the two groups of mourning apostles and saints are not just agglomerations of stock figures but assemblies of individuals, united and swayed by common sorrow. The two massive buildings at the sides are almost palpably three-dimensional. The entire composition is a homogeneous whole, not, as in earlier decorations, an "architectural" system made up of several units. But the greatest quality of the painting lies in the spiritual sphere. The expression in the face of Christ, his glance so full of love and compassion—this is the kind of thing which had hardly ever been realized before, at least not since the heyday of Hellenic art (Fig. 11). Other compositions are no less impressive: the Crucifixion, with its Holy Women in agitated groups, Mary collapsing in the arms of St. John, and its soldiers;[52] or the Anastasis, Christ stooping low to rescue Adam, the resurrected souls in a great mass, the angels chaining the devils.[53] Everything is full of new ideas, new motifs; everything is clad in new forms. It is as if we were present at the birth of a new art.

The most astonishing innovations, however, are to be found in the fields of architectural representation and of spatial composition. The floor on which the figures stand in the Presentation of the Christ Child in the Temple (Fig. 12) appears a horizontal surface; the ciborium and the other architectural motifs stand in a rational relation (of scale and distance) to the figures and to one another, so as to create almost the illusion of an interior. The semicircular colonnade

50 Ibid., PL. 23–27.
51 M. P.-S. [Panić-Surep], "Saštita Sopoćana," *Communications de l'Institut pour la Protection et l'Etude des Monuments*

Historiques, I (1956), pp. 15 f., esp. p. 23.
52 Millet and Frolow, *Peinture*, II, PL. 13.
53 Ibid., PL. 14, 15.

in the scene that shows the twelve-year-old Christ teaching in the Temple (Fig. 13) is curved in space, as in the Kariye scene of the Virgin Receiving the Skein of Purple Wool but much more convincingly and correctly.

Generally speaking, almost all the motifs—not only those of attitude, drapery, etc.—which characterize Palaeologan art in contrast to earlier Byzantine painting are already to be found in Sopoćani. What distinguishes these frescoes from later works, however, is the complete absence of any kind of exaggeration. The frescoes of Sopoćani represent, in fact, the classical phase of an art which, later on, was to ripen into precious mannerism and fulsome baroque.

However, with all their grandeur and with all their classical harmony, the Christological frescoes of Sopoćani do not yet constitute the highest achievement of the classical phase. Other parts of the same decoration show qualities that go still beyond. These are, in the main, single figures, located with few exceptions in the lower parts of the nave, figures (and compositions like Abraham's Hospitality) decorating those surfaces that offer themselves most conspicuously to the eye of the beholder looking eastward.[54] The figures in question are, thus, not only the latest parts of the decor to have been completed but also those which are exposed to the closest view in the most striking manner; and it was, quite obviously, for these reasons that they were entrusted to the best and the most "modern" painter available. Especially the apostles in the transepts (again those on the east walls) and some of the Old Testament personages on the piers (Fig. 14) are painted with all the technical refinements of Palaeologan art—the soft, liquid modeling and the bold, painterly lighting up of the relief with parallel white strokes.[55] The most impressive qualities of these truly heroic figures, however, are their statuesque grandeur, the rhythm and the harmony of their draperies, the suffused light that seems to surround them as with a shining atmosphere, and especially the human depth, the imposing greatness and serenity of their faces. There is no trace left in these images of the lyrical sentimentality that is one of the most appealing qualities of the Christological paintings of the church: it has been supplanted by a new dignity, a maturity of feeling and expression that is surely one of the highest manifestations of the classical ideal in post-antique painting.

It is likely that these latest parts of the Sopoćani decoration were painted in the 1270's, although, as stated above, we have no basis for an exact dating. The fact that the somewhat provincial frescoes of Gradac [56] seem to contain echoes of this style does not provide a terminus, since the dating of Gradac, "about 1275," is not at all firmly established. The decoration of Arilje, on the other hand, which is dependably dated at 1296,[57] is quite definitely later stylistically. The only thing that seems fairly certain is that the decoration of Sopoćani must have been completed before 1275–76, the year of Dragutin's accession to the throne: Dragutin would hardly have failed to have his own portrait as crown prince, next to that of Uroš I as king, altered into a likeness of himself as king, if he had had anything to do with the decoration of the church.[58]

The critical years are thus, in any case, the later sixties and the earlier seventies of the thirteenth century. This is important because it suggests an explanation of the sudden appearance

54 Ibid., PL. 32, 33 (3, 4). Generally speaking, the decoration is arranged with perfect regard to angles of vision. Thus, the ground in the dead angles behind the bema pillars is not treated with gold leaf, because it cannot be seen from the nave.

55 The parallel white strokes are to be found not only in the faces but also in the draperies: cf. the angel of the Annunciation, Millet and Frolow, *Peinture*, II, PL. 6.

56 Ibid., PL. 49–67; Dj. Bošković and S. Nenadović, *Gradac* (Belgrade, 1951).

57 Millet and Frolow, *Peinture*, II, PL. 68–97; N. L. Okunev, "Arilje," *Seminarium Kondakovianum*, 8 (1936), pp. 221 ff.

58 Millet and Frolow, *Peinture*, II, PL. 45. For the general question of rulers' portraits in Serbian wall paintings see Sv. Radojčić, *Portreti srpskih vladara u srednjem veku* (Skoplje, 1934), and Winfield, "Four Historical Compositions."

of the new style—that of the Christological frescoes and of the heroic single figures—a style that quite definitely did not grow out of the earlier styles of Serbian and Macedonian painting but must have been imported from outside.

4. THE ORIGIN OF THE CLASSICAL STYLE

A. *Constantinople*

The question of where this style came from allows of one answer only: its immeasurable superiority as regards both its progressiveness and the unequaled excellence of its products makes it quite certain that it came from Constantinople itself, which by that time must have regained its leading role as the capital of Byzantine art.[59] This raises, of course, the difficult and complex matter of the origin and genesis of this art. Could it have sprung up and developed in Constantinople itself during the Latin occupation, or did this happen after 1261, in the few years between the reestablishment of the empire in the capital and the date of the "export" of this art to Serbia, certainly earlier than 1275? And, if the latter was the case, where did the artists come from who created the new art, and what kind of tradition did they bring with them? Did they come, with the dynasty, from Nicaea, and had the new art thus had its roots in that "provisional" capital? Or did they come from Salonika, which had been regained by the Greeks more than a generation before? Or from Trebizond, where a Greek pigmy empire had led a rather secluded life? What did they owe to local developments, in Macedonia, in Epirus, in Hellas, in Cilicia, in the Crusading states? Did Oriental, did Italian, did Slav influences play an essential part in the formation of their artistic language? None of these questions can so far be answered with absolute certainty, but some suggestions can be proffered as to the direction in which the correct answers may lie.

Two things can, perhaps, be assumed at the outset: first, that a great many artists left the capital in 1204, when it fell to the Latins, or soon afterward; and, second, that there existed only a rather limited activity there during the foreign occupation. The process of emigration may have been gradual and even slow—for instance, we know from documents that as late as 1220 there were still fresco painters available in Constantinople who could be invited to Serbia to paint the church of Žiča;[60] and some painters may actually have found work in the capital itself even at a later date, especially in the fields of secular decoration,[61] of icon painting, and, perhaps, of manuscript illumination.[62] So far, however, we have no dependable proof of the exact dates and places of origin of such works, which have been suggested as representing the art of Constantinople during the Latin occupation. For instance, the group of illuminated manuscripts which has been presented as having originated in Constantinople during these decades is not as homogeneous as has been thought: the fact that they all derive from tenth-century prototypes— perhaps even from one common model—does not mean that they all hail from one workshop or were made at about the same time. One of these manuscripts, the Gospel Book of the British Museum, Burney 20, is dated (by colophon) 1285,[63] and others are even later, while one at least,

59 Demus, "Die Entstehung," pp. 54 f., with bibliography.
60 Radojčić, *Majstori*, pp. 5, 13.
61 There may have existed, in Constantinople, decorations similar to the destroyed decorations of the castle of St. Omer in Thebes, of the third quarter of the 13th century, which carried representations of the Crusade; see W. Miller, *The Latins in the Levant: A History of Frankish Greece (1204–1566)* (London, 1908), p. 165.
62 K. Weitzmann, "Constantinopolitan Book Illumination in the Period of the Latin Conquest," *GBA*, 6th series, 25 (1944), pp. 193 ff.
63 V. N. Lazarev, review of Weitzmann's article cited in preceding note, *VV*, 2 (1949), pp. 367 ff.; idem, "Novyj pamjatnik" (see above, n. 27), pp. 178 ff.

the cod. Athen. 118, must be considerably older. As a matter of fact, there is even proof that the copying of the tenth-century model which may have been the common prototype of the entire group began before 1235, because an echo of this copying activity seems to exist in German manuscripts (a model book and a Gospel) of that date.[64] But none of the preserved Byzantine manuscripts is likely to have been written at this early period. Nor do we have dependable indications where any one manuscript of the group originated. It is, however, not impossible that the Athens manuscript mentioned above, which is distinguished by an especially painterly style, was actually produced in Constantinople during or soon after the Latin occupation.

This is, of course, not sufficient evidence to provide a basis for "reconstructing" Constantinopolitan art in the time from 1204 to 1261. Nor are we better off in the field of icon painting. Here again, some icons, in tempera and in mosaic, may actually be Constantinopolitan works of the first half of the thirteenth century, but in view of the complete lack of sources or inscriptions we are thrown back on guesses. Nevertheless, a good case can be made for the two Washington icons (see below, p. 145 and Fig. 22), the mosaic icon of the Virgin on Mt. Sinai, the Bargello Christ, and the Louvre Transfiguration, because of their high quality and because they mix Comnenian and Palaeologan traits and thus seem to prepare the new movement.[65]

But, single attributions apart, it seems possible to draw certain conclusions as to the general effect which the Latin occupation must have had on Greek artists who remained in the capital. Since commissions for executing monumental paintings, especially mosaics, must have ceased, perhaps with the exception of an occasional secular decoration executed for Latin grandees, the activity of these artists was certainly restricted to small-scale paintings, especially icons, which were obviously the objects most in demand on the part of the Latin overlords. It is not unlikely that it was at this time that an entire new genre came to be, if not created (because forerunners exist) at least revived and expanded—the genre of miniature mosaic, which combined the technique of monumental mosaic with the preciousness and the small scale of fashionable jewelry.[66] Byzantine mosaicists out of work may have found there a new field for their skill. It would be quite logical to assume that, by concentrating on small-sized icons, the artists gradually lost both taste and capability for doing large-scale work—at least in the second generation—and that the preference of Palaeologan art for small-scale forms even in the field of revived ecclesiastical decoration was an outcome of this situation.

Other changes must have occurred too: the laborious technique of cloisonné enamel, already on its way out in the later twelfth century, seems to have been abandoned, in the thirteenth, in favor of simpler procedures;[67] likewise, weaving in favor of embroidery, the magnificent development of which seems to have begun at that period.[68] One art form that had long lain dormant in Byzantium came again into being, namely figural sculpture in stone; the revival has been traced in Greece and Constantinople and, rightly, connected with Latin patronage.[69]

The changing and mixing of techniques must have had far-reaching consequences in the sense

64 H. R. Hahnloser, *Das Musterbuch von Wolfenbüttel* (reprinted from *Mitteilungen der Gesellschaft für vervielfältigende Kunst*, Vienna, 1929); K. Weitzmann, "Zur byzantinischen Quelle des Wolfenbüttler Musterbuches," *Festschrift Hans R. Hahnloser* (Basel and Stuttgart, 1961), pp. 223 ff.

65 O. Demus, "Zwei konstantinopler Marienikonen des 13. Jahrhunderts," *JOeBG*, 7 (1958), pp. 87 ff., esp. p. 98 ff.

66 O. Demus, "Two Palaeologan Mosaic Icons in the Dumbarton Oaks Collection," *DOP*, 14 (1960), pp. 89 ff., with bibliography.

67 This does not mean, of course, that there are no 13th-century enamels: for examples, see the Dumbarton Oaks medallion reliquary of St. Demetrius, Catalogue No. 282, or the brooch from the tomb of P. de Courtenay in Orléans.

68 G. Millet, *La dalmatique du Vatican: Les élus, images et croyances* (Paris, 1945), and *Broderies religieuses de style byzantin* (Paris, 1947).

69 A. Xyngopoulos, Φραγκοβυζαντινὰ γλυπτὰ ἐν ᾿Αθήναις, in ᾿Αρχαιολογικὴ ᾿Εφημερίς (1931), pp. 69 ff.; O. Demus, *The Church of San Marco in Venice: History, Architecture, Sculpture* (Washington, 1960), p. 142.

that age-old traditions, dictates of taste, and, one might also say, inhibitions were loosened or thrown overboard. At the same time, the process of secularization, which seems to have begun in the twelfth century, must have been intensified: it is hardly likely that there were still many clerics or monks among the Constantinopolitan artists during the second quarter of the thirteenth century. Their places must have been taken largely by lay artists.

B. The Gothic West

In this way, new techniques, new attitudes, and new ideas may have gradually taken root in an otherwise reduced field of artistic activity. Even direct influences from abroad cannot have been lacking. Although we can hardly gauge the extent of these influences in Constantinople itself, or in Nicaea for that matter, we can draw certain conclusions from neighboring regions. In Bulgaria, for instance, Western influence has been shown to have been at work in costumes, attitudes, and iconographic details.[70] Several types of images new in Byzantium or reappearing there after long abeyance turned up in the Balkans and have been credited to Western influences: among them the tree of Jesse, the symbols of the Evangelists, the representation of Ecclesia and Synagogue in the Crucifixion, the Man of Sorrows, the Pietà, the Galaktotrophousa.[71] It is more difficult to trace Western influences in the style of Byzantine painting of the thirteenth century. However, it is not unlikely, for instance, that the great discrepancies in scale within one decoration—to be seen in Mileševo, Oropos, and the Kariye, with forerunners in Nerezi and Monreale—were, in the last resort, derived from Western models: the huge figures of St. Christopher or of angels in Romanesque decorations may have given the lead.[72] Otherwise, there is little likelihood of intense Western influences having gone into the shaping of Byzantine painting in the thirteenth century: it has been rightly emphasized that Western elements, as far as they are traceable in the "Byzantinizing" art of the border countries, must have had a rather retarding effect on the nascent Palaeologan style, since they were derived not so much from contemporary, "modern," Gothic art as from archaizing or outmoded Romanesque currents.[73] It was, indeed, only in the fourteenth century that genuinely Gothic forms penetrated the barrier of Byzantine idiosyncrasies; some of the Kariye's figures and certain miniatures painted in thin watercolors are the first examples of this—for Byzantium—exotic genre.[74]

How very little the Gothic (French) element contributed toward the fashioning of the Palaeologan style can be deduced from a study of the Crusaders' manuscripts, where Byzantine and Western elements can be found in a close symbiosis but in which nothing was produced that was in advance of other works originating in less strongly westernized regions. The first manuscript that contains features foreshadowing Palaeologan forms, the Psalter at Florence, Biblioteca Riccardiana 323, painted, according to Professor Buchthal, in Jerusalem between 1235 and 1237, is in the main still linked with the Sicilian development of the late twelfth century;[75] and the nascent sense of volume to be seen in its figures cannot compare at all with that of the much more devel-

70 A. Grabar, *La peinture religieuse en Bulgarie* (Paris, 1928), pp. 170 ff., and idem, "Un reflet du monde latin dans une peinture balkanique du 13e siècle," *Byzantion*, 1 (1924), pp. 229 ff.

71 Demus, "Die Entstehung," pp. 33 f.

72 Compare the Christophorus fresco in Gurk cathedral (13th cent.) and the angel in the cathedral of Le Puy (12th cent.).

73 Lazarev, *Istorija*, I, pp. 180 f.

74 Compare the Theocritus of Paris, Bibl. Nat. gr. 1832, and the leaves in the Walters Art Gallery (530 f, g) and the collection of H. R. Willoughby: The Walters Art Gallery, *Early*

Christian and Byzantine Art (Exhibition Catalog) (Baltimore, 1947), Nos. 735, 736.

75 H. Buchthal, *Miniature Painting in the Latin Kingdom of Jerusalem* (Oxford, 1957), pp. 39 ff., PL. 52–54; that the MS might even be Sicilian was suggested by H. Bober in his review of Professor Buchthal's book in *ArtB*, 43 (1961), p. 67. On the Sicilian development itself see H. Buchthal, "A School of Miniature Painting in Norman Sicily," *Late Classical and Mediaeval Studies in Honor of Albert Mathias Friend, Jr.*, ed. K. Weitzmann (Princeton, 1955), pp. 312 ff.

oped forms of the contemporary frescoes of Mileševo; nor can the later miniatures of the Perugia Missal, the Arsenal Bible, and the manuscripts of the Histoire Universelle, which were illuminated in Acre in the second half of the century,[76] equal the "progressive" features of Sopoćani.

Another part of the former Byzantine territory where Greek artists came into close contact with Western Gothic painters was Greece. Some decorations, e.g., that of the Evangelistria in Geraki, show Byzantine and Western Gothic painters working side by side: the point is that the two styles did not mix, that they remained absolutely unrelated.[77]

C. Italy

Thus, Palaeologan painting does not seem to have owed much to Western Gothic influence. Byzantine artists had to work out their own "Gothic." Nor was Italian art an important factor in this process, contrary to what was believed one or two generations ago.[78] The thesis of the Italian origin of the Palaeologan style, which found its most fervent advocates in Likhachev, Kondakov, and Ainalov,[79] is today practically abandoned except by some Italian authors.[80] As a matter of fact, this hypothesis cannot stand up to a confrontation of works and dates: any dated work in the Greek orbit surpasses by far any contemporary Italian painting, with regard not only to plastic modeling and spatial composition but also to its humane and humanistic qualities. And even if Professor Longhi's "giudizio sul Duecento" [81] seems too harsh, it must be admitted that neither Guido nor Coppo nor Giunta can in any way compete, in the respects just mentioned, with their Eastern contemporaries.[82] It was only the last generation of artists of the thirteenth century, the generation of the Maestro di San Martino, of Cimabue, Duccio, and the Romans, who, partly under the guidance of the new art of Byzantium, created a new and grand style—a style, however, which was in some respects (especially in those of spatial composition) still less "modern" than the Palaeologan style. Cimabue, for instance, in addition to using Greek manuscripts as models,[83] took his cue, as far as volume and monumental form are concerned, from prototypes as far back as the frescoes of Mileševo.[84]

This general verdict would not, of course, exclude the possibility that some impulses from Italian art were nevertheless taken up by Greek painters in Constantinople or in the diaspora, especially by those who lived in Italy itself. Sicily and Venice especially were centers where Greek artists working for Italian patrons may have been strongly influenced by their environment. As far as Sicily is concerned,[85] no convincing argument has been brought forward for the Sicilian origin of a group of painted and mosaic icons which do show early Palaeologan characteristics; these, we believe, should be regarded as Constantinopolitan because of their close relation to metropolitan works. On the other hand, those works that are definitely Sicilian, like

76 Buchthal, *Miniature Painting*, p. 48, PL. 57 *a*, 58, 59 *a* (Perugia, Biblioteca Capitolare 6, formerly 21); pp. 54 ff., PL. 62–81 (Paris, Bibliothèque de l'Arsenal 5211); pp. 68 ff., PL. 82–129 (Dijon, Bibliothèque Municipale 562 (323), Brussels, Bibliothèque Royale 1075, London, British Museum Add. 15268).

77 Demus, "Die Entstehung," p. 36.

78 Ibid., pp. 36 ff., with bibliography, esp. G. Millet, "L'art des Balkans et l'Italie au XIIIᵉ siècle," *Atti del V Congresso Internazionale di Studi Bizantini*, II (Rome, 1940) (=*Studi bizantini e neoellenici*, 6), pp. 272 ff.

79 N. P. Likhačev, *Istoričeskoe značenie italo-grečeskoj ikonopisi* (St. Petersburg, 1911), p. 30 and passim; N. P. Kondakov, *Ikonografija Bogomateri*, II (Petrograd, 1915), 15 ff.; D. V. Ajnalov, *Vizantijskaia živopis' XIV stoletija* (Petrograd, 1917), pp. 150 ff. and passim.

80 S. Bettini, "I mosaici dell' atrio di San Marco e il loro seguito," *Arte Veneta*, 8 (1954), pp. 22 ff., esp. pp. 37 f.

81 R. Longhi, "Giudizio sul Duecento, 1939," *Proporzioni*, 2 (1948), pp. 5 ff.

82 See Demus, "Zwei konstantinopler Marienikonen," pp. 87 ff.

83 See Demus, "Die Entstehung," Figs. 18, 32, p. 40; see also below, p. 146.

84 There is, as yet, no comprehensive study of the role of Byzantine influence in Italian Duecento painting; see Demus, "Die Entstehung," pp. 40 f., and Lazarev, "Duccio and Thirteenth–Century Greek Icons."

85 V. Lazarev, "Early Italo-Byzantine Painting in Sicily," *The Burlington Magazine*, 63 (1933), pp. 279 ff., and idem, "Costantinopoli e le scuole nazionali alla luce di nuove scoperte," *Arte Veneta*, 13–14 (1959–60), p. 7 ff.

the Messina mosaics,[86] have a typically Italian hardness and even harshness, which make them quite different from anything Byzantine and let them appear as forerunners of the strong and manly art of the great Italians of the late Duecento.

As for Venice,[87] we certainly find there Byzantine painters, and especially mosaicists, in the first half of the thirteenth century, some of them working in the basilica of San Marco. As a matter of fact, it has been thought that the characteristic landscape backgrounds of Palaeologan painting were actually evolved in San Marco,[88] the narthex domes of which are said to present a consecutive series of spatial compositions, culminating in the rocky, terraced landscapes and spatially designed, "winged" structures of the story of Moses, in the last bay (Fig. 15). The point is, however, that these domes are far from offering a progressive series of solutions. On the contrary, the "Palaeologan" landscapes and architecture of the last bay appear quite abruptly; they have no forerunners in the preceding bays. This change reveals itself thus as the effect of outside influence; the influence reached Venice suddenly in the late seventies or the eighties,[89] at a date somewhat later than that of the immeasurably more advanced motifs and compositional schemes to be found in the frescoes of Sopoćani.

Another hypothesis, namely that the decorative arrangement of the vault mosaics of the Kariye, involving the fitting together of several scenes to form a kind of circular frieze, with a central medallion in the zenith and with separate corner motifs, might derive from antique prototypes that were revived in Italy in the thirteenth century (Anagni, crypt; Venice, San Marco, narthex) and thence transferred to Constantinople,[90] raises a more complicated problem. The discovery of the fact that at least one of the domical vaults in Hagia Sophia, Constantinople, contained a true annular frieze of scenes in mosaic, created perhaps as early as the tenth century, disposes of the alleged priority of the Italian examples. In addition, the schemes to be found in the Kariye are in certain respects different from those of Anagni and Venice. The compositions of these two monuments—in so far as they are not subdivided by an inner framework, as are some in Anagni—are genuinely peripheral; that is, the figures stand or move on or along the periphery of an inscribed circle and the scenes unroll in the shape of an annular, isocephalic frieze (see Fig. 16), while the vaults of the Kariye are generally composed of (or divided into) two to four "pictures," only superficially adapted to the vaulted surfaces. However, of all the cupola schemes to be found in Italy, none corresponds so closely to the compositions of the Kariye vaults as the latest of the domes of the narthex of San Marco (Fig. 15), which is exactly that part of the decoration of the Venetian church that betrays direct (and sudden) Palaeologan influence. It seems, therefore, that there existed two independent but parallel traditions of cupola schemes, one in Italy and another in Byzantium, both derived from antique prototypes but developing in different ways; when they met, in Venice in about 1280, the Byzantine strain was the stronger one and superimposed itself on the Italian scheme.

Thus, in the relation between Greek and Italian painting before 1300, Byzantium was certainly the active partner; and even after that date, when Italian painting had reached its first climax, Byzantium took no notice of the creation of a new, great style by the painters of Rome and

---

86 Lazarev, "Costantinopoli e le scuole nazionali," Fig. 6.

87 O. Demus, *Die Mosaiken von San Marco in Venedig, 1100-1300* (Vienna, 1935), pp. 64 f.; V. Lazarev [Lasareff], "Über eine neue Gruppe byzantinisch-venezianischer Trecento-Bilder," *Art Studies*, Vol. 8, Part II (1931), pp. 1 ff.

88 Ajnalov, *Vizantijskaia živopis'*, passim; Bettini, "I mosaici dell' atrio," pp. 31 ff.

89 Demus, *Die Mosaiken von San Marco*, pp. 58, 64. For the date of the Moses dome in San Marco see idem, "The Ciborium Mosaics of Parenzo," *The Burlington Magazine*, 87 (1945), pp. 238 ff. For illustrations see Bettini, *Mosaici di San Marco*, PL. LXXX ff.

90 Grabar, "La décoration," pp. 111 ff.

Tuscany. It has been rightly pointed out that the fact that the painters of Byzantium did not let themselves be influenced by the greatest of these Italian painters, Giotto himself, practically rules out Italian influences perpetrated by his immeasurably weaker forerunners. It would be strange if these alleged Italian influences had ceased at the very moment in which Italian art reached its first maturity and its greatest power.[91]

The only possible effect of Italy on Greek painters and painting in the thirteenth century must be sought, it seems, in the same sphere as the effect of Western factors in general: it may have had a certain loosening and leavening influence, which may have been quite important but which was, on the whole, rather negative and, moreover, hardly allows of a clear-cut definition.

D. The Orient

The counterpart of the "Western" hypothesis, namely the belief that Palaeologan art owed some or most of its iconographic and stylistic innovations to oriental influences, has today been more or less abandoned.[92] Here again, the dates show that the modern traits to be found in oriental painting of the thirteenth and fourteenth centuries were, in fact, imported from Constantinople. As regards one alleged source of Palaeologan style and iconography, namely a group of much earlier Cappadocian frescoes in which still older Syro-Palestinian cycles and compositions were believed to have been preserved, as in cold storage, there is absolutely no reason to assume that these provincial, popular, and in many cases primitive paintings, in their secluded and remote cave churches, attracted in any way the attention of Palaeologan artists and patrons. Neither does the only vigorous branch of Eastern painting of the thirteenth century, Armenian book illumination, flowering in Cilicia, seem to have exerted any influence on nascent Palaeologan painting, although Toros Roslin, Constantine, and Barsegh must have been among the most gifted miniaturists of their time.[93] The stylistic changes that carried these artists to the forefront of "modernism" in the sense of the new plastic style occurred in the second half of the thirteenth century only, and here too the initial impetus was supplied by early Palaeologan painting in Constantinople.

E. The Slavs

It is more difficult to define the influence of the Slav factor on the crystallization of the Palaeologan style.[94] Russia, to begin with, is to be counted out because of the Mongol occupation.[95] Rumania, too, hardly produced anything of importance before the fourteenth century; it is only at that time that we find a development of interest, which, however, occurred entirely under the influence of Constantinopolitan painting. The frescoes of St. Nicholas in Curtea-de-Argeş, for instance, seem to have been inspired directly by the mosaics of the Kariye.[96]

The case is more complicated with regard to Bulgaria.[97] It might be supposed that Greek painters found refuge and work there during the Latin period, especially under John Asen II

91 Ch. Diehl, "La dernière renaissance de l'art byzantin," *Choses et gens de Byzance: Etudes d'histoire et d'archéologie* (Paris, 1926), pp. 143 ff.

92 Demus, "Die Entstehung," pp. 41 ff., with bibliography; esp. Lazarev, *Istorija*, I, p. 277, n. 14, and G. Millet, "Byzance et non l'Orient," *RA*, 4th ser., 11 (1908), pp. 171 ff. For the opposite view see G. de Francovich, "L'arte siriaca e il suo influsso sulla pittura medievale nell' oriente e nell' occidente," *Commentari*, 2 (1951), pp. 3 ff., 75 ff., 143 ff.

93 S. Der Nersessian, *Armenia and the Byzantine Empire: A Brief Study of Armenian Art and Civilization* (Cambridge,

Mass., 1945), pp. 124 ff. and bibliography on p. 140.

94 Demus, "Die Entstehung," pp. 43 ff.

95 Lazarev, *Istorija*, I, pp. 181 ff.

96 M. Beza, *Byzantine Art in Roumania* (London, 1940), with bibliography; the earlier literature in *L'art byzantin chez les Slaves. Dédié à la mémoire de Théodore Uspenskij*, I: *Les Balkans*, Pt. 2 (Paris, 1930), pp. 445 ff.

97 Demus, "Die Entstehung," p. 43, with bibliography, esp. Grabar, *La peinture religieuse*; N. Mavrodinov, *Starobŭlgarskata živopis* (Sofia, [1945]); K. Krestev and V. Sakhariev, *Alte bulgarische Malerei* (Dresden, 1960).

(died 1241), who stood in close (if not always friendly) contact with the Angeli of Salonika and Epirus and even concluded an alliance with Nicaea against the Latins; however, the most important cycle of wall paintings that has survived in Bulgaria, that of Boiana,[98] of 1259, does not support the idea of an essential Bulgarian contribution toward the shaping of the Palaeologan style. There is, in fact, little to be found in these frescoes that could be called Palaeologan,[99] either in the figures (types, attitudes, modeling) or in the architectural and landscape backgrounds. The paintings contain only the most meager attempts at spatial projection,[100] and the general impression is one of provincial archaism. If the painter was a Bulgarian (which seems likely) and if his work is at all typical of Bulgarian art on the eve of the Palaeologan re-establishment, Bulgaria can hardly have contributed much toward the fashioning of the new style.[101]

The most interesting problems are posed by the frescoed churches of Serbia.[102] There is no doubt that Serbian painters had a sizable share in decorating the numerous churches that were founded by kings and princes of the Nemanja dynasty. However, in portioning out among Serbian and Greek painters the various styles to be found in these frescoes it is hardly permissible to ascribe to the Serbs those styles which point forward to the new Palaeologan ideals. It is much more likely that the Slav element was responsible for the overemphasis on linear patterns than for the introduction of new plastic and spatial forms. This is at least suggested by the fact that the one form of art which can be called Serbian without any shadow of doubt, namely the illumination of Serbian manuscripts,[103] shows an almost exclusive preference for highly complicated abstract linear patterns, interlaces, and rinceaux that recall the excessive linear mannerisms of the group of Macedonian wall paintings (Kurbinovo, etc.) mentioned above. The really "modern" contribution to the decorations of Serbian churches was surely the work of Greek artists.

It is, of course, a different question what these Greek painters owed to their employment in the service of Serbian patrons: quite apart from the fact that they were thus given opportunities, on a scale not to be found anywhere else at that time, to try to develop their skill at monumental tasks, they could hardly help being impressed by the general atmosphere, the freshness and intensity of feeling natural to a young people, by a certain trend toward popular realism, and, at the same time, by the widespread gift of the Slavs for creating "decorative" effects. None of these factors, however, can have contributed greatly to the genesis of Palaeologan art.

F. Greece and Salonika

Thus it is the Greeks to whom credit must be given for developing the new style—the Greeks in the diaspora, in Constantinople, in Epirus and Macedonia and, finally, the Greeks in Anatolia, in Trebizond and Nicaea. Of the western bloc, Hellas,[104] mostly under Latin domination, does not seem to have played an important part. With few exceptions (Oropos, for instance),

98 Grabar, *La peinture religieuse*, pp. 117 ff., with bibliography; Ph. Schweinfurth, *Die Wandbilder der Kirche von Bojana bei Sofia* (Berlin, 1943); N. Mavrodinov, *Starobŭlgarskata živopis*, (Sofia, 1959), pp. 89 ff.; G. Stoikov, *Boyana Church* (Sofia, 1954).

99 With the exception, of course, of the Presentation of Mary in the Temple, which dates from the 14th century (Schweinfurth, *Die Wandbilder*, PL. 52).

100 E.g., the throne of the 12-year-old Christ in the Temple (Schweinfurth, PL. 48); as regards the figures, the most "modern" one is that of Adam in the Anastasis.

101 This must be emphasized against the exaggerated claims of Mavrodinov in *Starobŭlgarskata živopis* and *Starobŭlgarskoto izkustvo* (Sofia, 1959), and of A. Protić, "Les origines sassanides et byzantines de l'art bulgare," *Mélanges Charles Diehl* (Paris, 1930), II, pp. 137 ff.

102 Demus, "Die Entstehung," pp. 49 ff., with bibliography; and especially, on the share of Serbian painters in the decorations of the 13th century, Radojčić, *Majstori*.

103 Sv. Radojčić, *Stare srpske minijature* (Belgrade, 1950).

104 Demus, "Die Entstehung," pp. 48 f., with bibliography.

the style of the wall paintings to be found there is rather conservative; it is only in the north that more progressive trends can be found at work. But even in Thessaly (Trikkala, Panagia Porta, of 1285) [105] and western Epirus, frescoes and mosaics exhibit an uneven mixture of archaic and modern elements, right down to the close of the century. The recently cleaned mosaics of the Panagia Paregoritissa in Arta (1290), [106] for instance, impressive though they are, show quite clearly that Arta was hardly a creative center. They may well be imitations of Constantinopolitan works.

It has been claimed, on the other hand, that Salonika was such a center, even *the* creative center of the thirteenth century—and it was most probably just the passionate way in which this claim was made by Professor Xyngopoulos [107] that led a good many specialists toward contradicting it. The fact, however, that Salonika was in Greek hands from 1223 onward and that it became, in the later fifties, one of the centers of Palaeologan political propaganda—a propaganda the acrostic slogan of which (ΜΑΡΠΟΥ) is to be found even in much later Serbian wall painting [108]—these facts would by themselves suggest that Salonika played an important part in the rallying of the Greek forces during the Latin occupation of Constantinople. To these circumstances must be added the reports about the calling of artists from Salonika to Serbia [109] and the great density of monuments, some of them—like Studenica, of 1209—with Greek inscriptions, in a region which, though it cannot be called the hinterland of Salonika, was, in any case, its natural sphere of influence.

Thus, although no wall paintings of the thirteenth century have so far come to light in Salonika itself, Professor Xyngopoulos seems to be justified in assuming that the capital of Macedonia played an important role in keeping alive the tradition of Greek monumental painting and in preparing its great flowering in the second half of the thirteenth century.

G. Nicaea

However, Salonika was not the only, nor even the main rallying center of Greek forces before 1261; the most important role in this respect fell, of course, to Nicaea, the center of the eastern Greek bloc. It is as yet too early to say whether Trebizond had a certain share in this activity, as far as painting was concerned: [110] the frescoes of St. Sophia are in process of being cleaned, and, as regards the production of illuminated books, we so far lack dependable data. In any event, Nicaea must have been the leading center, politically and culturally. [111] There is no doubt, either, that it did produce wall paintings as well as illuminated manuscripts. Of the former, nothing is preserved in the town itself; but the remains of wall paintings which have come to light in Pergamon [112] and which, though not dated, must be ascribed to the second quarter of the thirteenth century on stylistic grounds are of the highest quality, if still somewhat conservative in their linear treatment. Conservatism is also the most outstanding characteristic of a group of illuminated

105 A. K. Orlandos, Ἡ Πόρτα-Παναγιὰ τῆς Θεσσαλίας, in Ἀρχεῖον τῶν βυζαντινῶν μνημείων τῆς Ἑλλάδος, 1 (1935), pp. 5 ff., esp. p. 33.

106 A. K. Orlandos, Ἡ Παρηγορήτισσα τῆς Ἄρτης, in Ἀρχαιολογικὸν Δελτίον, 5 (1919), pp. 1 ff. In a lecture at the Byzantine Congress of Munich, 1958, Professor Orlandos announced a new publication.

107 Xyngopoulos, *Thessalonique*. See also V. J. Djurić, "Origine thessalonicienne des fresques du monastère de Resava," *ZRVI*, 65, No. 6 (1960), pp. 111 ff.

108 Radojčić, "Die Entstehung der Malerei," p. 110.

109 Radojčić, *Majstori*, p. 13.

110 G. Millet and D. Talbot Rice, *Byzantine Painting at Trebizond* (London, 1936); Alpatov, "Eine Reise," pp. 73 ff. The frescoes of St. Sophia at Trebizond, color slides of which were presented by Professor Talbot Rice in a report at the Byzantine Congress of Ohrid, in 1961, seem to belong to the middle of the 13th century. They are of high quality but do not show especially "modern" forms.

111 Demus, "Die Entstehung," pp. 53 f., with bibliography.

112 Demus, "Zwei konstantinopler Marienikonen," p. 97.

manuscripts that, though ascribed by a number of scholars to Constantinople and to a date after 1261, ought in all probability to be regarded as Nicaean works of the first half of the thirteenth century.[113] The manuscripts of this group, exemplified by the Parisinus Coisl. 200, the Rocke-feller-McCormick New Testament (Gregory 2400) at Chicago, and the Leningrad Gospel Book gr. 105, from Karahissar, are not dated directly, but there are two dates connected with them that, if interpreted rightly, may help in assigning them their proper place. The first date is the year 1269, in which Paris. Coisl. 200 was sent by Michael VIII Palaeologos to Saint Louis of France, as a gift; the date marks a *terminus ante quem*. The colophon of the related manuscript at Mount Athos, Lavra 146 (B.26), gives the other date, 1084—quite clearly not the year of the writing of the book but the date of its prototype; apparently, the colophon was copied in the thirteenth century, together with the rest of the book, from a model dated 1084. This circum-stance is of great importance since it fits very well with what we know about the collecting and copying of earlier books in Nicaea, as reported by contemporary sources,[114] and since it helps to explain the conservative, even archaizing style of the manuscripts in question. As a matter of fact, the miniatures in these manuscripts contain not a single element that points to the future; not a single element, even, that goes beyond the average style of the later twelfth century. Their archaizing character makes it difficult to date them stylistically beyond a general attribution (mainly on technical grounds) to the first half of the thirteenth century.

This group of manuscripts, product of a very conservative court scriptorium, is, however, not the only one that can be ascribed to Nicaea. A related, but more modern, group contains a good many books, the most interesting (and perhaps also the latest) of which is a Commentary on the Psalms in the Seraglio Library of Istanbul, No. 13.[115] The miniatures of this group are characterized, among other things, by lateral ornamented bands in the place of proper frames, a feature which is also to be found in some Crusaders' manuscripts.[116] The Seraglio codex is especially important on account of a new sense of plastic values that is exhibited in its figures, a plastic style that seems to foreshadow (or is a parallel of) the style of the narthex frescoes of Sopoćani. However, since the manuscript is the most developed and therefore probably the latest known member of the whole group, it may have originated after the return to Constantinople.

It is thus very difficult, if not impossible, at this juncture to arrive at a well-founded estimate of the part played by Nicaea. From the few examples of Nicaean work that can now be recog-nized as such with a certain degree of probability, one might easily derive a one-sided picture—as if Nicaea had stood solely for conservatism and archaism, or in any case for re-establishing contact with the older tradition. This was certainly one of the trends of Nicaean art, perhaps even the most important one, because it revived knowledge and understanding of ancient models and thus prepared the Palaeologan "renascence"; but it cannot have been the only trend in the art of the provisional capital of the Empire. Life and art in Nicaea must have developed within the two generations from 1204 to 1261, and it is only logical to assume that the town which was the cradle of the new political concept was also, to a certain extent, the birthplace of the new art.

---

113 H. R. Willoughby, "Codex 2400 and Its Miniatures," *ArtB*, 15 (1933), pp. 3 ff., with bibliography. For additions to the group see Demus, *Norman Sicily*, pp. 435, 441 (n. 112), and Lazarev, *Istorija*, pp. 165 f. A date before 1261 and an origin in Nicaea have been suggested by S. Der Nersessian in E. C. Colwell and H. R. Willoughby, *The Four Gospels of Karahissar*, II (Chicago, 1936), p. xxvii, and Demus, "Die Entstehung," pp. 18 f.

114 Lazarev, *Istorija*, I, p. 168.

115 To the group belong, among others, Oxford, Bodleian Library, Laud. gr. 30 A; Oxford, New College 44; Paris, Bibl. Nat. gr. 1528. On the Seraglio Psalter, cod. 13, see A. Muñoz, "Tre codici miniati della biblioteca del Serraglio a Constan-tinopoli," *Studi bizantini*, I (1925), pp. 201 ff., Figs. 7, 8.

116 Buchthal, *Miniature Painting*, p. 11, where the Seraglio codex is dated in the 14th century.

5. THE PERIOD OF MICHAEL VIII (1261–1282)

The recovery of the capital in 1261 must have been the signal for the return of a good many artists from the diaspora to Constantinople, where great and new tasks would be waiting for them.[117] Naturally, the artists who returned to the capital were not the same ones, physically or psychologically, who had left the town at the beginning of the century; not physically, since hardly any of the refugees of 1204 could have been alive in 1261; and not psychologically, because the entire situation of the painter must have changed fundamentally during the two generations of the diaspora. The artist in 1261 was no longer part of an accepted order, upheld by sociological and spiritual forces, as he had been before. There was now no dependable code of iconographic or stylistic conventions. The artists themselves, on the other hand, had been through widely differing experiences, had received widely differing training. Some came from western, some from oriental countries: one from Serbia, where he had worked for a Slav prince, another from Nicaea, where he had either lived in the somewhat artificial atmosphere of retrospective conservatism or shared the endeavors of a national revival; it must indeed have been a motley crowd who came back to the capital which many of them had never seen. One thing, however, they must have had in common, as against their fathers and grandfathers of the beginning of the century: their outlook and their art itself must have been much more personal, much more individualistic. The growth of this new, personal element can be traced in the increasing number of artists' signatures (or rather, names) in works of the first half of the thirteenth century.[118]

Thus, the situation of Constantinopolitan art in 1261 was entirely different from that at the end of the iconoclastic controversy. In both cases, it is true, the result was the birth of a new religious art after a period of secularization; but in the ninth century, the emphasis was more on a new iconography, in the thirteenth, on a new style. After the victory of the iconodules, the secular element was completely eliminated from ecclesiastic decoration, while the thirteenth century produced a synthesis of secular and religious elements, perhaps the first synthesis of this kind in Byzantine art.[119] The ninth century saw a narrowing, the thirteenth a widening of the range of artistic possibilities: in the earlier period, the artists were the executants of programs worked out by ecclesiatics; in the later, they became the individual interpreters of ideas conceived by humanists.

With all this, it is very impressive to see how quickly the various tendencies and traditions that must have met, perhaps even clashed, in Constantinople after 1261 were molded into a more or less homogeneous whole. Such was the force—one might even say the genius—of this unique town that the process of amalgamation was completed within one generation and that a new koine, which in spite of a multiplicity of local styles and artistic currents dominated the art of painting from Georgia to Serbia, was in existence as early as the last quarter of the thirteenth century.

The number of works created under the first two Palaeologan emperors must have been gigantic; nevertheless, the period of Michael VIII, immediately after the reconquest, is still rather poorly documented. One of the few dated manuscripts, the Parisinus gr. 117, a Gospel

---

117 Demus, "Die Entstehung," pp. 55 ff., 62 f.

118 Radojčić, *Majstori*, passim. The names that appear in Mileševo are not, however, artists' names but the names of the saints to be represented on the respective surfaces.

119 L. Bréhier, "La rénovation artistique sous les Paléologues et le mouvement des idées," *Mélanges Charles Diehl*, II, pp. 1 ff.; Shmit, "La 'renaissance'."

Book of 1262–63, is still a derivative of the Nicaean "Karahissar group"; [120] bodies and structures are, however, much more voluminous, though the modeling is still emphasized by form-designing lines. To the same stylistic phase, combining graded modeling with form-designing lineament, belong the Sinai Psalter, St. Catherine's Monastery 38 (with some leaves in Leningrad, Public Library 269), [121] the Psalter at Mount Athos, Stauronikita 46, which has been found related to the frescoes of Sopoćani, [122] and the Vat. gr. 1153, which contains large pictures of prophets in full figure, whose somewhat barbaric magnificence seems to prefigure the mosaics in the dome of the Panagia Paregoritissa of Arta and may be the hallmark of provincial (Epirote?) origin (Fig. 17). [123] More likely to have originated in Constantinople itself are some manuscripts of the group discussed above that were thought by Professor Weitzmann to have been illuminated in the capital during the Latin occupation. As has been said before, this early date may hold true for one or two of these books, but others, like Leningrad, Public Library, gr. 101 and Mount Athos, Iviron 5, must surely be ascribed to the period of Michael VIII. [124]

All these manuscripts show the characteristic style of the period, a plastic style that produces the effect of forceful volume by a combination of vigorous shading and flexible lineament. The same combination can be found in a number of icons, both in mosaic and in tempera. A typical mosaic icon of this period is the Crucifixion, in Berlin (Fig. 18), [125] which is so near in style to the Leningrad Gospels, gr. 101, that it is tempting to regard the two works as products of the same workshop in two different techniques. Somewhat later, perhaps, is the Octateuch of Mount Athos, Vatopedi 602, which, as Professor Weitzmann has shown, was in all probability illuminated in the imperial scriptorium since it shows a direct dependence on the Joshua Roll, Vatican, Palat. gr. 431 (Fig. 57), which would hardly have been available outside Constantinople. [126] The plasticity of the figures and buildings places the work in the first rank of early Palaeologan manuscripts.

So far, we know of only one monumental painting in Constantinople that might be attributed to the time of Michael VIII, a work that can, indeed, be regarded as one of the chief masterpieces of the period—namely the great Deesis in the South Gallery of Hagia Sophia (Figs. 19–21). [127] If we gave rein to our imagination, we might even think that we have in this work the monument that Michael VIII caused to be made as a kind of thankoffering after his triumphal entry into Hagia Sophia. The mosaic shows the great art of Palaeologan painting in its early stage, when there was a new feeling for plastic values and for the importance of light and shade but the use of form-designing lineament continued. Characteristic of the early date, immediately after the return to the capital, is the employment, side by side, of three different methods of modeling.

120 Omont, *Plus anciens MSS grecs*, PL. LVI,2. Willoughby, "Codex 2400," p. 19, includes the MS in the Karahissar group: it stands between this and the group of the Seraglio Psalter, cod. 13.

121 K. Weitzmann, "Eine Pariser-Psalter-Kopie des 13. Jahrhunderts auf dem Sinai," *JOeBG*, 6 (1957), pp. 125 ff.

122 Radojčić, "Die Entstehung der Malerei," Fig. 1.

123 Lazarev, *Istorija*, I, p. 340, n. 31; A. Muñoz, *I codici greci miniati delle minori biblioteche di Roma* (Florence, 1905), pp. 29 ff., PL. 7 ff.

124 Weitzmann, "Constantinopolitan Book Illumination," with bibliography; Lazarev, review of Weitzmann's article, in *VV*, 2 (1949), pp. 367 ff.; idem, "Novyj pamjatnik"; see also below.

125 O. Wulff and M. Alpatoff, *Denkmäler der Ikonenmalerei in kunstgeschichtlicher Folge* (Dresden, 1925), Fig. 39; Demus, "Die Entstehung," p. 57, with bibliography (the St. Matthew of the Leningrad Gospels, gr. 101 is reproduced on PL. 19).

126 Weitzmann, "Constantinopolitan Book Illumination," p. 208, and idem, *The Joshua Roll* (Princeton, 1948), p. 37. Weitzmann has rightly characterized the illumination of the MS as a mixture of conservative and modern elements.

127 Th. Whittemore, *The Mosaics of Haghia Sophia at Istanbul: Fourth Preliminary Report* (Oxford, 1952); Demus, "Zwei konstantinopler Marienikonen," pp. 96 f., and "Die Entstehung," pp. 16, 56 f., both with bibliography. Lazarev (*Freski Staroi Ladogi*, p. 84) has recently reaffirmed his dating of the Deesis in the second quarter of the 12th century. See, however, R. Hamann-MacLean's review in *BZ*, 54 (1961), p. 396. The fact, observed by Professor Underwood, that the mosaic figures appear to have been set into an earlier golden ground would tend to support a date at the beginning of Michael VIII's reign: golden cubes would hardly have been in store at that time and their manufacture would as yet hardly have been resumed. Thus, Michael may have resorted to the device of usurping the golden ground of an earlier mosaic.

The most archaic is the use of lines following the form, as in the face of John the Baptist—a treatment which already had almost become an iconographic attribute of this figure and can still be found in much later representations of the Forerunner. Next, there is a very soft shading by tone and color arranged in lines, which, however, do not follow the plastic forms but seem to run across them; the finest example of this method, which was in use as early as the twelfth century,[128] is the modeling of the face of the Virgin, with its strands of small tesserae running through the whole gamut from olive brown (in the shadow of the nose) to ivory, pink, bluish green, and blue (at the contour of the cheek). And the third means is the introduction of cast shadows, to be found in the face of Christ: the shadow that crosses his throat represents one of the very first attempts at producing an optical effect of this kind since late antiquity. A new feature also is the "spatial" projection of the mouth of the Virgin, a new way of seeing and representing details which is foreshadowed in the late twelfth century [129] but which seems to have found its mature form only in the Deesis mosaic, unless the two Washington icons [130] that show the same peculiarity are one or two decades older. As a matter of fact, the face of the Kahn Madonna (Fig. 22) offers the closest parallel that can be expected to exist in two so widely different media, a near-identity of form that should be accepted as sufficient proof of the Constantinopolitan origin of the two Washington panels.

The style of Michael VIII reached its classical perfection in the later parts of the Sopoćani frescoes, which have been dealt with in detail above. And somewhat later still, perhaps in the eighties, was created, certainly in Constantinople itself, one of the most splendid mosaic icons that have come down to us, namely the icon of the Forty Martyrs, in Dumbarton Oaks, a work full of the classical spirit of early-Palaeologan art (Fig. 23).[131]

6. THE PERIOD OF ANDRONICUS II (1282–1328)

A. The End of the Thirteenth Century and the First Decade of the Fourteenth

The development of the pictorial style in the first half of the reign of Andronicus II seems to be characterized, at first, by a further increase of volume in bodies and architectural motifs, by a growing bulkiness and heaviness so marked that the term "cubism" does not seem too extravagant for certain characteristic products of the period. The difference between the plastic style of the epoch of Michael VIII and this cubist style can be seen very clearly by a comparison of earlier and later manuscripts of the group characterized by the Athens, Leningrad, and Iviron Gospels discussed above. London, British Museum, Burney 20, of 1285,[132] already shows the greatly increased heaviness of the figures, but a confrontation of Iviron 5 (Fig. 24) [133] and the related but later (and iconographically derivative) Gospel Book, Paris. gr. 54 (Fig. 25),[134] reveals the essential difference between the two phases. For instance, the treatment of the body of St. Luke in the Paris manuscript is wooden, the plastic values are overemphasized, the whole figure looks hard and frozen. The "cubism" of this figure is far removed

---

128 In the face of Alexios in the John and Alexios panel of the Hagia Sophia: Whittemore, *The Mosaics: Third Preliminary Report*, PL. 35 and color plate after p. 20.
129 Monreale: Demus, *Norman Sicily*, p. 432, PL. 76 *b*; Kitzinger, *Monreale*, PL. 4.
130 Demus, "Zwei konstantinopler Marienikonen"; see esp. the juxtaposition of Figs. 4 and 5.
131 Demus, "Two Palaeologan Mosaic Icons," pp. 89 ff.

132 Lazarev, "Novyj pamjatnik," pp. 178 ff. Reproduced also in idem, *Istorija*, II, PL. 256 *a*, *b*.
133 A. Xyngopoulos, Ἱστορημένα εὐαγγέλια μονῆς Ἰβήρων Ἁγ. Ὄρους (Athens, [1932]); Demus, "Die Entstehung," p. 16, with bibliography.
134 Omont, *Miniatures des plus anciens manuscrits grecs*, PL. XC ff.

from the spatial and painterly treatment of the Iviron, Leningrad, or Athens Gospels. The Paris codex seems, in fact, the *outré* product of the development which we have followed from the early thirteenth century. A little earlier than this ending phase, perhaps shortly before the turn of the century, should be dated a further example of the same iconographic group of manuscripts, the Princeton Gospel Book, gr. Garrett 2, formerly Athos, Andreaskiti 753 (Fig. 26), [135] which displays compact and sharply indented forms foreshadowing the extreme solution of the Paris. gr. 54 without attaining it. The trend is carried further in the Gospels at Mount Athos, Philotheou 5, which must belong to the turn of the century. [136]

Equally ample and massive are the Evangelists of Mount Athos, Pantokratoros 47, dated 1301, portrayed in a rather hard and sharp relief, [137] or those of Vatopedi 736 (938), another dated Gospel Book, of 1304. [138] Both these books may, however, be of provincial origin, but two Vatican manuscripts—gr. 1208 (Fig. 27), [139] containing magnificent figures of standing Apostles, and gr. 1158 (Fig. 28), [140] containing extremely fine seated Evangelists—are doubtless works of one of the best painters, perhaps even the leading one, of the metropolitan workshops. The figures are voluminous without being inflated. The extreme cubist stage seems to have been left behind by the artists of this court scriptorium: the relief is firm and precise, pointing the way toward an increasingly "graphic" differentiation of the surface, every stroke of the brush still signifying either a raised ridge or a concave furrow of the drapery.

Byzantine manuscripts of the time of Andronicus II must have traveled widely and fast, perhaps as imperial gifts; a book of the type of the Paris Gospel, gr. 54, for instance, must have been in the hands of Cimabue when he painted his Evangelists in the upper church of San Francesco in Assisi, certainly before 1290. [141] But not all early-Palaeologan influence that can be found in Italian painting toward the end of the thirteenth century is likely to have been transmitted by illuminated manuscripts. A good deal more important, surely, were monumental paintings, either works seen in Byzantium itself by itinerant Italian artists or, and this is more likely, works executed in Italy by Greek painters, like those perhaps not entirely mythical Greeks of Vasari's who are said to have worked in S. Maria Novella, in Florence. The poor remnants still to be seen there do not permit a well-founded judgment. [142]

However, a fair amount of monumental painting of the first half of Andronicus' reign is preserved in Byzantine lands, although nothing has so far become known in Constantinople itself. Outside the capital, the most impressive monuments of the "heavy style" are the fresco decorations of the church of St. Clement (Peribleptos) in Ohrid [143] and of the Bogorodica Ljeviška in Prizren, [144] the earliest known works of a pair of Greek masters who later on became the court

135 Weitzmann, "Constantinopolitan Book Illumination," pp. 201 f., with bibliography. The Evangelists are the work of two masters.

136 Ibid., p. 205, with bibliography.

137 Ibid., p. 213, with bibliography, and Fig. 13. The style of the Evangelists' portraits seems rather well developed for the date of 1301.

138 Ibid., p. 213, with bibliography, and Fig. 14. The Vatican Psalter, Pal. gr. 381 is very close in style.

139 Ibid., p. 207, with bibliography, and Fig. 10.

140 St. Beissel, *Vatikanische Miniaturen* (Freiburg, 1893), PL. X (with a date in the 11th–12th century); actually, the text and the canon tables are of the late 11th or the early 12th century, the miniatures having been added in the beginning of the 14th century.

141 Demus, "Die Entstehung," p. 40.

142 K. Frey, *Le vite . . . scritte da M. G. Vasari,* I (Munich,

1911), pp. 390 f. The frescoes cannot have been painted before 1278; this, of course, contradicts the Cimabue legend.

143 R. Hamann-MacLean, "Zu den Malerinschriften der 'Milutinschule,' " *BZ,* 53 (1960), pp. 112 ff., with bibliography; V. R. Petković, *La peinture serbe du Moyen Âge,* II (Belgrade, 1934), PL. CXXIII–CXXVII; St. Pelekanides, Ὁ ζωγράφος Μιχαὴλ Ἀστραπᾶς, in Μακεδονικά, IV (1955–60), pp. 545 ff.; Bihalji-Merin, *Fresken und Ikonen,* PL. 46 f. There is as yet no comprehensive study of this most important cycle; see, however, the album of reproductions by D. Čornakov, *St. Clement (Bogorodica Perivleptos)* (Skoplje, 1961), and R. Ljubinković and M. Ćorović-Ljubinković, "La peinture médiévale à Ohrid," *Zbornik du Musée National d'Ohrid* (ed. spec., 1961), pp. 101 ff.

144 R. Hamann-MacLean, *Aus der mittelalterlichen Bildwelt Jugoslawiens: Einzelheiten des Freskenzyklus der Kirche der Gottesmutter von Leviša in Prizren* (Marburg an der Lahn, 1955), with bibliography.

painters of King Milutin of Serbia: Michael (Astrapas) and Eutychios.[145] The reading of the inscribed date of this Ohrid church, 1295, has recently been challenged on the strength of a reputedly wrong indiction and has been altered to 1303–04 (according to Hallensleben, even 1310–11); a more recent examination, however, proved the date of 1295 correct.[146] The related cycles of Prizren (Bogorodica Ljeviška, 1307–09), Žiča (ca. 1309),[147] and Mount Athos (Protation and Vatopedi) are somewhat later.[148]

The leading painter of Ohrid (Fig. 29)—the placing of the inscriptions does not permit a clear identification of hands—must have come from a milieu intimately related to that of the illuminator of the Paris Gospel, gr. 54. The treatment of the drapery in hard and glassy folds, the cutting up of the draped bodies by straight lines into dark and well-lit parts, the entire "cubist" approach, the very ductus of the linear design, and finally the cold, transparent colors are very much alike in the two works. Common to both works is also the way in which space is suggested by the placement of figures behind ridges of the terrain so that their legs are hidden up to the knees; and in both works we find similar architectural motifs—extremely heavy, cubic masses, which outweigh everything in earlier Byzantine art. In spite of this heaviness and brittleness of the forms, there is nothing clumsy, nothing primitive about the Ohrid frescoes. The colors are highly refined (if somewhat loud), giving to the figures the transparent air of cut glass. The fact that the donor of the church, Progonos Sguros,[149] seems to have been related by marriage to the imperial family argues for the origin of the workshop, or at least the leading master, in one of the great centers of the period—possibly Salonika, the art of which shows a certain penchant for the heavy, plastic style. At least, this style is also to be found in other works in the neighborhood of Salonika, among them the fresco cycles of Mount Athos mentioned above, of the Protaton and of Vatopedi. These cycles are in some respects very close to the frescoes of Ohrid, for instance, with regard to the plastic heaviness of the extremely broad figures and to the cross-shaped structures made up of heavy blocks. True, the Athos paintings show a freer play of lines, a more painterly modeling, a somewhat more baroque exuberance of form—qualities, in short, that are characteristic of Millet's "Macedonian" school;[150] but there are figures and forms in these frescoes which could almost be interchanged with parts of the Ohrid cycle—for instance, some figures in the two representations of the Birth of the Virgin in the Protaton and St. Clement's (Fig. 30). The Ohrid frescoes are, however, earlier and better, the Athos paintings being clearly derivative. A more painterly variety of the heavy style is represented by the decoration of the Euthymios chapel in St. Demetrius, Salonika, dated by an inscription in 1303.[151] The two painters who worked at these small-scale paintings used an impasto technique that is quite different from the hard modeling of Ohrid, although somewhat nearer to the "liquid" treatment of the Protaton frescoes it; is, perhaps, the most painterly method to be found in frescoes of the period. An echo of this style and technique can still be found, a dozen years later, in the frescoes

145 The most recent study of the problems connected with Michael and Eutychios is a paper by P. Miljković-Pepek, "Les données littéraires, se rapportant aux peintres Mihail Astrapa et Eutihie" (Macedonian with French résumé), *Glasnik na Institutot za nacionalna istorija*, IV (1960), pp. 139 ff.

146 Hamann-MacLean, "Zu den Malerinschriften"; for a reading of the date as 1295 I am obliged to Professors I. Ševčenko and H.-G. Beck. Professor Radojčić has always upheld the earlier date: Radojčić, *Majstori*, pp. 19 ff.

147 Millet and Frolow, *Peinture*, I, PL. 62; Petković, *La peinture*, II, PL. XXXVIII.

148 Millet, *Athos*, PL. 5–58 and 81–94.

149 P. N. Miljukov, "Khristianskija drevnosti Zapadnoj Makedonii," *Izvestija Russk. Arkh. Inst. v Konstantinopolé*, IV (Sofia, 1899), pp. 90 f.

150 G. Millet, *Recherches sur l'iconographie de l'Evangile aux XIVe, XVe et XVIe siècles* (Paris, 1916; reprinted 1960), pp. 630 ff.; Xyngopoulos, *Thessalonique*, pp. 7–14, 29; idem *Manuel Panselinos* (Athens, 1956); idem, "Nouveaux témoignages de l'activité des peintres macédoniens au Mont-Athos," *BZ*, 52 (1959), pp. 61 ff.

151 G. and M. Soteriou, Ἡ βασιλικὴ τοῦ Ἁγίου Δημητρίου Θεσσαλονίκης (Athens, 1952), pp. 213 ff., PL. 82 ff.

of the church of Christ in Verria, of 1315,[152] by the painter Kalliergis, who betrays his belonging to the tradition of Salonika also by close affinities of motifs and iconography.

Of contemporary icon painting a good idea can be formed from a number of panels from the church of St. Clement in Ohrid.[153] These icons have been known for a long time, but their signal importance became clear only after their recent cleaning and restoration. Especially the older of the two Crucifixions (Fig. 31), with its swelling body and drapery forms, provides a perfect counterpart to the style of the frescoes of the same church. The expressive distortions of the faces, especially the deep triangular furrows under the eyes,[154] the overmodeling, and the somewhat monochrome treatment, distinguishing marks of a highly specialized workshop, are also to be found in an icon of the Twelve Apostles in the Tretiakov Gallery of Moscow (Fig. 32).[155] Both icons must have been painted toward the end of the thirteenth century or in the very first years of the fourteenth.[156] It is instructive to look back from the Apostles of the Moscow icon to those of the Dormition of Sopoćani: the soft voluminousness of the latter has turned into a hard compactness in the Moscow figures; the lights sit more abruptly on the surface and take on abstract shapes in graphic configurations.

B. The Later Years of Andronicus II (1310–1328)

The emphasis on graphic means for creating relief is, indeed, the main characteristic of the second and third decades of the fourteenth century, in contrast to the tendency toward overmodeling or "cubist" shading in the late thirteenth and the first years of the new century. Figures and forms now tend to spread out in increasingly flat reliefs; the architectural motifs lose a good deal of their plastic heaviness and of their "correct" suggestiveness as regards perspective representation. The growth of this style—which is the style of the Kariye Djami—can be followed in a series of dated works which, in its entirety, presents the picture of an irreversible development. A number of these works are products of the Greek workshop mentioned above, in the service of King Milutin of Serbia. Two of its leading artists, Michael and Eutychios, began their career, it will be remembered, at the end of the thirteenth century and were still active after 1320. Their *oeuvre* cannot, of course, stand comparison with the art of the Kariye, but at the beginning of the fourteenth century they seem to have been fully abreast of the metropolitan development; it was only in the later stages that they dropped behind and became really provincial.

Even in the capital, the style of the first decade is still far removed from that of the Kariye. For instance, compare the angel in an icon of the Annunciation from Ohrid (Fig. 33), which probably originated in Constantinople itself at about 1310,[157] and the angel in the fresco of the

152 Xyngopoulos, *Thessalonique*, pp. 27 f., PL. 9, 10.

153 For a general view of icon painting in Yugoslavia, see Sv. Radojčić, "Die serbische Ikonenmalerei vom 12. Jahrhundert bis zum Jahre 1459," *JOeBG*, 5 (1956), pp. 61 ff.; P. Miljković-Pepek, "Les auteurs de quelques icônes d'Ohrid du XIII–XIV S.: Mihailo ou Eutyhié," *Glasnik Soc. des musées et de l'institut de conservation de la R. P. Macédoine* I, 3 (Skoplje, 1954), p. 23 ff.; M. Ćorović-Ljubinković, *Les icônes d'Ohrid* (Print sets of "Jugoslavija," set 2; Belgrade, 1953); J. Macan, "Ohridskite ikoni," *Kulturno nasledstvo*, 5 (1959), pp. 61 ff.; Bihalji-Merin, *Fresken und Ikonen*, PL. 68 ff.; W. Felicetti-Liebenfels, *Geschichte der byzantinischen Ikonenmalerei* (Olten and Lausanne, 1956), PL. 87 ff.; D. Talbot Rice, *The Art of Byzantium* (London, 1959), PL. XLI ff. The icons of Ohrid and other Yugoslav centers were shown in 1961 in an exhibition at Ohrid, on the occasion of the 12th International Congress of Byzantine Studies; see the catalog, V. J. Djurić, *Icônes de Yougoslavie* (Belgrade, 1961).

154 Similar distortions are to be found in some of the works of Giunta Pisano, e.g., the crosses of S. Maria degli Angeli, in Assisi, and S. Domenico, in Bologna; see E. Carli, *Pittura medievale pisana* (Milan, 1958), PL. 32, 33, 35, 38, 40 (Ugolino). On the Ohrid Crucifixon and the Hodegetria (front of the panel) see Djurić, *Icônes de Yougoslavie*, No. 4, pp. 19 f., 85 f., PL. IV-VI.

155 Lazarev, *Istorija*, I, pp. 221, 361 (n. 22), PL. XLVI; II, PL. 305; Talbot Rice, *The Art of Byzantium*, p. 85, with bibliography; the latter work contains a good color reproduction, PL. XXXV.

156 A slightly later phase is represented by the icon of St. Matthew from Ohrid, ascribed to Eutychios: Radojčić, "Die serbische Ikonenmalerei," p. 72, Fig. 9; Felicetti-Liebenfels, *Geschichte der byzantinischen Ikonenmalerei*, PL. 102 A; Djurić, *Icônes de Yougoslavie*, No. 7, pp. 20 ff., 86 ff., PL. IX.

157 Talbot Rice, *The Art of Byzantium*, PL. XLI f.; Djurić, *Icônes de Yougoslavie*, No. 14, pp. 24 f., 91 f., PL. XVII–XXI; by the same hand, No. 15, p. 93, PL. XXII–XXV.

slaying of the Assyrians in the parecclesion of the Kariye (PL. 464)—two figures that, indeed, invite comparison because of the similarity of attitude, the vigorous stride so characteristic of the new pathos of mature Palaeologan art. How much more bulging, heavy, and overmodeled is the pictorial relief of the Ohrid icon and how much more graphic, with almost abstract patterns, flat, and sophisticated in posture is the rendering of the Kariye figure. Even stronger (partly because of the provincial character of the Ohrid frescoes and of the somewhat greater difference in date) is the contrast between two thematically identical compositions in the Kariye and in the Ohrid frescoes introduced above as the earliest work of Michael and Eutychios. The two renderings of the Birth of the Virgin in the two cycles (Fig. 30 and PL. 98) belong to the same iconographic tradition, but, apart from the fact that in the Kariye mosaic the number of figures has been greatly augmented, from six to eleven—an increase that is in accordance with the general trend toward enriching the story and lightening the tenor of the narrative, the trend from the hieratic toward the novelistic—and quite apart also from the greater liveliness in movement and linear patterns in the mosaic, the two works are also profoundly different in the treatment of relief, volume, and space. Not only has the heavy style been abandoned in the Kariye in the plastic representation of single figures and architectural motifs—the figure of St. Anne, for instance, has been changed from an immensely heavy, undifferentiated, and square mass into a slender, articulated figure, the block on which she sits into a proper bed—but the composition as a whole has been adapted to the new "relief style." The picture space has been unified: the low wall which cut right across the stage at Ohrid has been replaced in the Kariye by a higher wall farther back, a quiet, light foil for the visiting virgins, whose figures now appear outlined before it. This background wall, together with the curtain which indicates that the stage is set in an interior, replaces also the central pavilion, the solid, heavy mass of which encumbered the composition in Ohrid. What is left in the way of architectural setting is only the combination, familiar in Byzantine art, of two corner motifs connected by a wall, the whole forming the background and the frame for the frieze of figures. Thus, in spite of the greater depth and freedom of the stage, the composition in the Kariye has more the character of a relief and less that of an accumulation of heavy masses, as at Ohrid. The color composition too, which at Ohrid is dominated by sharp contrasts of cold colors, contributes in the Kariye to lightening and at the same time unifying the whole, with a bias toward pink at the left and top, toward blue at the bottom and right. In spite of all these changes, not only the general layout has been preserved but also some rather odd devices, like that of interpolating an obliquely placed object between the bed of St. Anne and the background wall: a table for the presents has taken over the spatial function of the Virgin's cradle.

The later works of the Milutin workshop show the gradual increase of the graphic element and the ebb in the use of cubic volume. In the "Royal Church" of Studenica, of 1314 (Fig. 34),[158] there is still a fair amount of graded modeling; the linear design is rounded and follows the curving of the body relief. Flying folds are still shell-shaped, enclosing space, as it were, and not pressed flat as in the Kariye. A juxtaposition, for instance, of the figure of Adam in the Anastasis frescoes of the two churches shows the much more plastic approach of the Studenica painter. However, there is already a marked increase of linear play at Studenica, in comparison with

---

158 V. R. Petković, *Manastir Studenica* (Belgrade, 1924); Bihalji-Merin, *Fresken und Ikonen*, PL. 28–30; Radojčić and Talbot Rice, *Yugoslavia*, PL. XXII–XXV.

earlier cycles. One feels the growing taste for graphic complication. The compositions tend to spread out laterally, in friezes, showing a lighter and flatter relief than the Ohrid paintings. In the church at Staro Nagoričino, of 1316–18 (Fig. 35),[159] the graphic element has become stronger; it expresses itself in numerous zigzags, the motifs crowding each other in mannerist patterns. Graded modeling, on the other hand, is disappearing, to be replaced by a technique in which three or four shades of one color are juxtaposed without any transitional shading—a technique of "layers" which is also the dominant technique of the Kariye.

The final result of the evolution of the Milutin workshop is the very dry, very mannered style of the frescoes of Gračanica (Fig. 36);[160] their brittle forms are rapidly painted, and they have some of the oddities that characterize the mosaics and frescoes of the Kariye—for example, the projection of figures as if seen from below.[161] Gračanica marks the end of the activity of the school, at least of its main branch, an activity drawn out too long and exhausted after having produced several thousands of figures: there are unmistakable signs of decomposition in the style of this late work. Thus it does not lend itself very well to a detailed confrontation with the work of the Kariye; although the two cycles are contemporary, the Kariye painters were, in addition to being immeasurably superior in force and finesse, also much more "modern."

In this time of rapid development, a few years must have mattered as much as half a century in more static periods. This can be seen by a comparison of the art of the Kariye with works that were created by the same metropolitan ateliers a few years earlier, namely, the mosaics of the Apostles church in Salonika.[162] The mosaics must be dated immediately before 1315—the date can be fixed with a margin of one or two years. It is true that this most important decoration was introduced by Professor Xyngopoulos as the chief monument of early-fourteenth-century Salonikan art as opposed to that of Constantinople. A closer analysis must, however, lead to the conclusion that the mosaics were undoubtedly made by Constantinopolitan artists—a conclusion that is further supported by the fact that the donor of the mosaics was a patriarch of Constantinople, Niphon I, whose deposition in 1315 put a stop to the not yet completed mosaic decoration of the church.[163] Since the greater part of the nave cycle of the Kariye is lost, the feast cycle of the Salonika church can be compared directly with only three compositions of the Kariye: the Nativity, the Anastasis, and the Dormition; to a certain extent also it can be compared with the Birth of the Virgin, which contains details that are directly comparable with motifs forming part of the Nativity of Christ at Salonika.

First let us consider the similarities, which show the close relationship of the two cycles. The two representations of the Nativity, for instance, have not only the general layout in common but also individual groupings, like those of the shepherds (Fig. 37 a, PL. 172), and the bathing of the Child (Fig. 37 b, PL. 169); in the latter the identical zigzag drapery appears on the seated figure in both mosaics—and is repeated, once more, in the fresco version of the scene in the

---

159 N. L. Okunev, "Crkva svetog Djordja u Starom Nagoričinu," *Glasnik Skopskog naučnog društva*, 5 (1929), pp. 87 ff.; *Staro Nagoričino, Psača, Kalenić* (Belgrade, 1933); Petković, *La peinture serbe*, II, PL. XLVII–LVII; Bihalji-Merin, *Fresken und Ikonen*, PL. 52, 53.

160 Dj. Bošković, *Gračanica* (Belgrade, n.d.); Petković, *La peinture serbe*, II. PL. LIX–LXXXI; Bihalji-Merin, *Fresken und Ikonen*, PL. 56, 57; Radojčić and Talbot Rice, *Yugoslavia*, PL. XXVI, XXVII; to the same period belong the frescoes of Chilandari (report by H. Hallensleben in *XIIᵉ Congrés International*

des Etudes Byzantines, Résumés des communications (Belgrade and Ohrid, 1961), pp. 43 f.).

161 Petković, *La peinture serbe*, II, PL. LXXV, David.

162 On the mosaics of the church see Xyngopoulos, Ἡ ψηφιδωτὴ διακόσμησις τοῦ ναοῦ τῶν Ἁγίων Ἀποστόλων Θεσσαλονίκης (Salonika, 1953). The frescoes are not yet published.

163 This conclusion was also reached by Professor P. A. Underwood in his review of Professor Xyngopoulos' book in *Archaeology*, 10 (1957), pp. 215–16.

Apostles church.[164] The two representations are, at the same time, different enough to show that they are not copies of one another or of a common model but free versions created by closely related masters. The Anastasis [165] follows different types in the two cycles, since the functions that the scene has to fulfill are different; nevertheless, the figures of Adam and Abel at Salonika show a strong resemblance to their counterparts in the Kariye. The most striking similarities are to be found in the Dormition:[166] some figures and heads in the two representations could easily be interchanged, and others are the reverse of each other; hands, the forms of heads and beards— the treatment in general—are identical (Fig. 38, PL. 322). Thus, there cannot be any doubt that the mosaicists of Salonika and those of the Kariye belonged to the same metropolitan workshop.

There exist, however, stylistic differences between the two cycles, differences which concern the interpretation of the material. One of the main discrepancies is in modeling. The prophets in the dome of the Holy Apostles church are much more plastic than the comparable figures in the Kariye:[167] their modeling is strongly reminiscent of that to be seen in the Moscow icon of the Twelve Apostles; compared with the ancestors of Christ in the Kariye, they appear inflated. A juxtaposition of the Jeremiah of Salonika (Fig. 39), the first Apostle on the left in the Moscow icon (Fig. 32), and the figure of Sala in the Kariye (PL. 51), three figures closely related in their layout, shows the swelling forms of the first two reduced to an almost concave relief in the Kariye; the bold draperies have been supplanted by sophisticated patterns, curved lines by straight and broken strokes.

Even more striking are the discrepancies between the mosaics of Salonika and the frescoes of the Kariye. A confrontation of the two shows that the difference consists not only in a reduction of the plastic form but also in an entirely new attitude toward the function of the figure in the spatial system of the entire decoration in the Kariye. For instance, the Evangelists in the pendentives of the Salonikan church (Fig. 40) are seated in stereotyped attitudes, very much as if the figures had been copied from a Gospel Book without reference to the place they were to occupy. In contrast to this, the figures of the Hymnographers in the similar pendentives of the parecclesion of the Kariye (PL. 432) were expressly composed for their places by a painter who knew, or at least felt, all the implications of the figures' position in space. Theophanes, for instance, is fitted diagonally into a space which, surrounded as it is by odd crystalline shapes, forms a perfect receptacle for the figure. There can be no doubt that the Kariye pendentive embodies a much more advanced phase than that in the Salonika church in the development away from the old, dignified forms toward a more mannerist style, as regards both the linear accentuations of broken surfaces and the spatial organization of shapes and compositions. At the same time, there was a movement away from forms imbued with the classical or renaissance spirit of the late thirteenth and the early fourteenth centuries. This change can be made clear by the comparison of almost any two figures in the church of the Holy Apostles in Salonika and in the Kariye, but it becomes still more striking if the Salonika mosaics are compared with those of the

164 Cf. Xyngopoulos, Ἡ ψηφιδωτὴ διακόσμησις, PL. 11, 12; for details see the confrontation in Xyngopoulos, *Thessalonique*, PL. 5, Figs. 1, 2. A similar zigzag drapery appears in the Birth of the Virgin at the Kariye, Vol. 2 of this work, PL. 101, 102.

165 Cf. Xyngopoulos, Ἡ ψηφιδωτὴ διακόσμησις, PL. 28, 29, 30, and Vol. 3, PL. 341 ff.

166 Cf. Xyngopoulos, Ἡ ψηφιδωτὴ διακόσμησις, PL. 31,

32; A. Grabar and M. Chatzidakis, *Greece: Byzantine Mosaics* (UNESCO World Art Series, 13 [Greenwich, Conn.], New York Graphic Society, 1959), PL. XXX, XXXI; and Vol. 2, PL. 320 ff.

167 Cf. the Prophets Elisha and Habakkuk, Xyngopoulos, Ἡ ψηφιδωτὴ διακόσμησις, PL. 2,1 4,1 and 2, and Vol. 2 of this work, PL. 46 ff.

Pammakaristos church, the Fethiye Djami, in Constantinople.[168] Of course, the Fethiye Djami mosaics cannot vie in quality with those of the Kariye: their technique is less differentiated, the color somewhat poorer. But the mosaicists drew from the same tradition and must have been quite closely associated with the Kariye workshop.

There is, however, a further decrease of plastic power, a further reduction of expressive force. For instance, a comparison of the two figures of Habakkuk at Salonika (Fig. 41) and in the Fethiye Djami (Fig. 42) shows that the same motif, the same attitude that lend a heroic effect at Salonika have become petty, insistent, and meaningless; a similar loss of functional strength and expression can be found in the Jonah of the Fethiye Djami as against the same figure at Salonika. But the most impressive contrast is provided by the juxtaposition of the two mosaic compositions of the Baptism at Salonika (Fig. 43) and the Fethiye Djami (Fig. 44). The figure of Christ is presented in the earlier of the two mosaics in a free, almost heroic *contrapposto*— the body is shaped and modeled after a prototype that, in the last resort, stems from Lysippian sculpture; the angels approach with an energetic stride. In the other mosaic the movement has lost all its strength, all its rhythm; the forms have lost all their plastic force. The statuesque posture of Christ has been changed to a somewhat constrained, timid, and self-conscious attitude, which is at the same time elegant and mannered. The angels make deep ceremonial bows, the Baptist is almost doubled up. The forms are neat, complicatedly carved and broken, the colors soft and milky; the whole represents a kind of courtly rococo compared to the humanist spirit of the Salonika mosaic. One cannot help feeling that this art has become overrefined and tired.

7. THE LATER DEVELOPMENT (1328–1450) [169]

The mosaics of the Fethiye Djami represent a style that is somewhat more mannered than the style of the Kariye. But even the art of the Kariye has some part in the overrefinement which heralds the crisis of the second quarter of the fourteenth century and which is so entirely different from the robust classicism of the earlier Palaeologan period. The crisis began even before the downfall of Andronicus II and his premier Metochites, but it came to a head in the next reign. One of the facts that seem to characterize this crisis is the bifurcation of the evolution of painting. One branch continues and further develops the "rococo" strain of the Fethiye Djami mosaics; the other begins with an attempt at preserving the style of the Kariye and ends with its complete petrification.

The conservative trend is represented, among many other decorations, by the frescoes of the church of St. Demetrius in Peč, after 1324, and of the great church of Dečani, of the thirties and forties of the century. Master Joannes, who signed the frescoes of Peč,[170] arrived at very charming solutions; in some of his frescoes, e.g., in the Birth of the Virgin (Fig. 45), he succeeded in recapturing something of the atmosphere that pervades the frescoes of the Kariye. He is at times even more correct than the Kariye's artist, archaeologically, in the imitation of classical details, as demonstrated in the "Alexandrian" striped glass vessel in the hands of one of the virgins, or

168 P. A. Underwood, "Notes on the Work of the Byzantine Institute in Istanbul: 1954," *DOP*, 9 and 10 (1956), pp. 298 ff. Michael Glabas, for whose burial the chapel was built, died in 1315.

169 Bibliography for the history of Byzantine painting in the 14th century is to be found in Millet, *Recherches*, and Lazarev, *Istorija*, I, pp. 358 ff.; text, p. 208. For the post-Byzantine development see A. Xyngopoulos, Σχεδίασμα ἱστορίας τῆς Θρησκευτικῆς ζωγραφικῆς μετὰ τὴν ἅλωσιν (Athens, 1957).

170 D. Bošković, "Osiguravanje i restoracija crkve manastira Sv. Patriaršije u Peči," *Starinar*, VIII–IX (1933–34), pp. 91 ff.: Bihalji-Merin, *Fresken und Ikonen*, PL. 36–38; Petković, *La peinture*, II, PL. LXXXVI–XCVI.

the large vase in the hands of another; but the forms are frail, thin, and refined to the point of decadence. The elegant warrior saints (Fig. 46) are so willowy that the comparable figures in the Kariye (PL. 488, 492) appear almost sturdy. The painterly element is almost wholly excluded from the technique of these paintings: every form appears hard, as if turned in ivory, and isolated. The compositions, though crowded, are falling to pieces for lack of rhythmical connection.

An even greater hardness and dryness is to be found in the acres of frescoes that form one of the richest ensembles of the fourteenth century, the decoration of Dečani (Fig. 47).[171] The drapery style of these wall paintings is still quite close to that of the Kariye; the technique uses the same superimposed layers of various shades. There is also the same sustained dignity; the difference of about fifteen to twenty years is visible mainly in an increase of dryness and hardness.

This survival of the Kariye style, in a dehydrated state, as it were, can be found in a great many paintings datable in the second quarter of the century, among them the frescoes of Curtea-de-Argeş,[172] the painters of which in some instances, perhaps, used the Kariye itself as a model. Examples in the field of book illumination are a Gospel Book in the collection of Sir K. Clark;[173] the Oxford, Bodl. Selden Supra 6 (Selden 5);[174] the Vienna, Nationalbibliothek theol. gr. 300;[175] the Sinai gr. 152, of 1346 (Fig. 48), which shows even the same flying folds with hooks at their ends that appear in the mosaics and frescoes of the Kariye; the Patmos 81, of 1345;[176] and many others. The production must have been very rich if somewhat stereotyped. There is again a lot of copying. In general, we find few new forms or ideas in the works that follow this conservative trend. The middle of the century probably saw the end of this traditional and somewhat sterile art.

In the meantime, however, another current had gained momentum, the trend which above has been called the rococo variety of the high Palaeologan style. The forms of this rococo trend are diminutive and complicated at the same time; there is an increase in decorative detail, the colors become very rich and somewhat sombre, the modeling more broken.

Quite a number of the works exhibiting this style seem to be products of a clearly definable metropolitan school. The Oxford menologion, Bodl. gr. theol. f. 1 (S.C. 2919),[177] for instance, is not only very close, stylistically, to the mosaics of the Fethiye Djami; the Baptism of this manuscript even seems to go back directly to the mosaic characterized above: the figure of Christ, especially, is almost identical. Related works, much more precious in technique and form, are the mosaic diptych illustrating the Twelve Feasts in the Florence cathedral [178] and the exquisite mosaic icon of the Annunciation in the Victoria and Albert Museum (Fig. 49),[179] by the same artist. The broken forms of the minute figures at Florence are presented in a very sophisticated color scheme. The icon, an elaboration of the same scene in the Florentine diptych, is rendered on a somewhat larger but still very small scale. In addition, the workshop seems to have produced a number of icons in tempera, some of them preserved in the Sinai monastery.[180]

171 V. R. Petković and Dj. Bošković, *Dečani* (Belgrade, 1941); Bihalji-Merin, *Fresken und Ikonen*, PL. 58–64.

172 O. Tafrali, *Monuments byzantins de Curtéa de Argeş* (Paris, 1931); compare, for example, PL. LXXV with Vol. 2 of this work, PL. 159.

173 J. Chittenden and Ch. Seltman, *Greek Art: A Commemorative Catalogue of an Exhibition Held in 1946 at the Royal Academy* (London, 1947).

174 O. Pächt, *Byzantine Illumination* (Oxford, 1952), Fig. 15.

175 P. Buberl and H. Gerstinger, *Die byzantinischen Handschriften* (Die illuminierten Handschriften und Inkunabeln der

Nationalbibliothek in Wien, IV), Pt. 2 (Leipzig, 1938), PL. XXXI,2; of the same hand is Lavra 113 A.

176 Photographs by P. Buberl, National Library, Vienna, Nos. 101.555–101.560.

177 Pächt, *Byzantine Illumination*, Fig. 16, right.

178 Good color plates in Talbot Rice, *The Art of Byzantium*, PL. XXXVI f.; for bibliography see Lazarev, *Istorija*, I, p. 360, n. 14.

179 Color plate in Talbot Rice, *The Art of Byzantium*, PL. XXXVIII; for bibliography see Lazarev, *Istorija*, I, p. 360, n. 15.

180 G. and M. Soteriou, *Icônes du Mont Sinai*, I (Athens, 1956), PL. 208–16.

Toward the middle of the century the rococo style was even exported to Venice: a Constantinopolitan master, following the trend, supervised at that time the brilliant decoration of the baptistery of San Marco (Fig. 50),[181] a decoration which, though it contains some Western features in iconography and figure material, is nevertheless predominantly Byzantine in style and technique. It is a very rich decorative ensemble, leaving behind even the Kariye mosaics in this respect, fully orchestrated with ornaments in rich color. The rococo of the early phases of the style has turned into baroque. Its boldness stands in strong contrast to the coolness and dryness of the conservative trend of Dečani.

This bold, baroque manner with its rich colorism seems to have been the basis of a new development which dominated the greater part of the second half of the fourteenth century (the time of John V, 1341–91)—a style that combines an agitated expressionism with an optical illusionism. The forms of the baroque style were not only tortured and twisted out of recognition in this new phase but also dissolved, liquefied into an almost impressionist luminarism by an exceedingly daring technique.

The expressionism of this style was sufficiently pliable to be employed for the display of widely differing qualities of content. The miniatures of the Moscow Gospel Book, Historical Museum gr. 407,[182] offer good examples of the wide range of the style in the hands of gifted and bold artists. The figures seem to be animated by a new, intense life, quite different from the affected elegance of the rococo phase. Time-honored figure types, like that of the Evangelist Luke, are interpreted in a novel way: the folds look as if they had been hewn out with a hatchet. In other miniatures in the same manuscript, the forms show a new fluidity: the two figures in the Visitation seem to melt into each other; it is as if the artist had taken his cue from the loving embrace of the two Holy Women. The manuscript is not dated but must have originated in the third quarter of the century. Roughly contemporary, belonging most probably to the sixties or seventies, are the frescoes of Ivanovo in Bulgaria (Fig. 51).[183] They show the expressionist, tormented style in its most uninhibited and most aggressive form. The contortions of the figures, with their dislocated limbs, are echoed by wild overstatements in the draperies and in the architecture. The sprawling scaffoldings that embrace the figure groups are elaborations of architectural motifs that appear in early-Palaeologan art; but they seem now to have freed themselves from all rational order. A spatial conception implied by one half of a building can suddenly be canceled, even reversed, in the other half, so that the spatial relief seems to snap forward or backward from convex to concave or vice versa (as in the Washing of Feet). The figures seem to be thrown about as if by an earthquake: everything is in turmoil, in tortured frenzy. But the elements, types of figures, costumes, and architectures are still those of the Kariye, the broken draperies those of the rococo phase, succeeding that of the Kariye. Professor Grabar is of the opinion that the frescoes of Ivanovo are the work of a painter from Constantinople. In any case, they were painted by a master who had gone through metropolitan schooling: a comparison with the similarly agitated forms of the Transfiguration in the Constantinopolitan manuscript of John Cantacuzenus, illuminated between 1372 and 1375 (Fig. 52), seems to bear this out.[184]

181 R. Tozzi, "I mosaici del battistero de S. Marco a Venezia e l'arte bizantina," *Bollettino d'arte*, 26 (1932–33), pp. 418 ff.; Bettini, *Mosaici di San Marco*, PL. C–CXIII.

182 M. Alpatov [Alpatoff], "A Byzantine Illuminated Manuscript of the Palaeologue Epoch in Moscow," *ArtB*, 12 (1930), pp. 207 ff.

183 A. Vasiliev, *Ivanovskite stenopisi* (Rusenski Arkhe-

ologičeski Muzej i Arkhiv: Materiali za istorijata na gr. Ruse i rusenskija okrŭg, I; Sofia, 1953); A. Grabar, "Les fresques d'Ivanovo et l'art des Paléologues," *Byzantion*, 25–27 (1955–57), pp. 581 ff.

184 Paris. gr. 1242: Omont, *Miniatures des plus anciens manuscrits grecs*, pp. 58 f., PL. CXXVI f.; for a color reproduction, see Talbot Rice, *The Art of Byzantium*, PL. XXXIX.

A variant of this style was transferred to Russia when Theophanes, the Feofan Grek of Russian sources, went to Novgorod before 1378.[185] His style is, of course, much more "civilized" than that of the painter of Ivanovo, but it is no less agitated and tortured (Fig. 53). In some respects it is even bolder, since the emphasis is even more on painterly freedom here than in Bulgaria. The technique of liberally splashed-on white highlights is a bold travesty of the so-called "Cretan" technique of the early fourteenth century. It seems that the extreme possibilities of this painterly variant of the agitated style were more fully realized in the provinces, some time after the transfer of the style from Constantinople: the metropolis seems to have exerted a certain restraint which gradually fell away after the painters had settled down in the provinces.[186]

A few years later the classicizing element, always latent in Constantinople, seems to have come to the fore again. The painters of the metropolis seem to have got tired of the wild contortions of the agitated style and reverted to the neoclassical ideals of about a century before. A dated example of this new metropolitan style has been preserved in Georgia, in Tsalendzhikha; it was painted between 1384 and 1396, as we know from contemporary sources, by Kyr Manuel Eugenikos, a painter expressly brought to Georgia from Constantinople (Fig. 54).[187] Although the "Cretan" technique of using white highlights modeling the relief out of the dark, is basically the same as that of Theophanes, the contrast between the actual handling of this technique in the two cases could not be greater. In place of the slapdash but ingenious brushwork of the earlier painter we find in the work of Manuel a new discipline, a new reserve, a new firmness, which are reminiscent of the style of the late thirteenth century. The frescoes of Tsalendzhikha are not the only witnesses of the reappearance, at the turn of the century, of the sculptural ideals of about one hundred years before: other examples are to be found in Serbian Macedonia, on Mount Athos, in Bulgaria, in Mistra (Peribleptos), and in numerous icons and manuscripts. The very grand but overloaded draperies in the decoration at Andreaš, on the Treska near Skoplje, of 1389 (Fig. 55),[188] and at St. George in Sofia,[189] are likewise elaborations of figure schemes developed about 1300, as are a good many iconographic compositions. The cycle of Kalenić, for instance, datable after 1415, follows in part the prototype of the Kariye (e.g., the Enrollment for Taxation and other scenes), in part even earlier models: some of the miracle scenes of this cycle repeat Comnenian patterns.[190] That the art of this period, from about 1390 to about 1420, was, in fact, again a kind of renascence, a new attempt to recall and revive something of the spirit of earlier times, is suggested by works like the icon from Poganovo, now in the National Museum of Sofia, which, as Professor Grabar has shown,[191] goes back to the early-Byzantine mosaic of Hosios David in Salonika; the number of such reprises could easily be multiplied. However, this new renascence, if we can call it thus, was short-lived: no trace of it can be found after 1420. The last decades before the fall of Constantinople are again characterized by a very nervous style, with violent movements, odd contrasts in color, broken and hard forms, and complicated spatial configurations, which look as if they were the result of a violent earthquake. The frescoes of the Pantanassa in Mistra (Fig. 56)[192] and the reliquary icon of Cardinal Bessarion

185 V. Lazarev, "Etjudy o Feofane Greke," I–III, *VV*, N.S., 7 (1953), pp. 244 ff.: 8 (1956), pp. 143 ff.; 9 (1956), pp. 193 ff.; idem, *Feofan Grek i ego škola* (Moscow, 1961).

186 V. Lazarev, *Iskusstvo Novgoroda* (Moscow, 1947), pp. 77 ff., PL. 58–68.

187 S. J. Amiranašvili, *Istorija gruzinskogo iskusstva*, I (Moscow, 1950), pp. 249 f., PL. 8, 163.

188 Petković, *La peinture serbe*, II, p. 57 f., PL. CLXXIII–CLXXV; Radojčić, *Majstori*, p. 42, PL. XXVII–XXIX.

189 A. Protić, "Le style de l'école de peinture murale de Tirnovo au XIIIᵉ et au XIVᵉ siècle," *L'art byzantin chez les Slaves. Dédié à la mémoire de Théodore Uspenskij*, I: *Les Balkans*, pp. 92 ff., PL. VI, and Fig. 17.

190 *Staro Nagoričino, Psača, Kalenić*; Petković, *La peinture serbe*, II, PL. CXCIX ff.

191 A. Grabar, "A propos d'une icône byzantine du XIVᵉ siècle au Musée de Sofia," *CA*, 10 (1959), pp. 289 ff.

192 G. Millet, *Monuments byzantins de Mistra* (Paris, 1910), e.g., PL. 138,2; 144,2; 145,2 and 3.

155

in Venice [193] are among the finest creations of this period—proofs that Byzantium was still able to create significant forms in the last hour of her existence.

8. THE PLACE OF THE KARIYE IN PALAEOLOGAN PAINTING

This brief sketch of some of the salient points and tendencies of Palaeologan painting—a sketch that should not be mistaken for an attempt at giving a history, even in outline, of its very complicated development—is aimed at giving to the mosaics and the frescoes of the Kariye their proper place within the larger context of Palaeologan art. This, of course, raises the question whether we are at all justified in thinking of Palaeologan art (or painting, for that matter) as a whole, as possessing a specific style with a development of its own—or whether we should regard it as the outcome of a series of attempts at stemming decay by numerous reprises, by borrowing and copying from the past. As a matter of fact, there should be no difficulty in answering this question. Even the very superficial review of the main trends of Palaeologan painting sketched out above must have shown that there was, indeed, a genuine development, as genuine as, and even more rapid than, that of any other period in Byzantine history. Naturally, as is unavoidable when dealing with a phenomenon related (and referring back) to late-antique art, we must anticipate a multiplicity of styles or of *modi* rather than one single, homogeneous way of expression.[194] It should be remembered that something like this multiplicity of styles existed already in Roman art;[195] in later periods, connected with the late antique through numerous reprises, this multiple structure must be more noticeable still. This does not mean, however, that there was no clearly traceable development. Indeed, such a development began in the last years of the twelfth or the first years of the thirteenth century with linear simplifications leading to a new monumental style; the middle third of the thirteenth century saw the growth of a plastic style with classical forms; and the end of the century saw the rise of a heavy style. Its heaviness and fullness gave way, in the first quarter of the fourteenth century, to a relief style relying more and more on graphic means of presentation. So far, there can be hardly any doubt that this pattern of stylistic changes is a typical evolutionary pattern of medieval art. It can be closely paralleled in the West: in French sculpture for instance, the Chartres transepts corresponding to Mileševo, Reims and Amiens to Sopoćani, and the St. Denis tombs of the turn of the century to the frescoes of St. Clement in Ohrid; or in Italian painting—from the Pisa Master of the Cross No. 20 to the Franciscus Master and, finally, to Cimabue, the Romans, and Giotto, whose immensely heavy seated or crouching figures have perfect counterparts in Ohrid or the Protaton. The growth of the graphic relief style too can be paralleled in Italy; it corresponds to the step from Giotto's art to that of his followers. With this phase, the parallel comes to an end: the thirteenth century was the last and perhaps the only period in which the evolution of the figurative arts in Eastern and Western Europe moved in more or less perfect concord. This concord was, perhaps, brought about as much by the infiltration of Western ideas into Byzantium through the medium of the Latin occupation as by Byzantine influences in the West, carried there through the loot of the Fourth Crusade and the diaspora of Greek artists.

From the beginning of the fourteenth century the two great branches of European art, the

193 At the Accademia: Felicetti-Liebenfels, *Geschichte der byzantinischen Ikonenmalerei*, PL. 131, p. 94.

194 E. Kitzinger, "Byzantine Art in the Period between Justinian and Iconoclasm," *Berichte zum XI. Intern. Byzantinisten-*Kongress*, IV,1, pp. 47 f.

195 P. H. von Blankenhagen, "Elemente der römischen Kunst am Beispiel des flavischen Stils," in H. Berve, *Das neue Bild der Antike* (Leipzig, 1942), II, pp. 315 ff.

Western and the Byzantine, separated for good; and even Western European art itself split up into national schools. Sporadic infiltrations of Byzantine art into Italy could not influence the general trend, which favored the architectural and sculptural as against the painteresque, and the few directly Byzantinizing schools of the *maniera greca* (Venice and southern Italy) [196] counted as little in the general picture as Italian influences did in Byzantine territory [197] (Crete, Cyprus; the growth of a late composite art on Mount Athos and in the Slavic countries is an altogether different chapter). In Byzantium the evolution divided: one trend elaborated the classicist and graphic relief style of the Kariye, and another led, by way of a kind of rococo, to an agitated expressionism with illusionistic effects; a new reprise of classical forms at the end of the fourteenth century provided the raw material for new complications.

The most outstanding factor in this history of stylistic change is the chain of reprises, the ever present possibility for Greek artists of going back to earlier styles and, in the last resort, of drawing, again and again, from the mainsprings of Hellenistic, of Greek art. One might even speak of a "renaissance in permanence"—if the term "renaissance" were really fitting for the phenomena that dominated the history not only of Palaeologan art but of Byzantine art in general. It would be more apropos to speak of a series of revivals connected by survivals; of periods in which the ever present memory of the classical past became especially intense and conscious. There was no Renaissance in the proper sense of the term in Byzantium: the Byzantines never got far enough away from the classical heritage to rediscover it, as was the case in the West. There was no chain reaction, consequently, which might have guided them from the rediscovery of classical art to the discovery of nature. In most cases they did not even go back to classical art itself—although Constantinople was until the very end full of antique works (of which Theodore Metochites himself had a collection)—but to examples that were already the results of some earlier revival. In the case of the Palaeologan renascence the particular question is whether the classical elements that play so large a part in its productions were drawn from Hellenistic-pagan art, from the art of the early-Byzantine revival of the fifth and the sixth centuries, or from the art of the Macedonian renascence of the tenth century. This question has been answered by Professor Weitzmann in favor of the tenth century, and Professor Grabar has reached similar conclusions.[198] Not only did the artists of the thirteenth and the fourteenth centuries choose from preference tenth-century manuscripts for copying and reproduction (to name only two groups: the Gospels of the Iviron 5 and Paris. gr. 54 type, and the Psalters of the so-called aristocratic version); not only did they use types of figures and architectural and landscape details of the tenth century (the curious profiles, figures seen from the back, even the oddly shaped feet, the characteristic shape of the clavi, block-shaped buildings with monochrome relief decor, splintery

---

196 S. Bettini, *La pittura di icone cretese-veneziana e i Madonneri* (Padua, 1933); Lazarev, "Über eine neue Gruppe"; Ph. Schweinfurth, "Maniera greca und italobyzantinische Schule: Abgrenzung und Wertung dieser Stilbegriffe," *Atti del V Congresso Internazionale di Studi Bizantini*, II (Rome, 1940) (= *Studi bizantini e neoellenici*, 6), pp. 387 ff.; V. Lazarev, "K voprosu o grečeskoj manera, italo-grečeskoj i italo-kritskoj školakh živopisi," *Ežegodnik Instituta Istorii Iskusstv* (Akademija Nauk SSSR; Moscow, 1952), pp. 152 ff.

197 P. A. Underwood, "Palaeologan Narrative Style and an Italianate Fresco of the Fifteenth Century in the Kariye Djami," *Studies in the History of Art, Dedicated to William E. Suida on his Eightieth Birthday* (London, 1959), pp. 1 ff.; G. Gerola, *Monumenti veneti nell'isola di Creta*, I (Venice, 1905); for Cyprus see, for instance, the Crucifixion, PL. 10, in A. and J. A. Stylianou,

ʽΗ μονὴ Ποδύθου παρὰ τὴν Γαλάταν, in Κυπριακαὶ Σπουδαί, 18 (1954), pp. 49 ff.

198 Weitzmann, "Constantinopolitan Book Illumination"; idem, "Eine Pariser-Psalter-Kopie"; and see Professor Grabar's essay in the present volume. M. Alpatov has also repeatedly (*REG*, 39 [1926], pp. 313 ff.; *Repertorium für Kunstwissenschaft*, 49 [1928], pp. 69 ff.) pointed to the Joshua Roll as a source of the Palaeologan style. An interesting parallel in religious thought is the harking back of 14th-century mysticism to ideas of Symeon the Young; see H.-G. Beck, *Kirche und theologische Literatur im byzantinischen Reich* (Munich, 1959), p. 585. The revival of 10th-century art in the 13th century was stressed in a communication by P. Miljković-Pepek at the Byzantine Congress of Ohrid in September 1961 (*Résumé*, p. 73).

rock landscapes, isolated trees, etc.[199])—they also adopted some of the characteristic modeling techniques of the Macedonian renascence, like that of superimposing layers of shades in abstract shapes, a technique that is fully developed in the Joshua Roll of the tenth century. All this does not exclude, of course, the possibility that at one time or other some genuinely antique object served as a model,[200] but generally speaking the models were provided by tenth-century art.

The question is now, at what time in the course of the thirteenth and fourteenth centuries did this revival of tenth-century art appear, at what time did the so-called Palaeologan renascence begin, reach its climax, and end? The question is not correctly put, because the process of revival seems to have gone through several phases; different aspects of "antiquity" were "revived" at different times, so that we might even speak of a series of revivals following each other. The plastic figure style of the tenth century, for instance, with its insistence on rounded forms brought out by tone and line, and with its statuesque and heroic dignity, was revived at an early period, soon after the middle of the thirteenth century. In Sopoćani, in the sixties and seventies of the century, we already meet with an elaboration of this style, bolder, more plastic, one might almost say more antique, more classical than the tenth-century prototypes which, it seems, had provided only the initial stimulus. This heroic phase of the revival was already a thing of the past at the time of the decoration of the Kariye;[201] the overrefined figure schemes of the mosaics and the frescoes seem to have been evolved from thirteenth-century figures without renewed recourse to the tenth-century models. There is one subject in the Kariye frescoes that is especially informative in this respect, namely the group of figures carrying the Ark of the Covenant (PL. 455). The somewhat affected attitudes, the halting and mincing steps, the way these figures are not really carrying the weight of the Ark, all this is very different indeed from the heroic vigor of movement displayed by the same figures in the Joshua Roll (Fig. 57), although the formula of the composition is still the same. Now, the painters of the Kariye did not go back in this case to the Joshua Roll or a related prototype of the tenth century; they used a model that was already couched in the language of Palaeologan art, a model of the late thirteenth century, something like the Vatopedi Octateuch (Fig. 58)—and even this model, so close in time, was reinterpreted and modified. The energetically moving and very amply modeled figures of the prototype were reduced in bulk by slicing off parts of the drapery—the folds at the back of the last figure at the left, for instance, were cut away and, without any substantial alteration of forms, given to another figure.

The artists of the Kariye, so it seems, were not interested in reproducing the classical and heroic figure style or the organic roundness and movement of tenth-century compositions; these had been the problems of their fathers and grandfathers. The new generation was, rather, fascinated by curious refinements and oddities, like the *sotto in sù* projections of figures, back views, fleeing profiles, upside-down faces; or by details of a neoclassical kind, quite often with an antiquarian flavor, like the monochrome reliefs decorating architectural forms.[202] Most of

199 Odd forms of profiles occur, for instance, in the Joshua Roll, the Leo Bible of the Vatican, the Paris Psalter, gr. 139; "Palaeologan" feet, in the Chloudov Psalter (Moscow, Historical Museum gr. 129); back views, in the Paris Psalter and the Leo Bible (Vat. Reg. gr. 1), where there are also splintery rocks; upside-down faces, in the Leo Bible. The special form of the clavi occurs in the Joshua Roll. Monochromata of simple form are to be found in the Paris Psalter and at Castelseprio, structures with oblique wings in the Paris Psalter, etc.
200 Sv. Radojčić, "Uloga antike u starom srpskom sli-

karstvu," *Glasnik Zemaljskog Muzeja u Sarajevu*, N.S., 1 (1946), pp. 39 ff.
201 Weitzmann, "Constantinopolitan Book Illumination," p. 213: "at the beginning of the 14th century, the phase of the closest contact with the models which had stimulated the new classical movement had already passed."
202 The finest monochromata are to be found in Salonika, Holy Apostles (Xyngopoulos, *Thessalonique*, frontis.), in the works of the Milutin school, and in Peć (Radojčić, "Die Entstehung der Malerei," Fig. 3, and idem, "Uloga antike").

these traits, again, can be found in tenth-century manuscripts; others were suggested by still earlier models.[203]

Thus, the attitude of the Kariye artists and their contemporaries toward classical antiquity was already somewhat antiquarian in character. The heroic phase of the revival had been superseded by a humanistic phase, of which the patron of the Kariye, Theodore Metochites, is the typical representative.

This humanistic phase of the Palaeologan revival was ultimately followed by one in which the optical, the illusionistic trends of the classical tradition seem to have been of paramount interest to the artists and their patrons. These qualities too had been revived before, in the tenth century, and preserved in manuscripts like the Psalters with marginal illustrations [204] or in works like the Leo Bible of the Vatican. It was only after the middle of the fourteenth century that the form-dissolving quality of late-antique illusionism was once more understood and appreciated—an understanding which would have been impossible to the painters of the thirteenth century.

Thus, the late-Byzantine renascence should not be taken for a simple phenomenon that appeared suddenly and attained its full growth within a short period. It was, rather, a long-drawn-out process, which went through several phases according to the shifting of interest with respect to various facets of the antique tradition. Considered within the larger contours of this process, the Kariye phase would correspond to a humanistic "Late Renaissance" with definite leanings toward mannerism.

Supplementary Bibliography, 1961–71

Art et société à Byzance sous les Paléologues, Actes du Colloque organisé par l'Association internationale des études byzantines à Venise en Septembre 1968 (Bibliothèque de l'Institut hellénique d'études byzantines et post-byzantines de Venise, No. 4; Venice, 1971)

H. Belting, Review of R. Hamann-MacLean and H. Hallensleben, *Die Monumentalmalerei in Serbien und Makedonien*, and H. Hallensleben, *Die Malerschule des Königs Milutin*, in *Kunstchronik*, 21 (1968), pp. 131 ff.

————, "Das illuminierte Buch in der spätbyzantinischen Gesellschaft." *Abh. der Heidelberger Akademie der Wissenschaften*, Phil.-Hist. Kl., 1970/1 (Heidelberg, 1970)

M. Chatzidakis, *Icônes de Saint-Georges des Grecs et de la collection de l'Institut* (Venice, 1962)

V. J. Djurić, "La peinture murale serbe au XIIIe siècle," *L'art byzantin du XIIIe siècle* (Symposium de Sopoćani, 1965; Belgrade, 1967), pp. 165 ff.

————, *Sopoćani* (Belgrade, 1963)

A. Embiricos, *L'école crétoise: Dernière phase de la peinture byzantine* (Paris, 1967)

A. Grabar and T. Velmans, *Gli affreschi della chiesa di Sopocani* (Milan and Geneva, 1965)

————, *Mosaici e affreschi nella Kariye Camii ad Istanbul* (Milan and Geneva, 1965)

H. Hallensleben, *Die Malerschule des Königs Milutin* (Vol. 5 of Hamann-MacLean and Hallensleben, *Die Monumentalmalerei in Serbien und Makedonien*; see below) (Giessen, 1963)

R. H. L. Hamann-MacLean, "Der Berliner Codex Graecus Quarto 66 und seine nächsten Verwandten als Beispiele des Stilwandels im frühen 13. Jahrhundert," *Festschrift K. H. Usener* (Marburg an der Lahn, 1967), pp. 225 ff.

203 A number of motifs are to be found in the Vienna Genesis, such as the upside-down face (p. 5), the fleeing profile (p. 29). The hands hidden in the garment, for example, occur in the marble relief from Bakirköy, in the Archaeological Museum, Istanbul; see Talbot Rice, *The Art of Byzantium*, PL. VIII.

204 A. Grabar, *L'iconoclasme byzantin: Dossier archéologique* (Paris, 1957), pp. 196 ff., with bibliography on p. 198, and Figs. 143–61.

————— and H. Hallensleben, *Die Monumentalmalerei in Serbien und Makedonien, vom 11. bis zum frühen 14. Jahrhundert* (Giessen, 1963)

E. Kitzinger, "The Byzantine Contribution to Western Art of the Twelfth and Thirteenth Centuries," *DOP*, 20 (1966), pp. 25 ff.

V. Lazarev, *Storia della pittura bizantina* (Turin, 1967)

C. Mango, Review of H. Hallensleben, *Die Malerschule des Königs Milutin*, in *ArtB*, 48 (1966), pp. 439 ff.

Medieval Art in Yugoslavia: *Dečani, Kalenić, Kurbinovo, Nerezi, Mileševa, St. Clement at Ochrid, Peć, Ravanica, Resava* (Belgrade, 1961 ff.)

P. Miljković-Pepek, *L'oeuvre des peintres Michel et Eutych* (Skoplje, 1967)

R. Naumann and H. Belting, *Die Euphemia-Kirche am Hippodrom zu Istanbul und ihre Fresken* (Berlin, 1966), pp. 112 ff., esp. 162 ff.

A. K. Orlandos, Ἡ Παρηγορήτισσα τῆς Ἄρτης (with abridged version in French) (Athens, 1963)

Sv. Radojčić, *Mileševa: Its History and Painting* (Belgrade, 1963)

—————, *Staro srpsko slikarstvo* (Belgrade, 1966)

—————, *Geschichte der serbischen Kunst von den Anfängen bis zum Ende des Mittelalters* (Berlin, 1969)

D. Talbot Rice, ed., *The Church of Haghia Sophia at Trebizond* (Edinburgh, 1968)

—————, *Byzantine Painting. The Last Phase* (London, 1968)

J. H. Stubblebine, "Byzantine Influence in Thirteenth-Century Italian Panel Painting," *DOP*, 20 (1966), pp. 85 ff.

—————, "Two Byzantine Madonnas from Calahorra, Spain," *ArtB*, 48 (1966), pp. 379 ff.

K. M. Swoboda, "In den Jahren 1950 bis 1961 erschienene Werke zur byzantinischen und weiteren ostkirchlichen Kunst: Das 13. und 14. Jahrhundert," *Kunstgeschichtliche Anzeigen* (Graz, Vienna, and Cologne), N.S., V (1961–62), pp. 132 ff.

St. Tomić and R. Nikolić, eds., *Manasija: L'histoire—La peinture* (in Serbian with French résumé) (Belgrade, 1964)

T. Velmans, "Les fresques d'Ivanovo et la peinture byzantine à la fin du moyen âge," *Journal des savants* 1 (1965), pp. 358 ff.

—————, "Les fresques de Saint-Nicolas Orphanos à Salonique et les rapports entre la peinture d'icônes et la décoration monumentale au XIVᵉ siècle," *CA*, 16 (1966), pp. 145 ff.

—————, "Le Parisinus Grecus 135 et quelques autres peintures du style gothique dans les manuscrits grecs à l'époque des Paléologues," *CA*, 17 (1967), pp. 209 ff.

—————, "Le rôle du décor architectural et la représentation de l'espace dans la peinture des Paléologues," *CA*, 14 (1964), pp. 183 ff.

K. Weitzmann, "A Fourteenth-Century Greek Gospel Book with Washdrawings," *GBA*, 62 (1963), pp. 91 ff.

—————, "Icon Painting in the Crusader Kingdom," *DOP*, 20 (1966), pp. 49 ff.

—————, M. Chatzidakis, K. Miatev, Sv. Radojčić, *Frühe Ikonen: Sinai, Griechenland, Bulgarien, Jugoslawien* (Vienna and Munich, 1965)

A. Xyngopoulos, Οἱ τοιχογραφίες τοῦ Ἁγίου Νικολάου Ὀρφανοῦ Θεσσαλονίκης (Athens, 1964)

Iconography of the Cycle
of the Life of the Virgin

JACQUELINE LAFONTAINE-DOSOGNE

This text was written in 1962. References to my *Iconographie de l'enfance de la Vierge* and small additions concerning the cycle of the Virgin in the Peribleptos church at Mistra were added in 1965.

J. LAFONTAINE-DOSOGNE

Iconography of the Cycle of the Life of the Virgin

IN ITS ILLUSTRATION of events from the Infancy of the Virgin—the period extending from before her birth to her marriage, preceding the Annunciation—Byzantine art was firmly based upon very early tradition. The narrative that forms the basis for figured representations is the first part of the Protevangelium of James, an apocryphal text composed in Greek at the beginning of the third if not the end of the second century, probably in Egypt. The first direct documentation is supplied by Papyrus Bodmer V, a beautiful Greek manuscript in uncial letters of the beginning of the fourth century, which contains the complete text, including title and colophon.[1] The book very early attained a considerable circulation and was soon translated into various oriental languages. Among the translations the Syriac text that has come down to us dates from before the year 500.[2] In addition to the translations, various paraphrases were produced in the eastern regions of the Empire and in the West—for example, the Armenian Gospel of the Infancy of Christ, the Syriac of Budge, and the Latin Pseudo-Matthew.[3] This last text is an adaptation from the Greek narrative and certain oriental paraphrases. I believe that it must have been composed in Rome, under the influence of Greco-oriental circles, very probably in connection with the establishment of the feast of the Birth of the Virgin by Sergius I, at the end of the seventh century.[4] As the Protevangelium in the Byzantine Empire and, more generally, among peoples of the Orthodox faith, so in the West the Pseudo-Matthew is the basis for the textual and iconographic tradition. The two traditions are markedly different, and cases of conflation are extremely rare. In considering a Byzantine cycle of images of the Life of the Virgin, it is entirely unnecessary to refer either to this text or to the Gospel of the Nativity of Mary, which is derived from it.[5]

The Protevangelium is an apocryphal book of markedly orthodox character. The aim of the redactor was to remedy the silence of the canonical Gospels in respect to the life of the Virgin and her parents, as well as to prove the fact of her virginity by more realistic arguments. It very soon made its way into the ecclesiastical tradition and supplied not only the material for a large

---

1 E. de Strycker, *La forme la plus ancienne du Protévangile de Jacques: Recherches sur le Papyrus Bodmer 5* (Subsidia Hagiographica, 33; Brussels, 1961). The work that served as the basis for the present study on the cycle of the Life of the Virgin, down to Joseph Taking Leave of the Virgin after the marriage [99], is my *Iconographie de l'enfance de la Vierge dans l'Empire byzantin et en Occident*, 2 vols. (Brussels, 1964 and 1965).

2 A. Smith Lewis, *Apocrypha Syriaca: The Protevangelium Jacobi and Transitus Mariae* (London, 1902); de Strycker, *Protévangile de Jacques*, pp. 35 ff.; Lafontaine-Dosogne, *Iconographie*, I, Ch. I,1.

3 See, for the first text, C. Michel and P. Peeters, ed. and tr., *Évangiles apocryphes*, II, 2d ed. (Paris, 1924); for the second, E. A. Wallis Budge, ed., *The History of the Blessed Virgin Mary and the History of the Likeness of Christ which the Jews of Tiberias Made to Mock at: The Syriac Texts* (Luzac's Semitic Text and Translation Series, IV–V; London, 1899). The Pseudo-Matthew has been published several times; see especially E. Amann, tr. and ed., *Le Protévangile de Jacques et ses remaniements latins* (Paris, 1910), pp. 272 ff. and 138 ff.

4 L. Duchesne, *Le Liber Pontificalis*, I (Paris, 1886), p. 371 ff. and esp. 381, n. 43. The 6th-century date proposed by Amann, p. 103, is not supported by convincing arguments. But this does not mean that some of these narratives were not known in the West at an earlier period. (I have re-examined the problem of the textual tradition in *Iconographie*, I, Ch. I,1, and II, Ch. I,1.)

5 The Gospel of the Nativity found its way in the 13th century into the *Golden Legend* of Jacques de Voragine. For the text, see, among others, Amann, *Protévangile*, pp. 340 ff. This narrative, together with the Protevangelium and the Pseudo-Matthew, appears in C. von Tischendorf, *Evangelia Apocrypha*, 2d ed. (Leipzig, 1876).

number of liturgical texts but also the occasion for a number of Marian feasts. The Birth of Mary was no doubt celebrated from the first half of the seventh century, her Presentation in the Temple in the first half of the eighth, and the Conception at the end of the eighth or the beginning of the ninth.[6] The establishment of liturgical feasts naturally encouraged the appearance of illustrations in religious manuscripts and on the walls of churches.

However, we need not come down to these late dates to find testimony to the relations between the liturgical cult and our narratives. Thus, Procopius tells us that in the time of Justinian Constantinople itself contained, in addition to several churches of the Virgin, a church dedicated to St. Anne (*De aedificiis*, I. iii. 11). The notable spread of the cult of the Virgin after the Council of Ephesus (431), in the course of which she was solemnly accorded the title of Theotokos, Mother of God, brought with it a marked interest in the events of her life, especially in the eastern parts of the Empire—a fact that contributed in no small degree to disseminating the texts that we are considering. As for the existence of figured representations, the archeological evidence, though scarce and sometimes dubious, is none the less eloquent. An ivory in the Hermitage Museum, Leningrad, probably dating from the sixth century and of Syrian or Egyptian provenance (Fig. 9),[7] represents the Annunciation to Anne in complete accordance with the text of the Protevangelium. Since this episode is a less important one than the Conception, the Birth, or the Presentation in the Temple, we may suppose that a fully developed cycle was already in existence at that time, an assumption that would seem to be confirmed by the detailed depiction of the narrative carved on column A of the ciborium in San Marco, Venice. Concerning this monument, which has given rise to considerable controversy and whose execution is perhaps medieval, I have elsewhere shown that at least the iconography of the scenes from the Life of the Virgin displayed on it stemmed from an Early Christian and orientalizing tradition.[8] Iconoclasm on the one hand and the Arab conquests on the other having deprived us of many images from these early periods, it is Rome that, for the eighth century, supplies representations of the Life of the Virgin—almost all of them, unfortunately, lost or extremely fragmentary—in the churches of Santa Maria Antiqua and San Saba, which belonged to the Greco-oriental groups of the city.[9] Among the surviving frescoes from the end of the ninth century, in the Roman temple known as that of Fortuna Virilis, transformed into a church in the early Middle Ages under the name Sancta Maria de Gradellis, some scenes in the Life of the Virgin derive not from the Protevangelium but from the Pseudo-Matthew, as is perhaps already true of earlier Roman representations.[10]

Thereafter the iconographic schemes of the two parts of Christendom exhibit their individual characteristics. For we have the good fortune to be able to contrast with the Sancta Maria de Gradellis ensemble the series in the small Cappadocian church at Kızıl Çukur,[11] which is con-

---

6 This appears from the examination of liturgical calendars and texts (my *Iconographie*, I, Ch. I,2).

7 W. F. Volbach, *Elfenbeinarbeiten der Spätantike und des frühen Mittelalters*, 2d ed. (Mainz, 1952), No. 129, PL. 40; J. Strzygowski, *Hellenistische und koptische Kunst in Alexandria* (Vienna, 1902), p. 87; and idem, "Zwei weitere Stücke der Marientafel zum Diptychon von Murano," *BZ*, 8 (1899), p. 680.

8 J. Lafontaine, "Iconographie de la colonne A du ciborium de Saint-Marc à Venise," *Actes du XIIᵉ Congrès International d'Etudes Byzantines, Ochride (1961)*, III (Belgrade, 1964), pp. 213–19. For a recent review of the question, see O. Demus, *The Church of San Marco in Venice: History, Architecture, Sculpture* (Washington, D.C., 1960), p. 167.

9 In Santa Maria Antiqua, the Meeting of Joachim and Anne and the Birth; J. Wilpert, *Die römischen Mosaiken und Malereien der kirchlichen Bauten vom IV. bis XIII. Jahrhundert*, 2d ed.

(Freiburg im Breisgau, 1917), IV, PL. 194, and II, p. 653 ff. In San Saba there remain only fragments of inscriptions, one referring either to Joachim's Offerings Rejected or to the Presentation in the Temple, the other to the Marriage of Mary and Joseph; P. Styger, "Die Malereien in der Basilika des hl. Sabas auf dem kl. Aventin in Rom," *Römische Quartalschrift*, 28 (1914), pp. 63–64.

10 J. Lafontaine, *Peintures médiévales dans le temple dit de la Fortune Virile à Rome* (Brussels and Rome, 1959), pp. 20–28, PL. II–VI.

11 N. and M. Thierry, "Eglise de Kizil-Tchoukour: Chapelle iconoclaste, chapelle de Joachim et d'Anne," *Mon Piot*, L (1958), pp. 105–46. I have restudied the whole problem of the Kızıl Çukur cycle in *Iconographie*, I, pp. 37, 186–87 and passim, and Figs. 13–17.

temporary or a little later and which illustrates an oriental version of the Protevangelium. It is the earliest example of a church in the Byzantine area whose decoration illustrates these subjects. It is, indeed, the only church which, because of its small size, is entirely devoted to the Life of the Virgin, to whom it was certainly dedicated. In addition, various indications warrant the conclusion that the models for these frescoes were pre-iconoclastic.[12] Such subjects are in any case well represented at an early date in the eastern regions of the Byzantine world, particularly in Cappadocia and Georgia. At the beginning of the eleventh century five scenes, obviously selected from a fuller series, appear on a gilded silver icon from Georgia;[13] at the end of the century we find an entire cycle painted in the cathedral of Ateni; more of these scenes will be found in other Georgian churches of the twelfth century (at Ahtala) and of the early thirteenth (at Bertoubani).[14]

From the end of the tenth century, however, Constantinople itself, in the famous Menologion of Basil II (ca. 986), supplies images of a liturgical nature illustrating the feasts of the Conception, the Birth, and the Presentation of the Virgin,[15] in an iconography thenceforth "classic." On the basis of the documents at our disposal, it does not appear that such subjects were illustrated earlier in the capital.[16] But the Constantinopolitan schemes would seem to have imposed their standard from then on, even in Cappadocia itself, where there is a striking contrast between the tentative iconography of the Presentation of the Virgin in the Chapel of the Theotokos at Göreme (tenth century) and the synthetic, "Byzantine" composition in Sarıca Kilisse (third quarter of the eleventh century).[17]

In the second half of the eleventh century, we find illustration of the Infancy of the Virgin fully at home on the walls of Byzantine churches, and by no means only the smallest of them—in St. Sophia at Kiev, about 1050–60, and, about 1100, in the Church of the Dormition of the Virgin at Daphni.[18] If the Kiev cycle, placed in a side chapel, appears to be made up of a comparatively arbitrary choice among illustrations belonging to a detailed cycle, the five compositions at Daphni, executed with the utmost refinement in the magnificent medium of mosaic and thoroughly classic, constitute a cycle in the full sense, even though a small one. They are located in the southern part of the narthex, except for the Birth of the Virgin, which is given a place of honor in the nave, among the Great Feasts.

---

12 In particular, the unusual image that precedes the Birth and doubtless symbolizes the Immaculate Conception of Anne derives from a detail in the original text that quickly disappeared from Greek manuscripts but had passed into the old Syriac version. The scheme of the Annunciation to Anne is like that on the Leningrad ivory and the San Marco column but differs from that of post-iconoclastic works.

13 G. N. Čubinašvili, Georgian Repoussé Work, VIIIth to XVIIIth Centuries (Tiflis, 1957), PL. 41 (general view) and 38 (details of our scenes): Joachim's Offerings Rejected, Annunciation to Anne, Annunciation to Joachim, Nativity, Marriage (the Meeting and the Presentation, two essential scenes, are missing).

14 For Ahtala, see S. J. Amiranašvili, Istorija gruzinskogo iskusstva, I (Moscow, 1950), p. 190. The scenes at Ateni are in the south apse (the church is a tetraconch); idem, Istorija gruzinskoj monumentalnoj živopisi, I (Sachelgami, 1957), pp. 82 ff. and PL. 62 (Birth). The Ateni frescoes cannot possibly be earlier than the end of the 11th century, although a 10th-century date has been proposed and defended by the author, p. 96 and n. 23 to pp. 97–98. For Bertoubani, see G. N. Cubinašvili, Peščernye monastyri David-Garedži: očerk po istorii iskusstva Gruzii (Tiflis, 1948), PL. 104–105 and p. 67; also Lafontaine Dosogne, Iconographie, I, Figs. 39, 62.

15 Vaticanus gr. 1613, published in facsimile in Il Menologio di Basilio II (Codice Vaticano greco 1613) (Codices e Vaticanis selecti, VIII; Turin, 1907); see Vol. II, pp. 22, 198, and 229. For the date, see S. Der Nersessian, "Remarks on the Date of the Menologium and the Psalter Written for Basil II," Byzantion, 15 (1940–41), pp. 104–25.

16 It is perhaps worth remarking in this connection that if 11th-century psalters are illustrated, at Psalm 45:15, by a Presentation of the Virgin, the same is not yet true of earlier psalters, such as the Chloudov Psalter (although its decorative program makes this manuscript rather an unusual case).

17 J. Lafontaine, "Sarıca Kilise en Cappadoce," CA, 12 (1962), pp. 270 f. and Figs. 9–11.

18 O. Povstenko, The Cathedral of St. Sophia in Kiev (New York, 1954), figs. on pp. 130–32, PL. 113, 120–27, 128–29, 131 (the text, p. 124, is very slight). For the date see, among other studies, V. Lazarev, "Novye dannye o mozaikax i freskax Sofii Kievskoj," VV, N.S., 10 (1956), pp. 161–77. More recently, in Mozaiki Sofii Kievskoj (Moscow, 1960), p. 51, he proposes the date 1050–51. For Daphni, see G. Millet, Le monastère de Daphni: Histoire, architecture, mosaïques (Paris, 1899), PL. XVIII–XIX and Fig. 66: Annunciation to Anne, Annunciation to Joachim, Birth, Blessing of the Priests, Presentation in the Temple. It is difficult to say if the cycle may have included other scenes.

From the first half of the twelfth century, a document of exceptional value for the Constantinopolitan tradition—the series of miniatures accompanying the Homilies of the Monk James Kokkinobaphos—has been preserved in two very similar manuscripts, one in the Bibliothèque Nationale at Paris, the other in the Vatican Library.[19] Since the author closely follows the apocryphal account, though accompanying it by an extremely verbose commentary, the numerous narrative images that illustrate the homilies on the Conception, the Birth, and the Presentation of the Virgin may be considered to be precisely those which would be found at the period in a manuscript of the Protevangelium.[20] It is a manuscript deriving from a similar tradition that inspired the mosaics in San Marco, Venice.[21] In Russia, where many churches are dedicated to the Virgin, frescoes illustrating the episodes of her infancy are numerous and usually placed in the prothesis. They display a certain oriental influence, particularly noticeable in the extensive cycle in the monastery of Mirož at Pskov (1156).[22] From this time on, the scenes of the Birth and the Presentation, having attained a liturgical significance, can be detached from the narrative cycle or even be the object of isolated representations.[23]

Without opening the question of iconographic motifs here, I will only say that, in so far as the choice of subjects is concerned, a distinction must be made between representations more or less directly connected with the art of the capital and those that we may call orientalizing. Thus, prior to the Palaeologan period—that is until about the middle of the thirteenth century—we find among the former neither the Return of Joachim and Anne from the Temple, nor the First Steps of the Virgin, nor the Virgin Caressed by Her Parents, all of which are represented very early in the eastern regions and, at least in part, in twelfth-century Russia; on the other hand, these regions offer no examples of the Virgin Blessed by the Priests, known to Byzantium from the time of Daphni.[24]

The Palaeologan age, so rich in extensive painted ensembles in countless churches, whether

---

19 The Paris manuscript is reproduced by H. Omont, *Miniatures des homélies sur la Vierge du moine Jacques (Ms. grec 1208 de Paris)* (Bulletin de la Société Française de Reproductions de Manuscrits à Peintures, 11, *Album;* Paris, 1927), the Vatican manuscript by C. Stornajolo, *Miniature delle omilie di Giacomo monaco (Cod. Vatic. gr. 1162) e dell' evangeliario greco urbinate (Cod. Vatic. Urbin. gr. 2)* (Codices e Vaticanis selecti . . . , Series Minor, I; Rome, 1910).

20 In addition to these scenes, others are inspired by Kokkinobaphos' text itself, which is full of typological allusions; some combine symbolic with narrative matter (Lafontaine-Dosogne, *Iconographie*, I, Ch. IV,2). No illustrated manuscript of the Apocrypha of the Virgin has come down to us.

21 The episodes of the Marriage and the cycle of the Infancy of Christ are represented in the western part of the north arm of the church; S. Bettini, *Mosaici antichi di San Marco a Venezia* (Bergamo, [1944]), PL. XLIV–XLV. All the episodes preceding the Marriage had been represented in the corresponding southern part, but the mosaics were completely done over in the Baroque period. Otto Demus, who formerly proposed a 13th-century date, now dates these mosaics in the 12th century—rightly, I believe. I had already indicated that the iconography of the scenes of the Virgin might go back to the 12th century if not to the end of the 11th (Lafontaine-Dosogne, *Iconographie*, I, p. 186).

22 In particular, the Return of Anne and Joachim and their Conversation at home, and the Caresses. This series has not been published in detail; see F. I. Uspenskij, *Očerki po istorii russkogo iskusstva*, I (Moscow, 1910); F. A. Ušakov, *Opisanie fresok xrama Preobraženija Gospodnja v Pskovskom Spaso-Mirožskom monastyre* (Pskov, 1903) (description, sometimes inaccurate, of the photographs in Parli's unpublished Album); Lafontaine-Dosogne, *Iconographie*, I, cf. Index, and mostly II, pp. 209–10.

The presence of scenes of the Virgin in the prothesis must be related to the idea of the Incarnation (Lafontaine-Dosogne, *Iconographie*, I, Ch. IV,3).

23 We saw that the Birth had already been detached from the cycle at Daphni to figure among the Great Feasts. In Russian churches of the 12th century the Birth and the Presentation are also frequently detached from the narrative cycle; the same procedure is found at the beginning of the 14th century at Snetogorsk (V. Lazarev, "Snetogorskie rospisi," *Soobščenija Instituta Istorii Iskusstv*, Akademija Nauk SSSR, 8 (1957), pp. 85 and 90. At Kalenić, in the fifteenth century, the Birth appears in the cycle in the narthex; the scene appears again in the nave with the Presentation, the two scenes illustrating the Great Feasts; V. R. Petković and Ž. Tatić, *Manastir Kalenić* (Vršac, 1926), plan, Fig. 73, p. 87. Apart from ensembles, the same two scenes are often represented alone on the walls of churches. The Presentation appears alone in the middle of the 11th century in St. Sophia at Ohrid; G. Millet and A. Frolow, *La peinture du Moyen Âge en Yougoslavie (Serbie, Macédoine et Monténégro)*, I (Paris, 1954), PL. 4,1–3. The two scenes are represented at Nerezi in 1164; ibid., II (Paris, 1957), PL. 17. Also in the 12th century they are found on an epistylion at Sinai; G. and M. Soteriou, *Icônes du Mont Sinaï*, I (Athens, 1956), Fig. 99, and II (Athens, 1958), p. 107 (also reproduced in my *Iconographie*, I, Figs. 58 and 86). In the post-Byzantine period the Great Feasts series often begins with the Birth and the Presentation of the Virgin on the panels of the iconostases.

24 It should, however, be mentioned that if the Return and the Virgin Caressed by Her Parents illustrate passages from oriental versions, the episodes of the Virgin Blessed by the Priests and the First Steps are common to the Greek Protevangelium and its versions. We are dealing here with purely iconographic customs, not with particular textual traditions.

new or restored, offers an abundant harvest of scenes from the Life of the Virgin. Many of these churches are dedicated to the Mother of God. The cycle often appears in the middle register of the nave, especially in the case of a small edifice (as at St. Clement's, Ohrid, originally consecrated to the Virgin Peribleptos); but it is also found in side chapels, especially in the prothesis (at Dečani, for example), and less frequently in the narthex (as at the Holy Apostles, Salonika). During this period, remarkable for the development of narrative painting and a certain taste for the expression of emotions, such subjects appear to enjoy a privileged situation. A koine, based on the various tendencies that had appeared earlier, takes shape, especially in the unusually homogeneous group of the cycles of the Virgin in Macedonia and Serbia and at Mount Athos. Nevertheless, in Greece proper and the islands the three scenes just mentioned (Return, First Steps, Caresses) remain extremely rare.[25] Even ensembles as detailed as those of the Peribleptos at Mistra (end of the fourteenth century) and the church of the Cross at Pelendri in Cyprus (end of the fifteenth century), which, especially the former, are closer to richly illustrated manuscripts than to the usual representations in churches, include only the first of the three scenes—while being in their entirety more complete than cycles of the same period in Macedonia.

What place do the mosaics of the church of the Chora hold in the history of the cycle of the Infancy of the Virgin? What part did the Constantinopolitan tradition, which they represent, play in the elaboration of the typical cycle of the Palaeologan period? An examination of the scenes themselves will allow us to attempt an answer to these questions, which are of all the greater interest since the cycle is the only one still extant in a church in the capital.[26]

At the Kariye Djami the cycle of the Virgin occupies the greater part of the inner narthex. It begins at the north end and continues along the east wall and in the domes of the second and third bays, then along the west wall, to end at the northwest corner.

As was traditional from the time of the earliest Byzantine examples, the cycle begins with the scene of Joachim's Offerings Rejected [82], at present reduced to the figure of the high priest, in the left pendentive above the northern lunette (Vol. 2 of this work, PL. 86).[27] The scene was certainly the fully developed one that is found as early as the eleventh century on the Zarzma silver icon (Fig. 1)[28] and in the twelfth century in Russian frescoes.[29] The high priest, clad in his sacerdotal vestments, stands behind the closed doors of the sanctuary (or behind the altar, at Staraja Ladoga), while Joachim and Anne, carrying lambs, respectfully approach him.[30]

25 However, the Virgin Caressed by Her Parents is found in Crete, but under the influence of the north; J. Lafontaine, "Deux notes à propos des fresques de Crète," in Κρητικὰ Χρονικά, 10 (1956), pp. 395–98, and K. D. Kalokyris, Αἱ βυζαντιναὶ τοιχογραφίαι τῆς Κρήτης: Συμβολὴ εἰς τὴν χριστιανικὴν τέχνην τῆς Ἑλλάδος (Athens, 1957), pp. 107 ff.

26 Byzantine writers or travelers whose descriptions of Constantinopolitan monuments have come down to us do not mention our scenes, except, perhaps, for Montconys, who speaks (in 1648) of scenes from the life of the Virgin in the refectory of the monastery of the Peribleptos; J. Ebersolt, Constantinople byzantine et les voyageurs du Levant (Paris, 1918), pp. 136 ff. The frescoes in the diaconicon of the Odalar Djami, which are now destroyed, included several scenes from the Life of the Virgin, among them a Marriage; see the articles by M. Alpatov and N. Brunov in BZ, 26 (1926), pp. 352 ff., and by P. Schazmann in Atti del V Congresso internazionale di studi bizantini, II (Rome, 1940) = Studi bizantini e neoellenici, 6, pp. 372–86. In my opinion this decoration may well go back to the 12th century.

27 For the inscriptions accompanying all these scenes, as well as their description, the reader will please refer to Vol. 1 of this work.

28 Čubinašvili, Georgian Repoussé Work, PL. 38. The fragmentary Kızıl Çukur fresco may have included the same motifs, although the presence of Anne is not certain. But the lacuna is large enough for Anne to have been depicted in it.

29 In particular at St. George's in Staraja Ladoga (after 1167); V. Lazarev, Freski Staroj Ladogi (Moscow, 1960), pp. 6–8 (or Lafontaine-Dosogne, Iconographie, I, Fig. 34, after N. Brandeburg, Staraja Ladoga [St. Petersburg, 1896]).

30 Lambs were the offering of the rich, in contrast to doves, the offering of the poor. Less frequently the Virgin's parents offer boxes, as in the Homilies of the Monk James (Stornajolo, Omilie, PL. 4; Omont, Homélies, PL. II,1). Anne may also carry a pitcher, or be empty-handed. The high priest is not named in the Protevangelium in this passage. However, the confusion with Reuben was made in certain manuscripts. The priest of the Offerings is usually anonymous, but he is sometimes called Zacharias as the result of an association either with the high priest of the Presentation of the Virgin in the Temple or with the priest of the Marriage, for example at Chilandar, where this name is embroidered on his vestment; G. Millet, Monuments de l'Athos (Paris, 1927), PL. 78,2.

However, the priest's attitude is exceptional in our mosaic. Not only is he presented in a frontal view rather than in the usual profile—which may well be due to the fact that the composition was cut in two—but what is still more remarkable, his gesture clearly indicates refusal (PL. 87). In the other representations, both early and contemporary, he holds out his hand toward the Virgin's parents—an ambiguous gesture; for he thus seems willing to accept their offerings, despite his stiff posture and the hostility signified by the closed sanctuary doors.[31] The reason is that originally the illustration of the narrative comprised both the reception of the gift-bearers by the high priest—well seen in the miniature for the Homilies of the Monk James (Fig. 2)—and Reuben's opposition to Joachim's presenting his gifts because of his shameful sterility; only the sculptor of column A in the ciborium of San Marco, Venice, represented the scene under this twofold aspect.[32] Reuben and the "sons of Israel" soon disappeared from church painting, which tends to simplify the narrative elements.[33] The high priest thus took over Reuben's function, but at the same time the original welcoming gesture was preserved. More rational or more independent, the Kariye Djami mosaicist preferred to indicate a refusal.

As for the presence of Anne in the theme of the rejected offerings, it was from a desire to create a more meaningful scene that she was given a place in it with her husband. Though contrary to the indications of the texts, her presence can also be explained by a passage in her Lament in the garden, in which she resents the affront to Joachim as if it had been an affront to herself,[34] or else by a formal influence from the theme of the Presentation of the Virgin in the Temple. The scene as created by these three characters conveys an expressive symbolism.

The composition in the northern lunette [83], which followed Joachim's Offerings Rejected, is now reduced to a building, preserved in the left section, at the entrance to which a young maid-servant stands, raising the door curtain (PL. 88). It might be supposed that the scene represented one of the episodes accompanying the Annunciation to Anne, more especially the reproof made to her by her servant Judith, or Anne's Lament in her garden (Protevangelium 2:1–3). This would seem to be the more likely since, as we shall see presently, Joachim's Lament (PL. 91) is represented in conjunction with the Annunciation. But in the episode of Judith's Reproof the maid offers a headband to her mistress and speaks with her; here, there is nothing to individualize the maid. Furthermore, the bird's nest, an essential element in Anne's Lament, is represented in the Annunciation scene: certainly it was not depicted twice in the cycle. So it is practically out of the question that either of these themes was given a place in the lunette. Moreover, not only do they very rarely appear in church painting of the period but they seem to be more or less foreign to the Constantinopolitan tradition. At the beginning of the twelfth century the mini-

---

31 In the 11th and 12th centuries the sanctuary doors are likewise very often closed in the scene of the Presentation of the Virgin. But later they are open, making Zacharias' attitude more cordial, whereas they remain closed in the scene of the Rejected Offerings.

32 Lafontaine-Dosogne, *Iconographie*, I, Figs. 1–4 (lower register); during this time the priest censes the altar. In the Latin Pseudo-Matthew, Reuben is regarded as a scribe of the Temple in some manuscripts, as a priest in others. But the two personages are not confused in Italian iconography; cf., among others, the composition of the icon at Pisa called the Madonna di San Martino, ca. 1270, or Giotto's fresco in the Arena Chapel at Padua; A. Venturi, *Storia dell' arte italiana*, V: *La pittura del Trecento e le sue origini* (Milan, 1907), Fig. 44, p. 57, and Fig. 248, p. 308. In other Western countries, on the contrary, the high priest is often represented alone. The earliest example is the

scene carved on the capitals of the Portail Royal of Chartres Cathedral, ca. 1150; Et. Houvet, *Cathédrale de Chartres, Portail occidental ou Royal, XIIe siècle* (Chelles, 1919), PL. 77.

33 In early church painting, or in that which is particularly faithful to the manuscript miniatures, we find a larger cast of characters, priests or bringers of offerings, for example at Ateni (Amiranašvili; *Živopis'*, pp. 83–84) and Pelendri in Cyprus (Lafontaine-Dosogne, *Iconographie*, I, Fig. 27).

34 Protevangelium 3:1. Anne is not represented on the San Marco column, where the narrative is illustrated with unusual fidelity (this is one of the reasons that led me to consider this column a work that in tradition, if not in execution, is Early Christian). Anne is depicted in Western art, doubtless under Byzantine influence, except in Italy, where the iconographic tradition developed in greater conformity to the texts.

aturist of the Homilies of the Monk James knows them, for he introduces the corresponding scenes in his cycle of illustrations, even though they are not justified by the text itself. But he handles them incorrectly. He combines the theme of the bird's nest, which belongs to the Lament, with the episode of Judith's Reproof—which in any case he seems not to have understood—and substitutes a young maidservant for the messengers who come to tell Anne of Joachim's return (Fig. 3, lower register).[35] The themes just mentioned, like those of Joachim Searching the Records of the Twelve Tribes and his Return after the Annunciation, illustrate episodes narrated in the Protevangelium (1:3–4:3); but they are rarely represented in churches, and when they are, the representations seem to derive directly from manuscript miniatures and not from the selective cycle proper to monumental painting.[36]

In point of fact, the subject is certainly Joachim and Anne returning to their house after the rejection of the offerings. This purely narrative theme is frequent in the larger ensembles of the Palaeologan period, especially in Macedonia and Serbia. It represents an intrusion of the oriental tradition into the cycle of the Infancy of the Virgin, for it is the Syriac and Armenian paraphrases of the Protevangelium that mention Joachim's return to his house before his departure for the mountain.[37] It is also in the Byzantine East that we find the earliest representations of the scene: in the Georgian church of Ateni (end of the eleventh century), then at Pskov (1156), in Russia,[38] then again in Georgia in the rock-cut church at Bertoubani (1213–22) (Fig. 4). The Bertoubani painter showed Joachim and Anne approaching their house. But the theme is thoroughly integrated into the iconographic koine of the Palaeologan period. We may mention in particular the fresco in the church of Milutin at Studenica (1314), an example close in time to our mosaic, or the Cypriote fresco at Pelendri (end of the fifteenth century) (Fig. 5).[39] In those examples where the scene forms part of a frieze, and sometimes even when it is isolated, Joachim and Anne are shown leaving the Temple instead of approaching their house.[40] In the Kariye Djami, the mosaicist has introduced a maidservant standing at the entrance to the house and drawing aside a curtain (PL. 89). This charming motif is frequent in the Byzantine art of Constantinople and Greece. It occurs especially in the Annunciation to Anne. There was all the more reason for including it here, since the composition was cut in two by the triple window introduced into the lunette. It was a good way to enliven the starkness of the isolated building to the left, while the larger space to the right gave room for the figures of Joachim and Anne returning with their offerings.

---

35 Stornajolo, *Omilie*, PL. 6; Omont, *Homélies*, PL. III,2. In addition to these two scenes the miniature includes the Annunciation to Anne and the Meeting of Anne and Joachim. The inscription mentions only the last two episodes; hence the artist would seem to have been comparatively unfamiliar with the first two.

36 Some of these scenes are found on the San Marco column, in the Cappadocian church of Kızıl Çukur, where the painter certainly employed pre-iconoclastic models (Lafontaine-Dosogne, *Iconographie*, I, Figs. 1–4, 13, and 15), as well as on two 15th-century Russian *aers* that are markedly orientalizing in tradition; V. N. Ščepkin, "Pamjatnik zolotogo šht'ja načala XV veka," *Drevnosti*, 15, 1 (1894), PL. V–VII and fig. on p. 44. In the church of the Patriarchate at Peć the scene of the messenger is represented; V. R. Petković, *La peinture serbe du Moyen Âge*, I (Belgrade, 1930), PL. 70 *b*. In the Peribleptos at Mistra we find Joachim Searching the Records of the Tribes, a scene that is probably Anne with her maidservant, and Anne warned by two angels; G. Millet, *Monuments byzantins de Mistra* (Paris, 1910), PL. 126. At Pelendri the maidservant of the Annunciation holds a double ribbon, an allusion to the incident of Judith's Reproof (see our Fig. 5).

37 Budge, *History of the Blessed Virgin*, p. 6; Michel and Peeters, *Evangiles apocryphes*, II (1:1). Actually only Joachim appears in these texts, but since Anne accompanies her husband on the occasion of the Offerings in the figured representations, she must obviously be present in this scene too. The primitive text says that Joachim retired to the desert. This theme, which is Egyptian in origin, was dropped by some redactors. In particular, the oriental paraphrases—and the Latin narratives—replaced it by the mountain, which seemed more logical since shepherds and flock appear later in the story.

38 For Ateni, see Amiranašvili, *Živopis'*, p. 84; for Pskov, Uspenskij, *Očerki*, I, p. 147. See also Lafontaine-Dosogne, *Iconographie*, I, p. 66 and II, pp. 209–10.

39 Petković, *La peinture serbe du Moyen Âge*, II (Belgrade, 1934), PL. XLIV.

40 This is the case in St. Clement, Ohrid (1295), and at Volotovo (ca. 1380); V. Lazarev, *Feofan Grek i ego škola* (Moscow, 1961), PL. 47 *b*. Later, at Lavra among other places (Millet, *Athos*, PL. 140,2), both the entrance and exit of Anne and Joachim may be grouped about the central figure of the priest, with their arrival to the left and their departure to the right.

The Annunciation to Joachim was treated in two episodes in the church of the Chora. Only one of these is extant today, the Lament or Prayer of Joachim in the Wilderness [84]. Joachim has withdrawn to the mountain in despair after the rejection of his offerings and his discouraging researches into the archives of the tribes, to await a sign from God (Protevangelium 1:4). He is seated in an aureole of foliage against a background of mountains, in the presence of two shepherds (PL. 90, 91). In painting of this period we usually find a synthetic representation combining the Lament and the Annunciation. At St. Clement's, Ohrid, for example, the scene offers the same elements, with the addition of the little flying angel bringing the good tidings, whom Joachim, seated and lost in thought, has not yet seen (Fig. 6). In the earliest examples of the Annunciation proper, Joachim is seated while the angel stands before him; this is the scheme found on the column in San Marco, Venice, at Kızıl Çukur, at Daphni (Fig. 7), and sometimes even later.[41] In the first two examples he is seated on a stool. At Daphni, however, as at the Kariye Djami and in many other representations, he is placed in a bush whose upper branches have been tied together to make a sort of hut, which is an interpretation of the σκηνή of the text; but he may also be seated on a rock (Fig. 8).[42] At Kızıl Çukur the painter has added to the central group a grazing flock watched by two shepherds. The combination of these various motifs is unique in Byzantine art. The flock and even the shepherds represent an orientalizing motif, which is explained by the emphasis given by the Armenian and Syriac paraphrases to their presence, from the moment of Joachim's departure for the mountain. In the Protevangelium shepherds and flock are mentioned only in connection with Joachim's Return after the Annunciation.[43] They would seem to be foreign to the Constantinopolitan tradition, for they are found neither at Daphni nor in the Homilies of the Monk James, though the Return is suggested there.[44] On the other hand, they are found in oriental and Russian works before the Palaeologan period. In any case, from then on the shepherds become a standard motif in the scene of the Annunciation to Joachim, but the flock is never represented in it at the same time.[45]

The composition of the scene at Ohrid, just described, is the most frequent one during this period; it is also found in the Holy Apostles at Salonika.[46] But it is not the only way in which the episode is illustrated. In the church at Vatopedi, Mount Athos, the painter has combined two scenes: in the background Joachim seated in the presence of his shepherds; in the foreground, Joachim standing to receive the angel's message. Lament and Annunciation, then, were still treated separately.[47] Joachim's standing position was adopted either in imitation of the theme of Anne or to differentiate the two episodes. At Studenica only the second episode was repre-

41 Lafontaine-Dosogne, *Iconographie*, I, Fig. 1 (second register) and Fig. 13. A later example: the *aers* mentioned in n. 36.

42 As on the Zarzma icon, of the 11th century (Čubinašvili, *Georgian Repoussé Work*, PL. 38), or the fresco at Chilandar (Millet, *Athos*, PL. 78,2). The motif of Joachim seated in a bush is old. It is found as early as the end of the 9th century in the Roman fresco in Sancta Maria de Gradellis, where, however, it is combined with the rock (Lafontaine-Dosogne, *Peintures médiévales*, PL. II, III).

43 The Latin texts also stress the themes of the flock and the shepherds; in Italy they are never omitted from representations of the Annunciation to Joachim. In other countries of the West, if the flock appears at an early date, notably at Chartres, the shepherds are later. The Protevangelium first dwells on Joachim's sorrow (1:4). The Annunciation comes further on (4:2); it is very briefly recounted at the moment when the messengers inform Anne of her husband's return. It is clear how

two themes arose from this narrative: the Lament and the Annunciation.

44 Stornajolo, *Omilie*, PL. 5; Omont, *Homélies*, PL. III,1.

45 In the few examples in which the flock appears, the shepherds are not represented, at least in the actual scene of the Annunciation. In the Peribleptos at Mistra the cycle of Joachim comprises four scenes, as in the Homilies of the Monk James (Joachim goes to the desert, his Prayer, the Annunciation, his Departure from the desert). But while the shepherds appear nowhere in the miniature, they are found even in the first scene at Mistra, together with the flock. But the Annunciation does not seem to include this last motif (Millet, *Mistra*, PL. 126,1, 125,3 and 131,1, upper left).

46 Of the Annunciation to Joachim all that remains is the seated figure of Joachim and one leg of a shepherd; Joachim is looking up toward the vanished angel.

47 Millet, *Athos*, PL. 87,1. The frescoes, repainted in the 18th century, seem nevertheless to have preserved their original forms (1312).

sented, with Joachim standing—which suggests that the fresco-painter's model also included the Lament.[48] At the Kariye Djami, since the angel was not shown in the picture of Joachim in the Wilderness—or, rather, on the mountain, ἐν τῷ ὄρει, as the inscription says [49]—the Annunciation must certainly have formed the subject of a separate picture. This scene was represented in the lunette, to the left of the Annunciation to Anne (PL. 92), the two representations being placed side by side both because of their meaning and because the artist probably followed the same solution as that employed at Daphni. I consider it certain that Joachim was in a standing position, not only in conformity with the examples cited above but also for reasons of form: symmetry with the adjacent scene of Anne was thereby assured, while the two figures in the eastern lunette corresponded to the four standing figures of the opposite western lunette [99]. The fact that the episode of Joachim was treated in two separate compositions may be considered here a refinement.

If at this time Joachim's Lament and the Annunciation to him can still be the subjects of two pictures despite the existence of a synthetic composition, the same is not true of the Annunciation to Anne [85] (PL. 93, 94). Such a distinction is observed in some few very detailed cycles (the San Marco column, manuscript miniatures or works directly inspired by these).[50] However, a synthetic composition appears as early as the pre–iconoclastic period on an ivory at Leningrad that probably dates from the sixth century (Fig. 9). On this document, as in the Kızıl Çukur fresco, which derives from an old tradition, Anne is seated beside a tree in which birds are nesting (illustration for the Lament), while the angel, whom she has not yet seen, approaches her with an animated movement.[51] Later representations, though combining the same episodes, are much different. In the Daphni mosaic (Fig. 7) we see Anne standing beside the birds' nest with her hands raised, a little half-length angel in the field, a charming fountain with several basins, and an edifice which, depicting Anne's house, reinforces the idea that she is in her garden. This scheme is typical of all the post-iconoclastic representations. However, it is to be observed that at Daphni the birds are perched all over the branches, whereas usually the mother bird is feeding her young in the nest; and that the high portal of the house is enlivened by the presence of a maidservant, a conventional motif or a reminder of Judith, which in any case is found only in the zone comprising Constantinople, Greece, and the islands.[52]

The element of the theme that undergoes the greatest evolution is the fountain (PL. 94). It does not appear in images of the pre–iconoclastic type. However, on the San Marco column a pool containing fish is represented under the birds' tree, an illustration of another passage in the Lament which remains a *hapax*. It was probably a memory of this motif, combined with the theme of the well in the Annunciation to the Virgin, that determined the appearance of the fountain in

48 A striking feature at Studenica is the contrast between the large amount of space given to the principal compositions (Birth, Presentation, Dormition), no doubt because of their liturgical significance, and the very limited space often allotted to the other scenes. For the Annunciation to Joachim, see Petković, *La peinture serbe*, II, PL. XLVI.

49 Such an indication is unusual. It is not taken from the apocryphal text but is adapted to the figured representation (but see above, n. 37).

50 For the Venice column, see my *Iconographie*, I, Figs. 3, 4; for the Homilies of the Monk James, our Fig. 3. It is possible that the Lament was represented separately from the Annunciation in the Peribleptos at Mistra (Millet, *Mistra*, p. 126). In

St. Sophia at Kiev only the Lament was represented, for the angel does not appear in the scene (the painter's model certainly included the two themes); see Povstenko, *St. Sophia in Kiev*, PL. 120.

51 The attitude of the angel and of Anne is the same on the ivory, on the San Marco column, and in the Cappadocian fresco. The iconography of these three documents, which are pre-iconoclastic in execution or tradition, is thus clearly distinguished from the iconography current from the 11th century.

52 The motif in the fresco at Pelendri (our Fig. 5) indicates that, at least in some cases, a memory of Judith is certainly involved. No maidservant is seen in the other representations of this theme; she is unknown in the Macedonian cycles.

the Annunciation to Anne. The pine-cone that surmounts the basins, at Daphni as in the Homilies of the Monk James, no doubt stems from a contemporary fashion. We know, for example, that the phial of the Triconchos, at the Great Palace, included this motif, which in any case is ancient.[53] The particular form of the fountain in Palaeologan art—two or three successive basins, with water flowing from one to another through a lion's mask—is probably to be connected with a new fashion rather than considered an archaizing motif. The fountain in our mosaic, however, differs slightly from those in the Macedonian representations, where it takes the form of a large basin behind two smaller basins placed side by side (Fig. 6).[54]

Anne's house, which is always depicted—most frequently as a building, but otherwise as a more or less abstract portico, such as is sometimes found in Macedonia [55]—is represented at the Kariye Djami with unusual lavishness that makes it a completely original feature. The elevated social condition of the Virgin's parents permitted the use of motifs drawn from the life of the Byzantine court or aristocracy. Though identification of this vast imaginary palace or portico is quite out of the question, its luxurious aspect may suggest the dwellings of the rich and highly-placed personages of the period.[56] On the other hand it is difficult to understand why a boy has taken the place of the maidservant in the portal of the building. It may be that the artist, no longer aware of the character of Judith, was fond of the motif of Joseph's son, which appears further on in his own compositions; possibly there is also an influence from such a representation of the Annunciation to the Virgin as that produced by the miniaturist of the Homilies of the Monk James, in which the part of a curious spectator is played by the boy James, the youngest of Joseph's sons.[57] This feature is rather troublesome to account for, coming from an artist who often gives evidence of a rational approach.

Of interest, too, is the detailed nature of the inscription, which is not content with the usual formula, Ἡ ἁγία Ἄννα προσευχομένη, or Ἡ προσευχὴ τῆς ἁγίας Ἄννης (Daphni), but adds ἐν τῷ παραδείσῳ, which is, moreover, in conformity with the texts. The inscription that accompanies Joachim's Lament is also more detailed than usual. These Annunciation scenes are the only ones in the Infancy of the Virgin cycle that take place outdoors. Anne's garden always provided artists with an excuse for a genre picture—trees, birds, and fountains—which is often delightful, while Joachim's shepherds add a rare touch of the picturesque.

After the angel's annunciation to him, Joachim goes home and meets his wife Anne, who, warned by a messenger, has been awaiting him before the entrance to their house [86] (PL. 96, 97) (Protevangelium 4:4). The mosaicist has charmingly rendered the gesture of Anne as she reaches out her hands to "hang on Joachim's neck." Joachim puts his arms around her shoulders; their heads press tenderly against each other. The kiss is the constant element of the theme from

53 Theophanes Continuatus, III.43, Bonn (1838), p. 141 ff.; J. Ebersolt, *Le Grand Palais de Constantinople et le Livre des Cérémonies* (Paris, 1910), p. 111. For this type of fountain, which is early, see J. Strzygowski, "Der Pinienzapfen als Wasserspeier," *Mitteilungen des Kaiserlich Deutschen Archaeologischen Instituts, Römische Abteilung*, 18 (1903), pp. 185–206. The pine-cone can also be considered a fertility symbol, which is particularly appropriate in the case of Anne. It is very rarely found after the beginning of the Palaeologan period.

54 In addition to its appearance at St. Clement, Ohrid, this type is found, among other places, in the Holy Apostles at Salonika.

55 For example, at St. Clement, Ohrid (Fig. 6). This edifice can assume very different forms.

56 An example of these palaces will be found in Theodore Metochites' description of his properties; R. Guilland, "Le palais de Théodore Métochite," *REG*, 35 (1922), pp. 82–95. But nothing warrants the supposition that the mosaicist was inspired by some particular building; the structure in our mosaic cannot, in fact, be compared with anything known in this field at Constantinople or at Mistra; L. de Beylié, *L'habitation byzantine: Recherches sur l'architecture civile des Byzantins et son influence en Europe* (Grenoble and Paris, 1902). In all likelihood our mosaic presents an amplification of a well-known formula.

57 Stornajolo, *Omilie*, PL. 49; Omont, *Homélies*, PL. XIX,2 (the subject is not the Annunciation proper but the arrival of the angel).

the earliest Byzantine representations;[58] it is found, moreover, in other scenes, especially the Visitation. Whereas the sculptor of the San Marco column and the fresco painter of Kızıl Çukur [59] rendered the scene without any setting, later images will always include Anne's house. Images of a more synthetic type—the miniature in the Menologion of Basil II (Fig. 10), the Kiev fresco [60]—will also show the mountain from which Joachim has come down, at the left of the composition, Anne's house being traditionally represented at the right. Anne and Joachim run toward each other, their bodies still separated but their heads already close together for the kiss. Representation of the mountain was soon abandoned, and the movement became less animated. Yet the illustrator of the Homilies of the Monk James shows Anne throwing herself ardently into Joachim's arms before the wall of their house (Fig. 3, upper register); since he had earlier represented Joachim leaving the mountain,[61] he felt no need to introduce this motif into his picture. At St. Clement, Ohrid (Demus' study, Fig. 30), however, a bush to the left may be a reminiscence of the mountain, unless the bush is simply an indication of Anne's garden, as in the Menologion miniature. In the Macedonian fresco Anne and Joachim embrace each other before a sort of portico closely resembling the one in the previous scene, the Annunciation to Anne, but suggesting more clearly the entrance to a house. The mosaicist at the Kariye Djami, having represented the house of the Virgin's parents with the lavishness which we noted, felt obliged to imagine a sumptuous setting for this scene too. He conceived it as a three-story portico, decorated with two rich columns and a drapery, and prolonged, at least to the left, by a wall of a garden suggested by a tall cypress—an elaborate interpretation of the setting of earlier images. In addition, since there was no space for the maidservant within the portico itself—a theme dear to our mosaicist as to the illuminator of the Homilies—she peers curiously over the garden wall; the effect is charming.

We have already dwelt on the liturgical significance of the kiss of Joachim and Anne.[62] The theme, in fact, represents Anne conceiving. It is illuminating in this respect to compare the inscription that accompanies the narrative images of the Homilies—Ἀσπασμός—with the one that identifies the scene in the Kariye Djami and gives it its symbolic character—Ἡ σύλληψις τ(ῆς) Θ(εοτό)κου. Scenes of the Birth are often preceded by an episode suggesting the conception, which may be presented in various ways.[63] In Christian art, however, it is most usually the theme of the kiss that plays this role. Since this theme is a faithful adaptation of the text in the case of Anne and Joachim, it is tempting, not to say reasonable, to find the origin of such a formula there.

However, it is not the Conception of the Virgin, though it begins the process of the Incarna-

58 Western representations, on the contrary, will usually avoid suggesting the kiss too strongly, and the embrace of Anne and Joachim is far more reserved, to the point where they sometimes do no more than touch each other's hands. Such a procedure is explained by the concept of the Immaculate Conception, which was often confused with the absence of any fleshly union. However, there are notable exceptions, especially the very affectionate kiss between the old husband and wife in the fresco in the Arena Chapel at Padua. Following a constant tradition in the West, Giotto set the scene in front of a monumental city gate suggesting the *Porta aurea* of the Latin texts; Venturi, *Storia dell'arte italiana*, V, Fig. 253, p. 314. This last motif, which is foreign to the Greco-oriental texts, does not appear in Byzantine iconography, despite assertions to the contrary.

59 Lafontaine-Dosogne, *Iconographie*, I, Fig. 7 (4th register) and Fig. 14.

60 D. V. Ajnalov and E. K. Redin, "Kievskij Sofijiskij Sobor, issledovanie živopisi—mosaik i fresok Sobora," *Zapiski Imperatorskogo Russkogo Arxeologičeskogo Obščestva*, N.S., 4 (1890), pp.

231–381, and the album *Drevnosti Rossijskogo Gosudarstva, Kievskij Sofijskij Sobor* (St. Petersburg, 1871–87), PL. 31,13 (sketch); a detail in Povstenko, *St. Sophia in Kiev*, PL. 113.

61 Stornajolo, *Omilie*, PL. 5; Omont, *Homélies*, PL. III.

62 See above, p. 164, and P. A. Underwood's discussion in Vol. 1 of this work. The edict of Manuel Comnenus (1166) stresses the importance of the feast. However, it never attained such a leading role in the Byzantine liturgy as those accorded to the feasts of the Virgin's Birth and Presentation in the Temple. I shall return to this.

63 I cite just two examples. On the textile of Dionysus in the Louvre, the birth of the god is preceded by a representation of Semele on her couch being struck by the lightning bolt (this first part does not appear in the reproductions). In the illustrations to Genesis in San Marco, Venice, which reproduce miniatures of the Early Christian 'Cotton' Bible, the birth of Abel is introduced by a realistic scene of the union of Adam and Eve (Bettini, *Mosaici di San Marco*, p. 4, or Lafontaine-Dosogne, *Iconographie*, I, Fig. 52).

tion, but rather her Birth which plays a liturgical role of the first importance. In the visual representations the theme of the Meeting of Anne and Joachim, which is most commonly restricted to two personages, often occupies a subordinate place in the ensemble. In the Palaeologan period and the following centuries, in fact, it is often reduced to occupying only a portion of the Birth composition.[64] It is the Birth theme that acquired the symbolic significance of the first stage of the Incarnation and as such was accorded considerable liturgical importance, which entitled it to a prominent place in the decorative program of churches.

The large composition that occupies the entire eastern lunette of the second bay [87] is typical of Palaeologan art in the various elements that go to make it up. However, the way in which they are treated and arranged is quite unusual, though remaining within the frame of the Constantinopolitan tradition (PL. 98).

Two types of scenes representing the Birth of the Virgin are found at this period. There is a simple type, comprising the following motifs: Anne on her couch, three or four women—servants or visitors—and in some cases the child's bath with the midwife seated by it and a standing maidservant pouring water into it, in others the cradle with the infant lying in it, watched over by a maidservant who is spinning. As examples we will cite two representations from the end of the thirteenth century: the fresco in St. Clement, Ohrid (Demus' study, Fig. 30), which includes the motif of the cradle, and that in St. Achillius at Arilje, where the bath motif has been preserved.[65] A more complex type combines these various elements and may even include others. The Birth of the Virgin in the church of Milutin at Studenica is an excellent example (Fig. 11). The central figure of Anne on her couch serves as connecting link between the left section (simple type with bath motif) and the right section (simple type with cradle motif); in each section three women stand about Anne or approach her, all but one of them behind a low wall; some offer dishes, one waves a flabellum, two others support the newly delivered mother. Joachim has been introduced into the theme of the cradle: he converses with the maidservant, who holds a fly-whisk as she attends the child. The presence of Joachim is a new feature in the iconography of our theme and does not appear until Palaeologan times. He may well have been given a place in it during a period marked by a considerable development of iconographic themes as well as by more intimate feeling, perhaps in imitation of the figure of Zacharias in the Birth of John the Baptist, a composition very close to the Birth of the Virgin, or perhaps of the figure of Joseph in the Nativity of Christ. At the Kariye Djami, indeed, he stands quite timidly in the doorway which in other instances is often occupied by the last of the visiting women.

The mosaic, however, differs from the Studenica fresco in more than one respect. Though

64 At Chilandar (Millet, *Athos*, PL. 78,1), as at Studenica, the theme is squeezed in behind the wall bounding a larger composition—the Birth at Studenica, the Blessing of the Priests (!) at Chilandar. There are many examples of this procedure. It is especially typical of icon painting, where bringing the two themes together is much more natural. It was principally John of Euboea who, in the 8th century, advocated the establishment of the feast in his discourses on the Conception and Birth of the Virgin (*PG*, 94, cols. 1459–1500).

65 For Arilje, see Petković, *La peinture serbe*, II, PL. XXXII. The bath is, in fact, the old and constant motif in the Birth of the Virgin down to this period, when it is strongly rivaled by the cradle. The cradle motif begins to appear in it during the 12th century (however, the motif is already found in church painting about the middle of the 11th century, in the Birth of John the Baptist in St. Sophia at Ohrid; see Millet and Frolow,

Peinture, I, PL. 1,2 and 87,1, where the scene is mistakenly interpreted as a Birth of the Virgin). The infant's bath is an antique formula that was widely adopted into Christian art. It forms an integral part of the Birth of the Virgin from the earliest documents (San Marco column; Lafontaine-Dosogne, *Iconographie*, I, Figs. 7, 6), with the exception of the Kızıl Çukur fresco (ibid., Fig. 14), where the artist followed instead a scheme that recurs several times in illustrations for the births in Genesis—that of the infant presented to its mother (Bettini, *Mosaici di San Marco*, PL. LI, and other representations in the narthex), which would seem to be unique in the Byzantine theme of the Virgin. Yet the presentation of the infant to the mother well illustrated the text of the Protevangelium (5:2); however, the motif of the bath was so current a formula that it imposed itself against all opposition.

adopting the double motif of bath and cradle as well as a larger number of young women than usual, our artist created a composition that adheres to the specifically Constantinopolitan tradition both in the simplicity of the whole and the lavishness and refinement of the details. In comparison, the Milutin fresco shows a certain provinciality in the overinsistence with which it evokes the ceremonial of the birth of porphyrogenite princes;[66] the infant Virgin is twice represented in it, once on the midwife's knees and again in the cradle. The Kariye Djami artist avoided this pitfall by employing a motif as unusual as it is charming—that of the young maidservant preparing the cradle (PL. 100).[67] Moreover, at the Kariye Djami the infant is naked, in accordance with the old tradition (PL. 101), whereas at the period it was generally thought preferable to wrap her in a garment, doubtless out of respect for the Mother of God. The gesture of testing the temperature of the water—also old at Byzantium since it is already found in the miniature in the Menologion of Basil II (Fig. 12)—is preserved in both scenes. But at the Kariye Djami it is performed by the maidservant who pours the water into the great gilded basin, and this seems to be an innovation. In the Menologion miniature the midwife, being unaccompanied, held the baby and at the same time dipped one hand into the water. This gesture was preserved despite the widely accepted addition of a second woman.[68] On the other hand, at the Kariye, Anne's posture is hardly logical, and the shape of the bed is ill adapted to her body (PL. 99). She has raised herself from the back rest and has no support. Doubtless the artists of the capital generally avoided suggesting the weakness of the newly delivered mother and showed a preference for the type of the Virgin who gave birth without pain.[69] But it is also possible that the mosaicist wished in this way to render the attitude of Anne welcoming her visitors. At Studenica she is assisted by two maid-servants, one supporting her from behind, the other holding her hand. This theme of support would seem to be foreign to the Constantinopolitan tradition. Presumably of oriental origin, it is found during the Palaeologan period only in Macedonia and Serbia and at Mount Athos.[70]

The center of our composition is gracefully occupied by five young women. The first, who crosses her arms, and the last two, one holding a dish and the other, seen in profile, raising a flabellum, make up the trio common to many representations of the period—as, for example, in St. Clement, Ohrid (Demus' study, Fig. 30). Two others have been added, one carrying a perfume flask, the other a large and costly vessel that suggests glass.[71] The woman with the flabellum is an old motif. Although it does not seem to belong to the antique birth scheme, it may represent a quite popular motif, for it is found at Kızıl Çukur. At Daphni, on the contrary, the girl who stands at the head of the newly delivered mother's sumptuous bed raises a costly fan made of peacock

---

66 See below, p. 176 and n. 73.

67 A similar arrangement is already found in the Birth of John the Baptist in the Gospel Book Vaticanus Urbinas gr. 2, from the beginning of the 12th century (Stornajolo, *Omilie*, PL. 88).

68 The bath is presented in various ways. In the early documents, as at Daphni or in the Lectionary Vaticanus gr. 1156 (fol. 246v), the infant is submerged in the basin and held there by the seated midwife, while the maidservant pours in water from a pitcher (an exact prefiguration of this type appears on a sarcophagus of the end of the second century in the Terme Museum at Rome; see D. Faccenna, "Roma (Via Portuense)—Monumento funerario," *Notizie degli Scavi di antichità*, 8th Series, Vol. V (*Atti della Accademia nazionale dei Lincei*, 348; Rome, 1951), p. 116, Fig. 2 (cf. Lafontaine-Dosogne, *Iconographie*, I, Figs. 54, 55). When the woman holds the infant in her lap, she tests the water with her hand (this gesture is also antique—it is found in the celebrated Aldobrandini Wedding; A. Maiuri, *Roman Painting*, tr. Stuart Gilbert [Geneva, 1953], pp. 24, 30, 31-32). The midwife's cap at the Kariye Djami repeats a motif that is especially frequent in miniatures of the

11th and 12th centuries. For the motif of the bath, see also below, in connection with the Nativity of Christ [102].

69 For the posture of the newly delivered Virgin—languishing Virgin and Virgin without pain—see G. Millet, *Recherches sur l'iconographie de l'Evangile aux XIVe, XVe, et XVIe siècles* (Paris, 1916; reprinted 1960), pp. 99 ff.

70 The earliest example seems to be the Georgian fresco at Ateni (Amiranašvili, *Živopis'*, PL. 62). The theme also appears at Nerezi (Millet and Frolow, *Peinture*, II, PL. 17), in 1164. It was no doubt because of a contemporary sensibility that this motif was so successful, under the Palaeologi, in the geographical area indicated. Its origin may be sought either in a symbolic scene such as that which precedes the Birth at Kızıl Çukur or, on the contrary, in realistic scenes of childbirth such as are found in some illustrations for the Old Testament. On Roman sarcophagi the (seated) mother is sometimes supported by a maid (see the example cited in n. 68).

71 The shape of the vases varies. Very beautiful examples will be seen in a fresco in the church of St. Demetrius, Peć (Petković, *La peinture serbe*, II, PL. XCVI a. See below Demus Fig. 45.)

feathers attached to a long handle (Fig. 13). The same figure appears in the Homilies of the Monk James—where it is the infant Virgin in the cradle who receives the benefit of her attentions [72]—and in several representations of the Palaeologan period, including that in the Kariye Djami. Yet we should expect this figure to be posted not beside the entrance door, as is often the case, but behind Anne, where the Studenica fresco painter had the good sense to place her. The women bringing offerings are an invariable feature of the Birth of the Virgin, at least in the post-iconoclastic period. And in fact they are not found on the San Marco column or in the Kızıl Çukur fresco, which must go back to a pre-iconoclastic model. On the other hand, they appear in the earliest Constantinopolitan representations, the miniatures in the Menologion of Basil II and the Daphni mosaic (Figs. 12, 13). In the former case they offer dishes containing eggs, in the latter a similar dish and fruits. These representations are to be connected with the ceremonial of imperial births, as described by Constantine Porphyrogenitus.[73] The word he uses to designate the presents offered to the empress on this occasion, ξένιον, indicates that the presents consisted principally of foodstuffs. However, the women also offer vessels, as in the fresco in St. Panteleimon's at Nerezi (1164). On the other hand, maidservants and women visitors are often mingled and confused. Rather than an invention, we have here the borrowing of an antique formula, which must have been especially relished in the circles of the capital. This formula has come down to us, in an example particularly close to the Byzantine images, on the textile from Antinoë in the Louvre illustrated with episodes from the life of Dionysus: maidservants stand to the right of the newly delivered mother lying on her couch, while to the left women come forward presenting vessels (Fig. 14). The offering of vessels on the occasion of a birth was, moreover, current practice in antiquity, and it may be supposed that the custom survived in Byzantium.[74]

We see, then, how very much such a composition owes to formulas elaborated in antiquity, whether in the case of the newly delivered mother on her couch, or the infant's bath, or the women, both servants and visitors. What strongly suggests a more concrete inspiration from the customs of the court in the Kariye Djami mosaic, however, is the presence of a table on which the offerings are placed. It is hardly surprising that this motif was not assimilated sooner, for multiplicity of motifs was little suited to the images of earlier periods. Undoubtedly it is in imitation of our mosaic that this motif, infrequent at the time, will reappear later.[75] In other representations of the period the women are generally isolated behind a low wall, an old procedure that competes with the probably Constantinopolitan device of showing the women full length, thus making them more graceful. The architectural frame at the Kariye Djami is very well suited for this.

72 In the Homilies the scene of the Birth is followed by a second scene of the infant Virgin in her cradle (Stornajolo, *Omilie*, PL. 9 and 14; Omont, *Homélies*, PL. IV,2 and VII,1). The Birth is replaced by the symbolic visit of the twelve representatives of the tribes to the newly delivered mother, while the episode of the bath is awkwardly relegated to the upper left corner of the composition. The second scene shows Mary in her cradle, attended by the maidservant with the flabellum and a young woman carrying a dish containing eggs; these motifs, which are usually attached to Anne, are here transposed into a new context. Anne and Joachim are seated, talking. The sumptuous cradle, which reminds us that the infant was present when Anne received the offerings of her women, as well as the figure of Joachim, may also have been introduced into the theme of the Birth when pictures such as these were combined.

73 In *De Ceremoniis*, II.21, Bonn (1829), I, pp. 615 ff. In particular he records that on the eighth day the wives of dignitaries pass before the empress one by one to do her homage,

each bringing a present καὶ ἐπεύχονται ἀπευχαριστοῦσαι καὶ εὐφημοῦσαι τὴν αὐγούσταν, καὶ τὸ προσῆκον ἀπονέμουσι σέβας, μία ἑκάστη εἰσάγουσα ξένιον, ὅπερ κατὰ προαίρεσιν ἔχει (p. 618 c).

74 For the antique custom, see G. Van Hoorn, *De Vita atque Cultu Puerorum Monumentis Antiquis Explanato* (Amsterdam, 1909), p. 5. For the Parcae, see F. Cumont, *Recherches sur le symbolisme funéraire des Romains* (Paris, 1942), PL. XXXVII,1 and p. 336. Finally, on the antique custom of the Amphidromia, see Ch. Daremberg and Ed. Saglio, *Dictionnaire des antiquités grecques et romaines*, I (Paris, 1877), s.v. "Amphidromia."

75 The table motif is earlier: it is introduced into the scene of the Birth of St. Nicholas in Bogorodica Ljeviška at Prizren, of 1307 (R. H. L. Hamann-MacLean, *Aus der mittelalterlichen Bildwelt Jugoslawiens: Einzelheiten des Freskenzyklus der Kirche der Gottesmutter von Leviša in Prizren* [Marburg an der Lahn, 1955], Fig. 33), but very awkwardly, only serving, in fact, to isolate the women bringing offerings (the table is bare).

The three following scenes are concerned with the early infancy of the Virgin. In antiquity, infancy cycles include various scenes following the birth. If the child's first steps are infrequently found, its education is often represented, as are its games.[76] The First Steps are, in any case, an old and widespread literary theme, found even in the legend of the Buddha. In the cycle of the Virgin the scene faithfully illustrates the text (Protevangelium 6:1). The other episodes, represented at the Kariye Djami as in other important cycles, are the Virgin Caressed by Her Parents and the Virgin Blessed by the Priests (e.g., Fig. 15). The latter theme is called for by a passage in the Protevangelium (6:2), but the same is not true of the theme of the Caresses, which appears only in the Syriac and Armenian paraphrases already mentioned above and is certainly an oriental creation of comparatively late date. The San Marco column does not represent this episode, though its iconography often indicates close connections with the tradition of the eastern parts of the Empire. It may be well to mention at this point that these three themes are completely alien to the Western tradition, whether textual or iconographic.

The scene of the First Steps (the inscription specifies the number, "seven," like the majority of the texts) is far from common [88] (PL. 104, 105). After a few early and oriental representations—on the San Marco column, at Kızıl Çukur in Cappadocia, and at Ateni in Georgia [77]—it is found, during the Palaeologan period, principally in a few Macedonian cycles, at Constantinople, and later at Mount Athos. The fact that this episode was not illustrated in the Homilies of the Monk James, though it is mentioned in the text, leads us to believe that it derives from an orientalizing rather than from a strictly Byzantine iconographic tradition.[78] But it is well integrated into Palaeologan art. All the representations of it that have come down to us from this period are similar:[79] the little Virgin, attended by a maidservant, goes to Anne, who, seated on a chair, prepares to receive her. They differ in their setting, or by a motif like the graceful coil of the maidservant's veil in the Kariye Djami mosaic, a Hellenistic motif that is perfectly in place in a composition as carefully calculated as it is exquisite (PL. 106).

The episode of the Caresses [90] is closely connected with that of the First Steps in the oriental paraphrases; it is in a sense its epilogue.[80] However, in this scene the Virgin appears in an infant's dress, and this is undoubtedly why artists often placed it after the Birth instead of after the First Steps, in which she is already dressed as a grown-up.[81] But they also often inverted the order of other scenes, as can be seen in St. Clement's, Ohrid (Fig. 15). In the case of the Kariye Djami it must further be supposed that the order was adopted to accord with the architectural arrangement. The two themes of the Caresses and the Blessing are more nearly alike from the point of view of form, and balance each other perfectly on the vault where they are displayed (PL. 108), while the First Steps found a most suitable place in the soffit of an arch.

---

76 All these themes are found on the Terme Museum sarcophagus already cited, Faccenna, "Monumento funerario," Figs. 3 ff, and Lafontaine-Dosogne, Iconographie, I, Fig. 70. For the child's instruction, see especially H.-I. Marrou's study, Μουσικὸς ἀνήρ: Etude sur les scènes de la vie intellectuelle figurant sur les monuments funéraires romains (Grenoble, 1938).

77 Lafontaine-Dosogne, Iconographie, I, Figs. 7, 8, and 14; Amiranašvili, Živopis, p. 85. In the first two documents Anne is standing. At Kızıl Çukur the infant Virgin is moving away from Anne and the lacuna to the right is quite large, leading me to think that a scene of caresses may have been depicted there.

78 Significantly enough, it is not represented in the Peribleptos at Mistra, where the cycle of the Virgin was illustrated with a profusion close to that of the manuscripts with miniatures; Millet, Mistra, PL. 125 ff.

79 It should be noted, however, that Joachim is present at Dečani (Petković, La peinture serbe, II, PL. CXXXIV), no doubt in imitation of the theme of the Caresses.

80 Michel and Peeters, Evangiles apocryphes, II, p. 76 (2:9); Budge, History of the Blessed Virgin, p. 14.

81 Our mosaic is a partial exception in this respect, for the child wears dark-colored garments; however, her veil does not completely cover her head. Obviously the artist was trying to avoid an excessive familiarity. Since the Caresses come after the Birth, the two themes are sometimes linked together. In some Russian representations, such as Dionissi's in the Therapontov monastery, for example, the Caresses is actually a complement to the Birth; V. T. Georgievskij, Freski Ferapontova Monastyrja (St. Petersburg, 1911), PL. XXXXI. See also an aer of the same period showing the same subject; ibid., Fig. 34, p. 83.

The iconography of the theme of the Caresses, especially as found from the end of the thirteenth century in Macedonia and Serbia, is remarkably constant: Anne and Joachim, sitting side by side, fondle the child. One or two maidservants are generally present also, in a setting that may vary; as always, the Kariye Djami artist has taken particular pains here (PL. 114); he shows a maidservant in half-figure reaching out from the building at the right as if to receive the baby—an unusual motif (PL. 116). The position of the child is subject to slight variation. Most often she sits on her mother's knees, but it is sometimes difficult, as in the present case, to determine which of the two she is closest to; she may fondly press her head against her mother's while caressing her father's chin with her hand. Here the case is the opposite, whether because Joachim was to be given greater importance or because it was considered touching that the mother should relinquish the child to its father for a few moments (PL. 115).[82] In the texts only Anne is mentioned. But in treating this subject Byzantine artists not only adapted the well-known type of the Virgin of Tenderness to Anne and Mary but also added the father himself, thus creating a charming scene of family affection.

Whereas the themes of the First Steps and the Caresses appear late in the Constantinopolitan tradition, that of the Virgin Blessed by the Priests is well represented in it from the time of the Daphni composition in the eleventh century (Fig. 16). On the other hand, in the more easterly regions it is not found until quite late. The Daphni mosaic is fragmentary, but it is easy to reconstruct it in imagination, since the theme is highly constant, at least in church painting; to the left of the group constituted by Anne and by Joachim carrying the child, we must picture the three priests seated behind a table and making a gesture of blessing. In passing from manuscript miniatures to the walls of churches, the episode was as it were sublimated, as we saw was the case in respect to Joachim's Offerings Rejected. In the miniatures for the Homilies of the Monk James, the two categories of guests mentioned in the texts, the laymen and the high priest, who symbolizes the clergy, are depicted; the table is laden with dishes and even knives and a fork. The inscription mentions the banquet of the priests: Ἑστία ἱερέων.[83] In the frescoes in the Peribleptos at Mistra, which are very close to the manuscript illustrations, the artist has also delighted in representing a real banquet, with many guests, a well-laden table, servants.[84] But if we look at the Kariye Djami mosaic, we shall find only three priests seated in hieratic pose around a table, the principal priest at one end of it; bare except for three nondescript dishes, the table may well suggest an altar [89] (PL. 109, 112). The character of the inscription has changed too: Ἡ εὐλόγησις τῶν ἱερέων. Joachim, alone, approaches respectfully, holding the child in his hands, which are concealed under a fold of his robe (PL. 110, 111). It is a composition of this type that is usually found in the cycles of the Palaeologan period. However, in other similar representations, in Macedonia (Fig. 15) or in the Metropole at Mistra,[85] Anne stands behind Joachim. She may even present the child, either because, as in the Homilies, a particular text attributes this function

82 This feature of the scene is not unique; a good example of its occurrence elsewhere is in the Bela Crkva at Karan; M. Kašanin, "Bela Crkva Karanska," *Starinar*, 3d series, IV (1926–27), Fig. 30, p. 203.

83 Actually, a whole minor cycle illustrates this episode in the Homilies (Stornajolo, *Omilie*, PL. 17, 18; Omont, *Homélies*, PL. VIII; the Vatican copy contains an additional scene, in which the High Priest hands the child back to Anne). Before returning the child to its cradle, Anne plays with it instead of giving it the breast, in accordance with the text of the Homily. In the Peribleptos at Mistra giving the breast is represented, in accordance with Protevangelium 6:3. This is the only example of this particular passage's being illustrated within a narrative cycle;

however, the same theme is found on the San Marco column, but after the Birth, which is also in conformity with the test of the Protevangelium (5:2) (Millet, *Mistra*, PL. 128,4, and Lafontaine-Dosogne, *Iconographie*, I, Fig. 6).

84 Millet, *Mistra*, PL. 125,4.

85 The fact that Joachim's hands are veiled is likewise a characteristic feature of church composition that does not appear in the Homilies miniature (this feature is indistinguishable at the Peribleptos because of the bad condition of the fresco). In the Metropole at Mistra we see a laden table that certainly does not suggest an altar (Millet, *Mistra*, PL. 75,3). The Kariye Djami composition is highly abstract in comparison.

to her or because the image is connected with her cult in a church dedicated to her.[86] At the Kariye Djami, only the father acts, an arrangement which literally illustrates the text of the Protevangelium but is only rarely found, one of the few examples being furnished by Studenica.[87] Anne's presence is so customary, even in the Constantinopolitan tradition, that it may be for reasons of balance that the artist adopted this particular composition, the Joachim of the Blessing corresponding to the Anne of the First Steps. The setting in our mosaic is remarkable. As I said earlier, it is explained by a desire to integrate the two scenes harmoniously into the vault and at the same time to create, as everywhere else, a beautiful and sumptuous frame.

With the Presentation of the Virgin in the Temple we have, as in the Birth of the Virgin, a most important theme, not only because it illustrates an essential episode in the Infancy of the Virgin but also because it is connected with one of the liturgical feasts that were celebrated in Byzantium with the greatest solemnity. For if the Birth of the Virgin constitutes the first stage of the Incarnation, her Presentation and her life in the Holy of Holies stamp her destiny with a divine seal. As in the case of the Birth, this circumstance powerfully contributed to the appearance and increasing extension of the iconographic theme even outside of the narrative cycles. The Birth and the Presentation are the only subjects from this cycle which gave occasion for isolated representations on church walls; they may even appear among the Great Feasts.[88]

In the Kariye Djami the Presentation of the Virgin occupies a favored position: it extends over the domical vault of the bay corresponding to the principal entrance to the nave [91] (PL. 119). Although it remains a part of the narrative cycle, the position of the scene and the fact that it is accompanied by three other representations whose central theme is the Temple (the episode of the Skein of Purple Wool having been intentionally shifted from its normal place to fit this arrangement) give it a special significance. We do not know for what particular liturgical reason the Presentation of the Virgin was here placed in such a context. We do know, however, that in Palamas' day the feast raised a problem, that it had its supporters and its opponents (among them Gregoras), but the reasons for this are obscure.[89] The controversy may have begun earlier and have affected the program of the church of the Chora to the advantage of the feast.

The very brief inscription, τὰ ἅγια τῶν ἁγίων, represents the most commonly adopted formula. However, we also find τὰ εἰσόδια τῆς Θεοτόκου. Actually, these are merely two parts of a single sentence, as found complete in the titular inscription in the Menologion of Basil II. It would seem that the second part is more popular or closer to the narrative cycles.[90] The first

---

86 The example of the "Kera" Panagia at Kritsa, in Crete, is particularly striking in this respect: Anne alone presents the child both in this scene and in the Presentation in the Temple (Lafontaine-Dosogne, *Iconographie*, I, Fig. 90 and pp. 132 and 159).

87 Petković, *La peinture serbe*, II, PL. XLII; later, notably at Kalenić (ibid., Fig. 50, p. 63) and at Mount Athos (Millet, *Athos*, PL. 204,2 and 205,2).

88 See above, p. 166 and n. 23.

89 J. Meyendorff, *Introduction à l'étude de Grégoire Palamas* (Paris, 1959), p. 391. Palamas wrote in his youth (in 1335) a "Discourse on the Entrance of the Mother of God into the Holy of Holies," addressed to the monks of Lavra. The subject was not chosen at random, for Philotheos reports, says Meyendorff, that certain people "dared to slander the mysteries of the feast." Nicephorus Gregoras "affirmed the legendary nature of the narratives of the Virgin's entrance into the Holy of Holies and was in consequence the object of a sentence of excommunication

pronounced by the metropolitan of Selymbria, Philotheos . . . ; he also opposed the feast itself. . . . Palamas' Discourse does not, however, attempt to prove the historicity of one or another narrative of the Presentation; it constitutes a long profession of piety and faith, giving the feast an interpretation very similar to that which Gregory of Nyssa gave to Moses' ascent of the mountain, the two events being only the expression of the soul's mystical rise toward God." On this subject see also above, J. Meyendorff's study, pp. 93–106.

90 The words Τὰ εἰσόδια τῆς Θεοτόκου, ὅτε προσήνεχθεν τῷ ναῷ καὶ εἰσῆλθεν εἰς τὰ ἅγια τῶν ἁγίων accompany the miniature, under the date of Nov. 21 (*Menologio di Basilio II*, II, p. 198). In the Homilies of the Monk James, the different moments of the procession that accompanies the child Virgin to the Temple are designated by the words ἡ πρόοδος or ἡ ὁρμή (εἰς τὸν ναόν). The inscription for the Daphni mosaic is, unfortunately, lost, the background having been reworked.

lays particular emphasis on the sacredness of the place where the Virgin spent her childhood, and hence on the symbolic aspect of the scene. It should be noted in this connection that on the textual plane this episode in the life of Mary is made to seem something entirely exceptional, at once a grace granted to her who will be the Mother of God and an assurance that her virginity is safeguarded.[91] On the plane of iconography it is for this reason that the motif of Mary fed by the angel in the Holy of Holies has been added to the theme of the Presentation proper.

The various elements of the Kariye Djami composition are traditional in church painting. But their arrangement is intimately subordinated to the architectural space that carries them. The composition unfolds on the vault in the most felicitous manner, with the sanctuary and the building opposite to it, which usually limit the composition, balancing each other, while the graceful procession of maidens carrying torches occupies the intervening space (PL. 120, 121). All the differences to be noted between the present composition and the traditional scheme are explained by this fact. The number of the maidens, usually seven, is increased to nine (the same thing occurs in the Homilies of the Monk James, where the maidens may be even more numerous). Usually the building in the western section represents the entrance to the Temple. In church painting, indeed, the entire scene takes place inside the Temple. No document, not even the detailed miniatures of the Homilies,[92] where the procession precedes the scene itself, shows the maidens leaving the house of the Virgin's parents, and it is not this house that the artist intended to depict. Since the building is connected with the sanctuary by long walls behind which rise trees, it would seem to represent the entrance to the Temple court rather than the Temple itself. The particular scheme chosen must also account for the attitude of the child Mary seated under the ciborium (PL. 122). The laws of symmetry demanded that she be placed on the axis of the vault, that is, above the figure of Zacharias. The angel, moreover, always appears on the side where the event occurs, in this case on the left. Obeying this twofold imperative, the artist has seated the child facing to the right, in order to provide space enough for Zacharias, but turning to the left to receive the loaf of bread that the small angel holds out to her. The pretty gesture of the left hand resting on the knee recalls that in the mosaic of the same scene at Daphni (Fig. 17). The little Mary, who in both images is traditionally clothed in a miniature replica of her adult garments, lacks, however, in the Kariye the childish charm that is an unusual and exquisite feature of the eleventh-century mosaic. Standing in front of the entrance to the sanctuary, as is usual at the period,[93] Zacharias receives the child, whom Anne and Joachim eagerly present to him. Mary approaches him holding out her hands, which are bare and not, as in most images of the period, hidden under a fold of her robe.

The gesture of presentation is made by the parents, in accordance with an old and unvarying tradition.[94] However, from the end of the thirteenth century and during the greater part of the fourteenth, another type of composition is current, which might well be termed Macedonian,

91 So the redactor of the Protevangelium and the Byzantine authors understood it. The Latin texts, on the contrary, present Mary in the Temple like a model nun in her convent. On this question, see especially Amann, *Protévangile*, pp. 209 ff.

92 A whole cycle of images is devoted to the events of the Presentation; Stornajolo, *Omilie*, PL. 23–29; Omont, *Homélies*, PL. X–XII.

93 In a number of representations from the 11th and 12th centuries—at Daphni, for example—the sanctuary gates are closed. But they open later, thus making Zacharias' reception of the child more cordial. This feature is not found, however, in the miniature in the Menologion of Basil II, in which Zacharias,

on the contrary, exhibits marked eagerness.

94 This scene can be compared with that of the Presentation of Christ as well as with scenes of children being dedicated or presented to saints by their parents, such as those to be found on the mosaic votive panels in St. Demetrius, Salonika; A. Grabar, *Martyrium: Recherches sur le culte des reliques et l'art chrétien antique* (Paris, 1946), II, p. 91, and III, PL. XLIX. It should be noted, however, that the iconographic scheme for the Presentation of the Virgin well illustrates the account in the Apocrypha and that the motif of the angel gives it a character peculiar to itself.

since it is found almost exclusively in Macedonia.[95] It consists in placing the group of maidens between Joachim and Anne on the one side and Zacharias and Mary on the other. In St. Clement, Ohrid, the maidens wait in expectation, but in the later representations it is their leader who makes the gesture of presentation while Anne and Joachim are in the act of conversing (e.g., Studenica, church of Sts. Joachim and Anne, Fig. 18). This procedure derives from a synthesis of the detailed cycle which was accomplished in a peculiar way and the key to which is provided by the miniatures for the Homilies of the Monk James. There we first see the procession in which, in accordance with the texts, the maidens precede the child "so that she will not turn back," then her presentation to the high priest by her parents.[96] A rather similar procedure is seen in the earliest Cappadocian frescoes (ninth-tenth centuries), where the various elements supplied by the detailed miniatures in manuscripts have not yet been integrated into a satisfactory whole, and where, in addition, the episode of Mary fed by the angel remains a separate presentation, as in the Theotokos at Göreme (Fig. 20). The synthesis was accomplished in representations of a liturgical nature, the earliest example being the miniature in the Menologion of Basil II, where the painter could not avoid a certain awkwardness in rendering so complex a subject (Fig. 19). But from then on the iconography of the theme is fixed, and it is the Constantinopolitan scheme that will thenceforth impose its standard. From the eleventh century it is adopted not only in monuments more or less directly linked with the capital, but in Cappadocia too—the Sarıca Kilisse fresco contrasts strongly with those of the preceding period.[97] It is this synthetic theme of liturgical character which was introduced unchanged into the narrative cycles of church painting. In this respect it is one of the most interesting themes among those illustrating the Life of the Virgin.

The Kariye Djami mosaic, then, is an adaptation of the traditional iconographic theme to a particular setting. When it became a matter of emphasizing the liturgical importance of the event and using the arch south of the dome for a second representation of the episode of Mary Fed by the Angel [92] (PL. 126, 127), the artist could easily find his model in a detailed cycle of miniatures. If he was nevertheless obliged to retain the same motif in the principal composition, it was because this motif had formed an integral part of the scene for several centuries. However, he did not adopt the arrangement found on the San Marco column and in the earliest Cappadocian frescoes, where Mary sits at the altar table and the angel serving her stands before her, while Zacharias witnesses the miracle, censer in hand (Fig. 20), nor even that of the Homilies of the Monk James, where the angel is flying.[98] From the point of view of form, the motif of Mary fed by the angel is here only a repetition of the one in the scene of the Presentation, with an inscription of the type of those found in the Cappadocian images,[99] while a seated maiden has replaced the censing priest who appears in narrative images (PL. 128).

95 This arrangement appears even earlier on an ivory at Berlin (No. 2551) of the beginning of the 11th century (W. F. Volbach, *Mittelalterliche Bildwerke aus Italien und Byzanz*, 2d ed. [Bildwerke des Kaiser-Friedrich-Museums; Berlin and Leipzig, 1930], PL. 16), in a 12th-century fresco in the church of St. Nicholas Rhodias near Arta in Epirus (G. Tsimas and P. Papahadzidakis, eds., album of photos, *Fresques des églises d'Arta*, III [Athens, n.d.], Figs. 15–19), and, at the beginning of the 13th century, at Bertoubani in Georgia (Čubinašvili, *David-Garedži*, PL. 105). Later, traces of it will be found in Cretan frescoes, under northern influence. But it is in Macedonia and Serbia that we find the greatest number of examples; it actually amounts to a fashion (we may cite Chilandar, Studenica,

Gračanica, St. Demetrius in Peć, Dečani, etc.).

96 Stornajolo, *Omilie*, esp. PL. 24, 27, and 28; Omont, *Homélies*, PL. XI–XII.

97 See above, p. 165 and n. 17.

98 Stornajolo, *Omilie*, PL. 31; Omont, *Homélies*, PL. XII,3.

99 See Vol. 1 of this work. The inscription for the mosaic is a title identifying the image, whereas that for the fresco in the Theotokos at Göreme is an almost direct transcription of the text of the Protevangelium (8:1): Ἡ παναγία ἐν τῷ ναῷ λαμβάνει τροφὴν ἐκ χειρὸς ἀγγέλου (completed and corrected by G. de Jerphanion, *Une nouvelle province de l'art byzantin: Les églises rupestres de Cappadoce* (Paris, 1925–42), I,1, p. 128). But their meaning is exactly the same.

The same maiden recurs in the following scene, where it seems likely that an angel presided over the child Virgin's Instruction [93] (PL. 129).[100] The scene has almost entirely disappeared. Fortunately the inscription, which is well preserved, tells us that the Virgin was "instructed in the temple." As in the preceding mosaic, the sanctuary enclosure is not represented. However, the steps on which the Virgin is seated, as in the Presentation and in Zacharias Praying [95], here too suggest the Holy of Holies. The elaborate setting in the background has no realistic significance; it depicts a sacred place by imitating some Early Christian mosaic decoration.

The image may perhaps be compared with that in the Homilies of the Monk James, in which the Virgin is seated beside the altar, holding a book, in the presence of the priests.[101] But the differences are considerable, and there is no question of "instruction," an idea not found in the Protevangelium. Then too, the personage of the maiden in our two scenes is an element foreign to the Byzantine iconographic tradition, taking the term in its broadest sense. However, some texts from the Christian East, marginal to the Protevangelium, mention both the instruction of the Virgin in the Temple and the presence of older virgins. This is outstandingly the case in the Armenian Gospel of the Infancy,[102] and we should perhaps at the Kariye see an unusual trace of this tradition. If we turn to the West, we shall there find quite a number of representations of Mary Fed by an Angel (independently of the Presentation scene, which does not include the motif), praying, or most frequently weaving, with her companions often beside her. These are illustrations for the lengthy account that the Pseudo-Matthew devotes to her life in the Temple (Ch. 6).[103] Such images, which appear at the beginning of the thirteenth century in a manuscript whose text paraphrases the Pseudo-Matthew, the *Wernherlied von der Magd*,[104] are not found again before the fourteenth century and then they are less frequent in Italy than elsewhere in the West. In this period one also occasionally finds a book in Mary's hands as she prays, whether or not in the company of other maidens. In a stained-glass window at Amelungsborn, Mary kneels at a *prie-dieu* and a small angel appears in the lower corner of the composition.[105] Is "instruction" really involved here? The Latin texts mention the Virgin's instruction in the Temple, although in rather vague terms. But the actual scene of instruction that is current in the West from the fourteenth century is independent of the textual indications and even contradicts them: it is Anne who teaches the child Mary her letters.[106]

Thus, though comparisons with Western works are not very conclusive, it could be argued that the elements that are foreign to the usual iconography in the Kariye Djami mosaics may be the result of an influence from the West. But it seems to me both more valid and more probable to admit that the artist created these two compositions to serve his purpose, which was to emphasize Mary's life in the Temple: in the first she is fed there with heavenly food, in the second she is instructed there. He could have fallen back on some little-known oriental tradition; to this end

---

100 See Vol. 1 of this work, pp. 75–76 for comments of P. A. Underwood. The tip of a wing remains on the first step.

101 Stornajolo, *Omilie*, PL. 36; Omont, *Homélies*, PL. XV,1.

102 Michel and Peeters, *Evangiles apocryphes*, II, pp. 78 and 85 (3:2 and 4:3); the title of Chapter 3 also includes the word "instruction."

103 Less frequently images of Mary spinning with her companions illustrate the episode of the Purple Skein (8:5). Generally they appear as a complement to the Presentation (Lafontaine-Dosogne, *Iconographie*, II, Ch. III,9).

104 The original version goes back to the end of the 12th century. See H. Degering, *Des Priesters Wernher drei Lieder von der Magd* (Berlin, 1925), figs. on pp. 58 and 60 (some are reproduced in my *Iconographie*, II, Figs. 55, 56).

105 H. Wentzel, *Meisterwerke der Glasmalerei*, 2d ed. (Berlin,

1954), Fig. 137. The comparison was made by Miss Rosalie Green. We may add a fresco by Tiberio of Assisi at S. Maria del Popolo in Rome, in which Mary reads, seated at a desk, while an angel stands at her right and another at her left and a few maidens occupy the background. But this document is late (beginning of the 16th century).

106 See Lafontaine-Dosogne, *Iconographie*, II, pp. 108–09. The Pseudo-Matthew (6:2), in reference to Mary's life in the Temple, says, after mentioning her being fed by an angel, that Mary was more *learned* than any of the other virgins in the wisdom of the law of God. The Gospel of the Nativity of Mary (see above, n. 5) refers to the purpose of her parents, who leave their daughter in the Temple to be instructed ("virginem . . . educandam dimiserunt," 6:3).

he may have adapted the familiar theme of the education of a child—which occurs, at this period, more especially among the scenes from the life of St. Nicholas—together with one or another image of the life of Mary in the Temple which he found in a detailed cycle, such as that in the Homilies of the Monk James. Thus it becomes completely unnecessary to introduce the idea of Western influence in an ensemble that is so purely Byzantine.[107]

The scene of the Virgin Receiving the Skein of Purple Wool [94] (PL. 131) completes the trilogy of Mary's life in the Temple. This scene is most uncommon. Yet the episode was not without importance in the eyes of the redactor of the Protevangelium (10:1–2), who sought by relating it to emphasize the fact that Mary had remained a virgin after being entrusted to Joseph, for only virgins could spin wool for the Temple veil. The fact that the scarlet and purple fall to her is an explicit recognition of her royal Davidian origin,[108] as well as a portent of her future destiny. The episode acquires its significance only after Joseph's departure and before the Annunciation, and it is at this point that we shall find it represented in the Homilies of the Monk James (Fig. 21)[109] and in the manuscript that served as the model for the twelfth-century mosaics in San Marco, Venice.[110] So, too, in the very few Western representations.[111] The Kariye Djami artist, then, completely disregarded the meaning of the scene when he changed its place in the series. What are we to conclude from this? Probably that outside considerations came into play: it was necessary to emphasize Mary's relations with the Temple by the most unusual procedure of grouping together all the episodes of her life that were connected with it.

In any case, the scene is exceptional in church painting. The only Byzantine representations of a similar iconography are the miniature in the Homilies and the fragmentary fresco in the Peribleptos at Mistra.[112] The purple skein that Mary is spinning at the moment of the Annunciation—a very old feature—must have seemed a sufficient reminder of this episode in the other instances. In the mosaic as well as in the miniature the setting for the scene is the Temple; exactly the same number of personages are introduced; the Virgin, still a child, occupies the center of the composition in both cases. She receives the purple skein from the hand of the first of the three priests seated on the synthronon. Two of the six maidens who stand to the right have

107 We may even question whether any more importance is to be accorded to the presence of a maiden in these two compositions than to the presence of the little boy in the Annunciation to Anne, which is likewise an exceptional feature.

108 It is here stated for the first time in the Protevangelium that Mary was of the line of David—a circumstance which, in any case, the redactor appears to take for granted. Other versions, especially the Syriac and Latin texts, emphasize the fact from the beginning of the narrative. Amann, *Evangiles apocryphes*, pp. 218–19, is of the opinion that the author also thus sought to answer the calumnies according to which Mary spun to earn her living. See Lafontaine-Dosogne, *Iconographie*, I, Ch. III, 10.

109 Stornajolo, *Omilie*, PL. 45; Omont, *Homélies*, PL. XVIII,2. The frontispiece for the Homily devoted to the Annunciation is decorated with an illustration of Gideon's fleece (Judges 6:36–40), put in typological relation to that of the Virgin Receiving the Skein of Purple Wool (Stornajolo, PL. 46; Omont, XVIII,3). This theme appears, also with typological significance, in church painting, in particular at Gračanica, Lesnovo, and Dečani (Petković, *La peinture serbe*, II, 34, 46, and 53), among other representations of the same nature, in connection, at Gračanica and Dečani, with a cycle of the Life of the Virgin.

110 At least we may suppose so. The scene is not represented, but the inscription QUO TINGAT VELA PARAVIT, mistakenly applied to the episode of the Trial by Water, seems to refer to it (Bettini, *Mosaici di San Marco*, PL. XLV).

111 Degering, *Des Priesters Wernher drei Lieder von der*

Magd, p. 97: the messengers from the Temple bring a skein to Mary and the maidens who live with her in Joseph's house (Pseudo-Matthew 8:5). On the steatite (?) plaque in Berlin (Volbach, *Mittelalterliche Bildwerke*, p. 122, No. 2721, PL. 2), the episode (which Volbach interprets as a Marriage and which is in any case iconographically aberrant) is linked with that of the Trial by Water, the two episodes together forming a counterpart to the Annunciation-Visitation group. See Lafontaine-Dosogne, *Iconographie* II, Figs. 1, 72.

112 The fresco at Kiev which authors have usually identified as the Virgin Receiving the Skein of Purple Wool (Povstenko, *St. Sophia in Kiev*, p. 306 and fig. on p. 130), even if with reservations (Ajnalov and Redin, "Kievskij Sofijskij Sobor," p. 306 and n. 3), illustrates Mary's Farewell to the priest after the Marriage (compare with the Homilies of the Monk James, Stornajolo, *Omilie*, PL. 42; Omont, *Homélies*, PL. XVII,3). See Lafontaine-Dosogne, *Iconographie*, I, pp. 182–83, 211; II, p. 208. The fresco at Mistra, which Millet did not publish nor even mention, was discovered by Miss Suzy Dufrenne. The figure of the Virgin, followed by at least two veiled maidens, to the right of a sort of table; the lower parts of the robes of two or three priests, to the left; and a nimbus in the center of the upper part, which may belong to another priest, allow that interpretation. The scene, which occupies the width of the back wall of the diaconicon, brought a solemn end to the cycle, although the iconography is very much the same as in the miniature.

already received their skeins (PL. 133, 134).[113] The illustrator of the Homilies, though accompanying his miniature by a shorter rubric, better conveys the intent of the narrative by giving Mary a second skein (for she receives "the purple and the scarlet"), while the virgins stand waiting in a compact group. The Kariye Djami artist has brought the synthronon out of the apse to occupy the left side of the composition (PL. 130, 132); he has deliberately omitted the table on which the skeins are placed, which would have broken its admirable rhythm. The decorated wall in the miniature becomes a severe surface of the utmost purity, against which the graceful silhouettes of the maidens stand out. The two buildings that flank the wall, here given the form of a lofty entrance tower and a spacious curved apse, support the two lateral groups and at the same time provide a frame for the figure of the Virgin, at once so slight and so present. Such a composition demonstrates to perfection how the artists of the period, while remaining faithful to the behests of tradition, succeeded, by a simple aesthetic transposition, in creating an art that is definitely "modern."

The episodes of the Marriage follow, illustrated at the Kariye Djami by four scenes: Zacharias Praying before the Rods of the Suitors, the Virgin Entrusted to Joseph, Joseph Taking the Virgin to His House, Joseph Taking Leave of the Virgin. The texts elaborate at great length on the events that accompany the union—purely formal, of course—between Mary and Joseph, which actually constitute a small cycle in themselves (Protevangelium 8:2–9). The miniaturist of the Homilies of the Monk James devotes eleven pictures to them,[114] and the painter of the Peribleptos—here, as always, closely dependent on manuscripts—nine.[115] A group of three scenes is still found in some cycles of the fourteenth and fifteenth centuries.[116] This is unusual. In the Palaeologan period the group of episodes is regularly reduced to two themes, classically associated: Zacharias' Prayer, and the Marriage or Mary Entrusted to Joseph. In any case, earlier representations are infrequent, for the theme of the Marriage, which lacks the liturgical autonomy of the Birth and the Presentation, appears in practice only within an extended cycle, where it provides the transition between the episodes of the Infancy of the Virgin and those of the Infancy of Christ. Even where a cycle of Christ follows a cycle of the Virgin, it is not necessarily represented; this is the case at Daphni, at Ateni, and, still as late as the beginning of the thirteenth century, at Bertoubani.[117] However, the theme was introduced into church painting already in the eleventh century, at Kiev, and a few examples are found in the twelfth century.[118] At this period the artists had not yet settled on a selection suitable for the decoration of churches.[119]

At the Kariye Djami, the first two images are those found in all extensive cycles from the end of the thirteenth century (Fig. 23). The first one [95] (PL. 135–37) is really the result of a

---

113 For the number of the maidens, which creates difficulties even in the text, see Vol. 1 of this work, p. 77, and de Strycker's remarks, *Protévangile de Jacques*, p. 111.

114 Stornajolo, *Omilie*, PL. 38–44 (seven miniatures); Omont, *Homélies*, PL. XV,2–XVIII,1.

115 Millet, *Mistra*, PL. 128–30. Several fragmentary scenes have not been identified by Millet; some of them were mentioned to me by Miss Dufrenne. See my *Iconographie*, I, p. 50, and II, pp. 212–13 (Prayer of Zacharias before the Oracle, and Gathering of the Widowers).

116 At Dečani, it would seem, Joseph is shown taking leave of Mary (Petković, *La peinture serbe*, II, p. 47, refers to Joseph Reproaching the Virgin, but the scene falls between the Marriage and the Annunciation and so it must represent Joseph's Leave-taking); at the end of the 15th century, at Pelendri, Joseph and Mary are seen seated and conversing in their house (Lafontaine-

Dosogne, *Iconographie*, I, Fig. 28), as in the Homilies (Stornajolo, *Omilie*, PL. 44; Omont, *Homélies*, PL. XVIII).

117 At Daphni, it is true, the cycle of Christ is made up principally of the Great Feasts. At Ateni, the second register in the south apse ends with the Presentation of the Virgin and the third begins with the Annunciation (Amiranašvili, *Živopis'*, pp. 85–86). At Bertoubani the Annunciation follows the Presentation of the Virgin in the same register (Čubinašvili, *David-Garedži*, PL. 105).

118 At San Marco, Venice (Bettini, *Mosaici di San Marco*, PL. XLIV, XLV); at Pskov (see above, n. 22).

119 Thus it seems that at Kiev the painter, in addition to the Marriage, represented Mary's Farewell to the priest, a most uncommon scene (often interpreted as a Distribution of the Skeins; see above, n. 112).

synthesis of three scenes—Mary in the Holy of Holies, Zacharias prone before the altar, receiving the oracle, and Zacharias Praying before the Rods of the Suitors—as they might have been found in an illustrated manuscript of the Protevangelium.[120] In the mosaic in San Marco, Venice, the priest is seen, as in the Homilies, standing before the altar on which the rods are laid, and Mary is absent. At the period with which we are concerned the painter of Curtea-de-Argeş is almost alone in omitting the motif of Mary.[121] Twelve rods lie on the altar in the mosaic. The end of one of them bears a few leaves, which designate it as that of the chosen suitor. In the following scene [96], the priest immediately hands this rod to Joseph, the others still remaining on the altar (PL. 138). We must therefore suppose that the rod bore some distinctive mark showing that it belonged to Joseph.[122]

Now, all this is at variance with the texts, according to which the rods reveal no miraculous sign until the moment when the priest distributes them to the suitors. He hands the last one to Joseph, and it is then that the miracle occurs: a white dove flies off the end of it. This is well illustrated in such an early work as the Zarzma icon, or in one closely following the narrative, such as the miniature in the Homilies (Fig. 24).[123] From the eleventh century, however, in the fresco at Kiev, we see the rod with the dove replaced by a flowering branch. And in the San Marco mosaic the suitors have no rods.[124] Nor will they have them in later representations, while in most cases the motif of leaves will be preferred to that of the dove. In a very few examples, later than the Kariye Djami, the two motifs will be combined.[125] How did such a deviation arise? Unquestionably it was under the commanding influence of the theme of Aaron's flowering rod, which illustrates Numbers 17:1–8 (Septuagint version, Num. 17:16–24). On the textual plane, the redactor of the Protevangelium had already been inspired by this episode, but he had chosen to bring in the dove, symbol of the Holy Spirit,[126] at the same time that he emphasized Joseph's modesty, illustrating the saying, "The last shall be first." The artists made the transposition all the more easily since Aaron's rod was often put in typological relation to the person of the Virgin. The fresco in St. Sophia, Kiev, where the Virgin carries her own symbol (it is she who hands the green branch to Joseph), is an extreme case of this. Even in the Homilies we find a large representation of the Aaron episode, independent from the text.[127] Here the priest is distributing seven rods, one of which is decorated with leaves, and the same number reappear in the scene

120 Stornajolo, *Omilie*, PL. 35, 38, and 40 (right side). The Homilies further present the themes of Zacharias' Discussion with the priests and the Summoning of the Suitors and their Reception by the High Priest (PL. 38, left, and 39); see also Omont, *Homélies*, PL. XIV,2, XV,2, XVI,2. In the miniature in the Gospel Book at Florence, Laurent. Plut. VI.23, fol. 5v (Lafontaine-Dosogne, *Iconographie*, I, Fig. 95), in which the episodes are grouped with the utmost economy, Zacharias is already kneeling. It is worth noting that this apocryphal image illustrates the genealogy of Christ according to Matthew (1:1–17), not the text of the Protevangelium.

121 O. Tafrali, *Monuments byzantins de Curtéa de Argeş* (Paris, 1931), PL. CIX,2 (No. 276). At Pelendri the whole motif of Mary fed by the angel was erroneously introduced into the Prayer of Zacharias, although it also exists in the Presentation (see Fig. 22). To the left stand the suitors, an unusual feature in church painting but one that is nevertheless already found at Gračanica (Petković, *La peinture serbe*, II, PL. LXX). In the Peribleptos (Millet, *Mistra*, PL. 129,2) the scene is preceded by Zacharias receiving the suitors' rods.

122 At the Kariye Djami it is the fourth rod from the right (the motif does not appear in black and white photographs). The motif of the miraculously designated rod in Zacharias' Prayer appears at Pelendri, but it is the dove, not leaves, that is

represented (Fig. 22). In any case this shows that the motif must have been fairly current. It is found again, for example, in the church of the Assumption at Volotovo, in the form of leaves (Lazarev, *Feofan Grek*, PL. 46 a).

123 The Marriage, or Mary Entrusted to Joseph, is represented on fol. 100 of Vaticanus gr. 1162, fol. 135 of Parisinus gr. 1208 (Stornajolo, *Omilie*, PL. 41; Omont, *Homélies*, PL. XVI,2). For the Zarzma icon, see Čubinašvili, *Georgian Repoussé Work*, PL. 38.

124 I am not at all sure whether it is a fleur-de-lis or a stylized dove that surmounts Joseph's rod at San Marco. At Kiev, by way of exception, the suitors are replaced by four personages of both sexes, the first two of whom might be Anne and Joachim, although the physical types are not very conclusive (Povstenko, *St. Sophia in Kiev*, PL. 128).

125 This is the case in the Peribleptos at Mistra (Millet, *Mistra*, PL. 130,2) and at Volotovo. So too in a certain number of Italian representations, notably Giotto's fresco in the Arena Chapel (Venturi, *Storia dell'arte italiana*, V, Fig. 258, p. 320).

126 Amann, *Protévangile*, pp. 214–15.

127 Stornajolo, *Omilie*, PL. 58; Omont, *Homélies*, PL. XXIII,1. It is the frontispiece to the Sixth Homily, devoted to the Visitation. Each homily is similarly preceded by an image typologically referred to the Virgin.

of the Marriage. The Kariye Djami artist, on the contrary, adopted the number of twelve, in accordance with the passage in Numbers. There is, in fact, no fixed rule in this respect for the Marriage of the Virgin.

On the other hand, so far as I know our representation is the only one in which the altar is laden with the rods of the other suitors. Everywhere else, either the sanctuary is not depicted because, since the scenes succeed one another, it has already appeared in Zacharias' Prayer, or it is not visible because the priest usually occupies the entrance to it, thus hiding the altar. At the Kariye Djami the artist has gone all the way in assimilating this theme with that of Aaron. Such a procedure must, however, have earlier origins: it explains why in monumental painting, except for the frescoes in the Peribleptos at Mistra, which are closely dependent on the illuminated manuscripts, the suitors have no rods. But nowhere else is this fact so emphatically evident.[128] For the rest, the iconography of the mosaic scarcely differs from that in use at the period, particularly in the numerous Macedonian and Serbian cycles. However, the symbolism of the theme is more strongly emphasized. Especially to be noted is Zacharias' solemnly protective gesture as he covers the little Mary's head with his hand (PL. 140, 142). Joseph comes forward to receive his leafy rod more eagerly than usual. The suitors, though astonished and displeased, stand behind him quietly, without looking at one another to exchange their feelings, as is commonly the case (PL. 139, 141).[129] In short, although the usual motifs of the composition have been preserved, the prevailing impression here is that the narrative elements have yielded to the symbolic aspect of the episode. Naturally, the meaning of the scene is never realistic. As the inscription reminds us, Mary is entrusted to Joseph; she is not united with him ('Η προς τον Ἰωσὴφ παράδοσις). The Byzantines always refused to represent a normal union, and to this end they adopted the iconographic scheme of the Presentation in the Temple. The small stature of the Virgin, which is a constant feature in Byzantium, strengthens this impression.[130]

In the following scenes Mary will gradually attain adult stature. This is a refinement peculiar to our mosaics, for in the Homilies of the Monk James and elsewhere she is represented as an adult, beginning with the episode of the Farewells,[131] in which the Virgin is seen taking leave of the high priest while Joseph, who has started away, looks back at her. The scene of Mary and Joseph leaving the Temple to go to Joseph's house is represented very simply in the Homilies: the betrothed pair walk against a neutral background, Joseph carrying his carpenter's tools on his shoulder. The Temple no longer appears. These various images are grouped in a single miniature (Fig. 25).[132] The following composition shows Joseph and Mary arriving at the house, where

128 The idea of drawing lots appears once again, in a marginal tradition represented by the Armenian Gospel, in which we are told that the suitors' names were written on tablets (Michel and Peeters, *Evangiles apocryphes*, II [4:3]); by the History of Joseph the Carpenter (Michel and Peeters, I, pp. 196 ff.); and by a few Coptic texts. The iconography of the Marriage scenes is obscure on the ninth and last register of the San Marco column, and the cycle seems to be incomplete; in any case, no rods are visible (Lafontaine-Dosogne, *Iconographie*, I, Figs. 9–12).

129 The priest's gesture recurs, I believe, only at Curtea-de-Argeş, perhaps in imitation of the Kariye Djami (Tafrali, *Curtéa de Arges*, PL. CIX,2, No. 276). In any case the suitors maintain their dignity in the Byzantine compositions. In the West, on the contrary, especially in Italy, they are shown in great agitation, sometimes even breaking their rods over their knees in their resentment.

130 In the Peribleptos at Mistra only, Joseph and Mary clasp hands; the use of this motif may be the result of a Western

influence, where the *dextrarum junctio* is generally adopted in representations of the Marriage. But in Italy itself the motif is replaced by that of the ring that Joseph puts on Mary's finger, which more strongly suggests "betrothal." The Mistra iconography, which may go back to early Byzantine images of marriage, remains a real anomaly in the theme of the Virgin.

131 Stornajolo, *Omilie*, PL. 41 and 42 (upper part); Omont, *Homélies*, PL. XVII. In the West a rather similar idea is found in the Arena Chapel frescoes: Mary is of adult stature in the Marriage, but wears her hair down; her hair is braided in the Annunciation and the Visitation; it is only from the Nativity onward that she wears the traditional veil (Venturi, *Storia dell'arte italiana*, V, Figs. 258 ff.).

132 Stornajolo, *Omilie*, PL. 42; Omont, *Homélies*, PL. XVII,3. Inscription: Τῆς παρθένου παράληψις ἐκ τοῦ ναοῦ, καὶ ἀπαγωγὴ εἰς τὸν οἶκον Ἰωσήφ. After the Leavetaking from the priests, Mary and Joseph greet a group of people standing before a city gate; so it seems that they go to another city.

they are greeted by the old man's four sons.[133] Elements belonging to these various episodes—the Temple, Joseph's attitude, the young lad—are brought together in the mosaic [97] (PL. 143–45). But the inscription is somewhat vague. The departure from the Temple should have been mentioned, as it is in the inscription in the Homilies, and not merely Joseph's taking Mary to his house. We should probably see here the effect of a settled procedure, traces of which are found in the twelfth century in the Pskov frescoes and in the Gospel Book at Florence, Laurentianus Plut. VI.23, and which consists in showing a building representing Joseph's house on the right side of the composition.[134] In any case the theme is extremely infrequent. It will reappear only in the Peribleptos at Mistra.[135] The fact that a bust of the Virgin appears in the tympanum above the door of the Temple gives our scene a symbolic value, the Temple being assimilated to the Virgin.

After taking Mary home, Joseph immediately takes leave of her—so that no suspicion may be cast on her virginity—and returns to his carpentry in another town [99] (PL. 148–50). This theme, which is rather more frequent than the preceding one, may be presented in two ways: Mary and Joseph either sit together in their house, quietly conversing (Homilies of the Monk James [Fig. 26], Snetogorsk, Pelendri), or they both stand while Joseph, ready to depart, addresses Mary for the last time (Kariye Djami, Peribleptos at Mistra).[136] The theme is the same at Mistra and in the Kariye Djami. However, in the Mistra fresco Joseph has already set his foot on the threshold, in a movement parallel to that of the preceding scene. The existence of the theme in the Mistra cycle, which is connected with a series of illustrations that are often quite different from those of the Constantinopolitan series, does not permit us to attribute to our artist the creation of a representation unrelated to that in the Homilies. Between two types of composition, he chose that which was most in accordance with the tenor of the narrative and, above all, appropriate to the area which he had allocated to it. The two standing figures of Joseph and Mary correspond to those of the same personages in the scene of the Reproaches on the right side of the lunette, while the figure of Joseph's son occupies the center (PL. 148, 150). By the same token the mosaicist secured an effect of decorative symmetry between this lunette and the one facing it [85].

The cycle of the inner narthex closes with the Annunciation to the Virgin at the Well, placed in the pendentive to the left of the lunette, and Joseph Reproaching the Virgin. Chronologically, the scene of the Reproaches follows the Virgin Receiving the Skein of Purple Wool, the Annunciation, and the Visitation. We saw above the reason for changing the order of the Skein [94]. As for the Visitation, it is missing from the cycle. Not that there was no room for it—the four episodes of the Marriage could easily have been reduced to two or three, four being exceptional

---

133 Stornajolo, *Omilie*, PL. 43; Omont, *Homélies*, PL.. XVII,2. To the right, little James, the youngest son, is laying the table. This realistic touch is particularly interesting in Constantinopolitan art, which is often accused of idealism and academicism. Joseph's four sons, who, except one, are not represented in this scene in the Kariye Djami, will appear further on in that of the Enrollment for Taxation [101].

134 For Pskov, see Uspenskij, *Očerki*, PL. LXI (III). For the Gospel Book miniature, see above, n. 120.

135 Millet, *Mistra*, PL. 128,2, center. But there Joseph is about to enter his house; he has one foot already on the threshold and is looking back at Mary.

136 In the Homilies the presence of the four sons is a *hapax*, as in the preceding scene. The inscription in the Peribleptos has disappeared (Millet, *Mistra*, PL. 128,2, right). The inscription in the manuscript is very eloquent: Ἡ πρὸς τὴν παρθένον ὁμιλία Ἰωσὴφ ὑποχωροῦντος. At Snetogorsk the scene has its place between the Marriage and the Trial by Water and could also depict Joseph's Reproaches; however, neither the Annunciation nor the Visitation was represented in the narrative cycle, and the seated posture of the personages more nearly suggests the scene of the Admonitions than that of the Reproaches (Lazarev, "Snetogorskie rospisi," sketch, p. 89).

in church painting. Moreover, since the Visitation includes only two or three personages (Mary, Elizabeth, and sometimes Elizabeth's maidservant), it could perfectly well have been represented in place of Joseph Taking Leave of the Virgin, in which case the latter could have replaced the very rare and scarcely necessary composition of Joseph and Mary leaving the Temple. The absence of the Visitation from the narrative cycle can be explained by the assumption that the theme was represented among the Great Feasts, in the nave. Yet it is missing in many contemporary decorative schemes, and it may well not have been represented at all in the Kariye Djami.[137] On the other hand, the Annunciation to Mary in her house, which, in the apocryphal text as in a certain number of narrative ensembles, follows the appearance of the angel at the well, certainly appeared in the nave. For it is this type of Annunciation—the first being purely apocryphal—that was introduced into the cycle of the Feasts, from which it is never omitted. Drawing the conclusions from this fact, we can say that the Birth and the Presentation of the Virgin, which are magnificently treated in the mosaics in the narthex, were not found in the Feasts cycle. Aside from the Annunciation, the Dormition was the only feast of the Virgin to be represented there (it is the only image from the Feasts cycle that still exists today [185]). The Birth and the Presentation of the Virgin do not necessarily form part of the series of Great Feasts. Hence there is little reason to believe that they were depicted a second time in the nave.[138]

The Annunciation and Joseph's Reproaches already form part of the cycle of the Nativity of Christ, as we find it in pre-iconoclastic documents, in the frescoes of Cappadocia in the following period, and, still later, in the Akathistos Hymn.[139] On the other hand, the Annunciation is the first fact in the life of the Virgin that is reported in the canonical Gospels, although the description differs markedly from the account in the Apocrypha. However, during the Palaeologan period the Annunciation at the Well is generally retained in the apocryphal cycle of the Virgin, while the Annunciation in the House is represented, as we said, among the Great Feasts, with the Nativity and the Presentation of Christ, these three scenes constituting the abridged formula for illustration of the Infancy of Christ. In many churches, especially in the Balkans, the Annunciation at the Well comes after the episodes of the Marriage and may be followed by such scenes as the Visitation, Joseph's Reproaches, his Dream, the Trial by Water. The situation that we find in the Kariye Djami is similar: the two scenes of the Annunciation at the Well and the Reproaches close the apocryphally inspired decoration of the inner narthex, dedicated to the Virgin.

The theme of the Annunciation to the Virgin at the Well illustrates the apocryphal version of the event [98]. According to the Protevangelium, the Virgin, having gone out to draw water, hears a voice saying: "Hail, thou that art highly favored; the Lord is with thee; blessed art thou among

137 The Visitation is sometimes included in the cycle of the Baptist, when that cycle is represented: this is the case, among others, in St. Clement, Ohrid (in the diaconicon) and at Curtea-de-Argeş (north aisle; see *Buletinul, Comisiunii Monumentelor Istorice*, 10–16 [1917–23], Fig. 231, p. 212).

138 We shall see that, like the Annunciation in the House, the Presentation in the Temple and the Baptism are absent from the cycle of Christ, for the same reason. Thus, as it had already occurred at Daphni and later would occur in Russia especially, the detachment of the scenes with liturgical significance from the narrative cycle had continued at Constantinople, sometimes to the point of seriously disordering the cycle. The

case of the Nativity of Christ is an exception, since it is found among the narrative scenes in the outer narthex even though it was doubtless also introduced into the series of Great Feasts in the nave. But this is an absolutely essential scene, which could not be omitted from either ensemble.

139 Cf. for example the cycle on the throne of Maximian at Ravenna, with the Annunciation, the Trial by Water, etc. The numerous Cappadocian cycles of the Infancy of Christ quite often present the scene of Joseph's Reproaches after the Visitation. We shall return to this question further on, in connection with the cycle of Christ.

women. And she looked about her upon the right hand and upon the left, so see whence this voice should be: and being filled with trembling she went to her house and set down the pitcher, and took the purple and sat down upon her seat and drew out the thread. And behold an angel of the Lord stood before her saying: . . . ." (11:1–2). Then follows the Annunciation proper. The first utterance is really only a salutation, and Mary does not see the angel. Naturally, the artists nevertheless represented him, in order to make visual the statement in the narrative. The images show Mary turning quickly around in fright and raising her eyes to the heavenly messenger; she lifts one hand toward him while she holds her pitcher in the other. In a certain number of narrative cycles in which this scene appears, the artists have also represented the Annunciation proper—as we see in mural painting at Kiev [140] or later at Pelendri (Fig. 22),[141] and especially in the miniatures in the Homilies of the Monk James [142] (Fig. 27). We here have an iconographic tradition that goes back to the detailed illustrations in the manuscripts of the Protevangelium. However, as indicated by the identical inscriptions of the two Annunciations at Pelendri, the artist may have believed that there was really a double Annunciation. This is so much the case that the scene at the well is sometimes represented to the exclusion of the Annunciation in the House, even in Early Christian documents such as the ivories at Milan and Werden or the clay phial at Monza.[143] The phial is especially interesting, for the theme appears on it alone. The rather obscure inscription, which mentions "the stone (B)oudiam"(?)[144] seems to indicate a reference to a place, more specifically a rock, which doubtless preserved the memory of the event. Hence the individualization of the theme, in relation to a cult site. In some manuscripts the Annunciation at the Well even illustrates the Gospel text.[145]

The three early depictions just cited display a very similar iconography: the young Virgin, half-kneeling beside a spring toward which she holds out her pitcher, turns back toward the angel, who has approached her from behind and addresses her. On the two ivories the rock from which the spring gushes is clearly represented. On the phial the pool is at the foot of a tree whose foliage spreads out in space; behind the tree there is what may be a sketch of a rocky landscape; the angel is flying, whereas on the ivories he stands. Later, the scene differs by the position of the Virgin and the angel, she standing, he flying; the spring has been replaced by a well, and the artists do not fail to depict the chain that serves to let the pitcher down into it; at Kiev and

---

140 Povstenko, *St. Sophia in Kiev*, PL. 127 and 114 (the Visitation follows; see PL. 115).

141 At Pelendri the angel stands beside the well and at the same time appears flying in the house. Inscriptions: Ὁ Γαβριὴλ λέγι τὴν Παρθένον τὸ μιστίριον. (Ὁ ἄγγ)ελος διαλέγι τὸ μιστίριον (sic). The Visitation, which follows, has an interesting peculiarity: the two fetuses are visible in their mothers' wombs, and the infant Baptist salutes the infant Jesus (Fig. 22).

142 Stornajolo, *Omilie*, PL. 50, 51; Omont, *Homélies*, PL. XX, 1–3. In the first picture (our Fig. 27) Mary is seen beside the well turning toward the flying angel, then, with a pitcher in each hand (an exaggeration peculiar to this miniaturist), returning to her house, where the purple skeins await her. In the second she sits spinning and turns to the angel, who walks toward her. Aside from the two essential images, a whole cycle is developed around the subject of the Annunciation: first, the Archangel Gabriel's departure from the Court of Heaven and his arrival in the house of the Virgin, whom he secretly contemplates (Stornajolo, PL. 48, 49; Omont, PL. XIX, 1–2); then, various moments in the dialogue between Mary and Gabriel; and finally, Mary's acquiescence and the angel's return to heaven (Stornajolo, PL. 53–57; Omont, PL. XXI, XXII). The almost unvaried iconography of the scenes of the Virgin and the angel shows that

the miniaturist found himself rather in difficulties in illustrating the prolix text of the monk James.

143 Volbach, *Elfenbeinarbeiten*, Nos. 118 and 119, PL. 36 and 37; A. Grabar, *Ampoules de Terre Sainte (Monza-Bobbio)* (Paris, 1958), PL. XXXI. F. Šmit, *Blagoveščenie* (Sofia, 1911; reprinted from *Izvestija Russkogo Arxeologičeskogo Instituta v Konstantinopolě*, 15 [1911]), cites, in addition to the two ivories, only a relief of the "Adelfia" sarcophagus in the Syracuse Museum; J. Wilpert, *I sarcofagi cristiani antichi*, I (Rome, 1929), PL. LXXXXII,2, upper left. Millet, *Recherches*, remarks that later, particularly in the illustrations for the Akathistos Hymn, it was especially the Russians and the Slavs who represented the Annunciation at the Well.

144 ΕΥΛΟΓΙΑ ΤΗϹ ΘΕΟΤΚΌ ΤΗϹ ΠΕΤΡΑϹ (Β)ΟΔΙΑΜ̊(?) appears around the periphery of the medallion and ΧΕΡΕ ΚΕΧΑΡΙΤΟΜΗΝΙ in the field; Grabar, *Ampoules*, p. 31. We may note that on the two ivories the Annunciation at the Spring is related with the scene of the Trial by Water, in which Mary is being guided to the Temple by an angel. From the 6th century, the theme was given a more realistic form, for example on the throne of Maximian; Volbach, *Elfenbeinarbeiten*, PL. 43.

145 See, among others, Paris. gr. 74, fol. 105v; Paris, Bibliothèque Nationale, Département des Manuscrits, *Evangiles avec peintures byzantines du XIe siècle* (Paris, n.d.), II, PL. 93 b.

in the Homilies the rock has become a decorative mountain. This last feature soon disappears; it is found neither in the San Marco composition nor in those of the Palaeologan period.[146]

At the Kariye Djami, as has already been emphasized,[147] the Virgin's attitude is especially noteworthy because of the agitation that is expressed in her gestures and the folds of her garment. If her face, turned toward the angel, and her raised hand are traditional, her posture, with one foot on the second step of the well and the other in the air, is quite unrealistic and decidedly exceptional. She is silhouetted against a wall, above which the heavenly messenger appears. The wall is flanked by two porticoes that, as always, combine lavishness and fantasy. The motifs of the tree and the buildings, besides those of the well, the Virgin, and the angel, are already found in the twelfth century in the San Marco mosaic, but arranged in quite a different way. The Kariye Djami mosaicist has made admirable use of these elements, placing them with great skill in the difficult form of the pendentive.

In the chronology of the narrative, Joseph Reproaching the Virgin follows the Visitation, which, as we saw, is missing from the cycle. Unfortunately, the scene is badly damaged [99] (PL. 148, 151). The standing figures of Joseph and Mary, turned slightly toward each other, suggest a conversation, though the upper part is destroyed; the inscription gives Joseph's question.[148] The theme is comparatively frequent in Palaeologan painting and typically Byzantine; its iconography is highly homogeneous. Even on the icon in the Byzantine Museum, Athens, of the beginning of the seventeenth century, the composition remains practically the same (Fig. 28, zone 4, far right): Joseph rests one hand on his long traveler's staff (the lower part of which is still visible in the mosaic) and extends the other toward Mary; she, with head slightly bowed, holds her hands before her chest, palms outward in token of denial. They stand in front of a wall flanked by two towers, a simplified version of the Kariye Djami type, in which the architecture is extremely elaborate. Only the low tree, which appears in the Kariye mosaics from Joseph's departure onwards and which constitutes a unique feature of this series of images,[149] is not represented.

The theme is comparatively rare in pre-iconoclastic documents. It seems sometimes to have been combined with that of the Trial by Water, for instance on ivories such as the diptych of St. Lupicin at Paris or a plaque at Moscow—whether, as in some cases, Mary holds the cup while Joseph, standing beside her, addresses her or, as in others, she raises her hands high while Joseph offers her the cup.[150] The theme of the dialogue, however, is found occasionally—on the column of the ciborium in San Marco or in the Codex Purpureus at Munich,[151] where the seated Joseph addresses Mary, who stands before him. An iconography of this type is also found in the Homilies, where the scene, however, takes place in the presence of Joseph's sons.[152] This must be the result

146 At Pelendri the angel stands beside Mary, who is leaving the well as if to return to the house; there is no background, but the house of the second Annunciation, to the right, may serve as a frame (Fig. 22). At Dečani the wall in the background is oddly surmounted by a ciborium; V. R. Petković and D. Bošković, *Dečani* (Belgrade, 1941), Album, PL. CCL,2. In my opinion, this scene always forms part of the apocryphal narrative cycle, not of the illustration of the Akathistos Hymn. For San Marco, see Bettini, *Mosaici di San Marco*, PL. XLV.

147 See Vol. 1 of this work [98], p. 82.

148 Ibid. [99], p. 83.

149 Ibid.

150 Volbach, *Elfenbeinarbeiten*, Nos. 130 and 145, PL. 41 and 47. On the Moscow plaque, Mary and Joseph stand on either side of the well (which doubtless suggests the Annunciation).

151 Clm. 23631, Cim. 2, fol. 24. In the upper part of the miniature; below, a personage who may be a priest draws Mary along by the wrist, doubtless for the Trial by Water (photo Index of Christian Art, Princeton University). For the ciborium column in San Marco, see Lafontaine-Dosogne, *Iconographie*, I, Fig. 6 (first register).

152 Stornajolo, *Omilie*, PL. 73; Omont, *Homélies*, PL. XXVI,4. The scene is preceded by three pictures illustrating Joseph reaching home after his work, Joseph questioning the Virgin, Joseph's lament in the presence of his sons; a Defense of Mary follows (Stornajolo, PL. 70–72, 74; Omont, PL. XXVI,1–3, XXVII,1). The iconography of the last scene is exactly like that of the Reproaches. In the 12th-century mosaic in San Marco, two of Joseph's sons are also present at the scene—an extremely rare motif (Bettini, *Mosaici di San Marco*, PL. XLV).

of a revival, for the new type of two standing figures was adopted at the same period in the San Marco mosaics and even earlier in Cappadocia.[153] The theme, rare in the classical Byzantine period, is widespread under the Palaeologi, particularly in the northern Balkans. It is found especially in illustrations for the Akathistos.[154] Like many of his contemporaries, the Kariye Djami artist here adopted a scene drawn from an old apocryphal tradition.

The cycle of the Virgin, although usually serving to introduce that of Christ, has a certain autonomy, despite the fact that the canon of the scenes constituting it is not completely fixed. Some cycles, such as those at Daphni and in the Metropole at Mistra, end with the Presentation, others, as in the Peribleptos at Mistra, with the Marriage.[155] Especially in the Palaeologan period scenes belonging to the Infancy of Christ are often added to it; as we have seen, these are always apocryphal scenes that precede the Nativity. On the whole, this series of pictures, though transposed and abridged, is the same as that in the Homilies of the Monk James, since the last Homily, devoted to the Visitation, ends with the episodes of the Trial by Water. It is possible, then, that illustrations for homilies on the Virgin gave rise to a cycle covering the Infancy and Life of Mary down to the events that accompany the Annunciation and the Visitation. However, side by side with this tradition we find another and more developed one, directly inspired by the illustrations for the Protevangelium, traces of which are preserved in the twelfth-century mosaics in San Marco, Venice.[156]

Frequently, too, the cycle of the Virgin continues with the episodes of the Dormition, thus constituting a series of pictures covering her entire life, with the exclusion of the scenes with Christ. This procedure has distant origins, since it is already found on some pre-iconoclastic ivory diptychs, one face being devoted to Christ, the other to the Virgin, though the division is not always strictly applied.[157] The most striking document of this type at an early period is a steatite (?) plaque at Berlin, of the eleventh-twelfth centuries, the iconography of which presents an unusual mixture of eastern and western features, but whose program is distinctly Byzantine: around the central figure of the Virgin with the Child, the scenes of the Life of the Virgin succeed one another, from the Meeting of Anne and Joachim to the Dormition, with the exception of the Nativity of Christ.[158] In a certain number of churches of the Palaeologan period the apocryphal

153 Jerphanion, *Cappadoce*, esp. PL. 75,1, and PL. 188,2.

154 After the various representations of the Annunciation and the Visitation: cf., for example, the frescoes in the refectory at Lavra (Millet, *Athos*, PL. 145, 146).

155 The front and back left columns of the ciborium in San Marco, Venice, provide a good example of the separation of the cycles: the back column is devoted to the Virgin, down to the Marriage; the front column carries scenes from the Life of Christ, beginning with the Annunciation. At Kızıl Çukur, the episodes of the Presentation were followed by one scene (destroyed) which may have been a Marriage or perhaps a Dormition. In Russian frescoes of the 12th century we find, as already at Kiev and Daphni, a narrative cycle of the Life of the Virgin introducing a cycle of Christ which is reduced to the Great Feasts; the Pskov cycle ends with the episodes of the Marriage, and the cycle at Spas–Neredicy with the Presentation; N. V. Pokrovskij, *Očerki pamjatnikov xristianskogo iskusstva i ikonografii*, 3d ed. (St. Petersburg, 1910), pp. 255 ff., and V. K. Mjasoedov, *Freski Spasa-Neredicy* (Leningrad, 1925), PL. XLIV. On the icon in the Pisa Museum called the Madonna di San Martino, the numerous lateral scenes of which illustrate the Pseudo-Matthew narrative, the cycle ends with the Presentation; the Annunciation appears above to the right, outside the cycle (Venturi, *Storia dell'arte italiana*, V, Figs. 25 ff; Lafontaine-Dosogne, *Iconographie*, II, Fig. 5).

156 The complete cycle in the north transept, which follows the scenes of the Infancy of the Virgin in the south transept, includes Zacharias' Prayer, Mary Entrusted to Joseph, Visitation, Joseph's Reproaches, Annunciation at the Well (out of order), Trial by Water, Joseph Dreaming (out of order), Journey to Bethlehem (Bettini, *Mosaici di San Marco*, PL. XLIV, XLV); then come the Flight into Egypt and Christ among the Doctors. The Annunciation in the House, the Nativity, and the Presentation of Christ must have been detached from the narrative cycle to figure in that of the Great Feasts (they have disappeared). In the 14th century we find a similar case at Kritsa, in Crete; K. D. Kalokyris, Ἡ Παναγία τῆς Κριτσᾶς, in Κρητικὰ Χρονικά (May–Aug. 1952), fasc. 2, pp. 211–70; diagram, Fig. 7.

157 Cf. Volbach, *Elfenbeinarbeiten*, Nos. 142 (Etschmiadzin diptych) and 145 (diptych of St. Lupicin, Bibliothèque Nationale, Paris), PL. 44 and 47. Both include, on the tablet of the Virgin, the Annunciation, the Visitation, and the Journey to Bethlehem; in addition, on the first we find the Nativity and the Adoration of the Magi, on the second the Trial by Water and Christ's Entry in Jerusalem.

158 Volbach, *Mittelalterliche Bildwerke*, p. 122, No. 2721, PL. 2: Meeting, Birth, Presentation, Purple Skein or Marriage, Annunciation, Visitation, Trial, Presentation of Christ, Annunciation *ante mortem*, and Dormition; see also Lafontaine-Dosogne, *Iconographie*, II, Fig. 1.

cycle of the Life of the Virgin (interrupted by the three liturgical scenes—Annunciation, Nativity, and Presentation, properly belonging to the Great Feasts—so that a discontinuity in tone is produced) continues with the episodes of the Dormition. The most striking example occurs in St. Clement, Ohrid, where the cycle extends along the middle register on the side walls of the nave and ends on the west wall, which is the traditional place for the Dormition.[159] The procedure continued to be used after the fall of Byzantium. We find it on post-Byzantine Greek or Russian icons.[160] Here too it may be connected with a textual tradition found especially in Syria, from a very early period, which consists in continuing the text of the Protevangelium with that of the Transitus Mariae, thus providing a complete narrative of the life and death of the Virgin.[161]

However this may be, what we have to consider above all here in connection with the mosaics in the inner narthex of the Kariye Djami is the illustrated cycle of the apocryphal Life of the Virgin before the Nativity of Christ. Of this the decoration in St. Clement, Ohrid, is an outstanding example, both for the large number of subjects depicted and for the judiciousness with which they were chosen: Rejected Offerings, Return of Anne and Joachim, Annunciation to Joachim, Annunciation to Anne, Meeting or Conception, Birth of the Virgin, Blessing of the Priests, Caresses, First Steps, Presentation in the Temple, Zacharias' Prayer, and Marriage. The following scenes show a certain lack of balance: Annunciation at the Well, Joseph's Reproaches, Trial by Water, Joseph's Dream (the cycle, which began in the diaconicon, ends in the prothesis with this last scene); the Visitation is placed in the upper part of the diaconicon, with scenes from the life of John the Baptist. With the exception of the Dream, the same series is found in the church at Dečani, the rich decoration of which, with its more than a thousand subjects, forms a sort of anthology of Byzantine iconography.[162] The fullness of the Dečani cycle is surpassed in the Balkans north of Greece only by that in the Kariye Djami. The representations preserved in Greece itself, especially at Mistra, are very different in spirit. Earlier by only a few years than the Ohrid cycle, that in the Metropole, although close to it in style, is distinctly different in its limited selection of scenes, which seems to go back to Daphni, as well as in the use of more traditional motifs.[163] As to the series in the Peribleptos, toward the end of the fourteenth century, not only is it outstanding in its very great number of scenes (twenty-four, including the Virgin Receiving the Skein of Purple Wool, a number never surpassed in church painting), but it remains extremely dependent on illuminated manuscripts. This is to be seen particularly in the scenes of the Marriage, which give the impression of being simply extracted from a highly developed series of miniatures instead of being reworked to achieve the synthesis necessary for church painting.[164]

159 The other examples that are most interesting by their inclusiveness are those in the churches at Staro Nagoričino and at Dečani, but in each case the cycle of the Infancy of the Virgin is placed in the prothesis, so that it is less conspicuous.

160 For example, the icon in the Byzantine Museum, Athens (our Fig. 28), where the Annunciation, Joseph's Reproaches (out of order), and the Visitation form the transition between the Marriage and the Prayer on Golgotha (followed by the Dormition and the Assumption), and a Russian icon of the 16th century reproduced by Georgievskij, *Freski Ferapontova Monastyrja*, PL. XXXXIV, where the Annunciation at the Well is followed by the Trial by Water.

161 The text is published by Miss Smith Lewis, *Apocrypha Syriaca*, under the title: "In the hope of the Holy Trinity, one in essence, we begin to write the book of the History of the Mother of God, Mary, from the day of her birth until the day of her exit from this world. May her prayer be with us! Amen, amen."

The first part of the text published by Budge, *History of the Blessed Virgin*, is a history of the Virgin and gives an account of her infancy, the Infancy of Christ, the sojourn of the Holy Family in Egypt, and the death of the Virgin, together with a list of her miracles.

162 Petković and Bošković, *Dečani*, Album, PL. CCXXXV–CCXXXVIII, CCL, CCLI. For that matter, see Lafontaine-Dosogne, *Iconographie*, I, Ch. IV,1 and 2.

163 It includes the Rejected Offerings in addition to the Daphni scenes: Annunciation to Anne and to Joachim (in the same picture), Birth, Blessing of the Priests, Presentation. In the Presentation the iconography is traditional, while the Birth is very close to the one in St. Clement, Ohrid.

164 Thus, Mary does not appear in Zacharias' Prayer. As in the Homilies, Mary in the Holy of Holies should have been represented in a separate composition, which the frescoist omitted (Millet, *Mistra*, PL. 130).

The Kariye Djami cycle is not guilty of this excess. Yet it is very complete, for it includes almost all the scenes represented in St. Clement at Ohrid (the Dream is placed among the Christ scenes, in the outer narthex; the Visitation was perhaps represented in the nave).[165] In addition, a few supplementary scenes were drawn either from an illustrated manuscript of the Protevangelium or from a collection of homilies similar to that by James Kokkinobaphos: the repetition of the Annunciation to Joachim, Mary Fed by the Angel in the Temple, the episodes following the Marriage, and the Distribution of the Skeins.[166] To the creative mind of the artist who conceived the ensemble must be attributed the scene of Mary's Instruction in the Temple as well as the symbolic character given to several compositions.

If themes of oriental derivation, absent in earlier Constantinopolitan representations, such as the Return of Anne and Joachim, the First Steps, and the Caresses, were adopted in the Kariye Djami, it is because they were at that time incorporated into the Palaeologan koine. Within the themes themselves, however, the iconography proves to be quite conservative, closely connected as it is to the old tradition of the capital. The motif of the spinning maidservant watching over the cradle in the Nativity, the unusual arrangement of the procession of virgins in the Presentation in the Temple, novelties so widely adopted in the Macedonian painting of the period, do not appear here. The young maidservant in the scene of the Return, and the small figure present at the Annunciation to Anne, are, on the other hand, features specifically Greek in the strictest sense of the word.

Thus the cycle of the Virgin in the Kariye Djami has a distinctive character. Though not directly related to the numerous slightly earlier or contemporary examples known in Macedonia, in Serbia, at Mount Athos, yet it is closer to them than are those at Mistra. Undoubtedly the art of those regions is more strongly influenced by Salonika. The only cycle preserved in this city, that in the Holy Apostles, though later (second quarter of the fourteenth century) and now only fragmentarily preserved, shows undeniable connections with the Macedonian cycles.[167] Later, in the churches at Curtea-de-Argeş and Kalenić, some portions of whose decoration are visibly and strongly influenced by that of the church of the Chora, the scenes of the Life of the Virgin nevertheless exhibit a greater autonomy.[168] We have to admit that the Kariye Djami cycle stands almost alone in Byzantine art. Moreover, it is most remarkable that the apocryphal legends were adopted into the art of the capital to the point of resulting in a series of images executed in the refined and magnificent technique of mosaic. The small cycle at Daphni remained strongly liturgical in spirit. That in the Kariye Djami, though often ennobled by a symbolic approach, is essentially narrative and based on apocryphal traditions that are sometimes distinctly of oriental

165 Some scholars have seen an allusion to the Trial in the scene of the Dream in the outer narthex, but I do not hold with this opinion; see below, p. 203.

166 It is perhaps worth noting that the scenes run from left to right in the Homilies, at least usually, and from right to left in the Kariye Djami. The fact is striking.

167 These frescoes have not been published; see Lafontaine-Dosogne, *Iconographie*, I, p. 47. I have found the following scenes in the portions that are still visible: Annunciation to Anne, Annunciation to Joachim, Blessing of the Priests, Presentation in the Temple, perhaps a Marriage. The lacunae may have included the Caresses and the First Steps to the south of the Presentation, and Zacharias' Prayer between the Presentation and the Marriage. As for the Birth, it was not represented, doubtless because it was included in the cycle of the Great Feasts, treated in mosaic in the nave. A. Xyngopoulos, Ἡ ψηφιδωτὴ διακόσμησις τοῦ ναοῦ τῶν Ἁγίων Ἀποστόλων Θεσσαλονίκης (Salonika, 1953), does not suggest this possibility. He supposes, however, p. 3, that there was a scene pendant to that of Lazarus; I think that it was the Birth of the Virgin, which would thus have been given a place on the north wall of the north barrel vault (cf. diagram, p. 7). The fact that the mosaics in the nave (ca. 1315) are close to Constantinopolitan productions does not prevent the frescoes from being more nearly in the Macedonian tradition.

168 See below, my "Iconography of the Cycle of the Infancy of Christ," *passim*. For the scenes of the Life of the Virgin at Kalenić, see the sketches by M. Bošković in Petković, *La peinture serbe*, II, Figs. 48–50, pp. 43 ff. For Curtea-de-Argeş, see Tafrali, *Curtéa de Argeş*, PL. CIX,2 (No. 276) and CX,2 (No. 275) (the motif mentioned above, in n. 129, is the only one that can be compared with the same scenes in the Kariye Djami); according to the plan in PL. I (lower right), it seems to me that there could have been a small cycle in the narthex, of which the images of the Presentation and the Marriage form the end.

inspiration. In this respect, too, it remains an outstanding and typical example of Palaeologan art.[169]

The place that the cycle occupies in the church, as well as the position of the equally well known example of Daphni, has led several scholars to affirm that cycles of the Virgin are usually placed in the narthex. If this is sometimes true, it is rather by way of exception, for in fact these subjects can be found in all parts of a church except the domes and conch of the central apse, as we have seen from the examples cited above.[170] To illustrate the Life of the Virgin in the narthex seems undoubtedly to have been a Constantinopolitan solution—although not the only one, since in the Odalar Djami some of these scenes were represented in the diaconicon [171]—and that displayed in the Kariye Djami is certainly its most brilliant example.

169 See also below, my "Iconography of the Cycle of the Infancy of Christ," p. 238.

170 See also Lafontaine-Dosogne, *Iconographie*, I, Ch. IV,3.
171 See above, n. 26.

Iconography of the Cycle of
the Infancy of Christ

JACQUELINE LAFONTAINE-DOSOGNE

This text was written in 1962. A few references were added in the notes in 1965.

Iconography of the Cycle of the Infancy of Christ

THE SCENES of the Infancy of Christ, grouped around the essential event of the Nativity, are among the earliest subjects to be represented in Christian art. Indeed, after the symbolic representations in the catacombs, they form the first narrative cycle drawn from the Gospels to be introduced into programs of church decoration—if we except the miracles of Christ depicted on the walls of the baptistery at Dura-Europos. The earliest documentation goes back to the time of Constantine, who, as is well known, erected sumptuous buildings in the Holy Land to commemorate the events of the Life of Christ. On the west facade of the basilica of the Nativity at Bethlehem, the Nativity and the Adoration of the Magi were depicted in mosaic.[1] These two representations would appear to have been symbolic rather than narrative in character: they were commemorative images, like similar representations in the catacombs.[2] As early as the fifth century, however, the mosaics fortunately preserved in Santa Maria Maggiore at Rome supply a well-developed cycle that is more narrative in character, though still mingled with symbolism. They include, for the subject with which we are concerned, the Annunciation, Joseph's Dream, the Presentation in the Temple, the Adoration of the Magi, the Flight into Egypt, Herod and the Massacre of the Innocents.[3] The lost mosaics of La Daurade at Toulouse (fifth or sixth century) displayed an extensive cycle of the Infancy of Christ.[4] In the church of the Holy Apostles at Constantinople these subjects seem also to have been treated in mosaic, already in the pre-iconoclastic period.[5] Choricius of Gaza, a sixth-century author, has left us a description of the church of St. Sergius at Gaza, in which he mentions several representations of the Infancy: Annunciation, Visitation, Nativity, Annunciation to the Shepherds, Presentation in the Temple, in a sequence that is definitely historical.[6]

1 We know this from the letter of the Melchite patriarchs to the Emperor Theophilus, published by L. Duchesne, "L'iconographie byzantine dans un document du IXᵉ siècle," *Roma e l'Oriente*, 5 (1912), pp. 283–84.

2 Especially the images of the Adoration of the Magi in the cemetery of Saints Peter and Marcellinus and in the catacomb of Domitilla; J. Wilpert, *Roma sotterranea: Le pitture delle catacombe romane* (Rome, 1903), p. 60 and PL. 161,1.

3 C. Cecchelli, *I mosaici della basilica di S. Maria Maggiore* (Turin, 1956), PL. XLVII ff.; J. Wilpert, *Die römischen Mosaiken und Malereien der kirchlichen Bauten vom IV. bis XIII. Jahrhundert*, 2d ed. (Freiburg im Breisgau, 1917), III, PL. 53 ff.

4 H. Woodruff, "The Iconography and Date of the Mosaics of La Daurade," *ArtB*, 13 (1931), pp. 84 ff.

5 The famous church, founded by Constantius and rebuilt by Justinian, seems to have been decorated with figured representations not by the latter but by his successor, Justin II; A. Heisenberg, *Grabeskirche und Apostelkirche, zwei Basiliken Konstantins* (Leipzig, 1908), II, pp. 167 ff. See G. Downey, "Constantine the Rhodian: His Life and Writings," *Late Classical and Mediaeval Studies in Honor of Albert Mathias Friend, Jr.*, ed. K. Weitzmann (Princeton, 1955), p. 220, for the attribution to Constantius. The church was completely restored by Basil I, and it is this state of the building which is treated in the Rhodian's descrip-

tion, ordered by Constantine VII Porphyrogenitus, the grandson of Basil I. For the text of Constantine of Rhodes, see E. Legrand, "Description des oeuvres d'art et de l'église des Saints Apôtres de Constantinople, poème en vers iambiques par Constantin le Rhodien," *REG*, 9 (1896), pp. 32–65, followed by an archeological commentary by Th. Reinach, pp. 66–103. The mosaics were also described by Mesarites; see Heisenberg, *Apostelkirche*, pp. 45–48 and 221 ff., for the subjects with which we are concerned. Some authors consider that the descriptions refer to 6th-century representations, others maintain that they refer to the 9th-century representations. It is possible that the Rhodian was inspired by earlier descriptions. The scenes from the Life of Christ that he describes have been connected with a series of epigrams in the Palatine Anthology which go back to the 6th century and which certainly seem to be inspired by figured representations of the Infancy of Christ; A. Salač, "Quelques épigrammes de l'Anthologie Palatine et l'iconographie byzantine," *Byzantinoslavica*, 12 (1951), pp. 1–28. See also below, n. 20.

6 *Laudatio Marciani*, I, *Choricii Gazaei Opera*, ed. R. Foerster and E. Richtsteig, Teubner (1929), §§48–56, pp. 14 ff.; Ch. Bayet, *Recherches pour servir à l'histoire de la peinture et de la sculpture chrétiennes en Orient avant la querelle des iconoclastes* (Paris, 1879), pp. 61 ff.

197

Even outside of churches, these subjects appear many times in all kinds of techniques, often in documents of very early date. Among illustrated books, the most famous example is the Rabbula Gospels, a Syriac work dated 586.[7] In sculpture, they are found on sarcophagi from as early as the fourth century; on the Salonika ambo, of the end of the fifth century;[8] on column B of the ciborium in San Marco, Venice, the iconography of which, if not its execution, goes back to the sixth century.[9] Among ivories, aside from a large number of plaques, diptychs, pyxides, etc., we shall mention particularly the throne of Maximian at Ravenna (sixth century), which still preserves five scenes from the Infancy.[10] Jewels—rings, for example—frequently carry representations of the Nativity.[11] Finally we must emphasize the importance of phials from the Holy Land, on which the Annunciation, the Visitation, the Nativity, the Annunciation to the Shepherds, the Adoration of the Magi, and other scenes are represented; these phials were disseminated throughout Christendom by pilgrims.[12]

From the sixth century to the ninth it is more often in fresco than in the costly and rich mosaic technique of the beginnings of triumphant Christianity that a number of highly interesting and widely scattered ensembles of the Infancy of Christ have been preserved. The example in the Red Church of Peruštica, in present-day Bulgaria, goes back to the sixth century, the one at Deir Abu Hinnis, in Egypt, to the sixth or the seventh.[13] The paintings in Santa Maria Antiqua, at Rome, date from the eighth century.[14] Those in Santa Maria di Castelseprio, though their date is still in dispute, I consider may also be of the eighth century from the iconographic point of view.[15]

The problem of the textual and iconographic traditions from which these representations stem

7 It includes (after the Annunciation to Zacharias) the Annunciation, the Nativity of Christ, the Massacre of the Innocents, followed by the Baptism, etc.; C. Cecchelli, G. Furlani, and M. Salmi, *The Rabbula Gospels: Facsimile Edition of the Miniatures of the Syriac Manuscript Plut. I.56 in the Medicaean-Laurentian Library* (Olten and Lausanne, 1959), fol. 4 a and 4 b, pp. 54–55. For the early representations of scenes from the Infancy of Christ, reference may be made, though with caution, to the numerous documents collected by J. Reil, *Die altchristlichen Bildzyklen des Lebens Jesu* (Leipzig, 1910); see the tables on pp. 82 ff.

8 J. Wilpert, *I sarcofagi cristiani antichi* (Rome, 1929–36), passim, and Text, II (1932), p. 279, and III (1936), p. 525 ff. For the ambo, see W. F. Volbach, *Frühchristliche Kunst: Die Kunst der Spätantike in West- und Ostrom* (Munich, 1958), PL. 78–79.

9 This column has not been studied from the iconographic point of view; my remark applies to the scenes of the Infancy of Christ (photos Böhm, Nos. 3234 and 3235, second register); for the difficult problem raised by the chronology of these monuments, see above, my essay "Iconography of the Cycle of the Life of the Virgin," p. 164.

10 The Annunciation, the Trial by Water, Joseph's Dream and the Journey to Bethlehem, the Nativity, the Adoration of the Magi; see, *inter alia*, F. W. Volbach, *Elfenbeinarbeiten der Spätantike und des frühen Mittelalters*, 2d ed. (Mainz, 1952), No. 140, PL. 43; G. Bovini, *La cattedra eburnea del vescovo Massimiano di Ravenna* (Faenza, 1957), fig. on p. 13 (for the arrangement of the scenes, pp. 8 and 12 ff.). The missing scene in the lower register may have been the Visitation, which should be exchanged with the Trial by Water. See also below, n. 224.

11 See especially the article "Nativité" in *DACL*, and the documents assembled by M. Rosenberg, *Niello bis zum Jahre 1000 nach Chr.* (Frankfurt am Main, 1924), p. 49, Figs. 36–38.

12 A. Grabar, *Ampoules de Terre Sainte (Monza-Bobbio)* (Paris, 1958), pp. 52–54 and PL. I ff., XLVI ff.; idem, *Martyrium: Recherches sur le culte des reliques et l'art chrétien antique* (Paris, 1946), II, pp. 169 ff., on the local nature of the creation

of these iconographic subjects.

13 See A. Frolow, "L'Église Rouge de Peruštica," *The Bulletin of the Byzantine Institute*, for the frescoes, 1 (1946), pp. 31 ff. and PL. X, XI; for the date, ibid., 2 (=*Coptic Studies in Honor of Walter Ewing Cram*; 1950), pp. 471 ff. (end of the 5th century; Grabar prefers a later date, end of the 7th century: Frolow, "Peruštica," *loc. cit.*, 1, p. 32, n. 1). The construction of the church dates from the reign of Anastasius (491–518); D. Panajotova, *Červenata cŭrkva pri Peruštica: opit za restavracija* (Sofia, 1956).

For Deir Abu Hinnis, see J. Clédat, "Notes archéologiques et philologiques," *Bulletin de l'Institut Français d'Archéologie Orientale*, 2 (1902), PL. I, II, and V, pp. 49, 50, and 54. Clédat did not recognize the scene on PL. I, representing the Flight of Elizabeth with the infant John, nor, on PL. II, the Murder of Zacharias in the Temple, which give these paintings their apocryphal character. All these scenes formed part of an ensemble in which the episodes of the Infancy of Christ must also have appeared, for they are followed by Joseph's Dream and the Flight into Egypt (PL. II). The Flight of Elizabeth is preceded by the Magi before Herod and the Massacre of the Innocents (the Nativity seems to have preceded these scenes, p. 9).

14 Fragmentary paintings of the Infancy of Christ are found in the choir (period of John VII) and on the south wall (a little later); W. de Grüneisen, *Sainte-Marie-Antique* (Rome, 1911), Figs. 101, 102, 115, and 119, pp. 134, 135, 158, and 160; PL. XXI and Fig. 83, p. 109. In addition, Grimaldi's drawings and a few scattered fragments prove the existence of a mosaic decoration in the oratory of John VII in St. Peter's, Rome, which included several of our scenes; Grüneisen, PL. IC.LXVI ff.

15 G. P. Bognetti, G. Chierici, and A. de Capitani d'Argazo, *Santa Maria di Castelseprio* (Milan, 1948). The paintings have been dated in the 7th to the 10th century. For a summary of the question, see Ch. Delvoye, bibliography, "L'art byzantin," *L'information d'histoire de l'art*, 5 (1960), p. 83, and Ph. Verdier, review of K. Weitzmann, *The Fresco Cycle of S. Maria di Castelseprio* (Princeton, 1951), in *AJA*, 63 (1959), pp. 220–23.

is complex. The Byzantine cycle of the Life of the Virgin has its origin in apocryphal legends that are mainly represented by the Protevangelium of James. As for the images of the Infancy of Christ, they illustrate both the canonical Gospels and various apocryphal texts, among them the second part of the Protevangelium (Ch. 11–21) and the versions and paraphrases of it enumerated earlier, as well as the Gospel of Pseudo-Thomas, the Arabic Gospel of the Infancy, etc., which are more especially concerned with Christ.[16] As for the Gospels proper, the artists drew from Matthew and from Luke, the one supplementing the other. It is already the synoptic Luke-Matthew that is illustrated in the basilica of the Nativity at Bethlehem, the details of the Nativity going back to the former and the episode of the Magi to the latter.[17] Apocryphal elements soon make their way into the themes through various iconographic motifs, and into the cycles themselves through episodes that only the Apocrypha report. I shall have occasion to discuss this subject in the course of the following study. Some of these elements appear in the fourth century, but it is in the fifth century, and especially in the sixth, that they become widespread.

Accordingly then, we know both from the sources and from archaeological evidence that the events of the Infancy of Christ gave rise to numerous narrative ensembles, some of them highly elaborated, in pre-iconoclastic Christian art. The iconoclastic crisis halted the production of such images for more than a century (730–843), at least in the capital and in the regions of the Empire that were most subject to the decisions of the iconoclastic emperors. In some places, such as Cappadocia, the iconographic habits of the preceding periods continued to prevail during the crisis. For there, in the following centuries, we find archaizing decorative ensembles that carry on the pre-iconoclastic tradition. And the Cappadocian churches are the only ones that have preserved narrative cycles of the Infancy of Christ, at least from the ninth century to the eleventh.[18] In the other decorative ensembles known to us such cycles are extremely infrequent. However, it is incorrect to state, as has sometimes been done, that cycles of the Infancy of Christ were not represented at all in Byzantine churches of the Macedonian and Comnenian periods. We find at least two developed examples from the twelfth century, at Monreale and at San Marco, Venice.[19] (It is true that here we are in the West and that, though the artists of Monreale were Byzantines, the decorative program may have been determined under the influence of local customs.) When Constantine the Rhodian speaks of images of the Infancy of Christ in the Holy Apostles church at Constantinople, he is probably referring to a work recently executed, that is, soon after the iconoclastic crisis, for it seems unlikely that the iconoclasts could have tolerated such images in the capital.[20] In any case, numerous manuscripts dating from the ninth century to the twelfth, but preponderantly of the eleventh century, preserved the tradition of images rendering the episodes of the Life of Christ, especially his Infancy.

16 For the first group, see above, "Iconography of the Cycle of the Life of the Virgin," p. 163; for the others, *Evangiles apocryphes*, ed. and tr. C. Michel and P. Peeters, 2d ed. (Paris, 1924), I, pp. 162 ff. and II, 1 ff. The Gospel of Pseudo-Thomas does not relate the episodes of the Nativity; Jesus is five years old at the beginning of the narrative. These texts are conveniently brought together, with bibliographical references, in A. de Santos Otero, ed. and tr., *Los evangelios apocrifos* (Madrid, 1956), Ch. III.

17 The *Diatessaron* of Tatian, usually dated in the second half of the 2nd century, arranged the episodes of the Life of Christ in chronological order. This text has been compared with a series of epigrams in the Palatine Anthology (Nos. 37–46) which are believed to describe a series of representations of the Life of Christ that goes back to the 4th century (Salač, "Quelques épigrammes").

18 G. de Jerphanion, *Une nouvelle province de l'art byzantin: Les églises rupestres de Cappadoce* (Paris, 1925–42), passim; J. Lafontaine-Dosogne, "Nouvelles notes cappadociennes," *Byzantion*, 33 (1963), pp. 141 ff., passim. The iconoclastic edicts were not adopted in Cyprus, but the island, which was possessed and frequently ravaged by the Arabs during the period, has preserved no representations of our subjects earlier than the 11th century.

19 O. Demus, *The Mosaics of Norman Sicily* (London, 1949), PL. 65 a, 65 b, 66 a; for San Marco, see S. Bettini, *Mosaici antichi di San Marco a Venezia* (Bergamo [1944]), PL. XLIV and XLV; see also above, "Iconography of the Cycle of the Life of the Virgin," n. 156.

20 However, it is possible that among the representations executed during the restoration by Basil I, the program of the 6th century was used again, at least in part. See above, n. 5.

There are reasons for the partial abandonment of such subjects in churches. The style of the period may be termed severe, and it was little suited to the rendering of narrative and homely subjects. The codification of calendars, the elaboration, during the tenth century, of iconographic themes closely connected with the liturgy, entailed a strict selection of subjects. Of the principal episodes of the Life of Christ, the tendency was to use only those that have a particular liturgical importance. Hence we witness the creation of images illustrating the Great Feasts, whose number varied but was stabilized at about twelve.[21] The cycle of Feasts traditionally opens with the Annunciation, the Nativity of Christ, and his Presentation in the Temple. It seemed unnecessary, as well as unsatisfying from the point of view of the decorative program, to represent a marginal narrative cycle embroidering on the chosen themes. In the Menologion of Basil II (from which the Annunciation, which would have figured in the second volume, is missing), we see the Nativity, the Adoration of the Magi, and Joseph's Dream, all illustrating the feast of December 25, the Flight into Egypt illustrating that of the 26th, the Massacre of the Innocents that of the 29th, the Circumcision that of January 1, and the Presentation that of February 2.[22] This ensemble was further reduced—apart from the Annunciation—to the two essential episodes, Nativity and Presentation, the former incorporating the episode of the Magi. While reduced in number, the iconographic themes were enriched, sometimes in a synthesis comprising a great many elements, by motifs borrowed from other themes. The architectural arrangement of the edifices, which most often adopted the inscribed Greek-cross plan, was little suited to the development of numerous images and entirely rejected the frieze compositions. At Daphni or at Hosios Loukas the walls are sheathed with marble up to the cornices, and the figured representations are given a place only in the upper zones.[23] Such a disposition is of Constantinopolitan origin; it is found in the capital in numerous churches of the period, which have unfortunately not preserved their figured decoration. The trend at the time was toward large representations—two or four in each vault.

For all these reasons our themes are little represented in narrative sequences in the painted decoration of middle-Byzantine churches. But the three traditional scenes of the Annunciation, the Nativity, and the Presentation are always found in them, incorporated into the series of Great Feasts figured in the nave. From the thirteenth century, perhaps under the influence of the development of narrative cycles illustrating the lives of the Virgin and of certain saints, such as St. Nicholas, the cycle of the Infancy of Christ begins to reappear in Byzantine churches. We find it first at Bojana (1256).[24] But this Bulgarian church, whose paintings were inspired by miniatures in manuscripts from the capital, which was then sunk in the morass of the Latin occupation, remains a special case. More pertinent is the cycle of the Infancy in the Metropole at Mistra, of the end of the century. It consists of the Annunciation (the Nativity is lost), Joseph's Dream and the Flight into Egypt, and the Massacre of the Innocents, in the choir; the Presentation in the Temple follows, on the south wall of the nave, with the Great Feasts; the scene of Christ among the Doctors, on the vault of the south nave, forms the prelude to the cycle of the miracles.[25] Like that of the Virgin, this cycle is moderately narrative in character, being limited to a small number of themes. In the church of the Virgin at Gradac the whole upper part of one wall of the nave

21 G. Millet, *Recherches sur l'iconographie de l'Evangile aux XIV*, XV*, et XVI* siècles* (Paris, 1916, reprinted 1960), pp. 16 ff.; O. Demus, *Byzantine Mosaic Decoration: Aspects of Monumental Art in Byzantium* (London, 1948), pp. 22 ff.

22 Vaticanus gr. 1613, published in facsimile in *Il Menologio di Basilio II (Codice Vaticano greco 1613)* (Codices e Vaticanis selecti, VIII; Turin, 1907), II, pp. 271–74, 281, 287, 365.

23 On the question see particularly Demus, *Byzantine Mosaic Decoration*, esp. pp. 14 ff.

24 A. Grabar, *L'église de Boïana: Architecture—peinture* (Sofia, 1924), p. 30 (diagrams), and Nos. 21–25 and 61, PL. IX–XI and XXVII; for the Byzantine character of the models, pp. 24–25.

25 G. Millet, *Monuments byzantins de Mistra* (Paris, 1910), PL. 65,2,3; 66,1,3, and 4; 73,2.

is occupied by a huge composition grouping more numerous episodes around the central theme of the Nativity. But the Annunciation is not included, and it has been pointed out that the arrangement of the subjects is determined by the order of the rubrics in the Synaxarion.[26] Rather than a narrative cycle, we here have an elaborate evocation of the Nativity. Such a procedure is not new in Byzantine art. A remarkable icon at Sinai, dating from the eleventh century (Fig. 40),[27] is executed with a similar intent. But the fact that these subjects reach the walls of churches is typical of the Palaeologan period. They are found a little later in the Brontochion at Mistra, where the cycle is an elaborate narrative inspired by the Apocrypha.[28] The very fragmentary frescoes in the building of centralized type near the old church of the Theotokos Chalcopratia, at Constantinople, likewise belonged to a cycle of apocryphal character (Figs. 45 and 59); unfortunately it is not possible to determine whether the cycle was of an earlier or later period than the one in the Kariye Djami.[29] Our scenes will also appear during the period in another category of illustrations, those for the Akathistos Hymn, in which the images follow one another in the order of the strophes of the chant.[30] Apart from these cases, the scenes of the Infancy of Christ continue to be restricted to the three traditional themes in most churches, as we have already pointed out above. These scenes may sometimes be removed from a narrative cycle, with the result that this becomes seriously disjointed: such a procedure, which we have already found in the Constantinopolitan tradition in connection with the cycle of the Virgin, recurs in the cycle of Christ in the Kariye Djami.[31]

The themes of the Infancy of Christ always had their place in Constantinopolitan art. They do not have the somewhat marginal character peculiar to the illustration of the Life of the Virgin in the capital, at least in the earliest times. The cycle of Christ, even when permeated by details taken from the Apocrypha, was felt to be canonical. We shall see furthermore that, with a single exception, the inscriptions that accompany the representations in the Kariye Djami are drawn from Luke and Matthew. Thus the whole cycle of Christ, placed in the outer narthex, seems to contrast with that of the Virgin, in the inner narthex. Not a single series of illustrations of an apocryphal Infancy of Christ has been preserved in Byzantine art proper. We have already noted that no illustrated copy of the Protevangelium has come down to us. If, for the chapters dealing

26 Millet, *Recherches*, Fig. 88 and pp. 142–43.

27 G. and M. Soteriou, *Icônes du Mont Sinaï*, I (Athens, 1956), Figs. 43–45, and II (Athens, 1958), pp. 59–62.

28 Millet, *Mistra*, PL. 93,3, 95,8; idem, *Recherches*, Ch. II passim.

29 These paintings certainly date from the Palaeologan period. Professor Underwood has uncovered some fragments near the Chalcopratia, of which one belongs to a scene involving the Magi and another to the Murder of Zacharias (Figs. 45 and 59). See my article, "Fouilles et découvertes byzantines à Istanbul de 1952 à 1960," *Byzantion*, 29–30 (1959–60), p. 367.

30 The Annunciation, the Visitation, Joseph Reproaching the Virgin, the Nativity, the Journey of the Magi, the Adoration, the Return of the Magi, the Flight into Egypt, the Presentation in the Temple, illustrating strophes 1–4, 5, 6, 7, 8, 9, 10, 11, 12. For the text, see Ὡρολόγιον (Rome, 1937), pp. 887–94; A. Papadopoulos-Kerameus, Ὁ Ἀκάθιστος Ὕμνος, οἱ Πῶς καὶ ὁ πατριάρχης Φώτιος (Athens, 1903). The Akathistos Hymn is an ode in honor of the Virgin, supposedly written on the occasion of the deliverance of Constantinople from the barbarians (Persians and Avars) in 626. The existing text may go back to the 9th century. The earliest known illustrations go back no further than the 14th century. The most important document is the manuscript in the Moscow Historical Museum, gr. 429, probably dating from the 15th century; see "Acathiste de la Très-Sainte-Vierge," Vol. I of *Copies photographiées des miniatures du manuscrit grec appartenant à la Bibliothèque du Saint Synode*

(Moscow, 1862); and N. P. Lixačev, *Materialy dlja istorii russkogo ikonopisanija* (St. Petersburg, 1906), II, PL. CCCLVI, CCCLVII, 700–707 (the reproduction is only partial; see also J. Strzygowski, *Die Miniaturen des Serbischen Psalters* (Vienna, 1906), pp. 129 ff., for the description. The Serbian Psalter at Munich (Staatsbibliothek, slav. 4), also of the 15th century, contains a series of miniatures illustrating the Akathistos; Strzygowski, pp. 75 ff., PL. LII ff. (fol. 205v ff.), and the Introduction by Jagić, pp. xliv ff. The Syrian hypothesis put forward by Strzygowski for this illustration seems to me absolutely unfounded (pp. 133 ff.). Among the frescoes of St. Nicholas Orphanos at Salonika, recently published by A. Xyngopoulos (Οἱ τοιχογραφίες τοῦ Ἁγίου Νικολάου Ὀρφανοῦ Θεσσαλονίκης [Athens, 1964]), are several scenes of the Akathistos, the oldest ones known (the author dates the paintings as of 1310–20; see Figs. 93 ff.). J. Myslivec, "Ikonografie Akathistu Panny Marie," *Seminarium Kondakovianum*, 5 (1932), pp. 97–130, rightly distinguishes two groups of images in the illustration of the Akathistos, those connected with the Life of the Virgin and those that illustrate the text in the features peculiar to it. But he is mistaken in believing that the first group was not adapted to the particular features of the Akathistos, as we shall more than once have occasion to see in the course of the present study.

31 See above, my "Iconography of the Cycle of the Life of the Virgin," nn. 136 and 138.

with the Virgin, the Homilies of the Monk James partly substitute for it, for Christ no work of this nature can be cited. However, an illustrated manuscript of the Arabic Gospel of the Infancy, dated 1299, exists in the Laurentian Library in Florence (Med. Pal. orient. 387).[32] The text is inspired by a Syriac narrative.[33] As for the line drawings that accompany it, despite the oriental appearance of the protagonists and of numerous details, they visibly imitate Byzantine models, unless they go back to early Syrian images.[34] Except for this paradoxical document, the various miniatures illustrating the Infancy of Christ that are known to exist today are found in manuscripts of the Gospels of Luke and Matthew or in liturgical books, particularly lectionaries.[35] Strictly canonical events are often illustrated in these manuscripts by images inspired by apocryphal narratives, proof that such narratives had been extensively illustrated. But doubtless we here have a very old iconographic tradition, which had in some sort become canonical by making its way into the illustration of the Scriptures.

We shall now consider whence the Kariye Djami artist drew his inspiration and how he interpreted and modernized his models. Our mosaic ensemble remains unique in Byzantine art in its elaboration and its narrative character—a uniqueness which undoubtedly poses a difficulty for the defenders of an academic tradition for Constantinopolitan art. The painters of the extensive later ensembles of Curtea–de–Argeş and of Kalenić made it their entire source of inspiration.[36] As in the case of that of the Virgin, it is the only such cycle that has been preserved in the capital itself;[37] hence its great importance.

Since the Annunciation, which normally opens the cycle of the Infancy of Christ, had been represented both in the apocryphal cycle of the Life of the Virgin and, probably, among the Great Feasts, it was not repeated here nor, by the same token, was the Visitation.[38] Our cycle begins with Joseph Dreaming ([100].1); this is the first dream attributed to him by the narratives. The scene, which occupies the left section of the northern lunette, includes, in the distance, an enigmatic figure of Mary with two women before the walls of a city; the right–hand section contains the Journey to Bethlehem (Vol. 2 of this work, PL. 152). The Journey is not the consequence of a dream, but of the order for enrollment put forth by Augustus. The Dream does not necessarily precede the Journey, but it follows the revelation of Mary's pregnancy, suggested by Joseph Reproaching the Virgin ([99].2), the last illustration of the Life of the Virgin in the inner narthex. The angel appears to Joseph to assure him of Mary's innocence. Since the Protevangelium (14:2) narrates the event before the episode of the Trial by Water (Ch. 16), the scene is sometimes introduced into the cycle of the Virgin, as in the mosaics in San Marco, Venice, or, at the period with which we are concerned, in the frescoes in St. Clement, Ohrid, or, a little later, in the church of the Holy Cross at Pelendri.[39] It seems that we here have an

32 I am grateful to Miss Sirarpie Der Nersessian, who pointed out the existence of this manuscript to me and put at my disposal the almost unobtainable study by E. K. Redin, "Miniatury apokrifičeskogo arabskogo Evangelija detstva Xrista Lavrencianskoj biblioteki vo Florencii," *Zapiski Imperatorskogo Russkogo Arxeologičeskogo Obščestvo*, N.S., 7 (1895), pp. 55–71. Redin did not reproduce all the drawings, but describes them. Description also in A. Baumstark, "Ein apokryphes Herrenleben in mesopotamischen Federzeichnungen vom Jahre 1299," *Oriens Christianus*, N.S., 1 (1911), pp. 249–71, without reproductions. See H. Buchthal and O. Kurz, *A Hand List of Illuminated Oriental Christian Manuscripts* (London, 1942), p. 25, No. 73.

33 Michel and Peeters, *Evangiles apocryphes*, II, Introduction and pp. 1 ff.

34 This last opinion, which I consider unwarranted, was propounded by Baumstark (see n. 32).

35 To cite the most important of them: Parisinus gr. 74, Vaticanus gr. 1156 (11th century), Florence, Laurent. Plut. VI.23 (12th century).

36 See below, passim, and P. A. Underwood's discussion in Vol. 1 of this work, pp. 87 n., 94, 94 n., 95–96.

37 But see above, n. 29.

38 See above, "Iconography of the Cycle of the Life of the Virgin," pp. 187–88.

39 For Venice, see Bettini, *Mosaici di San Marco*, PL. XLV. It is by mistake that the Dream follows the Trial by Water, instead of preceding it, at Ohrid and in San Marco (where it is followed by the Journey: there was confusion with the second

adaptation of manuscript miniatures to mural decoration, although the scene is strangely absent from the cycle of images in the Homilies of the Monk James.[40] But Joseph's dream is also narrated by Matthew (1:20–23), so that, if the artist has in mind the account in the canonical Gospels, and not that in the Apocrypha, the theme is found in a different context, though with the same meaning and the same iconography.[41] It still always follows Joseph's discovery of Mary's condition but is not followed by the scene of the Trial: it precedes the scene of the Journey to Bethlehem, or even that of the Nativity, as in the Sinai icon (Fig. 40).[42]

It is in this way that the Kariye Djami artist appears to have conceived Joseph's Dream, for he has even accompanied the scene with the actual text of the Evangelist (Matt. 1:20). Joseph lies on his couch, his head supported by his right hand, while the little angel comes flying down from the sky and addresses him (PL. 153). The iconography is traditional, though in this scene the angel often appears standing. But Joseph's open eyes, which suggest a tormented wakefulness rather than sleep, are an unusual feature.[43]

The group of women standing before the walls of a city, behind a rise in the ground ([100].2), since it has no inscription besides the sigla MP ΘΥ designating the Virgin (PL. 153–154), raises a problem difficult to solve. It has been supposed to be a reference to the Trial by Water, Mary having been sent to the mountain after drinking the bitter waters.[44] This event is reported by the Protevangelium (16:2); in this narrative the episodes of the Trial come after Joseph's first dream. The two women, then, would be Mary's companions; the city would be Nazareth. So this hypothesis appears to be tenable. Yet, tempting as it is, certain elements raise difficulties. First of all,

---

Dream, which leads to the Flight into Egypt). At Pelendri, the Dream is suggested by a little angel speaking to Joseph in the scene of the Reproaches, before the Trial, an arrangement that respects the chronology of the narrative. At Mavrucan (8th century?) the Dream is also correctly placed, before the Trial, contrary to Jerphanion's assertion, *Cappadoce*, II, 213. The iconography of the fresco at Tokalı Kilisse 2 is markedly different: the little angel is flying above Joseph; the fresco follows the Trial and precedes the Journey. It seems that this erroneous placement was widespread. It is already found earlier on the throne of Maximian (Volbach, *Elfenbeinarbeiten*, No. 140, PL. 43, or *Frühchristliche Kunst*, PL. 230), then at Castelseprio (Bognetti et al., *Castelseprio*, PL. XC), doubtless because the two scenes of the Dream and the Journey were connected in the illustration of the Gospels.

40 The illustrator of the *Homilies*, who devotes five miniatures to Joseph's return, his doubts, etc. (see above, "Iconography of the Cycle of the Life of the Virgin," esp. n. 152), devotes no fewer than eight to the episodes of the Trial, from the visit of the scribe Annas down to Mary and Joseph leaving the temple justified, but omits the dream; C. Stornajolo, *Miniature delle omilie di Giacomo monaco (Cod. Vatic. gr. 1162) e dell'evangeliario greco urbinate (Cod. Vatic. gr. 2)* (Rome, 1910), PL. 75–82; H. Omont, *Miniatures des homélies sur la Vierge du moine Jacques (MS. grec 1208 de Paris)* (Bulletin de la Société Française de Reproductions de Manuscrits à Peintures, 11 *Album;* Paris, 1927), PL. XXVII,2–XXX,1. It should be remarked that this plentiful illustration is not founded on James's text, which ends, so far as these events are concerned, with a reference to Mary's return to her house after her visit to Elizabeth (*PG*, 127, col. 693 ff.; the author cites Luke 1:56).

41 Paris. gr. 74, fol. 3 (Paris, Bibliothèque Nationale, Départment des Manuscrits, *Evangiles avec peintures byzantines du XIᵉ siècle* [Paris, n.d.], I, PL. 4) (Fig. 29); Florence, Laurent. Plut. VI.23, fol. 5v (G. Millet, neg. Hautes Etudes, Paris, C 375); Mount Athos, Dionysiou 587, fol. 128 (Index of Christian Art, Princeton University) are among the earliest documents that can be cited (11th–12th century). Joseph's Dream is found later, for example in the Gospel Book of John Alexander, British

Museum Add. 39627, fol. 8v (B. D. Filov, *Les miniatures de l'Evangile du roi Jean Alexandre à Londres* [Sofia, 1934], PL. 6, No. 9), whose illustrator closely followed Paris. gr. 74. It is also found in oriental manuscripts—an Armenian Gospel Book in the Walters Art Gallery at Baltimore, W. 539 (dated 1262), fol. 17 (Index of Christian Art, Princeton University), and two Syriac Lectionaries, one in the Vatican Library, syr. 559, of 1220, the other in the British Museum, Add. 7170, of 1216–20 (G. de Jerphanion, *Les miniatures du manuscrit syriaque no. 559 de la Bibliothèque Vaticane* [Codices e Vaticanis Selecti, XXV; Vatican City, 1940], PL. III,6, and H. Buchthal, "The Painting of the Syrian Jacobites in Its Relation to Byzantine and Islamic Art," *Syria*, 20 [1939], pp. 136–50, PL. XXIV,2).

42 The dream does not refer to the Flight into Egypt, for the angel says to Joseph: μὴ φοβοῦ παραλαβεῖν Μαρίαν τὴν γυναῖκά σου (Matt. 1:20).

43 The angel is standing in all the examples cited, with the exception of the Tokalı Kilisse 2 fresco and the two Syriac manuscripts cited above (in which it is possible, but not certain, that Joseph has his eyes open).

44 Underwood, Vol. 1 of this work, p. 87. The hypothesis of the Visitation, which has been proposed by F. Šmit, Kaxriè-Džami (=*Izvestija Russkogo Arxeologičeskogo Instituta v Konstantinople*, 11), I (Sofia, 1906), p. 75, seems to be untenable for reasons of iconography (Mary is accompanied by *two* women) and of placement. The motif of Mary on the mountain is not without analogies to the representations of the Virgin praying on Golgotha at the moment of the announcement of her death, the theme that opens the cycle of the Dormition. On some post–Byzantine icons the episodes of the Infancy of the Virgin are connected with those of the Dormition by certain scenes that may vary (see above, my "Iconography of the Cycle of the Life of the Virgin," n. 165). The Trial by Water, in the Russian icon reproduced by V. T. Georgievskij, *Freski Ferapontova Monastyrja* (St. Petersburg, 1911), PL. XXXXIV, is followed by Mary's Prayer on Golgotha (the angel is not represented though the rainbow remains, because the Annunciation is represented separately). The subject cannot be Mary sent to the mountain after the Trial. If the image in the Kariye Djami really represents this theme, it remains unique.

the scene would be a *hapax*—even in the Homilies of the Monk James, where the cycle of the Trial is very extensive, it is not represented.[45] Secondly—and I consider this the principal argument—the artist seems to have conceived this image not as an independent scene but as a motif connected with the Dream, since he gave it no inscription and put it in close relation with the figures of the reclining Joseph and the flying angel: the silhouettes of the women constitute the third side of a triangle the rest of which is formed by the other two figures.

I should therefore be tempted to see in the scene rather Mary's appearance to Joseph during his dream, though I am not unaware that such a hypothesis also raises difficulties. This theme goes back to Early Christian iconography. On a sarcophagus at Arles, Joseph sits sleeping, with his head in his hands; the angel appears behind him, pointing to the Virgin, who follows.[46] The Werden casket, whose date is unfortunately not established but whose iconography in any case appears certainly to be Early Christian,[47] presents a series of scenes that are especially interesting: the Annunciation at the Well, Joseph's Dream (Joseph is half reclining; the angel, standing beside him, is followed by Mary), probably the Visitation (out of order), then, beyond a church, Mary led to the temple for the Trial by Water (Fig. 30).[48] The Virgin was often depicted in Western representations of Joseph's Dream, during the Middle Ages and down to the sixteenth century.[49] If this feature is more unusual in Byzantium, it occurs nevertheless, though in a less clear form. In the Mavrucan fresco, the figure standing beside Joseph's couch and balancing that of the angel can only be the Virgin.[50] In Parisinus gr. 74, of the eleventh century (Fig. 29), as in the London Gospel Book of John Alexander (1356), which stems from the same tradition, Mary lies on a couch that seems to be the mirror image of Joseph's, the two sleepers on their couches being perfectly symmetrical.[51] Undoubtedly the artist would not have introduced Mary into the scene—even though she is supposed also to be sleeping, since it is night—if he had not thought of her as present in dream to Joseph's mind.

The fact that in the Kariye mosaic Mary is accompanied by two women is difficult to account for; even more so is her pointing gesture. Is it possible that she is pointing out the city of Bethlehem, whither they must go, as the result of a confusion with Joseph's second dream, which concerns the departure for Egypt? This is not unlikely, though it is not proved. As for the Virgin's two companions, they may be simply a genre motif, but it is also possible that they refer to some fact that escapes us. In a general way the scene of Joseph Dreaming, combined with that of the group before the city, is reminiscent of the images on the Werden casket, which include the figures of the sleeping Joseph, the angel, Mary, and three women (of whom one is certainly Mary and the two others are probably Elizabeth and a maidservant), then a building that suggests a church. It would, however, be hazardous to draw an elaborate parallel between two works so different in style and so far apart in date, when it is impossible to suggest any intermediate stages.

---

45 The miniaturist showed Mary drinking from a cup handed to her by the high priest, then leaving accompanied by a personage who may be a temple scribe (and not by women); next, the same personage brings Mary into Elizabeth's house, where the two women are seen conversing. Mary's short stay on the mountain is not depicted, nor is Joseph's (Stornajolo, *Omilie*, PL. 80, 81; Omont, *Homélies*, PL. XXIX,2, 3). A scene similar to the one in the Kariye Djami appears later at Kalenić, but it is practically a copy of the mosaic, though Mary's second companion, who is barely distinguishable, was not reproduced (Fig. 31 *a*).

46 Wilpert, *Sarcofagi*, I, PL. XXI, and III, pp. vii–viii.

47 Volbach, *Elfenbeinarbeiten*, No. 118, PL. 36, dates it in the 5th century, but J. Beckwith, "The Werden Casket Reconsidered," *ArtB*, 40 (1958), pp. 1–11, considers it to be a Carolingian copy, for essentially stylistic reasons.

48 The first and the last of these scenes also appear on the Milan diptych (Beckwith, "Werden Casket," Fig. 2, or Volbach, *Elfenbeinarbeiten*, No. 119, PL. 37). The last scene has sometimes been interpreted (wrongly, I believe) as a Presentation of the Virgin in the Temple.

49 Cf. Luini's fresco in the Brera, Milan; L. Beltrami, *Luini, 1512–1532, Materiale di studio* (Milan, 1911), fig. on p. 128.

50 It is possible in the very badly damaged painting to distinguish an angel beside Joseph and, at the left, another personage, whom Jerphanion was unable to identify; see Jerphanion, *Cappadoce*, II, p. 213.

51 Filov, *Evangile du roi Jean Alexandre*, PL. 6, No. 9.

In our mosaicist's model, the town could belong to the following scene of the Journey (cf. Fig. 32 and n. 60). Considering the silence of both the inscriptions and the texts, as well as the absence of similar representations that might be conclusive, we must admit that it is hardly possible to identify the scene with certainty. The fresco at Kalenić, which in a general way reproduces the Kariye Djami composition (Fig. 31 *a*), is of no help to us.

The next image, on the contrary, raises scarcely any problems. It is the Journey to Bethlehem, and is accompanied by a long inscription, this time drawn from Luke, Ch. 2:4 ([100].3) (PL. 155). The iconography is traditional: Mary, seated on the ass, turns toward Joseph, who follows her, while one of Joseph's sons precedes them. The theme is, nevertheless, infrequent in the Palaeologan period, for it had a competitor in that of the Flight into Egypt, the iconography of which is practically the same, differing only in the presence of the infant. In the Balkans it is found principally at Curtea-de-Argeş and at Kalenić (Fig. 31 *b*),[52] but such representations testify rather to the influence of the Kariye Djami decoration upon later monuments than to the frequency of the theme itself. The various elements composing the theme are found both in manuscript miniatures illustrating the text of Luke and in the apocryphal cycles of Cappadocia. These elements, in fact, go back to the apocryphal narrative, "And . . . [Joseph] saddled the she-ass, and set . . . [Mary] upon it, and his son led it and Joseph followed after" (Protevangelium 17:2); the Evangelist says nothing of the ass. The text is not certain, however, for some of the earliest of the Protevangelium manuscripts mention another of his sons in place of Joseph;[53] further on in the text, Joseph turns back toward Mary and converses with her. Illustrations preserving this last feature are extremely rare; almost nothing can be cited but the mosaic in San Marco, Venice, which may reproduce a miniature accompanying the apocryphal narrative.[54]

The theme was frequently represented in the pre-iconoclastic period, with ivories constituting the principal documentation that has come down to us. On them it appears with considerable variation. Joseph supports the pregnant Mary in especially realistic fashion on the panel of Maximian's throne;[55] the ass is led by an angel, as in other contemporary documents. On a plaque in Paris the angel, armed with a cross, leads the ass, but Joseph follows and Mary turns toward him, their gestures indicating a conversation.[56] The presence of the ass, so common a riding animal in the East, does not perhaps constitute a direct reference to the apocryphal narrative, but the conversation between Mary and Joseph is certainly inspired by it. Joseph's son may have replaced the angel when it became a matter of illustrating the narrative more faithfully, and it seemed natural to put him in front, guiding the animal. Sometimes, too, Joseph's sons are more numerous, especially in certain Armenian documents.[57] Toward the eighth century, in any case,

52 O. Tafrali, *Monuments byzantins de Curtéa de Arges* (Paris, 1931), PL. LXXXIII,1; V. R. Petković and Z. Tatić, *Manastir Kalenić* (Vršac, 1926), Fig. 43, p. 52. Unlike the preceding themes, this one never appears in the cycle of the Virgin.

53 Papyrus Bodmer 5 gives the following version: "And his son led, and Samuel followed." This Samuel is doubtless another of Joseph's sons; E. de Strycker, *La forme la plus ancienne du Protévangile de Jacques: Recherches sur le Papyrus Bodmer 5* (Subsidia Hagiographica, 33; Brussels, 1961), p. 143, nn. 7, 8. The manuscript tradition represented by Tischendorf's text gives the place of the follower to Joseph, and it is this tradition that influenced the iconography.

54 From this point on we unfortunately lack the valuable testimony of the Homilies of the Monk James. It is not impossible that, in certain manuscripts, the episode was illustrated by two images, one showing Joseph behind and then, in the episode of the conversation, in front of the ass. The San Marco mosaic is not very satisfying, for the Virgin turns toward Joseph's son: this suggests a confusion, doubtless with the Flight into Egypt (Bettini, *Mosaici di San Marco*, PL. XLV).

55 Volbach, *Elfenbeinarbeiten*, PL. 43, No. 140 (upper right: Mary is visibly pregnant); see also the Lupicin diptych in the Louvre, ibid., PL. 47, No. 145.

56 Ivory from the former Stroganoff collection; ibid., PL. 45, No. 128.

57 The sons number two on the cover of the Etschmiadzin Gospel Book (ibid., PL. 44, No. 142). In the miniature in an Armenian manuscript of the 13th century, the Baltimore W. 539 already cited (fol. 415), three sons are grouped behind Joseph, while Mary, seated on the ass, leads the way.

the traditional iconography was fixed, at Castelseprio as on the reliquary cross in the Vatican.[58] The most homogeneous representations are those in the rock-cut churches of Cappadocia, which always show one of Joseph's sons, designated James in the inscriptions and appearing as a young lad dressed in a short tunic and holding the halter in one hand, a stick bearing a bundle over his shoulder. Mary is seated full face on the white ass, turned toward Joseph, with whom she converses, both of them gesturing with their hands (Fig. 33).[59] Frequently the youth turns slightly toward the Virgin. One of the very few strictly Byzantine examples is supplied by Paris. gr. 74, fol. 108 (Fig. 32), accompanying the text of Luke. It has two variant features: Mary looks forward—hence there is no conversation with Joseph; and the scene is flanked by two representations of cities, an allusion to the text of the Evangelist, who names Nazareth and Bethlehem.[60] Such representations may have influenced our composition, in which a single city is represented, behind the hill.

It seems clear that the Kariye Djami artist took his model from an apocryphal cycle, akin to those found in Cappadocia, which might very well have existed in a manuscript of the Protevangelium to which he had access. However, he made certain changes in it, in accordance with the general refinement of the decoration and with the restraint which he often exhibits. These qualities are perceptible in the great modesty of Mary's attitude—perhaps her attitude even expresses the moment when she asks to dismount from the ass because, she says, "that which is within me presseth me, to come forth" (Protevangelium 17:3)—and the quietness of Joseph's gestures; the ass walks without being led, white and gentle; the son who leads the way is not the young lad dear to the Cappadocian painters but one of the older sons, brown-bearded, doubtless considered more suitable than a boy for such a mission (PL. 156–158).[61] The scene, set as it is against the background of a mountain with a rocky summit, in a pyramidal composition, has a grace and purity that are seldom attained.

The Enrollment for Taxation [101], which follows in the first lunette of the eastern wall, illustrates the purpose of the journey to Bethlehem, as is shown by the inscription, which continues the quotation from Luke (2:4–5) (PL. 159). No text describes the enrollment itself, though it is everywhere given as the reason for Joseph's undertaking the journey (Prot. 17:1). And indeed, in the Protevangelium (18:1) the birth of Christ interrupts the journey before the arrival at Bethlehem, and there is no mention of any enrollment after that. The same is true of the other apocryphal narratives.[62] The Evangelist allows the travelers to reach Bethlehem and tells us that Mary gave birth "while they were there" (2:6), which leads one to think that the enrollment may have taken place upon their arrival. Hence the theme—which in any case is extremely infrequent—never appears in an apocryphal context but always as an illustration for Luke.

58 *DACL*, III,2 (1914), Fig. 3416; Bognetti et al., *Castelseprio*, PL. XLVI (of the young lad walking toward the right nothing remains but a bare leg and a part of the tunic; Joseph leans on a stick).

59 Jerphanion cites numerous examples; see *Cappadoce*, PL. 65,1 and 2 (Tokalı Kilisse 1); 72,1 (Tokalı Kilisse 2); 36 a (St. Eustathius); 103,4 (Karanlık Kilisse); 147,1 (St. Theodore); 189,1 (St. Barbara, Soğanlı).

60 The same scene is repeated in British Museum, Add. 39627, fol. 141v; Filov, *Evangile du roi Jean Alexandre*, PL. 69, No. 184.

61 If the Curtea-de-Argeş fresco is very like the mosaic, the same is not true of the fresco at Kalenić (see above, n. 52), in which the son is a young lad in a shepherd's tunic and cap, turning toward the Virgin; he holds the ass by the bridle and leans on a long staff, a motif that recurs in the case of Joseph (it will be remembered that it appeared, at least for the latter, at Castelseprio). In the miniature in Paris. gr. 74 there is no sign of the staff and the son wears a long tunic; but he turns toward Mary in the same way, and she does not look at Joseph. Such a scene tends to substantiate the hypothesis put forward in n. 54.

62 In particular the Latin Pseudo-Matthew (13:1); the compiler of this text attributes the enrollment to the governor of Syria, Cyrinus (sic), following Luke 2:2. The theme never appears in apocryphal representations in the West either, not even in the *Wernherlied von der Magd*, which is so profusely illustrated.

It is as such that it is found in eleventh-century miniatures. In the one in Mount Athos, Dionysiou 587 (Fig. 34), only Joseph and two of his sons, together with another person at the opposite side of the composition, are dealing with the two scribes surrounding the governor, who is solemnly enthroned in the center and represented full face. The image in the Lectionary Vaticanus gr. 1156, which precedes the episodes of the Nativity, exhibits an iconography closer to that of the Kariye Djami, although in a form that is still very simple (Fig. 35).[63] The governor, wearing a chlamys and a crown, sits on a curule chair in front of the lofty entrance to a building, his feet resting on a small dais, one hand extended as if to greet the new arrivals. These are Joseph and Mary. They are conducted into the governor's presence by a scribe, who, turned toward him, writes their names on a long parchment scroll. The personage of the governor is copied from that of Herod ordering the massacre in the same manuscript.[64] The theme is sometimes reproduced in Latin manuscripts, where it appears as an adaptation of the Byzantine composition.[65]

If the Kariye Djami artist chose to represent a scene so little known and of such little use to the development of the narrative, it is undoubtedly because he found it suitable material for exercising his taste for display. The composition, which is magnificent, occupies the entire surface of the lunette; its beauty, its unusual character are reminiscent of the Virgin Receiving the Skein of Purple Wool, in the cycle of the Virgin [94]. The iconographic elements go back to earlier images in manuscripts, but two guards in splendid cuirasses have been added to the personages of the governor and the scribe, and behind Mary and Joseph—a touch taken from the Apocrypha—stand Joseph's four sons (at least we may suppose that it is they). Herod has again supplied the model for the figure of Cyrenius (compare PL. 175 and 177), but the artist has represented the governor in his civil function: he holds a scroll, not a sword; his chlamys bears no ornamental tablion; in addition, the royal crown has been replaced by one of the tall light hats affected by Byzantine dignitaries. Joseph, who walks behind Mary, makes the gesture of presenting her. Her exaggerated stature and the position she occupies give to Mary an importance that is entirely symbolic, for obviously in a matter of enrollment it is the head of the family who speaks for it. This was understood by the miniaturist of Dionysiou 587. It is only to be expected that in this art the realism of a situation should have yielded to the expression of a moral heirarchy.

This feature, which is peculiar to our mosaic, will be found later in the churches of Curtea-de-Argeş and Kalenić, two monuments whose decoration, so far as the cycle of Christ is concerned, is greatly influenced by that of the Kariye Djami. The Curtea painter was the most faithful in following the iconography of the mosaic, though he eliminated two of Joseph's sons and emphasized the condition of the Virgin, whose pregnancy is obvious (Fig. 36). But, with too small an area at his disposal, he produced only a mediocre picture. The Kalenić painter, on the contrary, sensitively rendered the succession of spaces and figures (in this respect he had the happy idea of eliminating the old guard).[66] Yet the Kalenić fresco does not produce the striking effect of the Kariye Djami mosaic. In his concern for realism the painter reduced the figures of Cyrenius and Mary to normal proportions. The mosaicist, for his part, had deliberately used two tall figures

63 The theme of the miniature in Dionysiou 587 is, strangely enough, the only one chosen to illustrate the entire passage.

64 Fol. 279, photo Index of Christian Art, Princeton University.

65 In Chorale VIII in the Biblioteca Civica at Gubbio, 13th century, fol. 29v, Bollettino d'arte, 22 (1928-29), Fig. 24, p. 544; in MS 410 at Corpus Christi College, Oxford, 14th century, Meditationes of the Pseudo-Bonaventura, unnumbered folio,

photo Index of Christian Art, Princeton University. Millet, Recherches, p. 128, interprets—rightly no doubt—an obscure scene preceding the Nativity in Laurent. Plut. VI.23 as an Enrollment (Fig. 78).

66 Petković and Tatić, Kalenić, Fig. 44, p. 53 (Joseph's sons, to the right of the composition, are not clearly distinguishable). Both painters filled the background with a velum and omitted the motif of the tree, a favorite with our mosaicist.

not only to indicate their importance but also to hinge his composition upon two strong accents, emphasized even more by their architectural frames. It is his knowledge of composition and his feeling for plastic values that led him to produce, in the scene of the Enrollment, the most impressive, if not the most beautiful, scene in the cycle of Christ.

The Nativity [102] is developed in a large composition in the next lunette (PL. 166). The impression of airy space is all the stronger because the artist did not include the Magi—indispensable in the synthetic compositions of the period but unnecessary here because several of the following scenes are devoted to them. Even so, our composition is already the result of adding a number of motifs to the basic nucleus, which consists of the newly delivered mother, the Child in the manger, the animals, the star, and Joseph. These motifs are the cave, the annunciation to the shepherds and their flocks, the midwives and the bathing of the Child, the adoration of the angels. Demanded by the texts, whether canonical or apocryphal, and by certain marginal iconographic traditions, all these elements—which are already found together, though in accordance with a simpler formula, in the miniature in the Menologion of Basil II (Fig. 38)—took a certain time to find a definitive place in figured representations.

What we have called the "basic nucleus" naturally derives from the earliest and most constant tradition. At the Kariye Djami it is iconographically very close to the images on the Palestinian phials (sixth century), except for two details: the form of the manger and the setting; in our mosaic the setting is the cave, in the phials it is an architectural ensemble suggesting the church at Bethlehem—this latter feature being peculiar to Palestinian imagery.[67] The manger is traditionally a quadrangular construction of brick or stone, which is already found on ivories of the sixth century.[68] In the Palaeologan period the manger tends to become decorated, especially in Macedonian painting. Usually we find a slight motif in relief, as in the mosaic in the Holy Apostles at Salonika (Fig. 41). At the Kariye Djami the manger remains classically simple (PL. 170). The ass and the ox appear from the earliest representations of the Nativity, on sarcophagi of the fourth century.[69] The Protevangelium, the only text to be taken into consideration at this period aside from the canonical Gospels, speaks of "a cave" and "a manger of oxen," whereas Luke mentions only "a manger in a stable."[70] The ass may be the one that appears in the Journey. The cave, which is not indicated on the phials, is suggested on ivories from as early as the fifth-sixth century.[71] In monumental painting it is found clearly indicated at Rome in the eighth century, under Byzantine influence.[72] The theme of the cave, already known to Justin in the second

67 Grabar, *Ampoules*, PL. VII and LII and pp. 52–53.

68 Volbach, *Elfenbeinarbeiten*, Nos. 119, PL. 37, and 127, PL. 39 (the manger is somewhat reminiscent of the Palestinian *soros*). One of its faces may be pierced by an opening which also, it seems, suggests the sanctuary at Bethlehem; this feature is also found even later, for example in the miniature in Vaticanus Urbinas gr. 2, fol. 20v, of the 12th century (Stornajolo, *Omilie*, PL. 84). On some very early ivories, and on sarcophagi of the 4th or 5th centuries, the manger is either a little wall with straw on it or a manger on legs, and the Child's head is raised; see E. Baldwin Smith's remarks, *Early Christian Iconography and a School of Ivory Carvers in Provence* (Princeton, 1918), p. 15.

69 Often in connection with the stable; see Wilpert, *Sarcofagi*, for example, I, PL. XXX, and II, PL. CCI,5.

70 Protevangelium 21:3 and 22:2 (nothing different appears in the variants). The Pseudo-Matthew distinctly refers to the worshipping ox and ass (14). But this narrative as we know it certainly did not exist at the period. Baldwin Smith's allegations, *Early Christian Iconography*, pp. 18 ff., are to be regarded with

suspicion, as is his system of the successive introduction of the various motifs. The animals always appear, except in the miniature in the Rabbula Gospels, fol. 4 b, where their absence may be explained by lack of space; Cecchelli et al., *The Rabbula Gospels*, fol. 4 b and p. 54. The words of Isaiah, "The ox knoweth his owner, and the ass his master's crib" (1:3), which are cited in the Pseudo-Matthew, could be applied to the Nativity of Christ; see also the article "Âne," in *DACL*. Such an assimilation is already found in Homily XXXVIII—apocryphal but early—of Gregory of Nazianz, *PG*, 36, col. 332.

71 On the Werden pyxis and on the panel of the throne of Maximian; Volbach, *Elfenbeinarbeiten*, No. 169, PL. 54 and No. 140, PL. 43.

72 In the representations of the period of John VII in Santa Maria Antiqua (Grüneisen, *Sainte-Marie-Antique*, PL. IC.XXI and Fig. 83, p. 109); a little later the rocky landscape is highly developed at Castelseprio (Bognetti et al., *Castelseprio*, PL. XLVIII and LI). The later Western tradition keeps the motif of the stable (the Pseudo-Matthew combines the two motifs).

century, did not necessarily come from the Apocrypha, for in these countries caves often serve as stables.[73] Thus we may say that the primitive elements, including the figures of Mary and Joseph as well, essentially illustrate the text of Luke, with a slight influence from the apocryphal tradition.

The figure of the newly delivered Mary is prominently placed in the center of our image (PL. 167). She is reclining, as already on the phials and, in general, in pre-iconoclastic representations from the sixth century onward or, later, in representations of an orientalizing nature. In the reliefs on sarcophagi and even on certain early ivories, on the contrary, Mary is seated, in imitation of the antique nativities (Fig. 37).[74] A return to this position is observable in post-iconoclastic Byzantine art: in the miniature in the Menologion of Basil II as in the mosaic at Hosios Loukas in Phocis (Figs. 38, 39), or as late as the middle of the twelfth century, at Pskov,[75] the mother sits on the rock. In the miniature in Vaticanus Urbinas gr. 2 (of 1122),[76] although she is on a pallet she is clearly sitting too. The artists thus rendered the concept of the Virgin who gave birth without pain.[77] However, even within the Constantinopolitan tradition, several schemes can coexist. At Daphni the Virgin's legs are extended, and she turns away from the manger, looking at the viewer.[78] In some images the Virgin holds out her hands toward the Child and even touches him. This gesture goes back to an Adoration of the Magi, as is clearly apparent in the Cappella Palatina at Palermo, where the Virgin contemplates the approaching Magi.[79] In the Palaeologan period Mary was traditionally placed on her pallet, with her legs slightly bent. But her attitude can vary considerably. Completely reclining at Sopoćani and Arilje (second half of the thirteenth century), she sits up in certain Macedonian compositions of the fourteenth century and sometimes, as at Studenica, touches or fondles her Child, who is always lying in the manger.[80] She may also turn away and look either at the Magi or at the bath. The newly delivered mother and the Child in the manger traditionally stand out against the dark background of the cave. However, the silhouette of the Virgin sometimes extends beyond this frame, when she is represented horizontally, as at Arilje and Sopoćani.[81] This is also the case in the mosaic in the Holy Apostles, Salonika (Fig. 41), and in the Kariye mosaic: the figure of the Virgin, emphasized by the outline of the pallet as by a border, is placed in front of the cave; only the manger and the animals are inside it. This position of the Virgin, more horizontal than usual, gives her greater importance. The two mosaics at Salonika and Constantinople show another common feature, which, however, is not rare: the Virgin is looking at the bathing of the Child.

Joseph sits in somber isolation on a little hill in the foreground (PL. 171). It is possible, however, that he is watching the bathing, his gaze and the Virgin's, therefore, converging on the Child, a fairly frequent theme at the period with which we are concerned.[82] In his attitude and his appearance, however, Joseph likewise derives from an iconography that goes back to the

---

73 For Justin, see *Dial. cum Tryph.*, 78 (*PG*, 6, col. 660); cf. de Strycker's remarks, *Protévangile*, pp. 416-17, and those of Leclerq in article "Âne," *DACL*, col. 2055.

74 Volbach, *Elfenbeinarbeiten*, Nos. 118, PL. 36, and 119, PL. 37; Wilpert, *Sarcofagi*, passim. In one instance the Virgin is placed on her couch with the child in an Adoration of the Magi, but this is exceptional in this art (Wilpert, II, PL. CCIV,2).

75 N. V. Pokrovskij, *Očerki pamjatnikov xrestianskogo iskusstva i ikonografii*, 3d ed. (St. Petersburg, 1910), Fig. 172, p. 259.

76 Stornajolo, *Omilie*, PL. 84.

77 For Mary's attitude in the Nativity of Christ, see Millet, *Recherches*, pp. 99 ff.; see also below, n. 104.

78 G. Millet, *Le monastère de Daphni: Histoire, architecture, mosaïques* (Paris, 1899), PL. XII.

79 Demus, *Norman Sicily*, PL. 17, and below, p. 222 and n. 168.

80 V. R. Petković, *La peinture serbe du Moyen Âge*, II (Belgrade, 1934), PL. XIX and XXXII; I (1930), PL. 36 *d*. At Studenica, Mary is turned toward the Magi; however, the relation between the two motifs does not seem to be very close.

81 Cf. also Millet, *Mistra*, PL. 95,8 (Brontochion), and 118,1 (Peribleptos). It is probably for this formal reason that Mary's bust is raised or that her pallet, even when she is reclining at full length, is represented on the bias, not horizontally (cf., among others, the fresco at Peć; Petković, *La peinture serbe*, I, PL. 71). The two formulas can coexist: this is the case in Mount Athos, Iviron 5, fol. 6 and 17 (13th century).

82 See, for example, the miniatures in Paris. gr. 54, fol. 13v, and in Paris. gr. 543, fol. 116v (Millet, *Recherches*, Figs. 42 and 43).

phials [83] and that changed little in the course of the centuries. But the place he occupies in the scene can vary considerably. Joseph is introduced into the Nativity without having any real share in it: the father has only a supernumerary role in the scene, and this is no doubt the correct explanation for the minor part that he plays, although his presence is obligatory. He is usually shown in an attitude of anxious concern, seated with his head resting on his hand. In the earlier images he is turned inward and faces Mary, and the manger is placed between them.[84] Later he often turns away from the manger; he may also raise his head toward the Virgin or toward the Child in the bath.[85] Why this somber appearance when the event should be a source of joy? Doubtless the participants are more struck by its solemn gravity and by a sort of sacred awe. Doubtless Joseph is overwhelmed by events that are beyond him. The artists, especially in the Palaeologan period, nevertheless sought to make use of this isolated figure. They tried to put Joseph into relation either with the bathing, which he approaches and contemplates, or with the shepherds—in which case he appears to be conversing with one of them. This last procedure, which is found as early as the end of the thirteenth century at Arilje, was frequently employed in Macedonian painting. It appears, for example, in the mosaic in the Holy Apostles at Salonika, which in this respect differs sharply from the Kariye mosaic.[86] The Kariye Djami mosaicist, by keeping Joseph in isolation, resolutely withstood the temptation to introduce any such picturesqueness.

The shepherds in our mosaic are three in number, as is traditional (PL. 172), but their attitude is rather different from that which was customary at the period and which was the result of a long evolution. The shepherds were represented from the sixth century onward. They are found on phials, as an element in a symbolic composition in which Mary is solemnly enthroned at the center with the Child, the Magi are at the left, and the shepherds at the right (Fig. 42):[87] the composition is, in fact, a sort of simultaneous double Adoration, the elements of which, however, derive from an Annunciation by the angel.[88] Beginning at this time there are more specific representations of the Annunciation to the Shepherds, based on a narrative formula [89] which we find again in the complex compositions of the eighth century, such as in the mosaics of John VII at Rome, and Castelseprio.[90] The shepherds and their flocks constitute a picturesque motif of a decidedly Hellenistic cast. They are even more intimately incorporated into the Nativity in post-iconoclastic representations, where the number of three, representing the three ages, is

83 Grabar, *Ampoules*, PL. VII. On the earlier sarcophagi, Joseph appears standing, clad in a short tunic and armed with a staff; Wilpert, *Sarcofagi*, I, PL. XXX; II, PL. CCI,5. Wilpert has in most cases interpreted Joseph as a shepherd and argued from this to prove the existence of the Adoration of the Shepherds at a very early date; but Joseph is represented in the same fashion in the scene of Joseph's Dream on a sarcophagus at Arles (I, PL. XX,1), in the Codex Purpureus at Munich (Clm. 23631, Cim. 2, fol. 24), and on the ivories cited in n. 74, where, however, he is seated. I do not believe that the Adoration of the Shepherds exists in Byzantine art, with such extremely rare exceptions as the miniature in the Armenian MS of the 13th century, Baltimore W. 539, fol. 208v (photo Index of Christian Art, Princeton University).

84 See the ivory at Milan, of the 5th century (Volbach, *Elfenbeinarbeiten*, No. 119, PL. 37), the textile in the Sancta Sanctorum (Grüneisen, *Sainte-Marie-Antique*, Fig. 114, p. 155), the Syriac Gospels in the British Museum, Add. 7169, of the 12th century (Millet, *Recherches*, Fig. 107). This scheme recurs, with the ordinary type, in the developed but rather sketchy cycle in Laurent. Plut. VI.23 (ibid., Fig. 79).

85 Joseph is always markedly turned away in Cappadocia, but too much must not be made of these differences, at least in the Palaeologan period. In the two miniatures in Iviron 5 already cited (n. 81), Joseph is seated facing outward, in a prone position,

on fol. 17 but turns to look at the scene on fol. 6. The miniature on fol. 6 is in general more archaic in type than the other.

86 For Arilje, see Petković, *La peinture serbe*, II, PL. XXXII: while one shepherd addresses Joseph at the left, the flute-player is seated to the right of the bath; higher up, a single shepherd receives the angel's annunciation. The personage of Joseph had already been used earlier to suggest either the following scene of the dream; the preliminary to the Flight into Egypt, as at Pskov (see n. 75); or, as on the Sinai icon (our Fig. 40), the first dream.

87 Grabar, *Ampoules*, PL. I, II, IV, VIII, etc., and pp. 53–54.

88 See, in particular, phial No. 1, reproduced in our Fig. 42, where the little angels dive down from either side toward the two groups and a large and lively flock is in motion at the bottom of the composition; the shepherd on the right appears to be seated.

89 See the description of the representation in St. Sergius at Gaza by Choricius (*Laud. Marciani*, I, §§53–54). On column B in San Marco, Venice, the angel addresses three gesturing shepherds (the flock was omitted); photos Böhm, Nos. 3234 and 3235, second register. A more specific Annunciation to the Shepherds is also found on an encolpion at Istanbul, likewise of the sixth century; H. Kehrer, *Die heiligen drei Könige in Literatur und Kunst*, II (Leipzig, 1909), Fig. 35, p. 51.

90 See above, n. 72.

traditional though not always adhered to.[91] The miniaturist of the Menologion of Basil II introduces only one shepherd, whereas the mosaicist of Hosios Loukas has increased the usual trio by a little seated flute-player, an idyllic motif that is especially frequent in scenes of eastern provenance,[92] but was not long preserved as an individual entity. The flute-player soon takes the place of one of the shepherds. Often he stands, leaning on his crook, beside his flock or sometimes facing Joseph and holding his instrument in his hand. In contrast, the two others form a compact group: the younger shepherd puts one arm reassuringly around the shoulders of the elder, clothed in a pelt, and points out the angel to him with the other arm; the theme is found at a very early date and without variation, especially in oriental works.[93]

The flock, on the other hand, becomes more dispersed and more numerous. Often, especially during the middle–Byzantine period, the animals are drinking at a stream.[94] The episode of the shepherds becomes again what it was at the outset, a genre scene. All these elements were assimilated into Palaeologan art, especially into Macedonian painting, and we find them in the mosaic in the Holy Apostles at Salonika (Fig. 41). The Kariye Djami mosaic is very different. The shepherds are grouped together, their animals lying peacefully at their feet. To be sure, the current motifs of the shepherd leaning on his staff, the flutist, and the old man in his pelt are represented, but in a different fashion. The youngest no longer plays his pipe; he simply lays his hand reassuringly on that of the old man seated beside him. Like the standing shepherd, he wears a short tunic and is bareheaded; these features give them both an unusually classical appearance. All three are listening with equal attention to the words of the angel, who, as usual, comes into view from behind the rocky hill in which the cave opens. These elements appear transformed both by a better rendition of the meaning of the scene and by the elegant restraint characteristic of the artist.

The bathing of the Child is an important element of the composition because of the place it occupies, its beauty, and the interest in it displayed by Mary and Joseph (PL. 169). It is a classic constituent of the theme of the Nativity and is found in all the post–iconoclastic representations with the exception of a few oriental compositions that follow an earlier tradition omitting the bath.[95] It is not until the beginning of the eighth century, in the mosaic of John VII at Rome, that this motif is found closely associated, apparently for the first time, with the Nativity of Christ. However, it is not impossible that it appeared earlier, in images of a cyclic nature. Thus in a developed ensemble of the Nativity on one of the silk fragments found at Akhmim, which may

91 In the well-developed cycles of certain 11th- and 12th-century manuscripts, the Annunciation to the Shepherds may form the subject of separate representations even when it is also incorporated into the Nativity itself (Paris. gr. 74, fol. 108 and 108v, *Evang. du XIe siècle*, II, PL. 96–97; and Laurent. Plut. VI.23 and Vat. gr. 1156, Millet, *Recherches*, Figs. 76–79). This practice goes back to early detailed cycles, of which Choricius' description may give us an idea; see Millet's remarks, pp. 125–26.

92 For this motif see Millet, *Recherches*, pp. 114 ff. and esp. pp. 131–32 and the figures. It is an old feature, habitual in the Cappadocian frescoes but also found in Laurent. Plut. VI.23 (Millet, Fig. 78). It exists earlier in Byzantine manuscripts, unconnected with the Nativity, in the charming bucolic scene of Taphou 14 (Jerusalem, Greek Patriarchate), fol. 33v (photo Library of Congress).

93 The earliest example is found in syr. 28 at Berlin (8th–9th century), fol. 9v (photo Index of Christian Art, Princeton University). In the Dêr es Suriân fresco (10th century), the shepherd seizes the old man's arm as he shows him the angel; H. G. Evelyn White, *The Monasteries of the Wâdi'n Natrûn*, Part III (Publications of the Metropolitan Museum of Art Egyptian Expedition, VIII; New York, 1933), PL. LXI; the reference is to the El Adra church. The group of two shepherds is standard in Cappadocia. It appears as early as the 12th century in a Byzantine miniature, that in Vat. Urbinas gr. 2 (Stornajolo, *Omilie*, PL. 84).

94 The dog, which was mentioned as being present with the flock in the paintings in St. Sergius at Gaza and which reappears at Castelseprio, is rarely represented during the post–iconoclastic period. It is seen in manuscript miniatures (Vat. gr. 1156, only in the scene of the Annunciation; Laurent. Plut. VI.23; Mount Athos, Rossikon 2); however, it reappears later in the frescoes in St. Paul, at Mount Athos (Millet, *Recherches*, Figs. 37, 76, 78, 81).

95 There is no bathing, for example, in the Syrian fresco at Dêr es Suriân or in the otherwise very complete composition at Iprari in Georgia (1096); Š. Ja. Amiranašvili, *Istorija gruzinskoj monumentalnoj živopisi*, I (Sachelgami, 1957), PL. 120. Nor is it represented in two oriental manuscripts of later date, Parisinus copt. 13 (Millet, *Recherches*, Fig. 80) and the Arabic Gospel of the Infancy in the Laurentian Library, Med. Pal. orient. 387 (Redin, *Miniatjury*, Fig. 1, p. 5). However, the bathing appears in other contemporary oriental works.

date from the sixth century,[96] we see Mary on her couch looking at the Child, who appears from the waist up in a chalice-shaped basin, with his arms extended. The iconography is unusual, for the scene does not represent the bath given by the midwives and the gesture of the open arms is symbolic, not realistic.[97] In the fresco at Mavrucan, which may date from the eighth century, the bathing, like the Annunciation to the Shepherds, is again the subject of a picture separate from that of the Nativity.[98]

We have here an element that owes nothing to the texts, either canonical or apocryphal, but derives from a marginal iconographic tradition. To be sure, its introduction into the composition was facilitated by the episode of the midwives in the Apocrypha and indeed the Cappadocian painters long inscribed the midwives' names, drawn from such narratives, beside the women engaged in washing the Child.[99] Moreover, it was necessary for Byzantine art to have reached the point of being able to increase the number of motifs in a scene already crowded by obligatory elements. We saw, in connection with the Birth of the Virgin, that the bathing was an essential feature of antique representations of nativities, on children's sarcophagi as well as in cycles of images illustrating the lives of gods and heroes (Figs. 14 and 37).[100] This motif, frequent in pagan representations of late antiquity, was very early introduced into imperial and Christian art,[101] at least for illustrations of the Old Testament.[102] If the same was not done for the Nativity of Christ, it is because it was not easy to incorporate the motif into compositions so simple and so dependent upon the texts as were those of the early times. The problem was different in respect to the birth of the Virgin and of other holy persons, for which the artists had merely to take over the antique iconography unchanged or only very slightly modified.[103] Then too, there may have been opposition in principle to representing Christ being bathed, since his birth had been without impurity as it had been without pain. At a certain moment, however, the wish to humanize the scene in order to make the idea of the Incarnation more real may well have influenced the incorporation of the bathing into the composition.[104] In any case, it is thenceforth a constant motif, similar to that

---

96 H. Peirce and R. Tyler, *L'art byzantin*, II (Paris, 1934), PL. 58 (upper right).

97 However, a parallel may be drawn between this scene and that of the birth of Dionysus on the printed veil in the Louvre; see our Fig. 14 (and above, "Iconography of the Cycle of the Life of the Virgin," p. 176). In particular, the Virgin's bed may be compared with Semele's, which is, however, more luxurious.

98 Jerphanion, *Cappadoce*, II, pp. 213–14 and PL. 173,2.

99 The name Salome appears at Rome, in the painting in the cemetery of St. Valentinus (article "Apocryphes," in *DACL*, col. 2564–65), and frequently in Cappadocia. The denomination ἡ μαῖα (in the form H or E MEA) is not specific: it is found on the Louvre veil for the birth of Dionysus (see Fig. 14), and at Kızıl Çukur for that of the Virgin (see above, "Cycle of the Life of the Virgin," n. 65), as well as at Castelseprio and in Cappadocia in the Nativity of Christ. Numerous 6th-century representations include the purely apocryphal episode of the withered hand of Salome, the woman who doubted the virginity of Mary (Protevangelium 20); Volbach, *Elfenbeinarbeiten*, No. 127, PL. 39, No. 140, PL. 43, etc. The motif is also found at Bawît (Baldwin Smith, *Early Christian Iconography*, Fig. 21, p. 27), and on column B of the ciborium in San Marco, Venice (photo Böhm, No. 3234). It reappears in the 8th century in Roman painting; Grüneisen, *Sainte-Marie-Antique*, PL. IC.XXI and Fig. 83, p. 109; PL. IC.LXVII. The motif is still perfectly preserved in an Ethiopian manuscript of 1400–1401, in the Pierpont Morgan Library; P. W. Skehan, "An Illuminated Gospel Book in Ethiopic," D. Miner, ed., *Studies in Art and Literature for Belle da Costa Greene* (Princeton, 1954), Fig. 269. It must go back to an ancient model. In Cappadocia a trace of it is found not in iconography but in an inscription; Jerphanion, *Cappadoce*, II, p. 31.

On the other hand, two works show the arrival of the two midwives guided by a figure that seems to be Joseph's son: the Sinai icon (Fig. 40) and the fresco in the Brontochion at Mistra (Millet, *Mistra*, PL. 95,8). The two women are clearly recognizable in the two figures who are bathing the Child on the icon. The image in the Brontochion thus appears as the product of an already long tradition of complex compositions centered around the Nativity, whose connections with the liturgy do not preclude the presence of apocryphal elements.

100 Cf. above, "Cycle of the Life of the Virgin," pp. 174–75 and nn. 65 and 68.

101 We know from the poet Claudian (*Carmina*, XXII.245–47) that a picture representing the Empress Maria, wife of Honorius, bearing a child included the motif of the bathing: he thought he could hear sounds coming from the picture, which were the laughter and wails of the child, whom flower-crowned nymphs were bathing in a golden basin (cited by A. Frolow, "Deux églises byzantines d'après les sermons peu connus de Léon VI le Sage," *REB*, 3 (1945), p. 80). This "golden basin" can be compared, at the period, with the one in the Nativity of Alexander in the mosaic at Beirut (cf. our Fig. 37).

102 In default of ancient documents, we have the testimony of the mosaics in the narthex of San Marco, Venice, which are medieval copies of the Early Christian Cotton Bible; Bettini, *Mosaici di San Marco*, PL. LXIII (birth of Ishmael).

103 On columns A and B of the ciborium in San Marco, whose iconography is in all probability Early Christian, it is interesting to observe that the bathing appears in the Birth of the Virgin but not in the Nativity of Christ (photos Böhm Nos. 3234 and 3227–3226).

104 As was well shown by Prof. E. Kitzinger, "The Hellenistic Heritage in Byzantine Art," *DOP*, 17 (1963), p. 104 and n. 41, citing Mesarites' commentary on the subject of the mosaics in the Holy Apostles.

in the Birth of the Virgin and presenting the same variants. There is one important difference, due to a realistic adaptation: usually the midwife is seated not on a chair but on a rock. It is perhaps also worth noting that during the Palaeologan period the Christ Child is often still submerged in the water (an antique motif), whereas the infant Virgin is no longer, or very seldom, represented in this way.[105] But at the Holy Apostles as at the Kariye Djami, he is naked in the midwife's lap (who, at Salonika, is testing the water), while the maidservant fills the great gilded basin from a pitcher of no less sumptuous material, the water flowing out of it like an undulating tress.

A choir of angels appears at the left, behind the hill, balancing the figure of the angel of the Annunciation to the Shepherds (PL. 168). The choir illustrates Luke 2:14, where, after the annunciation to the shepherds, we read: "And suddenly there was with the angel a multitude of the heavenly host praising God, and saying, Glory to God in the highest and on earth peace, good will toward men." These angels are introduced into the composition only in the post–iconoclastic period, but from then on they are a constant feature of it. To be sure, angels invade other themes —the Crucifixion, for example—but in the Nativity their introduction is quite natural, both because they are a reference to Luke and because, from the beginnings, in the symbolic scene on the phials discussed above two of them are addressing the Magi and the shepherds, and thus are already occupying the upper portion of the image.[106] It is long, however, before they are incorporated into Cappadocian compositions, with the exception—hence all the more striking— of Tokalı Kilisse 2;[107] they will be found again only in the second half of twelfth century, in the so-called columnar churches.[108]

Sometimes the angels are divided into two symmetrical groups, one on either side of the summit of the hill, with an angel emerging from each group, one addressing the Magi, the other the shepherds;[109] sometimes they are all grouped together on one side and the angel of the Annunciation to the Shepherds remains isolated; even when the Magi are represented, the angels can be completely separated from them. All these variants recur in Palaeologan painting. The Kariye Djami artist was content to depict a group of four beautiful angels; lost in adoration and quite apart from the scene, they contemplate the star from which a luminous ray falls to light the Child in the manger. A similar attitude recurs especially in manuscripts, among others in the miniatures of the Vatican manuscript of the Menologium of Basil II and those of Vat. Urbinas gr. 2, where the angels are unusually numerous. They are even more numerous in the Sinai icon (Fig. 40), where the different orders are represented. At the period with which we are concerned, they point to the Child with their hands, in accordance with another early type already found at Hosios Loukas (Fig. 39), or they bend toward him, their hands respectfully covered by a veil (at Studenica, for example). Here again the Kariye Djami artist has remained faithful to his taste for discarding nonessentials and to his respect for a certain tradition, which is doubtless Constantinopolitan.

The upper part of the Holy Apostles mosaic has unfortunately disappeared. But enough is left

---

105 See above, n. 100.

106 This origin is apparent in the Dêr es Suriân fresco, which may date from the 10th century (Evelyn White, *Monasteries of the Wâdi'n Natrûm*, Part III, PL. LXI): the Virgin on her mattress, the Child in the masonry manger (the animals are lacking), Joseph seated; the three Magi with their offerings and the three shepherds with their flocks flanking the composition; on either side, an angel speeding down from heaven toward them. Two new motifs: the group of adoring angels above, and the flute-playing shepherd (the composition is crowded into the right side of the apse, the left being occupied by the Annunciation).

107 Jerphanion, *Cappadoce*, PL. 73,2 and 74,2: a compact group to the left, two angels to the right, in addition to the angel addressing the shepherds.

108 Jerphanion, *Cappadoce*, PL. 100,2, 127,2, and 129,2 (Jerphanion dates these churches 11th cent.).

109 See the mosaic in Hosios Loukas (Fig. 39) or the fresco in St. Demetrius, Peć (Petković, *La peinture serbe*, I, PL. 71).

of it to enable us to gauge the differences and the similarities between the two nearly contemporary compositions. The composition at Salonika seems to stand halfway between the classic elegance of the Constantinopolitan mosaic and the keen love of picturesque elements of Macedonian painting. The Kariye Djami mosaicist, if he does not omit these elements, yet accepts them with restraint and handles them with supreme moderation and distinction. In any case, the absence of other renderings of the theme in Constantinople does not warrant the affirmation that his work represents the only iconographic tradition current in the capital. It should also be emphasized that the theme of the Nativity of Christ, though marked by the novelties introduced into the Palaeologan koine, appears perfectly canonical, the apocryphal reminiscences having been sifted out in the course of time.[110]

The episodes of the Magi, this time narrated by Matthew (2:1–12), formed the subject of five compositions in the Kariye Djami: the Journey of the Magi [103].1, the Magi before Herod [103].2, Herod Inquiring of the Priests and Scribes (fragmentary) [104], the Adoration of the Magi (lost), and the Return of the Magi to the East (fragmentary) [105].[111] Such an ensemble is exceptional in earlier or even contemporary monumental painting. To be sure, all these scenes are also found in the large composition of the Nativity at Gradac, but, aside from the fact that there they do not have the same autonomy, they also do not possess the same narrative character: the arrangement of the motifs in the Gradac fresco is determined by the rubrics of the Synaxarion.[112] Some of the scenes recur at Curtea-de-Argeş and at Kalenić—narrative cycles that are of the same type as ours, and, though less extensive, are clearly inspired by it.[113] On the other hand, in the illustrations to the Akathistos Hymn, quite frequently painted in churches from the fourteenth century but more especially later, in the fifteenth and sixteenth centuries, the episodes of the Magi are reduced to three: the Journey, the Adoration, and the Return (strophes 8–10),[114] which may be compared with the first series of subjects at Gradac, though their iconography is somewhat different. On the other hand, almost the same iconography is employed for these three themes in the complex composition in the Brontochion at Mistra.[115]

Certain themes from the cycle of the Magi are not unknown in earlier mural painting. In Constantinople itself we can cite a famous precedent, the mosaics in the Holy Apostles. Whatever their date, in the ninth century at least, the visitor to the church saw the Journey and the Adoration of the Magi treated autonomously beside the Nativity.[116] In the mosaic decoration of

110 For the branch growing from the stump of a tree that appears in this image, as in all the preceding ones from Joseph Taking Leave of the Virgin [99] on, see P. Underwood's discussion, Vol. 1 of this work, p. 84.

111 Vol. 1 of this work [103]–[105].

112 Millet, *Recherches*, Fig. 88 and p. 143. The painter has put the Arrival of the Magi, the Adoration, and the Departure in direct relation to the Nativity; in the lower part of the composition, in relation to the Massacre of the Innocents at the right, he has represented at the left Herod addressing both the scribes and the Magi (who seem to be leaving the palace, as in Paris. copt. 13; ibid., Fig. 84).

113 At Curtea-de-Argeş, the Journey of the Magi, the Magi before Herod, and Herod Inquiring of the Priests and Scribes (the Adoration was not represented within the cycle; if it appeared in some other part of the church, no traces of it are left); see Tafrali, *Curtéa de Argeş*, PL. LXXV,2 (No. 173), or *Buletinul Comisiunii Monumentelor Istorice*, 10–16 (1917–23), Fig. 282, p. 238, and PL. VI *b* (the first two scenes in color). At Kalenić, only the Adoration and the Return of the Magi; Petković and Tatić, *Kalenić*, Fig. 45, p. 54, and Fig. 46, p. 55.

114 See, for example, the frescoes at Matejić and at Markov monastery (Petković, *La peinture serbe*, I, PL. 137 *b* and 145 *a*), in the Pantanassa at Mistra (Millet, *Mistra*, PL. 151), and at Athos, in the refectories of Lavra and of Chilandar (Millet, *Monuments de l' Athos* [Paris, 1927], PL. 145,2–146,1 and 100–101). In a Serbian psalter of the 15th century, Munich, slav. 4, there is a rather extensive cycle illustrating the Akathistos: Arrival of the Magi on horseback at the cave of the Nativity (fol. 214); Adoration of the Magi before Mary enthroned with the Child (the angel and Joseph are present—fol. 214v); Return of the Magi, who have dismounted in their city (fol. 215); Strzygowski, *Die Miniaturen*, PL. LIV,132, 133.

115 Millet, *Mistra*, PL. 95,8. In the mosaic in the baptistery of San Marco, Venice (14th century), we see the Magi before Herod, then the Adoration. The iconography is very Byzantine in general, but such motifs as the clothing and the Mongol servitors in charge of the camels derive from the Italian tradition; Bettini, *Mosaici di San Marco*, PL. C, CI.

116 According to the description by Constantine the Rhodian; see above, n. 5.

Monreale, of the twelfth century, the episodes of the Nativity, which had been the subject of a crowded synthetic composition in the Palatine Chapel at Palermo, were produced as a series of separate images, among them the Journey and the Adoration of the Magi.[117] These two themes are incorporated into the Nativity at Pskov, where they nevertheless constitute two autonomous little pictures.[118] In church painting, then, the choice of subjects remains restricted. In Cappadocia itself, the Magi Observing the Star is found at Tokalı Kilisse 2 alone, while only two problematical scenes at Münşil Kilisse may represent the Magi Guided by the Angel and the Magi before Herod. The Adoration, on the other hand, is often the subject of a separate scene there.[119] But if church painting is poor in representations of such subjects, the manuscripts provide numerous, often quite extensive cycles, from the ninth to the twelfth century, as do some icons.

Before considering these documents, we must briefly examine how the cycle developed in the pre-iconoclastic period. Already in Early Christian works the cycle of the Magi, closely connected with the Nativity of Christ, is not only frequent but also quite extensive. The symbolic importance attached to the episodes is considerable, for the Adoration of the Magi is the figuration of the calling of the Gentiles.[120] Aside from the Adoration proper, the theme most frequently represented in the earlier periods is that of the Search for the Star, suggesting the Journey, which is found sometimes separately, sometimes combined with the Adoration (in which case it is referred to by the gesture of the Magi pointing to the star), on numerous sarcophagi and ivories.[121] The two scenes are also found on the ambo at Salonika and on column B of the ciborium in San Marco, Venice.[122] Although the Magi are always on foot, the camels that serve as their mounts frequently appear on the sarcophagi and suggest the Journey in a more narrative fashion;[123]

117 Demus, *Norman Sicily*, PL. 17 and 66 a.

118 Pokrovskii, *Očerki*, Fig. 172, p. 259.

119 At Mavrucan the theme of the Magi Observing the Star is connected with the Adoration (Jerphanion, *Cappadoce*, II, p. 216), in accordance with the ancient tradition of the sarcophagi; at Tokalı Kilisse 2 (ibid., PL. 75,2) the group of the Magi is represented twice: seeking the star, and bringing their presents to the Child. For Münşil Kilisse, see ibid., II, p. 377 (the Adoration itself was not represented or has disappeared). Some of these scenes are also found in the newly published rock-cut churches in the valley of Belisirma: the Journey in the so-called church of Daniel (where the names of the Magi are inscribed according to the orthography of the Armeno-Syriac narratives, as at Tokalı Kilisse 1; Jerphanion, *Cappadoce*, I, p. 273, and the Armenian Gospel, 11:1), and at least three Adorations; see my "Nouvelles notes cappadociennes," pp. 141 ff.

120 St. Augustine found it possible to write of the star that, with it "serving as guide, Christ manifested himself to the nations" (cited by Millet, *Recherches*, p. 138). For the question of the Magi in its literary, liturgical, and iconographic aspects, reference may always profitably be made to Kehrer's *Drei Könige*, which remains indispensable, as well as to the article "Mages" in *DACL*, which contains an important discussion of the opinions expressed by the Church Fathers. Gilberte Vezin's *L'Adoration et le cycle des Mages dans l'art chrétien primitif* (Paris, 1950) has the advantage of supplying a recent, though incomplete, bibliography. On the oriental legends of the Magi, some of which were absorbed in the Middle Ages into the work of John of Hildesheim (second half of the 14th century), see U. Monneret de Villard, *Le leggende orientali sui Magi evangelici* (Studi e testi, 163; Vatican City, 1952). It goes without saying that F. Cumont's studies are of the first importance. I shall use especially "L'Adoration des Mages et l'art triomphal de Rome," *MemPontAcc*, 3d series, Vol. 3, (1932–33), pp. 81–105. See below pp. 217–18 and nn. 137 and 140, for an unpublished homily by John of Damascus, preserved in the 11th-century manuscript, possibly Constantinopolitan, Taphou 14 at Jerusalem.

121 See Volbach, *Elfenbeinarbeiten*, No. 119, PL. 37 (the theme by itself, left-hand leaf of ivory diptych at Milan, 5th

century), and Wilpert, *Sarcofagi*, passim, especially the sarcophagus in the Lateran also reproduced in Kehrer, *Drei Könige*, Fig. 13. For the earliest representations, see Kehrer, Figs. 1 ff.

122 Volbach, *Frühchristliche Kunst*, PL. 78–79 and p. 59; G. de Jerphanion, "L'ambon de Salonique, l'arc de Galère et l'ambon de Thèbes," *MemPontAcc*, 3d series, Vol. 3 (1932–33), pp. 107–32; the article "Mages" in *DACL*. However, the scene on the Venice column, second register (photo Böhm, No. 3236), is of a different nature: even before the Annunciation to the Shepherds, we see the three Magi, one consulting a globe, the other unrolling a scroll, the third pointing to the sky with uplifted arm. As certain authors have noted, the scene is an illustration of the tradition represented in Basil's Homily on the Nativity, where the Magi observe the stars, or examine the prophecy concerning the star—the prophecy of Balaam, which the Persian astrologers were held to have transmitted from generation to generation (*PG*, 31, col. 1469, and Millet, *Recherches*, p. 139). A somewhat similar episode occurs in the oriental paraphrases of the Protevangelium, especially the Armenian Gospel of the Infancy, 11:22–24, where the "Book of Adam" is mentioned. In the Search for the Star in Tokalı Kilisse 2 (Jerphanion, *Cappadoce*, PL. 75,2 and text Vol. I,2, pp. 329 f.), the three Magi hold the opened scroll of Balaam's prophecy, but this is exceptional. A mention of this legend appears in the *Menologio di Basilio II*, II, p. 57. Thus, contrary to what might be supposed, in the case of the Cappadocian fresco we have a Constantinopolitan feature.

123 See the works of Wilpert and Kehrer cited above and the article in *DACL*. Whereas the mounts of the Magi are always horses in Byzantine art of the post-iconoclastic period, and often in the West as well, camels remained very popular in Western art, particularly in Italy: Giotto himself represented them in the Arena Chapel; A. Venturi, *Storia dell' arte italiana*, V: *La pittura del Trecento e le sue origini* (Milan, 1907), Fig. 266, p. 329, or Vezin, *Cycle des Mages*, PL. XXXVI. On the problem of the mounts in Cappadocian images, reference may also be made to the article by M. Chatzidakis, "A propos d'une nouvelle manière de dater les peintures de Cappadoce," *Byzantion*, 14 (1939), pp. 95–113.

however, the Magi are not shown arriving at Jerusalem. The two themes of the Magi before Herod and Herod Inquiring of the Priests and Scribes are already depicted in the mosaics of the triumphal arch in Santa Maria Maggiore, where they are combined in a single composition.[124] But they remain comparatively infrequent. The first is represented at an early date in the mosaics of La Daurade at Toulouse,[125] and on a few sarcophagi; it becomes more frequent in Carolingian art. Both are found on an ivory of the School of Metz from the middle of the ninth century.[126] The Dream of the Magi, which is often treated in Western art, appears for the first time in the ninth century, in the Homilies of Gregory of Nazianz, Parisinus gr. 510.[127] The Departure of the Magi, in consequence of their Dream, is found in the tenth century, on an ivory at Lyons.[128]

Certain new themes also appear in Byzantine manuscripts of the ninth century, the most frequent being the Arrival of the Magi before the Walls of Jerusalem and the Magi Inquiring after the Birthplace of Christ. The cycle then becomes greatly extended in miniature painting. Obviously such a development could take place only in books. To illustrate the text of Matthew, the artists found their inspiration in various iconographic sources. Seven episodes can be distinguished in the Evangelist's account: Arrival of the Magi at Jerusalem, seeking information; Herod interrogating the scribes, who reveal Micah's prophecy to him; Herod summoning the Magi and making them promise to tell him where the newborn King is to be found; the Magi proceeding to Bethlehem, having found the star again; the Adoration and offerings; the Dream of the Magi; their Departure by another road. The most important ensembles of a canonical nature, those of Paris. gr. 74, Vat. gr. 1156, and Laurent. Plut. VI.23, show considerable differences. The first [129] comprises four scenes: the Magi before Jerusalem (Fig. 46 *a*), Herod Interrogating the Scribes (Fig. 46 *b*), the Magi before Herod, the Magi Arriving on Horseback at the Cave. The second [130] has three (after the episodes of the Nativity and the shepherds): the Magi before Herod, the Adoration with the Virgin enthroned, the Departure of the Magi; this manuscript being a lectionary, the order followed in it is not that of the Gospels but that of the feasts (lectionary illustrations seem to have influenced the introduction of the themes of the Journey, the Adoration, and the Departure into the complex composition of the Sinai icon, Fig. 40). The third [131] comprises six images: Herod Questioning the Scribes, the Magi before Jerusalem, the Magi before Herod, the Magi on the Road to Bethlehem, the Magi Hastening on Foot to the Cave, their Departure on Horseback (Fig. 43 *a* and *b*). It is this manuscript that affords the most complete example of the cycle of the Magi according to Matthew, though it departs from the Evangelist's account by putting the Arrival of the Magi after the Questioning of the Scribes. In this respect Paris. 74 is more faithful to the order of events, but it is less complete.[132]

The Protevangelium presents a narrative similar to that in Matthew, but replaces the Dream by the appearance of an angel (21:4)—which, though a perfect equivalent, sometimes caused the

124 Cecchelli, *S. Maria Maggiore*, PL. LXI; Wilpert, *Mosaiken und Malereien*, III, PL. 61, 62.

125 Woodruff, "La Daurade," p. 85 and Fig. 2 (upper left).

126 The ivory is at Frankfurt, Stadtbibl.; A. Goldschmidt, *Die Elfenbeinskulpturen* (Denkmäler der deutschen Kunst, hrsg. vom Deutschen Verein für Kunstwissenschaft), I (Berlin, 1914), PL. XXXI,75. See also Vezin, *Cycle des Mages*, PL. VIII *a* and IX.

127 H. Omont, *Miniatures des plus anciens manuscrits grecs de la Bibliothèque Nationale du VIᵉ au XIVᵉ siècle* (Paris, 1929), PL. XXXII (fol. 137).

128 Kehrer, *Drei Könige*, Fig. 106 (the plaque, which is divided into three registers, includes in descending order: the

Adoration, the Dream with the angel, and the Departure, with the Magi leaving the city on horseback).

129 *Evang. du XIᵉ siècle*, I, PL. 5, 6; the last scene also in Millet, *Recherches*, Fig. 100.

130 Millet, *Recherches*, Figs. 93–95.

131 Ibid., Figs. 85, 86.

132 We may further cite Parisinus gr. 115, which includes the scenes of Herod summoning the scribes, Herod summoning the Magi, and the Adoration; in Paris. copt. 13 the first two scenes are combined in one composition, a procedure already found much earlier. See Millet, *Recherches*, p. 138 and Figs. 82–84 on p. 139.

artists not to represent the sleeping Magi.[133] Mention in the Akathistos Hymn of the return of the Magi to Babylon and their revelation of the Christ to its inhabitants led to the creation of the theme of the Arrival of the Magi in their city (strophe 10), the theme being parallel from the iconographic point of view to that of their Arrival in Jerusalem.[134] The illustrator of the Arabic Gospel of the Infancy in the Laurentian Library (Med. Pal. orient. 387), like the text he follows (Ch. 8), goes even further and represents the returned Magi telling the story of their journey and exhibiting Christ's swaddling clothes, which Mary has given them.[135] This theme, which derives from a Syriac textual tradition, does not appear in Byzantine art. In the manuscript at Florence the passage referring to it is preceded by the Adoration.[136] In Byzantine art itself, a particular text, a homily of John of Damascus, gave rise to especially copious illustration, more than one of its miniatures remaining a *hapax*. The text is preserved in the eleventh-century manuscript at Jerusalem, Greek Patriarchate, Taphou 14.[137] In addition to the Journey to Bethlehem and the Nativity, together with the Journey of the Magi and their Offerings in connection with this last scene (Fig. 50 a and b), it is accompanied by an autonomous cycle of the Magi comprising fifteen images![138]

Independently of these unusual or distinctly oriental images, then, the Kariye Djami mosaicist had at his disposal within the Constantinopolitan tradition itself a very large selection of subjects from which he could draw to decorate the spaces assigned to him. The first scene ([103].1) (PL. 173) represents the Journey of the Magi—in fact, their Arrival at Jerusalem—in an iconography which is not peculiar to this theme [139] but is inspired by that of the more usual Arrival at Bethlehem. This last theme appears not only in cycles but also frequently, from the eleventh century on, as an element in the complex representations of the Nativity (Figs. 40 and 41), where the motif competes with that of the Offerings (Fig. 39). The Magi advance, on foot or on horseback, partly hidden or not by an undulation of the ground or by the rocky hill that contains the cave; they are on a slope, and one of them points with his arm to the star that shines above the manger. When the scene is autonomous, they are on horseback and the star appears in the sky only for them. However, this iconographic theme was sometimes used to represent the Journey

133 This is the case in Taphou 14; see below. Elsewhere the angel and the Magi usually appear, the artists having amalgamated the accounts of Matthew and the Protevangelium. In any case, not only is the angel an excellent transposition of a dream, but use of the motif for other themes, such as Joseph's Dream, was well known.

134 See below, same page.

135 Redin, "Miniatiury," Fig. 2, p. 58 (fol. 5 a of the MS); two of the Magi stand before three seated personages; one is unrolling Christ's swaddling cloths (see the accounts in the Arabic Gospel, 8, and in E. A. Wallis Budge, ed., *The History of the Blessed Virgin Mary and the History of the Likeness of Christ which the Jews of Tiberias Made to Mock at: The Syriac Texts* [London, 1899], pp. 38–39).

136 The Adoration is illustrated in fol. 4 b, but is not reproduced by Redin.

137 The text is unpublished. My knowledge of it is due to the kindness of Miss Sirarpie Der Nersessian, who permitted me to work from photographs in her possession. Millet, *Recherches*, p. 141 and n. 1, mentions this MS after A. Papadopoulos-Kerameus, Ἱεροσολυμιτικὴ βιβλιοθήκη, I (Petropolis, 1891), p. 53, and further cites the Menologion of Mount Athos, Esphigmenou (11th century), which also includes our text and is very copiously illustrated; see S. P. Lambros, *Catalogue of the Greek Manuscripts on Mount Athos* (in Greek), I (Cambridge, 1895), p. 172.

138 The first images are at fols. 97, 98, 99v, the fifteen images of the autonomous cycle at fols. 105, 105v, 106, 107, 107v, 108v (numbering according to the Library of Congress photographs). These images prove that artists illustrated the texts faithfully, not hesitating to create new themes when necessary, though they drew from a repertory of familiar motifs. In other words, the miniaturist employed motifs, if not themes, supplied by the iconographic tradition, in order to create original illustrations.

John Damascene's principal innovations were in respect to the relations of the Magi with Persia: it is their sovereign who sends them with presents (it should be noted that they are called "Magi-Kings"), and they order the making of an icon of the Virgin and Child to be installed in their temple, where it will be venerated. On the other hand, the metamorphoses of Christ—the infant whom the eldest of the Magi picks up from the ground becomes bearded in the arms of the second and an old man in those of the third (fol. 107v)—are distantly reminiscent of the various visions of Christ attributed to the Magi in the Armenian Gospel, 11:19 (see also my "Nouvelles notes cappadociennes," p. 169). The caresses that they bestow on the Child are peculiar to the manuscript. The offerings of the Magi, represented earlier (fol. 99v), are not repeated in the little autonomous cycle.

139 Which is known from manuscripts of the 11th century; cf. above, p. 216.

of the Magi before their arrival at Jerusalem, as we see in Taphou 14.[140] In our mosaics the solid walls that form the background to the following scene doubtless also serve to suggest Jerusalem in the scene of the arrival.

Usually the Magi succeed one another in the following order: the eldest leads the way and raises his hand toward the star; the second turns toward the third, who is the youngest—for, like the shepherds, though more systematically, they represent the three ages. However, this order is not unalterable.[141] Although the youngest is in the foreground in the Kariye mosaic, the eldest may be considered to be leading, for the Magi are proceeding toward the background of the composition, where the road—which, contrary to the usual practice, is represented as running through a mountain landscape—disappears behind a hill. The relative lack of space in comparison with the following scene, the need to adhere to a similar scale, or a deliberate desire to achieve a compositional effect by grouping the figures together in both scenes, prevented the artist from representing the Magi in single file. The youngest was thus shifted forward, and it is he who points to the star (PL. 176). The Curtea–de–Argeş painter reproduced the same group (Fig. 44), but, with only a very limited space at his disposal, he depicted them, without showing the road, as reaching the summit of the hill on far too steep a slope (a treatment reminiscent of the similar motif in the complex compositions of the Nativity). Even the second Magus' robe, which floats freely at the Kariye Djami, is strangely pressed up against the edge of the picture at Curtea. Once again the fresco painter, following his model too closely and having a different space at his disposal, was able to produce only an awkward transposition. In the substructure of a building of centralized type near the Early Christian church of the Theotokos Chalcopratia, the arrangement of the mounted Magi is more traditional. Even though all that remains is the figure of the old man and, to his left, a fragment of that of the mature man, the three Magi were certainly represented side by side, seen from below as is customary in the complex compositions of the Nativity (Fig. 45).

Brought before Herod, in the following scene ([103].2) (PL. 173), the three Magi have resumed their sequence in order of age. The old man, his hands covered by a part of his robe, holds a precious gilded casket, an unusual feature (PL. 174). The gifts that the Magi will offer the Child never appear earlier than the scene of the Adoration,[142] and it is difficult to see why the travelers should be so imprudent as to show them to Herod. This casket might represent a present intended for the King himself, which would be in conformity with custom although, doubtless out of hostility to Herod, no text mentions any such gift. This hypothesis, however, is difficult to maintain, for, in the scene of the Adoration at Kalenić, which presumably reproduces the lost

140 Fol. 105 *b* (second miniature). At fol. 105 *c*, the Magi next arrive at the gate of a city, where they are greeted by a personification. The same scene appears in Laurent. Plut. VI.23, but there the Magi are grouped and no longer traveling (Millet, *Recherches*, Fig. 85, and our Fig. 43 *a*); in Paris. gr. 74, they have dismounted (the horses have disappeared) and are talking with a group of people from the city, asking where Christ has been born (fol. 3v; *Evang. du XIᵉ siècle*, I, PL. 5). The illustrations for the Akathistos, strophe 5, show the Magi on horseback guided by an angel, who in the Serbian frescoes (and even in the refectory of Chilandar) may appear on horseback (see n. 114 for the references). Elsewhere they are guided by the star. At the Pantanassa, the city is depicted at the top of the composition (strophe 8; see Millet, *Mistra*, PL. 151,1).

141 Thus, in the Holy Apostles at Salonika (Fig. 41) the youngest leads, followed by the eldest, who turns to the mature man. The youngest is often placed between the other two in

Cappadocia; at Monreale (Demus, *Norman Sicily*, PL. 66 *a*) or at S. Apollinare Nuovo at Ravenna (Kehrer, *Drei Könige*, Fig. 34), the order is different again, in the Journey and in the Adoration.

142 Except in the baptistery of San Marco, Venice, where, in the scene of the interview with Herod, two of the Magi carry objects, one a casket, the other a decorated cylindrical box (Bettini, *Mosaici di San Marco*, PL. C). In the scene of the Adoration (PL. CI), each of the Magi presents a casket. The gifts are seldom indicated in the course of the Journey. The image in the London Psalter (British Museum, Add. 19352, fol. 92), where the Magi on horseback are followed by a mule laden with a bale, is an exceptional example; Millet, *Recherches*, Fig. 87. In a miniature of the Armenian manuscript at Jerusalem, of 1260, Armenian Patriarchate 251, fol. 15v (Millet, *Recherches*, Fig. 103), the Magi are followed by an escort of men of Mongol type, a feature not unique in oriental manuscripts.

one at the Kariye Djami (Fig. 48), the old man is offering the Child the same casket, while the other two display other gifts. Whatever the explanation, this action prevents the old man from leading the conversation, and it is again the youngest who makes the ritual gesture of the hands. The second, rather crowded between his two companions, merely raises one hand to his chest. Usually in this scene the artists show all three Magi speaking and gesturing (Fig. 43 b).[143]

Herod is sumptuously garbed as a military chief, wearing a diadem and chlamys, his left hand on the sheath of his sword and his right open toward his visitors in a gesture of welcome or conversation. (PL. 175). He sits imposingly on a great backless throne, his feet resting on a footstool. This attitude and costume, except perhaps for the sword, are traditional and go back to the Early Christian period.[144] The same is true of the motif of the guard who stands behind him. The number of guards may vary. In richly illustrated manuscripts of the eleventh and twelfth centuries there is only one—or even none.[145] The fresco painter of Curtea-de-Argeş (Fig. 44) outdid all others by grouping about the King not only the guard of our mosaic but also three armed and helmeted soldiers, who are obviously borrowed from the scene in which Herod orders the Massacre of the Innocents [107], which is omitted at Curtea. Herod's attitude is indeed very similar in the two cases.

It will have been observed that the appearance of the Magi is somewhat different in our two scenes. When mounted, they retain more of the appearance of oriental horsemen. With their trousers tucked into their boots, they resemble certain Old Testament characters who figure in the Genealogy of Christ in the inner narthex, particularly Daniel and Mishael (PL. 80). When they are before Herod, their tunics are longer and embroidered at the bottom, so that they resemble another type of Old Testament figure, that of the priest (PL. 86, 467). In Early Christian representations, on sarcophagi, the Magi are beardless and wear the Phrygian cap, anaxyrides, a short tunic, and a cloak that sometimes hangs loose. Their appearance and their number are decidedly reminiscent of the Three Hebrew Youths.[146] From the sixth century, at least in the eastern regions, they are of different ages.[147] The cap assumes a more abstract form, or is replaced by a tiara or a rounded turban.[148] Later the Magi usually wear a cap shaped like a truncated cone and wrapped at the bottom in a sort of small turban—the headgear given by the Byzantines to Jewish priests. If in the Menologion of Basil II [149] or at Daphni (Fig. 49) they are decidedly Persian in appearance, from the eleventh century, in the Vatican Lectionary (gr. 1156), for example, they sometimes wear a long, embroidered tunic.[150] The fact that the lower part of their

143 See Millet, *Recherches*, Fig. 93, for Vat. gr. 1156, and *Evang. du XIᵉ siècle*, I, PL. 6, for Paris. gr. 74. In Paris. copt. 13, the Magi are leaving the palace, while Herod continues to gesticulate; a rather similar scene is the subject of a badly damaged representation at Gradac (Millet, *Recherches*, Figs. 84 and 88, and pp. 142 ff.). The miniature in Taphou 14, fol. 105, shows the three Magi before the king of Persia, who is charging them with their mission, not before Herod.

144 Cf. especially a sarcophagus at Ancona (Vezin, *Cycle des Mages*, PL. V b) as well as the mosaics of Santa Maria Maggiore and La Daurade (see nn. 3 and 4). The attitude is typical of antique representations of military leaders. See, for example, the Emperor Galerius surrounded by his guards on the Salonika arch (Jerphanion, "Ambon de Salonique," Fig. 8, p. 114).

145 See our Figs. 43 a and b; no guard in Vat. gr. 1156 (Millet, *Recherches*, Fig. 93).

146 Wilpert, *Sarcofagi*, passim; Vezin, *Cycle des Mages*; Kehrer, *Drei Könige*. In the beginning, the costume of the Magi is that of the Hellenistic-Roman representations of "barbarians," particularly of the Persians, and not necessarily a priestly costume, as Cumont, "Adoration des Mages," has well demonstrated. See a reproduction of a sarcophagus at Arles showing Daniel's three companions, in Vezin, PL. IV b.

147 This is the case on the phials from the Holy Land (Fig. 42), in the miniature in the Etschmiadzin Gospel Book 229, in S. Apollinare Nuovo at Ravenna, etc. (Kehrer, *Drei Könige*, Figs. 32 ff.). So too in Roman painting of the 8th century (Grüneisen, *Sainte-Marie-Antique*, Fig. 119, p. 160) and at Castelseprio (Bognetti et al., *Castelseprio*, PL. LIII). The Magi are still beardless on certain documents of the 5th century (Kehrer, Fig. 30—Santa Sabina; Volbach, *Elfenbeinarbeiten*, No. 119, PL. 37—ivory at Milan). In the 6th century the feature is variable: only one Magus is bearded on certain ivories (Kehrer, Figs. 36 and 37) but all three are bearded on the column in San Marco, Venice (photo Böhm, No. 3236).

148 For example in Paris. gr. 510 (Omont, *Miniatures des plus anciens manuscrits grecs*, PL. XXXII) and later in the London Psalter, British Museum, Add. 19352, fol. 92 (Millet, *Recherches*, Fig. 87).

149 *Menologio di Basilio II*, II, p. 272.

150 Millet, *Recherches*, Figs. 93, 94.

bodies is often hidden by the rock in the complex images of the Nativity may have contributed toward depersonalizing them. In the beginning the Magi wore the Persian costume made widely familiar by priests of oriental religions, particularly the priests of Mithras.[151] Later their appearance tends to conform to the Byzantines' conception of oriental priests in general and of Old Testament priests in particular.

In the scene of Herod Inquiring of the Priests and Scribes [104], Herod is dressed as in the preceding scene and adopts a similar pose; the young guard standing behind him is viewed directly from the back, his head slightly turned to the right (PL. 179).[152] The group at the right which the King was addressing is completely destroyed in the mosaic (PL. 177). It can, however, be reconstituted, with the help of the fresco at Curtea-de-Argeş, in which Herod, the guard, and even the architectural background reproduce the motifs in our scene so exactly that the same must have been true of the priests and scribes (Fig. 47). They form a compact group of fourteen persons of different ages, most of them bearded, bareheaded or with head hooded by a fold of the robe; the leader addresses Herod, the others look at the King or at each other—all are attentive and animated. This is the classic group, which, though often less numerous, is found in the extensive manuscript cycles. In Paris. gr. 74 (Fig. 46 b), however, it is still more numerous and suggests the group at Curtea, though it is less animated; the figures of Herod and the guard are very similar. Since the conclusion of this interview is the revelation of Micah's prophecy,[153] we should expect that at least one of the scribes would be unrolling a parchment in witness to it, as was already the case in the fifth century in the mosaic in Santa Maria Maggiore, then in the twelfth century in Paris. copt. 13, and, again in the Palaeologan period, at Gradac.[154] But the motif seems to have fallen into disuse in post–iconoclastic Byzantine art, and our mosaicist was probably unaware of its existence. For even in Palaeologan art this feature is extremely infrequent.

The Adoration has completely disappeared (see PL. 180 a). Here again we can fall back on a later painting that probably reproduces the mosaic, this time at Kalenić (Fig. 48). Against a complex architectural background, the three Magi advance in order of age, respectively presenting the casket that has already appeared in the Magi before Herod in the Kariye Djami ([103].2) and two large and precious vases. They approach the throne on which the Virgin is seated, almost frontally, holding the Child on her knees; he makes the gesture of blessing, she that of welcome. Joseph's bust appears behind the high back of the throne. This is the solemn type of the Adoration or Offerings of the Magi, which coexists with that of the Magi honoring the Child in the manger or approaching him, laden with gifts, in combination with the Nativity.

The autonomous theme of the Adoration of the Magi is one of the oldest creations of Christian art. Frequently represented during the pre–iconoclastic period, it tends to fall into disuse later because it is generally incorporated into the complex compositions of the Nativity. At the end of the Byzantine epoch, it receives separate treatment, more especially in the illustrations for the Synaxarion or for the Akathistos Hymn. From an early period the autonomous type shows considerable variation. Thus, on many sarcophagi Mary sits in profile, holding the Child in her

---

151 See the documents assembled by Kehrer, *Drei Könige*, and the justifiable reservations expressed by Cumont, "Adoration des Mages," pp. 85 ff. See also P. A. Underwood's remarks, Vol. 1 of this work, pp. 92–93.

152 For this interesting attitude, see Underwood's remarks, Vol. 1 of this work, p. 94, and Demus' study in this volume,

above.

153 Micah 5:1 ff.; M.-J. Lagrange, *Evangile selon Saint Matthieu*, 4th ed. (Paris, 1927), pp. 25–26; see also Millet, *Recherches*, pp. 138 ff., and above, n. 122.

154 Cecchelli, *S. Maria Maggiore*, PL. LXI; Millet, *Recherches*, Figs. 84 and 88.

lap, while the three Magi advance in single file and Joseph is often shown beside her.[155] But in the composition of a symbolic nature that appears especially in oriental representations of the sixth century, the Virgin is enthroned frontally, surrounded by the Magi, to whom an angel has been added.[156] The solemn aspect of this last theme suggests that it may have its origin in the mosaic in the basilica of the Nativity.[157] Some images combine the frontal figure of the Virgin with the Magi in single file and even the angel, as is the case on the Salonika ambo.[158] However, the iconography that is to become traditional already appears in the sixth century, on the throne of Maximian at Ravenna.[159] It recurs in works of the eighth and ninth centuries, at Santa Maria Antiqua, at Castelseprio, in Paris. gr. 510.[160] The angel, standing or flying, presents the Magi to the Child on the Virgin's knees; she sits on a decorated throne, turned toward the new arrivals, and Joseph stands behind her; the eldest Magus bows before the Child, the second turns toward the third. Such a scheme can be considered a worthy final development of the earlier iconographic trends.

The independent theme of the Adoration is still frequent in post-iconoclastic Byzantine art of the tenth and eleventh centuries. In the narrative cycles of Cappadocia, the theme combines the same elements, but the Magi are shown in stiff single file.[161] In the Constantinopolitan tradition, Joseph seems to figure less frequently. He appears neither in the miniature in the Menologion of Basil II [162] nor at Daphni (Fig. 49). In the miniature in Taphou 14, fol. 99v (Fig. 50 b), however, he stands timidly behind the cave, while the Magi approach to do homage to the Child and Mother. The angel is represented in the first two of these documents—in the Menologion he is given a prominent place in the center of the composition. In the two miniatures the Virgin is seated before the cave, on a rock. This rock is a special motif, the result of a preoccupation with

---

155 Cf. in particular two sarcophagi in the Lateran (Kehrer, *Drei Könige*, Figs. 13 and 14) and Wilpert, *Sarcofagi*, passim. For the personage of Joseph, see above, n. 83. Joseph is absent from a certain number of separate representations of the Adoration (Kehrer, Figs. 28 ff.). He is seldom represented seated in this scene, as he is on the cover of the Etschmiadzin Gospel Book: in this case the figure is taken from the Nativity; he also appears seated at Castelseprio (Volbach, *Elfenbeinarbeiten*, No. 142, PL. 44, and Bognetti et al., *Castelseprio*, PL. LIII). It has been pointed out that the attitude of the Magi does not correspond with the narrative accounts, according to which they prostrated themselves before the Child (Kehrer, pp. 2 ff., and especially Cumont, "Adoration des Mages," pp. 100 f.; the latter relates our theme with that of conquered barbarians offering presents to the conqueror). It is the Arrival rather than the Adoration of the Magi which is in fact represented; the gesture by which one of them sometimes points to the star is, however, more specific, at the same time that it suggests the Journey.

156 See the miniatures in the Etschmiadzin Gospel Book 229 (D. V. Ainalov, *The Hellenistic Origins of Byzantine Art*, tr. Elizabeth and Serge Sobolevitch, ed. Cyril Mango (New Brunswick, N. J., 1961), Figs. 45 and 46, and his remarks on p. 91) and the ivory plaques at Manchester and in the British Museum (Volbach, *Elfenbeinarbeiten*, No. 127, PL. 39, and No. 131, PL. 41, or Kehrer, *Drei Könige*, Figs. 36, 37). On the two ivories the lower border comprises a small Nativity, which all the more strongly emphasizes the importance of the great frontal image of the Adoration; the Magi present their offerings on veiled hands, an "oriental" theme (Cumont, "Adoration des Mages," pp. 93 ff.). The composition of the Monza phials also derives from the solemn type, with the Virgin enthroned frontally with the Child, between the Magi to the right and the shepherds to the left—in particular the phial reproduced in A. Grabar, *Ampoules*, PL. VIII; that of our Fig. 42 is of a more animated type.

157 Cf. above, n. 1. It must be admitted, however, that the text of the Melchite bishops does not explicitly warrant such an

interpretation. But it is a scheme of this sort that appears in the paintings in the catacombs; Kehrer, *Drei Könige*, Figs. 1 and 10.

158 Volbach, *Frühchristliche Kunst*, PL. 79. The angels may be more numerous, to indicate a particular solemnity. This is the case in the mosaics of Santa Maria Maggiore at Rome and of S. Apollinare Nuovo at Ravenna (Cecchelli, *S. Maria Maggiore*, PL. XLIX, and Kehrer, *Drei Könige*, Fig. 34). The angels, numbering four in these two cases, flank the throne, mounting guard beside it.

As for the number of the Magi, though it is not specified in the primitive narratives, it was soon fixed at three, doubtless because Matthew mentions three different offerings: gold, frankincense, myrrh (2:11), and because three is a sacred number. In certain paintings in the catacombs the artists sometimes represented two Magi (Sts. Peter and Marcellinus) or four (Domitilla), for reasons of symmetry; Kehrer, *Drei Könige*, Figs. 1 and 10. The angel may have replaced the star as the celestial messenger. On the angel's deriving from the motif of the Nike, see Cumont, "Adoration des Mages," p. 102. See also the article "Mages" in *DACL*.

159 The scene was divided between two plaques; the second, showing the Magi, has disappeared; G. de Jerphanion, "La véritable interprétation d'une plaque aujourd'hui perdue de la chaire d'ivoire de Ravenne," *Rendiconti della Pontificia Accademia Romana di Archeologia*, 14 (1938), p. 31.

160 Grüneisen, *Sainte-Marie-Antique*, Fig. 119, p. 160; Omont, *Miniatures des plus anciens manuscrits grecs*, PL. XXXII. At Castelseprio the Virgin is enthroned on a high rock, rather as at Santa Sabina; the setting is particularly elaborate in this fresco, with a landscape to the right and a building to the left; Bognetti et al., *Castelseprio*, PL. LIII.

161 Jerphanion, *Cappadoce*, particularly in PL. 35,3, 75,2 and 182,1. Joseph alone is represented in certain images (PL. 37,3 and 47,1). Neither the angel nor Joseph appears in the chapel of the Forty Martyrs (13th century), PL. 161,2, nor in Pürenli Seki Kilisesi, in the valley of Belisirma; see my "Nouvelles notes cappadociennes," p. 165.

162 *Menologio di Basilio II*, II, p. 272.

realism not unusual in the refined works of Byzantine art.[163] Generally the Virgin sits on a more or less sumptuously decorated throne, but in this case she appears either against a bare background (Daphni, Cappadocia) or against a background of architecture (Taphou 14, fol. 107 ff.) [164] The miniaturist of the Menologion tried to render the proskynesis by a violent movement of the three Magi, the first being almost flat on the ground. But this is an isolated attempt. On the whole, the choice lies between two procedures: either the three Magi approach on foot; or all three have stopped, and the eldest bows or kneels, while the two others stand behind him, the second turning toward the third.[165] The Magi offer large round dishes filled with what are probably gold pieces and decidedly reminiscent of the dishes containing eggs carried by the offering-bearers in contemporary representations of the Birth of the Virgin. In Cappadocia, however, they usually present caskets, though they carry vases at Tokalı Kilisse 2, a church whose decoration is markedly Byzantine.[166]

The Adoration of the Magi, which is not among the Great Feasts, was soon reduced to being only a motif in the Nativity. The autonomous theme becomes simply an intrusion in complex compositions, such as those of the Sinai icon (Fig. 40) and the fresco at Pskov.[167] From the tenth century the Magi may be incorporated into the Nativity in other ways, either in an attitude suggesting the Journey (they approach on foot or on horseback, watching the star) or near to the Child with their offerings. Many twelfth-century representations achieve this incorporation very effectively, the Virgin raising the Child in the manger and sometimes even holding out one hand toward the Magi, who advance, respectfully bowing, with their gifts.[168] The formula is earlier, for the attitude of the Virgin at Hosios Loukas certainly seems to derive from it, though without the artist's understanding it, since he represented the Magi to the left while the manger faces right (Fig. 39). The gesture, whose meaning is sometimes forgotten, recurs in a certain number of representations during the Palaeologan period. It is frequent in Serbian and Macedonian frescoes, though it is not always clearly expressed. At Studenica, as earlier at Palermo, the angel has been retained.[169]

At Gradac, and later in the Brontochion at Mistra,[170] the artists resumed the practice of

---

163 In the Menologion a lower rock serves as the Virgin's footstool. In the illustration for the Akathistos at Moscow, Hist. Mus. gr. 429 (Lixačev, *Materialy*, PL. CCCLVI, 703), the Virgin's seat is her couch, set before the cave; a building is represented to the left (the cave seldom appears in church representations of the Akathistos).

164 In certain Armenian manuscripts of the 13th century, however, the Virgin is enthroned on a decorated chair before the cave; see especially Millet, *Recherches*, Fig. 103. As we see, several traditions coexist in regard to the place of the Adoration. Matthew has the Magi go "into the house" (2:11), the Protevangelium, into the cave (21:3). But the term οἰκία is not incompatible with the idea of a cave; see Lagrange's remarks, *Evangile selon Saint Matthieu*, pp. 29–30, n. 11. Nor do the other texts of the Byzantino–oriental tradition mention a "house." However, the passage in Matthew influenced the artists, the more so since an architectural setting was better suited to the solemnity of the scene. On the other hand, the account in the Pseudo-Matthew (16:1), according to which Christ was two years old at the time of the visit of the Magi, contributed to showing the child as older. But the artists most often combined the Nativity and the Adoration, since this was convenient. We may note that, in Byzantine church art, an architectural setting already appears at Peruštica; Frolow, "Peruštica," I, PL. X.

165 For the order of the Magi, see above, p. 218 and n. 141.

166 The caskets illustrate well the passage in Matthew (2:11, καὶ ἀνοίξαντες τοὺς θησαυροὺς αὐτῶν; Cumont, "Adoration des Mages," p. 101). But the offerings, whether in the case of our

theme or of another, such as the Birth of the Virgin (see above, "Cycle of the Virgin," pp. 175–76), doubtless derived from motifs in Byzantine art that were sterotyped, not peculiar to a theme.

167 Pokrovskij, *Očerki*, Fig. 172, p. 259.

168 In the Palatine Chapel at Palermo, Demus, *Norman Sicily*, PL. 17; in the columnar churches of Cappadocia, Jerphanion, *Cappadoce*, PL. 100,2, 104,3, 127,2, 129,2. Another interesting but much rarer type—that of the Virgin who, having taken the Child from the manger, holds him on her knees—appears on an ivory from the Stroganoff collection, now in the Walters Art Gallery at Baltimore (11th-12th century); P. Verdier, "A Byzantine Ivory Relief of the Adoration of the Christ Child," *Bulletin of the Walters Art Gallery*, 14, 3 (Dec. 1961). The text of Chrysostom cited by Millet, *Recherches*, p. 146, agrees particularly well with this type of representation. The feature appears in the Armenian Gospel of the Infancy, 11:16.

169 V. R. Petković, *Manastir Studenica* (Belgrade, 1924), Fig. 81, p. 64, or Petković, *La peinture serbe*, I, PL. 36 d. The Virgin's gesture is at the same time a gesture of tenderness, for she presses her cheek against the Child's. At Sopoćani an angel moves swiftly ahead of the Magi, but the Virgin does not turn toward them; at Arilje, however, she looks at them as they offer vases of different shapes (Petković, *La peinture serbe*, II, PL. XIX,1 and XXXII).

170 Millet, *Mistra*, PL. 95,8; idem, *Recherches*, Fig. 88 (Gradac).

incorporating the autonomous theme into a complex composition. In both instances Joseph stands behind Mary, still in a very humble attitude, and the angel appears sometimes standing, sometimes in half-length, between the Magi and the Virgin. In the Akathistos cycle the Adoration of the Magi is the subject of a separate scene, illustrating strophe 9. If in the Moscow manuscript (Hist. Mus. gr. 429) and the fresco in the Pantanassa the scene takes place in front of the cave,[171] elsewhere Mary is enthroned against an architectural background and the Magi advance with their caskets (in other representations the gifts assume various forms, vases or coffers of different sizes) in front of a wall, behind which the servant in charge of their horses sometimes appears.[172] The miniature in Munich, slav. 4 includes also the double motif of Joseph and the angel.[173]

It seems odd that at Kalenić the angel should have been omitted, for his presence gives the scene a more markedly symbolic character, which is suitable in a separate representation and in accordance both with a long tradition and with the most usual contemporary practice. In the Kariye Djami, the Virgin, the Child, and Joseph must have been placed in the left and smaller part of the lunette, while the Magi were given the larger space to the right.[174] An angel could easily have been introduced here. Yet, if the Kalenić fresco accurately reproduces our mosaic, the latter did not include an angel. The effect was doubtless deliberate. For we must take into account the particular rhythm of the procession of the Magi, all three of them adopting similar attitudes and advancing, slightly bowed, to present their offerings on veiled hands. Instead of the close, animated group found in most contemporary images, the artist would seem to have preferred showing the Magi deployed in procession to express a solemnity that is in the spirit of the Early Christian images. The architectural background, which is rare in early works and never as elaborate as in this composition, even in the illustrations for the Akathistos, is doubtless a reflection of the taste of the period, and so are the large and precious vases brought as offerings. The three doorways punctuate the rhythm of the processional Magi in a felicitous manner at Kalenić, and this quality must doubtless be attributed to the mosaicist of the Kariye Djami.

It is again a fresco at Kalenić (Fig. 51), that enables us to reconstruct the fragmentary scene in the eastern lunette of the seventh bay, which represented the Return of the Magi to the East [105] (PL. 181). This time the reconstruction is beyond doubt, for the remaining fragment in the Kariye Djami was copied almost exactly at Kalenić, and the entire composition, which is unusual, is also best explained as a copy from the mosaic.[175] The Magi are on horseback on a slope; at the top of the mountain a city is schematically represented. The subject, then, is the Return of the Magi to the East (see Fig. 53 *a*), not their Departure from Palestine, a theme that is fairly frequent in Byzantine miniature cycles of the eleventh century and that shows the Magi leaving the city, sometimes guided by an angel (allusion to the Dream; see Fig. 52).[176] The iconographic type of the scene at Kalenić was also used for the Arrival of the Magi at Jerusalem,

171 Millet, *Mistra*, PL. 151,2 and above, n. 163. For the representations of the Akathistos at Mount Athos, see Millet, *Athos*, PL. 146,1, 238,1 and 101,1.

172 Cf. in particular the fresco at Matejić (Petković, *La peinture serbe*, I, PL. 137 *b*); in the so-called columnar churches, at Göreme, the Magi are seen approaching the cave, while their horses are tied to a tree; Jerphanion, *Cappadoce*, PL. 104,3 and 129,2; see also the article by Chatzidakis, "A propos d'une nouvelle manière de dater les peintures de Cappadoce."

173 Strzygowski, *Die Miniaturen*, PL. LIV,132 (fol. 214v). Joseph is represented in it seated, as in a Nativity. In the illustration of the Akathistos at St. Nicholas Orphanos at Salonika,

only the angel is represented (Xyngopoulos, Ἅγιος Νικόλαος Ὀρφανός, Fig. 99).

174 Underwood, Vol. I of this work, pp. 95–96.

175 Ibid., p. 96.

176 See in particular the miniatures in the Vatican Lectionary, gr. 1156 (Millet, *Recherches*, Fig. 95), in which the Magi quietly leave the city on horseback, and the miniature in Taphou 14, fol. 108v (our Fig. 52), where the Magi, departing by a very similar gate, are extremely animated: the first points with raised arm to the angel, who flies above showing them the road; as the mature man watches from the steps, the youngest leaps on his horse—one may suppose it is running and that the movement indicates his haste.

particularly in the illustration for the Akathistos in the Pantanassa at Mistra.[177] In determining its meaning, however, we must relate it with another composition for the Akathistos Hymn, the Return of the Magi, in which the Magi approach their city, where a group of people often waits to greet them (strophe 10).[178] Our theme must be compared with the representations of this scene. Like Matthew, the apocryphal Greek narratives are silent on the episode, but their oriental versions are not. The text of the Akathistos may have been influenced by these latter narratives, though it does not go as far as they do.[179] The theme is rare. At Gradac it is clearly the Departure of the Magi from Bethlehem that is depicted, in close connection with the Adoration and the Nativity and in accordance with the tradition of compositions of the complex type from which that fresco derives.

The space available to the Kariye Djami mosaicist forced him to torture his composition, and, doubtless in order to justify the pose of the horsemen, he gave it a more mountainous setting than usual. The last Magus, the only one preserved in the mosaic, is the youngest; he raises his arm, and his whole body is violently tensed on his rearing horse. The Kalenić fresco painter lessened the expressiveness of this figure; he made it more elegant—the head well set off, the cloak sweeping back—but also less vigorous. The outline of the second Magus is barely discernible in the fresco, but the eldest, who leads the way, clearly turns to his companions, pointing out the road to them with a broad gesture. There was certainly no angel at Kalenić, and doubtless there was none at the Kariye Djami either, any more than in the Palaeologan illustrations for the Akathistos. In representations of the Departure of the Magi, the angel suggested the Dream, which seems no longer to have been treated after the twelfth century. He showed the Magi the road they must take to escape Herod's search, but had no role to play in the subsequent events.[180]

The cycle of the Magi at the Kariye Djami, then, draws from a Constantinopolitan tradition that was especially alive in the eleventh and twelfth centuries and is represented by an important group of richly illustrated manuscripts. Yet it is difficult to connect our cycle to any particular one of these manuscripts. The attempt has been made to show a relationship between Laurent. Plut. VI.23 and our images,[181] but I believe that this view is without foundation. If the mosaicist, like the miniaturist, did not completely abide by the order of the Gospel narrative, it was in a different way and for a better reason. It seemed more satisfactory to group the two scenes of the Magi—the Journey and the Magi before Herod—in one lunette and to devote the other lunette to Herod Inquiring of the Priests and Scribes. The Adoration and the Return of the Magi felicitously completed a well-balanced cycle, the model for which may, in the last analysis, have been a contemporary illustration of a more specific nature, such as one for the Synaxarion or the Akathistos Hymn, but which in our case was presented in a narrative sequence unusual at the period.

The Presentation of Christ in the Temple, or Purification of the Virgin (ἡ Ὑπαπαντή) should have been given a place at this point in the cycle of the Infancy. Actually, the place of this

---

177 See above p. 218 and n. 140.

178 See Xyngopoulos, Ἅγιος Νικόλαος Ὀρφανός, Fig. 100, and the references above, n. 171. The Magi can already have dismounted, as in the Pantanassa, before the city, at the gate of which stands a group of people. Similarly, in the Serbian Psalter at Munich they advance on foot toward a man seated before a building representing the city (fol. 215; Strzygowski, *Die Miniaturen*, PL. LIV,133).

179 See above, p. 217. The Armenian Gospel of the Infancy

(10:2) mentions a numerous army accompanying the Magi. In the scene of the Return in the Armenian manuscript W. 539 at Baltimore (1262), the Magi, returning to the East on horseback, are followed by their army: the men are of Mongol type, as in the Jerusalem manuscript (see above, n. 142).

180 However, he is still retained in the fresco at Dochiariou (Millet, *Athos*, PL. 238,1), but no doubt the motif is purely mechanical here.

181 Millet, *Recherches*, pp. 141 ff.

episode, which is narrated at length by Luke (2:22–38) but of which Matthew says nothing, is subject to variation. The Protevangelium does not mention it. The oriental paraphrases, which tend to combine the various sources, put the Presentation between the Visit of the Magi and the Flight into Egypt.[182] The Cappadocian painters most often defer it until after the close of the Protevangelium narrative, that is, even after the Flight into Egypt, but sometimes they depict it after the Nativity.[183] In the Synaxaria it comes after the episode of the Flight and the Massacre.[184] In any case, there is no place in the narthex of the Kariye Djami for such a scene; for, as we saw was the case with the Annunciation in the House and perhaps also with the Visitation,[185] it would have been placed in the cycle of the Great Feasts which decorated the central nave. The Presentation was indeed one of the episodes from the Infancy of Christ that were chosen to figure among the representations of a liturgical nature which constituted the ensemble of Great Feasts.[186] The same is certainly true of the Baptism, which should have appeared in the narthex before the scenes of Christ's public life, but of which no trace is to be found.

The scene of the Presentation traditionally includes the figures of Mary presenting the Child, of Simeon receiving him or preparing to do so, of Joseph following Mary and carrying two doves, and of the prophetess Anne, who stands behind the aged Simeon; in the center an altar, surmounted by a ciborium, may be represented. This is the most classic scheme, which in the Palaeologan period is found, for example, at Curtea–de–Argeș, where the fresco painter may have imitated the Kariye's vanished mosaic (Fig. 54).[187] Sometimes Anne is placed behind Mary, with Joseph— this is her position at Dečani, for example;[188] or again she may not appear at all, as in Paris. gr. 510 and some Cappadocian frescoes.[189] Sometimes too, in Palaeologan art, for example in the Holy Apostles at Salonika, the scene is divided between the opposite sides of an arch: in this case only the principal actors are represented.[190] Since we do not know what position the scene occupied in the Kariye Djami, any speculation on its possible iconography is precluded.

The right–hand side of the eastern lunette of the seventh bay was certainly occupied by Joseph's Dream ([105].2), the prelude to the Flight into Egypt (Matt. 2:13). We are justified in sup-

182 Armenian Gospel, 12; Budge, *History of the Blessed Virgin*, pp. 40 f. The Arabic Gospel of the Infancy, however, puts the event before the arrival of the Magi (5–6). The Pseudo-Matthew does likewise, for, according to this text, the Magi did not reach Bethlehem until two years later (15).

183 Jerphanion, *Cappadoce*, I, pp. 79–80. In decorations of the archaic period, the scene occurs only in extensive ensembles.

184 The Presentation is celebrated on February 2 (after the Circumcision, January 1); the episodes from the Nativity to the Flight are commemorated on December 25, and the Massacre of the Innocents on the 29th.

185 See above, p. 188.

186 Millet, *Recherches*, pp. 17 ff. The earliest selections seem not to have retained the theme; even later it is not obligatory, if not in the canons at least in figured representations. Millet did not include a study of this theme among the Gospel scenes. In the Byzantine tradition, however, it is always present in the cycle of Great Feasts painted in churches. The scene is uncommon in the pre-iconoclastic period. However, Choricius mentions its occurrence in St. Sergius at Gaza (*Laud. Marciani*, I, §56), and Constantine the Rhodian in the Holy Apostles, Constantinople (Legrand, above n. 5).

187 The traditional arrangement is already found in early monuments, for example in the fresco at Castelseprio (Bognetti et al., *Castelseprio*, PL. LVII and LVIII) or on the reliquary cross in the Sancta Sanctorum (*DACL*, III, 2, PL. facing col. 3116). At Curtea-de-Argeș, Simeon has the Child in his arms (the scene is divided in two by a window).

188 V. R. Petković and D. Bošković, *Dečani* (Belgrade, 1941), PL. CCXLVI (the scene here does not form part of the Aka-thistos cycle). This arrangement is also early; it was seen in the frescoes of John VII at Santa Maria Antiqua: Grüneisen, *Sainte-Marie-Antique*, PL. IC.LXVII,2.

189 Omont, *Miniatures des plus anciens manuscrits grecs*, PL. XXXII, and Jacqueline Lafontaine, "Sarıca kilise en Cappadoce," *CA*, 12 (1962), p. 277 and n. 1. Like Jerphanion, I had at the time seen no explanation for the fact. This explanation is supplied by the miniatures illustrating the Circumcision and the Presentation in the Menologion of Basil II; *Menologio di Basilio II*, II, p. 287 and 365. The first theme, most infrequent in Byzantine art (though it is extremely widespread in the West), involves the same personages as the second, except for the prophetess. The act of circumcision must have been distasteful to the Byzantines. Certain artists kept this image, but replaced the act by that of the Presentation, without adding Anne to it.

190 A. Xyngopoulos, Ἡ ψηφιδωτὴ διακόσμησις τοῦ ναοῦ τῶν Ἁγίων Ἀποστόλων Θεσσαλονίκης (Salonika, 1953), p. 15 and PL. 14; the author rightly compares such an arrangement with the one in the Palatine Chapel at Palermo (Demus, *Norman Sicily*, PL. 11 b). On the other hand, the Monreale mosaicist, having more space at his disposal, represented the full traditional composition; see ibid., PL. 65 b). The mosaics in the Holy Apostles, extremely damaged in this section of the church, preserve only the head of the Virgin and the lower part of her figure, together with some of the architectural setting in the background.

posing so because at Kalenić the episodes of the Return of the Magi and of Joseph's Dream are grouped together (Fig. 51).[191] If in the Early Christian period Joseph's second dream seems to be less frequently represented than the first, although it is well documented and at a very early date,[192] it appears in the detailed post-iconoclastic cycles, both in manuscripts—the Menologion of Basil II (Fig. 55 a) and numerous manuscripts of the eleventh and twelfth centuries [193]—and in the frescoes of Cappadocia, where it occurs especially in archaizing cycles.[194] It is quite seldom that the two Dreams are represented in one and the same cycle, because of their great similarity, and they are not necessarily both represented, even in copiously illustrated manuscripts. But they do both appear in the mosaics of San Marco, Venice,[195] which reproduce the images of a manuscript of Constantinopolitan origin or inspiration. Joseph's second dream is found in other decorative ensembles of the twelfth century, especially in Sicilian mosaics.[196] It may be incorporated into certain complex compositions of the Nativity, as at Pskov or, still later, at Gradac, where it precedes the Flight.[197] It is found in the Metropole at Mistra, one of the very few extensive cycles of the Infancy in the Palaeologan period.[198] But since it does not occur in the illustration of the Akathistos, it remains exceptional during this period and even later.

The two Dreams are represented in accordance with the same iconographic scheme, with the angel approaching Joseph, who lies on his couch. The angel is sometimes standing, sometimes half-length and flying. The first procedure is the earlier, and the second is found chiefly in Palaeologan art, in correspondence with the general evolution of annunciatory angels.[199] The setting, when it exists, is either a rocky background, as in the Menologion of Basil II, where the Adoration also takes place before the cave, or an architectural setting that suggests rather than represents Joseph's house, for example in the fragment of Taphou 14 at Leningrad.[200] In the case of the Kalenić fresco, and also most certainly in that of our mosaic, the scene takes place in the same rocky landscape that forms the background for the Return of the Magi.

The Dream led to the Flight into Egypt [106], which is placed in the lunette in the south wall of the seventh bay. Unfortunately, the scene is fragmentary, but what remains of it enables us to determine to a certain extent its iconographic type (PL. 182). This type is defined both by the presence of the young lad guiding the ass and by the Egyptian city where the idols fall. The lad is one of Joseph's sons—the one who appears in the scenes following the Marriage ([97] and [99]), not the older son, who leads the way in the Journey to Bethlehem ([100].3). It is the young lad who plays this role from the time of such pre-iconoclastic representations as the one at Peruštica,[201] and in numerous Cappadocian images, where the inscriptions name him

---

191 Underwood, Vol. 1 of this work, p. 96.

192 It is represented on the triumphal arch in Santa Maria Maggiore (Cecchelli, *S. Maria Maggiore*, PL. LIII), then in the frescoes at Deir Abu Hinnis (Clédat, "Notes archéologiques," PL. II) and perhaps also at Peruštica (Frolow, "Peruštica," I, p. 32).

193 Millet, *Recherches*, Figs. 90, 96, 110.

194 Jerphanion, *Cappadoce*, PL. 37,4, 51,1, etc.

195 F. Ongania, ed., *La basilica di San Marco in Venezia*, I (Venice, 1881), pl. XV *b* (north transept, west wall, second zone).

196 Demus, *Norman Sicily*, PL. 18 (Palatine Chapel) and 65 *a* (Monreale): the angel is standing in the latter, flying in the former. We may also note Paris. suppl. gr. 27, of the 12th century, fol. 173, where Joseph's Dream follows that of the Magi; Omont, *Miniatures des plus anciens manuscrits grecs*, PL. C,10.

197 Pokrovskij, *Očerki*, Fig. 172, p. 259; Millet, *Recherches*, Fig. 88.

198 Millet, *Mistra*, PL. 66,3. The Dream does not appear in the Serbian Psalter at Munich (slav. 4), where the Flight comes immediately after the Return of the Magi to the East (fol. 215, 215v), in accordance with the illustration of the Akathistos.

199 The angel is seen flying, however, in much earlier compositions, as in the Georgian fresco of Ateni; Amiranašvili, *Živopis'*, (see above, n. 95), PL. 67.

200 This is a single leaf from the Jerusalem MS, now in the Public Library at Leningrad; V. N. Lazarev, *Istorija vizantijskoj živopisi*, II (Moscow, 1948), PL. 130. Joseph sometimes lies on a simple mattress, sometimes on a more elaborate couch that is supposed to be in a house, as in the Vatican Lectionary, gr. 1156; Millet, *Recherches*, Fig. 96. The scene is not in Paris. gr. 74.

201 Frolow, "Peruštica," I, PL. XI. The young lad probably led too in the fragmentary fresco at Deir Abu Hinnis; Clédat, "Notes archéologiques," PL. II. Jerphanion, "Véritable interprétarion," pp. 32 ff., is right in saying that the Flight into Egypt is not found on ancient ivories nor, in general, in Syro-Palestinian

IAKOBOC.[202] As in the Journey to Bethlehem, several of Joseph's sons sometimes appear in the scene of the Flight—for example at Matejić (Fig. 53 *b*) and in the Kalenić fresco, which this time differs considerably from our mosaic, where only one lad must have been represented.[203]

The arrangement of the persons involved, which is not indicated in the texts, simply derives from an adaptation of the theme of the Journey, and consequently the same formulas are used: in illustrations that strictly follow the Gospel account, Joseph alone leads;[204] in those that are inspired by the Apocrypha, it is one of his sons. But the apocryphal son, still imitated from the Journey, often is introduced into images that accompany the actual Gospel text. Numerous examples are found in the Constantinopolitan tradition, such as the miniature in the Menologion of Basil II (Fig. 55 *b*) or that in Paris. gr. 74,[205] the mosaics in Venice and Sicily,[206] or the Sinai icon (Fig. 40), where, however, it is Joseph who leads the way. In the majority of representations, the Child sits in the Virgin's lap; in the Sicilian mosaics, however, he is carried on Joseph's shoulders. This conception appears for the first time to our knowledge in the Laurentian Gospel Book, Plut. VI.23.[207] The artists of the Palaeologan period delighted in representing Joseph in this attitude, perhaps more particularly in Macedonia and Serbia, in the illustrations for the Akathistos at Matejić and at Dečani (Figs. 53 *b* and 56), in the Serbian Psalter at Munich,[208] and also at Kalenić. In these images, Joseph is behind the ass and Mary turns back toward the Child or even holds out her arms to him. It is probably a similar iconography that was adopted at the Kariye Djami. For we may assume that the artist wished to produce an effect of symmetry between the Flight and the Return from Egypt, in which Joseph carries the Child on his shoulders (PL. 200). In the course of the fourteenth century, then, in Macedonia and perhaps in Constantinople (the frescoes in the Metropole at Mistra and at Gradac still adhered to the middle–Byzantine scheme [209]) the artists had decided in favor of an apocryphal and picturesque iconography which

---

works (though this is not absolutely certain), but he goes too far in doubting the very existence of the scene in Early Christian or at least pre-iconoclastic art. The scene at Deir Abu Hinnis which follows the Murder of Zacharias is certainly a Flight. The event must have been commemorated at an early date in Egypt. In the case of Peruštica, where there is no justification for it, the illustration of the narrative is itself the reason for the scene. In addition, the child guiding the ass already appears there: hence, contrary to Jerphanion's contention, this is not a Cappadocian or Anatolian invention.

202 Jerphanion, *Cappadoce*, PL. 47,2 (church of Kılıclar, where the inscriptions are clearest), 38,4, 66,2, 76,1, 142,1, etc. The lad holds the donkey by a chain and carries over his shoulder a stick bearing a bundle. Joseph follows, holding a slender staff in his right hand and raising the left; Mary sits up very straight on her mount; the Child usually sits on her knees in the same fashion; sometimes he hangs from her neck (Kılıclar). The name James is also given to the lad in the London Psalter, Add. 19352; Millet, *Recherches*, Fig. 119.

203 The scene is not found at Curtea-de-Argeş. At Matejić (Fig. 53 *b*) one lad leads, another walks between Joseph and the ass. At Kalenić (Petković and Tatić, *Kalenić*, Fig. 47, p. 56, and sketch in Millet, *Recherches*, Fig. 112), the three lads are together in front, one holding the animal's bridle. As we know, the compiler of the Protevangelium ends his account before the Flight. The oriental paraphrases mention it, but without reference to the presence of Joseph's sons (in the *History of Joseph the Carpenter*, Ch. 8, the Holy Family is accompanied by "Salome," a name that does not correspond to any of those previously given—Ch. 2—to Joseph's children). In the second part of the Pseudo-Matthew three boys are mentioned as traveling with Joseph, and a girl with Mary (18:1). However, we need not necessarily seek the origin of the Kalenić or the Matejić motif

here, for it is a fact to be emphasized that the Protevangelium mentions the "sons of Joseph" at the moment of the arrival at the cave of the Nativity (18:1), and it could well have occurred to artists to represent one or more of them in both the Flight into Egypt and the Return from it [111].

204 This is the case on the Adana encolpion in the Istanbul Museum and the lost encolpion known from a drawing at Windsor (Jerphanion, "Véritable interprétation," p. 32 and Fig. 4), which are pre-iconoclastic works, as also in a certain number of illustrated Byzantine Gospel Books; see, for example, Millet, *Recherches*, Figs. 97, 110, and 111, and p. 158, n. 2.

205 *Evang. du XIe siècle*, I, PL. 7 *a* (fol. 4v).

206 Ongania, ed., *San Marco*, I, PL. XV *b*; Demus, *Norman Sicily*, PL. 18 (Palatine Chapel) and 65 *a* (Monreale). The mosaicists of these two churches represented the group journeying beside the sea—we see fish in the water—or along a river, which, so far as I know, is exceptional (but cf. the undulating ground in the miniature in Paris. gr. 74, which may have given rise to such an interpretation).

207 Millet, *Recherches*, Fig. 111. It occurs again in Paris. suppl. gr. 914 (ibid., Fig. 108). In the badly damaged fresco at Peruštica (Frolow, "Peruštica," I, PL. XI), something round can be made out above Joseph's head, which might suggest that this motif had already been represented there, but the dimensions are very small; the Child, if he was in Mary's lap, has disappeared in the lacuna. Joseph usually carries the Child on his shoulders in the scene of the Return from Egypt [111].

208 Slav. 4, fol. 215v; Strzygowski, *Die Miniaturen*, PL. LIV, 134.

209 Millet, *Mistra*, PL. 66,3 (Joseph leads, the Child is on his mother's knees, the lad follows; to the right, a vanished building; the scene takes place against a background of rocky hills). For Gradac, see Millet, *Recherches*, Fig. 88, or Petković, *La peinture serbe*, II, PL. XXXIII.

differed from the ancient tradition and which, once again, had been adopted for the illustration of the Akathistos.

At the right side of the lunette an Egyptian city is depicted, with its gates partly open.[210] From its high walls fall the statues of the pagan divinities (PL. 183). Such an image illustrates not the Protevangelium, whose account ends before the Flight, still less the Gospel itself, but rather oriental paraphrases in the Syrian tradition, which narrate the event with a certain emphasis and with a decided inclination toward the miraculous.[211] It must be stressed, however, that the episode had been introduced into the text of the Akathistos Hymn, undoubtedly under the influence of such accounts.[212] Figured representations of it are hardly found in Byzantine art before the Palaeologan period, although they may have existed earlier in Syriac manuscripts.[213] Even so, they appear preponderantly in illustrations for the Akathistos, from the fourteenth century on. The motif itself, however, is known to artists in connection with other subjects, especially certain episodes in the lives of St. Nicholas or St. George, for which we have slightly earlier documents.[214] The idols are always represented as curious pallid silhouettes, naked and almost featureless.[215]

In the majority of cases, and even when the idols are represented, the artists depicted Egypt personified welcoming the Holy Family before the gates of the city. This is a regular motif of the Flight theme, found in numerous Byzantine manuscripts from the tenth (see Fig. 55 b) to the twelfth century,[216] on the Sinai icon (Fig. 40) and others of the same type, and in all the Cappadocian representations. It was already a pre-iconoclastic motif, for, though it is not found in Peruštica, it does appear on two encolpia of the sixth-seventh century decorated with scenes from the life of Christ.[217] It is comparatively infrequent in the strictly Byzantine church painting of the Macedonians and the Comneni; among the Sicilian and Venetian mosaics it was depicted only in the Palatine Chapel at Palermo.[218] Elsewhere only the walls of the city are represented.

210 As also in the Menologion of Basil II (our Fig. 55 b). But this is quite unusual. Sometimes the gates are closed, sometimes there is simply an opening being entered by the young lad or by Joseph, according to which of them is leading (cf. the mosaic in the baptistery in San Marco, Venice, Bettini, *Mosaici di San Marco*, PL. CII; and Millet, *Recherches*, Fig. 97, for the Vatican Lectionary). The opening may also remain empty, as at Monreale; Demus, *Norman Sicily*, PL. 65 a.

211 Armenian Gospel of the Infancy, 15:16 (city of Mesrin); Budge, *History of the Blessed Virgin*, p. 46 (the city is not named); Arabic Gospel 10 (likewise); also in Pseudo-Matthew, 23 (the city is named Sotinen).

212 Strophe 12: Λάμψας ἐν τῇ Αἰγύπτῳ φωτισμὸν ἀνηθείας, ἐδίωξας τοῦ ψεύδους τὸ σκότος· τὰ γὰρ εἴδωλα ταύτης, Σωτήρ, μὴ ἐνέγκαντά σου, τὴν ἰσχὺν πέπτωκεν· οἱ τούτων δὲ ῥυσθέντες, ἀνεβόων πρὸς τὴν Θεοτόκον . . . .

213 There is an illustration of it in the Arabic Gospel in the Laurentian Library, Med. Pal. orient. 387, of the end of the 13th century, which derives from the Syrian tradition. While Mary and the Child are on the ass, Joseph converses with a man; the idol is seen to the right—a nude statue, falling. The preceding scene represents the Flight proper, with Joseph behind the ass and an angel showing the way (fols. 7 a and 8 b; the Arrival in Egypt is reproduced in Redin, *Miniatiury*, Fig. 3, p. 7).

The motif of the idols never appears in Cappadocia. I do not think it justifiable to suppose, with K. Weitzmann, *The Fresco Cycle of S. Maria di Castelseprio* (Princeton, 1951), p. 78, that it existed at Castelseprio. In Western art—especially, it seems, in the art of France—the motif is found from the 12th century (stained glass at Chartres, sculpture at Moissac) and becomes more frequent in the 13th and 14th centuries: the occasion is the illustration of the Pseudo-Matthew; the statues usually fall from pillars (see Index of Christian Art, Princeton University). The

motif of the statues falling from their pillars is known in Byzantine art from the 11th century, in connection with subjects other than ours (see in particular the miniatures accompanying the text of Chrysostom in Taphou 14, fol. 104).

214 First the fresco at Bojana, illustrating an episode in the life of St. Nicholas (Grabar, *Boïana*, PL. XXXIV, No. 81); later the fresco at Dečani (Petković and Bošković, *Dečani*, PL. CCXCII,1). For St. George, see the fresco at Staro Nagoričino (1313-18), Petković, *La peinture serbe*, I, PL. 114 a.

215 This nudity no doubt is to make them appear similar to antique statues. Moreover, in the case of Nicholas, as in that of Christ according to the Armenian Gospel of the Infancy, the scene is a sanctuary of Apollo.

216 Paris. gr. 74 (*Evang. du XIᵉ siècle*, I, PL. 7), Taphou 14 (Lazarev, *Istorija*, II, PL. 130), the Vatican Lectionary, gr. 1156 (Millet, *Recherches*, Fig. 97). On the other hand, it is found in neither Laurent. Plut. VI.23 nor Paris. gr. 115 (Millet, *Recherches*, Fig. 111).

217 See above, n. 204. The figure stands on top of the city walls; this is also the case in the Vatican Lectionary, perhaps because of lack of space. Elsewhere it appears before the gate, either standing with a gesture of welcome or prostrate in token of respect (the second procedure is less frequent; cf. particularly Taphou 14).

218 E. Kitzinger, "The Mosaics of the Cappella Palatina in Palermo," *ArtB*, 31 (1949), Fig. 7 (facing p. 290). It is an angel who points out the city to the Family. On the symbolic meaning of such a scene, in relation to triumphal and imperial iconography, see ibid., pp. 279 f., and the works cited in n. 57. The presence of the angel is uncommon. It is Joseph or the young lad who usually points to the city, depending on which of them is leading.

But the motif becomes more frequent in the painting of the Palaeologi. At Gradac the young woman wearing the turreted crown bows before the gate of the city: the iconography goes back to the Menologion of Basil II (Fig. 55 *b*), where, however, the woman advances swiftly toward the approaching Holy Family, with her hands covered in token of respect [219] (in the miniatures the gate is partly open, a feature that is repeated in the Kariye Djami). Although in the Cappadocian frescoes as in certain miniatures in Byzantine manuscripts of the eleventh century the woman is represented in ordinary garments, the painters of the Palaeologan period often depict a personage dressed as a high Byzantine dignitary, yet with a feminine aspect, as at Dečani (Fig. 56). I consider it certain that, in all these cases, we are dealing with a personification of the city or the country, rather than with a particular personage such as a priest or the governor Affrodisius mentioned in the Pseudo-Matthew.[220] Sometimes, at Dečani, at Matejić (Fig. 53 *b*), or in the Munich Psalter, a group of men stands at the entrance to the city.[221]

In view of such a long tradition of welcome to the Holy Family in the land where they found safety, it is strange that the Kariye Djami artist did not choose to represent this personification, the more so as it would have made the scene all the more solemn. Doubtless he was confronted by problems of space. The narrow dimensions of the portion of the lunette available to the right of the window prevented him from grouping too many elements there. To be in proper relation in size to the statues falling from the walls and to the figures in the group at the left, the personification would have had to occupy most of the space. The artist could have effected this, but at the expense of the statues of the pagan gods. It is difficult to say whether he chose his solution for a mechanical reason—to suppress an awkward element in an ensemble of traditional motifs— or in order to emphasize the symbolic nature of the fall of the idols. If the latter explanation is correct, and there is reason to believe that it is, we have yet another indication of the influence of the Akathistos Hymn on the iconographic program adopted at the Kariye Djami.

Now follow five scenes that constitute an unusually extended cycle of the Massacre of the Innocents: Herod Ordering the Massacre, together with the soldiers beginning it, in the large southern lunette of the sixth bay [107]; various phases of the Massacre in the western lunette of the same bay [108]; the Mothers Mourning Their Children in the western lunette of Bay 5 [109]; finally, closing the series, the Flight of Elizabeth and John, in the western lunette of the fourth bay [110]. This ensemble can be compared with that of the Magi, which we have studied above and which in any case is closely related to it, for it is the visit of the Magi that makes Herod uneasy and their stealthy departure that arouses him to fury. In order to represent the episodes of the Magi the artist had drawn from extensively developed sources of images. In the cycle of the Massacre of the Innocents his approach was different, for he isolated motifs traditionally

---

219 The woman wears the same headdress in Vat. gr. 1156 and the Sinai icon, but she is bareheaded in Taphou 14 and in Paris. gr. 74 (her hair is sometimes decorated with a row of pearls). In the Cappadocian frescoes, where the inscriptions designate her as ΕΓΥΠΤΟC, she is clad in ordinary garments, without a crown, and she stands within the frame of the gate. A particular feature is that she often carries a torch, doubtless because it is night (Joseph leaves Bethlehem by night, and the artists put the Departure and the Arrival together; see Jerphanion's remarks, *Cappadoce*, I, p. 78).

220 On the triumphal arch in Santa Maria Maggiore the personage wearing the chlamys and heading the group of men before the city is doubtless Affrodisius: the scene, which illustrates a narrative preserved in the Pseudo-Matthew (24), occurs after the episode of the fall of the idols. It remains highly unusual.

221 The arrangement appears to be peculiar to the illustration of the Akathistos, where the motif also occurs in the scene of the Return of the Magi (see pp. 223–24). The Kalenić fresco is influenced by this scheme. In the MS in the Historical Museum at Moscow, gr. 429, strophe 12 is illustrated by an image showing Mary standing by a city from which the statues fall and before which are two figures, one with a high coiffure—doubtless a turreted crown—the other with a broad hat (these silhouettes suggest neither a priest nor a governor). Only Mary is interpreted in strict accordance with the text of the Hymn, where the salutations are addressed to the Virgin (see n. 212).

belonging to only one or two compositions in order to fill the four lunettes he had to decorate. The elements appearing in the first three lunettes are usually combined in a single image, into which sometimes even the Flight of Elizabeth may be incorporated. Naturally, while engaging in this spreading-out process, the artist padded the motifs so as to create convincing scenes. His inventiveness thus proves to be considerable, as does his skill in composition.

The subject is well known and existed in the Early Christian period. The earliest representations show Herod, sometimes accompanied by guards, directing the Massacre, which often weeping mothers attempt to resist.[222] The motif of the mothers foreshadows that of Rachel, who is personified only at a later period. In the frescoes at Deir Abu Hinnis and at Peruštica two purely apocryphal episodes were introduced at the end of the Massacre: the Flight of Elizabeth with the infant John, pursued by a soldier (Fig. 57), and the Murder of Zacharias [223] (the theme of the Flight of Elizabeth is old—it is found as early as the sixth century, for example on the Bobbio medallion [224]). The same subjects, with the exception of the weeping mothers, are grouped together in a single miniature in Paris. gr. 510 (Fig. 58). In the Cappadocian frescoes, where inscriptions name her as Rachel, the mother is always present. All these episodes were the more easily represented in Cappadocia where they were depicted in frieze decorations. They are frequent, though not obligatory, in the so-called archaic cycles. In properly Byzantine art—if indeed Paris. gr. 510 belongs to a different tradition—the scenes of the Flight of Elizabeth and the Murder of Zacharias are extremely rare. For this art illustrates canonical texts with some apocryphal influences, rather than the Apocrypha themselves. In all the known manuscript miniatures from the tenth to the twelfth century the episodes of the Massacre are combined in a single composition and do not include these two themes. Nevertheless, the Murder of Zacharias can be found in the Synaxaria even in Constantinople; hence it was not unknown there.[225] The Flight of Elizabeth was introduced at this period into certain complex compositions of the type of the Sinai icon; placed above the Massacre, it effectively creates the illusion of a mountain (Fig. 40). An Armenian miniature of the thirteenth century shows a similar arrangement; the motif of the Flight of Elizabeth is less fully treated, in a lower corner.[226] It seems that it was through images of this kind that the complete cycle was preserved. For, during the middle-Byzantine period, the Massacre was hardly ever represented in churches. It is found only at Monreale, in Sicily.[227]

These subjects are more frequent in churches during the Palaeologan period. They do not form part of the illustration for the Akathistos Hymn, a fact which diminished the likelihood of

222 See, among others, Volbach, *Elfenbeinarbeiten*, No. 119, PL. 37; Wilpert, *Sarcofagi*, I, PL. XXXIX,2; the article "Innocents" in *DACL*.

223 Clédat, "Notes archéologiques," PL. I and II (Clédat had not identified these two scenes; see pp. 9–10); Frolow, "Peruštica," I, PL. XI (lower register) and pp. 33–34. The Peruštica inscription in the scene of the Massacre is certainly to be read "Herod"; the red headdress of one of the personages is reminiscent of the red crest at Deir Abu Hinnis: he must be a soldier, not a notary (see below).

The event is narrated in Protevangelium 22:3 and 23. The passage in the Protevangelium might be read on the occasion of the feastday of Zacharias; de Strycker, *Protévangile*, p. 45 and n. 2. The reference to Zacharias' murder recurs in the synaxaria; H. Delehaye, *Propylaeum ad Acta Sanctorum Novembris: Synaxarium Ecclesiae Constantinopolitanae* (Brussels, 1902), col. 16, under Sept. 5. For the texts concerning Zacharias, see A. Berendts, *Studien über Zacharias-Apokryphen und Zacharias-Legenden* (Leipzig, 1895).

224 Grabar, *Ampoules*, PL. LVI; Jerphanion, "Véritable

Interprétation." The latter holds that the subject was depicted on one of the lost plaques from the throne of Maximian; see also idem, *Cappadoce*, II, p. 440. The event is reported in the synaxaria under the date of the commemoration of Zacharias (see preceding note), but not under the date of the Massacre of the Innocents (Dec. 29, col. 353).

225 In the Menologion of Basil II, under the date of Sept. 5; *Menologio di Basilio II*, II, p. 14.

226 In the Rockefeller McCormick New Testament at Chicago, of ca. 1265, a curious miniature groups Herod enthroned, a soldier raising his sword, and Elizabeth, carrying John in her arms, entering the rock that will close behind her. The following miniature shows John the Baptist Preaching in the Desert: the artist presumably wished to show the only incident from the episode of the Massacre that concerned the life of the saint; fol. 9v, in E. J. Goodspeed, D. W. Riddle, and H. R. Willoughby, eds., *The Rockefeller McCormick New Testament* (Chicago, 1932), I, color fac-simile.

227 Demus, *Norman Sicily*, PL. 66 a.

their being represented. But they must have been illustrated in synaxaria. For they appear in the cycle of the Nativity at Gradac, which in any case follows an older type of complex composition.[228] The Massacre was represented in the Metropole at Mistra, where only a fragment of it is still extant.[229] In the Brontochion at Mistra an entire dome of the south gallery was decorated with a crowded composition, today fragmentary, which comprised a large number of motifs connected with the Massacre, including the Flight of Elizabeth, and which was independent of the representation of the Nativity. In another dome the Murder of Zacharias was also represented.[230] In the Theoskepastos at Trebizond, this last theme was depicted with the Massacre, an arrangement that goes back to an old Cappadocian tradition.[231] Even in Constantinople, however, traces of a representation of the Murder of Zacharias have been recognized among the fragmentary frescoes of the Palaeologan period in the building near the Early Christian church of the Theotokos Chalcopratia (Fig. 59).[232] At Curtea-de-Argeş the composition that combines the episode of Herod Ordering the Massacre with that of the Flight of Elizabeth forms part of the cycle of the Infancy which shows such pronounced imitation of the Kariye Djami cycle; however, marked iconographic differences appear in the motifs themselves.[233] In the monastery of Markov, in Serbia, the theme of Rachel weeping for her sons received a prominent place within the composition of the Massacre.[234] Also in the fourteenth century, the mosaicist of the baptistery in San Marco, who was inspired by Byzantine models, in addition to the soldiers massacring the children introduced the themes of Elizabeth and of Rachel, but not that of Herod, undoubtedly because of its resemblance to that of Herod receiving the Magi, which he has already represented.[235] Finally we may add that the frescoes at Mount Athos of the first half of the sixteenth century provide a certain number of representations of our theme which always include the motifs of Elizabeth and Rachel.[236]

Thus the Kariye Djami mosaicist did not invent any new themes, and those that he represented were in fashion at the period. But the way he treated them is worthy of careful examination, for it is here that his originality is most outstanding.

The southern lunette of the sixth bay, the first of the series, contains, as I said, two scenes: Herod Ordering the Massacre and the Beginning of the Massacre, grouped under an inscription taken from Matthew 2:16 [107] (PL. 184). The first theme, however, is rather an illustration of the text of the Protevangelium (22:1), where Herod's order to the assassins is more clearly expressed. Such a distinction between order and execution had already been made in the mosaic in Santa Maria Maggiore, and again in the miniature of the Munich Codex Purpureus.[237] In certain representations—the miniature in Paris. gr. 510 (Fig. 58) and the Cappadocian frescoes—

228 Millet, *Recherches*, Fig. 88.

229 Millet, *Mistra*, PL. 66,4.

230 Ibid., PL. 93,3 (second dome); on the first dome there was the history of Salome, on the third, the Murder of Zacharias; on the walls, the episode of the Magi (*Recherches*, p. 162, n. 3, without reproduction). The development of the episode of the Massacre is due, according to Millet, to the sermon attributed to Gregory of Nyssa (p. 162).

231 G. Millet and D. Talbot Rice, *Byzantine Painting at Trebizond* (London, 1936), p. 49 and PL. XIX,1–2; Millet, *Recherches*, pp. 162 f. and Fig. 117 (Millet proposes a 14th-century date).

232 See above, n. 29. The inscription has been read by Underwood as: Ὁ ἅ(γιος) Ζαχαρίας ἀναιρούμενος ἐν τῷ θυσιαστηρίῳ. The Murder of Zacharias is also reported later in the

Serbian church of Sisojevac; V. R. Petković, *Pregled crkvenih spomenika kroz povesnicu srpskog naroda* (Srpska akademija nauka, Posebna izdanja, 157; Odeljenje društvenih nauka, N.S., 4; Belgrade, 1950), p. 297.

233 Tafrali, *Curtéa de Argeş*, PL. LXIX,1, and text, p. 128 (No. 135). The fresco is damaged and has been tampered with; the episode of Elizabeth is represented in it.

234 Petković, *La peinture serbe*, I, PL. 146 b.

235 Photo Anderson, No. 22668 (for Herod and the Magi, see Bettini, *Mosaici di San Marco*, PL. C).

236 Cf. below, 234 and n. 251.

237 Clm. 23631, Cim. 2, fol. 24v. Reproduced in Grüneisen, *Sainte-Marie-Antique*, Fig. 260, p. 313. For Santa Maria Maggiore, see below, p. 234 and n. 254.

Herod giving the order for the massacre is surrounded by what would seem to be civilian officials ("notaries"), who will transmit it.[238] Nevertheless the massacre takes place before his eyes. At Monreale the theme of the order has been preserved, but the order is given to the soldiers themselves (the scenes at Monreale are accompanied by inscriptions recalling the account in the Protevangelium).[239] Aside from these examples, in the majority of Byzantine representations earlier than the Palaeologan period the distinction is not made between the order and its execution: Herod watches the massacre, which has already begun, as on the Sinai icon of the eleventh century (Fig. 40). In the manuscripts of the same period [240] his aspect is military, and he may be surrounded by guards.

At the Kariye Djami the figure of the King is represented with magnificence (PL. 185). Though he wears a rich cuirass, the highly elaborate gold crown and the absence of a sword give him a civilian aspect and differentiate him from the very military-looking personage of the scene of the Magi before Herod. The artist thus reveals a concern for decorative effect which makes him reject a realistic but sterile repetition. Herod is enthroned on a seat resembling the one in the previous composition, but is placed against an architectural background that here suggests a room in a palace rather than the city walls. In other documents this background may be a dais (Fig. 40). Even in the early images of the Rabbula Gospels [241] and of the church at Deir Abu Hinnis Herod's silhouette stands out against a rounded form—a dais or an exedra—and he is flanked by two guards (Fig. 57). In the pre-iconoclastic fresco, as well as in the Sinai icon and other still later documents, the guards wear fanciful helmets with scalloped crests. The guard who stands behind Herod in our mosaic—a handsome figure of baroque design—also differs from the guard in the scene of the Magi before Herod by his helmet. The artist has animated the often static group of the guards. A soldier arrives from the left, his bare arm extended in a lively gesture. His figure balances that of the soldier standing before Herod and receiving his orders. This soldier is one of a group of four armed men that serves to link the two parts of the composition with consummate art: it forms the transition between the order and its execution—renders its transmission concrete, as it were. Two of the men are listening to the King's words; the other two are already setting off in search of victims, one toward the background, the other toward the right, in an alarming manner. This procedure is an amplification of that which had already appeared in the Metropole at Mistra.[242]

The two motifs in the right section of the lunette appear to be a generalized version of the themes of the weeping Rachel and of Elizabeth pursued to the mountain with John (PL. 186–89). It is striking to observe the kinship between these two motifs and those which, in the Sinai icon and many other documents, represent these episodes in detail. In mosaics that follow ([109] and [110]), the artist treated them specifically; here he has taken his inspiration from them to synthesize the Massacre as if by anonymous symbols.

---

238 Jerphanion, *Cappadoce*, PL. 37,4, 66,1–2, 142,2, 147,1, 153,3–4, 174,1. The term νοτάρις sometimes accompanies the person standing close to the King, who is no more military in appearance than he; Herod may hold the tablets on which the order is written.

239 Demus, *Norman Sicily*, PL. 66 *a*. Inscription: *Ite occidite omnes pueros a bimatu et infra—Iussu Herodis trucidant pueros—Rachel plorat filios suos.*

240 In the Menologion of Basil II (*Menologio di Basilio II*, II, p. 281); in Paris. gr. 74, fol. 5 (*Evang. du XIe siècle*, I, PL. 7 *b*); in Vat. gr. 1156, fol. 280v (Millet, *Recherches*, Fig. 98); and in

Laurent. Plut. VI.23, fol. 7, the London Psalter (British Museum, Add. 19352), fol. 123, Paris. copt. 13, fol. 6v, etc. (Millet, *Recherches*, Figs. 113 ff.).

241 See Cecchelli et al., *The Rabbula Gospels*, fol. 4 *b*. Herod often holds a sword in this scene, and sometimes even a whip, as in syr. 28 at Berlin (8th-9th century), fol. 24v; photo Index of Christian Art, Princeton University.

242 Millet, *Mistra*, PL. 66,4: the two soldiers are back to back in the center of the picture, one receiving the order, the other starting off toward the right (where the episodes of the Massacre, vanished today, must have appeared).

Various episodes of the Massacre are grouped together in the western lunette of the sixth bay [108]. No fewer than nine soldiers and three mothers—some fragmentary—can be seen in the portions that have been preserved (PL. 190). Such a number is exceptional. However, almost all the motifs involved are well known. Thus the motif of the soldier who seizes a child by the leg to cut it in two is found in very early works and, moreover, is taken from the iconography of the Judgment of Solomon.[243] It is frequent in manuscript illustrations of the middle-Byzantine period. The same is true of the soldier who raises his sword, on which a little corpse is spitted; the theme is repeated twice here—to the right the child is transfixed by a sword, to the left by the point of a lance. No less familiar are the motifs of the child whom the soldier pins to the ground with his foot in order to cut its throat, and that of the soldier tearing the baby from its mother's arms.[244] The role assigned to the mothers, of whom there were at least three, is more important than usual, especially in church painting. Even in miniature painting the mothers are rarely represented in this number (but see Fig. 60 a). The hands so touchingly reaching out in the left-hand section, at the edge of the lacuna, and, below, the woman from whom her child has been torn belong to well-known motifs.[245] But the beautiful group to the right (PL. 193) seems to me to have no precedent in the theme of the Massacre. In spite of the subject, of the soldier's threatening attitude as he unsheathes his sword, and of the mother's frightened gesture as she clasps the child, it breathes a tranquil beauty that contrasts with the horrible episodes in the rest of the composition. The lithe carriage of the soldier has a Hellenistic appearance. Again, it is antique sculpture that is brought to mind by the magnificent green figure of the mother silhouetted against the background of gray, barren hills. Whether we have here an original creation or the adaptation of an antique theme, the mosaicist has given proof of an extremely subtle artistic sense. An interesting refinement in the rendition of movements and postures is seen in the other figures.[246] These different motifs show a taste for horror that is rather disturbing, but they are sublimated by the elegance of the forms and the beauty of the colors, and if the faces of some of the soldiers tend to express a primitive brutality, their outline remains none the less elegant. The entire scene—which, as such, is a new artistic creation—provides the occasion for an extraordinary formal virtuosity.

The episode of the mothers mourning for their dead children was the subject of a large composition in the western lunette of the fifth bay [109] (PL. 194). It is uncommon for this theme to be treated separately. Even at Markov, though it has a certain autonomy, it is incorporated into the composition of the Massacre. It is not likely that it was accorded an unusual development in the Metropole at Mistra. On the other hand, it may have been more amply treated in the Brontochion. The Kariye Djami mosaic is in any case the earliest, and probably the only, example of the theme treated separately in Byzantine art.[247] The subject of the weeping mother tearing her hair is very old, although the idea of connecting it with the Rachel of the texts may not have

243 Compare Paris. gr. 510, fol. 137 (our Fig. 58), with the miniature at fol. 215v (Omont, *Miniatures des plus anciens manuscrits grecs*, PL. XXXIX, upper register), where Solomon and his guard have a military appearance. Herod presides like a judge at his tribunal; on this question, see Grüneisen, *Sainte-Marie-Antique*, Figs. 248 ff.

244 Millet, *Recherches*, pp. 158 ff. (especially Laurent. Plut. VI.23, Fig. 113).

245 Ibid., and the manuscripts cited in n. 240.

246 See Underwood's description, Vol. 1 of this work, pp. 100–101.

247 Fol. 280v of the Vatican Lectionary (gr. 1156) comprises three motifs: Herod seated and speaking, the Massacre, Rachel seated, weeping; photo Index of Christian Art, Princeton University. In the West, the miniature in the *Wernherlied von der Magd* must be mentioned as a separate representation; in it seven mothers give way to their despair in various attitudes (there are no children); the scene follows one in which two soldiers massacre children beside a heap of little corpses (H. Degering, *Des Priesters Wernher drei Lieder von der Magd* (Berlin, 1925), pp. 214 and 216, fols. 87 and 88 of the MS). These images seem to be drawn from an extensive cycle, unless, as at the Kariye Djami, it is a case of dividing up the usual complex composition.

arisen at first.[248] It appears in the majority of post-iconoclastic representations. While it does not appear in the Sinai icon (Fig. 40) and in certain manuscripts,[249] it formed the subject of an admirable image in the Vatican Lectionary, gr. 1156, and in Paris. gr. 74 the name Rachel is inscribed in large letters above the woman who stands tearing her hair.[250] The passage in Matthew (2:18) refers, of course, to Jeremiah (31:15). The later representations at Mount Athos, of the sixteenth century, often include, besides the figure of Rachel, that of the Prophet unrolling a phylactery on which his words are inscribed.[251]

The theme of the weeping woman or women is often represented together with children's corpses. A heap of little corpses is introduced into many illustrations of the Massacre (cf. our Fig. 60 a). It is frequent in Cappadocia and in general in post-iconoclastic representations. It inspired the pathetic image at Markov: depicted frontally the crouching Rachel raises her arms in despair, surrounded by a score of little bodies wrapped in their swaddling clothes or in shrouds (Fig. 61).[252] In the case of the Kariye Djami, since this motif does not appear in the preceding images it has been supposed that it may have been represented in the left half of our composition, which is lost, and even that Herod or an executioner may also have figured there.[253] The attitude of the rising woman in the center of the composition in any case confirms the presence of an important element to the left. The women of the group to the right clasp the bodies or severed heads of their dead children to their bosoms (PL. 195–96), an indication that the massacre is ended. They press against each other, seeking comfort in their common grief, and their sad, tender mourning is without dramatization. The reticence of this scene, the beauty of invention in the group of mothers, in which there is an admirable variety of attitudes, are, it seems, to be credited entirely to our artist. The group recalls that of the mosaic in Santa Maria Maggiore, which, however, represents a different moment.[254]

The episode of the Flight of Elizabeth [110], the last of the series connected with the Massacre of the Innocents, occupies the western lunette of the fourth bay (PL. 197). It is the only purely apocryphal theme in the cycle of the Infancy of Christ in the Kariye Djami. The inscription is not taken, as were the others, from Luke or Matthew, since the episode is not recounted in these gospels; nor is it from the Protevangelium, on which the theme is based (22:3). Traditionally known and incorporated centuries earlier into the Massacre, the theme was not felt to illustrate any particular text. Thus the artist simply entitled it "The Flight of Elizabeth."

As was the case with the Mourning, the episode forms here the subject of a separate composition, an unusual occurrence in church painting. However, the Flight of Elizabeth is more independent in character than the Mourning. In the Early Christian period there are not only several representations of it in cycles of illustrations of the Apocrypha, as at Deir Abu Hinnis (Fig. 57) or at Peruštica,[255] but also separate images, such as that on the Bobbio medallion. Such images

248 This is the case in the majority of pre-iconoclastic images; cf. among others the figures for the article "Innocents" in *DACL*.

249 There is no Rachel in the miniature in the Laurentian Gospel Book, Plut. VI.23 (Millet, *Recherches*, Fig. 113), where the artist nevertheless represented three soldiers in various attitudes but only one mother. There is no mother at all in the miniature in the London Psalter (British Museum, Add. 19352; ibid., Fig. 119).

250 Millet, *Recherches*, Fig. 99, for Vat. gr. 1156; *Evang. du XIe siècle*, I, fol. 5, PL. 7 b, for Paris. gr. 74.

251 Millet, *Athos*, PL. 122,1 (Catholicon of Lavra); 159,2 (Koutloumous); 198,1 (Cath. of Dionysiou); 224,2 (Dochiariou).

252 Cf. Petković, *La peinture serbe*, I, PL. 146 b.

253 Underwood, Vol. 1 of this work, p. 103.

254 Cecchelli, *S. Maria Maggiore*, PL. LX. The Massacre itself is not represented; Herod, surrounded by guards, gives the order, which a soldier, advancing toward the group of women, prepares to carry out. The women are numerous, and they stand in various poses, holding their children in their arms.

255 See above, n. 223.

have been connected with a cult site where the miracle was commemorated.[256] Later, however, the scene is found only in connection with that of the Massacre, either in the cycle of the Infancy of Christ or, more rarely, in that of John the Baptist.[257] It is of course more frequent in an apocryphal context: it precedes the Murder of Zacharias in Paris. gr. 510 (Fig. 58) and several times in Cappadocia,[258] but does not appear in the Byzantine manuscripts from the tenth to the twelfth century. The Flight of Elizabeth, a moving subject, soon begins, however, to make its way into the compositions of the complex type of the Nativity cycle, such as that of the Sinai icon (Fig. 40). We have seen that during the Palaeologan period it frequently figures in the Nativity cycle, as it does in the later frescoes at Mount Athos. In the Kariye Djami, therefore, we must not view this subject as the deliberate introduction of an apocryphal theme but simply as a motif of the Massacre cycle which, like the other motifs, was accorded separate treatment.

The Kariye Djami mosaicist has condensed two episodes: the pursuit of Elizabeth by the assassin (PL. 198) and the mountain opening to receive the mother and child (PL. 199). The apocryphal narrative includes a third episode: an angel appearing in the cavern, which his presence illuminates. The theme of Elizabeth and John in the cavern is found in Paris. gr. 510 (Fig. 58) and in the Cappadocian frescoes, where the angel too is sometimes depicted.[259] But elsewhere it is the iconography used at the Kariye Djami, which had become traditional in Byzantine art, that is found from the eleventh century. Such an iconography better renders the anguish conveyed by the narrative and is more closely connected with the episodes of the Massacre. In our mosaic the soldier was unsheathing his sword when the mountain opened—which proves the imminence of the danger. This gesture, it would seem, must be credited to the artist. The theme is rendered in a slightly different way in the Sinai icon (Fig. 40) where the man, here also bareheaded (he must have lost his helmet in his haste), extends his right hand toward Elizabeth as if to seize her, while he holds his lance in his left. In the Brontochion at Mistra the assassin holds his sword raised.[260] We see that, on the whole, the iconography of the theme remained almost unvaried in the tradition from which our artist drew.

In fact, from the point of view of iconography, the scene of Elizabeth is the least original in the cycle of the Massacre, in which the artist has shown so much inventiveness in dividing the subject into different scenes and in creating new compositions such as the separate themes of the Massacre and of the Mourning Mothers, and such extraordinary virtuosity throughout in rendering a variety of attitudes.

With the Return of the Holy Family from Egypt, depicted in the western lunette of the second bay [111], we are brought back to the story of Christ itself, according to the account in Matthew (2:19–23). Two scenes are represented: Joseph Dreaming and the Holy Family arriving before Nazareth (PL. 200). The Dream is the third in the Kariye Djami cycle but the fourth in the narrative, for as the inscription indicates, citing Matthew 2:22–23, it takes place when the Holy Family has already left Egypt [261] and immediately precedes the arrival at Nazareth. Thus the relation to the following scene is very close, as is the connection between the second Dream

---

256 Indeed, the Bobbio medallion bears the following inscription: ΕΥΛΟΓΙΑ ΚΥ ΑΠΟ ΤΗC ΚΑΤΑ(ΦΥ)ΓΗC ΤΗC) ΑΓ(ΙΑ)C ΕΛΙCΑΒΕΘ (Grabar, *Ampoules*, PL. LVI and p. 44). Jerphanion, *Cappadoce*, II, p. 440, is of the opinion that three images were painted in the Aïn Qarem chapel (6th century): (1) Flight of Elizabeth pursued by the assassins; (2) Elizabeth in the cavern, which has closed on her; (3) Appearance of the angel to John in the same cavern.

257 For example, in the Rockefeller McCormick New Testament at Chicago, cited in n. 226.

258 Jerphanion, *Cappadoce*, PL. 41,2, 142,2, 148,2.

259 See above, nn. 256, 258.

260 Millet, *Mistra*, PL. 93,3.

261 Cf. Underwood, Vol. 1 of this work, pp. 104–105.

and the Flight into Egypt in certain documents. We have seen that the first Dream is not directly connected with the Journey to Bethlehem but that the two scenes were often grouped together ([100]), either because they succeed each other in the narrative or because of their analogy to those of the Flight. Indeed, the two compositions at the Kariye Djami are on the whole very similar, allowing for the difference in setting. This Dream is rendered in the same way as the one that precedes the Journey to Bethlehem (cf. PL. 201 and 153), but this time the old man's eyes are closed, and there are subtle differences in the treatment of his garments.

The return journey, in meaning as well as in iconography, is a counterpart to the Flight. The correspondence between the two is striking in certain illustrations, such as that in Paris. gr. 74 (Fig. 60 *b*), where the Holy Family approaches the city of Nazareth personified by a woman who welcomes the approaching travelers, while the other end of the miniature shows the Egyptian city and Joseph's third Dream depicted therein. The miniaturist put the scene in a wider context, covering the entire story in Matthew; Joseph carries on his shoulders the Child, already older, a feature which is seldom found in the Flight but is frequent, if not habitual, in the Return; Mary is seated on the ass, as in the Journey to Bethlehem, and turns back to Joseph's young son, who brings up the rear. The theme of the Return is seldom illustrated, and apparently was never treated in church painting before the Kariye Djami. Later it appears, in imitation of our mosaic, at Curtea–de–Argeş (Fig. 62). Its rarity is explained by the fact that it is not directly connected with the central episode of the Nativity. It exists only as an illustration for the passage in Matthew in certain manuscripts from which our artist may have taken his model.[262] However, in addition to those noted above, there are marked iconographic differences between the mosaic and the middle–Byzantine miniatures, especially in the attitude of the Virgin; in the mosaic the Virgin is on foot, following close behind the advancing Joseph bent beneath the weight of the Child (PL. 204–205). Mary's position is not a new creation, since she already assumes it in an Armenian Gospel Book of the thirteenth century,[263] but Joseph's attitude exhibits a realism that is very rare. Joseph's son—doubtless the youngest, apparently the same one who accompanied them on the Flight—is leading the ass by the bridle up a steep hill from behind the crest of which it has just emerged (PL. 202). The group is in the center of the composition; it has reached a sort of plateau, whence the view extends to the walled city of Nazareth with its variously and exquisitely colored houses and its trees (PL. 203). It is the crescent form of the lunette which obliged the artist to present the scene in this fashion, and he has utilized it in a most elegant manner, with the figure of Joseph stretched on his couch to the left and Nazareth to the right, balancing each other. The use of the corners of the lunette is less successful. The motifs of the tree and the small mausoleum are charming, but they are not well integrated into the ensemble.

The scene of the Holy Family arriving at Jerusalem to celebrate the Passover [112] is placed in the last lunette of the western wall and thus closes the cycle of the Infancy (PL. 206). The episode carries us several years forward in time. Although the inscription quotes Luke 2:41, it

---

262 In addition to our Fig. 60 *b*, I will mention the miniature in the Gospel Book of John Alexander, London, Brit. Mus., Add. 39627, which in any case copies Paris. gr. 74 (Filov, *Evangile du roi Jean Alexandre*, PL. 9, 16), and that in the Armenian Gospel Book at Baltimore, W. 539, fol. 20v (1262). The scene does not seem to have been illustrated in the Laurentian Gospel Book, Plut. VI.23. In church painting it is possible that the theme is represented at San Marco, Venice, for the Dream and the scene of the Holy Family arriving at a city, which come before that of Jesus among the Doctors, may refer either to the Flight into Egypt or to the Return (Ongania, ed., *San Marco*, I, PL. XV *b*). According to the Index of Christian Art, Princeton University, the scene of the Return is found in the West from the 11th century.

263 See the preceding note. Millet, *Recherches*, p. 650 and n. 9, points out that Mary is on foot, carrying the Child, in the Flight into Egypt on a Carolingian ivory casket in the Louvre.

is really verse 42 that is illustrated here, since Jesus, now twelve, accompanies his parents.[264] Such a representation is almost a *hapax* in Byzantine art. It is found only in very few manuscript illustrations as the first episode in the narrative of Jesus and the Doctors—for example in Laurent. Plut. VI.23 (Fig. 63), where it is treated rather simply.[265] In view of this, the Kariye Djami composition appears all the more to be an original creation. It is based, to be sure, on certain familiar elements, and it repeats some features of the preceding scene, so that the two compositions have much the same general appearance. The fresco painter of Curtea-de-Argeş, in copying them one after the other in a rectangular space (Fig. 62), has awkwardly emphasized the resemblance.[266]

However, a different spirit pervades the two scenes. The tired group approaching Nazareth in the hope of finding peace and a refuge there has little in common with the figures of Joseph and the twelve-year-old Jesus, now clad in a golden robe, advancing in a manner both eager and solemn toward the imposing walls of Jerusalem. The haste of Jesus and Joseph, who signals to the boy to follow him (PL. 210), is indicated by a *knielauf* of entirely antique tradition. One of Joseph's two sons who have halted on the road and seem to be waiting for Mary, who has some difficulty in maintaining such a pace, extends one arm toward the city. Jerusalem, in which two of the most celebrated monuments in Christendom—the rotunda of the Holy Sepulchre and the basilica of Constantine—are recognizable (PL. 207), is the journey's end toward which the whole group advances eagerly on the rising ground (PL. 208). The composition is more successfully adapted to the difficult setting of its lunette than the preceding one, for here but one event is depicted. The corners are soberly occupied by the green carpet of the ground. To the right the artist has not foregone the representation of a tree—a leitmotif, as it were, for him—its green foliage softening the starkness of the walls and at the same time counterbalancing the dark figure of the Virgin.

Luke (2:43–49) next tells how Jesus lingered in the temple at Jerusalem, arguing with the doctors, and how his parents, who had already left the city, came back to seek him. The various episodes occupied a large part of the vault of the first bay, the decoration of which has almost entirely disappeared [113] (PL. 211). On the basis of the fragments preserved on part of the lower slopes of the vault it has been possible to produce a convincing reconstruction of the scenes represented.[267] Under these conditions, an iconographic study is hardly possible; it is, however, permissible to determine what place in the tradition was held by the theme of Jesus and the Doctors, which forms the connecting link between the events of the Infancy of Christ and those of his Ministry, and thus begins a new cycle.[268] The connecting role of the episode has sometimes caused artists to be uncertain as to the place that the scene should occupy. If in certain illustrated Gospel Books it naturally follows the episodes of the Infancy (Fig. 63),[269] the same is not always the case in churches. It may occupy its chronological place, as at Monreale or in San Marco, Venice.[270] But at Bojana it is isolated in the narthex,[271] and in the Metropole at Mistra it is

264 Underwood, Vol. 1 of this work, p. 106.
265 The miniature at fol. 106 (photo Index of Christian Art, Princeton University) perhaps also illustrates the episode; to the right Mary and Joseph are seen approaching a city.
266 Tafrali, *Curtéa de Argeş*, PL. LXII,2, (No. 132). The fresco painter has introduced further personages, who appear behind the hills: doubtless they are other people traveling to Jerusalem.
267 Underwood, Vol. 1 of this work, pp. 108–10.
268 For the cycle of Christ's Ministry, see P. A. Underwood's study in this volume.

269 I may further cite Paris. gr. 74, fol. 110 (*Evang. du XIe siècle*, II, PL. 98), and Vat. gr. 1156, fol. 283v (photo Index of Christian Art, Princeton University). In Paris. gr. 510, the episode of Jesus and the Doctors is illustrated further on, at fol. 165 (upper register; Omont, *Miniatures des plus anciens manuscrits grecs*, PL. XXXV).
270 Demus, *Norman Sicily*, PL. 65 *b*; Ongania, ed., *San Marco*, I, PL. XV *b*.
271 Whereas the beginning of the cycle is in the nave; Grabar, *Boïana*, diagram on p. 30 and PL. XXVII–XXVIII (No. 61).

represented in the south aisle.[272] In the Brontochion and the Pantanassa it is found in the narthex.[273]

The theme, which already appears in Early Christian art,[274] nevertheless remains rare in the early periods, and is seldom represented in Cappadocian decoration.[275] It is illustrated, in a group of three narrative scenes, in Paris. gr. 510, where there is a remarkable representation of the scene of Mary finding Jesus again, with the boy kissing his Mother.[276] Apparently it took some time for the traditional iconographic scene to take shape, since in a manuscript of the tenth century, Atheniensis 211 (fol. 226),[277] as well as on the Milan ivory, Christ is seated in profile and the doctors are all grouped on one side. However, in the central scene of Paris. gr. 510 Jesus is enthroned frontally between two pairs of doctors who are seated below him. This is the scheme that is thenceforth classic, varying only in the number of figures and the architectural setting. Mary and Joseph are usually depicted in it, approaching the group but remaining outside of the action.[278] Narrative instances of the type of the Paris manuscript are rare.

The theme is not particularly frequent in Macedonian painting of the Palaeologan period. It appears in the Protaton, with the representations of two feasts of the Infancy of Christ, the Nativity and the Presentation.[279] Later it recurs in numerous decorations at Mount Athos, of the sixteenth and seventeenth centuries. The narrative tradition of Paris, gr. 510, still illustrated, though differently, in the twelfth century in Laurent. Plut. VI.23 (Fig. 63), is found again in the fresco in the Brontochion at Mistra,[280] where Jesus kissing his Mother is represented after the "classic" scene. The Kariye Djami mosaic constituted a stage between these representations and was probably the first example of detailed treatment of the episode in church decoration.

We may now attempt to define the iconographic characteristics of the cycle of the Infancy of Christ at the Kariye Djami. It must first be emphasized that the case of this cycle differs from that of the Virgin. Illustrations of the infancy and life of Mary down to the Annunciation are very frequent in the Palaeologan period, and the existence of a series of comparatively homogeneous ensembles has even made it possible to define a cycle type, with which we have compared the cycle at the Kariye Djami.[281] The same is not true of the images of the Infancy of Christ. The practice of representing its chief episodes among the Great Feasts led to the almost complete abandonment of narrative sequences of the events of the Infancy in programs of church decoration, from the middle–Byzantine period on.

Outside of Cappadocia, it is in works of Constantinopolitan tradition, such as the mosaics at Monreale or those in San Marco, Venice, that we find examples of the Infancy cycle in the twelfth century.[282] In these we must see an influence from illustrated manuscripts, which were especially numerous in the eleventh century and which perpetuated the practice of representing these events. It is with this same tradition that we must connect the frescoes at Bojana, of the middle of the thirteenth century, the first important narrative cycle in pre-Palaeologan painting. The

272 Millet, *Mistra*, PL. 73,2.
273 Ibid., PL. 98,2 and 149,4.
274 As in the 5th-century diptych at Milan; Volbach, *Elfenbeinarbeiten*, No. 119, PL. 37.
275 Jerphanion, *Cappadoce*, esp. PL. 76,1 and 151,2.
276 Omont, *Miniatures des plus anciens manuscrits grecs*, PL. XXXV (fol. 165), upper register.
277 A. Grabar, "Miniatures gréco-orientales: II, Un manuscrit des homélies de Saint Jean Chrysostome à la Bibliothèque

Nationale d'Athènes (Atheniensis 211)," *Seminarium Kondakovianum*, PL. XX,2 and pp. 268–69.
278 The theme has been well studied by A. Grabar, *La peinture religieuse en Bulgarie* (Paris, 1928), pp. 146 ff.
279 Millet, *Athos*, PL. 35.
280 Millet, *Mistra*, PL. 98,2.
281 See above, "Cycle of the Life of the Virgin," pp. 192–93.
282 The mosaics in the Holy Apostles at Constantinople included, beside the "classic" scenes, only the Journey and the Adoration of the Magi.

ensemble in the Metropole at Mistra, of the end of the same century, more extensive but still limited, constitutes an admirable church cycle, which, however, will have no progeny. In Macedonian painting the cycle of the Infancy of Christ remains rare. Or better, it appears there in a different light, being connected with the rubrics of the Synaxarion and especially with the strophes of the Akathistos Hymn. It is indeed the Akathistos which, from the fourteenth century (we possess no earlier documents, although they must have existed) takes over the themes of the Infancy of Christ, though subjecting them to iconographic modifications in accordance with the text. In the following centuries the same applies to all art in the Byzantine tradition. As for the strictly apocryphal tradition, after the representations at Venice and in Cappadocia, it reappears in the Brontochion at Mistra, in an exceptional, crowded cycle that recalls the cycle of the Virgin in the Peribleptos.

Thus, as a narrative sequence, the cycle of the Infancy at the Kariye Djami stands more or less alone. We may, however, note again that it exercised a direct influence on two later ensembles, those at Curtea-de-Argeş and at Kalenić,[283] whereas it will be remembered that the Kariye Djami cycle of the Virgin, precisely because it was in competition with a flourishing tradition, seems to have had no descendants in church decoration. The themes represented at the Kariye Djami which are not found in contemporary or slightly earlier painting are the Journey to Bethlehem, the Enrollment, the Return from Egypt, Christ Taken to Jerusalem for Passover. Furthermore, Joseph's three Dreams do not appear anywhere else in a single ensemble; the five compositions of the Magi are exceptional in number; the episodes of the Massacre had never been the subject of a comparable series of autonomous scenes. Thus the cycle is characterized by its fullness, which is also determined by the architectural arrangement of the building. It was in order to cover all the surfaces of the outer narthex suitable for decoration that the artist elaborated such a detailed sequence; he drew not only upon the comparatively scanty contemporary tradition but also upon the rich material supplied by the sequences of miniatures in middle-Byzantine manuscripts. In this respect, certain scholars were justified in connecting our mosaics either with Laurent. Plut. VI.23 or with Paris. gr. 74, but they went too far in their hypotheses. Millet related them to the Laurentian Gospel Book, which provides the most extensive of these cycles, and sought to connect our mosaics with what he called the Alexandrian tradition.[284] Shmit thought rather of manuscripts of the type of Paris. gr. 74 and Vat. gr. 1156 for the scenes of Christ, and, for those of the Virgin, of frescoes allegedly executed in the earlier, ninth-century church of the Chora, at the time of Michael Synkellos; thus he proposed a Syrian origin[285] for the cycle of the Virgin. These "archeological games," which, on the one hand, restricted the Palaeologan renaissance to imitating the art of the Macedonian renaissance and, on the other hand, sought at all costs to determine the geographical origin of one or the other iconographic tradition, were very rightly denounced by Diehl, among others.[286] Even if Diehl's arguments are not exactly the same as ours, he is certainly correct in viewing the Kariye Djami decoration as a product of the high culture of Constantinople under the Palaeologi.

---

283 See also, on this question, Underwood, Vol. 1 of this work, pp. 87 n., 94, 94 n., 95–96.

284 Millet, *Recherches*, pp. 649 ff. and 688. Millet rejects Shmit's hypothesis (see below). Now, the example of the Enrollment is far from convincing, since the Kariye Djami composition is much closer to the miniature in Vat. gr. 1156 than to that in Laurent. Plut. VI.23 (p. 650).

285 Shmit, *Kakhrie-dzhami*, pp. 184–85 (for Michael Synkellos, pp. 24 ff. and 224 ff.).

286 Ch. Diehl, *Manuel d'art byzantin*, 2nd ed., II (Paris, 1926), pp. 744 ff. However, we cannot accept some of this author's arguments concerning the iconographic originality of the cycle of the Virgin: themes such as that of the First Steps are in no sense a creation of the Palaeologan period (p. 801). What is new is the integration of all these themes into the Palaeologan cycle, as we have seen above.

It is true, in respect to both the scenes of the Virgin and the scenes of Christ, that our artist drew upon old manuscripts of Constantinopolitan tradition—for, as we have remarked more than once, the iconography of the cycle of the Infancy of Christ is more closely linked to the refined and elegant miniatures of the Paris Gospel Book than with those of the Gospel Book in the Laurentian Library, while that of the Virgin is related to the illustrations of the Homilies of the monk James. But within the compositions themselves, the motifs are far from being derived from such manuscripts only. In particular, unmistakable connections with the iconography employed in illustrating the Akathistos in the Palaeologan period sound a modern note. These concordances with, or borrowings from, the Akathistos cycle certainly demonstrate the eclecticism of our artist, but they also reveal a certain perplexity, caused by the absence of a well-established tradition in church painting for a narrative cycle of the Infancy of Christ.[287] As a result, our ensemble breathes a boldness of conception that is truly remarkable. The greater freedom accorded the artist in this situation was propitious for his genuinely creative activity—which is especially striking in the autonomous compositions into which he has divided the complex schemes then in use in illustrating the episodes of the Magi and the Massacre. Such qualities are far less perceptible in the cycle of the Virgin, which, however, in its density and homogeneity may seem more satisfying intellectually.

The cycle of the Infancy of Christ is certainly intended to be canonical. All the compositions are accompanied by inscriptions taken from Luke and Matthew, with the single exception of the Flight of Elizabeth, which is given a title, not a quotation. Similarly, in the inner narthex the compositions of essentially apocryphal derivation are accompanied by inscriptions that define them without precisely relating them to the texts from which they originally proceeded. The apocryphal nature of these images, which had long before become part of the tradition, was hardly felt. The same applies to the motifs of apocryphal inspiration which are interspersed through the scenes of the Infancy of Christ. Some of them are already found in the miniatures in Gospel books of the eleventh century, which are influenced by illustrations for the Protevangelium. Others, especially the figures of Joseph's sons, who form a sort of apocryphal counterpoint in several compositions, seem to be connected with more distinctly oriental traditions, since they are akin to Armenian images of the thirteenth century. It is the particular nature of Palaeologan art to mingle various influences—some of them very old—in a koine that then establishes a true kinship in all art of Byzantine tradition. In the presence of the Kariye Djami mosaics it is at any rate impossible to deny to the art of the capital the right of being narrative and apocryphal with the utmost elegance.

Finally, the role that the Virgin continues to play in the cycle of the Infancy of Christ is remarkable, not only because of her presence in a whole series of compositions but also because of the importance given to her figure. The homage to the Virgin which is expressed by the decoration of the inner narthex is continued here as well. This is another specific characteristic of a period that saw the flowering, in honor of the Mother of God, of new compositions or compositions new in their development, illustrating typological themes or the strophes of the Aka-

---

287 Dionysius of Fourna, in his chapter on how to represent the festivals of the Lord and other actions and miracles of Christ according to the Holy Gospels, establishes the following list of the themes of the Infancy of Christ (Ἑρμηνεία τῆς ζωγραφικῆς τέχνης, ed. A. Papadopoulos-Kerameus [St. Petersburg, 1909], pp. 85 ff.): Annunciation, Joseph's Reproaches, Visitation, the Magi and Herod, Nativity, Adoration of the Magi (and their Departure), Presentation of Christ in the Temple, Flight into Egypt, Massacre of the Innocents, Jesus among the Doctors. He refers each time to the text of the Evangelist, despite the apocryphal motifs introduced into his descriptions. This list appears to be the result of a compilation rather than a faithful reflection of a cycle used in churches.

thistos.[288] Above the entrance door to the inner narthex there is a representation of Christ Pantocrator, χώρα τῶν ζώντων, "dwelling-place of the living." Responding to this image, the image of the Virgin Blachernitissa, occupying the lunette above the entrance door to the church exactly opposite the Pantocrator, is accompanied by an inscription that truly rivals that of Christ: χώρα τοῦ ἀχωρήτου—the Virgin, "dwelling-place of the uncontainable." [289]

[288] For the typological representations, see Sirarpie Der Nersessian's study in this volume on the frescoes of the parecclesion. In respect to the Akathistos, the scenes at the Kariye Djami that I have compared with the illustrations of this Hymn attest that similar illustrations certainly existed from the beginning of the 14th century; this fact is confirmed by the recent publication of the frescoes of St. Nicholas Orphanos at Salonika (see above, n. 30).

[289] See [1] and [2], PL. 17 and 20.

Some Problems in Programs
and Iconography of Ministry Cycles

PAUL A. UNDERWOOD

Some Problems in Programs and Iconography of Ministry Cycles

A MURAL CYCLE of Christ's Ministry might comprise a greater number of scenes than other Christological cycles, for, in theory at least, any of the events of the life of Christ between his Infancy and Passion might be depicted. Indeed, they were so numerous that the mural painters, restricted as they were by considerations of space and the higher priority usually accorded to certain other cycles, were forced to be highly selective. Moreover, in a Ministry cycle there was nothing traditionally canonical regarding the selection, grouping, and disposition of subjects. In these respects the artists had considerable freedom and opportunity to bring out meanings of special significance if they were to do more, as many did, than present a random series of narrative representations. In formulating this cycle, then, the artists were confronted with certain types of decisions and problems that were unique to it.

In this study the attempt will be made to observe some of the problems that faced Byzantine muralists in constituting their Ministry cycles and to discover some of the ways in which they took advantage of opportunities to infuse them with meaningful content.[1] Since we will be dealing primarily with cycles, that of the Kariye Djami and others, it follows that manuscript illuminations or illustrations in others of the minor arts will not figure prominently, for by their nature they seldom present subjects in cyclical form and in general the problems of the painters of monumental cycles were of quite a different order from those of the book illuminators.

In their iconography some of the individual subjects, in both monumental and miniature art, had developed rather stereotyped forms which, in the context of this study, offer little of art historical interest or significance. No attempt, therefore, will be made to analyze the iconography of a number of the scenes in a systematic way. But for those individual subjects that raise pertinent questions or, as units within a group of subjects, throw light upon the significance of the group as a whole, a more purely iconographic analysis and detailed comparisons will sometimes be made and recourse taken to manuscript illumination or other media of art.

With few exceptions the monuments containing well-developed Ministry cycles, which will be of main concern here, are from the Comnene and, more especially, from the Palaeologan era, during which there was a general tendency to be excursive in the proliferation of cycles, in individual cycles, and in the subjects that comprise them. Attention will not be limited to those subjects depicted in the cycle of the Kariye Djami, but in general this cycle will serve as the focal center from which investigations will proceed.

1 My warm thanks are due to Fanny Bonajuto, Associate in Research for the Dumbarton Oaks Faculty, for her able and generous assistance during the preparation of this study.

The cycle of the Kariye Djami is presented *in extenso* in the mosaics of the narthexes,[2] immediately succeeding the Infancy and preceding the now-missing festival cycle of the nave. More precisely it occupies the successive domical vaults of the seven bays of the outer narthex and the vaults, the pendentives, and two lunettes beneath the southern dome of the inner narthex.[3] Although these mosaics have suffered severe losses, they give evidence of having been among the most extensive in existing monuments of Byzantine mural decoration. Originally there must have been at least thirty-two scenes. If, as we believe, four subjects were placed in the pendentives of the vault of the seventh bay, in an arrangement comparable to that in the pendentives of the sixth vault, the cycle consisted of thirty-six subjects.[4]

In theory a Ministry cycle could include any of the events celebrated as Great Feasts prior to the Passion cycle or events that immediately anticipated it. Thus, the Baptism, Transfiguration, Raising of Lazarus, and Entry into Jerusalem, all of them normally to be found among the so-called Twelve Feasts, might appear in such a cycle. But when a distinct Ministry cycle was attempted in a late-Byzantine church, as at the Kariye Djami, where these particular scenes formed part of the festival cycle of the nave, the scenes had to be either repeated in the Ministry cycle or omitted from it. The evidence provided by the twenty-eight extant or fragmentary subjects of the Ministry in the Kariye shows that the Great Feasts and events associated with the Passion were omitted, and it appears also that none of Christ's parables were represented. The mosaicists of the Kariye conceived the Ministry as extending from the appearance of Christ among the Doctors up to, but not including, those subjects which relate to the Betrayal and the awesome events culminating in the final fulfillment of his mission—the Passion itself. A Ministry cycle might, thus, include as its last event Christ's Anointment in the House of Simon.[5] Although I shall continue to regard the scene of Christ among the Doctors as the starting point of the Ministry, as I did in Volume 1,[6] I will not discuss its iconography, which has been treated in the preceding study by Jacqueline Lafontaine-Dosogne.[7]

Such a definition of the scope of a Ministry cycle is roughly comparable to that of the *Hermeneia*.[8] Part Three of that work is entitled "How one depicts the feasts and other works and

---

2 Scenes [113]–[141]. See Vol. 2 of this work, PL. 211–81.

3 See Plans and Sections, *Figs. 2–8*, at end of volume.

4 At Monreale there are 27 subjects, including miracles, in what could be called a Ministry cycle—certainly one of the most extensive of such cycles. However, 3 of these subjects (Christ among the Doctors, Cana, and Baptism) are in the crossing (otherwise devoted to the Infancy); 4 (Temptation, Paralytic, Blind Born, and Samaritan Woman) are in the south arm (otherwise assigned to festival subjects and the early part of the Passion); and 20 are in the side aisles, 10 in each. The 27 subjects are thus so scattered that the unity of the cycle, as such, is sacrificed, and parts are mixed in with other cycles.

5 Matt. 26:6–13; Mark 14:3–9.

6 P. 108 f.

7 "Iconography of the Cycle of the Infancy of Christ," pp. 237–38.

8 Dionysius of Fourna, Ἑρμηνεία τῆς ζωγραφικῆς τέχνης, ed. A. Papadopoulos-Kerameus (St. Petersburg, 1909), pp. 88–103 (Nos. 10–76); French version, A. N. Didron, ed., *Manuel d'iconographie chrétienne grecque et latine*, tr. P. Durand (Paris, 1845), pp. 162–88. In the present study our interest in this very late manual for use by painters is limited to the chronology of events it established in the Ministry of Christ. We are not concerned with the iconographical instructions it contains, for it is immaterial whether they do or do not correspond to the iconography of the specific existing paintings with which we shall deal. See also p. 247 and n. 11. For studies of the editions of the *Hermeneia* of Dionysius of Fourna, their dates, and editions

of other manuals independent of it, see V. Grecu, "Eine kritische Ausgabe der Ἑρμηνεία τῆς ζωγραφικῆς τέχνης," *Bulletin de l'Institut archéologique bulgare*, 9 (1935) = *Actes du IVᵉ Congrès international des études byzantines, 1934*, I, pp. 224–37; idem, "Byzantinische Handbücher der Kirchenmalerei," *Byzantion*, 9 (1934), pp. 675–701. In the form that appears under the name of Dionysius, the *Hermeneia* must have been compiled in the first half of the eighteenth century (Grecu, "Byzantinische Handbücher," p. 677). Fragments of shorter manuals, independent of the *Hermeneia*, exist, and several Russian manuscripts of the eighteenth and nineteenth centuries are translations of them. They contain lists (but not descriptions) of Biblical subjects and many texts and legends to accompany the scenes; the lists are in orders entirely different from those of the *Hermeneia*. In Papadopoulos-Kerameus' edition of the latter, two such fragments are published as appendixes: Parartemata Γ (pp. 265 ff.) and Δ (pp. 274 ff.). In both of these, beginning respectively on p. 265 and p. 278, it can be observed that with regard to the subjects which would comprise a Ministry cycle they do not agree with one another or with the *Hermeneia* in their order, which is very haphazard, as if someone had jotted down subjects, regardless of their position, represented in some church he had visited. Grecu ("Eine kritische Ausgabe," p. 236) concludes that Dionysius' compilation was taken, with the exception of the descriptions, from material already existing in earlier painters' guides, but he suspects that some earlier examples also contained descriptions.

miracles of Our Lord according to the Holy Gospels." The first section of Part Three extends from the Annunciation to Christ's Anointment in the House of Simon. In actual practice, however, the artist would normally assemble the first nine subjects—from the Annunciation to the Massacre of the Innocents—and treat them as an Infancy cycle, but from subject No. 10 (Christ among the Doctors) to the end of the first section of Part Three, No. 76 (Christ's Anointment), the subjects comprise a Ministry cycle that includes the festival events which occurred during that period of Christ's life. The second section of Part Three (subjects 77-98),[9] which does not concern us, is entitled "The Passion of Christ"; it begins with the incident of Judas receiving his pieces of silver and ends with the Descent of Christ into Limbo (the Anastasis). This is followed by a third section dealing with events after the Resurrection (subjects 99-111). Part Four, section one, consists of Christ's parables. Part Three, section one, of the *Hermeneia*, which, as we shall see, almost exhausts all possible depictable events, describes sixty-seven Ministry subjects. Obviously, in no single monument could all of them be depicted, for reasons of space, and it was always necessary, therefore, to make a selection.

Although only about half of the possible subjects were depicted in the cycle of the Kariye Djami, its compass, but not its sequence, generally accorded with the scope of the Ministry in the *Hermeneia;* it should be noted again, however, that because the nave of the Kariye undoubtedly contained a festival cycle, festival subjects were omitted, as were the parables. But the Ministry as described in the Gospels comprised events which were susceptible of division into several categories, such as those which chronologically preceded Christ's first miracle; his conversations with individuals for purposes of teaching; his formal teaching of groups in temples, synagogues, or elsewhere; his miracles of healing; and other miracles. In some monuments, as at the Kariye Djami, the Ministry might run the gamut of all types, but in others it might be limited to one or more categories, and even include a few parables. In a generally comprehensive cycle, as that of the Kariye Djami, some scenes from an individual category could be assembled as a group to form one part of the cycle or, as at Monreale, could be dispersed among other cycles and placed in various parts of the church.[10]

One of the major concerns here is to try to discover what rationale was in the mind of the artist in the selection and disposition of his subjects within the cycle and what meanings he may have attempted to convey. Mere narration was by no means the sole, or even the major, intention in depicting the Ministry, but in some cycles no content other than narration or decoration can be definitely detected or defined.

Many ways were open to artists and iconographers in selecting the subjects and arranging them in a cycle of the Ministry. One was to attempt a general historical chronology. It will be seen, however, that this method was truly feasible only for the beginning of the Ministry, up to the performance of the first miracle; thereafter an arbitrary chronology would have to be attempted through an artificially created "harmony" of the Gospels, because the accounts of the four disagree drastically as to the sequence of events and even as to events themselves. Such a chronological sequence did seem to exist earlier than that of the *Hermeneia* as we know it in the very late manuscripts that have come down to us, for it will be seen that a chronological "harmony" of that sort was probably employed in the layout of some cycles.[11] But always, in minor

9 Papadopoulos-Kerameus, pp. 103-10.
10 See n. 4 above.
11 Efforts to establish a harmony of the Four Gospels go

back to the second century, when Tatian, a Syrian, wove them into a single version known as the *Diatessaron*, probably written in Syriac but translated into Greek (see *New Catholic Encyclo-*

ways and for various reasons, that sequence was never strictly followed, for it was often affected by considerations other than chronology. Even when dealing with events from the appearance of Christ among the Doctors to the first miracle, for which the chronology was clearly established in the Synoptic Gospels, the Kariye Djami was not one of those monuments which attempted a chronological approach to the layout.

The Kariye Djami, like other monuments, affords evidence of a prevalent method in which the layout of the Ministry was at times influenced by the liturgical calendar. That is to say, here and there subjects were selected and grouped together to illustrate the lections from a given Gospel and from days within a limited number of successive weeks. We shall see, for example, that all subjects depicted in the south bay of the inner narthex, comprising eight healing miracles, and the set of three in the pendentives of the sixth bay of the outer narthex,[12] were chosen in order to illustrate the Gospel lections read in the services in successive weeks of the liturgical calendar.[13]

At times still other devices might be used. For example, scenes might be juxtaposed, or paired, to establish analogies between them that would recall the holy rites or the allegorical meaning of the events depicted. Such allegories might be drawn from exegetes of the Scriptures, from hymns, or from other familiar allusions to be found in the liturgies. Now and again, a few subjects were grouped because the events they depict occurred in the same place; or subjects were paired or placed in opposition to one another to demonstrate that in fulfilling his mission to mankind Christ displayed impartiality between man and woman, between the lowly or despised and those who were not.

Other possibilities that must be kept in mind are artistic, or at least compositional, in nature. Large areas such as the domical vaults of bays three, six, and seven of the outer narthex at the Kariye Djami were too extensive to receive a single episode of one subject. In such cases the artist might create a small cycle of a single subject by depicting a series of episodes, or he might decide to treat the perimeter of the whole vault as an annular frieze and compress many individual subjects without strongly delineated boundaries to make of them a single composition. Again, he might assign a given subject to a rather large area because it would feature a large number of persons; such a subject at the Kariye Djami was Christ Healing a Multitude [141], which was assigned to the largest lunette in the south bay of the inner narthex.

All these devices, and doubtless others that are less apparent, are to be found in various monuments. If at first sight the layout of the cycle in the Kariye Djami, after the Miracle of Cana, appears to be chaotic or whimsical because of the lack of chronology, such an impression, though not entirely overcome, is nevertheless reduced when we take into account a number of alternative methods which could have been, and were, used in the layout. We should now turn to the various procedures described above and see to what extent they were used not only at the Kariye Djami but in other monuments as well. We should begin with the device of chronology and the problems it posed.

---

pedia, Vol. 4 [New York, 1967], p. 853). In early centuries it was widely known and commented upon, but only a few fragments in Greek are extant. Ammonius of Alexandria (early 3rd c.) supposedly composed another harmony of the same kind, which is now lost (see P. A. Underwood, "The Fountain of Life in Manuscripts of the Gospels," *DOP*, 5 [1950], pp. 121 f.). For a bibliography on Tatian's *Diatessaron*, see C. Nordenfalk, "An Illustrated Diatessaron," *ArtB*, 50, 2 (1968), p. 137, n. 100. In

the end, the system of harmonizing the Gospels that was to remain in common practice was that of the Eusebian sections that were incorporated in the Canon Tables, a method of cross-referencing that is frequently found in Gospel manuscripts. For use by painters, the *Hermeneia* is an example of another sort of "harmony," one that may well have had antecedents during the earlier Middle Ages.

12 The fourth pendentive contains foliate ornamentation.
13 See below, pp. 258 ff. and 263 f.

The great majority of subjects in a Ministry cycle were miracles or events that were commonly classed as such even though they were not miraculous in the strict sense.[14] For convenience I shall refer to the list compiled in the *Hermeneia* (see below) in which sixty-one are listed (Nos. 16–76), from Cana, the first miracle, to Christ's Anointment in the House of Simon. The subjects were far too numerous to be encompassed in any one monument, for in the total iconographic program of a typically Byzantine church of the middle and late periods much of the space was preempted by other essential or traditional cycles or elements that were considered *de rigueur*. If the iconographer were to follow a chronological pattern he could, of course, arrange them in the artificially created "harmony" that was at times employed, or limit himself to the account of a single Gospel. To my knowledge, the latter practice was never followed consistently, one reason being that no single Gospel included all the miracles that were thought to be the most important or significant ones. For example, John, who records far fewer miracles (only fourteen) than any of the Synoptics, is the sole authority for such important subjects as the Marriage at Cana, the Samaritan Woman, the Paralytic at the Pool of Bethesda, the Blind Born, and the Raising of Lazarus, among others.

Any attempt to establish a chronology that would embrace all acts and miracles described in the four Gospels had to be an artificial and arbitrary written compilation, such as we find in the *Hermeneia*. Gabriel Millet [15] long ago observed that the sequence in the *Hermeneia* was based on the chronology of Matthew and that wherever events were missing from that Gospel the compiler interspersed those related in other Gospels. To demonstrate that this was indeed the case, and to reveal the method used by the compiler in weaving in events from other Gospels, I present herewith the subjects listed in the *Hermeneia* and references to the passages in the Gospels in which they occur, beginning with the *Hermeneia*'s No. 10, Christ among the Doctors.[16]

A glance at the columns of Gospel references reveals that the *Hermeneia* (henceforth referred to as H) builds a chronological sequence based on Matthew, whose order is followed consistently. For reasons to be explained below, and with only one exception, which cannot be explained, the relatively few events recounted in John are also in the sequence of his Gospel. But if we follow the references in Mark and Luke we find that at numerous points they jump back and forth out of the order given in the first Gospel. Matthew was chosen as the basis not only because it is the first of the Gospels but primarily because out of a list of sixty-seven events it describes a greater number, forty-two, than any other; five of these are unique to it. Mark describes thirty-seven, only two of which occur solely in his Gospel. Luke mentions thirty-nine subjects, of which eight are unique. John recounts only seventeen events, but twelve of these are unique in his version.

If we examine the lacunae between listed Gospel passages it becomes evident that H ignored all but one (No. 20) of the numerous verses referring to Christ in the act of teaching. It also omitted the parables (listed in Part Four, first section), the sermons, and all but two (Nos. 26 and 44) of the many healings of multitudes that are mentioned in the Gospels, usually in a casual way and without details. The second of Matthew's healings of two blind men (Matt. 20:29–34) was not listed by H probably because it was pictorially so similar to No. 34. In short, H omitted passages where there is no specific action that might be classed as works and miracles, such as

---

14 Some cycles that were obviously intended as miracle cycles, as at Monreale for example, include such subjects as Christ purging the Temple or Mary Magdalen anointing Christ's feet.

15 *Recherches sur l'iconographie de l'Evangile aux XIVe, XVe, et XVIe siècles* (Paris, 1916, reprinted 1960), p. 59.
16 The first nine subjects concern the Infancy.

LIST OF SUBJECTS IN THE MINISTRY CYCLE ACCORDING TO THE HERMENEIA
(ed. Papadopoulos-Kerameus, pp. 88–103; ed. Didron, pp. 162–88)

No.	Subject	Matthew	Mark	Luke	John
10	Christ among the Doctors			2:43–48	
11	Christ Goes to Jordan to be Baptized	3:13–15			1:29
12	Baptism	3:16–17	1:9–11	3:21–22	
13	Temptations	4:1–11	1:12–13	4:1–13	
14	John Baptist Witnesses of Christ before John and Andrew, Latter Presents Peter and Philip, who Presents Nathaniel				1:35–49
15	Christ Calling Disciples at Shore of Lake	4:18–22	1:16–20	5:3–11	
16	Miracle at Cana				2:1–11
17	Nicodemus Seeks out Christ				3:1–2
18	Christ and the Samaritan Woman at Well				4:5–27
19	Healing of Nobleman's Son at Capernaum				4:46–53
20	Christ Teaching in Synagogue at Nazareth	4:23	1:21	4:16–22	
21	Christ Casts out Demon in Synagogue at Capernaum		1:23–28	4:33–37	
22	Healing of a Leper	8:1–4	1:40–44	5:12–14	
23	Healing of Centurion's Servant at Capernaum	8:5–13		7:1–10	
24	Raising of Widow's Son at Nain			7:11–16	
25	Healing of Peter's Mother-in-Law at Capernaum	8:14–15	1:29–31	4:38–39	
26	Healing of Various Diseases	8:16–17	1:32–34	4:40–41	
27	Christ Stilling the Tempest	8:23–27	4:35–41	8:22–25	
28	Healing of Two Demoniacs in Land of Gadarenes	8:28–34	5:2–17	8:26–37	
29	Healing of Paralytic at Capernaum	9:1–8	2:1–12	5:18–26	
30	Calling of Matthew	9:9	2:14	5:27–28	
31	Christ Eating in House of Publican	9:10–13	2:15–17	5:29–32	
32	Healing of Woman with Issue of Blood	9:20–22	5:25–34	8:43–48	
33	Raising of Daughter of Jairus	9:23–26 cf. 18–19	5:35–43 cf. 22–24	8:49–56 cf. 41–42	
34	Healing of Two Blind Men	9:27–31			
35	Healing of Dumb Demoniac	9:32–33		11:14–15	
36	Christ Questioned by John's Disciples	11:2–6		7:18–23	
37	Christ and Disciples Passing through Field of Corn	12:1–8	2:23–28	6:1–5	
38	Healing of Man with Withered Hand	12:9–13	3:1–5	6:6–10	
39	Healing of Blind and Dumb Demoniac	12:22–23			
40	Christ Sought by His Mother and Brothers	12:46–50	3:31–35	8:19–21	
41	Healing of Paralytic at Pool of Bethesda in Jerusalem				5:2–15
42	Feeding of Five Thousand	14:15–21	6:35–44	9:12–17	6:5–13
43	Christ Walking on the Water	14:22–33	6:45–52		6:16–21
44	Healing of Various Diseases by Touching Hem of Christ's Garment	14:34–36	6:53–56		
45	Healing of Daughter of Canaanite Woman	15:21–28	7:24–30		
46	Healing of Deaf and Dumb Man in Decapolis		7:31–35		
47	Feeding of Four Thousand at Sea of Galilee	15:32–38	8:1–9		
48	Healing of a Blind Man at Bethsaida		8:22–26		
49	Transfiguration	17:1–13	9:2–13	9:28–36	
50	Healing of Lunatic Son of an Archon	17:14–21	9:14–29	9:37–42	
51	Christ and Peter Paying Tribute Money	17:24–27			
52	Christ Blessing Small Child	18:1–6	9:36–37	9:47–48	
53	Christ Questioned by Doctor of Law			10:25–29	
54	Christ Visits Mary and Martha			10:38–42	
55	Healing of Bent Woman in Synagogue on a Sabbath			13:10–17	

LIST OF SUBJECTS IN THE MINISTRY CYCLE ACCORDING TO THE HERMENEIA (Cont.)

No.	Subject	Matthew	Mark	Luke	John
56	Healing of Dropsical Man in House of a Ruler of Pharisees on a Sabbath			14:1–6	
57	Christ Heals Ten Lepers in Passing through Samaria and Galilee			17:11–19	
58	Christ Blessing Little Children	19:13–15	10:13–16	18:15–17	
59	Christ Questioned by Young Rich Man	19:16–23	10:17–23	18:18–25	
60	Christ Instructs Sons of Zebedee Not to Seek Preeminence	20:20–28	10:35–45		
61	Christ Heals a Blind Man before Entering Jericho			18:35–43	
62	Christ Calls to Zacchaeus			19:1–10	
63	Christ Heals a Blind Man (Bartimaeus) on Leaving Jericho	[20:29–34]	10:46–52		
64	Christ and Woman Taken in Adultery				8:3–11
65	Christ about to be Stoned by Jews				8:21–59
66	Healing of Blind Born in Jerusalem				9:1–38
67	Christ, a Second Time, about to be Stoned				10:22–39
68	Raising of Lazarus				11:38–45
69	Mary, Sister of Lazarus, Anoints Christ's Feet				12:1–8
70	Entry into Jerusalem	21:1–11	11:1–11	19:28–38	12:12–19
71	Christ Purging Temple	21:12–13	11:15–17	19:45–46	2:13–16
72	Christ in Temple Heals Blind and Lame	21:14			
73	Christ Curses Fig Tree	21:18–21	11:12–14 11:20–23		
74	Christ in Temple Again Questioned by Doctor of Law	22:35–40			
75	Widow's Mite		12:41–44	21:1–4	
76	Christ's Head Anointed (in House of Simon)	26:6–13	14:3–9	[7:36–50]	

those just referred to, or descriptions of Christ's travels to and fro in Galilee and Judaea. Let us see, now, what methods the compiler used in inserting into the framework of Matthew's sequence the subjects that were not included in his Gospel.

Subjects that are missing from Matthew but present in Mark, or Luke, or both are inserted into the sequence of H immediately *after* the subject in either or both of those Gospels which is also recorded in Matthew. No. 21, for example, is missing from Matthew, but No. 20 (common to all three) refers to Mark 1:21 and Luke 4:16–22. For No. 21, therefore, H inserted Mark 1:23–28 and Luke 4:33–37, both of which immediately follow the references in those Gospels for No. 20. Again, in the case of No. 46, the miracle is missing from Matthew; H therefore inserted that miracle after No. 45 (common to Matthew and Mark) because Mark 7:31–35 (No. 46) follows immediately after Mark 7:24–30 (No. 45). The same procedure was followed in Nos. 24, 48, 53–57, 61, 62, and 75, all of them subjects that are missing from Matthew but described in Mark, or Luke, or both.

The method of introducing events described in John is quite different from that used for Mark and Luke and not entirely consistent. In fitting some of the twelve unique subjects into his sequence, the compiler of H withholds them until a point is reached where John records an event that is also in Matthew. Working backward from that subject the compiler then enters the subjects unique to John which precede it in that Gospel. This system is clearly evident if we look at No. 70 (John 12:12–19), which is present also in Matthew (and the other Gospels). The following subjects, all unique in John, are inserted in reverse order as Nos. 69 to 64: John 12:1–8 (No. 69);

11:38–45 (No. 68); 10:22–39 (No. 67); 9:1–38 (No. 66); 8:21–59 (No. 65); and 8:3–11 (No. 64). Again, No. 42 is present in John (6:5–13) and Matthew (and also in the other two Gospels). Working backward the compiler inserts the verses from John 5:2–15 (No. 41). Of the remaining subjects unique to John, Nos. 14 and 16 are in positions dictated by chronology: Nos. 17 (3:1–2), 18 (4:5–27), and 19 (4:46–53) are placed immediately after 16 (2:1–11). The result is that the references to John, with the sole exception of No. 71 (2:13–16), appear in chronological order.

The sequence in H should now be compared, first, with that of the Kariye Djami. From Christ among the Doctors through the Temptation, the order is clearly established in the Synoptic Gospels; at the Kariye it does not depend upon H, but the sequence is logical if we take into account the fact that the festival subject of the Baptism was omitted. In its stead we find two scenes of John Bearing Witness of Christ, taken from the Gospel of John, into which the artist incorporated the Calling of the First Disciples according to John's version—that is, Andrew and the youthful John. At the Kariye Djami the witnessings are followed by the Temptation. For the beginning of the Ministry cycle, therefore, chronology was followed. Thenceforward, in the miracles and other acts the order is not at all that of H. If we have correctly reconstructed the sequence in the Kariye, it can be described, in terms of H, as 16; 42; 22 or 57 (depending upon whether scene [119], which shows only one leper, was a "shorthand version" of the Healing of Ten Lepers); 27?; first episode of 41; 56; 29; 28 or 39; 18; second episode of 41; 66; 73?; 20?; 62; 39; 34; 25; 32; 38; 22; and 26. It is obvious that at the Kariye the principle of chronology was not applied in the layout of the Ministry after the Miracle at Cana. We shall see, however, that in some parts other principles of layout played a part in the disposition of the subjects.

One principle that is said to have governed the distribution of miracle subjects in mural decoration is that of separating events which occurred in Galilee from those which occurred in Judaea and Jerusalem.[17] Cited as examples of this usage are Monreale (late twelfth century) and the Metropole at Mistra (fourteenth century). At Monreale, with only three exceptions, which are placed elsewhere and in a different context, the cycle of miracles is placed between the windows of the side aisles, the scenes in the south being said to have occurred in Galilee, those in the north in Judaea and Jerusalem. To attribute this distribution to geographic considerations is not quite correct and is rather misleading.

To understand the arrangements at Monreale, it is necessary to place the miracles in context with the narrative cycles of the Infancy and the Ministry in the central square, the south transept, and the aisles of the great cruciform basilica.[18] The New Testament cycles begin in the upper and continue in the lower of the two zones of the central square, beginning on the south wall and running clockwise along the west and north walls (the great arch in the east wall, opening into the forechoir and sanctuary, left no space for more than decorative and figure compositions). In that order, in the central square, we find the Infancy, which consists of thirteen subjects, arranged in chronological order, from the Annunciation to Zacharias to Christ among the Doctors.

The Ministry cycle then begins with the last two scenes in the central square: the Miracle of Cana and the Baptism. It continues in the uppermost of three zones on the south wall of the southern transept, where we find the Temptation. At the same level, but on the west wall, are

---

17 Millet, *Recherches*, pp. 62, 63.
18 See E. Kitzinger, *The Mosaics of Monreale* (Palermo, 1960),

the Index of Principal Cycles on pp. xii–xiv at the back of the volume and section drawings (based on Gravina) II, III, IV.

the miracles of the Healing of the Paralytic at Bethesda and the Blind Born;[19] in the second register of the south wall the first subject is the Samaritan Woman.[20] As we shall see, the latter three miracles are also grouped in many other monuments, as they are in the Kariye Djami, but at Monreale they are placed out of context with the miracle cycle to which they belong. Special notice should be taken of this group of three miracles at Monreale, for they illustrate the influence of the liturgical calendar and symbolic content on the layout of miracles—a phenomenon that will be discussed below.

The remaining subjects on the south and west walls of the transept comprise festival subjects (Transfiguration, Raising of Lazarus, and Entry into Jerusalem) and the beginnings of a Passion cycle. We then come to the miracle cycle, in the two aisles.

The distribution of the twenty miracles at Monreale, equally divided between the two aisles, is surely made on the basis of early versus late miracles and is not due primarily to geographic considerations. It is true that, assuming that the list of H represents a medieval conception of the chronological order of events, the sequence of the miracles within the south aisle (to be read from east to west) is not chronological; it corresponds to H's numbers 45, 35, 22, 38, 43, 24, 32, 33, 25, and 42. But, with the exception of the first, which will receive further explanation, they are early miracles and fall within the range of the 20's to early 40's of H. The miracles of the north aisle, on the other hand, fall mainly in the upper 50's and 60's of H. Reading from west to east the first three correspond to H's numbers 55, 56, and 57; then comes Matthew's second account of the Healing of Two Blind Men (20:30–34), which was omitted by H because it was indistinguishable from the first (9:27–31); it is followed by Nos. 71, 64, 41; next comes one of the many healings of multitudes omitted in H (where only two (Nos. 26 and 44) were taken as typifying all); and the series ends with Nos. 69 and 23. This last again is an exception, which calls for special explanation.

The first and last scenes, which are based not on chronology or geography but on a different principle, are peculiarly situated with respect to the others; each, in two parts, is on the arcade side and the eastern wall of its respective aisle. They depict, in the south aisle, the Healing of the Daughter of the Canaanite Woman (see Figs. 2 a, b) and, in the north aisle, the Healing of the Centurion's Son (see Figs. 3 a, b).[21] This arrangement at Monreale is an example of a principle that can be observed elsewhere, that is, the playing off of two miracles one against the other to illustrate Christ's impartiality toward all of mankind, his equal treatment of the two sexes, of individuals from different stations in life, and of those who were despised as pagans for not possessing the true faith of the children of Israel.

It is true that of the events in the south aisle one (No. 45) occurred in Phoenicia and the rest in Galilee; those of the north, with few exceptions, in Samaria, Judaea, or Jerusalem. But similar results would ensue from a selection based on chronological grounds, for Christ began his mission in his home territory of Galilee, where he urged secrecy after his miracles; only later, as his fame spread, did he go into the Judaean stronghold of the Pharisees and Sadducees and publicly proclaim that his powers were a divine manifestation—that he was the Messiah, son of David, son of God—and openly perform his miracles.

The Ministry or rather, in this case, the Miracle cycle painted in the aisles of the fourteenth-

19 See W. Krönig, *Il duomo di Monreale e l'architettura normanna in Sicilia* (Palermo, 1965), PL. 46.
20 Ibid., PL. 37.

21 See below, p. 268. Illustrated courtesy of Professor Ernst Kitzinger.

century Metropole at Mistra was also said by Millet [22] to be an example of the laying-out of scenes in the two aisles according to a geographical principle. The disposition of these scenes [23] again shows a general chronology comparable to that of H.

The northern side aisle of the Metropole includes, in the eastern end of the barrel vault and in its east tympanum, a series of scenes from the lives of Sts. Demetrius and Nestor. Most of the space in the barrel vaults of both side aisles, however, and the south wall of the southern aisle are devoted to two cycles: one, a restricted cycle of the Virgin and the Infancy of Christ; the other, a cycle of Christ's Miracles.[24] In the north side of the southern barrel vault are the Miracle at Cana (H 16), Christ Teaching in the Synagogue (H 20), the Healing of the Demoniac at Capernaum (H 21), the Healing of Peter's Mother-in-Law (H 25). In the west tympanum of the aisle is the Healing of Various Diseases (H 26). The sequence then continues in the southern half of the same vault, from east to west, with the Raising of the Widow's Son (H 24), the Healing of the Paralytic at Capernaum (H 29), and the Healing of the Gadarene Demoniac (H 28), which completes the series in the vault. There followed, on the south wall of the southern side-aisle, the story of Jairus and his daughter in three episodes: Jairus imploring Christ to raise his Daughter (H 33), the Healing of the Woman with the Issue of Blood (H 32), and the Raising of the Daughter (also H 33).

In the north aisle, where most of the vault at the east end was devoted to the lives of Sts. Demetrius and Nestor, space was available for only five miracles. Moving westward from the cycles of the two Saints, we find the Paralytic at Bethesda (H 41) confronted by the Samaritan Woman (H 18); the Dropsical Man (H 56) opposite the Blind Born (H 66); and in the west tympanum a curious scene of the healing of two lepers which may be, so to speak, a shorthand version of the Ten Lepers (H 57). In the layout of the miracles in the north aisle, chronology was not the operative principle. Rather, it would seem, the painter was intent on grouping the three miracles of the Paralytic, the Samaritan Woman, and the Blind Born, which form a triad in a number of other monuments, and, since space was available, he added two others. At Monreale we have already encountered the gathering together of the three miracles; others will be discussed below in connection with the influence of the liturgical calendar on the layout of miracle cycles.

It can be said, therefore, that in the major part of the Miracle cycle at the Metropole (i.e., in the south aisle) the general principle was to follow a chronology that is remarkably close to that of the *Hermeneia* and not one that is based on geographical grounds.

That a medieval "harmonized" chronology for the events of the Ministry, similar to that of H, did exist and was actually used in mural decoration is even more evident in the nave frescoes of Sant'Angelo in Formis,[25] of the last quarter of the eleventh century. This simple three-aisled basilica, its plain wall surfaces above the two nave arcades unbroken save for the relatively small windows just below the ceiling, lent itself admirably to a treatment of continuous friezes

---

22 *Recherches*, pp. 62, 63.

23 Determined from G. Millet, *Monuments byzantins de Mistra* (Paris, 1910), section drawing, PL. 17,1; from the locations of the paintings as listed in his "Table explicative des planches," p. 12; and from PL. 71–73, 75–78.

24 Christ among the Doctors (H 10) was badly misplaced, for it is among the scenes of the Life of the Virgin.

25 See F. X. Kraus, "Die Wandgemälde von S. Angelo in Formis," *Jahrbuch der Königlich Preussischen Kunstsammlungen*, 14 (1893), pp. 3 ff., 84 ff., with composite photographs of south

and north walls of the nave; G. de Jerphanion, "Le cycle iconographique de Sant'Angelo in Formis," *La voix des monuments: Notes et études d'archéologie chrétienne* (Paris and Brussels, 1930), pp. 273 ff.; J. Wettstein, *Sant'Angelo in Formis et la peinture médiévale en Campanie* (Geneva, 1960), pp. 40 ff.; O. Morisani, *Gli affreschi di S. Angelo in Formis* (Naples, 1962), pp. 36, 82 ff.; A. Moppert-Schmidt, *Die Fresken von S. Angelo in Formis* (Zurich, 1967), pp. 47 ff., 139 (diagram of south wall), 140, 142.

of narrative cycles. In contrast to Monreale, whose nave walls were decorated with two continuous friezes of Old Testament subjects, Sant'Angelo contains three zones of New Testament Christological subjects. Between the windows of the upper register of the south wall, where the story began, the paintings are now entirely destroyed, but they undoubtedly depicted events of the Infancy from the Annunciation to and including the Flight into Egypt. The cycle continued in the upper register of the north wall, to be read from west to east, with two scenes of the Massacre of the Innocents followed immediately by the beginning of Christ's Ministry: Christ among the Doctors (H 10), John the Baptist Preaching (not in H but substituted for H 11, Christ Goes to Jordan to be Baptized), the Baptism (H 12), and three episodes of the Temptation (H 13).

The cycle continues in the south wall, second zone, where only the lower third of the paintings still exists. From the remaining portions of the paintings and the Latin inscriptions beneath them the ten subjects can be identified. They correspond to the subjects listed in H as Nos. 15, 16, 22, 27, 29, 32, 33, 39, 42, and 45, in that order. The miracles of the second register of the north wall present some confusion caused by the introduction of parable scenes. In that register we find H 49; H 51; the Parable of the Unmerciful Servant (Matt. 18:23–35, which is No. 10 of H's list of parables); H 75; the Parable of the Good Samaritan in three scenes (Luke 10:30 ff., H's parable No. 21); the Parable of Dives and the Beggar Lazarus in two scenes (Luke 16:19–31, H's parable No. 25); a miracle that is probably the Healing of the Gadarene Demoniac (H 28); and finally, the upper part of the Ascension, which intrudes into the second zone from the lower, where it belongs.

In the third, or lowest, register of the south wall we find a few minor inconsistencies with the order of H, for the subjects correspond to H Nos. 62; 18 (Samaritan Woman); 64, 66, 68, 60; the Supper in the House of Simon the Pharisee (Luke 7:36–50), which was conflated with H 76; and finally No. 70 (Entry into Jerusalem). The two remaining scenes in the lower zone of the south wall inaugurate the Passion cycle, which continued in the lower zone on the opposite side of the nave.

In the three monuments—Monreale, the Metropole at Mistra, and especially Sant'Angelo in Formis—we find the miracles and other cycles laid out in continuous narrative friezes, and the scenes of the miracles of the Metropole and Sant'Angelo arranged in a chronological order quite close to that of H. All three churches are basilical structures. Two of them fall within the Latin-Byzantine orbit of medieval architecture, where the Latin tradition of the basilical church remained strong and accounts for the Latin predilection for the continuous method. The decorators of such western churches, from early times, tended to represent in one or more friezes a cycle of Old Testament subjects in the continuous method on one side of the church, and it was only natural to depict New Testament Christological scenes on the opposite side, thus confronting the Old with the New dispensation. In contrast, in the Byzantine central type of building with its short stretches of walls and vaults it was difficult, though not impossible, to arrange extensive series of paintings in the continuous method and in clearly chronological order. This type of building did, however, lend itself to the juxtaposition of a number of subjects to illustrate a liturgical or an allegorical content.

That is not to say, however, that, aside from chronology, liturgical considerations did not also play a part in the selection and arrangement of subjects in the decoration of basilical churches. One such is the basilica of Sant'Apollinare Nuovo, Ravenna, of the early sixth century, where a

Christological cycle is found in the mosaics of the upper registers of the north and south walls of the nave. The subjects on the north wall, which constitute a Ministry cycle, mainly of miracles,[26] are not arranged chronologically, in contrast to the cycle of the Passion and Resurrection on the south. A theory that all these mosaics illustrate Gospel lections from the liturgy of Ravenna was advanced by Anton Baumstark,[27] who thought this liturgy to be influenced greatly by that of the Syrian Jacobites. The subjects on the north wall, which concern us, were thought by Baumstark and others to illustrate the pericopes from the First Sunday of Lent to the Wednesday of Holy Week.

It has been shown by Nordström,[28] however, that the theory of the Syro-Jacobite influence on the mosaics of the north wall is not convincing, since one of the scenes was wrongly interpreted and, together with four others, is absent from the pericopes. But he does retain the suggestion that the program reflects a liturgy, and he shows that better parallels can be drawn between the mosaics and certain manuscripts connected with the Roman liturgy, the closest being a sixth-century manuscript of the Gospels (MS C. 39 inf.) in the Ambrosiana Library at Milan,[29] in whose margins are later notes of the seventh–eighth century which indicate the days when certain passages should be read, making it possible to use this Gospel Book as a lectionary for Gospel lessons.

The fact that the passages designated as pericopes in the Ambrosiana manuscript are not very numerous makes it all the more significant that the thirteen subjects in the Ravenna cycle of the Ministry are to be found among them. The subjects of the mosaics, the notations as pericopes, and Gospel references are as follows:[30]

Mosaics, east to west	Marginal notations of feasts	Lections
1. Cana (much restored)	*In vigiliis epiphaniae domini*	John 2:1–11
2. Bread and Fishes { Five Thousand	*In laetanias prima die*	Matt. 14:14–21
	In letanias die secundo	John 6:5–14
{ Four Thousand [31]	*In letania tertia*	Matt. 15:32–38
3. Calling of Peter and Andrew	St. Andrew's Day	Matt. 4:18–[22]
4. Two Blind Men (The Blind Born) [32]	*Domenica de caeco* (4th Sunday of Lent)	John 9:1–38
5. Woman with Issue of Blood [33]	*Cottidiana* (text for any Sunday or weekday not otherwise specified)	Mark 5:21–34
6. Samaritan Woman	[*Dom.*] *de Samaritana* (2nd Sunday of Lent)	John 4:4–[?]
7. Raising of Lazarus	*Dominica de Lazaro* (5th Sunday of Lent)	John 11:38–45
8. The Pharisee and the Publican	*Cottidiana*	Luke 18:10–14
9. Widow's Mite	*Cottidiana*	Mark 12:41–44
10. Separation of Sheep and Goats	(No indication of day, but with the note F[init] at Matt. 25:46)	Matt. 25:31–46
11. Paralytic at Capernaum	*Cottidiana*	Luke 5:18–26
12. Gadarene Demoniac	*Cottidiana*	Mark 5:1–20
13. Paralytic at Bethesda	*In dedicatione* (anniversary of dedication of church)	John 5:2–15

26 For illustrations, see F. W. Deichmann, *Frühchristliche Bauten und Mosaiken von Ravenna* (Baden-Baden, 1958), PL. 154–79.

27 "I mosaici di Sant'Apollinare Nuovo e l'antico anno liturgico ravennate," *Rassegna Gregoriana*, 9 (1910), pp. 33 ff.; cf. idem, *Festbrevier und Kirchenjahr der syrischen Jakobiten* (Paderborn, 1910), pp. 177, 187 f., 208 f., 220 f., 223 f., 234, 252, 256.

28 C. O. Nordström, *Ravennastudien* (Uppsala, 1953), pp. 63–78.

29 G. Morin, "Un système inédit de lectures liturgiques en usage au VIIe/VIIIe siècle dans une église inconnue de la haute Italie," *Revue Bénédictine*, 20 (1903), pp. 375 ff.

30 Based on Nordström, *Ravennastudien*, pp. 76 ff., and Morin, "Un système inédit de lectures liturgiques," pp. 376–80.

31 Scene 2 could represent either the Feeding of the Five

On the whole, Nordström's theory that the selection of the Sant'Apollinare Nuovo mosaics of the north wall, at least, was based on the liturgy seems quite convincing. It is true, however, as Nordström says, that the sequence of the mosaics does not correspond to the sequence in the Ambrosiana Gospel–Lectionary, nor to that of any other known early Western system of biblical lections. The idea which led to the selection and distribution of the scenes so far remains unknown; the one exception may perhaps be the first scene, Cana, which is placed appropriately at the east end, facing the Last Supper (on the south wall), to which it is a symbolic counterpart because of the eucharistic signification of both.

Before taking up other instances of liturgical influences in the layout of monumental cycles, especially of miracle cycles, we should consider the examples to be found in the Kariye Djami. In the next study, Professor Der Nersessian presents the evidence of the influence of the lections in the composition of the cycle of the Prefigurations of the Virgin in the parecclesion and in works elsewhere. These Old Testament scenes and their inscriptions are taken from the Old Testament lections for the various Feasts of the Virgin as they appear in liturgical works.[34]

A series of three miracles that stand out as a group among the mosaics of the outer narthex of the Kariye is an equally clear instance of selection and arrangement based on the liturgical calendar and, as we shall see, on the symbolic content of the scenes. The three miracles, Nos. [127], [121] and [128], and [129],[35] are placed in the only pendentives of the sixth bay in which scenes were depicted. It is, I think, of some significance that the fourth pendentive, at the southwest, contains only some foliate ornament, a fact that can be explained only on the grounds that the miracles of the three pendentives should clearly stand as a group. The subjects of the three are Christ and the Samaritan Woman [127]; the Paralytic at the Pool of Bethesda [128] and [121] above it; and the Healing of the Blind Born [129]. The scenes are clearly so grouped not because of chronology, for a chronological system was not used at the Kariye in arranging the miracles, but rather because they depict the three Feasts celebrated on the fourth, fifth, and sixth Sundays of the period between Easter and Pentecost. In the *Pentekostarion* and the Lectionaries the fourth Sunday is entitled the Sunday of the Paralytic (κυριακὴ τοῦ παραλύτου); the fifth is the Sunday of the Samaritan Woman (κυριακὴ τῆς Σαμαρείτιδος); and the sixth is the Sunday of the Blind Born (κυριακὴ τοῦ τυφλοῦ).[36] The order of the three subjects in the Kariye, if read in a clockwise direction (Samaritan Woman, Paralytic, Blind Born), is not

---

Thousand or the Feeding of the Four Thousand. Both are noted in the Ambrosiana Gospel-Lectionary and the former appears in both Matthew and John.

32 According to Nordström this is the weak point in his theory because the mosaic shows two blind men whereas the MS has the lection from John 9:1–38 dealing with the Blind Born. The discrepancy is not significant, for the system of Biblical lections in use of Western churches before the adoption of the definitive Roman rite, as Morin pointed out (p. 375), could vary greatly. Compare, for example, the Ambrosiana MS; the early Roman lectionary of about 700 (Th. Klauser, *Das römische Capitulare Evangeliorum*, I [Liturgiegeschichtliche Quellen und Forschungen . . . , 28; Münster i. W., 1935], pp. 13 ff.; W. H. Frere, *Studies in Early Roman Liturgy*, II: *The Roman Lectionary* [Oxford, 1934], pp. 1 ff.); a MS at Cividale of the sixth-seventh century (D. De Bruyne, in *Revue Bénédictine*, 30 [1913], pp. 208–18; *DACL*, V.1, cols. 883–94, s. v. "Evangiles"); and a MS of the Missale Ambrosianum of the ninth century (*Missale Ambrosianum Duplex*, ed. M. Ceriani and others [Milan, 1913]). Incidentally, both the Missale Ambrosianum and the early Roman lectionary, the latter overlooked by

Nordström, contain the lection on the Two Blind Men for the Saturday after Pentecost. For the Roman lectionary, see Klauser, *Capitulare*, p. 28, No. 129, and Frere, *Studies*, p. 14, No. 142. Thus the hypothetical Ravenna liturgical book which may have served as a guide for the selection of the mosaic subjects was not necessarily a duplicate of, but similar to the Ambrosiana Gospel-Lectionary used in an unknown north-Italian church.

33 Scholars disagree as to whether this represents the Woman with the Issue or the Canaanite Woman, or even the Adulteress. In any case all three are noted in the Ambrosiana Gospel-Lectionary (Canaanite Woman: *Cottidiana*, Matt. 15:21–28; Adulteress: *Tertia dominica post pascha*, John 8:3–11).

34 S. Der Nersessian's study in this volume, pp. 334–49.

35 See Vol. 1 of this work, pp. 126–29, 135–37; diagrams Figs. 2–6 at end of volume; and Vol. 2, PL. 250, 251 *a* and *b*, and 257 *a* and *b*.

36 See any modern edition of the *Pentekostarion*. For early lectionaries, see E. C. Colwell and D. W. Riddle, eds., *Prolegomena to the Study of the Lectionary Text of the Gospels* (Studies in the Lectionary Text of the Greek New Testament, I; Chicago, 1933), pp. 87 f.

that of the three successive Sundays of the calendar. However, it restores the order in which they appear in John's Gospel.

The grouping of these three miracles is a phenomenon that recurs in several monumental cycles of the miracles.[37] We have already seen that at Monreale they were grouped together in a context outside that of the main miracle cycle in the side aisles. There, in the upper zone of the west wall of the southern transept, we find, at the left, the Paralytic, and next to it, as the only other scene in that register, the Healing of the Blind Born. At the far left (east) in the second register of the south wall of the transept, which follows immediately in the sequence of mosaics in the transept, is the Samaritan Woman.[38] These have no contextual relation to the other mosaics of the south transept, which is otherwise devoted to the Temptation, scenes from the festival cycle, and the beginnings of the Passion.[39]

It is quite possible that the fact that the three events were celebrated as feasts on the middle Sundays between Easter and Pentecost was sufficient to explain the grouping of the three scenes. It is also possible that the explanation of this phenomenon lies in the fact that from a very early tradition the three were associated because they share still another context whereby they were interpreted in terms of Christian baptism. In each instance water is the healing or life-giving instrument and was therefore interpreted in terms of baptismal waters. To the Samaritan Woman Christ said: "If thou knewest . . . who it is that saith to thee, Give me to drink; thou wouldest have asked of him, and he would have given thee living water"; and again, "whosoever drinketh of the water that I shall give him shall never thirst; but the water that I shall give him shall be in him a well of water springing up into everlasting life."[40] Of the paralytic lying beside the pool of Bethesda, whose waters were troubled at a certain season by the angel—as the Holy Spirit was to descend upon the water of baptism at the *benedictio fontis*—Christ asked, "Wilt thou be made whole? . . . Rise, take up thy bed, and walk" (John 5:6–8). Hymns chanted at matins on the Sunday of the Paralytic compare the miracle to Christ's holy baptism. After Christ had anointed the eyes of the Blind Born with clay, he told him to wash himself at the pool of Siloam (which is often depicted as a baptismal font). As early as the fourth century the passage John 9:1–38 (Healing of the Blind Born) was read in connection with the *scrutinium* of the catechumens in preparation for baptism.

At least two of the three subjects, the Paralytic and the Samaritan Woman, were deemed to be appropriate for the decoration of the early-third-century baptistery at Dura-Europos.[41] The miracle of the Paralytic at Bethesda is on the upper part of the north wall near the west end, the Samaritan Woman at the west end of the south wall. Altogether only three miracle scenes have survived among the paintings of the baptistery, the third being the scene of Christ and Peter walking on the water (Matt. 14:22–33; see also Mark 6:45–52 and John 6:16–21). So many of the paintings have been entirely lost that one cannot say conclusively that the third of

37 See above, pp. 252 f., 254; and below.

38 See nn. 19 and 20.

39 See the sequence given in Kitzinger, *The Mosaics of Monreale*, p. XIII of his Index of Principal Cycles.

40 John 4:5–27. For textual evidence that from early times these words of Christ were taken to refer to baptism, see the comments and references of J.-L. Maier, *Le baptistère de Naples et ses mosaiques: Etude historique et iconographique* (Fribourg, 1964), pp. 80 ff.

41 *The Excavations at Dura-Europos*, Final Report VIII, Part II (ed. C. Bradford Welles), C. H. Kraeling, *The Christian Building*

(New Haven, 1967), pp. 34 ff. (the date); pp. 145 ff. (the identification of one of the rooms as a baptistery); pp. 177–203 (interpretation of the paintings of the baptistery). This final work of the late Professor Kraeling admirably summarizes the problems and controversies that have arisen since the publication of *The Excavations at Dura-Europos . . . Preliminary Report of Fifth Season of Work, October 1931–March 1932* (New Haven, 1934). For illustrations see Kraeling, Plans V and VIII and PL. XVII–XLVI; Fifth Preliminary Report, plans, PL. XL and XLI; PL. XLII, XLIV, and L (Paralytic); PL. XLVI and XLVII,1 (Woman at the Well).

our group of miracles, the Blind Born, was not depicted. It is apparent, however, that at Dura the three would not have been placed in close conjunction with one another.

Several scholars who have studied the mosaics of San Giovanni in Fonte at Naples,[42] of the end of the fourth century, have expressed the opinion that originally the three miracles with which we are concerned were depicted among those which decorate the segments of the octagonal dome. Of the mosaic scenes in the eight compartments four, and a fragment of a fifth, are preserved and three are totally destroyed. Among the extant scenes is that of the Samaritan Woman (partly preserved); it is combined with an abbreviated version of the Miracle at Cana.[43]

Maier suggests that the program of the biblical scenes at Naples began at the east, where only a small fragment still exists. At the northeast is the Samaritan Woman - Cana; the mosaics at the north, northwest, and west are missing. At the southwest is the Holy Women at the Sepulcher, and at the south, in two registers, are the partly preserved scenes of Christ Walking on the Water and the Miraculous Draught of Fishes. Finally, at the southeast is the Traditio Legis. In his discussion of the lost mosaics, Maier,[44] like Wilpert and Stuhlfauth,[45] makes a case for the inclusion of the Paralytic at Bethesda and the Blind Born in two of the three empty segments following immediately after the Samaritan Woman. In the case of the Paralytic, he does so partly on the basis of its presence at Dura, which he sees as an iconographic parallel to the Naples baptistery in its program. Indeed, he also is of the opinion that Dura, as well as Naples, once contained the miracle of the Blind Born. He points out, furthermore,[46] that these two earliest baptisteries have in common the following iconographic elements of their programs: the Good Shepherd,[47] the Samaritan Woman, Christ Walking on the Water,[48] and the Women at the Sepulcher.[49] Since neither the baptistery of Naples nor that of Dura contained an extensive series of biblical subjects, it is striking that four should be present in both.

The *capitula* of the early liturgy of Naples show also that the three miracles were commemorated in a baptismal context. The text relating to the Paralytic at Bethesda was read as the pericope, according to the *capitula* of Naples, "*in dedicatione fontis,*"[50] and the pericope of the Blind Born, on Saturday of the third week in Lent, "*post scrutinium*" of the catechumens in conjunction with the baptismal rites.[51] The Naples *capitula* also show, by means of the liturgical calendar, still another baptismal connotation, though somewhat less directly; the pericope of the Samaritan Woman was read "*post III dominicas de epifania* [sic] *de muliere samaritaniae.*"[52] The feast of the Epiphany was celebrated on January sixth to commemorate both the Nativity and the Baptism of Christ; in the West it was celebrated on that date beginning in the early fourth century, but in the East there is evidence that the feast was introduced on that date at a still earlier time. The baptismal aspect of the feast, however, assumed more importance than the Nativity, for it was at Christ's baptism that the Holy Spirit "manifested" (the principal meaning of the word ἐπιφάνεια) that Christ was God's beloved son in whom he was well pleased.[53]

42 Maier, *Le baptistère de Naples*, p. 57; J. Wilpert, *Die römischen Mosaiken und Malereien der kirchlichen Bauten vom IV. bis XIII. Jahrhundert*, 2d ed., (Freiburg im Breisgau, 1917), I, p. 230; G. Stuhlfauth, "Das Baptisterium San Giovanni in Fonte zu Neapel und seine Mosaiken," *Reinhold Seeberg Festschrift*, II (Leipzig, 1929), p. 199.

43 Maier, PL. IV.

44 Ibid., pp. 57–62.

45 See n. 42, above.

46 *Baptistère de Naples*, pp. 79 ff.

47 At Naples, this is in one of the spandrels of the niches (Maier, PL. XI); for Dura see Kraeling, *The Christian Building*, PL. XVII, XXX, XXXI, and XXXII.1.

48 At Naples, Maier, PL. VII; at Dura, Kraeling, PL. XVIII, XXXVI–XXXVIII.1.

49 At Naples, Maier, PL. V b and VI; at Dura, Kraeling, PL. XX, XXVII, XXVIII, XLIV, and XLV.

50 Maier, p. 60, n. 3. See also *DACL*, XII.1, s. v. "Naples," under the heading "Capitula disposés suivant l'ordre des manuscrits," col. 760, no. 132 (Brit. Mus., Cotton Nero D.IV), and col. 767, no. 201 (Würtzburg, Burchard Gospels).

51 Maier, p. 61, n. 2; *DACL*, XII.1, s. v. "Naples," col. 760, no. 145 (Cotton Nero D.IV).

52 Not mentioned in Maier, but see *DACL*, XII.1, s.v. "Naples," col. 760, no. 129 (Cotton Nero D.IV).

53 *DACL*, V.1, s. v. "Epiphanie," col. 197 ff.

Among the lectionary systems of the early church, according to Sir Edwyn Hoskyns,[54] there are close similarities in the liturgical use of the sections of St. John's Gospel that are commonly denominated "Of the Samaritan Woman," "Of the Paralytic," and "Of the Blind Man." Two treatises of the end of the fourth or the beginning of the fifth century which are attributed to St. Ambrose—*De mysteriis* and *De sacramentis*[55]—consist of addresses pronounced during Easter Week to those who had been baptized on the previous Easter. The *De sacramentis* assumes that the narrative of the Healing of the Paralytic had been read on Easter Tuesday. It also mentions that at some time during their preparation the catechumens had heard the narrative concerning the Blind Born and that Christ wished to prefigure the mystery of baptism in that miracle. Thus, the narrative of the blind man was also read in Easter Week.

The *Manuale Ambrosianum*, again according to Hoskyns, contains the cycle of lessons used in the church of Milan in the eleventh century. In it the first Sunday in Lent is called the Sunday of the Samaritan Woman and the lection is John, chapter four. The third Sunday in Lent is called the Sunday of the Blind Man; and on Tuesday in Easter Week there was the mass for the newly baptized, at which the fifth chapter of John was read (the narrative of the Paralytic). We are thus reminded of the three successive Sundays in the Greek *Pentekostarion* midway between Easter and Pentecost (the fourth, fifth, and sixth Sundays), the feasts of which are called those of the Paralytic, of the Samaritan Woman, and of the Blind Born.[56] In both East and West the rites of baptism had been performed in the early centuries at both Easter and Pentecost.[57] In the modern Greek calendar these feasts have lost their specific relation to baptism, but it seems assured that the origin of this phenomenon is to be explained in terms of early usage, in which the feasts did make reference to baptism.

It should also be pointed out that in Syriac biblical manuscripts of the sixth and seventh centuries, used in churches of the Euphrates valley, the Gospel lessons for Lent, in a context of baptism, were chosen mainly from St. John's Gospel: the lesson of the Blind Born was read on the mid-Lent Sunday.[58] This evidence suggests that the use of two of the three miracles from John in the paintings of Dura, on the Euphrates river, already had a liturgical connection. Since Roman catacomb paintings depict the three miracles in question as baptismal symbols, the liturgical, baptismal use of these passages from John's Gospel may perhaps go back into the second century, even before the paintings of Dura were executed.

According to Oscar Cullmann,[59] the author of the Gospel of John consciously attempted to demonstrate that many events in Christ's life were brought about in order that they might be prefigurations of certain liturgical feasts and sacraments, and that these were already in use in the liturgy and rites in the time of the Gospel's author.[60] Prefigurations of the sacrament of baptism were Christ's Baptism,[61] the three miracles with which we are especially concerned,[62] and other events, such as Jesus addressing Nicodemus with the words "Except a man be born again, he cannot see the kingdom of God" (John 3:3).[63] The miracles of Cana and the Feeding of the Multitudes,[64] as we shall see later, were prefigurations of the sacrament of the Eucharist.

---

54 *The Fourth Gospel* (London, 2d ed., 1947), pp. 363–65: "The Use of the Fourth, Fifth, and Ninth Chapters of Saint John's Gospel in the Early Lectionaries."

55 *De mysteriis*, IV.22, *PL*, 16, col. 412; *De sacramentis*, ibid., cols. 443–45.

56 See above, p. 257 f.

57 See L. Duchesne, *Origines du culte chrétien: Etude sur la liturgie latine avant Charlemagne*, 2d ed. (Paris, 1898), pp. 281–328.

58 Hoskyns, *Fourth Gospel*, pp. 364, 365.

59 *Urchristentum und Gottesdienst* (Zurich and Stuttgart, 1962).

60 Ibid., pp. 39 ff.

61 Ibid., pp. 58 ff.

62 Ibid., pp. 80 ff., 84 ff., 97 ff.

63 Ibid., pp. 74 ff.

64 Ibid., pp. 65 ff., 88 ff.

It is, I think, more than mere coincidence that in the thirteenth-century Gospel at Mount Athos, Iviron 5,[65] between chapters four and ten of John's Gospel only the Samaritan Woman (fol. 371), the Paralytic at Bethesda (fol. 377v), and the Blind Born (fol. 405v) were illustrated.[66] No other miracles or events recorded in this portion of John were illustrated despite the fact that five other events are described therein.[67] This is quite evidently attributable to the long tradition with respect to these particular miracles and their relation to liturgy and rites.

In turning again to mural decoration in churches we might recall that at the Kariye Djami, Monreale,[68] and the Metropole at Mistra[69] the three subjects were set apart and placed in conjunction with one another. In addition to these, there are several other monuments where the same phenomenon occurs. These are not in all cases churches that contained true miracle cycles, for the number of extant monuments containing cycles of miracles, as such, is not great; some present a number of miracle scenes not grouped as a cycle within the framework of the architectural setting.

One example of the arrangement of the three miracles so as to indicate a distinct relation between them is to be found in the Catholicon of the Serbian monastery of Chilandar on Mount Athos, whose paintings are basically of the thirteenth century and are closely reproduced in the repainting carried out in 1804.[70] Placed in the lunette of the recessed southern wall, zone one, of the southwest bay is the Paralytic at Bethesda.[71] To the left of it, and at the same level on the face of the engaged pier of the wall, and thus adjacent to the Paralytic, is the Samaritan Woman.[72] The counterpart to the Paralytic, in the north wall of the northwest bay, and again in zone one, is the scene of the Blind Born,[73] depicted in two episodes: Christ anointing the eyes of the blind man, and the latter washing his eyes at the pool of Bethesda, which has the form of a cruciform baptismal font.

The Serbian church of the Trinity at Sopoćani has no miracle cycle. However, in its outer narthex, built shortly before 1346[74] in front of the narthex of the original church of the late thirteenth century,[75] the three miracles, and only they, were painted in the upper zone on the eastern slope of the barrel vault. To the north of the portal leading into the narthex of the original church are a small fragment of a bust of Christ, in the top of the vault above the portal, and side by side the scenes of the Paralytic at Bethesda and the Healing of the Blind Born. To the south of the portal, and at the same level as the other miracles, is the scene of Christ and the Samaritan Woman, which is equal in width to its counterparts at the north.[76]

At Dečani[77] a great number of miracles are depicted. They are distributed in scattered parts of the church[78] but are mainly concentrated in the apse and bema and in the area of the northeast

65 Millet, *Recherches* (pp. 8, 9), classes this Gospel manuscript as one of a group in which the illustrations were selected because of their relation to the liturgy. See A. Xyngopoulos, Ἱστορημένα εὐαγγέλια μονῆς Ἰβήρων Ἁγίου Ὄρους (Athens, 1932), Nos. 47–49.

66 It is interesting to note that in the short list of subjects appearing in Parartema Γ, published as an appendix in Papadopoulos-Kerameus' edition of the *Hermeneia*, p. 265, the three subjects are presented in succession.

67 The Healing of the Nobleman's Son (John 4:46–53), the Jews persecuting and seeking to slay Christ (John 5:15–18), Christ Teaching in the Temple (John 7:14–15), The Woman Taken in Adultery (John 8:3–11), and Christ about to be stoned by the Jews (John 8:21–59).

68 See above, p. 252 f.

69 See above, p. 254.

70 G. Millet, *Monuments de l'Athos* (Paris, 1927), Répertoire des monuments, p. 61.

71 Ibid., PL. 71,2, 77,1.

72 Ibid., PL. 71,2, 77,1.

73 Ibid., PL. 73,2.

74 V. J. Djurić, *Sopoćani* (Belgrade, 1963), with Serbian text and a resumé in English, pp. 11–120. For the date, p. 113. There is a more recent German edition of this work (Leipzig, 1967).

75 Ibid., p. 112.

76 For a drawing illustrating their disposition, see Djurić, *Sopoćani*, pp. 138 and 139. For a plan of the church, see p. 36; for photographic reproductions of the scenes see N. L. Okunev in *Byzantinoslavica*, I (1929), Fig. 21 (Paralytic and Blind Born) and Fig. 20 (Samaritan Woman).

77 R. Hamann-MacLean and H. Hallensleben, *Die Monumentalmalerei in Serbien und Makedonien vom 11. bis zum frühen 14. Jahrhundert*, I (Giessen, 1963), p. 38, date the paintings of Dečani in the first half of the fourteenth century.

78 On the apse wall; on the south wall of the bema; in the cross vault of the northeast bay of the main body of the church

bay of the main body of the nave. The cross vault of this bay, divided into four triangular segments by ribs, contains two episodes of the Samaritan Woman at the Well in the north and east segments: in the north segment Christ and his disciples at the left face the Woman at the right, with a cruciform well-head between them; in the east segment, the Woman calls others of the Samaritans to come out of the walls of a city. In the south segment is the Paralytic of Bethesda carrying his bed, a colonnaded structure behind him. Finally, in the west segment is the Blind Born, in the usual two episodes. Thus, the entire vault is devoted to our three miracles.[79]

Still another example of the juxtaposition of our three miracles in the decoration of churches is that of the sixteenth-century frescoes in the parecclesion of St. John the Theologian in the monastery of the Virgin Mavriotissa at Kastoria.[80] Placed in succession within a series of miracles on the north wall, middle register, are the Paralytic, the Samaritan Woman, and the Blind Born.[81] This is exactly the order of the successive Sundays between Easter and Pentecost in the *Pentekostarion*. There can be little doubt that the layout of the three at Kastoria was influenced by tradition, which, in turn, was based on liturgical considerations.

The subjects depicted at the Kariye Djami in the vaults, pendentives, and lunettes beneath the dome in the south bay of the inner narthex ([134]–[141], Vol. 2, PL. 260–81) comprise a group of eight miracles whose selection, but not their distribution, can be explained in one of three ways: they could have been taken from the Gospel of Matthew, from a painter's manual, or from the liturgy. Before considering these alternatives I must emphasize that the eight subjects are exclusively miracles of healing which would provide a deliberate and coherent theme for the program in that area of the narthex. In the sequence in which these mosaics have been catalogued in Volume 1, the subjects of the healings are as follows: (1) the Blind and Dumb Man [134]; (2) Two Blind Men [135]; (3) Peter's Mother-in-Law [136]; (4) the Woman with the Issue of Blood [137]; (5) the Man with the Withered Hand [138]; (6) the Leper [139]; (7) an unidentified miracle of healing [140] (both the inscription and the scene are only partly preserved); (8) the Healing of a Multitude [141].

The seven identifiable scenes illustrate verses from Matthew, Chapters 8, 9, and 12 [82] (though five are common to the Synoptic Gospels). If the mosaicist was inspired to make his selection from these three chapters of Matthew, eleven true *healing* miracles would have been available to him. In other words, the chapters contain four more healings, in addition to the seven just listed. One of the four (the Healing of the Paralytic at Capernaum) is illustrated in the sixth bay of the outer narthex ([124], PL. 253). One of the remaining three—the Centurion's Servant, Two Gadarene Demoniacs, and the Dumb Demoniac—which come within the same portion of Matthew's text could have been the subject of the unidentified mosaic [140], and the other two might possibly have been among the lost mosaics of the outer narthex, or might not have been used at all.

(just to the north of the domed bay of the nave) and on its east and north walls and piers; and in the western bays of the outer south aisle, where miracles are mixed with scenes of teaching and parables.

79 For the ensemble of the vault, see V. R. Petković and D. Bošković, *Dečani* (Belgrade, 1941), PL. CXCII. For details of the two episodes of the Samaritan Woman, ibid., PL. CCXXV and CCXXIX.

80 There are doubtless other examples that could be cited, and many in which the three are present but have only two of the three in close relation to one another. However, the instances

referred to here are sufficient to show the strength of the tradition binding the three in both liturgy and art.

81 The paintings are dated in 1552. For illustrations of the three see N. K. Moutsopoulos, Καστορία, Παναγία ἡ Μαυριώτισσα, in Greek and English (Athens, 1967), PL. 18–20. For their location in the parecclesion see ibid., Diagram VII, p. 20, Nos. 7–9, and the identification of the subjects listed on p. 18 (in Greek) and p. 71 (in English). For plan of the monastery, see diagram on p. 10, and for the church, p. 12. See also S. Pelekanides, Καστορία, I (Salonika, 1953), PL. 208 *b*, 209 *a* and *b*.

82 No miracles are described in Matt. 10 and 11.

Of course, if the mosaicist had consulted a painters' manual which, like the *Hermeneia*, was based on Matthew, much the same situation would have existed: he could have selected eight healing miracles from the eleven that fall between Nos. 22 and 39 of the *Hermeneia*.

However, it is probable that the iconographer selected his healing miracles for the area in question by referring to a liturgical work—specifically, a lectionary—rather than to the Gospels or a manual. We should bear in mind that this is the case in the cycle of the Old Testament prefigurations in the parecclesion, where the inscriptions quote from the *Prophetologion* and where the paintings illustrate the lections of the feasts of the Virgin.[83] Again, we have found that the selection in the pendentives of the sixth bay of the outer narthex derived from the lections for three successive Sunday services. Other examples of liturgically inspired scenes depicted in monumental art will be mentioned below.

Let us return to the healing miracles in the south bay of the inner narthex. A glance at the Gospel lections for the period from the third Saturday to the seventh Sunday *after* Pentecost [84] will show that all the twenty-nine daily Gospel lections were from Matthew. If we eliminate from the twenty-nine all lections which concern Christ's teachings and parables as well as incidents that were not miracles (in other words, lections that would not in any case be illustrated in a cycle of miracles), there remain twelve miracles, all of them healings of afflicted persons. The following table [85] gives, in chronological order according to the calendar, the days, the lection references from Matthew, and the subjects of the twelve miracles described by the lections on eleven of the days during that period (one of the lections included the two related miracles of Jairus' Daughter and the Woman with the Issue of Blood). The key numbers of the eight mosaics in the south bay ([134]–[141]) are given as I have assigned them in Volumes 1 and 2 of this series on the Kariye Djami. The short titles of the eight mosaics are italicized.

3rd Saturday after Pentecost	Matt. 8:1–4	*The Leper* [139]
4th Saturday after Pentecost	8:14–23	*Peter's Mother-in-Law* [136]
4th Sunday after Pentecost	8:5–13	Centurion's Servant [140]?
5th Monday of Matthew	12:9–13	*Withered Hand* [138]
5th Tuesday of Matthew	12:22–30	*Blind and Dumb Man* [134]
5th Sunday after Pentecost	8:28–9:1	Two Gadarene Demoniacs [140]?
6th Saturday after Pentecost	9:18–26	Raising of Jairus' Daughter; *Woman with Issue of Blood* [137]
6th Sunday after Pentecost	9:1–8	Paralytic at Capernaum
7th Wednesday after Pentecost	14:35–15:11	*A Healing of a Multitude* [141]?
7th Friday after Pentecost	15:29–31	*A Healing of a Multitude* [141]?
7th Sunday after Pentecost	9:27–35	*Two Blind Men* [135]

From this list of twelve lections of miracles in the section of the calendar with which we are concerned, seven were definitely depicted in the mosaics of the south bay. However, [140] may well have illustrated one of the five remaining lections. The five subjects in question are the Healing of the Centurion's Servant (4th Sunday after Pentecost), the Gadarene Demoniacs

83 See Der Nersessian in the succeeding study in this volume, pp. 334–49; and Vol. 1 of this work, pp. 190, 223–24, 228, 234, and 237.
84 For the lections of this period of the calendar, see Colwell and Riddle, eds., *Prolegomena*, pp. 91–93. The calendar, as they present it, is based on a collation of four lectionary manuscripts dating from the tenth to twelfth centuries. While the readings for the period from Easter to Pentecost Sunday with very few exceptions are taken from John, those for the period of about

sixteen weeks after Pentecost are from Matthew.
85 Extracted from Colwell and Riddle, *Prolegomena*, pp. 91–93, excluding all lections that were not miracles. The typicon of the Great Church of St. Sophia gives the same Gospel lections for Saturdays and Sundays only and thus confirms at least those lections. See J. Mateos, *Le Typicon de la Grande Eglise*, II (Orientalia Christiana Analecta, 166; Rome, 1963), pp. 147–51; his list is based on manuscripts of the typicon of the ninth to twelfth and fourteenth centuries.

(5th Sunday after Pentecost), the Raising of Jairus' Daughter (one of two miracles in the lection for the 6th Saturday after Pentecost), the Paralytic of Capernaum (6th Sunday after Pentecost), and one of two healings of multitudes (7th Wednesday and Friday after Pentecost).

The five can immediately be reduced to four, because it would be highly unlikely that the mosaicist would illustrate two healings of large numbers of people which would appear to be so similar to one another; rather, he would depict a single Healing of a Multitude that could encompass the two lections on the seventh Wednesday and Friday. This he did in the large and final mosaic of the series of eight healing miracles ([141], PL. 277–81), which he placed in the largest space in the area, the western lunette of the bay—a summing up, as it were, of the entire miracle cycle in a scene that does not correspond in detail to any single text and has only one relatively close iconographic counterpart in extant monuments.[86]

Since there were twelve possible lections to choose from for the eight available spaces, four would be eliminated or placed in the series of the outer narthex. One such was the Healing of the Paralytic of Capernaum, which was depicted in the sixth bay of the outer narthex ([124], PL. 250, 253–55). As an illustration of the lection for the sixth Saturday, which refers to two miracles—the Raising of Jairus' Daughter and the Woman with the Issue of Blood—the mosaicist chose the latter to be placed among the eight in the inner narthex. The Raising of the Daughter, which was not a miracle of healing in the strict sense, was inappropriate to the iconographic program of depicting eight healings. Moreover, it was obviously reserved to accompany the Raising of the Widow's Son in the program of the eastern part of the parecclesion, which was devoted to the theme of Resurrection and Judgment.[87] That leaves us with two possible subjects for the unidentifiable, partly destroyed mosaic No. [140]: the Centurion's Servant, and the Gadarene Demoniacs; the one not chosen may have appeared among the lost mosaics of the fifth, sixth, or seventh bays of the outer narthex, or may not have been depicted at all.

Whichever of the three sources—Chapters eight, nine, and twelve of Matthew; a painter's manual such as H; or the Gospel lections for the period between the third and seventh weeks after Pentecost—was the one actually used in selecting the subjects of the south bay, it is very evident that chronology played no part in their distribution or sequence. However, it will be shown that the four miracles in the pendentives were selected and placed where they are for didactic [88] and compositional [89] reasons.

The mastermind who established the layout of an iconographic program sometimes resorted to the device of juxtaposing scenes in order to symbolize by means of analogy various rites of the church, especially the holy sacraments. In a way, the grouping of the three scenes of the Paralytic, the Samaritan Woman, and the Blind Born was a case in point, and it originated, as we have seen, in the earliest periods of Christian art as a means of symbolizing the sacrament of baptism. In later periods, it is possible that the original meaning was lost, but the scenes continued to be grouped together because of their liturgical connections.

An even clearer instance of drawing analogies, by pictorial means, between events in the life of Christ and the rites of the church is found in the Kariye Djami in the juxtaposition of the miracles of Cana and the Multiplication of Loaves ([117], [118], PL. 228–45). Here, simply stated, the purpose was to indicate that when Christ performed these miracles he was prefiguring

86 See below, p. 299.
87 See Vol. 3 of this work, nos. [202] and [203], PL. 360–67; Vol. 1, pp. 196–99; and Der Nersessian, in this volume, pp. 308–309.
88 See below, pp. 267–68.
89 See below, p. 271.

the holiest of all sacraments of the church—the Eucharist—which lay at the very heart of the doctrines concerning the redemption of man, for the elements of the wine and the bread, when administered to all Christians, become the very blood and body of Christ.

Significant of the importance that was attached to these two miracles at the Kariye Djami is the prominence that was given to them in the program of the Ministry cycle and, indeed, in the church as a whole. Not only do they fill the large domical vault of the outer narthex that falls on the axis of the church, but the bay in which they are placed is that into which one first enters and the subjects are more elaborated than the others. In addition, their position between the two lunettes above the entrance doors, where the dedicatory figures of Christ as the Land of the Living and the Virgin of the Incarnation are placed, lends further importance and significance to the miracle scenes.

It is a curious fact that among extant monuments of middle and late Byzantine art the confrontation of these two meaningful subjects should be so extremely rare, for in several of the Early Christian catacombs and in minor arts of the first Christian centuries one rather frequently finds the subjects used to express this very theme. Early Fathers, and other exegetes, so often made reference to these miracles as prefigurations of the institution of the Eucharist that their meaning must have been known to all Christians.

That the two miracles came to typify the blood and flesh of the eucharistic sacrifice stems, in the first instance, from Christ's own words as they are recorded in the fourth Gospel. At the wedding feast Christ said to his Mother, even before he performed the miracle, "mine hour is not yet come" (John 2:4). The "hour" was to be his death, when, through the offering of his flesh and blood, eternal life was to be bestowed on man. That phrase occurs time and again in John's Gospel and it always refers to his future sacrifice.[90] The words imply that Christ and the author of the fourth Gospel saw the miracle as a prefiguration of Christ's sacrifice. They also carry the connotation that Christ, in his first miracle, knew the foreordained plan of his Father and knew that the hour when the water would be truly changed to wine would come after his death, when the foundations would be established for the institution of the Eucharist.[91] The form of the Eucharist, however, was established, before the liturgies of the church took shape, by Christ himself at the Last Supper.

In the case of the Multiplication of Loaves, Jesus again gave the explanation of its significance.[92] This he did, according to John's version (Ch. 6:22–58), when he addressed the multitudes on the day after the miracle and clearly associated the bread fed to them (John 6:26) with the eucharistic sacrifice, for he said, in several variations, that eternal life would be gained by him who was to eat his flesh (the true meaning of the bread given them) and drink his blood (a reference to the wine).

Origen, along with other early commentators, viewed the bread of the miracle as a type of the eucharistic feast. Addressing in the third century a community of the faithful to whom this symbolism was well known, he said, "And I believe, up to the present time and until the consummation of time, the twelve baskets remain filled with the fragments of the living bread."[93] Writing "on the Body and Blood of Christ," Cyril of Jerusalem, referring to the Cana miracle but expanding his thought to include also the Multiplication of Bread, says "Wherefore with

90 Hoskyns, *Fourth Gospel*, p. 188; Cullmann, *Urchristentum und Gottesdienst*, pp. 66 f.

91 Cullmann, *Urchristentum und Gottesdienst*, p. 68.

92 See J. Wilpert, *Fractio panis: La plus ancienne représentation du sacrifice eucharistique à la "Capella Graeca"* (Paris, 1896), pp. 8–11.

93 *Commentaria in Evangelium secundum Matthaeum*, XI.2, PG, 13, col. 908B.

full assurance let us partake as of the body and blood of Christ: for the *typos* of bread, his body, is given to thee; and in the *typos* of wine, his blood."[94] The two miracles were again coupled in a Latin source of the fourth century. Addressing Marcellina, sister of St. Ambrose, as she assumed the veil and thus became the "bride" of Christ, Pope Liberius said, "It is [Christ, your bridegroom] who . . . changed water into wine. . . . It is he again who, with five loaves and two fishes fed . . . four thousand men. He has invited more [men] . . . to feed them not with barley bread but with his divine flesh."[95]

In the mosaic of the Cana miracle attention should be called to the motif in the pendentive illustrating the slaying of what was called the "white bullock" in Volume I (p. 118). It should better be called the "fatted calf"[96] because it was derived from the parable of the Prodigal Son. Exegetes took it to symbolize the sacrifice of Christ and hence saw it as a prefiguration of one of the elements of the Eucharist. Cyril of Alexandria, for example, commenting on the parable, says, "But what else is the fatted calf if not surely Christ, the unblemished victim, who takes away the sins of the world, who is sacrificed and eaten."[97]

It is not necessary to cite further textual examples, which are abundant,[98] to illustrate similar ideas. More pertinent here are some of the examples of Early Christian art which reflect the same thought. The miracle of the bread is represented more frequently than that of Cana. From the third century it is formulated in a highly schematic manner. Christ touches the baskets with a rod, or—less frequently in painting but quite commonly on fourth-century sarcophagi [99]— he blesses the bread and fishes carried by two disciples at each side. In at least two instances the miracle of the bread is coupled with that of the wine in the catacomb paintings. In the Roman catacomb of Petrus and Marcellinus, in the soffit of a fourth-century arcosolium in the Regione delle Agapi,[100] there is depicted, at the right, Christ changing water into wine and, at the left, Christ blessing the bread, both scenes representing the consecration of the eucharistic sacrifice, according to Wilpert. In the badly damaged lunette is a banqueting scene containing a Sigma-shaped table, which Wilpert interprets as a symbol of eternal bliss, the result of having partaken of the Eucharist. Again in the same catacomb, in the center of the *monumentum arcuatum* III, dated by Wilpert in the first half of the fourth century,[101] is a tondo, in which Christ stands holding a partly unrolled scroll in his right hand, his left hand raised in blessing (?); at his right are three amphorae and at his left a square cist filled with loaves. Wilpert connects this painting with the relief on the lid of a square silver reliquary in San Nazaro Maggiore, Milan (Fig. 1), and relates both to the *durus sermo* of John, Chapter 6, especially to verses 52–58. On the lid of the reliquary Christ sits frontally on a throne, right hand raised in speaking, left holding a codex; at his right are five apostles above five baskets filled with bread, and at his left, six disciples above six jars.[102] On the famous wooden doors of the Roman church of S. Sabina, the second panel from the top

94 *Catechesis*, XXII, *Mystagogica*, IV, *PG*, 33, col. 1100A.

95 Reported by Ambrose, *De virginibus*, II.1, *PL*, 16, col. 231. For further discussion of the connection in art and Christian thought between the two miracles, see *DACL*, II.2, s. v. "Cana," pp. 1802 ff.

96 Luke 15:23.

97 *Comment. in Lucam*, XV.5.18, *PG*, 72, col. 809B. Again Christ is the "calf" in Cyril of Alexandria, *De adoratione*, III, *PG*, 68, col. 292C; and in *The Epistle of Barnabas*, VII.2, in *The Apostolic Fathers* (Loeb), I (London and New York, 1930), p. 368: "The calf is Jesus," etc.

98 E.g.: Cyprian (*Epist.*, LXIII [87], *PL*, 4, col. 383 ff., especially col. 395); Augustine (*Tract. in Iohannem*, VIII.3, *PL*,

35, col. 1450).

99 The two miracles are often represented on fourth-century sarcophagi. For two examples where they are coupled, see the sarcophagi of Tarascon (E. Le Blant, *Les sarcophages chrétiens de la Gaule* [Paris, 1886], PL. IX.3) and of Arles (idem, *Etude sur les sarcophages chrétiens antiques de la ville d'Arles* [Paris, 1878], PL. V,9).

100 J. Wilpert, *Die Malereien der Katakomben Roms* (Freiburg im Breisgau, 1903), text, pp. 302 f., and PL. 186,1.

101 Ibid., pp. 306 f. and PL. 166,1.

102 W. F. Volbach, *Frühchristliche Kunst: Die Kunst der Spätantike in West- und Ostrom* (Munich, 1958), Fig. 111, dated by Volbach at end of the fourth century.

of the leaf at the far left depicts three miracles, one above another: at the top is the Raising of Lazarus, and beneath it are the miracles of the bread and the wine. In the first of these Christ stands at the right touching one of the seven baskets with a rod, and in the second he stands at the left and touches one of seven jars.[103]

When we come to the coupling of the two miracles in extant Byzantine churches of the middle or late period, aside from the mosaics at the Kariye Djami we have, to my knowledge, only one other instance where they appear together in the context of the eucharistic sacrifice. That remarkable case is in the eleventh-century frescoes in the gallery of St. Sophia at Kiev.[104] On the south wall of the gallery is depicted the miracle at Cana, divided into two registers: above, Christ is at table with three of the participants in the feast, and to the right of them is a servant; below, Christ approaches the amphorae and changes the water into wine. On the north wall, below a scene of the Last Supper and opposite the Cana scene, is the Multiplication of Loaves.[105] On the south and north walls are the Old Testament scenes of Abraham's Hospitality and the Sacrifice of Isaac, both of which were considered in the Middle Ages as prefigurations of the eucharistic sacrifice. Two other Old Testament scenes—Abraham meeting three angels and the three Hebrew youths in the fiery furnace—are also grouped on the north and south walls of the tribune. Since the scenes of the Last Supper and the two miracles were placed entirely out of context with the Christological scenes in other parts of the church and are accompanied by those particular Old Testament subjects, it is clear that the tribune paintings were grouped for the purpose of symbolizing the Eucharist.

Another device used for didactic purposes by the artist in arranging scenes within a cycle, especially in a cycle of miracles, is the confrontation of events concerning men with similar ones concerning women. As "Theophanes Cerameus" said in one of his homilies,[106] humanity consists of males and females, both of whom share guilt in the fall of man; consequently, Christ showed that both enjoyed his beneficence and forgiveness. The writer cited several pairs of miracles to illustrate his point, among them the Man Sick with the Palsy and the Bent Woman; Zacchaeus and the Sinful Woman; the Centurion's Son and Jairus' Daughter.

A few examples of the application of this principle appear in the iconographic layout at the Chora. A notable instance, but one that does not occur in the cycle which concerns us here, is the confrontation of the Raising of the Widow's Son [202] with the Raising of Jairus' Daughter [203], in opposite sides of the bema arch of the pareclesion,[107] immediately in front of the great scene of the Anastasis [201] in the apse conch. The purpose here was to show that just as Christ raised both Adam and Eve in the Anastasis,[108] he displayed impartiality toward men and women in the resurrections he performed during his earthly mission.

Another example of this usage at the Kariye Djami is to be seen in the pendentives in the

---

103 See Volbach, *Frühchristliche Kunst*, Fig. 103, dated by him at the year 432 (p. 64 of notes); S. Bottari, ed., *Tesori d'arte cristiana*, I: *Dal paleocristiano al romanico* (Bologna, [c. 1966]), Fig. 2, p. 91.
104 The frescoes were painted over repeatedly in oils, and in 1955 only parts of what was still preserved of the originals had been uncovered. See V. N. Lazarev [Lazareff], *Nouvelles découvertes à la cathédrale Sainte-Sophie de Kiev*, in Russian and French (Moscow, 1955), pp. 27 f., pp. 31 ff. See also idem, "Novye dannye o mozaikax i freskax Sofii Kievskoj," *VV*, N.S., 10 (1956), pp. 172–77 and diagram Fig. 6; and especially idem, *Old Russian Murals and Mosaics from the XI to the XVI Century*, tr. B. Roniger (London, 1966), p. 45; p. 230, Fig. 10

(miracle at Cana); and p. 232.
105 This scene, according to Lazarev, *Nouvelles découvertes*, p. 34, was arbitrarily transformed in the 1840's into a scene of Judas' Betrayal.
106 Homily 44, *PG*, 132, col. 828C–829B. On the identity of the author, see G. Rossi Taibbi, *Sulla tradizione manoscritta dell'Omiliario di Filagato da Cerami* (Istituto Siciliano di Studi Bizantini e Neoellenici, Quaderni, 1; Palermo, 1965), pp. 79 ff.
107 Vol. 1 of this work, pp. 196–99; Vol. 3, PL. 360, 363; and, in this volume, Der Nersessian's study, pp. 308–309.
108 A version of the subject that differs in this respect from the more usual one in which Christ is shown raising Adam alone. Cf. Der Nersessian, pp. 320–21.

south bay of the inner narthex.[109] Facing one another in the two eastern pendentives are the healings of two women: Peter's Mother-in-Law [136] and the Woman with the Issue of Blood [137]. Opposing them in the western pendentives are two healings of blind men: the Blind and Dumb Man [134], and the Two Blind Men [135].[110] We shall see below, furthermore, that in these pendentive scenes, which may be called a "cycle within a cycle," the mosaicist has used compositional means to enhance the unity of the group of four healing miracles.

As has already been pointed out,[111] the Chora was not the only monument in which this procedure was used. At Monreale, for example, are two miracle scenes at the eastern ends of the side aisles [112] which represent the first and last of the cycle of twenty miracles and are thus pendant to one another. The two depict the healings of the Daughter of the Canaanite Woman (Figs. 2 a and b) and of the Centurion's Son (Figs. 3 a and b). Here the contrast is not alone between the sexes but also between persons of widely divergent stations in life, that is, between one who was a lowly and despised Canaanite and one of lofty official position; the element common to both of them, however, was that they were pagans.

Comparable also, in the sense that distinct categories of persons are juxtaposed or grouped together, are the figures from the Genealogy of Christ in the Kariye Djami in the two zones of the north dome, inner narthex. There the royal ancestors filled the upper zone above the spiritual, or priestly, "ancestors" portrayed below.[113] The latter group, moreover, is broken up into two subgroups of persons who shared certain experiences and were therefore arranged in sequence. The three Hebrew youths (Hananiah, Azariah, and Mishael), followed by Daniel [68]–[71], form the first group; they were fellow princes of the house of Judah, captives in the court of Nebuchadnezzar, and magi (wise men) wearing the oriental priestly garb. They are followed, in order, by Joshua, Moses, Aaron, and Hur, the military and priestly leaders of the Israelites in their journey to the promised land. Thus again the categorizing of personages played a part in determining the disposition of figures within an iconographic layout.

As an example of a miracle cycle in which only compositional considerations seem to have played a role in the distribution of scenes, I cite that which is found in the important but seldom illustrated twelfth-century Russian church of the Mirozh monastery at Pskov.[114] The naos contains a well-thought-out iconographic program of frescoes, which includes the festival cycle, mainly in the barrel vaults and tympana; a cycle of Passion and post-Resurrection scenes, which omits all festival subjects, placed in the fourth, or upper, register of the three walls in the south

109 PL. 260 and 262; 264 and 268. See above, pp. 262–64, where the attempt was made to discover by what principle the artist selected the miracles of healing which appear there as a group of eight.

110 The two miracles in which women are healed and the two in which blind men are healed are the only ones (aside from the resurrection of Jairus' daughter, which was reserved by the painter for illustration in the parecclesion) which appear in the three possible sources from which the group of eight healing miracles was selected; i.e., Chs. 8, 9, and 12 of Matthew's Gospel (Chs. 10 and 11 contain no miracles of healing); the list of H between Nos. 22 and 39; and the pericopes concerning healings for the services between the third and seventh weeks after Pentecost. This fact gives added weight to the evidence, presented above (cf. n. 109), that one of the three sources was used in the selection, but not in the distribution, of the eight subjects in the south bay, inner narthex.

111 See above, p. 253.

112 Ibid.

113 See the discussion of the Genealogy mosaics, their symbolism and sequence, in Vol. 1 of this work, pp. 54–56, and illustrations in Vol. 2, PL. 67, 71–84.

114 According to I. Tolstoj and N. Kondakov, *Russkie drevnosti v pamiatnikax iskusstva*, VI: *Pamjatniki Vladimira, Novgoroda i Pskova* (St. Petersburg, 1899), p. 178, the church was built and painted under the patronage of Niphon, bishop of Novgorod, in 1156. This publication illustrates the building and a selected number of paintings in line drawings, Figs. 216, 218–231. For the most complete and best illustrations of the paintings see the extremely rare album of photographs taken by O. I. Parli which accompanies a brief text of F. A. Ušakov, *Opisanie fresok xrama Preobraženiia Gospodnja v Pskovskom Spaso-Mirožskom monastyre* (Pskov, 1903). I wish to thank the Director of the M. E. Saltykov-Ščedrin State Public Library, Leningrad, for providing photographic prints of the album illustrations, and my colleague, Professor Ernst Kitzinger, for making some of his notes available to me.

and north arms; and a miracle cycle of fourteen scenes, which is distributed symmetrically in the third register of the south and west walls of the southern arm and the west and north walls of the northern arm (Figs. 4–6).

Whereas the Passion and post-Resurrection cycles are arranged in chronological order, the miracles are not. Furthermore, one is unable to discover influences of the liturgical calendar on the distribution of the miracles, nor are there juxtapositions of subjects to illustrate a symbolic or allegorical meaning. On the other hand, some scenes in a frieze on a given wall appear to have been composed and placed where they were to relate with, or reflect, compositions or motifs which appear in the Passion cycle immediately above, or to repeat in an entire frieze of three or four scenes the sequence of compositional motifs which appear in the miracles in a corresponding position in the opposite arm of the nave. To show these relationships we must list the subjects and describe the distribution of scenes, sometimes in the fourth as well as the third register.

On the south wall, south arm, of Pskov there were originally four miracles (Fig. 4, lower zone); the second and third have been partly destroyed by the insertion of a window.[115] From left to right, the scenes are the Stilling of the Tempest;[116] part of a damaged scene of a woman on a bed, which surely represented the Daughter of the Canaanite Woman;[117] a miracle, probably a representation of the Healing of the Man with the Withered Hand, of which only the afflicted man remains;[118] and the Healing of the Ten Lepers.[119] The first and last of the four may very well have been selected and placed where they are to provide compositional similarities to the two scenes in the zone immediately above them which represent successive post-Resurrection events based on John 21:4–14. Above the Stilling of the Tempest, with its boat filled by Christ and his disciples, is depicted the Miraculous Draught of Fishes, the event which took place when Christ, after the Resurrection, appeared to the disciples at the Sea of Tiberias (Fig. 4, upper zone). Both are strongly horizontal compositions and they depict similar boats at sea as their main elements. At the far right in the third register is the miracle of the Ten Lepers, a composition with markedly vertical elements—the lepers stand in a group before a standing Christ—that is almost a mirror reversal of the post-Resurrection scene above it, namely, Christ Feeding the Disciples immediately after the Draught of Fishes, in which the disciples stand erect in a line as they await their turn to receive food. As compositions the first and last miracles thus respond to those above them.

Again at Pskov, the two friezes of miracles, each with three subjects, on the western walls of the south and north arms, across the nave from each other, are meant to be compared and to be read in succession from south to north (left to right).[120] In the frieze of the south arm (Fig. 5) are the Healing of Peter's Mother-in-Law;[121] the Healing of the Blind Born,[122] in which the

115 The remains of the two were doubtless repainted to some extent.

116 Matt. 8:23–27; Mark 4:35–41; Luke 8:22–25.

117 There are only three miracles involving a woman on a bed: those involving Peter's Mother-in-Law, Jairus' Daughter, and the Canaanite's Daughter. The first two are depicted elsewhere in the Pskov cycle. According to the Gospel accounts of the third (Matt. 15:21–28; Mark 7:24–30), the Canaanite's Daughter was not brought before Christ. However, at Monreale (east end of south aisle) the Canaanite's Daughter is depicted in bed with a devil issuing from her mouth, which is not the case at Pskov, and in the *Hermeneia* (No. 45) the description specifies that the Daughter was present and on a bed. The illumination on fol. 79r of Paris. gr. 74 (Paris, Bibliothèque Nationale, Départe-

ment des manuscrits, *Evangiles avec peintures byzantines du XIe siècle* [Paris, n.d.], I, PL. 71), is the closest parallel to the parts that can be seen at Pskov. Not only is the Daughter lying on a bed in the presence of Christ, but no demon is depicted. As at Pskov and Monreale, architecture is depicted to indicate that the setting was within a house.

118 Matt. 12:9–13; Mark 3:1–5; Luke 6:6–10.

119 Luke 17:11–19.

120 Adding to the respondences between the two friezes are the paintings of two stylite saints, one at the end of the frieze in the south arm, west wall, the other at the beginning of the frieze in the north arm, west wall.

121 Matt. 8:14–15; Mark 1:29–31; Luke 4:38–39.

122 John 9:1–38.

man is shown being touched by Christ and a second time as he washes his eyes at a font; and the Healing of the Paralytic,[123] in which the healed man carries his bed. Because of the juxtaposition to the Blind Born this is probably the Paralytic in the miracle at Bethesda. The corresponding frieze in the north arm (Fig. 7) again begins with a scene of a woman on a bed—the Raising of Jairus' Daughter [124]—which is compositionally the almost exact counterpart of the Healing of Peter's Mother-in-Law. There follows the scene of the Healing of Two Demoniacs;[125] the two figures in a general way are the compositional equivalents of the double representation of the Blind Born. The third scene is the healing of a man who wears only a short skirt from hips to knees, has an emaciated torso, and raises his right forearm vertically but carries no walking stick. Except for the lack of a stick one would say he was blind, for Christ reaches forth close to the man's face. Although one cannot be certain solely from a study of photographs, the subject is possibly that of the Blind and Dumb Demoniac.[126]

With the exception of the scene which terminates the miracle cycle at Pskov, the frieze of four miracles on the north wall, north arm [127] (Fig. 6) is not very convincingly related in terms of composition or similarity of motifs to the scenes from the Passion above it, and not at all to the other friezes of the miracle cycle. The striking feature of the two Passion scenes on the north wall—Christ before Annas and Caiaphas,[128] and Christ before Pilate [129]—is the two groups of frontally enthroned, imposing personages before whom Christ stands at the left. In the miracle frieze below, from left to right, are Christ and the Samaritan Woman; an unidentifiable miracle of which only the figure of Christ is preserved; the partly destroyed Healing of the Woman with the Issue of Blood, identifiable by the unusual stance of Christ that is peculiar to this scene;[130] and the final scene of the miracle cycle, which, in its massing of imposing frontally seated men, does bear a general similarity, compositionally, to the Passion scene above it. For other reasons the final scene of the miracle cycle calls for special comment.

At the left, Christ is seated on a curious throne-shaped mattress—a poorly understood version of a dining couch—which seems to rest on the left front corner of the table at which a group of five men are dining. Below Christ, a woman anoints his *feet*. Four of the other five diners are behind the table and the fifth, the host, is at the far right in front of the table, seated on a bench with a footstool. The exact identification is problematical. In each of the Gospels there is described an anointment of Christ at a meal in a private house. According to Matthew (26:6–13) and Mark (14:3–9) Christ's host is Simon the leper, and the sinful woman anoints Christ's *head*. In both, the event immediately precedes the Betrayal and Passion, and Christ foretells his anointment at his death. In John's version (12:1–8) the host is Lazarus, his sister Mary anoints Christ's *feet*, and Christ again foretells his final anointment. In John, however, the event precedes the Entry into Jerusalem, and again it is very close to the beginning of the Passion. The fourth anointment, that of Luke (7:36–50), is an earlier event in Christ's life, the host is Simon, described as a Pharisee, and the woman anoints Christ's *feet*. But here Christ does not liken the anointment to that after his death. The painter of Pskov, it would seem, has conflated the accounts of Matthew, Mark, and John and from the last has taken the anointment of the feet; and for this there is ample precedent. For example, in the miniatures of the four anointments in the

123 John 5:2–15.
124 Matt. 9:23–26; Mark 5:35–43; Luke 8:49–56.
125 Matt. 8:28–34.
126 Matt. 12:22–23.
127 As in the south wall, the second and third scenes were

largely sacrificed when a window was cut through the wall.
128 John 18:12–14.
129 Matt. 27:11 ff.
130 For example, see the same pose, in reverse, in the Kariye; Vol. 2 of this work, PL. 268.

Gospel Book Parisinus gr. 74,[131] the woman in each case anoints Christ's feet, and little distinction is made in the garb of the host. The dining couch, incidentally, is better represented than in the scene at Pskov.

I had occasion above to speak of the group of four miracles in the Kariye Djami pendentives of the south dome, inner narthex ([134]–[137]), as an example of the choice and arrangement of certain subjects to contrast two categories of persons—men versus women—for didactic purposes. The same four also serve to illustrate a compositional formula that would enhance their unity as a group. To see how this was done it is first necessary to note that it was the almost invariable rule in depicting events, and especially miracles, to give the compositions a sense of movement from left to right by placing Christ and his accompanying disciples at the left facing or striding toward the afflicted at the right. But in this case it is quite apparent that the mosaicist wished, by compositional means, to orient the group as a whole by giving the scenes in the two southern pendentives (PL. 260 and 268) a sense of movement from right to left and those in the two northern pendentives (PL. 262 and 264) a sense of movement from left to right, thus causing all four to converge toward the axis of the eastern side of the bay. This meant that the two scenes of blind men in the western side turned their backs, so to speak, on one another while the two in the eastern pendentives faced one another.[132] Thus subjects [134] and [137] in the southern pendentives violated the rule that scenes should read from left to right. However, scene [137] (the Woman with the Issue of Blood), though reading from right to left, still adhered to the rule that Christ and his disciples should be at the left, for it is the one subject, as usually depicted, in which Christ and his disciples are at the left and yet direct their movement from right to left, contrary to the general practice. This is inherent in the subject itself, for the Gospel texts state that as Christ was on his way to Jairus' house the woman pressed through the crowd behind him. As normally depicted all figures in the scene follow Christ and his disciples as they stride toward the left, but Christ, and his disciples too, turn the upper parts of their bodies to look back at the woman, who touches the hem of Christ's garments.

Before undertaking an iconographic analysis of a select number of subjects in the Kariye Djami and other monuments [133] which best serve to indicate the extent to which the iconographic formulae were common to or, on the contrary, distinct from one another, or which indicate the sources of some seemingly irrelevant motifs appearing in our mosaics, it is necessary to say a few words about the layout in the first three bays of the Kariye Djami, where the Ministry cycle begins.

It is obvious that one of the salient purposes in the layout of the Ministry cycle at the Kariye Djami was to arrange the sequence in such a way that the miracles of Cana and Multiplication of Loaves would appear in confrontation with one another in the third bay of the outer narthex, where they and their symbolic content might have the utmost prominence for the beholder entering the church.[134] This disposition, however, meant that space for only four subjects would

---

131 See n. 117 above for reference to the published miniatures. The four are on folios 52v, 94, 122, and 193, PL. 42, 82, 108, and 166 respectively. See also Monreale: O. Demus, *The Mosaics of Norman Sicily* (London, 1949), PL. 89 *b*.

132 The orientation of these miracles follows the general practice in the representation of figures in pendentives of domes: for example, among the hymnographers in the dome of the pareeclesion at Kariye Djami and the Evangelists in the pendentives of the Holy Apostles, Salonika, the pair in the south face to

the left and those in the north face to the right. See Vol. 3 of this work, PL. 408, 430, 432, and 426, 428; A. Xyngopoulos, ῾Η ψηφιδωτὴ διακόσμησις τοῦ ναοῦ τῶν ῾Αγίων ᾿Αποστόλων, Θεσσαλονίκης (Salonika, 1953), PL. 8,1 and 10,1 and 2.

133 For a statement on the extent to which I will engage in an iconographic study of the scenes in the Ministry, see above, p. 245.

134 See above, pp. 264–67.

be available in the first two bays for the earlier events of Christ's Ministry, between the final scene of the Infancy cycle (the Journey of the Holy Family to Jerusalem for Passover) and the beginning of the miracles. Space was further restricted by the need to begin the Ministry cycle in the domical vaults with the scene of Christ among the Doctors, which could not be omitted since the Journey to Jerusalem, the last Infancy subject on the walls of the narthex, was only a prelude to the much more important episode of the disputation with the doctors.

The mosaic in the Kariye Djami of Christ among the Doctors (PL. 211–14) is so fragmentary that its reconstruction cannot be carried further than was attempted in Volume 1 of this series (pp. 108–10). Mme. Lafontaine-Dosogne quite legitimately regarded it as the final event in the cycle of Christ's Infancy and included it in her study, which precedes this one.[135] As she there noted, however, it can also be considered the first event of the Ministry, as the mosaicist seems to have done. But considering its fragmentary state and the discussions of it both in Volume 1 and in the preceding study, it is hardly profitable to dwell further on this subject. I shall, therefore, proceed to consider the iconography of some of the succeeding subjects.

The nine events from which the mosaicist could choose his illustrations for the three remaining spaces between the disputation with the doctors and the miracle of Cana—events, moreover, in which Christ appeared—are the following: John Baptizing (Matt. 3:5–6; Mark 1:4–5; Luke 3:3); the three occasions, on successive days, when John the Baptist bore witness of Christ and Andrew and John chose to follow Christ (John 1:24–28; 29–34; and 35–37); Christ coming to John at the Jordan to be baptized (Matt. 3:13); the Baptism (Matt. 3:16–17; Mark 1:9–11; Luke 3:21–22); the Temptation (Matt. 4:1–11; Mark 1:12–13; Luke 4:1–13); Christ calling Peter and Andrew (Matt. 4:18–20); and Christ calling James and John (Matt. 4:21–22; Mark 1:19–20). The first five of these were anticipatory to the Baptism itself, and we shall see that by the fourteenth century they and other subjects relating to John and baptism were treated in monumental art as subsidiary to the Baptism and, with the Baptism as the central element, were sometimes gathered together in a single composition which formed, as it were, a baptismal cycle.

Christ's Baptism was universally regarded as the most important of the early events of the Ministry, for it was nearly always numbered among the great feasts of the church and in the typical Byzantine iconographic program of decoration it took a prominent place in the festival cycle of the nave. That this was the case also in the Chora is proved by the fact that it was omitted from the Ministry cycle, where its absence is conspicuous. In the Gospels, after the Baptism, the next important event was the Temptation. Surprisingly, this subject was seldom included in monumental Ministry cycles, but in the Chora it was depicted in the position immediately preceding the first of the miracles. Having declined to represent the Baptism a second time, the mosaicist chose two of the three episodes of John Bearing Witness of Christ as his subjects for the spaces preceding the Temptation, but in them he added motifs which were derived from other elements of the baptismal cycle. In a sense the two Witnessings substitute for the missing scene of the Baptism. In the following discussion of the cyclical treatment of the Baptism, I will be concerned not with the Baptism itself but with the subsidiary episodes with which it was surrounded in monuments of the early fourteenth century and later, whose traces can be observed in the two scenes of John Bearing Witness ([114] and [115]). It will be my purpose to show that the two Witnessings of John at the Kariye Djami were, at least in part, derived from subsidiary elements of a composite baptismal cycle that already existed in the

135 Pp. 237–38.

repertory of Byzantine art when the Chora mosaics were installed, but were used there as independent subjects.[136]

The first of John the Baptist's Witnessings of Christ [114] (John 1:19–28) is definitely represented, and in the same compositional form as that of the Kariye Djami, in the murals of only two other churches.[137] The identification in Volume 1 (pp. 110–11) of the fragmentary mosaic as a representation of this subject is based in part on the painting of the subject in the Protaton of Mount Athos (Fig. 8),[138] which is used as a subordinate detail to fill the spandrel to the left of the Baptism, the first of the illustrations of the festival cycle on the south wall of the nave. Above the Baptism itself is the usual titulus, but to the left, above the figure of John bearing witness, the text of John 1:26–27 is inscribed, definitely identifying the subject of the subsidiary scene: "I baptize with water: but there standeth one among you, whom ye know not," etc. The scene at the Protaton is composed with John at the right, separated by a narrow, vertically curving stream from the massed group of Pharisees and Levites in whose midst stands the dominant figure of Christ. At the foot of the stream is a small bridge on which three young boys, fully clad, hold hands as they appear to dance. This detail invites comparison with the two young boys wrestling at the very edge of the river bank in the pendentive at the far left of scene [114] at the Chora. Nearby, to the right, is part of the group of Pharisees and Levites, in whose midst there doubtless stood the figure of Christ in parts that are now destroyed.

Excepting that it is composed in reverse, the scene in the Protaton is very much like one of five identifiable subjects that surround the Baptism in the south conch of the Catholicon of Chilandar monastery, Mount Athos (Figs. 9, 9 a and b),[139] the six scenes comprising a baptismal cycle. The first Witnessing is in the lower left part of the composition and contains the same elements as that in the Protaton: the Baptist gesticulating, his right hand extended toward a group in which Christ stands; at the base of the stream the same group of three young boys on the bridge. That the scene is indeed John's first Witnessing is evident not only from the painting itself but from the inscription on the scroll held by John, which, in garbled form, quotes the words of John 1:26. At the far lower left, in the angle formed by the conch, seemingly as a space-filler, the artist has added a large group of men (one places his hand on the head of a boy) who stand quite apart from the scene of witnessing and seem to direct their gaze at the activities of young boys who undress and enter the stream of Jordan; the stream with the swimmers extends the full length of the base of the conch. Also in the stream are the usual personifications pertaining to the central scene of the Baptism.

Above the hillocks that form a background for the first scene in the Chilandar conch is another scene in which are the figures of the Baptist, at the left, and Christ with two disciples, at the right, dressed in the usual tunic and himation. The foremost of the disciples is clearly of the type of Peter; the second may be of the type of John, or of James, depending on whether he is depicted as beardless or not. This fact, and the lack of inscription, make the scene difficult to identify. The presence of disciples again recalls the two scenes of John Bearing Witness at

136 In manuscript illumination the individual episodes of the Kariye Witnessings appear as independent scenes. See Laurent. Plut. VI.23, fol. 169, right half, where the composition of Kariye Djami, Witnessing II [115], is reversed, as it also is in Paris. gr. 74, fol. 168.

137 One of the panels in Sant'Angelo in Formis may possibly represent this subject, but its inscription is effaced (fourth panel from west, first register, north wall of nave). See Jerphanion, *Voix des monuments*, p. 275, and Wettstein, *Sant'Angelo in Formis*,

pp. 41, 43. In a very simple hieratic composition John is at the left, separated by a tree containing the axe from a double-arched building at the right; in the first arch is a crowd of Jews, in the second Christ stands alone. The scene is simply one of a narrative series of New Testament scenes, not part of a cycle of the Baptism.

138 Cf. Millet, *Athos*, PL. 6,1 and 3; 7,2; and 11,2.

139 Cf. ibid., PL. 66,1; 66,2; 67,2.

the Kariye Djami, in which two disciples, Andrew and John, are depicted in close proximity to Christ.[140] The textual passages on which the first Witnessing at the Chora is based do not mention disciples, but the passage describing John's third Witnessing (John 1:35–42) says that two disciples, Andrew and, by inference, John the Evangelist himself, were present and followed Jesus (John 1:40). At the Kariye, this fact was made retroactive to include the first two Witnessings. Was it the third Witnessing that inspired the second subject in the Chilandar cycle? If so, the artist depicted the wrong disciples. On the other hand, the text of John continues, in 1:41–42, with the words "[Andrew] first findeth his own brother Simon . . . and . . . brought him to Jesus." Perhaps this induced the representation of Simon Peter, but the second disciple should have been Andrew. It is more likely that the scene in question depicts a conflation of textual passages and in fact simply represents, in addition to John's Witnessing, the general theme of the calling of disciples as is the case, in a different manner, at the Kariye Djami. We can only conjecture that at the Kariye, space being available in the two scenes of witnessings, the mosaicist wished to introduce, at least in a minor way, the important subject of the calling of some of Christ's disciples, for which no separate provision was made in the program.

To the lower left of the central subject of the Baptism at Chilandar, and close to the tree with the axe which so commonly figures in compositions of the Baptism, John the Baptist points to the axe and turns to look back at a group of the Jews who are with him. The open scroll in his left hand bears a very much corrupted version of Luke 3:9 (and Matt. 3:10): "And now also the axe is laid unto the root of the trees," signifying that already the Judgment is beginning.

At the upper right of the conch is one of the episodes of John teaching—in this instance he is speaking to a group of soldiers, as described in Luke 3:14, instructing them to "Do violence to no man," etc. Beneath the figure of John in this scene, Christ is shown standing in the center of a circular disc and holding a winnowing fan in his right hand. To the right, the Baptist points to Christ as he turns to speak to a large group of Jews in the lower right angle of the conch. This scene refers to Matthew 3:12 (or to Luke 3:17), which speaks of the winnowing fan in Christ's hand, his purging of the threshing floor, and the gleaning of the wheat.[141]

As fully developed as the Chilandar cycle of Baptism, but differing from it in a number of details, is the composition in the central cross vault of the outer narthex of the Serbian church of the Bogorodica Ljeviška at Prizren [142] (Figs. 10 a and b). This time the cycle consists of seven scenes, including the Baptism in the east side of the vault, surrounding a central circular glory in which are angels and an open door containing the hand of God; from the door emerges a ray of light leading to a star-shaped glory in which is the dove of the Holy Spirit.[143] Near the dove above the Baptism is an Old Slavonic inscription (Mark 1:9–10) which refers to Jesus' coming to be baptized and to the Spirit-dove descending upon him.

In the northeast quadrant, more or less centered on the groin, is a scene which can be en-

---

140 See Vol. 1 of this work, pp. 111, 113; Vol. 2, PL. 215, 217.

141 At Dečani some of these elements are depicted as isolated, framed scenes. See Petković and Bošković, *Dečani*, PL. CCLXXXV.1 and 2 for Christ on the threshing floor holding a winnowing fan, and John preaching in the midst of Jews; PL. CCLIV.2 for John addressing the soldiers (to which is added the axe at the root of the tree and flames which consume it). At Gračanica (V. R. Petković, *La peinture serbe du Moyen Âge*, II [Belgrade, 1934], PL. LXIII) the episode of John teaching the soldiers is clearly visible in the upper left corner of the scene of Christ's Baptism.

142 Hamann-MacLean and Hallensleben, *Die Monumentalmalerei*, I, pp. 29 f., and others date the building as a work of King Milutin to the years 1306–09 and thus earlier than the Kariye Djami. Because the paintings in the narthex were so severely damaged many details in the western half of the vault do not appear clearly in photographs and I am unable to provide adequate illustrations. For many details described here, and for the identification of the inscriptions, I am greatly indebted to Mrs. D. Panić-Surep.

143 The same features are present also above the Baptism in the conch of Chilandar.

titled John Preaching Repentance (Matt. 3:1–5) (Fig. 10 a).[144] The Baptist stands on a rock holding an open inscribed scroll as he preaches to a group of people who are at the left, on the opposite bank of a narrow stream, standing before a city gate. Above John is an inscription quoting from Matthew 3:3, and above the gate is another based on Matthew 3:5. John's scroll bears an inscription from Matthew 3:2.

Moving around to the left, to the northwest quadrant, we find a composition depicting two of John's Teachings (Fig. 10 b). At the left, again centered on the groin, John teaches a group of soldiers and holds a scroll quoting Luke 3:11; above the soldiers an inscription quotes Luke 3:14. To the right is a group of Jews, beside whom is the axe referred to in the inscription of Luke 3:9 placed above the figure of John.

Continuing in a clockwise direction we come to the scene at the west side of the vault, opposite the Baptism. Here Christ stands frontally in the center holding a closed scroll. At the lower left two young men (possibly followed by others) look up at him. A partially preserved inscription seems to quote from Luke 7:19 and thus identifies the subject as Christ being questioned by some of John's disciples.

Painted on the groin at the southwest is the figure of John, at the left, standing on a rock and holding an open inscribed scroll in his left hand as he speaks to a group of men at the right. The subject is John Bearing Witness of Christ, for the inscriptions quote John 1:30 and 33.[145] The verses are from John's second testimony, but the painting may be intended as a representation of John's witnessings in general, as is suggested by the fact that Christ is not depicted.

In the scene on the southern axis of the vault Christ stands frontally in the center on a circular winnowing floor on which is chaff at the left and wheat at the right; he holds a fan in his hand. John, in profile at the left, holds an illegibly inscribed scroll and points to Christ as he addresses a group of people at the right. The scene is superscribed with the words from Matthew 3:11–12 and therefore represents John Preaching in a composition that is almost exactly like its counterpart at Chilandar and comparable to one of the scenes at Dečani.[146]

The last of the scenes at Prizren is that in the southeast (Fig. 10 a), in which Christ comes to John to be baptized. John is at the left in profile holding an inscribed scroll as he faces Christ, who is standing on slightly higher ground at the right. John's scroll quotes Matthew 3:14.

Extending across the east side of the vault at Prizren is the stream of Jordan, represented in a manner comparable to that in the conch of Chilandar. Beneath the northeast quadrant, where the scene of John preaching repentance and baptism in water is represented, there are at least four children, of whom one is undressing and two are swimming. Lacking is the motif of the boys wrestling, which we have seen at the Kariye, or on the bridge as in the Protaton and especially at Chilandar, where it is part of a well-developed theme of aquatic activities along the banks of Jordan.

In line with the baptismal iconography of the Protaton, Prizren, and Chilandar are the fresco of the Baptism in the Peribleptos, Mistra (Fig. 11), and the almost identical version in the icon of the Baptism in the Medieval Section of the National Museum, Belgrade, No. 4348.[147]

---

144 What may be a simplified version of this subject is found at Staro Nagoričino (see Petković, La peinture serbe, II, PL. 49), added to the right of a painting of the Baptism from the series of menologies for Jan. 6.

145 The inscription above scene [115] at the Kariye Djami quotes the first of these verses.

146 Petković and Bošković, Dečani, PL. CCLXXXV.

147 Published by M. Tatić-Djurić, "Le Baptême de Jesus-Christ, icône datant de l'époque de la renaissance des Paléologues" (in Serbian with French résumé), Zbornik radova Narodnog Muzeja, IV (Belgrade, 1964), pp. 267–81, and PL. 1–7. I am indebted to Mrs. Doula Mouriki for calling this to my attention and for the photograph of the Peribleptos fresco in the vault of the south transept, west side. See Millet, Mistra, PL. 118,3.

In each case, above the scene is an arc of heaven very much like that at Chilandar. The Jordan flows vertically through the center of the composition, and Christ is in the stream, John with the tree and the axe is on the left bank, and the angels are in the upper part of the right bank. In the upper left a small John the Baptist bows before Christ; in the lower left is a group of Jews, one man in the group holding a naked infant and another, a clad and an unclad infant. Below them at the edge of the river stand three youths fully clad. A similar group of men, women, naked infants, and young boys is at the lower right. In the stream surrounding Christ are fish, at the top five naked boys either swimming or about to dive, and below them the usual personifications.

In addition to the examples in monumental painting of scenes containing large numbers of unclad and disrobing children, groups of adult Jews, and John the Baptist, but not Christ, such a scene is depicted in an eleventh-century manuscript now in the State Historical Museum, Moscow [148] (Fig. 12), as a composition in its own right and not as a Baptism of Christ. Above, on the left bank of the vertically depicted river, John the Baptist stoops forward in profile, his right hand extended toward a nude boy in midair who is diving into the river from the opposite bank; behind John is the tree with the axe "laid to the root." At the same level on the right bank is a group of standing men, fully clad, facing toward the Baptist. Below them, on both sides of the river, are boys undressing themselves or being assisted by their mothers; a second boy dives from the left bank and five others swim in the river. At the upper left, two of Christ's future disciples, who seem to be of the type of Andrew and John, peer around the peak of a mountain, and the latter points to the Baptist.

The miniature appears in the Moscow manuscript in illustration of *Oratio XL* of Gregory of Nazianz, on Holy Baptism.[149] In this homily Gregory teaches that there are three births for mankind: "the natural birth, that of Baptism, and that of Resurrection," and since the subject of the sermon was baptism, the illuminator depicted not the Baptism of Christ but that of the populace of "Jerusalem, and all Judaea, and all the region round about Jordan" who went out to John to be baptized, confessing their sins (Matt. 3:5–6; Mark 1:4–5; Luke 3:3). It is notable that in the Moscow miniature, the lower parts of the Chilandar and Prizren vaults, the Protaton Baptism, and the Kariye Djami Witnessing [114], those who are being baptized by actually plunging into the river, preparing to do so, or swimming in it are all depicted as children. Is this by way of expressing the thought that through the "birth" by baptism one becomes a child, as in natural birth? This is to be inferred from Matthew 3:9 and Luke 3:8, where the Baptist says that "God is able of these stones [on the banks of the Jordan] to raise up children unto Abraham."[150] The frequent recurrence of at least some of the elements depicted along the banks of the Jordan in mural paintings of baptismal cycles and in manuscript illumination raises the question whether they are simply extraneous, genre motifs or illustrations of the Gospel texts mentioned above with reference to John's activities in baptizing those who came to him. Viewing them simply as accessories to the Baptism in Chilandar and Prizren, one might be tempted to consider such representations of children dancing and undressing on the banks of the river and swimming in it as mere survivals of the tradition of representing aquatic creatures and persons

148 Vlad. 146 (Sabba 61), a manuscript of the Homilies of Gregory of Nazianz. The miniature (fol. 145) is illustrated in V. Lazarev, *Istorija vizantijskoi živopisi*, II (Moscow, 1948), PL. 135 g. In Lazarev's revised edition of this work, *Storia della pittura bizantina*, tr. G. Fossati (Turin, 1967), it is illustrated as Fig. 227 and designated as John baptizing the people in Jordan.

149 *PG*, 36, cols. 360 ff.

150 The Moscow miniature includes the tree with the axe mentioned in Matt. 3:10 and Luke 3:9, so that it is evident that the miniaturist illustrated the Gospel accounts of Matt. 3:5–10 and Luke 3:3–9, passages that also included John's statement regarding children.

engaged in swimming in scenes involving streams of water—a survival, that is, of "nilotic" elements from antiquity. But the miniature from the Moscow manuscript cannot derive from such traditions, for it is obviously an illustration of John baptizing the populace in general as described in Matthew and Luke.

It is evident that by the first decade of the fourteenth century or even much earlier, before the mosaics of the Kariye Djami were executed, a cyclical iconography of baptism was already in existence in monumental art. Moreover, we have seen that, although the mosaicist of the Kariye was obliged to omit the scene of Christ's Baptism from the Ministry cycle, in its stead he used some of the subordinate themes or motifs from the baptismal cycle, namely, the first and second Witnessings of Christ by John the Baptist; the motif of the children at the river's edge; and the portrayal of two of Christ's future disciples—Andrew and John.

Representations of the Temptation in fresco or mosaic cycles of the Ministry are surprisingly few in number and vary considerably in type and details. There are some minor variations also in the accounts given in the three Gospel texts. Mark's version (1:12–13) can be disregarded as a major influence in the monumental paintings of the subject, for it merely states that Christ was "tempted of Satan; and was with the wild beasts; and the angels ministered unto him." Beasts never figure in the monumental representations, but angels are sometimes depicted, because in their accounts of the challenge that Christ cast himself from the pinnacle of the temple both Matthew and Luke say angels would attend him. Except for the sequence of the episodes, the accounts of Matthew and Luke are much alike. Both agree that there were three temptations. According to Matthew (4:3–10), Christ was tempted as follows: (1) to turn stones into bread to satisfy his hunger; (2) to cast himself down from the pinnacle of the temple after being taken by the devil "up into the holy city"; (3) to worship the devil in return for "all the kingdoms of the world, and the glory of them" after being taken "up into an exceeding high mountain." For convenience, I shall refer to these as the temptations of the stones; of the pinnacle of the temple; and of the kingdoms of the world. The temptations according to Luke (4:3–12) are essentially the same, but their order is: the stones; the kingdoms; and the pinnacle—that is, 1, 3, 2 in the order of Matthew. The principal points of difference among the various representations of the Temptation are these: the number, choice, and sequence of episodes; the type of creature used in representation of the devil; and the means by which the stones, pinnacle, and especially the kingdoms were symbolized.

By far the most detailed and compositionally unified version of the Temptation is that of the Kariye Djami,[151] which is also unique in presenting four rather than three episodes, for it contains the additional representation of Christ being taken up into an exceeding high mountain, which both Matthew and Luke had given as the setting for the offer to give Christ all the kingdoms of the world. It is difficult to say which order, Matthew's or Luke's, was followed in arranging the four incidents in the southern half of the domical vault of the second bay, outer narthex ([116]), for we cannot assume that they were to be read continuously from left to right; the mosaicist may have intended to employ the method of alternating from left to right beginning with the two extremities and working back and forth between them. His system could be either one of the two, but whichever he used he misplaced the incident of Christ being led

---

[151] Vol. 1 of this work, pp. 114–17; Vol. 2, PL. 216, 222–27.

to the high mountain, which was a prelude to the offering of the kingdoms and should have come to the left rather than to the right of that temptation (PL. 222).

A description of the Temptation at the Kariye Djami is given in Volume 1 of this work, but for convenience in making comparisons with other monuments the devil and the attributes of each temptation should be briefly described here. The devil (PL. 227) is a dark, energetic, winged anthropoid with sharp features and wild hair, wearing a sleeveless short garment about his torso; the stones (PL. 223), in a rectangular open box, are quite realistic; the kingdoms (PL. 226) are represented as a group of six figures wearing fanciful crowns and rich vestments adorned with gold and red and holding batons, all enclosed within turreted walls; the pinnacle of the temple (PL. 224) is a rectangular, flat-roofed tower, and to show that the tower pertains to a temple an altar covered with a ciborium is placed nearby.

In two Cappadocian churches the Temptation was included in a Ministry cycle. At Tokali Kilisse,[152] the subject is dealt with through only one of the three episodes: the third one of Matthew (4:8–10), i.e., the kingdoms and their glory. At the left is a small, winged devil of the type found in the Chora, who stands in near-profile high up and relieved against a great rock, looking away from Christ. The kingdoms are represented by three containers of various types (the treasures of the earth) placed below the devil. Christ, at the right, strides animatedly away but looks back at the devil and extends his right arm in a gesture of refusal. The other example in Cappadocia is in the church of St. Theodore at Sousam Baïri.[153] Here two temptations are depicted. In each Christ faces the tempter, represented in the form of a winged, monstrous giant who wears a short skirt-like garment; between them are the objects of the temptation. In the first scene these are the kingdoms, symbolized by a chest (the treasures of the earth), and in the second, the stones—a container filled with round objects that could represent either stones or small loaves.

At Sant'Angelo in Formis, at the eastern end of the upper register in the north wall, in the cycle of the Ministry, the Temptation is depicted in three episodes (Figs. 13, 14, 15). In them are certain peculiarities that have not been noted in previous, quite inadequate descriptions.[154] The first of the temptations (Fig. 13) seems to be that of the stones.[155] Standing at the left between two palm trees, Christ faces and makes speaking gestures toward Satan at the far right. At the foot of the tree between them is a large, chalice-like bowl filled with stones, and slightly above it are a flask (filled with water?) and two small "chalices" also filled with stones; a second flask is on the ground. The figure of Satan (seated?) at the right is that of a nude man, nearly as large as Christ, at whose shoulders are rather small wings. The flasks are extraneous to the texts and presuppose Christ's thirst in addition to his hunger. The containers of the stones, because they are encrusted with gems, are anomalous and perhaps allude to the precious objects by means of which the riches of the world (the temptation of the kingdoms) are sometimes symbolized.

The second temptation painting is clearly the pinnacle scene (Fig. 14). At the far left are a curious highly stylized mountain and a palm tree. A little to their right Christ stands on the domical covering of a ciborium-like structure facing and gesticulating toward Satan, who stands to the right, facing and gesturing toward Christ. As before, Satan is nude and winged.

152 G. de Jerphanion, *Une nouvelle province de l'art byzantin: Les églises rupestres de Cappadoce* (Paris, 1925–42), Text, I,2, p. 335, and Plates, II, PL. 77,2 and 81,4.
153 Ibid., Text, II,1, pp. 35 f., and Plates, III, PL. 148,1.
154 For example, Jerphanion, *Voix des monuments*, p. 275;

Wettstein, *Sant'Angelo in Formis*, p. 43; Morisani, *Gli affreschi di S. Angelo in Formis*, p. 83. To my knowledge these have not been adequately reproduced in publications, and it is with this lack in mind that I publish them here.
155 The effaced inscription is illegible.

In the final scene (Fig. 15), which should be the kingdoms, Christ, with at least two angels to the right and possibly another behind, stands [156] facing toward the right, addressing Satan, who plunges over backward. In the lower left part an area of painting is completely destroyed; if objects symbolizing the kingdoms had ever been painted in this area, they could not have been very prominent or of large dimensions. The motifs of the angels and the "plunging" Satan, which are also found at Monreale, are probably attributable to Matthew's version of the final temptation, in which Christ rejects Satan with the words, "get thee hence . . . " and which says that the devil left him and angels came. The falling attitude of Satan may have been a means of indicating Christ's triumph over Satan.

The Temptation at Monreale [157] has these features in common with that at Sant'Angelo in Formis: the three temptations in the same order (Matthew's); the nude Satan of relatively large size who, in the final scene, plunges downward; and the angels in the temptation of the kingdoms. Points of difference are that, excepting in the scene of the temple pinnacle, depicted as a colonnaded building with a slate roof, Christ stands on a rather flat-topped, rocky hillock; Satan is given a small tail; the stones of the first temptation are one large square and three large circles floating in air and having wavy lines; and the "kingdoms" consists of an oblong cloth, floating in air, on which are golden attributes of royal power: the orb (?), crown, scepter, baton, faldstool, goblets, and a number of circles representing gold coins.

At San Marco, Venice, there is no Ministry cycle, as such, but the mosaics of three arches are devoted to eleven miracles.[158] The only other subjects that could pertain to the Ministry are Christ among the Doctors, the Baptism, the Temptation, and the Entry into Jerusalem. The first of these is grouped with two others as part of the Infancy,[159] and the second is in an arch with Infancy and festival subjects.[160] The Temptation and the Entry into Jerusalem, curiously enough, are grouped in an arch with subjects that more properly belong to the Passion.[161]

The Temptation [162] at San Marco (Fig. 16), in three parts and in the order of Matthew (stones, pinnacle, kingdoms), which is the order also at Sant'Angelo in Formis and Monreale, depicts the angels and the fall of Satan in the final temptation,[163] and, in the second temptation, as at Sant'Angelo, places Christ on the roof of a ciborium. The Temptation at San Marco differs from that of the other two Italo-Byzantine versions primarily in the temptation of the stones, where Christ is shown seated on a throne-like rock while Satan holds the stones in his veiled hands as though they were the bread of the Holy Eucharist. The attributes of the kingdoms are also different, but somewhat akin to those of Monreale: Christ stands on a rocky peak on which are scattered coins and three goblets; when shown in this guise, the scene of the kingdoms connotes the riches of the world. The type of Satan used throughout the Temptation at San Marco is also different, for except that he seems to wear a diadem from which two horns project, he more closely resembles the Satan of the Kariye Djami than is the case in others of the monumental

156 Not seated, as is said by Demus, *Norman Sicily*, n. 178, p. 338.

157 It fills the upper register of the south wall of the south transept. See Kitzinger, *The Mosaics of Monreale*, Figs. 44, 46 (offerings of the kingdoms). Although the Temptation mosaics are restored, they preserve the original iconography.

158 Central bay, N. arch; north bay, N. arch; and south bay, E. arch. Thus, they are widely dispersed. The subjects of other cycles are also poorly defined and illogically laid out.

159 In the tympanum on the south wall of the north bay, with Joseph Dreaming and the Flight into Egypt.

160 Central bay, E. arch, with Annunciation, Adoration, Transfiguration, and Presentation in the Temple.

161 Central bay, S. arch, with Last Supper and Washing of Feet. For the layout of the mosaics see the plan, O. Demus, *Die Mosaiken von San Marco in Venedig, 1100–1300* (Vienna, 1935), p. 6.

162 Demus, *Die Mosaiken von San Marco*, Fig. 5; S. Bettini, *Mosaici antichi di San Marco a Venezia* (Bergamo [1944]), PL. XII.

163 This third temptation is unusual in showing Satan twice, first tempting and then falling or departing.

representations of the subject: he is dark and small and wears the type of garment of the Satan at the Kariye.

As at San Marco, no Ministry cycle exists in the chapel of St. John the Theologian at the church of the Virgin Mavriotissa at Kastoria, although this chapel, too, presents many miracles.[164] Placed entirely out of context in the south wall is a rectangular panel in which the three elements of the Temptation are combined in a single composition.[165] Here is the only other mural representation of the kingdoms depicted like the one at the Kariye Djami; that is, as a group of kings (three in number) seated and enclosed. Satan is small and winged, with disheveled hair, but unlike his counterpart at the Kariye, he is nude and has a rather long tail.

With the Temptation, the early phase of Christ's Ministry was concluded and he began to teach and perform miracles. At the Kariye Djami, as in the Gospel of John, the first miracle was that performed during the Marriage Feast at Cana. Before we can place the Kariye version of the Cana scene [117] in the general iconographic development of the subject, it is first necessary to reconstruct the missing parts, which occur mostly in the episode of the Feast. If we recall that all seven scenes in the friezes of the upper zone of the south, west, and north walls of the nave in the church of St. Nicholas at Curtea-de-Argeş [166] are almost identical to their counterparts at the Kariye Djami,[167] it comes as no surprise that a close relation can be detected between the original parts of the banqueting episode at Curtea (Fig. 17, left half) [168] and the fragmentary parts of the mosaic at the Kariye (PL. 229 left, 230, 232, and 233). So close are they that we can conclude that in this scene, too, the Curtea painter copied the Kariye mosaic. That being the case, the original parts of the painting provide a reliable basis for reconstructing the missing parts of the mosaic. It is for this purpose that I must discuss the Curtea painting in considerable detail and also consider two other paintings of the subject which bear a remarkable similarity to Curtea's.

If we compare the Kariye fragments of the lower extremities of Christ, seated on a bench at the left end of the table, and of Peter, who sat on a lower bench behind him (PL. 232) with the corresponding parts of the same figures at Curtea (Fig. 17), we see that the legs of Christ are disposed in exactly the same way and that the details of the feet of Christ, the drapery of both Peter and Christ, the cushion on which Christ sits,[169] and the legs of the two benches in each version are alike.[170]

It was remarked in Volume 1 (pp. 118-19) that the use of the motif of the slaying of a calf at the Kariye has no textual authority [171] and that except for its appearance at Curtea it is unique

164 Ten panels in the frieze of the second register running westward from the middle of the south wall, across the west wall at the same level, and eastward on the north wall for half the length of the chapel. See Moutsopoulos, *Kastoria*, Diagram VII, Nos. 17-19; Diagram VI, K, L, M; and again, Diagram VII, Nos. 6-9.

165 Moutsopoulos, *Kastoria* (see above, n. 81), Diagram VII, No. 21, and Fig. 34; Pelekanides, Καστορία, PL. 212 a.

166 See I. D. Stefanescu, *La peinture religieuse en Valachie et en Transylvanie depuis les origines jusqu'au XIXᵉ siècle* (Paris, 1930), Album, PL. 7, south wall (Journey to Bethlehem, Enrollment for Taxation, Magi before Herod, Herod Inquiring of the Priests and Scribes); PL. 8, west wall (Joseph Dreaming and Return of Holy Family from Egypt, and Christ Taken to Jerusalem); and PL. 6, north wall (Multiplication of Loaves). For more detailed illustrations, see *Buletinul Comisiunii Monumentelor Istorice*, 10-16 (1917-23), pp. 237, 238, Fig. 282 a; pp. 220, 221, Fig. 250; pp. 229, 230, Fig. 266 (our Fig. 22). For the date of the frescoes, see below, n. 225.

167 Compare with our PL. 155, 159, 173 right half, 177, 200, 206, 238.

168 Reproduced here from a composite print of the same negatives used in *Buletinul*, p. 225, Fig. 260. The Miracle of Cana at Curtea is in the second register below the cornice on the south wall of the western arm of the nave, immediately above the arch leading to the southwest corner bay.

169 Red, both at the Kariye (see Vol. 1 of this work, p. 120) and at Curtea (O. Tafrali, *Monuments byzantins de Curtéa de Argeş*, Text (Paris, 1931), p. 129).

170 The bench of Christ at Curtea has a higher end rail, but the same type of ornament appears in the end rails of Peter's bench.

171 It was suggested that the motif derived from the representations of the fatted calf in illustrations of the Prodigal Son. For the significance of the calf in the pendentive at the Kariye, see above, p. 266 and nn. 96, 97.

in representations of the Marriage Feast. Its presence at Curtea again supports the dependence of the painting on the mosaic. Of course, the painter had to place the motif in his rectangular composition and so lifted it up, as it were, from its position in the pendentive at Kariye, inserting it at the right end of the table. If we compare each detail of the painting of the calf and the drapery of its slayer with its counterpart in the mosaic (PL. 233), we see how extraordinarily close a copy the painting is of the mosaic.

Above the slaying of the calf at Curtea, we have the figure of Peter, who at the Kariye (PL. 234) was the first of four figures in the episode of the conversion of the water to wine. When we compare this latter figure of Peter with that in the painting we again encounter great exactitude of copying. In the painting Peter's lower extremities are obscured by the introduction below him of the sacrificed calf. In the episode at the Kariye, John stands between Peter and Christ, and at first glance he seems to be omitted from the painting. But when we note that in the latter, immediately to the right of Peter, there is a vertical suture running the entire height of the painting, and observe the great difference between the two versions (painting and mosaic) from that point onwards, as well as the very marked change in style in the painting to the right of the suture, we must deduce that the right part of the original painting was destroyed and re-painted in an entirely different iconography and style. However, immediately to the left of the suture, in the original paint near Christ's foot we see that a fragment of the second disciple—his right foot and parts of the drapery above it—still exists. We can, therefore, conclude that John also was present originally, and by extension we can safely assume that the original painting of the miracle episode at Curtea was also copied from the Kariye; the only features that were retained from the Kariye by the restorer of the painting, although rendered in a different style, are the figures of Christ and Mary, which are in very much the same poses and positions as at the Kariye (PL. 231).

Considerable damage was done in the feasting episode at Curtea in the area of the heads of the figures, other than Peter, who sat or stood in a group at the left end of the table. We have already noted that the Kariye fragment gives evidence only of Peter and Christ. Tafrali, however, states that at Curtea a second disciple (head destroyed by the circular reinforcing disc and damage done below it) stood between Peter and Christ.[172] It would be surprising if Mary were not also present near Christ at the table, but Tafrali says nothing of this. However, between Christ and the groom, the first of three figures seated behind the table, there is a rather wide space, and in its lower parts the photograph (Fig. 17) shows drapery that belongs to a fourth person at the head of the table. The upper parts of this area, like the heads of Christ and the second disciple, are badly damaged, but we can be certain that the drapery must belong to Mary, who is nearly always present at the table near Christ, as we shall see. However, it is rare if not unique to have two disciples as well as Christ and Mary depicted at the head of the table.

There is one other point where we seem to have evidence that still another figure, present at the table in Curtea, was also depicted in the mosaic of Kariye. Seated at the rear right corner of the table in the painting is the "governor of the feast," who holds up a glass in his right hand; he is clad in a headdress and a mantle beneath which is a tunic with a bordered hem. In exactly the same relation that the "governor's" tunic and hem in the painting have to the right back corner of the table, in the mosaic in Kariye there is a small fragment of a garment with a decor-

172 *Monuments byzantins de Curtéa de Argeş*, p. 129.

ated hem (PL. 230).[173] It may well be that this detail is all that remains of the "governor" at the table in the Kariye, and that this is still another feature that is common to both versions. It is well also to note how very similar the "governor" in the feast episode at Curtea is to the same official in the miracle of the jars at Kariye (PL. 236), who stands behind the boy filling the water jars. This suggests that at the Kariye the "governor" was represented in each of the two episodes. At Curtea also the "governor" may have been present, originally, in the episode of the conversion of the water to wine, for there can be little doubt that the restored area at the far right in the episode of the jars bears little similarity to the original painting, or to any other extant representation of the subject.

Granting the similarities described above between the Curtea and Kariye feasting scenes, we may gain further information about other details, now lost in the mosaic, by examining the furnishings of the banquet table and the personages who sat or stood behind and to the right of it in two other representations that are remarkably similar to those of Curtea and hence, in all probability, to those of the Kariye. These are the miniature on folio 363v of MS 5 in Iviron Monastery, Mount Athos (Fig. 18),[174] which illustrates both the feast and the miracle of the wine, and the painting of the subject in the church of St. Nicholas Orphanos, Salonika (Fig. 19),[175] which, on the other hand, illustrates only the feast. Although the rectangular tables in these versions are depicted with slight differences they all have an edging of drapery in swags along the back edge of the table top. Each has three large bowls with flaring bases, aligned near the front edge, the corresponding bowls in each version filled with food of a particular sort. On all the tables are round loaves of bread; at St. Nicholas they are unrealistically, but perhaps symbolically, depicted as circles on which pairs of vertical and horizontal parallel lines form crosses. All versions have one or two knives laid on the table. At both Curtea and St. Nicholas, root vegetables with their leaves, which resemble white radishes, are laid out near the forward edges of the tables. At Curtea there seem to be two or three eggs, a triangular piece of cheese, and two glass goblets. Among the personages behind the table the groom and bride (the *neogamoi*),[176] seated in that order, from left to right, are strikingly similar in all three paintings in matters of dress, especially in the costumes and crowns which both wear in Iviron 5 and at St. Nicholas, and in the crown worn by the bride at Curtea [177] and St. Nicholas, where pendants hang from each side. The bearded *architriclinos* ("governor of the feast") at Curtea, holding up a glass and seated on a throne at the rear right corner of the table, in costume, features, and attitude very closely resembles the Kariye "governor" in the episode of the jars (PL. 231). At St. Nicholas he is again enthroned, but at the right end, and holds up a glass; however, he more nearly resembles his counterpart in the Iviron miniature (Fig. 18), who is the third personage at the back of the table. The last of the "cast of characters" at the table is the *diakon*,[178] who is not mentioned in the Gospel text. It is interesting to note that in Iviron 5 he is a young man who stands at the right of the table and wears the deacon's *orarion*, a narrow scarf, over his left shoulder. At St. Nicholas and Curtea he is also young but is seated in the third position behind the table. Finally, in one important point Iviron 5 and St. Nicholas are alike but differ from Curtea and Kariye,

173 See Vol. 1 of this work, p. 120, under "Colors and Materials."

174 Cf. Xyngopoulos, Ἱστορημένα εὐαγγέλια, No. 46.

175 Eastern end of the second register of the north wall, southern narthex. Cf. A. Xyngopoulos, Οἱ τοιχογραφίες τοῦ

Ἁγίου Νικολάου Ὀρφανοῦ Θεσσαλονίκης (Athens, 1964), Figs. 91, 92, and 178.

176 For nomenclature see below.

177 The groom here does not wear a crown.

178 For this personage see the inscription on the fresco at Tokali, Old Church, Göreme; see below, p. 283 and n. 180.

as we know from its existing fragments: at the left end of the table the two versions represent only Mary and the enthroned Christ, in rather similar attitudes and poses.

In Early Christian art the episode of the transformation of the water into wine was emphasized, often to the exclusion of the feast, and was rendered in simple, symmetrical compositions that suppressed the narrative element in favor of the symbolic. Sometimes only three figures and a varying number of jars were depicted.[179] But in Middle and Late Byzantine mural representations both scenes were nearly always represented and the feast took on increasing importance and became the dominant feature, even to the occasional exclusion of the miracle of the jars. The titles of most of the "cast of characters," other than Christ, Mary, and disciples, that appear at the feast are inscribed on a fresco in the "Old Church" of Tokali at Göreme.[180] The bride and groom are called the newlyweds (ΝΕΟΓΑΜΥ, sic); the functionary who is usually with them is inscribed the ΔΙΑΚΟΝ;[181] the "governor of the feast," who holds a glass, is called Ο ΑΡΧΙΤΡΙ-ΚΛΙΝΟC; and the youth who pours the water into the jars is Ο ΑΝΤΛΙΟΝ.[181a] In more developed representations in other, and later, monuments these figures are usually present but are augmented by others.

In monumental art the table in the wedding feast may be either rectangular, as at the Kariye and Curtea-de-Argeş,[182] or semicircular;[183] the two types are about equal in numbers of representations. The use of one or the other fits no pattern of chronology or locale, but the semicircular, or sigma, table may have been used in allusion to the Last Supper, where the sigma form was traditional. In the scene of feasting there is great variation in the number of personages who are *seated* at table and participating in the feast. Examples exist in which four,[184] five,[185] six,[186] eleven,[187] and even as many as thirteen[188] people, as in St. Nikita, Čučer (Fig. 20), are seated

179 To cite a few: the Andrews ivory diptych in the Victoria and Albert Museum, London (left to right, a boy pouring water into jars, Mary in the center, and Christ touching a jar with a rod), J. Beckwith, *The Andrews Diptych* (London, 1958), PL. 2; the diptych in Berlin, Staatliche Museen (a boy pouring water, Christ blessing, and a disciple), ibid., Fig. 7, p. 11; a gold medallion in the Berlin museum (Christ touching a jar with a crossed staff, a figure with hand raised in astonishment, and an attendant pouring water), *Amtliche Berichte aus den Königl. Kunstsammlungen*, 35 (1913), Fig. 47; Maximian's chair at Ravenna (a man holding a cup, a bearded disciple, and Christ holding a long crossed staff and extending his hand toward one of the jars), C. Cecchelli, *La cattedra di Massimiano ed altri avorii romano-orientali* (Rome [1936–44]), fasc. I, PL. 29.

180 Jerphanion, *Cappadoce*, Text, I,1 (Paris, 1925), pp. 276–77, and Plates, I (1925), PL. 65,2 and 66,1, middle register.

181 Probably the Christian title for the Jewish religious official who performed "the Jewish rites of purification," rites that are mentioned by John (2:6) as having been performed at the Cana marriage.

181a Possibly an error for Ο ΑΝΤΛωΝ, "the one who draws" (a liquid), with ω taken for ΙΟ.

182 Also at Göreme, Tokali, Old Church, Jerphanion, *Cappadoce*, Plates, I, PL. 65,2; Sousam Baïri, St. Theodore, ibid., Plates, II, PL. 148,1; Gračanica, Petković, *La peinture serbe*, I (Belgrade, 1930), PL. 49 *a*; Ljuboten, ibid., II, PL. 149; St. Nikita near Čučer, Hamann-MacLean and Hallensleben, *Die Monumentalmalerei*, Fig. 242; Salonika, St. Nicholas Orphanos, Xyngopoulos, ῎Αγιος Νικόλαος ᾿Ορφανός, Fig. 91.

183 Tokali, New Church, Jerphanion, *Cappadoce*, Plates, II, PL. 77,3; Kiev, St. Sophia, Lazarev, *Old Russian Murals and Mosaics*, p. 230, Fig. 10; Monreale, Demus, *Norman Sicily*, PL. 66 *a*; Kalenić, Petković, *La peinture serbe*, I, Fig. 153 *b*; Dečani, ibid., PL. 105 A; Mistra, Metropole, Millet, *Mistra*, PL. 75,4 (drawing); Kastoria, chapel of St. John the Theologian, Moutsopoulos, *Kastoria*, PL. 17.

184 In this and the following notes, the figures are always listed from left to right. Kiev: Christ, three unidentifiable men (possibly disciples or two disciples and the *diakon*); as at Tokali, New Church, the newlyweds are not present. Curtea-de-Argeş and possibly Kariye Djami as described above. Mistra, Metropole: a unique type in which the jars are at the left and Christ is seated between them and the table but facing the jars, with arm extended performing the miracle, while Mary and another person stand behind him; at table, in addition to Christ, are the groom, the bride, and the *architriclinos*.

185 Tokali, Old Church: Christ, *diakon*, groom, bride, *architriclinos*. Ljuboten: Christ, Mary, bride and groom (both crowned), *architriclinos* holding glass and richly clad. Dečani: Christ, Mary, groom, bride (crowned), *architriclinos*. Salonika, St. Nicholas Orphanos: Christ, groom, bride, *diakon*, *architriclinos*.

186 Tokali, New Church: Christ, Mary, four disciples (Peter and Andrew and possibly James and John). Sousam Baïri, St. Theodore: Mary, Christ, two disciples, groom presenting a vessel to bride. Monreale: Christ, Mary, groom, bride (crowned), *diakon*, *architriclinos* holding a glass. Kalenić: Christ, Mary, groom, bride (crowned), *architriclinos* with glass, *diakon*. Kastoria, Mavriotissa: Christ, Peter, groom (crowned), *diakon*, *architriclinos*, a young beardless man (not a disciple).

187 Gračanica: left end of table, Christ; far side of table, groom and bride (both crowned), three men (not disciples); near side of table, left to right, two men richly garbed, man with headdress holding up glass (*architriclinos* ?), two unidentifiable men.

188 St. Nikita, Čučer (south arm, south wall, second zone from the floor): left end of table, Christ; far side of table, five men all holding food, goblets, glasses, but none dressed as disciples; right end of table on throne-like seat, bride and groom; near side of table, five men, three with headdresses, none of whom seem to be disciples, all of them conversing and holding food or drink. See Hamann-MacLean and Hallensleben, *Monumentalmalerei*, I, PL. 242.

while others stand or are seated behind those at table. At St. Nikita the feast, but not the miracle of the wine, was depicted. Mary is nearly always present in scenes of the Cana miracle, for, according to John, she was its instigator. Cana is the only miracle at which she is said to have been present, or in which she was depicted. When she is not seated at table she stands near Christ conversing with him, and even when she is seated she seems to be urging that the wine be provided by miraculous means. In a majority of examples a few servants stand about in the background, and often one or more disciples, when not depicted sitting down, are also present.[189] Some of the representations of the feast depict the occasion as a solemn one, in which the participants do not eat although the table may be laden with loaves of bread, roasted animals in vessels, and various utensils. In a few instances, however, especially in some of the Serbian paintings, the event is convivial and animated; the scene at St. Nikita, Čučer, is presented as an unusually festive event with genre motifs. Christ is always seated at the left on a distinctive piece of furniture, which sometimes resembles a reclining banqueting couch, his feet on a footstool. As background there is nearly always elaborate or even quite fanciful architecture.

The three Cappadocian examples of the transformation of the water into wine (Tokali, Old Church and New Church; and Sousam Baïri, St. Theodore) have several iconographic points in common. The two episodes are physically separate from one another;[190] only three figures are represented: Christ, the *architriclinos* holding a glass, and a youth pouring water into a jar;[191] in all three examples Christ holds a rod that is dipped into one of the jars;[192] and in none are Mary or any of the disciples depicted. Aside from the Cappadocian group, the mural of the miracle at Dečani (Fig. 21) is the only one in which Christ uses a rod in performing the transformation of the water.[193] Here the miracle is in a panel separate from the feast, but adjoining it. Christ is at the left before three jars; Mary is present for the second time (a rare feature) and speaks to Christ, and a servant carries a jug on his shoulder while another pours water into one of the jars.

In a group of three paintings of the Cana wedding the miracle is so closely integrated with the feast that the two episodes become a single, simultaneous one. At Kalenić[194] six jars are close to the right end of the table; one servant is about to serve the wine from a jug to the guests and another pours water into a jar. At the Metropole, Mistra, as remarked above, a servant with a jug (?) on his shoulder stands at the left with six jars while Christ, seated at the table to the right, turns toward the jars with arm extended toward them as though performing the miracle while seated at the feast. Finally, in the painting of the miracle in St. John the Theologian at Kastoria[195] six jars are lined up in front of the table and a servant pours water while another carries a jug on his shoulder.

In only one instance—the Brontochion at Mistra[196]—is the miracle of the jars depicted but not the scene of the feast. Peter (?), Christ, and Mary approach the six jars, and two men stand behind them; one man holds a glass, the other pours water into a jar. Conversely, it is possible

189 For the position of others see above, nn. 184–88.

190 At Tokali, Old Church (Jerphanion, *Cappadoce*, Plates, I, PL. 64–66), they are opposite one another in a barrel vault but in corresponding registers; at Tokali, New Church (ibid., Plates, II, PL. 72.1 and 73.1), they are on the north wall and adjoining east spandrel, at same level; and at Sousam Baïri, St. Theodore (ibid., Plates, III, PL. 148,1), the miracle is in a register below the feast.

191 At Tokali, Old Church, he is inscribed the ANTΛION. At Tokali, New Church, Christ is on the north wall.

192 Said by Jerphanion (*Cappadoce*, Text, I,1, p. 277) to be a "primitive" or archaic iconographic feature since the motif is common in Early Christian art. See above, n. 179.

193 Petković, *La peinture serbe*, I, PL. 105 a.

194 *Staro Nagoričino, Psača, Kalenić* (Belgrade, 1933), Kalenić, PL. XXI; S. Radojčić, *Kalenić* (Belgrade, 1964, one of the small volumes from the series entitled Medieval Art in Yugoslavia), Fig. 41.

195 Moutsopoulos, *Kastoria*, PL. 17.

196 Millet, *Mistra*, PL. 98,3.

that only the feast was represented at St. Nicholas Orphanos.[197] As at Curtea-de-Argeş, Dečani, and possibly the Kariye Djami, the miracle episode at Gračanica [198] includes Mary, this being another of the few examples where she appears in both scenes. Here, the only other figures in the miracle itself are Christ and a servant, before five jars. At the Kariye, Peter and John are also present, as they probably were also at Curtea. Indeed, the presence of even one disciple in the miracle episode is rare, the Kariye, Brontochion, and Curtea being the only examples.

The close relationship between the Multiplication of Loaves at the Kariye Djami and the fresco of that subject at Curtea-de-Argeş (Fig. 22) was pointed out in Volume 1.[199] Because of that relationship it was possible to reconstruct in the mind's eye the destroyed portions of the mosaic. As depicted at the Kariye, the subject comprised the four principal episodes described in the Gospels: the blessing of the bread;[200] Christ breaking bread,[201] and handing it to the disciples; the disciples, in turn, distributing the bread;[202] and the twelve baskets full after the multitudes have eaten. Although all the Gospels speak of both loaves and fishes, the Kariye version and some others depict only the bread. Some versions are more literal and present both bread and fishes. The fact that only the bread is represented suggests that it was the desire of the Kariye mosaicist to make clear the symbolic analogy between the eucharistic bread in this scene and the wine depicted in the companion mosaic representing the Miracle at Cana.[203] In addition to the four principal episodes, there is at least one point in the various accounts of the Gospels that in rare instances was alluded to or used as a motif in manuscript representations of the subject, that is, the conversation between Christ and the disciples regarding the problem of feeding the multitude.[204]

We have already mentioned a few of the Early Christian representations of the miracle of the Feeding of the Five Thousand that were coupled with the Cana miracle.[205] Because it was viewed as a symbolic prototype of the Eucharist, the early examples of the Feeding were not narrative in character but highly schematic, simple compositions with very few figures aside from Christ and a few of his disciples, one bearing loaves and another a container of fish. The representation of the Feeding on the Andrews ivory diptych is representative of the type.[206] Almost equally simple and symmetrical are the compositions on the ivory panel of the Cathedra of Maximian and the mosaic panel of S. Apollinare Nuovo, Ravenna.[207] The miniature of the Sinope Gospels [208] has, at the left, a symmetrical group of three figures (Christ, flanked by two disciples, touching the bread and the fish held by them) and somewhat detached from them, at the far right, at least eight baskets and two companies of the multitude, one above the other.

197 Since the feast is the last scene in zone 2 of the north wall, southern narthex, the miracle episode could have adjoined it on the east wall, where all paintings were destroyed.

198 To my knowledge, there is no published illustration of this part of the Cana scene.

199 Pp. 121–23. Compare PL. 238–42, 244, 245 in Vol. 2 of this work with Fig. 22, below. Either Kariye and Curtea were drawn from the same model or, it is possible, the Curtea painter copied the mosaics at the Kariye. See the discussion above, p. 280 and n. 166, for evidence of the close dependence of the Curtea painter on a number of other mosaics at the Kariye. The illustration of the Multiplication of Loaves is from prints of the same negatives used in *Buletinul*, 10–16 (1917–23), Fig. 266, pp. 229, 230. The Multiplication of Loaves at Curtea occupies the entire upper frieze, below the cornice, on the north wall of the nave.

200 The Synoptics say Christ blessed both bread and fishes,

but John speaks of blessing only the bread, although he, like the other three, says there were two fishes; John also says the disciples distributed both bread and fish.

201 John implies Christ broke fishes as well.

202 Only Matthew says the disciples distributed simply bread; according to all others they distributed fishes as well.

203 See above, pp. 264–67, for a discussion of the miracles of Cana and the Multiplication of Loaves as prefigurations of the institution of the sacrament of the Eucharist.

204 Matt. 14:15–18; Mark 6:35–38; Luke 9:12–14.

205 Above, pp. 266–67.

206 Beckwith, *The Andrews Diptych*, PL. 4.

207 Both of the sixth century. See Cecchelli, *La cattedra di Massimiano*, fasc. I, PL. XXIX, and fasc. VI–VII, at p. 174.

208 Parisinus Suppl. gr. 1286, also of the sixth cent.; Cecchelli, *La cattedra di Massimiano*, fasc. VI–VII, at p. 175.

The late-ninth-century miniature in the Constantinopolitan manuscript of the Homilies of Gregory of Nazianz [209] still subordinates the narrative to the symbolic purpose.[210]

From the eleventh century onward the narrative, episodic treatment of the subject came increasingly to the fore in manuscript illumination, and, as we shall see, this was also the case, with a few provincial exceptions, in its treatment in monumental painting. We have only to compare some of the miniature paintings of the subject with the mosaic at the Kariye Djami (and the painting at Curtea and other closely related frescoes) to realize that Gospel Book illustrations lie behind this as well as a number of other Kariye mosaics. The number of manuscripts illustrating the Feeding is great, but only a few, dating from the eleventh to fourteenth centuries, are relevant to the mosaic of the Kariye Djami and related versions in monumental art.

The Feeding of the Five Thousand is recounted in each Gospel, that of the Four Thousand only in Matthew and Mark; thus, in some manuscripts one finds six separate accounts, but no significant distinctions are made in those cases where the two miracles are illustrated. The manuscript that presents them in the fullest detail, in one instance devoting two folios to one account (the Matthew version of the Five Thousand), is Laurentianus Plut. VI.23, of the eleventh century.[211] Here the illustrations are unframed friezes introduced in spaces left between lines of the text, and the illustration always precedes the text on which it is supposedly based. Much attention is given to the conversations between Christ and the disciples regarding what should be done to feed the multitudes (fols. 29v, 77v, 123v, and 179). In no instance in the manuscript is there a distinct blessing of the bread, and in one (fol. 29v) no distribution is shown. Some do not depict the twelve or seven baskets (fols. 29v, 77v, 123v, 179v), but in the miniature on folio 30 the filled baskets are the source from which the food is distributed, contrary to the narrative accounts. In one instance the companies of the multitude are omitted (fol. 29v). Characteristic of all the miniatures is the division into three distinct groups of persons (fols. 29v, 30, 32v, 77v), or even two (fols. 123v, 179v). Indeed, the episodes depicted do not very faithfully adhere to the verses of text beneath them. Nevertheless, Laurent. Plut. VI.23 is episodic and narrative in intent and seems not to allude to the miracle as a eucharistic prefiguration.

Somewhat more akin to the Kariye mosaic of the Feeding are the eleventh-century illuminations in Parisinus gr. 74 [212] and its copy, British Museum, Add. 39627, dated 1356.[213] The compositions of all six miniatures of the Feeding in Paris. gr. 74 are much alike. Depicted in the following order are three distinct episodes: the blessing of the five, or seven, loaves and two fishes; the group of twelve, or seven, baskets with disciples behind them, one of whom sometimes gives food to a youth or a man; and either one or two companies of the multitude—the figures are usually seated but occasionally some are standing. In the miniature on folio 29v [214] (Fig. 23), lower right, is a detail that clearly anticipates the group of six young boys, scrambling about on the ground and eating crumbs, which appears in the southeast pendentive (PL. 243) at the Kariye Djami.

A feature that should be noted in all the miniatures of the Feeding in Paris. gr. 74 is that the episode of the baskets is the second of the three and occupies the center of the frieze between the

209 Parisinus gr. 510, fol. 165; H. Omont, *Miniatures des plus anciens manuscrits grecs de la Bibliothèque Nationale du VI⁰ au XIV⁰ siècle* (Paris, 1929), PL. XXV.

210 S. Der Nersessian, in *DOP*, 16 (1962), p. 206 and Fig. 6.

211 Fols. 29v and 30 (Matthew, Five Thousand); 32v b (Matthew, Four Thousand); 77v (Mark, Four Thousand); 123v (Luke, Five Thousand); 179v (John, Five Thousand).

212 Fols. 29v, 32, 76v, 80, 127v, 178v; see *Evang. du XI⁰ siècle*, I, PL. 26, 28, 70, 72; II, PL. 112, 153.

213 Fols. 45, 48v, 104, 108, 165, 228; B. D. Filov, *Les miniatures de l'Evangile du roi Jean Alexandre à Londres*, in Bulgarian and French (Sofia, 1934), PL. 22, 23, 50, 52, 80, 110.

214 See *Evang. du XI⁰ siècle*, I, PL. 26.

blessing and the companies of the multitudes. In Volume 1 of this publication (p. 123) it was argued that the fresco at Curtea-de-Argeş (Fig. 22) was a copy of the mosaic at the Kariye (PL. 238) but that its painter misunderstood the sequence of episodes at the Kariye when he placed the twelve baskets between the last two companies and not at the very end as the final episode. It would seem that the painter simply pushed the episode of the baskets (which occupies the pendentive at the Kariye) upward, as it were, thus removing it from its proper position.[215] The result was that at Curtea the baskets are in the midst of the distribution of the bread, as in Paris. gr. 74, and on folio 30 of Laurent. Plut. VI.23. However, the Kariye mosaicist clearly intended the episode of the twelve baskets as the final one, thus adhering to the narrative accounts, but for symbolic reasons he regarded the baskets full of bread as the prefiguration of the eucharistic bread, the bread that remained after the miracle, which was to be fed to all mankind through the sacrament of the church. Such an interpretation of the twelve loaves was commonly understood from the teachings of the church and goes back to the beginnings of Gospel exegesis.[216]

The blessing in Paris. gr. 74 differs greatly from that at the Kariye; the loaves and fish are on the ground between Christ and Peter and two of his fellow disciples. Christ does not look up to heaven or hold food in his hand. In four of the miniatures (fols. 32, 76v, 80, 178) there is in the lower right corner a small body of water,[217] usually triangular, from which in one instance (fol. 76v) a man fills an amphora. Still another unusual detail, on folio 127v, is a group of four men seated on the ground around a circular table, on which are bread and fish, and flanked by two standing men, one of whom is a disciple.

Iconographically, but not in formal composition, the Kariye mosaicist followed a tradition in the Multiplication of Loaves that is much closer to that found in two thirteenth-century manuscripts, namely, Iviron 5,[218] and Parisinus gr. 54 [219] (Figs. 24 and 25). Both miniatures are oblong, framed compositions in which the narrative is presented in three zones, each separated by undulating hillocks which, in the two lower zones and part of the upper, obscure behind them the lower parts of the figures. This arrangement is comparable to that of four figures partly concealed behind mountain peaks in the Curtea painting (Fig. 22) and probably also at Kariye. Excepting that Iviron 5 lines up the twelve baskets in a row along the lower edge while Paris. gr. 54 stacks them in two columns at the right edge, the two are almost identical and can be described together.

In the upper zone, in the first episode Christ stands alone facing left and, unlike the Christ in the Kariye version, without disciples facing him. As at Curtea (and probably Kariye) he holds a stack of five loaves (but with two small fish on top); this scene obviously represents the blessing of the bread. No baskets appear in the upper or lower zones, but the second episode, again as at the Kariye, illustrates the breaking of the bread and Christ handing it to four (rather than two) disciples with veiled hands. There follows the first of a total of six companies of the multitude seated on the ground, a disciple distributing bread to each—a much more profuse illustration

215 Compare Kariye (Vol. 2 of this work, PL. 238 and 244) with Curtea (Fig. 22, below).

216 See above, p. 265 and n. 93, for a quotation from Origen referring to precisely this point.

217 Probably depicted in anticipation of the miracle of Christ Walking on the Water, which in Matthew, Mark, and John follows immediately after the Feeding.

218 Fol. 63v. Cf. Xyngopoulos, Ἱστορημένα εὐαγγέλια μονῆς Ἰβήρων Ἁγ. Ὄρους (Athens [1932]), No. 20, dated on p. 7 in the twelfth century; Millet, Recherches, Fig. 655 and p. 9, where it is dated thirteenth century. See also the succeeding note.

219 A manuscript in both Greek and Latin, fol. 55. Cf. Omont Miniatures des plus anciens manuscrits grecs, PL. XCII,4; Millet, Recherches, Fig. 654 and p. 9, where it is dated thirteenth century. For bibliography see K. Weitzmann, "Constantinopolitan Book Illumination in the Period of the Latin Conquest," GBA, 6th series, 25 (1944), pp. 200–205; Weitzmann assigns it to Constantinople, dates it and Iviron 5 within the limits of the Latin conquest, thirteenth century, and suggests that Paris. gr. 54 is a direct copy of Iviron 5; H. Buchthal, Miniature Painting in the Latin Kingdom of Jerusalem (Oxford, 1957), p. 69, dates it first half of the thirteenth century.

of the distribution than at the Kariye. Finally, as on folio 29v of Paris. gr. 74 (Fig. 23), we find, in the lower right, the motif of the young boys which appears in the southeast pendentive of the Kariye (PL. 239, 243). However, in the two miniatures the gathering of the fragments into baskets is not narratively illustrated as at the Kariye, but merely symbolized.

To turn to mural decoration, the scenes of the Feeding in the rock-cut churches of Cappadocia conform, in the main, to the early traditions in what de Jerphanion calls "primitive" iconography.[220] Aside from these, surviving examples of the miracle in monumental art are surprisingly few in number. Regrettably, the painting of the subject at Sant'Angelo in Formis [221] has perished except for its inscription. Also lost, but attested by Lazarev,[222] is the eleventh-century fresco in the gallery of St. Sophia, Kiev. In the late-twelfth-century mosaic in the miracle cycle at Monreale,[223] only the breaking of the bread and the handing of it to the disciples, their distribution of the bread to a single large company of the seated multitude, and the twelve baskets are represented. John's version is followed to the extent that Andrew and Philip play an important role. Thus, the Monreale mosaic adheres to the narrative rather than the symbolic treatment. On the other hand, the later mosaic in San Marco, Venice,[224] reverts to the earlier formulae; its iconography is like that of Paris. gr. 510, fol. 165.

For the rest, in addition to the Kariye mosaic (PL. 238), supplemented by the painting at Curtea-de-Argeş (Fig. 22),[225] we have only a few fresco representations of the Multiplication of Loaves in late Serbian churches: those at the church of the Savior, Ravanica; Sisojevac; Kalenić; and the church of the Trinity, Manasija (Resava). For Ravanica and Sisojevac I have no published illustrations, photographs, or descriptions.[226] The Multiplication of Loaves at Kalenić (Fig. 26) obviously employed a model very much like that of the scene at Curtea-de-Argeş and at Kariye.[227] Like them, the Kalenić painting includes, at the far left, the blessing of the loaves, in which Christ faces right (instead of left) and holds stacked in his hands the five loaves surmounted by a few fish, as he looks up to an arc of heaven from which rays of glory shine down. However, no disciples stand before him. There follows the episode of Christ handing pieces of bread to two disciples, as at Kariye, but with two instead of three baskets on the ground between them.[228] Notable differences occur to the right. Two disciples, each carrying a basket,

220 Jerphanion, *Cappadoce*, Text, I,1, pp. 278 f., and Plates, I, PL. 66,1, 66,2, and 36,4 (Tokali, Old Church, the most fully developed version of the Cappadocian paintings). For Sousam Baïri, St. Theodore, see ibid., Text, II,1, pp. 37 f., and Plates, III, PL. 148,1 and 148,2; Mavroudjan, Cruciform Church, ibid., Text, II,1, p. 221, and Plates, III, PL. 175,1. The first two of these present the miracle in two parts: the blessing of the fish and bread (held respectively by Peter and Andrew, inscribed), and the distribution of bread and fish.

221 South wall, register 2, panel 9; cf. above, n. 25, for bibliography.

222 See above, p. 267 and n. 105.

223 In south aisle, west end of south wall and on west wall in the miracle cycle. See Demus, *Norman Sicily*, PL. 87 a and b.

224 South transept, east aisle, upper zone. The mosaic is much restored. Photograph Alinari, No. 32402. See F. Ongania, ed., *La basilica di San Marco in Venezia*, Vol. III (Venice, 1881), PL. XXX, line drawing. In ibid., Text Vol. (Venice, 1888), p. 377, it is classified as "mosaici in stile antico," but the author adds that the disciple at the left was done in the fifteenth century and signed "Vincenzo B(astian) F(ecit)."

225 The date of the Curtea paintings is controversial. See Stefanescu, *La peinture religieuse en Valachie et en Transylvanie*, Album, PL. 6, and Text, pp. 27 f.; Stefanescu points out (as does Tafrali, *Curtéa de Argeş*) that the paintings are much restored and that there are three periods; the earliest paintings, of

which the Feeding is a part, are dated ca. 1340–60 (p. 387). *Buletinul*, fasc. 34, pp. 31 ff. and 49 ff., presents them as works of the second half of the fourteenth century. On the other hand, Tafrali, *Curtéa de Argeş*, pp. xvii ff., unconvincingly attempts to date them in the thirteenth century.

226 Petković, *La peinture serbe*, II, p. 60, lists the Feeding at Ravanica along with eight other miracle scenes in the nave. In Vol. I, p. ix, the paintings are dated 1381; in V. J. Djurić, "Origine thessalonicienne des fresques du Monastère de Resava," *ZRVI*, 65, No. 6 (1960) (in Serbian with French résumé), p. 128, Ravanica is dated 1385–87. For Sisojevac, Petković, *La peinture serbe*, II, p. 61, lists the Feeding with five other miracles in the upper zones of the south wall. Djurić, "Resava," p. 128, dates the Sisojevac paintings in the apse in the last decade of the fourteenth century and believes the frescoes in the upper zones of the nave, and thus the Feeding, were executed by the painters of Ravanica (1385–87).

227 The Feeding at Kalenić is best illustrated in Radojčić, *Kalenić*, Fig. 32. On p. v, the construction is dated 1407–13. See also V. R. Petković and Z. Tatić, *Manastir Kalenić* (Vršac, 1926), Fig. 51, p. 60 (a photograph of poor quality and taken before cleaning).

228 Millet, *Recherches*, p. 648, Fig. 652, gives a line drawing of the Kalenić fresco but shows at this point only one basket; the cleaned fresco illustrated by Radojčić shows faint traces of the second.

are moving to the right toward one, or possibly two, seated companies; in the background behind them three disciples also carry baskets in the distribution to the people. It is obvious that the two published illustrations of this painting are incomplete at the right side, where we might expect to find, as at Kariye and Curtea, the twelve baskets and perhaps another seated company. We have only a line sketch as illustration for the Feeding at Manasija (Resava), which exists in fragmentary state.[229] Because it is composed in zones and seems to have depicted a large number (four) of seated companies, the Manasija version superficially resembles the type in the manuscripts Iviron 5 and Paris. 54. At the upper left, before a high mountain and partly obscured behind a hillock, are what appear to be two disciples with veiled hands facing left, and before them are two baskets.[230] Below them, from left to right in the middle zone, are a seated company facing left; the blessing of the bread, very much like that at Kalenić but with three baskets between Christ and three disciples who face him, two with veiled hands and one with a basket on his shoulder; and Christ again, facing toward a destroyed area of the painting. In the lower zone, left side, are two companies back to back, each facing a disciple who distributes the bread, and finally, two companies with disciples holding baskets. In the sketch of the existing parts of the painting there is no trace of the twelve baskets.

Over the centuries, the depiction of the Multiplication of Loaves underwent great transformation both in the minor arts and in mural painting. In the latter category it reached its highest state of development at the Kariye, both as a logically conceived narrative representation adhering more strictly than others to the Gospel accounts and as a didactic painting in which the sacramental implications of the subjects were clearly brought out. That the Kariye version and its model, which draw upon the traditions of Laurent. Plut. VI.23 and Paris. gr. 74 on the one hand, and on the type of Iviron 5 on the other hand, were followed by so nearly identical a composition at Curtea and an only slightly less precise replica at Kalenić, is a most unusual phenomenon in mural painting. Manasija, however, represents a different mixture of the sources that produced the version at the Kariye Djami.

Two subjects in the Ministry cycle that raise iconographic problems are the two Healings of a Paralytic, which, in the Kariye Djami, are on opposite sides of the domical vault of the sixth bay in the outer narthex.[231] The first is depicted in two episodes, one above the other ([121] and [128], PL. 251), and the second in a single composition ([124], PL. 253). In Volume I (pp. 126–29, 132–33) they are respectively designated as the Paralytic at the Pool of Bethesda (based on the account in John 5:2–15) and the Paralytic at Capernaum (which is described in the Synoptics[232]).

In each of the four accounts, and thus in both miracles, the paralytic is commanded to take up his bed and walk. It is this motif that was usually depicted in Early Christian art to indicate symbolically the remission of sins;[233] the paralytic was represented with his bed on his back (mostly in catacomb painting) either alone, or in the presence of Christ (mainly on sarcophagi).

229 S. Tomić and R. Nikolić, eds., *Manasija: L'histoire— La peinture* (in Serbian with French résumé) (Belgrade, 1964), PL. II, Fig. 2, and details of figures on PL. XVI and XVII. The authors date Manasija (p. 96) in the year 1418. Millet, *Recherches*, p. 648, Fig. 652, gives what purports to be a sketch of the same fresco; it is wholly erroneous and depicts the subject from some other church or perhaps from a manuscript.

230 The sketch of Tomić and Nikolić is not sufficiently detailed to enable one to describe a number of the features of this painting with certainty.

231 Among other monuments in which the two miracles are represented are S. Apollinare Nuovo, Ravenna; Dečani; Ravanica; the Metropole at Mistra; the chapel of St. John the Theologian at Kastoria.

232 Matt. 9:1–8; Mark 2:1–12; Luke 5:18–26.

233 The Synoptics all quote Christ as saying to the paralytic, "thy sins be forgiven thee," and John implies the remission of sin with Christ's words, "sin no more."

When the narrative aspect was suppressed in this way, it is not always clear whether the artists distinguished between the Bethesda and the Capernaum miracles. It is a question whether the Early Christians really—or always—believed that two separate miracles were performed on paralytics. In the *Diatessaron* of Tatian, at least in the Arabic version, the Johannine miracle and that described by the Synoptics were thought to be distinct from one another.[234] But John Chrysostom, although believing there were two miracles involving paralytics, says that "some believe them to be one and the same."[235] In the numerous instances in the ivories, mainly of the fifth or sixth centuries, in which the simple composition of the paralytic carrying his bed appears in conjunction with representations of the Samaritan Woman at the Well and/or the Blind Born,[236] the composition can be assumed to represent the Paralytic at the Pool of Bethesda because of the symbolic, liturgical, and sacramental connotations that bound these subjects as a group and that have been discussed above.[237] The abbreviated manner of representing the Bethesda Paralytic in monumental art of the early period is to be observed in one of the thirteen mosaic panels of the upper register, north wall, in S. Apollinare Nuovo, Ravenna, where there are also represented the Samaritan Woman and the Paralytic at Capernaum.[238] Since the miracle of the Paralytic in the third panel can only be that of Capernaum (see below), the Paralytic with his bed in the first panel at S. Apollinare Nuovo is certainly that of Bethesda. Even in some manuscripts, ranging in date between the ninth and thirteenth centuries, the subject is depicted simply as the paralytic carrying his bed.[239]

In some of the Late Byzantine renditions of the healing at Bethesda, especially in monumental painting, the miracle was elaborated by the introduction of the episode of Christ healing the man ahead of that of the carrying of the bed. The essential points in John's account of the actual healing are the following. The locale was the κολυμβήθρα (a pool or reservoir) by the sheep market in Jerusalem called Bethesda. The pool is said to have had five stoas, or covered colonnades, which were interpreted by most artists, including the mosaicist of the Kariye Djami, as a structure with five vaulted units supported on columns. The pool, John tells us, was a place where the afflicted were cured if they were in the water at the moment when an angel "troubled" it. Being unaccompanied, and unable to enter at the proper time, the paralytic was thereupon cured by Jesus as he lay on his bed by the pool. At Christ's command, the man took up his bed and walked, and he was then questioned by the Jews.

We can best reconstruct the fragment of the Healing in the Kariye (PL. 250, lower left, and 251 *a*) to something close to its original form by comparing it with the miniature on folio 377v of Iviron 5 (Fig. 27),[240] in which we again see the close affiliation of the Kariye iconography with that of the manuscript. Both show the paralytic in the act of arising in his bed, probably at the moment of being healed; the bed he is sitting on is covered by a mattress in a reclining position, and has draped sides; the man's legs are bent downward over the edge and both arms are extended toward Christ, who stood at the left. It should be noted that in the mosaic version (PL. 251 *a*)

234 See Kraeling, *The Christian Building*, p. 58 (see above, n. 11).

235 Homily 36.1, *In Joannem*, PG, 59, col. 208.

236 A few examples are: Paris, Cluny Museum, pyxis, W. F. Volbach, *Elfenbeinarbeiten der Spätantike und des frühen Mittelalters*, 2d ed. (Mainz, 1952), p. 83, No. 180, PL. 56; Rome, Vatican, Museo Sacro, pyxis, ibid., p. 83, No. 181, PL. 56; Milan, Cathedral Treasury, five-part diptych, ibid., p. 61, No. 119, PL. 37; Cambridge, Fitzwilliam Museum, plaque, ibid., p. 74, No. 152, PL. 50; London, Victoria and Albert Museum, the Andrews diptych, Beckwith, *The Andrews Diptych*, frontispiece.

237 Pp. 257–62. The three miracles are, moreover, unique to John.

238 Respectively, west to east, in the first, eighth, and third panels. See G. Bovini, *Mosaici di S. Apollinare Nuovo di Ravenna: Il ciclo cristologico* (Florence [1958]), PL. 13, 6, and 11. Bovini arranged the sequence to read from east to west.

239 Paris. gr. 510, fol. 143v; Vienna, National Library, gr. 154, fol. 233v; Chicago, the Rockefeller McCormick New Testament (Gregory 2400), fol. 89; Leningrad, Public Library, gr. 105, fol. 185; Vat. Barb. gr. 372, fol. 181v.

240 Cf. Xyngopoulos, Ἱστορημένα εὐαγγέλια, No. 48.

behind the bed there were five equally spaced, slender columns. The second column from the left is obscured by the body of the paralytic and is otherwise invisible because the fragment is broken off at too low a level, and the fourth, of which only the base is visible, is obscured by the head of the bed; the fifth rises to the right of the bed and marks the division between this scene and the fragment of the next on the right [122]. Parallel to the left edge of each of the green columns is a narrow vertical strip of a more neutral, paler green; these represent a row of five columns in a back row, each partly obscured by its counterpart in the front row. In the miniature of Iviron 5 (Fig. 27) there are ten slender columns supporting five domical vaults; it would seem, then, that the miniaturist intended to depict two parallel rows of five columns to carry the front and back sides of the five vaults. We may imagine, therefore, that both the mosaicist and the miniaturist intended to depict the five stoas mentioned by John, and interpreted the term "five stoas" to mean a five-vaulted structure supported by colonnades. Unlike the mosaicist, however, the miniaturist has depicted the pool as a rectangular basin filled with water and placed it either behind or within the stoa. Since the pool is an important element in other examples, as we shall see, the Kariye artist may have placed a small circular or quatrefoil pool to the left of the bed. In the mosaic, of course, Christ followed by a few disciples must have stood further to the left, as in Iviron 5 and many other versions of this miracle. At the right in Iviron 5 the episode of the paralytic carrying his bed is depicted in very much the same manner as in the Kariye Djami's second episode [128] (PL. 251 b). In both, some Jews dispute with the paralytic (John 5:10 ff.) and not with Christ; in the passage describing the Capernaum miracle the dispute is with Christ, and this sometimes serves as an indication in the identification of the particular miracle. The fully developed iconographic type of the Bethesda paralytic consisted of five elements: the paralytic on his bed; the stoa; the pool; Christ and disciples; and the healed man carrying his bed, sometimes accompanied by Jews. In all probability the Kariye mosaic, like the Iviron 5 miniature, included them all. Another example which has all these elements is the scene in a cross vault of the church at Dečani.[241]

Some versions show the first four elements but omit the episode of the paralytic carrying his bed. In the scenes at Ravanica (Fig. 28) and Sisojevac,[242] which are very much alike, the man on his bed is in the same pose as at Kariye, the bed is very similar to that of Iviron 5, but in the background, behind the bed, the stoa seems to be a square building with five columns in the façade. In these, the pool, unlike its counterpart in Iviron 5, is a rather small, circular structure, like a well-head, with a step at its base; this is placed immediately to the left of the bed. An added element is a group of three men behind the foot of the bed, who extend their hands either in entreaty to Christ or in awe of the miraculous healing. Christ, followed by numerous disciples, stands to the left of the pool.

Still another manner of representing the miracle was to omit the healing itself and depict only the episode of the paralytic carrying his bed, but with some features of setting taken from the first episode: Christ and disciples; the stoa; and sometimes the pool. At St. Nikita (Čučer) [243] Christ and disciples at the left face the paralytic, who is turned toward Christ, as he carries his bed in the usual manner (Fig. 29). The element that proves this to be the Bethesda rather than the Capernaum miracle is the presence of the stoa with five tile-roofed arches carried on two

---

241 Petković and Bošković, *Dečani*, PL. CXCII.
242 Djurić, "Resava," Figs. 12 and 11 respectively. Both paintings are late fourteenth century.

243 G. Millet and A. Frolow, *La peinture du Moyen Âge en Yougoslavie (Serbie Macédoine et Monténégro)*, III (Paris, 1962), PL. 40,4; Petković, *La peinture serbe*, I, PL. 34 b.

rows of five columns; the columns rest on the coping of a rectangular pool filled with water. Very similar to the scene at St. Nikita is the fresco in the outer narthex of Sopoćani.[244] Here, the principal differences are that the stoa is a series of five arches on columns and the pool is represented as a quatrefoil basin placed in front of the stoa and behind the paralytic carrying his bed. The fragmentary painting in the chapel of the Theotokos at the monastery of John the Theologian, Patmos,[245] must have been of the type of Sopoćani. At Chilandar, Mount Athos,[246] at opposite sides of a window in a tympanum are Christ and Peter (left), and the paralytic (right) facing Christ and bearing his bed; behind him is a five-arched stoa, partly on the tympanum and partly in the soffit of the adjoining arch. No pool is shown. Essentially the same type is found also in the parecclesion of St. Euthymius at the church of St. Demetrius, Salonika.[247] Similar to these, but with the pool beneath the stoa, is the painting in the church of St. Catherine, Salonika.

Belonging to this general iconographic category, which concentrates on the second episode, is a fresco in the Metropole, Mistra,[248] which, however, adds a group of Jews. Here, all the other elements are depicted: Christ and some disciples in front of a vaulted structure, which in the sketch resembles a ciborium but may have been a stoa; a quatrefoil pool; the healed man carrying his bed; and, at the far right, a group of the Jews questioning the healed man, and a young boy. In some manuscript illuminations, placed in conjunction with the text of John's description of the Bethesda miracle, the first episode is also omitted. In Laurent. Plut. VI.23, folio 176v, the paralytic with his bed is shown walking away from Christ; then comes a group of three paralytics reclining on their pallets, a five-lobed pool, and finally the paralytic, still with his bed, speaking to three Jews before a tower. A still more abbreviated miniature of this type is in the Armenian Gospel in the Walters Art Gallery, Baltimore;[249] it simply depicts the paralytic carrying a bundle (possibly his pallet or bed-covering) on his shoulder as he speaks to a group of Jews. The motif of the Jews in all these instances is with reference to John 5:10 ff. A fresco which probably omitted the first episode and illustrates only the healed man and his bed is that at St. Nicholas Orphanos.[250] What we have of this incomplete painting depicts the paralytic with his bed looking backward to the left toward persons in the destroyed left part of the panel, probably Christ with disciples. Again, to the right of the paralytic is a large group of Jews. Although it seems unlikely that the first episode could have been accommodated in the lost area at the left, the pool, as well as Christ and some disciples, may have been represented.

It is most probable that the paralytic scene at Pskov (Fig. 5), which shows only Christ, two disciples, and the healed man with his bed, is an illustration of the Bethesda miracle, for it follows immediately after the Healing of the Blind Born. Some manuscript illuminations that depict only the man with his bed indicate that the miracle is that at Bethesda by occurring at or near the beginning of John's account, but iconographically they could apply to either miracle.[251]

One element in the description of the Bethesda miracle which I have not discussed and which

244 See Okunev in *Byzantinoslavica*, I (1929), pp. 119–50, Fig. 21, upper left. The frescoes of the outer narthex date ca. 1345–50.

245 A. K. Orlandos, in *Byzantine Art, an European Art: Lectures* (Athens, 1966), Fig. 48 and pp. 73, 77. Orlandos has noted that the placing of this scene in a chapel dedicated to the Theotokos may be connected with the legend that the home of Joachim and Anne, where the Theotokos was born, was in the same place as the pool of Bethesda and cites John of Damascus (*PG*, 96, col. 677), who called the pool "the sacred temple of the Theotokos."

246 Millet, *Athos*, PL. 77,1.

247 G. A. and M. G. Soteriou, Ἡ βασιλικὴ τοῦ Ἁγίου Δημητρίου Θεσσαλονίκης, Vol. of Plates (Athens, 1952), PL. 87 b.

248 Millet, *Mistra*, PL. 72,1 (line drawing).

249 W. 539, fol. 137, a marginal illustration.

250 Xyngopoulos, Ἅγιος Νικόλαος Ὀρφανός, Fig. 88. Somewhat more than a third of the painting, at the left, is destroyed.

251 Such as Vienna, National Library, gr. 154, fol. 233v; Leningrad, Public Library, gr. 105, fol. 185; or Chicago, the Rockefeller McCormick New Testament (Gregory 2400), fol. 89. Nor can one be certain of the miniature in the Vatican Psalter, Barb. gr. 372, fol. 181v, where the subject is used to illustrate Ps. 107:20, or the miniature in Paris. gr. 510 (Homilies of Gregory of Nazianz), fol. 143v.

is rarely illustrated is the angel who troubled the waters of the pool. In monumental art this feature is presented in the mosaic at Monreale (Fig. 30),[252] where only the second episode is depicted: Christ and his disciples face toward the healed man with his bed; in the center behind them are a circular pool and a flying angel touching the water. In the background is an architectural façade of five arches (the stoa?). In a very complicated presentation the angel appears also in the sixteenth-century fresco in the chapel of St. John the Theologian at Kastoria.[253] In the foreground the paralytic stands with a ladder-like bed on his shoulders in the midst of three other afflicted people lying on the ground; to the right an angel kneels behind a quatrefoil pool stirring the water. In the background, behind a wall, is a five-arched stoa in front of which Christ stands with his disciples; at the left is a domed ciborium.

The motif of the angel appears also in a few manuscripts. The miniatures on folio 176 of Paris. gr. 74 and its copy, folio 225 of London, British Museum, Add. 39627,[254] composed of two registers, have in the center of the upper register a large quatrefoil pool, in which are bathing figures; an angel above stirs the water with a wand, and at each side are three figures on reclining beds. At the left in the lower register, both manuscripts show Christ leading two disciples as he extends his hand to the paralytic on his bed, and at the right the healed man carries his bed. Finally, in a thirteenth-century Syriac lectionary at the Vatican,[255] the pool, seen from above in a lozenge with lobes at each side, is being troubled by an angel descending toward it. The paralytic with his bed is at the left and Christ and two disciples are at the right. In the background the stoa is represented as a double portico consisting of two arches and a half in front and again two arches and a half at the back, seen at an angle so that they seem to interlace and form five pointed arches.

The accounts of the healing of a paralytic in the Synoptic Gospels,[256] it is universally agreed, refer to one and the same miracle—that at Capernaum—although only in Mark is the place specified.[257] While the three descriptions have points of variance which at times account for differences in the iconography of the scene, there are sufficiently close textual resemblances to establish the fact that they refer to the same miracle. It will be useful to summarize the narratives to see both their likenesses and their differences.

> Matthew (9:1–8): Jesus came to his own city; a paralytic [258] was brought lying on a bed; Jesus seeing the faith of the sick man and his companions forgave sins; scribes accused Jesus of blasphemy and they argued; at Jesus' command the paralytic took up his bed and walked; the multitudes marveled.
>
> Mark (2:1–12): Jesus, in Capernaum, was preaching in a crowded house; the paralytic was brought on a bed (vs. 4) carried by four men; because of the crowd, the roof of the house was uncovered and the sick man was let down before Jesus; Jesus saw their

252 The mosaic is somewhat restored. Illustrated courtesy of Professor Kitzinger. For its context see above, p. 252 f.

253 Moutsopoulos, *Kastoria*, Diagram VII, No. 7, and Fig. 18.

254 For Paris. 74, see *Evang. du XIe siècle*, II, PL. 152; and for Br. Mus., Add. 39627, Filov, *Evangile du roi Jean Alexandre*, PL. 109.

255 Vat. syr. 559, fol. 121v. See J. Leroy, *Les manuscrits syriaques à peintures conservés dans les bibliothèques d'Europe et d'Orient* (Paris, 1964), Album, PL. 87,2.

256 Matt. 9:1–8; Mark 2:1–12; Luke 5:18–26.

257 In Matthew 9:1 it is said that Christ "came into his own city." There is reason to believe that this meant Capernaum,

for, as W. Sanday says in *A Dictionary of Christ and the Gospels*, ed. J. Hastings et al., I (Edinburgh, 1906), p. 270, "So far as our Lord had any fixed headquarters during his Galilean ministry, they were in Capernaum."

258 It has been my observation that when an inscribed titulus accompanies a clearly identifiable representation of the Capernaum miracle the paralytic is called ὁ παραλυτικός. On the other hand, in inscriptions of scenes of the Bethesda miracle the paralytic is referred to as ὁ παράλυτος. The Kariye representations observe this distinction, one that may be regarded as a means of differentiating between the two healings.

faith and forgave sins; scribes accused him of blasphemy; at Jesus' command the man took up his bed and walked; all were amazed.

Luke: (5:18–26): The paralytic was brought in a bed; finding no way to lay him before Jesus, his friends let him down through the roof; Jesus seeing their faith forgave sins; scribes and Pharisees accused him of blasphemy; at Jesus' command the paralytic took up his bed and walked; all were amazed.

Common to all three are the bringing of the paralytic lying on a bed; Christ forgiving sins; the accusation of blasphemy by a crowd of scribes and/or Pharisees; the command and the afflicted walking with his bed; and the marveling of the beholders. The principal differences are that whereas Matthew says nothing about the house, the crowd, or how the sick man was presented to Jesus, both Mark and Luke tell of the necessity to lower him through the roof.

The mosaic at the Kariye Djami ([124], PL. 253) is obviously based on Matthew's version, but it reduces the narrative to four elements: Christ with four disciples standing at the left; the paralytic supine on his bed; a group of four men gathered around the head of the bed; and a small building in the background at the right. Omitted are the accusation of the scribes, the marveling crowd, and, most conspicuously, the episode of the paralytic carrying his bed.[259] It seems improbable that the four men at the head of the bed are scribes disputing with Christ, or that they represent the marveling spectators. On the contrary, their number, attitude, and position with relation to the sick man suggest an iconographic conflation with the passage in Mark which says that the paralytic was carried by four men.

Illustrations that approximate the iconography of the miracle as depicted in the Kariye Djami are quite rare, and no extant mural is of the same type, but two miniatures of the Rockefeller McCormick New Testament[260] are generally comparable. On folio 16 the composition is reversed and there are only three attendants, one disciple, and no house; on folio 38v Christ is seated, with no disciples, the bed is reversed, and the attendants are more numerous.

Among earlier mural representations of the miracle, we cite the mosaic panel in S. Apollinare Nuovo, Ravenna,[261] of the sixth century—the second of the two paralytic scenes in the frieze of the north wall, which definitely depicts the Capernaum miracle. As in all such early representations, the narrative quality is minimal and hence the mosaic presents a much simplified version of the miracle. Based presumably on Luke's account, because of the connection between these mosaics and the pericopes of the Gospels at Milan,[262] it depicts the episode of the paralytic being lowered from the roof. Christ and one disciple, on a rather large scale, stand at the left as two men on the roof of a most simple structure hold the ropes by which the sick man is being lowered. The latter elements are on a greatly reduced scale.

An eighth-century fresco in the lower church of S. Saba, Rome,[263] based on either Mark or Luke, is a more literal and narrative version; in it the house and the lowering of the afflicted form the background of the painting (Fig. 31). The house is a skeletal structure of columns, has no walls and a roof in which is a great hole. Two men with ropes lower the bed on which the paralytic lies supine. In the left foreground is Christ followed by four disciples and at the right is a

259 It will be seen, however, that this omission is usual in the mural representations of the subject.

260 At Chicago (Greg. 2400), published in facsimile in E. J. Goodspeed, D. W. Riddle, and H. R. Willoughby, eds., *The Rockefeller McCormick New Testament* (Chicago, 1932), I. See S. de Ricci, *Census of Medieval and Ranaissance Manuscripts*

in the United States and Canada: Supplement (originated by C. V. Saye, continued and edited by W. H. Bond; New York, 1962), p. 163.

261 Bovini, *S. Apollinare Nuovo*, PL. 11.

262 See above, p. 256.

263 Wilpert, *Mosaiken und Malereien*, IV, PL. 188.2.

crowd of scribes and Pharisees. Between Christ and the latter group is the paralytic carrying his bed. Thus the paralytic, in two episodes, occupies the center of a composition that is a remarkably complete depiction of most of the details of the textual source.

An eleventh-century painting of the Capernaum miracle once formed part of the Ministry cycle on the south wall of the nave of Sant'Angelo in Formis. So little, other than the inscription,[264] now survives that one is unable to determine its iconography, and we shall have to be content in merely recording this as one of the relatively few examples of the Capernaum miracle in monumental art.

In a majority of the mural representations of the miracle in Middle and Late Byzantine, or byzantinizing, art, even in works as late as the sixteenth century, the iconography tended to conform to a single type that admitted only minor differentiations. That iconography can be observed most typically in the mosaics of Monreale (Fig. 32)[265] and of San Marco, Venice (Fig. 33),[266] and in the fresco in the Catholicon of the Grand Lavra, Mount Athos.[267] The type is characterized, first of all, by its formal, symmetrical composition, in which the elements are depicted, so to speak, in flat elevation; that is, they are placed in flat planes that are parallel to the picture plane. The center foreground is occupied by the paralytic on his bed and the center background by a house on whose roof are two or four men[268] holding ropes with which they lower the afflicted. All the examples have the head of the bed or pallet to the right, and on it the paralytic lies supine, except at Monreale, where, uniquely, he sits upright on his bed. One can suggest that the mosaicist confused this posture with that in the Bethesda miracle, or that he combined the two miracles on this point. In all three examples Christ is seated in near-profile on a throne at the left, a varying number of disciples standing behind him. Balancing this group, a crowd of scribes and Pharisees stands at the right.[269] An important point about these representations is that the episode of the paralytic walking away with his bed is not represented. At San Marco (Fig. 33), despite the fact that the inscription reads *Ponunt languentem, fit sanus, fertque ferentem*, the paralytic does not walk with his bed. Indeed, with the exception of the fresco of S. Saba and a late example at the Metropole, Mistra, no extant monumental representation of what can be definitely identified as the Capernaum miracle depicts this second episode.

An iconography essentially the same but less formal in its composition was used in the fresco at Dečani,[270] a monument that is more nearly of the period of the Kariye Djami. Even here, frontality is applied except in the presentation of the bed, which is diagonal—the result, perhaps, of the wish to indicate that the foot of the bed rests on the ground while the head is still being lowered. Exceptional to the type, however, is the figure of Christ, who is not seated but walks toward the afflicted. Somewhat more lavish than others, this painting presents a truly great number of scribes and Pharisees, some of whom are very clearly engaged in disputing with Christ. It is interesting to note that the type of house, with a great square opening in its roof, is much like that of the Lavra painting.

---

264 Jerphanion, *Voix des monuments*, p. 276, transcribes the inscription as *Tolle vadens lectum: facit hoc spes firma parentum* and points out its allusion to Matt. 9:2 and 6, which suggests that the painting was of the Capernaum paralytic.

265 Cf. Demus, *Norman Sicily*, PL. 91 *b*; this is a work of the late twelfth century.

266 Cf. Ongania, ed., *La basilica di San Marco* (see above, n. 224), I, PL. XVI, a line drawing; also Text Vol., p. 375, where the San Marco mosaic is classed as being "di stile antico," an

expression used for those mosaics which are no longer of the "Byzantine" period but date before the mid-fifteenth century.

267 Millet, *Athos*, PL. 126,3, and p. 61 of the Répertoire des Monuments, where he dates the fresco at about 1535.

268 San Marco has four, the others two; the paralytic here lies on a pallet.

269 At the Lavra, perhaps owing to the narrow confines of the painting, the five men in this crowd are aligned behind the entire length of the bed; with two exceptions they are seated.

270 Petković and Bošković, *Dečani*, PL. LXXXV.

The interest in the minutiae of narrative painting and profusion of details that one often ob-serves in the paintings of Mistra are evident in the representation of the Capernaum miracle in the Metropole.[271] While the emphasis is still centered on the theme of the lowering of the para-lytic through the roof, the painting presents some unusual features. Christ, standing with his disciples, is at the left as usual. The disputing Pharisees have been placed as a tight group im-mediately to the right of Christ. Most unusual is the fact that the paralytic in this painting is represented three times. In the right background he is literally being brought into the house through a hole in the roof. Two ladders are used, one against the right exterior side, the other inside the house, which, as in the S. Saba painting, has no walls. On the first ladder two men climb as they raise the head of the pallet on which the paralytic lies supine. Another man, on the roof, supports the foot of the pallet and transfers his burden to two men near the top of the second ladder, inside the house, who prepare to bring the man down. In front of the house the afflicted is borne toward Christ by four men. Finally, as was rarely done, the paralytic is shown again, at the right, as he carries his pallet after being healed; to the right is another group of Jews. Obviously, this last element is what we usually find in representations of the Bethesda paralytic, where, in accordance with John's words,[272] the healed man is questioned by Jews. With this excep-tion, however, the scene meticulously depicts events as they were described in Mark and Luke.

A final, quite late fresco of the subject, that in the chapel of St. John the Theologian at Kastoria, of 1522,[273] need not be discussed in detail. It is sufficient to say that Christ is seated and that, aside from the Jews disputing with Christ and some figures kneeling in amazement, the episode depicted is that of the lowering of the supine man by two men on the roof of the house. Again, the incident of the walking paralytic is omitted.

Examination of most of the extant mural representations of the Capernaum miracle has shown that the dominant features were the house, the lowering of the supine paralytic through the roof, and the group of Jews charging Jesus with blasphemy for proclaiming his power to forgive sin. At the Kariye Djami, to return to that unique rendition, none of these major and characteristic components appears, aside from the small piece of architecture at the right edge of the mosaic, which is presented more as an accent between adjoining scenes than as the house in which the miracle was performed. One might say that in composing this scene our mosaicist used the simple formula—Christ attended by disciples confronting the protagonist and his attendants—which was typical of all but a few miracle scenes from the fourth bay onward to the conclusion of the cycle in the inner narthex. Most of those scenes, as I have said, are not considered here because they offer too little of iconographic significance to merit detailed study and comment beyond that to be found in Volume 1.

Before leaving the subject of the two healings of a paralytic, however, I would make one gen-eralization that is perhaps valid and, if so, of considerable importance. This concerns the nu-merous instances in which only the episode of the paralytic carrying his bed is represented. Is it not likely that, with a few possible exceptions, these refer to the Johannine miracle at Bethesda rather than that at Capernaum despite the fact that all three Gospel versions of the Capernaum miracle include the walking paralytic? When illustrated in that manner are they not likely to be representations intended to epitomize or symbolize a well-understood dogma that reflects the liturgy or the sacramental rites of baptism, as was discussed above?[274] This was cer-

---

271 Millet, *Mistra*, PL. 76,3, center (a line drawing).
272 John 5:10 ff.
273 Moutsopoulos, *Kastoria*, PL. 13.
274 Pp. 257–62.

tainly the case in the numerous Early Christian examples where the subject was placed in conjunction with equally simple and symbolic representations of the Samaritan Woman and the Blind Born,[275] or even stood alone, in catacomb painting or on sarcophagi, as symbols of ultimate redemption. Moreover, in many of the Late Byzantine renderings of the Bethesda miracle which were treated as fully developed narrative paintings, the scene, while giving prominence not only to the healing of the paralytic but to the components of the locale (stoa and pool), includes much more often than not as an essential element of the narrative the paralytic walking. On the other hand, the Capernaum miracle cannot be clearly identified in any symbolic version early or late, and in its narrative development it emphasized the house and the incident of the roof, very rarely including the walking of the paralytic. When this latter motif was represented, moreover, it became a minor incident and at times seems to involve a conflation with the Bethesda iconography.

There is one other subject—The Healing of a Multitude ([141], PL. 277–81)—that deserves consideration because of iconographic problems it posed, not only to our mosaicist, but to any muralist who wished to depict it as part of a miracle cycle. Indeed, it will be seen that not many undertook its representation at all, if we can judge from examples in extant monuments.

The four Gospels record about ten occasions when Christ healed large numbers of diseased or afflicted persons. There are, actually, some eighteen references to such miracles, but by examining their relative chronology or topographical locale one may reduce the number of such events to ten, for some of the events are recorded in more than one Gospel.[276] Not only was there a multiplicity of textual passages from which, in theory, the artist might choose, but for the most part they were couched in such vague terms that they were lacking in sufficient narrative detail to serve as sources for clearly recognizable depictions of specific texts. Most of the accounts simply dismiss the miracles as healings of "all manner of sickness and all manner of disease," "every sickness and every disease," or "divers diseases." The most nearly explicit description is that of Matthew 15:29–31, where mention is made of those afflicted by a number of specific maladies—the lame, blind, dumb (or deaf), maimed—"and many others." (The Greek word κωφός, used in Matthew 15:30, means both dumb and deaf.)

Under such circumstances a distinct iconographic type for use in mural decoration in churches was not developed for the subject of the Healing of a Multitude. We shall see that the only extant examples have little in common iconographically and that each artist appears to have devised his own ensemble of variously afflicted persons, sometimes using motifs from other miracles which had iconographic traditions of their own.

I observed above [277] that the group of subjects in the inner narthex of the Kariye Djami was probably selected to illustrate the miracles, all in Matthew and all miracles of healing, whose accounts were read as lections for the period from the third Saturday to the seventh Sunday after Pentecost. I also noted that two of those lections concerned the healing of multitudes and, further, that the one for the seventh Friday after Pentecost was Matthew 15:29–31. In theory, therefore, our mosaicist may be thought to have illustrated that passage in his panel [141]. I have no doubt that this rarely depicted subject was chosen mainly because it, with the others in

275 See above, passim, where some of these are mentioned, as well as the extraordinary number of later miracle cycles in which the three are grouped.

276 The ten are: (1) Matt. 4:23–24; (2) Matt. 8:16–17; Mark 1:32–34; Luke 4:40–41; (3) Matt. 9:35; (4) Matt. 12:15–16; Mark 3:8–12; Luke 6:17–19; (5) Matt. 14:14; Luke 9:11; John 6:2; (6) Matt. 14:34–36; Mark 6:53–56; (7) Matt. 15:30–31; (8) Matt. 19:2; (9) Matt. 21:14; (10) Mark 6:5.

277 Pp. 262–64.

the south bay of the inner narthex, fell within that period of the liturgical calendar, but in any case it was a most suitable one with which to sum up Christ's miracles of healing. Although some, if not all, of the maladies mentioned by Matthew are represented among the figures in our mosaic, there was no attempt on the part of the artist to limit himself to the illustration of any particular text. One gains the impression that he introduced one or two well-known types derived from specific miracles of healing which, perhaps, he had not represented elsewhere in his cycle, and combined them with inventions of his own in a kind of synthesis of healings in general.

In the consideration of representations of Christ Healing a Multitude distinctions must be made between them, on the one hand, and what we might term "multiple" healings which are recognized subjects in their own right but which, because of inconsistencies on the part of the artist, might be mistaken for healings of multitudes. If one looks through the exhaustive list of miracles in the *Hermeneia*, it is rather surprising to find that except for one entitled the Healing of Various Diseases (H 26), and another called the Healing of Various Diseases by Touching the Hem of Christ's Garment (H 44),[278] only four miracles were performed on more than one person: those relating to the Two Gadarene Demoniacs (H 28); Two Blind Men (H 34); Ten Lepers (H 57); and the Blind and Lame in the Temple (H 72). These subjects were sometimes represented in miracle cycles in monumental art.[279] The monumental illustrations of the Blind and Lame in the Temple are especially a source of confusion; sometimes they may be interpreted as conflations of two or more miracles or as illustrations applicable to more than one miracle, or erroneously taken as depictions of the Healing of a Multitude. For example, the mosaic at Monreale (Fig. 32, right) is inscribed "Christ healing the blind (*caecos*) and the lame (*claudos*)," each category in the plural, and might therefore refer to Matthew 21:14. The mosaic depicts a lame man with hand-crutches, a blind man pointing to his eyes, and another who is not only blind but also a hunchback. But since it does not place the miracle in the temple, but in open country at the foot of a mountain, it might be thought, rather, to refer to some of the afflictions of Matthew 15:30 and, iconographically, to be a synthesis of one of the healings of multitudes. However, I take it to be a rather free rendition of the Lame and the Blind.[280]

Another instance of a painting that may be interpreted in more than one way because of its ambiguous content is that at Dečani (Fig. 34),[281] which is a possible representation of the Two Blind Men or of the Blind and Lame. The painting presents two almost identical figures, wearing identical hats, who are obviously lame or maimed and unable to stand since they crouch on the ground and possess hand-crutches; they are also depicted as blind. However, the inscription reads: "Christ healing a blind and a deaf man," which hardly corresponds to what is painted; moreover, no miracle such as is described in the inscription is recorded in the Gospels. The first of the two men is almost exactly duplicated in the first of the lame men in the painting at St. Nicholas Orphanos, Salonika,[282] which is inscribed as the healing of two maimed, or crippled

---

278 Respectively based on Matt. 8:16–17, Mark 1:32–34, Luke 4:40–41; and Matt. 14:34–36, Mark 6:53–56. Note that because H limited itself to only two such general healings, it omitted the one that was most likely the inspiration for the Kariye mosaic—that of Matt. 15:30–31.

279 For representative examples see the following: Ten Lepers: Monreale (Demus, *Norman Sicily*, PL. 90 *b*); Pskov (our Fig. 4); Dečani (Petković and Bošković, *Dečani*, PL. CCXXVI). Two Blind Men: Monreale (Demus, *Norman Sicily*, PL. 90 *b*); Kariye Djami (our PL. 262); and possibly Dečani (Petković and Bošković, *Dečani*, PL. CCXXIV). The Blind and Lame in the Temple: Monreale (Demus, *Norman*

Sicily, PL. 91 *b*); and again possibly Dečani (our Fig. 34). The Two Gadarene Demoniacs: Dečani (Petković and Bošković, *Dečani*, PL. CCXXVII); Kastoria, chapel of St. John Theologian (Moutsopoulos, *Kastoria*, PL. 32).

280 The painting at the Sts. Anargyroi, Kastoria (Pelekanides, Καστορία, I, PL. 30 *b*), which Pelekanides calls the Healing of the Blind Men may be another of the healings of the Blind and Lame (Matt. 21:14), for the foremost of the four kneeling men has a pair of hand-crutches before him.

281 Cf. Petković and Bošković, *Dečani*, PL. CCXXIV.

282 Xyngopoulos, Ἅγιος Νικόλαος Ὀρφανός, PL. 45, Fig. 87, and pp. 16, 17.

men (δύο κυλούς); the first lame man at St. Nicholas, in turn, as we shall see, is like one of the figures in the foreground of the Healing of a Multitude, also at Dečani. Xyngopoulos thinks the St. Nicholas painting a synthesis of Matthew 15:30 (a healing of a multitude), for again, despite the inscription, no healing of two cripples, or maimed men, is mentioned in the Gospels. In my view it is a free invention, taking motifs from the healing of the Blind and Lame but omitting any indication of blindness, and has been given a freely invented titulus.[283]

As true examples of the Healing of a Multitude in monumental art, there are, to my knowledge, only three extant representations: that of the Kariye Djami ([141], PL. 277); the painting at Dečani (Fig. 35),[284] which is inscribed "Christ heals those afflicted with various diseases," a titulus that is almost exactly that given the mosaic of the Kariye;[285] and the fresco in the west lunette of the south aisle at the Metropole of Mistra.[286] As will be seen, the first two have a number of iconographic features in common, although no individual figures are closely paralleled; the third is altogether different, and it cannot be said that an iconographic type had been developed for this subject.

In the mosaic of the Kariye Djami, aside from Christ and three of his disciples, there are eight figures involved in the miracle, four men and four women. Two of the women are placed in a background plane and hold infants in their arms. In the foreground we have, from left to right: a man seated on the ground, who not only may be said to be lame (or, in fact, maimed), since his posture and his hand-crutch suggest this, but who also is blind; another seated man, wearing a short tunic, who is blind; a third seated man, who has a large growth between his legs;[287] a fourth man, standing, holding a stick, and clad in tight-fitting trousers and a tunic, who is not blind even though a stick is often an indication of blindness; the Bent Woman,[288] leaning on a stick, who might be termed maimed; and a woman just behind the latter whose blindness is depicted. As for the women in the back row, both of whom hold infants, the implication is that although they themselves may not be afflicted they have brought sick infants to be cured. The inclusion of women and children serves to make the miracle more comprehensive and in this summation of healing miracles points up again Christ's impartiality between the sexes, which was observed in the scenes of the four pendentives. Some of the eight persons might qualify as being deaf or dumb, or both, but unless the person so afflicted points to his ear or his mouth, which is not the case in the mosaic, those maladies are difficult to identify.

In the right half of the painting at Dečani (Fig. 35), the afflicted are again lined up in parallel zones, one behind the other, but this time in three registers. Those who are definite supplicants for healing are the following: In the lower foreground is a lame or maimed man with hat, hand-crutches, and even posture almost exactly like those of the lame men referred to above in the scene at Dečani erroneously inscribed as the healing of a blind and a deaf man[289] (Fig. 34),

---

283 The fresco in the church of St. Theodore, Sousam Baïri, which Jerphanion (*Cappadoce*, Text, II,1, pp. 38 f., and Plates, III, PL. 148,2) calls "The Healing of the Withered Hand and other Infirmities," is an instance in which the artist has deliberately expanded a healing of a single disease (the Withered Hand) into one involving a number of other diseases. At St. Theodore, however, the artist has proceeded to include a healing of a multitude because the textual sources for the Withered Hand in the Synoptics are immediately followed by a healing of a multitude which is lacking in details.

284 Cf. Petković and Bošković, *Dečani*, PL. CCXXIII. The painting is placed on the apse wall, second register from the bottom, to the west of the south window, in conjunction with two other healing miracles.

285 Vol. 1 of this work, p. 149.

286 Millet, *Mistra*, PL. 76,1 (line drawing). See also above, p. 254, where the sequence of the miracles of the Metropole is compared to the order of the *Hermeneia* and this miracle is listed as No. 26.

287 This appears to be his only affliction. To my knowledge, no parallel can be found in Byzantine art, nor are there any references in any of the accounts of healing miracles to such an affliction.

288 In numerous representations of the Healing of the Bent Woman (Luke 13:10–17), the woman is shown in just this way (see for example Monreale, Demus, *Norman Sicily*, Fig. 89 *a*) and thus represents the most clear-cut example of the insertion of a specific miracle into a multiple healing.

289 Cf. Petković and Bošković, *Dečani*, PL. CCXXIV.

and those of the first lame man at St. Nicholas Orphanos, Salonika, in the scene entitled the healing of two crippled men.[290] In the same zone is an old man, bent over and leaning on a T-stick, who is a male counterpart of the Bent Woman in the Kariye version. The third and last figure in the foreground, at the far right, has only a superficial similarity to the fourth man at Kariye; both are bearded and lame, but their costumes differ, and whereas at the Kariye the man holds a long stick in front of him, the Dečani figure has a T-crutch placed under his left shoulder. In the middle register is a young cripple using two T-crutches; he is curiously placed, for he appears to be raised quite far off the ground. Behind him, to the right, is a bearded man, fully clad, who leans backward, his belly protruding, and who is supported from the rear by two men; except for the costume he resembles the afflicted in the miracle of the Dropsical Man.[291] In the background, as at the Kariye, are two women holding infants; the foremost, somewhat in the manner of the first woman at the Kariye, extends her infant toward Christ, while the second carries her child on her shoulders, pickaback. Finally, it should be noted that in the far background is a crowd of persons who seem to be mere onlookers.

In summation, the elements which the two representations of the Healing of a Multitude have in common are: the same inscribed titulus; the arrangement in zones; a cripple placed in the lower left foreground; the depiction of both men and women as supplicants, with two of the women bringing sick infants;[292] the use of figures taken from other well-established and independent miracles (in the Kariye, the Bent Woman for whom, at Dečani, a bent man is substituted, and in the latter church, a version of the Dropsical Man); and what appears to be a freedom of invention that does not correspond to any particular text of the Healing of a Multitude, not even that of Matthew 15:30, which, though lacking in narrative detail, is more likely than any other to have been the textual source of inspiration.

The chief differences are that the Kariye version is limited to Christ, the disciples, and the afflicted, whereas Dečani introduces a crowd of accompanying beholders and friends of the afflicted; that the Kariye version depicts three persons who suffer from blindness, some of whom are also otherwise afflicted, whereas at Dečani no figure is clearly portrayed as blind; and that the setting in each case is different, the Kariye version depicting a landscape with two small structures in the background, whereas Dečani presents a city wall with a turret and a gate approached by a flight of steps.

The third, and last, of the murals of the Healing of a Multitude is that of the Metropole, Mistra.[293] Above the head of Christ is an inscription, based on Luke 4:40, which serves as titulus: "Christ healing those sick [or weak] with diverse diseases." Two other inscriptions, one high up at the center of the lunette, the other between Christ's halo and a figure to the right, quote verbatim consecutive phrases from Luke 4:41: "And devils also came out of many, crying out, and saying, Thou art Christ the Son of God. And he rebuking them suffered them not to speak." As was noted above, this is one of two healings of multitudes listed in the *Hermeneia* (No. 26). In front of a wall and some fanciful architecture Christ, to left of center and followed by two disciples, faces those who have been brought to him for healing. In the front row are two figures lying on their pallets (those who are sick, or weak—ἀσθενοῦντας, as the text has

---

290 Xyngopoulos, Ἅγιος Νικόλαος Ὀρφανός, PL. 45, Fig. 87.
291 Cf. Petković and Bošković, *Dečani*, PL. CCXXV; Xyngopoulos, Ἅγιος Νικόλαος Ὀρφανός, PL. 44, Fig. 85, where the Dropsical Man also uses two T-crutches; Millet, *Mistra*, PL. 73,1, 83,1 (Metropole), etc.

292 This feature is present also in the fresco at St. Theodore's in Cappadocia (see above, n. 283), where the Healing of the Withered Hand was transformed into a multiple healing.
293 Millet, *Mistra*, PL. 76,1 (line drawing).

it). Behind them stand three men in a row turned toward Christ. They appear to have open mouths and doubtless represent those from whom the devils, mentioned in the uppermost inscription, have come forth. Finally, at the right are two men, probably those who brought the sick to Christ. This example, as we see, is totally different from the other two and again serves to demonstrate that for the Healing of a Multitude no formula had been developed, as there had been for many of the other healing miracles. The major distinction between this presentation and the other two is that it is based upon, and fairly literally illustrates, the text of Luke 4:40–41 describing a healing of a multitude, whereas the other two, even if they were inspired by the only other text to speak of particular illnesses—Matthew 15:30—used utmost freedom and were not literal reflections of any text.

Among extant monuments the Kariye Djami possessed what was probably the most comprehensive of true Ministry cycles. It included events preparatory to Christ's Ministry, namely, the testimony of John the Baptist that Christ was the divine Son of God, the acquisition of the first disciples, and Christ's rejection of the temptations of mortal man. Depicted also, but not gathered together as a group, were some of his non–miraculous acts.[294] All other existing scenes appear to have been miracles. However, excepting the group of healings in the inner narthex, the miracles were not assembled as an independent cycle as they sometimes were in the other monuments.

Having avoided any attempt to narrate the Ministry chronologically, except at the very beginning, the mosaicist at times grouped scenes not by categories but for didactic or liturgical reasons: twice to express the significance of Christ's acts as prefigurations of sacraments; twice as illustrations of pericopes from specific periods in the liturgical calendar.[295] Like the artists of some other monuments the Kariye mosaicist and painter consciously opposed and contrasted certain subjects that would illustrate Christ's teachings of impartiality between man and woman; he also, but rarely, grouped subjects to establish compositional relationships. In general, it might be said that the iconographic mastermind of the Kariye mosaics exhibited a great interest in, and knowledge of, the symbolic significance of Christ's acts, and perhaps in a more learned way than others successfully conveyed this significance by the various means that have been pointed out above.

The iconographic program in the church as a whole was devoted exclusively to Christological and Marian subjects. The mosaicist placed the cycle of the Great Feasts, and probably of the Passion and post-Passion, in the nave. In the two narthexes he arranged a succession of cycles that form a logical and physical continuity. The Marian, Infancy, and Ministry cycles are in a continuous relationship to one another. A location in the narthex for a Ministry cycle is extremely rare. Its presence there at the Kariye Djami may be explained on the grounds that being a "luxury" church, as befitted the traditions of Constantinople, the Kariye had to be richly decorated with marble-covered walls and the mosaic scenes had to be restricted to the vaults above. No space was available for the Ministry except in the narthexes, for the nave could not have accommodated more than the Festival and Passion cycles.

There can be no denying that the iconography of many of the scenes of the Ministry and other cycles at the Kariye Djami was inevitably within the main currents of fourteenth-century

---

294 Such as his conversation with the Samaritan Woman; his calling of Zacchaeus; and possibly his reading in the Synagogue—the mosaic is very fragmentary. There may also have been others, now lost.

295 The group of the Samaritan Woman, the Paralytic, and the Blind Born figures in both categories, that is, as prefigurations of a sacrament and as illustrations of feasts celebrated during a period of the liturgical calendar.

Byzantine art. On the other hand, in so far as existing monuments permit us to judge, the designer seems to have given a number of subjects original treatment, introduced features that remain unparalleled, and endowed some scenes with iconological significance that is not to be found elsewhere.

There is also one general characteristic that sets the works of the Chora apart from other monuments of its period, a characteristic which may possibly be attributable to the traditions of monumental art in Constantinople, which are so little known owing to the lack of sufficient comparative material in the capital city. The master of the Chora can be seen to have exercised a restraint that contrasts with the profusiveness of much of the work in other areas, where the artists indulged in the introduction of unessential figures and in a multiplicity of detail that often produced overly crowded, complex compositions. Indeed, the mosaicist of the Chora, as a rule, employed the bare minimum of figures and motifs called for by his textual source, sometimes rendering them in even more concise terms than the source suggests. The result is that his compositions always possess spaciousness of setting that contrasts with compositions elsewhere.[296]

On certain points of iconography rather close parallels to the Kariye Djami have been found in some of the frescoes of Dečani, especially in matters of details, and, in several striking instances, in miniatures of MS Iviron 5. There is, however, no conspicuous, over-all iconographic affiliation between the Constantinopolitan Kariye mosaics and extant work elsewhere,[297] except possibly the Holy Apostles in Salonika.[298] Lacking, as we do, representations of the same subjects in other Palaeologan churches in Constantinople itself, with only two exceptions,[299] it may be rash to say, as I would be tempted to do, that in iconography the Constantinopolitan school of the Palaeologan era stood somewhat apart from the currents that were at work in other parts of the Orthodox world, especially in the Serbian kingdoms.

296 As an extreme case, compare the Cana Wedding Feast of the Kariye, as we have been able to reconstruct it (above, pp. 280–85), with that at St. Nikita, Čučer (Fig. 20). Or, to take an example that is not from the Ministry cycle, compare the version of the Dormition at the Kariye Djami (PL. 320) with that at St. Nicholas Orphanos, Salonika (Xyngopoulos, Ἅγιος Νικόλαος Ὀρφανός, Fig. 32). The former is quite faithful to its textual source (see Vol. 1 of this work, pp. 164 ff.) and therefore depicts only eleven Apostles and a few other persons named in the source, while the latter adds almost countless persons and is, as a result, a highly crowded, rather complex composition. Despite these differences, the two conform to the same general iconographic tradition of the day.

297 The presence of copies of a number of the Kariye scenes at Curtea-de-Argeş and Kalenić does not of itself indicate their close affiliation with the iconography of Constantinople as it is represented in the Kariye Djami. Aside from the copies there is little in common between them.

298 To my mind the iconography of the lost festival cycle in the Kariye Djami may have reflected that of the Holy Apostles. The style of the two monuments is so similar as to suggest that both were products of the Constantinopolitan school. Iconographic comparisons, unfortunately, can be made only between some of the frescoes in the narthexes of the Holy Apostles and in the pareccelsion of the Kariye Djami. In these we do find points of iconographic affiliation; see S. Der Nersessian in the study that follows.

299 Compare, first, the fresco of the Priests before the Altar in the pareccelsion of the Kariye (PL. 466) and its only known counterpart, in the Constantinopolitan church of the Pammakaristos, now known as the Fethiye Djami, of which Professor Der Nersessian speaks in the study that follows (p. 346 f and her Fig. 18). See also C. Mango and E. J. W. Hawkins, "Report on Field Work in Istanbul and Cyprus, 1962–1963," DOP, 18 (1964), Figs. 10 and 11 and p. 324. A second instance is found in the only mosaics thus far uncovered in the Kilisse Djami, Istanbul, where two if not all three of the fluted or ribbed domes of the outer narthex are devoted to the Genealogy of Christ, as are the two domes of the inner narthex at the Kariye Djami (PL. 43, 67). The plaster covering the mosaics of the north dome in the Kilisse Djami has not been removed. The fact that in the only two Constantinopolitan churches where mosaics have survived in fluted domes in the narthex the subject is the Ancestors of Christ may well suggest a local usage. Nowhere else, to my knowledge, are Genealogies thus disposed. For illustrations of the Kilisse Djami mosaics, see A. Ogan, "Bizans mimari tarihinde: Istanbul kiliseleri ve mozaikler," Güzel Sanatlar, 5 (1944), figures on pp. 105, 112, 113.

Program and Iconography of the Frescoes
of the Parecclesion

SIRARPIE DER NERSESSIAN

Program and Iconography of the Frescoes of the Parecclesion

The Program

THE PARECCLESION, the chapel erected by Theodore Metochites on the south side of the Kariye Djami, consists of two square bays—the western one covered with a ribbed dome on pendentives, the eastern one with a domical vault—and a large apse extending the full width of the nave.[1] The principal entrance is through an arched opening in the east side of the seventh bay of the outer narthex (PL. 335). A small door in the north wall of the parecclesion leads by way of a narrow passage into the main church (PL. 532 a); a second door in the north wall, close to the bema, opens into the small chamber that was originally the diaconicon of the church. Except for the disappearance of several single figures and minor injuries in the larger compositions, the paintings of the parecclesion are in a good state of preservation, and we thus have one of the rare religious edifices of Constantinople which have retained almost intact their original decoration. The decoration of the parecclesion must have been executed immediately after the completion of the mosaics in the two narthexes, for on the arched opening into the seventh bay of the outer narthex one can see the point of juncture where the mosaics stop and the frescoes begin.

Leaving aside the paintings of the tombs, which were executed later,[2] the figural representations of the parecclesion may be briefly indicated as follows. The lower zone comprises only single figures: six Church Fathers on the semicircular wall of the apse (PL. 476–85); the Virgin and Child on the south end of the bema (PL. 486, 487); and a row of saints and martyrs around the walls (PL. 488–520). The Anastasis (PL. 340–59) fills the conch of the apse, and the Raising of the Widow's Son at Nain and the Raising of the Daughter of Jairus decorate the bema arch (PL. 340, 360–67). The Last Judgment is developed on the domical vault and on the lunettes of the eastern bay (PL. 368–407). The western bay is given over to the Virgin; her image surrounded by angels occupies the dome (PL. 408–25), and Old Testament scenes in which she is prefigured are depicted on the vaults and on the lunettes (PL. 437–68).

In his dedicatory poem Metochites referred to the *trapeza*, or refectory, which he had built alongside the church and adorned with paintings that recounted the mysteries and miracles of

---

[1] Illustrations of all the frescoes in the parecclesion are to be found in Paul A. Underwood, Vol. 3 of this series of volumes, PL. 335–520. Plans and Sections of the parecclesion with numbers indicating location of all paintings are placed at the back of each volume (*Figs. 9–12*). For general views of the interior of the parecclesion see PL. 335–39.

[2] The tombs of the parecclesion are discussed in Vol. 1, pp. 269–99; for the illustrations of their decoration see Vol. 3, PL. 533–39.

Christ. On the basis of these passages Feodor Shmit identified the parecclesion with the *trapeza*, and his views have been shared by some scholars.[3] Several points are in favor of this identification. There is no other reference in the poems to a structure decorated with paintings, and although an argument *ex silentio* is not always valid, if the south annex is not the *trapeza*, then Metochites has failed to speak of one of the major additions he made to the monastery, on the adornment of which he lavished so much care.[4] The passing reference to the paintings which represented "the mysteries and miracles of Christ" does not entirely agree with the subjects we now see, but it may be argued that Metochites spoke in very general terms and did not intend to give an exact description. In themselves the compositions that adorn the parecclesion are not inconsistent with the function of the building as a refectory, as can be seen by reference to the programs developed in later periods in the refectories of Mount Athos. The Last Judgment is represented at the Lavra, at Dionysiou, and at Xenophon, and the eschatological theme is further stressed at Dionysiou and at Dochiariou through the cycle of the Apocalypse.[5] The scenes related to the Virgin occupy an important place in these refectories: in addition to the narrative cycles we find illustrations of the hymns celebrating the Virgin—the Akathistos Hymn at the Lavra and at Chilandar,[6] and the sticheron of Christmas at Chilandar and Dionysiou.[7] At Chilandar the sticheron is represented on the same wall as the Tabernacle of Moses, one of the scenes considered a prefiguration of the Virgin; at Dionysiou it faces the Last Judgment.[8] The Tree of Jesse at the Lavra should be mentioned, as well as the composition depicting the prayer before the icon of the Virgin at Chilandar.[9] This latter scene and, in general, all those related to the Virgin find their explanation in the services of the refectory, in particular the Elevation of the Panagia, that is the bread blessed in honor of the Virgin. Before the meal the bread marked with the sigla of Christ and a cup filled with wine were placed before the icon of the Virgin, and, in the prayers asking for her intercession, the Virgin was invoked as the Mother of God, in whom Christ, our God, condescended to dwell.[10] In raising the Panagia, the monks invoked first the holy Trinity and next the most holy Mother of God, asking God to have pity on them through her prayers.[11]

Thus the two principal themes developed in the parecclesion figure among those selected for the decoration of refectories, and the choice of the subjects, in itself, is not a sufficient reason for excluding the possibility that this annex was destined to be the *trapeza* mentioned in the dedicatory poems. However, other considerations favor the hypothesis that it was erected as a funerary chapel.

The evidence available so far shows that the refectories were independent, autonomous buildings, often built at a short distance from the church. Even at the fortified monastery on the island of Patmos, where space was restricted, the refectory, although adjoining the church, had a separate entrance and there was no passage connecting it with the church, as there is at

3 F. Šmit, Kaxriè-Džami (= *Izvestija Russkogo Arxeologičeskogo Instituta v Konstantinopolě*, 11), I (Sofia, 1906), pp. 92–98. M. Alpatov [Alpatoff], "Die Fresken der Kachrie Djami in Konstantinopel," *Münchner Jahrbuch der bildenden Kunst*, 6 (1929), 345–64; O. M. Dalton, *East Christian Art: A Survey of the Monuments* (Oxford, 1925), p. 255; V. N. Lazarev, *Istorija vizantijskoi živopisi*, I (Moscow, 1947), p. 216. For a contrary view, see Underwood, Vol. 1, pp. 188–89.

4 But see Vol. 1, p. 188, at note 8, where verses of Metochites are cited which may refer to the two lateral annexes of the church, one to the north, the other (the parecclesion) to the south.

5 G. Millet, *Monuments de l'Athos* (Paris, 1927), PL. 149,

210,2; H. Brockhaus, *Die Kunst in den Athos-Klöstern* (Leipzig, 1891; 2d ed., 1924), pp. 283, 285. For the Apocalypse, see Millet, *Athos*, PL. 206–09, and J. Renaud, *Le cycle de l'Apocalypse de Dionysiou: Interprétation byzantine de gravures occidentales* (Paris, 1943).

6 Millet, *Athos*, PL. 99–103, 145–47.

7 Ibid., PL. 104,3, 201,1.

8 Ibid., PL. 104,1, 210.

9 Ibid., PL. 150–151,3, 104,2

10 F. Mercenier and F. Paris, *La prière des églises de rite byzantin*, I [Gembloux, 1937], pp. 191–93 and 46, 86.

11 Ibid., p. 191.

the Kariye Djami.[12] More important are the structural elements: as already indicated by P. A. Underwood: "Four wall tombs, in the form of arcosolia, were built within the thickness of the walls and were actually used for sepulchral purposes . . . and in addition two long vaults were built parallel to one another beneath the floor of the parecclesion, probably to serve as the ossuaries of the monastery."[13]

But even though the parecclesion of the Kariye Djami was, in all probability, erected as a mortuary chapel, the similarities between its decorative program and that of the refectories should be observed for their general implications. For they show that analogous systems could be adopted for buildings which had essentially different functions, because of the similarity of certain services. This is even more noticeable in the case of the narthexes, where commemorative services for the dead were held, and their decorative program, as we shall see below, offers many points of similarity with that of the parecclesion. We need only mention here, as an example, the outer narthex of the church of the Virgin Ljeviška at Prizren, in Yugoslavia, where the scenes of the Last Judgment appear in the groin vault over the south bay, and the prefigurations of the Virgin in the vault over the north bay.[14]

As a second observation of a general order I should like to call attention to the diversity of the iconographic programs of mortuary chapels or of crypts. In the crypt of the church of Hosios Loukas in Phocis, where the important members of the monastic community were buried, the Deesis is represented in the apse, whereas scenes from the Passion and the Resurrection (from the Entry into Jerusalem to the Incredulity of Thomas) and the Dormition of the Virgin decorate the walls.[15] In the crypt of the mortuary church of Bačkovo, in Bulgaria, erected in 1083 by Gregory Pakourianos, the Deesis again occupies the apse, Ezekiel's vision of the dry bones is painted on the west wall, and the figures of holy bishops and other saints appear on the vaults and on the lower register of the walls. The narthex of the crypt is entirely decorated with the composition of the Last Judgment.[16] The typicon of the Monastery of Christ Pantocrator, in Constantinople, written in 1136, contains interesting information about the central church, dedicated to the archangel Michael. This was the funerary chapel of the Comnenian rulers; later, some of the Palaeologi also were buried there.[17] In the apse, above the altar—designated in the typicon as the holy sepulcher of the Lord—Christ appearing to the Holy Women was represented; the Crucifixion and the Anastasis were depicted in the side apses.[18] All these paintings stressed, in different ways, the funerary character of the building; but no such intent can be discerned in the mosaics of the parecclesion of the Pammakaristos in Constantinople, which was erected after the death of the Protostrator Michael Glabas Doukas Tarchaniotes, before 1315, by his wife Maria as a mausoleum in which to place his tomb, and later the tombs of other members of the family.[19] Once again the Deesis is at the east end, but for the rest the iconographic program is the one normally used in churches. The Pantocrator

12 A. K. Orlandos, "Fresques byzantines du monastère de Patmos," *CA*, 12 (1961), pp. 285–302; idem, Ἡ τράπεζα τῆς ἐν Πάτμῳ μονῆς Ἁγίου Ἰωάννου τοῦ Θεολόγου, Part I: Ἀρχιτεκτονική, Δωδεκανησιακὸν Ἀρχεῖον, 3 (Athens, 1958), pp. 3–8.
13 Vol. I of this series, p. 189.
14 R. Hamann-MacLean and H. Hallensleben, *Die Monumentalmalerei in Serbien und Makedonien, vom 11. bis zum frühen 14. Jahrhundert*, I (Giessen, 1963), plan 23; H. Hallensleben, *Die Malerschule des Königs Milutin* (Giessen, 1963), pp. 44–45.
15 G. A. Soteriou, "Peintures murales byzantines du XIe siècle dans la crypte de Saint Luc," *Actes du IIIe Congrès international des études byzantines* (Athens, 1932), pp. 389–400.

16 A. Grabar, *La peinture religieuse en Bulgarie* (Paris, 1928), pp. 55–57, 59–60.
17 Al. Dmitrievskij, *Opisanie liturgičeskix rukopisej*, I. Τυπικά (Kiev, 1895), pp. 680–81.
18 Ibid., p. 678.
19 The year of Michael's death is not precisely known. See C. Mango and E. J. W. Hawkins, "Report on Field Work in Istanbul and Cyprus, 1962–1963," *DOP*, 18 (1964), p. 330 and n. 35, 36. See also P. A. Underwood, "Notes on the Work of the Byzantine Institute in Istanbul," *DOP*, 9 and 10 (1956), pp. 298 ff.; idem, *DOP* 14 (1960), pp. 215 ff.; and A. H. S. Megaw, *DOP*, 17 (1963), pp. 367 ff.

and the prophets appear in the dome; the "feast cycle," of which only the Baptism now remains, was represented in the lunettes of the vaulting bays of the arms; and the remaining part of the decoration consists of single figures of bishops, *hosioi*, and the four archangels.

The variety in the decorative schemes of funerary chapels or crypts, evidenced by the examples just examined, shows that there was considerable freedom in the elaboration of an iconographic program. The one devised for the parecclesion of the Kariye Djami is remarkable for its inner cohesion, and I shall examine it more closely now, considering the choice of subjects and the places assigned to them in the building, leaving for the end the iconographic study of the different themes.

The decoration of the lower zone (PL. 474, 475) conforms, in its main features, to the system adopted in churches when fresco paintings replaced mosaics: the entire surface of the walls was covered and the images of the saints were transferred from the vaults and arches to the lower register of the nave walls. The Church Fathers are, as usual, on the semicircular wall of the apse, and in the absence of piers (between which the iconostasis was customarily placed) the Virgin embracing the Child is painted on the south end of the bema wall. On the north end there must have been the corresponding figure of Christ, now destroyed.

The Anastasis (PL. 341) or Harrowing of Hell is rarely represented in the apse, although in some symbolical interpretations of the church, as well as in the liturgy, the apse is considered as an image of the sepulcher of Christ and the altar is said to figure his tomb.[20] The paintings of the New Church of Tokali, in Cappadocia, reflect these ideas: the Crucifixion is in the conch of the apse, and four scenes of the Passion and the Resurrection, namely the Descent from the Cross, the Entombment, the Holy Women at the Sepulcher, and the Anastasis, are painted on the semicircular wall.[21] At the church of the Holy Sepulcher in Jerusalem, restored by the Crusaders, the Anastasis was in the apse of the Rotunda.[22] The influence of the Holy Sepulcher may be detected in two small edifices of the Latin Orient: the church of Abou Gosh, about 12 kilometers to the west of Jerusalem, erected during the second half of the twelfth century;[23] and the church of St. Phocas at Amioun, south of Tripoli, in Lebanon, where the Harrowing of Hell was represented in the apse.[24] This influence is even more likely in the case of the monumental composition that once adorned the apse of the cathedral of Ravenna, dedicated to the Resurrection and commonly designated as the Ursiana from the name of Bishop Orso, who restored it in 1112. The engravings made in 1741 by Gian-Francesco Buonamici show that the Anastasis, flanked by the representations of the Holy Women at the Sepulcher and the Visit of Peter and John to the Sepulcher, filled the conch of the apse.[25]

These medieval examples show the survival of the early tradition of the martyria of the

20 F. E. Brightman, "The *Historia Mystagogica* and Other Greek Commentaries on the Byzantine Liturgy," *The Journal of Theological Studies*, 9 (1907–08), p. 258; *PG*, 98, col. 388C-D; S. Petrides, "Traités liturgiques de Saint Maxime et de Saint Germain traduits par Anastase le Bibliothécaire," *ROC*, 10 (1905), pp. 309–10; A. Grabar, *Martyrium; Recherches sur le culte des reliques et l'art chrétien antique* (Paris, 1946), II, p. 273.

21 G. de Jerphanion, *Une nouvelle province de l'art byzantin: Les églises rupestres de Cappadoce* (Paris, 1925–42), I,2 pp. 312, 345–49. and PL. 84, 85. At the Catholicon of Lavra, the Anastasis fills the conch of the north transept; Millet, *Athos*, PL. 129.

22 H. Vincent and F. M. Abel, *Jérusalem: Recherches de topographie, d'archéologie et d'histoire*, II (Paris, 1914), pp. 253, 262; description given by Theodoric in his *Libellus de locis sanctis*, ibid., p. 288. The Anastasis may already have been represented in the eastern apse of the rotunda if the mosaics mentioned by the Russian pilgrim Daniel (who visited Jerusalem

in 1107), which include an "apotheosis of Adam," are those executed during the restorations undertaken by Constantine Monomachos and completed in 1048, rather than those of the Crusaders; S. P. de Khitrovo, ed. and tr., *Itinéraires russes en Orient* (Société de l'Orient Latin, Publications, Série géographique, V; Geneva, 1889), p. 12. Vincent and Abel (pp. 252–53) also interpret as an Anastasis the scene described by the Persian traveler Nâsiri Khosrau, who visited Jerusalem in 1047.

23 Ch. Diehl, "Les fresques de l'église d'Abou-Gosch," *Comptes-rendus des séances de l'Académie des Inscriptions et Belles-Lettres* (Paris, 1924), pp. 89–96.

24 Ch. Virolleaud, "Les travaux archéologiques en Syrie en 1922–23," *Syria*, V (1924), pp. 117–18.

25 G. Gerola, "Il mosaico absidiale della Ursiana," *Felix Ravenna*, No. 5 (1912), pp. 177–90. G. Galassi, *Roma o Bisanzio*, I (Rome [1930]), pp. 250–57, PL. CXXXIV-CXXXVI, and Fig. 145.

holy sites, where the particular event in the life of Christ that was commemorated was represented in the apse.[26] But since the apse and the altar symbolically represent the sepulcher and Golgotha, an image of the Crucifixion or of the Anastasis could be represented in the apse of any church; and this symbolism is specifically recalled in the typicon of the church of the Pantocrator, as we have seen. Moreover, an image of the Resurrection was particularly suited to a mortuary chapel. At the parecclesion of the Kariye the Resurrection theme has been further developed by the placing on the bema arch of the Raising of the Widow's Son and the Raising of the Daughter of Jairus (PL. 360, 363).

These two scenes seem not to have been included among the many miracles in the narthexes, a large number of which are miracles of healing. Byzantine commentators of the Gospels marked the distinction between the different kinds of miracles. In the Homily on the Widow's Son, published under the name of Theophanes Cerameus, it is stated that Christ began his ministry by performing simple miracles in order to arouse the faith of the people, and he gradually led them to the mystery of the Resurrection, which was revealed by the raising of the widow's son.[27] The patriarch John IX Agapetus (1111–39) considered the relation of the miracles of resurrection to the final Resurrection.[28] He first listed three Old Testament miracles: the widow's son raised by Elijah (III Kings 17:17–24); the son of the Shunammite woman raised by Elisha (IV Kings 4:32–37); and the resurrection of the man whose body touched the bones of Elisha (IV Kings 13:21). He next mentioned five miracles of resurrection from the New Testament: those of the widow's son at Nain; the daughter of Jairus; Lazarus; the dead who came to life at the time of the Crucifixion; Christ's resurrection. These eight miracles mean, he added, that the general resurrection of the dead will take place in the eighth age.

The grouping of the scenes at the parecclesion corresponds to these ideas. Frescoes of two of the resurrection miracles performed by Christ flank the representation of his own resurrection —that is, his descent to Hell to redeem the souls of the righteous—and these two scenes lead to the final resurrection of the dead, deployed on the vault and on the lunettes, bringing a message of hope to the faithful who walk in the paths of God. Because of the inner association between the events which had taken place in the past and those which were to take place at the end of time, the Last Judgment, usually represented in the western end of the nave, or in the narthex, was brought over to the eastern bay.

The promise of salvation is echoed in a composition placed above the arched passageway to the narthex (PL. 469, 470): infants in swaddling clothes are held in the Hand of God issuing from the arc of heaven. This literal interpretation of the words of Solomon, "the souls of the righteous are in the hand of God" (Wisd. of Sol. 3:1), is sometimes introduced into the composition of the Last Judgment, as we shall see in the iconographic study; at the parecclesion it has been placed where it could be seen by anyone leaving the chapel. A troparion sung at the beginning of Lent also suggests this association with the Last Judgment. "Every thing is in Thy hand, O Lord, every thing that Thou hast ordained in advance. Those who have been dissolved into the four elements, mayst Thou recompense at Thy coming and raise up, forgiving them all their trespasses, whether unknowingly, or knowingly committed."[29]

---

26 Grabar, *Martyrium*, II, pp. 159–68 and passim.

27 *PG*, 132, cols. 217–35.

28 *PG*, 120, cols. 1201–09, under the name John Xiphilinus. For the attribution to John Agapetus cf. H.-G. Beck, *Kirche und*

theologische Literatur im byzantinischen Reich (Munich, 1959), pp. 630–31.

29 G. Millet, *La dalmatique du Vatican: Les élus, images et croyances* (Paris, 1945), p. 60; Τριώδιον κατανυκτικόν (Rome, 1879), p. 22.

The idea of redemption, developed in the eastern bay, is also implicit in the decoration of the western bay, which is entirely devoted to the Virgin. For salvation came to mankind through the Incarnation, and the Virgin, "the instrument of the Incarnation," is exalted as such in the prayers recited during the feasts of the Birth of the Virgin, the Annunciation, and the Nativity; her pre-eminent role in the redemption of mankind—the "new Eve" wiping away the sin of the "old Eve"—is constantly recalled. It is by her that insolent Hell has been trampled under foot so that, together with all her race, Eve will enter a life without perils.[30] Mary is hailed as the reconciliation of Adam and the consolation of Eve; in one of the Odes, Mary herself is made to exclaim: "Let the condemnation of Eve be now abolished by me; let the debt be now remitted by me." [31] In the prayers recited on the feast of the Nativity thanks are rendered to her, the Mother of God and Virgin, who, having given birth to the Savior, has wiped away the ancient curse of Eve.[32]

In the dome of the western bay the celestial host surrounds the medallion figures of the Virgin and Child; four hymnographers, placed in the pendentives, hold scrolls that bear excerpts from the hymns they composed in her honor (PL. 408). Her role in the reconciliation between God and man is recalled on the scroll held by Joseph the Poet (PL. 430, 436 c), "Propitiation of the world, hail, spotless Virgin," while the other inscriptions refer to the funerary function of the parecclesion. On the scroll held by John Damascene are written the opening words of his Idiomela for the Funeral Service: "What joy of life remains without its share of sorrow"; and the inscription on the book of Theophanes is taken from the sixth Ode of his Canon for the Funeral Service for Laymen: "We were turned back to the earth after having transgressed God's divine commandment." [33]

The Painter's Manual of Mount Athos recommends decorating one of the domes of the narthex with the medallion of the Virgin and Child, borne by angels and surrounded by the prophets, and placing on the pendentives the hymnographers with appropriate words written on their books or scrolls.[34] But already in the twelfth century, and frequently from that time on, the portraits of the hymnographers appear next to the portraits of the Virgin or scenes from her life. John of Damascus and Cosmas of Maiuma, each carrying a long scroll inscribed with excerpts from the canon he has written for the death of the Virgin, stand at the sides of the composition of the Dormition.[35] In the outer narthex of the Kariye, in the soffit of the arcosolium of Tomb E, the portraits of these same two hymnographers flank the Virgin with the Christ Child and the inscriptions on their scrolls quote the incipits of their chants for the funeral services for monks.[36]

The medallion of the Virgin and the Christ Child in the northern dome of the inner narthex at the Kariye Djami (PL. 66–84) is surrounded by the Virgin's kingly ancestors in the upper zone and, in the lower zone, by prophets and other righteous men who foretold the Incarnation or who have been considered as prefigurations of Christ and for this reason were designated as

30 F. Mercenier and G. Bainbridge, *La prière des églises de rite byzantin*, II,1, 2d ed. [Gembloux, 1953], p. 83.

31 Ibid., pp. 350, 363.

32 Ibid., pp. 217, 228.

33 P. A. Underwood, Vol. 1 of this series, p. 217.

34 Dionysius of Fourna, Ἑρμηνεία τῆς ζωγραφικῆς τέχνης, ed. A. Papadopoulos-Kerameus (St. Petersburg, 1909), p. 220.

35 For instance at Bačkovo and Boïana in Bulgaria; Grabar, *La peinture religieuse*, pp. 79–80 and PL. IV; idem, *L'église de Boïana: Architecture, peinture* (Sofia, 1924), p. 48 and PL. XXIX,2. Such examples occur more frequently in later periods, for in-

stance at the Holy Apostles in Salonika and the church of the Savior at Verroia (A. Xyngopoulos, Ἡ ψηφιδωτὴ διακόσμησις τοῦ ναοῦ τῶν Ἁγίων Ἀποστόλων Θεσσαλονίκης [Salonika, 1953], pp. 49–50 and PL. 321, and idem, *Thessalonique et la peinture macédonienne* [Athens, 1955], PL. 10); in numerous churches in Bulgaria (Grabar, *La peinture religieuse*, PL. XL, L, LVIII); and on Mount Athos (Millet, *Athos*, PL. 132,1, 133,2, 163,1, 170–71, 176,2, 197,2, 226,1–2, 261,1).

36 Underwood, Vol. 1 of this series, pp. 282–83, and Vol. 3, PL. 540, 544, 545.

"other ancestors who are outside the genealogy." Two of these figures carry attributes that are "types" of the Virgin: Moses, a vessel with the image of the Virgin, a vessel that represents the stamnos or pot of manna; and Aaron, the flowering rod (PL. 82). The typology of the Virgin merely suggested in these mosaics of the dome is fully developed in the frescoes of the parecclesion by means of biblical scenes.

This cycle begins in the eastern bay, on the western half of the southern lunette, and it continues in the vaults and on the southern and northern lunettes of the western bay. Four consecutive scenes show the ark of the covenant and the sacred vessels brought into Solomon's temple, in the presence of the King and all Israel, and placed in the Holy of Holies (PL. 454–60). These are followed by other typological representations: Isaiah prophesying the slaughter of the Assyrian army (PL. 461–65); the high priests before the altar (PL. 466–68); Jacob's vision of the ladder and his wrestling with the angel (PL. 437–43); and finally Moses before the burning bush (PL. 444–52).

From the very beginning of Christian exegesis the events recounted in the Old Testament were frequently interpreted as prefiguration of what was to be fulfilled with the coming of Christ. Many of the heroes of the Old Testament were considered as types of Christ, and in the monumental art of the Early Christian period biblical scenes referring to Christ and to his Passion, for instance the Hospitality of Abraham and the Sacrifice of Isaac, were represented in the bema, as we see them at S. Vitale in Ravenna. Monuments such as St. Sophia at Ohrid in Yugoslavia and some of the Cappadocian churches show the survival of this type of symbolic representation during the Middle Byzantine period;[37] in the Palaeologan era this practice was further developed. However, the pictorial counterparts of the Mariological typology do not appear in monumental art before the age of the Palaeologi, although from the fourth century on, and increasingly as the special feasts of the Virgin were established, the biblical typology was also applied to Mary in homiletic texts, in the hymns and canons composed in her honor.[38]

The earliest preserved examples of an imagery corresponding to the ideas expressed in these writings occur in the psalters with marginal illustrations of the ninth century, where Mary is identified with Mount Sion and with Jerusalem. The medallion figure of the Virgin and Child is painted on the summit of Mount Sion or next to a church erected on this mountain; or again in front of the walls of Jerusalem, above which rise a tower and a large church designated as the Holy Sion.[39] As an illustration of Psalm 68[67]:16, "this is the hill which God desireth to dwell in; yea, the Lord will dwell in it for ever," the artist has represented David pointing to the image of the Virgin and Child on the summit of Mount Sion, while Daniel, reclining on a bed, looks at the stone that has fallen from the mount.[40] This composition refers to Daniel's explanation of Nebuchadnezzar's dream (Dan. 2:34–35), interpreted in Christian exegesis as

37 P. Miljković-Pepek, "Matériaux sur l'art macédonien du moyen-âge: Les fresques du sanctuaire de Sainte-Sophie d'Ochrid" (in Serbian with French résumé), *Recueil des travaux (1955–1956)* (*Publications du Musée Archéologique—Skopje*), I (1956), pp. 37–70 and PL. I–XXXI; A. Grabar, "Les peintures murales dans le choeur de Sainte-Sophie d'Ohrid," *CA*, 15 (1965), pp. 257–65; Jerphanion, *Cappadoce*, I, pp. 325, 384, 409, 441, 461, 530, and PL. 128,1, 139,1; II, pp. 133, 257.

38 Dom B. Capelle, "Typologie mariale chez les Pères et dans la liturgie," *Les questions liturgiques et paroissiales*, 35 (Louvain, 1954), pp. 109–21; G. G. Meersseman, "Virgo a Doctoribus Praetitulata: Die marianischen Litaneien als dogmengeschichtliche Quellen," *Freiburger Zeitschrift für Philosophie und Theologie*, I (1954), pp. 129–78; R. Laurentin, *Maria, Ecclesia, Sacerdotium: Essai sur le développement d'une idée religieuse*,

I (Paris, 1952)—see especially the bibliography of the early sources in the footnotes of pp. 34–39; Th. Maertens, "Le développement liturgique et biblique du culte de la Vierge," *Paroisse et liturgie*, 1954, No. 4, pp. 225–49; A. Kniazeff, "La Théotokos dans les offices byzantins du temps pascal," *Irénikon*, 34 (1961), No. 1, pp. 21–24. For a list of the epithets of the Virgin in Byzantine hymns, see S. Eustratiades, Ἡ Θεοτόκος ἐν τῇ ὑμνογραφίᾳ (Paris, 1930).

39 A. Grabar, *L'iconoclasme byzantin: Dossier archéologique* (Paris, 1957), Fig. 148. S. Dufrenne, *L'illustration des psautiers grecs du moyen âge*, (Paris, 1966), PL. 18, fol. 121.

40 Grabar, *L'iconoclasme*, p. 199 and Fig. 147. The corresponding miniature of the Psalter at Mount Athos, Pantocratoros 61, does not have the image of the Virgin; Dufrenne, *Psautiers grecs*, PL. 11, fol. 83v.

a type of the Incarnation. For instance, John of Damascus wrote in his first homily on the Dormition of the Virgin: "What is this mountain of Daniel, from which the cornerstone, Christ, was detached without the intervention of a human instrument? Was it not you who conceived without impregnation and always remained a virgin?" [41] In the Psalter of the British Museum, known as the Bristol Psalter, the image of the Virgin does not appear on the mountain; but one of the accompanying inscriptions explains that the mountain is the Theotokos, and the stone, Christ.[42]

Typological images of the Virgin appear more frequently in the following centuries. In the two illustrated copies of the Homilies on the Virgin, composed by the monk James of the monastery of Kokkinobaphos (Parisinus gr. 1208 and Vaticanus gr. 1162), the full-page miniatures, placed as frontispieces before each one of the homilies, differ from the narrative scenes which illustrate the text, and they represent each time a biblical scene.[43] Jacob's vision of the ladder precedes the sermon on the Birth of Mary; Moses before the burning bush, the sermon on the Presentation of the Virgin. Moses distributing the rods to the high priests and Aaron's blossoming rod are used as a frontispiece for the sermon on the Visitation; and the miracle of Gideon's fleece, for that of the Annunciation. The last miniature of this series, placed before the homily on the Betrothal of the Virgin, represents Christ reclining on a bed and surrounded by angels in military costume, an image inspired by the Song of Solomon, 3:7: "Behold his bed, which is Solomon's; threescore valiant men are about it, of the valiant of Israel." As we shall see in the iconographic study of those scenes which also occur in the parecclesion, the Marian symbolism is not always stressed in the actual details, but the intent is obvious in the selection of the subjects, and particularly in the last miniature, where Christ and not Solomon has been represented.[44]

The illustrations of the *Topography* of Cosmas Indicopleustes as seen in the manuscript of the Evangelical School in Smyrna, a manuscript destroyed by fire in 1922, bear evidence of the growing interest in the typological imagery of the Virgin.[45] According to Cosmas, the tabernacle erected by Moses was the model of the universe; he therefore gave a detailed description of the ark, the tabernacle, and all the sacred vessels. In the ninth-century manuscript of the Vatican Library, and in the later copies in Florence and on Mount Sinai, the miniatures depict the objects as they are described and no symbolical meaning is attached to them or to the personages and events of the Old and New Testaments represented in the other sections, beyond what is already set forth in the text. However, in the Smyrna manuscript the symbolic image sometimes accompanies that of the object itself or replaces it. Three miniatures of the enthroned Virgin and Child follow one another, and the meaning of this image is explained each time by the accompanying verses or by the title inscribed above it. In the first Mary is the antitype of Noah's ark, for she gave birth to Christ, who washed away sin and stilled the waves.[46] In the second she is the "tabernacle of God and the Logos, the ark gilded by the Holy Ghost." [47] In the third she is the τράπεζα, the costly table "that bore the celestial bread of life." [48] In the two miniatures which

41 *PG*, 96, col. 713B (see also col. 756B); V. A. Mitchel, *The Mariology of Saint John Damascene* (Kirkwood, Mo., 1930).

42 Dufrenne, *Psautiers grecs*, p. 60 and PL. 53, fol. 105v.

43 C. Stornajolo, *Miniature delle omilie di Giacomo monaco (Cod. Vatic. gr. 1162) e dell' evangeliario greco urbinate (Cod. Vatic. Urbin. gr. 2)* (Codices e Vaticanis selecti . . . , Series Minor, I; Rome, 1910), PL. 7, 21, 32, 46, 58; H. Omont, *Miniatures des homélies sur la Vierge du moine Jacques (ms. grec 1208 de Paris)* (Société Française de Reproductions de Manuscrits à Peintures, Album, 11; Paris, 1927), PL. IV,1, X,1, XIV,1, XVIII,2, XXIII,1.

44 S. Der Nersessian, "Le Lit de Salomon," *ZRVI*, 8,1 (1963) (= *Mélanges Georges Ostrogorsky*, I), pp. 77–82 and Figs. 1–3; A. Xyngopoulos, "Au sujet d'une fresque de l'église Saint-Clément d'Ohrid," ibid., pp. 301–06 and Figs. 1–3.

45 J. Strzygowski, *Der Bilderkreis des griechischen Physiologus des Kosmas Indikopleustes und Oktateuch nach Handschriften der Bibliothek zu Smyrna* (Leipzig, 1899).

46 Ibid., p. 56 and PL. XXV.

47 Ibid., pp. 56–57 and PL. XXVI.

48 Ibid., p. 57 and PL. XXVII.

follow, her image is added to that of the object itself. In the first, as the "lamp of living light shining upon those in darkness," she is seated with the Christ Child, above the seven-branched candlestick; in the second her image appears above the altar on which Aaron's rod is placed.[49] In the composition of Moses before the burning bush, once again the image of the Virgin and Child is depicted above the scene,[50] The enthroned Hodegetria is represented above the stamnos, the vase which contained the manna, since she is hailed as the "gold stamnos . . . which contains Christ, the celestial manna and the pure nourishment of the world." Finally, in the miniature that groups several of the sacred objects of the tabernacle—the stamnos, the tables of the law, and Aaron's rod, the Virgin with the infant Jesus on her left arm is depicted in the lunette of the architectural frame.[51]

A beautiful icon at the Monastery of St. Catherine on Mount Sinai, which may be dated in the twelfth century, provides us with an early example of the iconographic theme of the Virgin and Child surrounded by prophets (Fig. 1), designated in the Painter's Manual as Ἄνωθεν οἱ προφῆται (the prophets of old), from the opening words of the chant.[52] The composition of the icon is rich in symbolic ideas, but we shall consider here only the images of the prophets painted on the side compartments, holding inscribed scrolls and accompanied almost always by the objects which were considered as types of the Virgin.[53] In the second compartment on the left we see Aaron and Moses, the latter pointing to the burning bush. Ezekiel and David are represented in the fourth compartment; the "closed door" is placed next to Ezekiel, and a small building in front of David. Balaam pointing to the star and Habakkuk standing next to a mountain occupy the last compartment on the left. Jacob and his vision of the ladder fill the second compartment on the right; in the fourth compartment we see the cherub touching Isaiah's lips with the live coal and Daniel standing next to the mountain from which a stone has been detached. The last compartment has portraits of Solomon and of Gideon; next to the latter the fleece has been represented. All these figures are the ones mentioned in the Painter's Manual, and the accompanying objects are the types by which each one of the prophets announced the Virgin, although judging from the inscriptions on the scrolls held by Aaron and Moses, which can be deciphered on the reproduction, the texts themselves differ from the distichs given in the Painter's Manual.[54]

It is possible that during the eleventh and twelfth centuries, when the narrative cycle of the Virgin was developed in monumental art, there were some typological compositions as well, as there were in Western Europe. No such scenes are known so far, but the possibility may be envisaged, in view of the existence of this type of imagery in manuscripts and on icons. However, it is during the Palaeologan period that such representations do appear. The enlarged iconographic programs of the churches and the renewed fervor of the cult of the Virgin explain the spread of these typological scenes, as well as of the illustrations of such hymns as the Akathistos or the Christmas sticheron. The decree promulgated in 1297 by Andronicus II, whereby the feast of the Dormition was to be celebrated throughout the month of August in the principal churches of Constantinople, is one of the many indications of the development of the cult of the Virgin during the Palaeologan period.[55]

49 Ibid., p. 57 and PL. XXVIII.
50 Ibid., p. 58 and PL. XXIX.
51 Ibid., p. 59.
52 Ἑρμηνεία, p. 146.
53 G. and M. Soteriou, Icônes du Mont Sinaï, I (Athens, 1956), Figs. 54–55, and II (Athens, 1958), pp. 73–75.

54 It should be noted that the inscriptions listed on p. 146 of the Painter's Manual also differ from the verses listed on p. 282.
55 V. Grumel, "Le mois de Marie des Byzantins," Echos d'Orient, 31 (1932), pp. 257–61; J. Verpeaux, Nicéphore Choumnos, homme d'état et humaniste byzantin (ca. 1250/1255–1327) (Paris, 1959), p. 94.

The earliest extant example of the biblical prefigurations of the Virgin known so far appears to be the decoration of the north porch of the church of St. Sophia in Trebizond. The paintings are in the same style as those of the nave, which have been assigned a date ca. 1260.[56] The Tree of Jesse decorates the eastern half of the vault and most of the east wall. Jacob's vision of the ladder, his struggle with the angel, and the burning bush have been represented on the north wall, and below are the portraits of Job and of Gideon. The paintings of the south wall are less well preserved, but among the fragments it has been possible to recognize the Hospitality of Abraham. On the west wall there is a large composition which it has not been possible to identify exactly. The Hospitality of Abraham is more directly connected with the typology of Christ himself, but Jacob's vision and the burning bush are two of the prefigurations of the Virgin most frequently represented, and the Tree of Jesse also occurs in other ensembles connected with Mary.

If the fragmentary condition of the paintings of St. Sophia prevents us from getting a clear idea of the general program, we have, in the narthex of the church of St. Clement in Ohrid, a church formerly dedicated to the Virgin Peribleptos and decorated in 1295, a complete example of a coherent ensemble. The large figure of the winged Christ, or *Christos–Angelos*, enclosed in a mandorla borne by four angels, occupies the crown of the domical vault, and the prophets Ezekiel and Habakkuk stand in two of the pendentives. Christ holds a scroll with the inscription, "Today salvation to the world, to the visible and to the invisible." [57] The salvation thus announced has come to mankind through the Incarnation, and the painting above the door leading into the nave illustrates the Christmas sticheron, which begins with the words: "What shall we offer, O Christ, to thee who hast appeared on earth as a man." The entire creation offers its gifts to the enthroned Virgin and Child, in accordance with the words of the sticheron: "The angels bring thee the hymn; the heavens, the star; the magi, their gifts; the shepherds, the admiration; the earth, the cave; the desert, the manger; and we, the Virgin Mother." [58]

The scenes painted above the entrance door and on the walls of the narthex honor Mary, through whom Christ assumed a human body, and symbolically recall her role in the economy of salvation as the instrument of the Incarnation. These scenes are Moses before the burning bush; Jacob's vision of the ladder;[59] Nebuchadnezzar's dream of the stone detached from the mountain and Daniel explaining its meaning;[60] the Tabernacle of Moses; the "closed door"; Wisdom who has built her house and invited all men to eat of her bread and drink of her wine;[61] and the icon of the Virgin and Child placed on a bed around which stands a company of armed men. Several of these typological compositions had been represented in manuscripts, as already mentioned, though according to different iconographic formulas: the stone detached from the mountain appears in the Psalters; the burning bush, Jacob's ladder, and the Tabernacle in the Homilies of the Monk James Kokkinobaphos. But the greater emphasis on the Marian typology in the paintings of St. Clement's becomes apparent when the last composition listed above is compared with the miniature of the Homilies representing Christ on Solomon's bed. For the

56 D. Talbot Rice, ed., *The Church of Haghia Sophia at Trebizond* (Edinburgh, 1968), pp. 149–55, 182–83, 243–44; Figs. 112, 114, 115; PL. 63–66.

57 S. Der Nersessian, "Note sur quelques images se rattachant au thème du Christ-ange," *CA*, 13 (1962), pp. 209–16; G. Millet and A. Frolow, *La peinture du Moyen-Âge en Yougoslavie (Serbie, Macédoine et Monténégro)*, III (Paris, 1962), PL. 15.

58 Millet and Frolow, *Peinture*, III, PL. 14; Millet, *Recherches sur l'iconographie de l'Evangile aux XIVᵉ, XVᵉ, et XVIᵉ siècles*

(Paris, 1916, reprinted 1960), pp. 163–69.

59 D. Kiornakov [Čornakov], *The Frescoes of the Church of St. Clement at Ochrid* (Belgrade, 1961), Fig. 6.

60 Millet and Frolow, *Peinture*, III, PL. 13,1. V. R. Petković, *La peinture serbe du Moyen Âge*, II (Belgrade, 1934), PL. CXXII-CXXIII.

61 Millet and Frolow, *Peinture*, III, PL. 13,2; J. Meyendorff, "L'iconographie de la Sagesse divine dans la tradition byzantine," *CA*, 10 (1959), pp. 259–77.

icon placed on the bed expresses the idea that Mary is the nuptial bed where the union between the divine Logos and the human nature took place.[62]

A different program was adopted in 1308 at the church of Bogorodica Ljeviška at Prizren, in Yugoslavia. In the north bay of the outer narthex the following scenes are painted on the vault and the lunette: the Tree of Jesse; Jacob's vision of the ladder and his struggle with the angel (Fig. 2); a composition inspired by the canon of Cosmas sung on the feast of the Dormition. Next to the empty tomb from which the Virgin has risen and ascends to heaven stand groups of maidens holding musical instruments and singing.[63] In addition to these scenes the portraits of the prophets, accompanied each time by the type of the Virgin by which they prophesied her, decorate the soffit of the arch, next to the image of the Virgin painted in the lunette of the door leading to the church. In the southern half of the arch appear Aaron, with the vase and the flowering rod; Solomon and a temple with seven columns; Jacob and the ladder; Jeremiah and the closed door; Zechariah with a censer; Zechariah again and the seven-branched candlestick. On the northern half of the arch are Moses and the burning bush; David and the tabernacle adorned with the image of the Virgin; Daniel and the mountain; Habakkuk and a small boat with the Christ Child inside it; Isaiah and the seraphim; Balaam and the star.[64]

Still another selection of biblical scenes decorates the south arm of the outer narthex of the Holy Apostles in Salonika. The Tree of Jesse covers the entire height of the east wall. The Tabernacle of Moses (Fig. 3) is painted in the north lunette of the east bay, and opposite, on the small tympanum above the windows, is Gideon wringing the fleece on which the dew has fallen.[65] The domical vault of this bay is divided into four sections by means of red lines radiating from the central medallion of the Virgin and Child. Jacob's vision of the ladder fills the northeast section. In the southeast section Moses is represented first loosening the strings of his sandal and next standing, turned to the right. The paint has fallen off from the area where the burning bush was most probably depicted. The compositions of the two western sections are greatly damaged, but, as we shall see below, they may have represented the high priests before the altar and Solomon's temple.

It is possible that in other parts of the south arm of the outer narthex there were additional biblical scenes or figures which are either destroyed or still under the coat of plaster. In the northwest pendentive of the south dome is a painting of Habakkuk holding a scroll,[66] like the portrait of the same prophet in the pendentive of the narthex vault of St. Clement at Ohrid; in the southwest pendentive two men stand in front of an architectural background. In the south lunette of this bay a man, kneeling, raises his hands to receive an open scroll which projects from the arc of heaven; the composition suggests Ezekiel's vision by the river Chebar, during which he was told to eat the roll (Ezek. 2:9–3:3). The illustration of the Christmas hymn, which at Ohrid was grouped with the prefigurations of the Virgin, has been moved to the north arm of the

62 Der Nersessian, "Le Lit de Salomon," pp. 79–80.

63 Hamann-MacLean and Hallensleben, *Die Monumentalmalerei,* I, plan 23, Nos. 218, 219; R. Hamann-MacLean, *Aus der mittelalterlichen Bildwelt Jugoslawiens: Einzelheiten des Freskenzyklus der Kirche der Gottesmutter von Leviša in Prizren* (Marburg an der Lahn, 1955), Figs. 16 and 36. The troparion of the first Ode of the Dormition says that all the faithful are assembled in joy, Miriam intones, and all, with choirs and tambourines, sing the Only Son. In the troparion of the second Ode, the young virgins are called upon to sing, with Miriam, a farewell ode to the Virgin, the only Mother of God, who is carried away to her celestial heritage; F. Mercenier and G.

Bainbridge, *La prière,* II, 2, 2d. ed. [Gembloux, 1953], pp. 427–28.

64 I wish to thank Miss Gordana Babić for the information concerning these portraits. The names of the prophets are those inscribed next to them, but these identifications and the inscriptions on the scrolls do not always agree with the biblical text or with the legends prescribed by the Painter's Manual; G. Babić, "L'image symbolique de la porte fermée à Saint Clément d'Ohrid," *Synthronon: Art et archéologie de la fin de l'antiquité et du moyen-âge* (Paris, 1968), p. 150.

65 Xyngopoulos, *Thessalonique,* PL. 19.

66 Ibid., PL. 3,2.

narthex at Salonika and painted above the side door of the south wall, which opens into the nave.[67]

In the outer narthex of the church of the Virgin at Peć, in Yugoslavia, decorated around 1334, six prophets, holding scrolls and pointing to the symbols by which they predicted the Virgin, stand in the soffit of the arch to the south of the entrance door, above which appears the image of the Virgin Hodegetria. These prophets and their symbols are Aaron and the vase; Solomon and the temple with seven columns; Jacob and the ladder; Ezekiel and the closed door;[68] Zechariah and the burning bush; Zechariah, again, and the seven-branched candlestick.

In the narthex of the church of Lesnovo in Yugoslavia, decorated immediately after its construction in 1349, all the prefigurations of the Virgin, with the exception of Gideon wringing the fleece depicted on the north face of the southwest pier, are grouped on the east piers and the east vault, at the sides of the image of the Virgin, Fountain of Life (Πηγὴ τῆς Ζωῆς). They represent Jacob's vision and his struggle with the angel; the tabernacle; Moses before the burning bush; the interpretation of Ezekiel's vision of the closed door (44:2–3); and the sacred vessels of the tabernacle.[69]

A fragmentary composition representing Ezekiel's prophecy of the closed door was recently discovered on the south facade of the church of St. Mary Pammakaristos (Fethiye Djami) in Istanbul; this scene probably formed part of a cycle of biblical prefigurations that has been destroyed.[70]

In this general survey I have considered only those monuments in which these typological images appear in the narthex or on the facade. For when they are represented in the prothesis or in the bema, as at the Protaton and Dochiariou on Mount Athos, or at Dečani and Gračanica in Yugoslavia, their connection with Christ has been stressed rather than that with the Virgin.[71] Sometimes, for instance at Asinou in Cyprus and St. Nicholas Orphanos in Salonika, such images are placed in the nave.[72] On the other hand the Marian typology is stressed in such representations as the Dormition in the church of Staro Nagoričino in Yugoslavia, where prophets holding inscribed scrolls and pointing to the Marian symbols, as at Peć or on the icon of Mount Sinai, are represented above the group of angels standing around the couch of the Virgin.[73]

In comparing the choice of biblical prefigurations at the Kariye with that of other churches, one is impressed by the close adherence of the former to the liturgy, for with the exception of the Slaughter of the Assyrians, which will be discussed below, all the compositions illustrate lessons that are read on Marian feasts. The pericope of the dedication of Solomon's temple (III Kings 8:1–6) is read on the feast of the Presentation of the Virgin. The composition of the priests

67 Ibid., PL. 17.

68 Babić, "L'image symbolique," p. 150 and Fig. 3. I also owe to the kindness of Miss Babić the information concerning the images of the other prophets.

69 N. L. Okunev, "Lesnovo," L'art byzantin chez les Slaves. Dédié à la mémoire de Théodore Uspenskij, I: Les Balkans, Pt. 2 (Paris, 1930), pp. 236 ff. and PL. XXXIV–XXXVII.

70 Mango and Hawkins, "Report on Field Work . . . 1962–1963," pp. 324, 326–27 and Figs. 10, 11.

71 Millet, Athos, PL. 32, 218, 219; V. R. Petković and D. Bošković, Dečani (Belgrade, 1941), Album, PL. CCLXV–CCLXXI. Wisdom who has built her house and Nebuchadnezzar's Dream are in the western bay of the south aisle; the tabernacle of Moses and Gideon's fleece are in the prothesis; Jacob's vision and his struggle with the angel are on the northwest pier of the nave; the Tree of Jesse is on the west wall. Petković, La peinture serbe, I (Belgrade, 1930), PL. 53 a, 54 b, 63 a, II, p. 34 and PL. LX; I. D. Stefanescu, L'illustration des liturgies

dans l'art de Byzance et de l'Orient (Brussels, 1936), pp. 138–39.

72 Rt. Rev. the Bishop of Gibraltar, V. Seymer, W. H. Buckler, and Mrs. W. H. Buckler, "The Church of Asinou, Cyprus, and Its Frescoes," Archaeologia, 83 (1933), p. 344 and PL. XCIV,1; Moses before the burning bush and Ezekiel's prophecy of the closed door are on the east face of the western arch at Asinou, on either side of the Mandylion. At St. Nicholas Orphanos, Moses before the burning bush, represented in the south aisle, is the only extant scene of the prefigurations of the Virgin; A. Xyngopoulos, Οἱ τοιχογραφίες τοῦ Ἁγίου Νικολάου Ὀρφανοῦ Θεσσαλονίκης (Athens, 1964), p. 20 and Fig. 118.

73 Millet and Frolow, Peinture, III, PL. 99; Babić, "L'image symbolique," p. 147, Fig. 2. The prophets and their symbols are, on the left, Gideon and the fleece, Isaiah and the live coal, Ezekiel and the closed door, Moses and the burning bush. On the right are represented Daniel and the mountain, Balaam and the star, David and a boat, Solomon and the temple.

before the altar illustrates the opening verse of the lesson from Ezekiel (43:27–44:3), read on all the Marian feasts. The pericope of Jacob's vision (Gen. 28:10–17) is read on the feasts of the Birth and the Dormition of the Virgin, as well as on the feast of the Annunciation, which is also a Marian feast. The pericope of the burning bush (Exod. 3:1–8) is read twice during the services of the Annunciation. Moreover, the inscriptions that accompany these paintings reproduce the text of the liturgical books and not the wording of the Septuagint.[74]

In the other churches mentioned above, we find, on the contrary, several biblical prefigurations based on texts that are not read on the Marian feasts. The subjects of these scenes are: Gideon's fleece (Judges 6:36–40); Nebuchadnezzar's dream (Dan. 2:31–35); the Tree of Jesse (based on Isa. 11:1); and the icon of the Virgin on Solomon's bed (inspired by the Song of Sol. 3:7–8). The tabernacle of Moses is based on Exodus 25–27; it can however be considered as an illustration of the Epistle to the Hebrews 9:1–7, read on the feast of the Presentation of the Virgin.

Another characteristic feature of the iconographic program of the Kariye is that the dedication of Solomon's temple, which illustrates the pericope read only on the feast of the Presentation, has been depicted in four consecutive scenes (PL. 454–60), and thus developed more than any of the other biblical scenes. One of the underlying ideas of the program thus becomes clear. The ark brought into Solomon's temple and placed on the altar is the type of the Virgin brought into the temple and introduced into the Holy of Holies. The hymns sung on the feast of the Presentation of the Virgin hail Mary as the temple of God, the celestial tabernacle brought into the material temple, the spiritual ark that encompasses the Logos, which cannot be encompassed (τὸν ἀχώρητον λόγον); they celebrate her as the pure Virgin, the only one blessed among women who was offered to the temple of the old dispensation to reside in the Holy of Holies.[75] These same ideas are repeated in the homilies on the Birth or the Presentation of the Virgin, with special insistence on the sanctity of Mary, who, though a woman, resided in the most sacred precinct of the temple, which the high priest himself was allowed to enter only once a year.[76]

The emphasis on Mary as the spiritual ark brought into the material temple, expressed symbolically in the parecclesion, is paralleled by the images and narrative scenes grouped in the central axis of the two narthexes (PL. 119 ff., 228 ff.), where they were immediately seen by the faithful coming into the church. Over the entrance door appears the image of the Virgin with the epithet ἡ χώρα τοῦ ἀχωρήτου (PL. 20). The Presentation of the Virgin occupies the domical vault of the inner narthex. On the eastern half of the southern supporting arch of this vault the scene of Mary being miraculously fed in the temple, already depicted in the Presentation, has been repeated (PL. 126); and on the western half of this same arch we see the Virgin being instructed in the temple (PL. 129), a composition of which no other example is known and which was probably added in order to introduce another temple scene. Mary receiving the skein of purple wool (which is also a "figure" of the Virgin) has been taken out of the proper sequence of events and placed in the lunette above the door from the outer narthex, so that it is close to the other temple scenes (PL. 131).[77]

It is obvious that the basic idea in all Marian typology is that of the Incarnation, and if it has

74 G. Engberg, " 'Aaron and His Sons'—A Prefiguration of the Virgin?" *DOP*, 21 (1967), pp. 279–83.

75 Mercenier, *La prière*, II,1, pp. 81–91.

76 Laurentin, *Maria*, pp. 80–83. See especially Patriarch Germanus, *PG*, 98, col. 293C, 304D, 309C, 311C.

77 Underwood, Vol. 1 of this series, p. 76, and, in the present volume, J. Lafontaine-Dosogne, "Iconography of the Cycle of the Life of the Virgin," p. 183.

seemed to us that a slightly greater stress has been placed on Mary, the spiritual ark brought into the material temple, we have not lost sight of the fact that she is, above all, the dwelling-place of the One above the seraphim, the tabernacle of God and the Word. But a difference, in degree, in the decorations of the parecclesion may be observed if we turn once again to the representations at St. Clement in Ohrid. There the entire cycle is dominated by the figure of *Christos-Angelos*, the incarnate Logos, the "messenger" of God bringing salvation to the world. In the large composition of the Repast of the Holy Wisdom, although the small image of the Virgin on the pediment of the temple recalls that she is the true temple in which the Son of God has come to dwell, the winged figure seated at the table has a cruciform nimbus, showing clearly that he represents Christ, and a eucharistic interpretation has been given to the passage of the Proverbs that has been illustrated.[78]

As already mentioned, the Slaughter of the Assyrians (PL. 461), based on Isaiah 37:21–36, is the only scene of the parecclesion that does not illustrate a lesson read on the Marian feasts. We shall see in the iconographic study how, by means of the image of the Virgin painted above the gate of Jerusalem (PL. 463), the painter has connected this composition with the prefigurations of the Virgin.[79] The reason for selecting this scene, which does not occur in any of the other cycles of biblical prefigurations, should be sought in the personal devotion of Theodore Metochites to the archangel Michael. Among his unpublished works there is an Address to the Archistrategos and the Angelic Essences, probably written in the earlier period of his literary career, the knowledge of which I owe to the courtesy of Ihor Ševčenko. After general consideration of the archangels and of Michael's special role as protector of Israel, Metochites reviews Michael's apparitions to men, and in the long enumeration of these miracles he specially dwells on the slaughter of the Assyrians. One may therefore suppose that it was at Metochites' personal request that this event was represented at the Kariye. Metochites ends his Address by quoting a verse from the First Epistle to the Thessalonians (4:16): "For the Lord himself shall descend from heaven with a shout, with the voice of the archangel, and with the trump of God: and the dead in Christ shall rise first." The iconographic study of the Last Judgment will provide us with another example of the important place assigned to the archangel Michael.

Iconographic Study

FIGURES ON THE WALLS

(PL. 474–520)

In the frieze of Church Fathers painted on the semicircular wall of the apse, the two authors of the liturgy, St. John Chrysostom and St. Basil, stand at the center, on either side of the triple window; on the right are St. Gregory of Nazianz, or the Theologian, and St. Cyril of Alexandria, on the left St. Athanasius; the figure on the extreme left is destroyed (PL. 476–85). All five bishops stand frontally, holding the closed book of the Gospels in the left hand; they are clad in the typical episcopal vestments of the period, namely the polystavrion (or chasuble marked with crosses), worn over the tunic, and the omophorion; also, as is usually the case, St. Cyril alone wears a headdress.[80] The frontal attitude, however, is at variance with the current practice.

---

78 Meyendorff, "L'iconographie," p. 266.
79 See below, pp. 343–45.

80 According to a tradition devoid of historical foundation the patriarchs of Alexandria celebrated the liturgy with covered

From the twelfth century on, except in a few provincial monuments or some where earlier types have been retained, the bishops depicted in the apse, or in the prothesis, are represented as officiants; turned in three-quarter view toward the center, they carry scrolls bearing excerpts from the prayers of the liturgy, and as a rule the center of the composition is occupied by an altar on which is placed the paten with the Christ Child, the *Amnos*.[81] Adoption of the iconic instead of the officiating type at the Kariye is an indication that the regular liturgy, including the communion service, was not celebrated in the parecclesion.

The Virgin and Child painted on the south end of the apse wall corresponds, as already mentioned, to the templon image of the churches, placed on one of the pilasters of the bema, opposite the image of Christ (PL. 486, 487). The iconographic types usually adopted are the Hodegetria, standing frontally or in a slightly three-quarter pose, as in the nave mosaic of the Kariye (PL. 329, 330), or else the interceding Virgin, sometimes hands raised like the Hagiosoritissa, at other times holding a scroll on which a prayer is inscribed.[82] The Eleousa, that is the Merciful or Compassionate Virgin, used in the parecclesion, although frequently depicted from the eleventh century on in panel paintings and in manuscripts,[83] is rarely chosen for the templon image. We find an example in the fourteenth century at the church of Nagoričino, in Yugoslavia, where the half-figure of the Virgin embracing the Child, designated there as the Pelagonitissa, is painted on the iconostasis, to the right of the central door (Fig. 4);[84] the full-length figure of the Eleousa may be seen in a monument of later date, at the church of St. Alypios in Kastoria.[85]

A row of saints, some represented as bust figures but the greater number standing in full size, girds the parecclesion on all three sides (PL. 474, 475, 488–520). There must have been originally twenty-six portraits; six of these have been destroyed, and of the remaining twenty a few are in a fragmentary condition or have lost their inscriptions, and their identification remains uncertain.[86] It is not possible, therefore, to have a clear idea of the guiding principle in the choice of saints, but certain observations can still be made. The painters did not take into consideration the mosaic decorations of the outer narthex but looked upon the parecclesion as a self-contained unit and repeated the portraits of some of the saints who had already been represented. These are among the well-known saints whose iconographic types were firmly established, and there are only minor differences between the mosaics and frescoes. In the narthex St. George and St. Demetrius, each dressed in a long tunic and chlamys, hold in one hand a sheathed sword and in the other a cross, symbol of their martyrdom (PL. 304–05), whereas in the parecclesion their military role has been emphasized: each wears a cuirass over a short military tunic and carries

head because Pope Celestine had sent a miter to Cyril of Alexandria when he asked the latter to preside at the Council of Ephesus (Balsamon in *PG*, 138, col. 1048B–C; Symeon of Thessalonica, *PG*, 155, cols. 716C and 872C–D; Nicephorus Callistus, *PG*, 146, col. 1169B; J. Braun, *Die liturgische Gewandung im Occident und Orient* [Freiburg im Breisgau, 1907], pp. 490–91). In the 11th-century Menologion of the Walters Art Gallery in Baltimore (W. 521, fol. 151) Cyril's head is covered with a short, transparent white veil. In mosaics and paintings of the middle Byzantine period his headdress is a close-fitting white cap with small dots arranged in the shape of a cross, for instance at Hosios Loukas in Greece, at the Monastery of St. Cyril near Kiev, and at the church of the Mother of God at Studenica in Yugoslavia. From the late 13th century on the close-fitting cap sometimes is slightly pointed and is adorned with gammas or checkers arranged to form a cross; at other times the headdress looks like a cowl made of a soft material; Petković, *La peinture serbe*, I, PL. 50,1; II, PL. III,1; idem, *Manastir Studenica* (Belgrade, 1924), p. 70 and Fig. 88; St. Stanojević,

L. Mirković, and Dj. Bošković, *Le monastère de Manasija* (Belgrade, 1928), PL. XI,1; Petković and Bošković, *Dečani*, Album, PL. 149; O. Tafrali, *Monuments byzantins de Curtéa de Argeş* (Paris, 1931), pl. XLI,1; and other examples.

81 G. Babić, "Les discussions christologiques du XIIème siècle et l'apparition de nouvelles scènes dans le décor absidal des églises byzantines," *Zbornik za likovne umetnosti*, 2 (1966), pp. 11–31; M. Chatzidakis, Βυζαντινὲς τοιχογραφίες στὸν Ὠρωπό, in Δελτίον τῆς Χριστιανικῆς Ἀρχαιολογικῆς Ἑταιρείας, 4th series, 1 (1959), pp. 87–107.

82 S. Der Nersessian, "Two Images of the Virgin in the Dumbarton Oaks Collection," *DOP*, 14, pp. 78–86.

83 V. N. Lazarev [Lasareff], "Studies in the Iconography of the Virgin," *ArtB*, 20 (1938); see pp. 36–42, The Eleousa Type, and bibliography in the footnotes.

84 Millet and Frolow, *Peinture*, III, PL. 119,1.

85 St. Pelekanides, Καστορία, I, (Salonika, 1953), PL. 178; A. K. Orlandos, Βυζαντινὰ μνημεῖα τῆς Καστορίας (Athens, 1939), pp. 173–74 and Fig. 117.

86 Underwood, Vol. 1 of this series, pp. 249–52.

a spear and a shield in addition to the sword (PL. 488–89, 492–93). There are slight variations in the costumes of some of the other saints; for instance, in the narthex Florus wears a chlamys decorated with a tablion while in the parecclesion his simple, unadorned outer garment is draped over his right shoulder (PL. 301 b, 490). In the mosaic portraits of Samonas and Gurias the chlamys of each, adorned with two tablia, is clasped under the chin, while in the fresco it is attached on the right shoulder, so that the brocaded ornaments of the tunic are revealed (PL. 307b–08, 510–11). But the similarities between the two groups of portraits are far more striking than these minor variations and clearly show the work of the same workshop.

A second observation that can be made despite the loss of some portraits is that by far the greater number represented military saints. This situation is in keeping with the general practice in churches of this period, and it reflects the importance attached to the military saints in Greek hagiography [87] and in the liturgy. In the rite of the Proskomide, when the priest detaches particles of the eucharistic bread, invoking in turn the Virgin, archangels, prophets, apostles, and saints, the warrior saints Demetrius, George, and Theodore are mentioned immediately after the Church Fathers and before the other saints.[88] The prominence given to them in the liturgy finds its expression in a number of Byzantine works of art, such as the ivory triptychs in Rome and Paris, the reliquary at the cathedral of Limburg on the Lahn, or the reliquary at the Marciana Library in Venice.[89] In all these examples, either the military saints are represented immediately after the Church Fathers or they are the only ones to have been selected, apart from the apostles.

In the group of military saints a kind of hierarchic order was established in the Byzantine tradition, and the foremost in rank were George, Demetrius, the two Theodores, Mercurius, and Procopius.[90] In the normal system of decoration these saints are usually placed as pendant figures on either side of the nave, but the architectural plan of the parecclesion, whose north wall is cut up by doors and niches, precluded such an arrangement.[91] The chiefs of the military saints have therefore been placed, in the order just mentioned, along the south wall, starting with the area closest to the bema.

THE ANASTASIS

(PL. 340–59)

In the traditional iconographic schemes of the Anastasis in the Middle Byzantine period, Christ, holding the cross, advances toward Adam and Eve and takes Adam by the hand, or else he walks in the opposite direction, pulling Adam with him.[92] In a few representations, closely connected with the liturgy, Christ stands frontally, with both hands extended, and Adam and Eve are on either side.[93]

87 H. Delehaye, ed., *Les légendes grecques des saints militaires* (Paris, 1909).

88 F. E. Brightman, ed., *Liturgies Eastern and Western* (Oxford, 1896), p. 358.

89 E. Kantorowicz, "Ivories and Litanies," *Journal of the Warburg and Courtauld Institutes*, V (1942), pp. 70–72; A. Goldschmidt and K. Weitzmann, *Die byzantinischen Elfenbeinskulpturen des X.–XIII. Jahrhunderts*, II (Berlin, 1934), Figs. 31–33, 38, 78, 121, 195; J. Rauch, "Die Limburger Staurothek: Herkunft und Schicksale," *Das Münster*, 8 (1955), p. 216; A. Pasini, *Il tesoro di San Marco in Venezia*, Vol. VIII,2 of F. Ongania, ed., *La basilica di San Marco in Venezia* (Venice, 1885), PL. IX and XI,12. On the enamel book cover of the Treasury, around the central figure of Michael, the ἀρχιστράτιγος, stand the leaders of the army of Christ: the two Theodores, Procopius,

George, Demetrius, Nestor, Eustathius, and Mercurius; Pasini, PL. II.

90 Delehaye, *Les légendes grecques*, pp. 2–3.

91 Underwood, Vol. 1 of this series, p. 252.

92 G. Millet, "Mosaïques de Daphni: Adoration des Mages, Anastasis," *MonPiot*, 2 (1895), pp. 204–14; Ch. R. Morey, *East Christian Paintings in the Freer Collection* (New York, 1914), pp. 45–53; K. Weitzmann, "Das Evangelion im Skevophylakion zu Lawra," *Seminarium Kondakovianum*, VIII (1936), pp. 87–89; J. Villette, *La Résurrection du Christ dans l'art chrétien du IIe au VIIe siècle* (Paris, 1957).

93 A. Xyngopoulos, Ὁ ὑμνολογικὸς εἰκονογραφικὸς τύπος τῆς εἰς τὸν Ἅδην καθόδου τοῦ Ἰησοῦ, in Ἐπετηρὶς Ἑταιρείας Βυζαντινῶν Σπουδῶν, 17 (1941), pp. 113–29; K. Weitzmann, "Aristocratic Psalter and Lectionary," *Record of the Art Museum*,

The compositional scheme of the parecclesion, where Christ raises at the same time both Adam and Eve, must have already been used in the early thirteenth century. The evidence is furnished by the Sketchbook of Wolfenbüttel, in which a German artist, working around 1230–40, faithfully copied Byzantine models.[94] The figures which formed part of the Anastasis are distributed over three different pages. The central group appears on folio 92v: Christ, trampling over Satan, is turned to the right and raises Eve; a bearded man stands behind Eve, in the attitude of prayer. Christ's head is slightly turned to the left, and his right hand is half closed, as if he were grasping the wrist of a person who has not been represented on this page.[95] This person is Adam, as can be seen from the drawing on folio 90v, where Adam kneeling extends his left arm, on the wrist of which one can see the outline of Christ's hand which grasped it.[96] A group of kings and prophets stand behind Adam; other righteous men, preceded by John the Baptist, are represented on folio 90.[97]

In the Anastasis painted in 1313–14 at the church of Joachim and Anne at Studenica, in Yugoslavia (Fig. 5), the central group of Christ, Adam, and Eve is very similar to the one in the Sketchbook; the German artist must have copied an earlier example, closely related in type to this fresco.[98] In the parecclesion Christ's movement is reversed, but in this symmetrical type, frequently used from the fourteenth century on, Christ sometimes walks toward Adam, sometimes away from him, as he did in the earlier representations, where Adam and Eve were on the same side.

The distinguishing feature of this symmetrical composition is that Eve shares with Adam the honor of being raised by Christ. This equality was already suggested in the iconographic variant mentioned above, where Adam and Eve appeared on either side of Christ; it is also apparent in some compositions of the Last Judgment, where Adam and Eve kneel on either side of the throne of the Etimasia. The preference accorded to the symmetrical type in the Palaeologan and later periods [99] may be due in part to the development of the cult of the Virgin. Its choice is particularly appropriate at the parecclesion, where part of the decoration is devoted to the Virgin, for, as already mentioned, the antithetical theme of Eve, because of whose sin humanity was condemned, and Mary, the "New Eve," through whom it was redeemed, frequently developed by the Church Fathers, was recalled in the hymns sung on the Marian feasts.[100]

Except for the changed position of Eve this later type did not introduce any new elements into the composition. John the Baptist continues to occupy a prominent place, standing behind the kings or slightly detached from them as at the Kariye; he points to Christ, indicating that he was the first to bear witness to Christ, and he turns his head toward the kings and other righteous

Princeton University, XIX (1960), pp. 98–107 and Fig. 1. In the Psalter at Mount Athos, Vatopedi 760, Christ exceptionally holds the cross; Weitzmann, "Aristocratic Psalter," Fig. 4. Icon of the Hermitage Museum in Leningrad: Lazarev, *Istorija*, II (Moscow, 1948), PL. 200.

94 Herzog-August-Bibliothek, codex 61.2.Aug.oct.; H. R. Hahnloser, *Das Musterbuch von Wolfenbüttel* (reprinted from *Mitteilungen der Gesellschaft für vervielfältigende Kunst*, Vienna, 1929); K. Weitzmann, "Constantinopolitan Book Illumination in the Period of the Latin Conquest," *GBA*, 6th series, XXV (1944), pp. 193–214; idem, "Zur byzantinischen Quelle des Wolfenbüttler Musterbuches," *Festschrift Hans R. Hahnloser* (Basel and Stuttgart, 1961), pp. 223–50.

95 Hahnloser, *Musterbuch*, Fig. X; Weitzmann, "Zur byzantinischen Quelle," Fig. 6.

96 Hahnloser, *Musterbuch*, Fig. VI; Weitzmann, "Zur by-

zantinischen Quelle," Fig. 5.

97 Hahnloser, *Musterbuch*, Fig. V; Weitzmann, "Zur byzantinischen Quelle," Fig. 7.

98 Millet and Frolow, *Peinture*, III, PL. 63,2.

99 See for instance Xyngopoulos, Ἅγιος Νικόλαος Ὀρφανός, Figs. 27, 28; St. Pelekanides, Βυζαντινὰ καὶ μεταβυζαντινὰ μνημεῖα τῆς Πρέσπας (Salonika, 1960), PL. X; K. D. Kalokyris, Αἱ βυζαντιναὶ τοιχογραφίαι τῆς Κρήτης: Συμβολὴ εἰς τὴν χριστιανικὴν τέχνην τῆς Ἑλλάδος (Athens, 1957), PL. XXVII,2; G. A. Soteriou, Τὰ βυζαντινὰ μνημεῖα τῆς Κύπρου (Athens, 1935), PL. 102 b; Pelekanides, Καστορία, PL. 221 b; Grabar, *La peinture religieuse*, PL. LXIII; Petković, *La peinture serbe*, I, PL. 38 b; L. Mirković and Ž. Tatić, *Markov Manastir* (Novi Sad, 1925), Fig. 50; Millet, *Athos*, PL. 69,3, 129,1, 154.2.

100 Mercenier, *La prière*, II,1, pp. 82, 83, 92, 94, 99, 217, 350; R. Laurentin, *Court traité de théologie mariale*, 1st ed. (Paris, 1953), pp. 37–39 and bibliography in footnotes.

men standing next to him, for according to the apocryphal Gospel of Nicodemus, on which the composition of the Anastasis is based, he was the first to tell them that the Son of God would soon come down to save them. This is made quite clear in some monuments where John holds a scroll with the inscription, "Behold Him of whom I spoke to you that He will come to raise us from Hades." [101] Abel is not mentioned in the Gospel of Nicodemus, but his name occurs in homiletic texts. For instance, in the Homily for Easter Eve, ascribed to Epiphanius of Cyprus, he is mentioned immediately after Adam as in the group assembled in Hell; he is called the first dead and the first shepherd, the image of the unjust death of Christ, the shepherd. [102] The oldest representations of the Anastasis do not include Abel. One of the earliest examples, in which he stands next to Eve, is the miniature of the Lectionary of Lavra, of the beginning of the eleventh century, [103] and from the thirteenth century on he is almost always present in the group of the righteous. But he is rarely given as prominent a position as at the parecclesion, nor is he clad in such sumptuous garments; in this representation his shepherd's crook contrasts strangely with his tunic, which is decorated with bands of gold brocade. [104]

Despite the barren crags rising on both sides of the composition at the Kariye, the black chasm of the foreground, the broken gates of Hell, the locks and keys scattered on the ground, the fettered figure of Satan—all of which are integral parts of this theme—the painter has tried to attenuate the vision of the dark abyss and to stress, on the contrary, the light which filled it when Christ appeared. The luminous figure of Christ is one of the noblest created by Byzantine artists (PL. 343). His white garments have a diaphanous aspect; the aureole of light is painted in three zones of blue, and although they vary in value, a light tonality prevails and the gold stars which covered it must have created a glittering effect. This emphasis on light destroying the darkness which prevailed until then carries with it the idea of the enlightenment and salvation brought to the souls by the Sun of Righteousness, an idea expressed by the Church Fathers and in the liturgy. [105]

THE RAISING OF THE WIDOW'S SON   (PL. 360–62)

The miracle of the Raising of the Widow's Son (Luke 7:11–17) was represented in the sixth century at the church of St. Sergius in Gaza. According to the description of Choricius of Gaza one saw the young man carried to the grave accompanied by a group of weeping women; then, when the young man was recalled to life by the Savior, the women ran forward, rejoicing. [106] The mosaic at the church of the Holy Apostles in Constantinople, described by Constantine the Rhodian, represented the young man bedridden and brought to the grave, and then returning to the house alive, walking full of joy. [107] These two iconographic types, comprising two different moments, reappear in the narrative cycles of illustrated Gospels of the eleventh and twelfth centuries, [108] but in monumental art (as well as in some manuscripts) there is usually only one

101 Soteriou, Τὰ βυζαντινὰ μνημεῖα, PL. 70 a, 88 a; Millet and Frolow, Peinture, II (Paris, 1957), PL. 14,1.
102 PG, 43, col. 452C.
103 Weitzmann, "Das Evangelion," PL. II,1.
104 At the church of the Holy Apostles in Salonika Abel's tunic has a gold band around the neck (Xyngopoulos, Ἡ ψηφιδωτὴ διακόσμησις, PL. 28–30). Although the iconographic scheme differs from that of the Kariye, the facial type of Abel bears a striking resemblance to that of the Kariye fresco.
105 J. A. MacCulloch, The Harrowing of Hell: A Comparative Study of an Early Christian Doctrine (Edinburgh, 1930), pp.

248–50. Mercenier, La prière, II,2, pp. 220–21.
106 Choricii Gazaei Orationes, ed. J.-F. Boissonade (Paris, 1846), p. 91.
107 A. Heisenberg, Grabeskirche und Apostelkirche, zwei Basiliken Konstantins (Leipzig, 1908), II, pp. 239–40.
108 Millet, Recherches, p. 570 and Figs. 601–03. The two moments also occurred in the Latin Gospels of Corpus Christi: F. Wormald, The Miniatures in the Gospels of Corpus Christi, Corpus Christi College MS 286 (The Sandars Lectures in Bibliography, 1948; Cambridge, 1954), PL. VIII.

scene, as at the parecclesion. Christ, accompanied by the apostles, stands near the bed; the young man, wrapped in a shroud, sits up; and a numerous crowd comes out of the gates of the city of Nain.[109] Differences occur in minor details. Sometimes the bed is placed on the ground and the carriers are omitted, as at Kalenić (Fig. 6); at other times, as at the Kariye, the men are shown bearing the bier. As at the Kariye also, the widowed mother usually stands somewhat apart from the group of mourners and bends forward, raising her hands in a gesture of supplication. The painter of the parecclesion has retained the reserved attitude of some of the earlier monuments, and in this respect his composition differs from the dramatic scene described in the Painter's Manual, in which the mother is said to be weeping and tearing out her hair.[110]

THE RAISING OF THE DAUGHTER OF JAIRUS
(PL. 363–67)

The narrative illustrations of Gospel manuscripts show the successive moments of the story of the Raising of the Daughter of Jairus (Matt. 9:18, 19, 23–26; Mark 5:22–24, 35–43; Luke 8:41, 42, 49–56): Jairus, the ruler of the synagogue, beseeches Jesus; while Jesus is on his way a woman with an issue of blood touches his garment and is healed by him; Jesus enters the house and raises Jairus' daughter.[111] This entire cycle is developed in the south nave of the Metropole at Mistra,[112] but ordinarily, in monumental art, the two miracles are separated from one another. This separation is sharply marked at the Kariye, where the subject of Christ and the woman with an issue, a healing miracle, occupies the southeastern pendentive of the southern dome of the inner narthex and the resurrection miracle is reserved for the parecclesion.[113]

The general scheme of this composition resembles that of the Raising of the Widow's Son, except for minor differences imposed by the Gospel text: Christ takes the young girl by the hand instead of making the gesture of speech; two buildings, joined by a wall to indicate an interior scene, are substituted for the mountains and the city of Nain.

The iconography of this miracle does not present marked variations. In most examples the parents stand at the head of their daughter's bed and only two or three apostles accompany Jesus,[114] in accordance with the Gospel narrative which states that "he suffered no man to go in, save Peter, and James, and John, and the father and the mother of the maiden" (Luke 8:51). At the Kariye the number of the apostles has been increased and two women stand behind the mother. This larger number of secondary figures may be due to the desire of the painter to balance the groups in the two pendant scenes of the bema; however, they may be seen in other monuments as well, for instance at the cathedral of Monreale, at the Metropole, and at Kalenić (Fig. 7).[115]

109 V. R. Petković and Ž. Tatić, *Manastir Kalenić* (Vršac, 1926), Fig. 52. This composition, which is very close to the Kariye painting, is designated in the caption and on p. 67 as the Healing of the Daughter of the Syrophenician woman (Mark 7:24–30). But the large city, the group of men emerging from the gate, the figure reclining on the bed in the foreground, clearly indicate that the Raising of the Widow's Son has been represented. For the daughter of the Syrophenician woman was not present when the latter begged Christ to cast out the devil, and it was only when she returned home that she discovered that her daughter had been healed. For other representations of the Raising of the Widow's Son see O. Demus, *The Mosaics of Norman Sicily* (London, 1949), PL. 86 a; Millet, *Athos*, PL. 126,1; idem, *Monuments byzantins de Mistra* (Paris, 1910), PL. 76,3; Petković and Bošković, *Dečani*, Album, PL. CCXX; Tafrali,

Curtea de Argeş, text, p. 101; H. Omont, *Miniatures des plus anciens manuscrits grecs de la Bibliothèque Nationale du VIe au XIVe siècle* (Paris, 1929), PL. XLVI, XCVI,22; E. J. Goodspeed, D. W. Riddle, and H. R. Willoughby, *The Rockefeller McCormick New Testament* (Chicago, 1932), I, fol. 65v; III, pp. 175–77.

110 Ἑρμηνεία, p. 92.

111 Paris. gr. 74; Paris, Bibliothèque Nationale, Département des Manuscrits, *Evangiles avec peintures byzantines du XIe siècle* (Paris, n.d.), I, PL. 18 b, 67; II, PL. 111. Florence, Laurentianus Plut. VI.23, fols. 18, 71v, 122.

112 Millet, *Mistra*, PL. 77,1, 78,2.

113 Underwood, Vol. 1 of this series, pp. 146–47; Vol. 2, PL. 268–71.

114 Demus, *Norman Sicily*, PL. 86 b; Millet, *Mistra*, PL. 77,1; Petković and Tatić, *Manastir Kalenić*, Fig. 61.

115 See preceding note.

At the Kariye, Jairus is separated from the mourning women: he stands in the background between his daughter and Christ, his body partly masked by the rectangular building, and he raises both hands as he does in the scenes where he beseeches Christ to come and heal his daughter. At Curtea-de-Argeş the intrusion of the earlier incident into the miracle scene is even more marked: Jairus kneels at Christ's feet, the maiden is lying in her bed, and the mother has not been represented.[116] The mother is also absent from the composition at Dečani, where Jairus is represented twice—first kneeling before Christ, as at Curtea-de-Argeş, a second time in the background, turned to the right and giving thanks with raised hands for the healing of his daughter.[117]

The painter of the Kariye has introduced an element of pathos, but without exaggerating the expressions of grief one sees in later monuments.[118] The mother bends forward and, in a gesture full of tenderness and solicitude, gently touches the young girl's head; one of the mourning women turns her eyes away as if she could hardly bear to watch the spectacle.

THE ARCHANGEL MICHAEL

(PL. 472, 473)

At the center of the bema arch, between the two resurrection scenes and immediately above the Anastasis, is a large medallion containing the bust figure of the Archangel Michael. In his right hand he holds a staff and in his left a discus, surmounted by a small cross and inscribed with the letters chi, delta, and kappa (XΔK). This discus is the "seal" of Christ, held by angels as the "ministers" of God. The archangels in the western dome of the parecclesion hold a discus that supports a small cross and is inscribed with the letter chi.[119] In other examples, the discus is sometimes inscribed with the sigla of Christ, or with the cross, as in the mosaic of Parenzo, or even with the image of Christ, as on a steatite tablet of the Bardini Museum in Florence.[120] At the parecclesion Christ's image, in a medallion, is painted at the center of the soffit of the western arch of the eastern bay, that is, in a position corresponding to the medallion portrait of the archangel (PL. 338, 471 c).

The three letters of the discus, XΔK, stand for Christos Dikaios Krites, that is, Christ the Equitable Judge; the letters stress the connection of this image with the Last Judgment, for the Painter's Manual of Mount Athos recommends writing the words Ἰησοῦς Χριστός, ὁ δίκαιος κριτής next to the figure of Christ in the representation of the Last Judgment.[121] It was thus most appropriate to inscribe these three letters on the discus in the image of Michael placed between the resurrection scenes of the bema and immediately below the Last Judgment. As another example of Michael holding a discus with the same letters, one may mention an icon in the Byzantine Museum in Athens (Fig. 8), closely related in style to the fresco of the parecclesion.[122] Other representations stress the connection of Michael with the Last Judgment, for he is the "psychopompos" angel par excellence, the one who conveyed the souls of the deceased and also weighed them on the day of the final resurrection.[123] On an icon at the Museo Civico in Pisa, Michael holds a discus displaying the image of Christ Emmanuel and at the same time

116 Tafrali, *Curtéa de Argeş*, PL. XXXVI,1.
117 Petković and Bošković, *Dečani*, Album, PL. CCXV.
118 Millet, *Athos*, PL. 213,3; Pelekanides, Καστορία, PL. 252 b.
119 Underwood, Vol. 1 of this series, p. 214; Vol. 3, PL. 412, 422.
120 Grabar, *L'iconoclasme*, p. 252 and Figs. 137, 138.
121 Ἑρμηνεία, p. 141.

122 M. Soteriou, Παλαιολόγειος εἰκὼν τοῦ Ἀρχαγγέλου Μιχαήλ, in Δελτίον τῆς Χριστιανικῆς Ἀρχαιολογικῆς Ἑταιρείας (Athens, 1959), pp. 80–86 and PL. 31, 32. The letters XΔK are interpreted here as Χριστὸς Δεσπότης Κόσμου; S. Der Nersessian, *Byzantine Art, a European Art* (Publications filmées d'art et d'histoire; Paris, 1965), pp. 63–64.
123 *DACL*, I,2, cols. 2130–41, "Les anges psychopompes".

the scales on which the souls are weighed, and in his right hand he carries a long lance, with which he pierces a demon who is trying to lower one of the trays of the balance scale.[124]

THE LAST JUDGMENT   (PL. 368–407)

By the early fourteenth century, when the parecclesion was decorated, the fully developed iconographic scheme of the Last Judgment had long been established and there existed numerous examples in monumental art as well as in the minor arts. It is not my purpose to discuss here the origin or the development of this theme;[125] I shall consider the fresco of the Kariye only in relation to other monumental examples in order to see to what extent it conforms to the usual scheme and what innovations, if any, were introduced. The composition, developed vertically in several registers, could be represented in churches with a basilical plan, such as Torcello, the west wall of which offered a large surface, or on the pages of a manuscript, as in the two miniatures of the Gospel Paris. gr. 74, or again on icons like the two icons of Mount Sinai.[126] No similar area was available in domed churches, and the Last Judgment rarely appears in these as a unified composition. In Russian churches of the twelfth century the central group is placed on the west wall and the other scenes on the adjoining walls and vaults.[127] At the church of Ateni, in Georgia, the Last Judgment is painted in the west apse and walls.[128] In Byzantine monuments, as well as in those in Bulgaria and Yugoslavia, the Last Judgment is usually relegated to the narthex and the component elements are distributed over the vault, the walls, and the lunettes.[129] The oldest extant example of the fully constituted type is that of the church of the Panagia Chalkeon in Salonika (Kazandjilar Djami) decorated in the early eleventh century.[130] From the following century there are interesting examples at the church of the Panagia Mavriotissa in Kastoria,[131] at Bačkovo,[132] and at the church of the Mother of God in Studenica, and from the thirteenth century, at Sopoćani and at St. Sophia in Trebizond.[133] At Mileševo, where the large outer narthex is entirely given over to the Last Judgment, the scenes are more fully developed than in any other contemporary monument.[134]

124 Lazarev, *Istoriia*, II, PL. 274.

125 The latest study is that of B. Brenk, *Tradition und Neuerung in der christlichen Kunst des ersten Jahrtausends: Studien zur Geschichte des Weltgerichtsbildes* (Vienna, 1966). See also idem, "Anfänge der byzantinischen Weltgerichtsdarstellung," *BZ*, 54 (1964), pp. 106–26.

126 G. Lorenzetti, *Torcello: La sua storia, i suoi monumenti* (Venice, 1939); *Evang. du XIe siècle*, I, PL. 41, 81; G. and M. Soteriou, *Icônes*, I, Figs. 150, 151. The same arrangement may be seen on an ivory: M. H. Longhurst, "A Byzantine Ivory Panel for South Kensington," *The Burlington Magazine*, 49 (1926), pp. 38–43.

127 Novgorod, Saint Nicholas, erected in 1113: D. Ainalov, *Geschichte der russischen Monumentalkunst der vormoskovitischen Zeit* (Berlin and Leipzig, 1932), p. 31 and PL. 17 *b*. Kiev, Monastery of Saint Cyril: ibid., p. 31; *Istorija Russkogo Iskusstva*, ed. I. E. Grabar, I (Akademija Nauk SSSR, Institut Istorii Iskusstv; Moscow, 1953), pp. 215–16. Church of Saint George in Old Ladoga: V. N. Lazarev, *Freski Staroj Ladogi* (Moscow, 1960), pp. 47–53 and PL. 62–69. Novgorod, Spas Nereditca, V. K. Mjasoedov, *Freski Spasa-Neredicy* (Leningrad, 1925), PL. LXVII–LXXVII. Vladimir, Cathedral of Saint Demetrius: I. E. Grabar, *Die Freskomalerei der Dimitrij Kathedrale in Wladimir* (Berlin, [1925]).

128 S. J. Amiranašvili, *Istorija gruzinskoj monumentalnoj živopisi*, I (Sachelgami, 1957), pp. 90–93 and PL. 72–80.

129 In the Cappadocian churches of Karche Kilisse, Damsa, and Timios Stavros there are fragmentary scenes of the Last Judgment in the nave; Jerphanion, *Cappadoce*, II, pp. 12–16, 101, 182 and PL. 145, 146, 194,4. At Djanavar Kilisse the Last Judgment is painted in the funerary chapel; ibid., pp. 364–67, and PL. 207, 208.

130 K. Papadopoulos, *Die Wandmalereien dex XI. Jahrhunderts in der Kirche Παναγία τῶν Χαλκέων in Thessaloniki* (Graz and Cologne, 1966), pp. 57–76 and Figs. 19–22. The first layer of paintings at the church of St. Stephen at Kastoria (Pelekanides, Καστορία, PL. 87, 88), and the frescoes of Yilanli Kilisse in Cappadocia (N. and M. Thierry, *Nouvelles églises rupestres de Cappadoce* (Paris, 1963), pp. 93–98, 140; PL. 40–50), may be earlier than the paintings of Salonika, but the schemes of these provincial examples differ from the usual Byzantine iconographic scheme.

131 Pelekanides, Καστορία, PL. 78–82.

132 Grabar, *La peinture religieuse*, pp. 60–61, 82–85.

133 Studenica: Millet and Frolow, *Peinture*, I (Paris, 1954), PL. 91,1; II, PL. 23, 24,1. Sopoćani: Petković, *La peinture serbe*, II, PL. XX. Trebizond: Talbot Rice, *Trebizond*, pp. 146–49 and Figs. 109–11.

134 Sv. Radojčić, "Etudes sur l'art du XIIIe siècle," extract from *Glas*, 234 (Académie Serbe des Sciences, Classe des Sciences Sociales, No. 1, 1959), pp. 23–32 and PL. LVI–LXX. At Manastir, exceptionally, the Last Judgment occupies the upper register of the south wall of the north aisle; D. Koco and P. Miljković-Pepek, *Manastir* (Skoplje, 1958), pp. 76–77 and Fig. 92.

This rapid enumeration of some of the monumental examples prior to the fourteenth century shows that in placing the Last Judgment in the east bay of the parecclesion, for reasons already mentioned above, the painters of the Kariye not only departed from the usual practice but had to rearrange the composition in order to adapt the principal sections to a domical surface. The skill with which this rearrangement was achieved becomes all the more apparent when the paintings of the parecclesion are compared with others for which a domical surface was also used, entirely or in part. At the church of Asinou, in Cyprus, the secondary scenes are painted on the lunettes and arches of the narthex, but the painter was not able to adjust the group of the Deesis and the apostles to the shape of the dome. Instead, he placed the usual bust of Christ Pantocrator at the crown of the dome, surrounded by the Virgin and angels in medallions, and he represented the apostles in the pendentives, by groups of three.[135] At Prizren, where the Last Judgment occupies the south bay of the outer narthex, the traditional iconography was not modified, but the awkward shape of the double groin vault prevented the painters from creating a closely knit, unified composition.[136]

This unity was achieved, to a large degree, at the Kariye, for although some of the scenes are distributed in the pendentives and lunettes, they are skillfully arranged around the central groups, and these are brought into special prominence by being placed in the domical vault.

The principal figures of the composition, consisting of the Deesis, the seated apostles, and the angels standing behind them, have been placed slightly lower than the crown of the domical vault, on the curved surface of the eastern half, in such a way that they are immediately visible as one enters the parecclesion—framed, as it were, by the contour of the western arch of the bay. The enthroned Christ appears directly above the Christ of the Anastasis (PL. 338). In order to mark the crown of the domical vault the painter transferred there the beautiful figure of the flying angel; the angel's scroll, studded with stars, sun, and moon, winds in a spiral almost as large as the mandorla of Christ and forms a focal point around which the groups of the elect are deployed (PL. 368, 371). In earlier and contemporary representations this scroll, inspired by the words of the Apocalypse, "and the heaven departed as a scroll when it is rolled together" (Rev. 6:14), is usually a narrow band, and the angel stands below the apostles, or in an arch of the vault. Occasionally, as at the church of the Virgin Ljeviška at Prizren, two flying angels, facing one another, hold the scroll, which passes behind the enthroned Christ.

Amid the angelic host two archangels, standing on either side of the Deesis, are distinguished from the others by their imperial costume and the open book in the hands of each (PL. 373). These books, which are not represented in other examples where archangels in imperial dress also stand guard next to the throne, should probably be explained with reference to those mentioned in the Apocalypse: "And I saw the dead, small and great, stand before God; and the books were opened: and another book was opened, which is the book of life: and the dead were judged out of those things which were written in the books, according to their works" (Rev. 20:12). In the Last Judgment scene of the Metropole, at Mistra, the Book of Life is given great prominence; on the south pier of the west wall, an angel reads out of a large book placed on a lectern.[137] At a much earlier date we find, in the Utrecht Psalter, as an illustration of

---

135 Seymer et al., "The Church of Asinou" (see above, n. 72), pp. 336–40 and PL. XCIII–XCV.

136 Christ, seated in a large, circular mandorla, fills the central section of the vault; the Virgin, John the Baptist, and the apostles are destroyed, and so are the representations of paradise and some of the choirs of the elect. The resurrection of the dead, the weighing of the souls, the torments of the sinners occupy the north and south sections of the vault and the lunettes of the west wall.

137 Millet, *Mistra*, PL. 80,2.

Psalm 69[68]:28, "Let them be blotted out of the book of the living, and not be written with the righteous," a figure with an open book.[138] An angel opening the Book of Life has also been represented in the manuscript of the Homilies of John Chrysostom at Athens, National Library 211, in connection with his commentary on the Parable of the Steward.[139]

Below Christ we see, as usual, the throne of the Etimasia, inspired by the words of the Psalmist: "Justice and judgment are the habitation of thy throne" (ἐτοιμασία τοῦ θρόνου σου; Ps. 89[88]:14); "The Lord hath prepared his throne in the heavens; and his kingdom ruleth over all" (Ps. 103[102]:19). The book of the Gospels is placed on the throne, behind it are the instruments of the Passion, and at each side, in front, Adam and Eve kneel in supplication. The seraphim, the cherubim, the wheels are not represented as usual close to Christ enthroned; instead, two cherubim appear at the sides of the throne of the Etimasia, and their position, in addition to the simple rectangular shape of the Etimasia throne, recalls the composition of the Ark of the Covenant with the two golden cherubim, one at each end (PL. 374, 386).

In the western half of the domical vault five choirs of the elect form a ring around the angel with the scroll; the sixth choir is brought forward to the eastern half, below the apostles seated on the right hand of Christ (PL. 368). The fact that the elect are supported by clouds serves to emphasize the idea that the event takes place in Heaven. The ultimate source of inspiration for this detail is to be found in the First Epistle to the Thessalonians: "For the Lord himself shall descend from heaven with a shout . . . and the dead in Christ shall rise first: Then we which are alive and remain shall be caught up together with them in the clouds, to meet the Lord in the air" (I Thess. 4:16–17). In his homily *De fine extremo* Ephraem the Syrian also speaks of the righteous flying in the sky: *Justi volabunt in caelum et peccatores comburentur in igne, volabunt martyres in thalamum et exibunt mali in tenebras*.[140] Unlike the sedate groups who usually advance solemnly toward the throne of God, the elect of the Kariye are depicted, for the most part, in a half-running attitude, almost in proskynesis, no doubt an attempt, somewhat unsuccessfully carried out, to show them flying through the air.

In the choir of the martyrs, in the central part of the western section, several figures stand in a frontal position, and it is possible that in the adjoining area, where the paint has fallen, there were others also in a frontal position. But from this central area the movement diverges in opposite directions, leading to the Judgment throne. A converging movement toward Christ may be seen in other works of art, such as the so-called Dalmatic of Charlemagne and a triptych in the Vatican, where for compositional reasons the choirs of the elect form a semicircle around the central figure.[141] We must take this movement into consideration so as to understand the order of precedence of the different choirs at the Kariye. Although there is considerable variety in the number and categories of the elect mentioned in the liturgy and other texts, or represented in art, there is a fair agreement on their hierarchic order.[142] The prophets and the apostles come first, and at the Kariye also they precede the others: the choir of the prophets is represented in the eastern half of the dome, below the seated apostles, and that of the apostles immediately after them in the northwestern section of the domical vault (PL. 385). The martyrs

138 E. T. DeWald, ed., *The Illustrations of the Utrecht Psalter* (Illuminated Manuscripts of the Middle Ages; Princeton, London, and Leipzig [1932]), fol. 38v, PL. LXIII.

139 A. Grabar, "Miniatures gréco-orientales: II, Un manuscrit des homélies de Saint Jean Chrysostome à la Bibliothèque Nationale d'Athènes (Atheniensis 211)," *Seminarium Kondakovianum*, 5 (1932), pp. 264, 281–82, and PL. XIX,1.

140 Th. J. Lamy, ed., *Sancti Ephraem Syri Hymni et Sermones*, III (Mechelen, 1889), col. 212.

141 G. Millet, *Broderies religieuses de style byzantin* (Paris, 1947), PL. CXXXV-CLI; idem, *La dalmatique*, p. 81, Fig. 4; see also PL. I,2, an icon from the monastery of Karakallou on Mount Athos with the representation of "All the Saints."

142 Millet, *La dalmatique*, p. 85.

and the hierarchs are usually the next two choirs; at the Kariye the martyrs stand next to the apostles, and the hierarchs are the first choir in the southwestern section (PL. 384). The "hosioi," or anchorites, and the women martyrs are the last groups; they have been represented in the western axis between the martyrs and the hierarchs, that is, in the section from which the diverging movement started (PL. 384 *b*).

The Judgment itself takes place in the eastern half of the vault, where the souls—or rather their acts—are weighed. The balance scale hangs from the footstool in front of the throne of the Etimasia instead of being held by an angel, or by a hand issuing from the segment of sky or from the mandorla of Christ (PL. 386). Two angels approach from the left, their arms laden with scrolls in which are recorded the virtues; the angels are ready to place the scrolls on the left-hand tray, which is already weighted in their favor. A small demon, armed with a hooked stick, who tries to pull down the scale on his side, is much less conspicuous than is usually the case. A soul awaiting judgment stands under the balance scale. Others have already been judged and have been condemned; some of these stand with sorrowful expressions while their companions, a cord tied around their necks, are pulled and pushed by other demons (PL. 387–90). A soul awaiting his fate had already been represented in the twelfth century at Nereditsa, where he was placed next to the angel, and also at Bačkovo;[143] in the fourteenth century at Prizren, Gračanica, and Dečani the nude figure was depicted immediately under the balance scale as at the Kariye.[144] The souls who are being driven toward the river of fire but are not yet in it also occur at Bačkovo and Gračanica, and they are repeated in paintings of the fifteenth and sixteenth centuries.[145]

The river of fire issues from Christ's throne, in conformity with Daniel's vision, "A fiery stream issued and came forth from before him" (7:10). It broadens into the lake in which, according to the Book of Revelation, were cast the false prophets, the idolaters, the unbelieving, in short "whosoever was not found written in the book of life" (19:20; 20:14–15; 21:8). This area has suffered considerable damage, but one can distinguish the angel who pierces the sinners with his lance, the men attired in different costumes or wearing different types of headdress and representing the various categories of the damned, and, in the lower section, the front quarters of a beast (PL. 390–91). The group of old men above the lake of fire is in a slightly better state of preservation: they wear long mantles and scarfs that cover their heads and shoulders (PL. 390). Similar groups may be seen in the two Last Judgment icons of Mount Sinai;[146] in one of them the group consists of young men; in the other, of older men. One of those older men in the front row is dressed in a long tunic and mantle, and his head seems to be covered by a scarf; the man next to him has an Oriental costume consisting of a close-fitting bodice buttoned down the front, a wide skirt, and a pointed, helmet-like headdress. The inscription, οἱ κατάκριτοι, refers to all the sinners in general, but in the *Hortus Deliciarum* illustrated by Herrade of Landsberg in the twelfth century, eight separate groups, depicted in three registers above the river of fire, are identified as false prophets, false apostles, impious bishops, abbots, and so forth, and the last one as Jews and pagans.[147] Similar groups appear in Rumanian paintings of the Last Judgment; the foremost men, usually led by Moses, are the Jews; the others

143 Mjasoedov, *Freski Spasa-Neredicy*, PL. LXXII; Grabar, *La peinture religieuse*, p. 85.

144 Petković and Bošković, *Dečani*, Album, PL. CCLXXVIII. At Prizren the nude figure has two small wings.

145 Millet, *Athos*, PL. 149,2, 244,2; Soteriou, Τὰ βυζαντινὰ μνημεῖα, PL. 109.

146 Soteriou, Τὰ βυζαντινὰ μνημεῖα, PL. 150–51.

147 Herrade de Landsberg, *Hortus Deliciarum*, ed. J. Walter (Strasburg and Paris, 1952), PL. XLIII.

are designated as Armenians, Latins, Ethiopians, Turks, and Tatars.[148] The men with scarfs over their heads represented at the Kariye are therefore the Jews who did not recognize Christ.

In passing from the wide surface of the domical vault to the pendentives and to the lunettes, the decorators of the Kariye were forced to separate from one another figures which should have been represented together, though in almost every instance they found an interesting solution to their problem. Ordinarily the elect, led by St. Peter, advance from right to left toward the gate of paradise guarded by the cherubim. On the northern lunette of the parecclesion the direction is reversed, but by this means the Good Thief, and the Virgin enthroned between two angels, represented in the right half of the lunette, adjoin the composition of the northeastern pendentive, in which Abraham is seated in an arbor with Lazarus on his knees and other souls standing at his sides (PL. 368, 394–96, 404, 405, 407).

On the southeastern pendentive, thus facing the group of Abraham and Lazarus, the rich man burning in the fires of hell touches his parched lips, as usual, begging for a drop of water (PL. 369, 397). The Torments of the Damned are developed in the left half of the adjoining lunette (PL. 398–403). Thus the representations of paradise and hell are placed, as usual, on the right and left sides of Christ.

In several compositions of the Last Judgment the painters have depicted the punishments reserved for those guilty of different sins, such as avarice, usury, and lust;[149] in others, separate compartments of hell enclose standing figures surrounded by flames, or skulls being devoured by worms. At Mileševo, where the representation of hell was probably developed over the entire surface of the south wall of the outer narthex, a considerable section is still preserved and one can see, in four consecutive scenes of the upper register, angels pushing, or piercing with their lances, groups of false prophets and apostles, kings, bishops, and monks. The torments of hell occupy the lower register, where, according to the available space, either the sinners are full-size or three-quarter figures, or only the skulls eaten by worms are shown.[150]

At the Kariye the individual punishments, as well as the simpler images of the skulls, have been omitted; instead, on the southern lunette are depicted four groups of the damned, enclosed in separate compartments. Despite the absence of inscriptions, which sometimes accompany similar representations, one can easily recognize the different torments mentioned in the Gospels (Matt. 8:12; Mark 9:43–48). On the lower left is the "worm that sleepeth not" (PL. 400–401); on the next panel, painted in a very intense yellowish red, is the "unquenchable fire" (PL. 402–403). The panel above it, in which figures in deep black stand against a slightly lighter background, represents the "outer darkness" (PL. 399). Finally, the panel on the upper left, which is almost completely effaced, must have depicted the "gnashing of teeth" (PL. 398).[151]

The scene of the resurrection of the dead, compressed into the narrow surface of the southwestern pendentive, contrasts with the more elaborate compositions of other churches of the

148 P. Henry, *Les églises de la Moldavie du Nord des origines à la fin du XVIe siècle* (Paris, 1930), p. 242 and PL. XLII,1, XLV,1–2, LXI; S. Der Nersessian, "Two Slavonic Parallels of the Greek Tetraevangelion: Paris. 74," *ArtB*, 9 (1927), p. 266 and Fig. 55; idem, "Une nouvelle réplique slavonne du Paris. gr. 74 et les manuscrits d'Anastase Crimcovici," *Mélanges offerts à M. Nicolas Iorga* (Paris, 1933), pp. 699–702 and Figs. 6, 8.

149 Yilanli Kilisse: N. and M. Thierry, *Nouvelles églises*, p. 100 and PL. 49 *b*, 50 *a*. Panagia Mavriotissa: Pelekanides, Καστορία, PL. 81. Sopoćani: Millet and Frolow, *Peinture*, II, PL. 23. Prizren: Hamann-MacLean, *Aus der mittelalterlichen*

Bildwelt Jugoslawiens, Fig. 18. Asinou: Seymer et al., "The Church of Asinou," p. 334 and PL. XCIII, XCVII,1. Dečani: Petković and Bošković, *Dečani*, Album, PL. CCLXXIX,2. Metropole: Millet, *Mistra*, PL. 80,1; Herrade de Landsberg, *Hortus Deliciarum*, PL. XLIV.

150 Radojčić, "Etudes," PL. LVII–LXIV, LXIX.

151 The two groups of sinners on the southwest pier of the nave at Dečani representing the "outer darkness" and the "worm that sleepeth not" closely resemble those of the Kariye except that the figures are partly veiled; Petković and Bošković, *Dečani*, Album, PL. CCLXXIX,1, CCLXXX,1.

fourteenth century, such as Prizren, Gračanica, and the Metropole at Mistra. It would have been possible to distribute this scene on the two western pendentives, representing separately the land and the sea giving up their dead, as did for instance the painters of Asinou and Dečani.[152] But the painter of the Kariye has reserved the northwestern pendentive for two figures which will be discussed below; thus only one pendentive was available for the resurrection scene. At the sound of trumpets blown by two angels the dead awaken: some rise from the ground, and two other groups stand in sarcophagi (PL. 392). This part of the composition follows the text of John: "for the hour is coming, in the which all that are in the graves shall hear his voice, And shall come forth; they that have done good, unto the resurrection of life; and they that have done evil, unto the resurrection of damnation" (5:28-29). The dead standing in sarcophagi had been represented in the eleventh century in Paris. gr. 74, and the illustrator had also added, as a pendant to the sea giving up its dead, wild animals disgorging the men they had eaten.[153] This last scene, frequently represented in later centuries, has been omitted at the Kariye, but in the lower half of the pendentive we see the sea giving up "the dead which were in it" (Rev. 20:13), called forth by the angel on the left. Heads, hands, feet issue from the mouth of the fish; in the center a dolphin carries on his back a partly draped figure seated in a shell; lobster claws, which look like horns, arise out of her head, and she raises her right hand (PL. 392). The classical personification of the sea, Thalassa, represented in Byzantine manuscripts of the ninth and tenth centuries, was introduced at an early date into the composition of the Last Judgment; seated on a sea monster, she usually carries an oar or a boat, or both at once, and sometimes a trident as on the icon of Sinai.[154] At Nereditsa, at Kakopetria in Cyprus, and at Sopoćani her attribute of crab or lobster claws at the sides of her head is omitted; at Torcello she has two short horns; and at Gračanica long lobster claws come out of the sides of her head and a pointed object from the top.[155]

While the resurrection scene is thus crowded into a narrow space, only two figures occupy the northwestern pendentive: an angel bends slightly and touches the head of a nude soul (PL. 393). In Christian exegesis the idea of souls carried by angels has its origin in the parable of the rich man and Lazarus, where it is said that when the beggar died he "was carried by the angels into Abraham's bosom" (Luke 16:22). The legendary lives of saints recall instances in which the soul of a saintly hermit or of a martyr was seen being borne to heaven by angels, and such a scene is represented in two miniatures of the Menologion of Basil II.[156] At the church of St. Neophytos, in Cyprus, two angels, standing on either side of the saint, carry him up to heaven (Fig. 9).[157] In the art of Western Europe an angel carrying a soul occasionally appears in the large compositions of the Last Judgment. On the tympanum of the cathedral of Autun an angel lifts a soul in his arms and introduces him into the mansions of heaven.[158] At St.-Trophime in Arles and at the portal of St. Denis there is a closer connection with the parable of the rich man and Lazarus. In the former, an angel carrying a soul approaches the three patriarchs, seated with other souls

152 Seymer et al., "The Church of Asinou," PL. XCV,1; Petković and Bošković, *Dečani*, Album, PL. CCLIX,2, CCLXXVI-CCLXXVII.

153 *Evang. du XIᵉ siècle*, I, PL. 41.

154 Papadopoulos, *Die Wandmalereien*, Fig. 5 in the text; Soteriou, Τὰ βυζαντινὰ μνημεῖα, PL. 151.

155 Mjasoedov, *Freski Spasa-Neredicy*, PL. LXXV; A. and J. A. Stylianou, Ὁ ναὸς τοῦ Ἁγίου Νικολάου τῆς Στέγης παρὰ τὴν Κακοπετριάν, in Κυπριακαὶ σπουδαί, 10 (1946),

p. 122 and Fig. 7; Millet and Frolow, *Peinture*, II, PL. 98,4; Petković, *La peinture serbe*, I, PL. 60.

156 Codex Vaticanus gr. 1613, published in facsimile in *Il Menologio di Basilio II (Codex Vaticanus gr. 1613)* (Codices e Vaticanis selecti, VIII; Turin, 1907), II, PL. 90, 170.

157 C. Mango and E. J. W. Hawkins, "The Hermitage of St. Neophytos and Its Wall Paintings," *DOP*, 20 (1966), plate opp. p. 166.

158 D. Grivot and G. Zarnecki, *Gislebertus, sculpteur d'Autun* (Paris, 1960).

in their bosoms; in the latter an angel holding two souls in his arms is carved on the voussoir, under the figure of Abraham with the souls in his bosom.[159]

Such representations are absent from the Byzantine compositions of the Last Judgment, and the painting of the Kariye Djami expresses a slightly different idea. The angel does not carry the soul in his arms, but lays a protective hand on the soul's head and raises the other hand as if in speech; his attitude is that of an intercessor before the throne of the Almighty. In considering this exceptional group, and the importance that the artist has given to it by placing it alone in a pendentive, one is reminded of the closing paragraphs of Theodore Metochites' Address to the Archistrategos, in which he begs Michael to intercede for him on the day of the final Judgment.

Except for this group, there are no new elements in the composition. Some of the modifications noted above were dictated by the necessity of adjusting the component elements to the shape of the domical vault; exigencies of space explain some of the simplifications, but in one instance there may have been another reason as well. The groups of the sinners in hell occupy only the eastern half of the lunette, perhaps in order to make room for the extensive, typological cycle of the Virgin, which begins in the western half of this lunette. However, the relatively small space devoted to the representation of hell, in contrast to the greater development of the scene in paradise, which faces it, makes one wonder whether it was not intentional that more emphasis was laid on the rewards of the faithful than on the punishments reserved for the sinners, just as in painting the Anastasis the idea of light destroying darkness was stressed.

THE SOULS OF THE RIGHTEOUS IN THE HAND OF GOD (PL. 469–70)

The image of a large hand holding three infants in swaddling clothes, painted in the western arch above the opening leading into the outer narthex, conveys the promise of salvation for the righteous, already developed in the paradise scenes of the Last Judgment; the theme is based on a passage in the Book of Wisdom, "But the souls of the righteous are in the hand of God, and the tortures of death shall not touch them" (Wisd. of Sol. 3:1). Of the figures that were placed below, on the tympanum, there only remains, on the right, the lower part of a man shod in red buskins. He appears to have been turned toward the center and must have faced, originally, a similar figure standing on the left.

At the Holy Apostles in Salonika the Hand of God holding the souls, without any figures under it, is painted above the door leading from the north arm of the outer narthex into the church.[160] In other instances, this image is associated with the Last Judgment. At Gračanica, Christ, seated in judgment, appears in the tympanum of the western groin vault, and the Hand of God holding the souls is painted at the summit of this vault, enclosed in a mandorla surrounded by angels; a ray of light descends from the Hand to shine on Christ.[161] At the cathedral of the Dormition in Vladimir, redecorated in 1408 with a detailed composition of the Last Judgment, the Hand with the souls occupies the center of the western arch of the nave; it is flanked by two medallions enclosing the bust figures of David and Solomon; two trumpeting angels stand below.[162] Later still, at the church of Voroneţ, in Rumania, the Hand of God with the souls of the righteous holds at the same time the balance in which other souls are weighed.[163]

159 E. Mâle, *L'art religieux du XIIe siècle en France: Etude sur les origines de l'iconographie du moyen âge* (Paris, 1922), p. 29 and Fig. 27; S. McK. Crosby, *L'abbaye royale de Saint-Denis* (Paris, 1953), PL. 9.

160 Xyngopoulos, *Thessalonique*, PL. 18,1.

161 Millet, *La dalmatique*, pp. 22 and 60.

162 *Trudy VI arkheologicheskago s'ezda v Odesse III* (Odessa, 1887), PL. 80 facing p. 330.

163 Henry, *Les églises de la Moldavie*, p. 242. At Suceviça it has been represented in the tympanum of the door; Henry, p. 260.

This iconographic theme also occurs in other contexts. At the church of the Assumption, at Volotovo, the Hand with the souls is represented in the vault of the apse, under the Descent of the Holy Spirit.[164] At Manasija it is painted in the arch above the tympanum of the western door of the nave, and David and Solomon, in imperial dress, stand at the sides (Fig. 10).[165] The phrase inscribed on the scroll held by Solomon, "the souls of the righteous are in the hand of God," refers to this image, while the inscription on David's scroll, "Awake, why sleepest thou, O Lord?" (Ps. 44[43]:23), refers to the composition of the tympanum. Here Christ Emmanuel is lying on a mattress, and at his sides stand the Virgin and two angels carrying the instruments of the Passion. This composition, designated in Byzantine iconography as "Jesus Christ the sleepless one," is a symbolic representation of Christ's messianic mission,[166] but for our particular purpose it is important to call attention to the presence here, as at Vladimir, of David and Solomon. These two kings must have been represented at the Kariye Djami also, Solomon probably carrying a scroll with the same inscription as at Manasija, while David may have held a scroll inscribed with a passage from another psalm, more closely connected with the Hand of God.

A last example of the Hand of God, represented in yet another context, should be mentioned. It appears in the Serbian Psalter of Munich, in the Creation scene that illustrates Psalm 24[23]:1-2: "The earth is the Lord's, and the fulness thereof; the world, and they that dwell therein. For he hath founded it upon the seas, and established it upon the floods." [167] The scene itself is different, but the presence of the Hand of God evokes an idea similar to the one expressed by Solomon, for to say that "the world and they that dwell therein" are the Lord's is almost equivalent to saying that "the souls of the righteous are in the hand of God."

MEDALLION PORTRAITS   (PL. 336-339, 471)

Four medallion portraits are painted in the crowns of the transverse arches of the parecclesion. I have already spoken of the medallion on the soffit of the bema arch, which contains the bust figure of the Archangel Michael holding the "seal" of Christ; the portrait of Christ which decorated the soffit of the eastern arch is a pendant to it. As far as can be determined, the mature Christ was represented here, and the same type is repeated in the medallion placed at the center of the vertical face of this arch, between the seated hymnographers. This second portrait forms a pendant to the medallion figure of Melchizedek painted on the vertical face of the western arch (PL. 471).

In both instances symbol and portrait are coupled: in the first, Christ is depicted opposite his "seal," held by Michael; in the second, Christ faces his antitype, for such was the interpretation given in Christian exegesis to the enigmatic figure of Melchizedek, King of Salem, "priest of the most high God."

The artists of the Early Christian period brought out the eucharistic symbolism of Melchizedek offering bread and wine to Abraham (Gen. 14:18), recalled in the prayers: "Thy holy priest, Melchizedek, offered unto Thee, a holy sacrifice, an immaculate Host." At S. Vitale in Ravenna Abel offers a lamb and Melchizedek a wafer, typifying the sacrament of the Last

---

164 *Monuments de l'art ancien russe publiés par l'Académie impériale des Beaux-Arts*, IV (St. Petersburg, 1912), Fig. 24.

165 Cf. Stanojević et al., *Le monastère de Manasija*, PL. XVIII, XIX.

166 For a study of this theme see Grabar, *La peinture religieuse*, pp. 257-62.

167 J. Strzygowski, *Die Miniaturen des serbischen Psalters* (Vienna, 1906), pp. 27-28 and PL. XI,25.

Supper.[168] At S. Apollinare in Classe, Melchizedek officiates behind the altar table; on the left Abel again offers a lamb, and on the right stand Abraham and Isaac.[169] The theophanic vision painted in the apse of chapel 51 at Bawit has been interpreted as an image of the foundation of the New Alliance; the figure on the left who carries a pyxis and a censer is most probably Melchizedek, and the one on the right, St. Paul, "author of the Christian interpretations of the kingly priesthood of the Messiah." [170]

The Byzantine artists of later centuries did not repeat these typological scenes; they usually represent Melchizedek among the group of prophets and other biblical figures, but at times an artist will suggest the symbolism by showing Melchizedek holding a bowl which contains three loaves of bread, for instance, in the narthex of the Kariye (PL. 84 b), at Prilep in Yugoslavia, and at the Protaton on Mount Athos.[171] A parallelism between Christ and Melchizedek is probably suggested at St. Sophia in Kiev. The medallion placed on the face of the east arch encloses the bust of Christ, represented with a tonsure,[172] an iconographic type figuring Christ as priest which also occurs in the churches of Nerezi and Nereditsa. The Communion of the Apostles appears on the semicircular wall of the apse, and on the pier to the left of this scene Aaron stands holding a censer and an incense box. It has been suggested that the destroyed figure on the right pier depicted Melchizedek.[173] These figures are associated here with the Communion of the Apostles, where Christ is officiating, as well as with the medallion portrait of Christ-priest placed above, at the center of the arch.

The poor condition of the Kariye fresco prevents us from seeing whether Christ was depicted with a tonsure, but its typological relation with the portrait of Melchizedek is conveyed through the places assigned to the two figures, facing one another.

THE DOME OVER THE WESTERN BAY   (PL. 408-36)

A medallion of the Virgin and Child adorns the crown of the dome, and angels, dressed in court costumes, stand between the ribs of the dome, offering their worship to the incarnate Christ and to his Mother, the instrument of the Incarnation (PL. 408-25). Four hymnographers occupy the pendentives (PL. 408, 426-36).

During the Palaeologan period, and later, saints other than evangelists were sometimes represented in the pendentives. In the small chapel of Sts. Peter and Paul, next to the monastery of Vlattades in Salonika, the Church Fathers occupy this position;[174] occasionally, as in the narthex of Lesnovo, these Church Fathers are depicted as the "Sources of Wisdom" and the people drink the water that flows from the desk at which they are seated, writing.[175] It has already been mentioned above that the Painter's Manual recommended placing the hymnographers in the pendentives of the narthex dome decorated with the image of the Virgin and Child surrounded by angels and the prophets,[176] and this became common practice during the late period. Many of the prophets surrounding the Virgin hold "symbols" of the Virgin, such as the burning

168 F. W. Deichmann, *Frühchristliche Bauten und Mosaiken von Ravenna* (Baden-Baden, 1958), Figs. 322, 323.
169 Ibid., Fig. 407.
170 Grabar, *Martyrium*, II, pp. 216-19, and III, PL. LV.
171 Millet, *Athos*, PL. 8,2.
172 V. N. Lazarev, *Mosaiki Sofii Kievskoj* (Moscow, 1960), PL. 17-18.
173 Ibid., pp. 97-99 and PL. 26.

174 Xyngopoulos, *Thessalonique*, PL. 20,1.
175 Okunev, "Lesnovo" (see n. 69), pp. 236-37 and PL. XXXIII; T. Velmans, "L'iconographie de la 'Fontaine de Vie' dans la tradition byzantine à la fin du moyen-age," *Synthronon: Art et archéologie de la fin de l'antiquité et du moyen-âge* (Paris, 1968), pp. 119-34.
176 See above, p. 310.

bush or the fleece, and in the outer narthex of the church of Suceviţa, in Rumania, biblical prefigurations of the Virgin have been painted on the walls, as in the parecclesion of the Kariye.[177]

The choice of hymnographers varies but little, being largely confined to the ones who composed the principal canons in honor of the Virgin, and their iconographic types also show only slight modifications. In the Menologion of Basil II, John of Damascus and Cosmas of Maiuma, dressed as monks, are bare-headed,[178] but by the fourteenth century the type used in the parecclesion had been firmly established. John, who lived at Damascus and in Palestine under Arab domination, always wears a turban, and he is represented as an old man (PL. 426, 427). Cosmas, a younger man with a dark beard, wears a cowl the ends of which are wound around his neck, and the folds of this cowl give it the appearance of a turban (PL. 428, 429). Joseph and Theophanes are bare-headed (PL. 430–33), as they are usually represented, although Joseph sometimes wears a turban, for instance at the church of Lagoudera, in Cyprus, of the twelfth century.[179]

The painter has varied the attitudes of the hymnographers: John Damascene sharpens his pen; Cosmas is about to dip his pen into the ink pot; Joseph reads from a long scroll, which he holds with both hands; Theophanes writes on the open book resting on his knees. These attitudes repeat those of the Evangelists painted in churches or in manuscripts. As in many examples of the Palaeologan period, the desk, the lectern placed behind it, the buildings depicted on either side fill all the available space, and in these particulars, as well as in the attitudes of the hymnographers, the artists have introduced considerable variety.

JACOB'S LADDER; JACOB WRESTLING WITH THE ANGEL   (PL. 438–43)

Jacob lies asleep at the foot of a monumental flight of stairs with wide treads, which curves with a sweeping movement following the contour of the lunette and leads to the half-length figures of the Virgin and Child in the arc of heaven; two angels are ascending the stairs, and two descending. Jacob's struggle with the angel is depicted to the right of the stairs, in front of a rocky mountain.

The pericope of Jacob's vision (Gen. 28:10–17) is read at the Great Vespers on the feasts of the Birth of the Virgin, the Annunciation, and the Dormition, and in the odes sung on those days, as well as in the numerous homilies, the Virgin is celebrated as the spiritual or the living ladder between God and men, the bridge leading to the Creator.[180] In the Akathistos Hymn she is acclaimed in the following words: "Hail! heavenly ladder by which God came down. Hail! earthly Bridge carrying the earthborn into heaven." [181] The account of Jacob wrestling with the angel (Gen. 32:24–30) does not form part of the lessons read on the feasts of the Virgin, but this incident has been represented almost always in the churches where Jacob's Ladder forms part of the Marian cycle. At St. Sophia in Trebizond (Fig. 11), at St. Clement in Ohrid (Fig. 12), and at Prizren the two scenes appear side by side, as at the Kariye;[182] at Lesnovo (Fig. 13) they are one under the other; and at Dečani they are separated because the narrow surface of the arch or the pier did not provide sufficient room for both scenes at once.[183] The connection of Jacob's

177 J. D. Stefanescu, *L'évolution de la peinture religieuse en Bucovine et en Moldavie* (Paris, 1928), pp. 149–50.

178 *Menologio di Basilio II*, II, PL. 213.

179 A. and J. A. Stylianou, *The Painted Churches of Cyprus* (Cyprus, 1964), p. 84 and Fig. 38.

180 Y. M.-J. Congar, *Le mystère du temple* (Paris, 1958), pp. 308–09; Mercenier, *La prière*, II,1, pp. 98, 102, 168, 347, 367; II,2, 14, 21; Eustratiades, Ἡ Θεοτόκος, s.v. κλίμαξ.

181 *PG*, 92, col. 1337C.

182 Kiornakov, *The Frescoes of the Church of St. Clement at Ochrid*, Fig. 6; Hamann-MacLean, *Aus der mittelalterlichen Bildwelt Jugoslawiens*, Fig. 36.

183 For placement of scenes at Lesnovo see Okunev, "Lesnovo," PL. XXXIV; for Dečani, Petković and Bošković, *Dečani*, Album, PL. CCLXVI, CCLXVIII.

struggle with the Marian typology is not as clear as that of his vision, but in some writings the two events are recalled together and a Marian symbolism is suggested. In his first Homily on the Dormition John of Damascus writes that just as Jacob saw the sky and earth united by the ladder, by which the angels descended and ascended, and saw "Him, who is truly the strong and invincible, engage in a symbolic struggle with him," so also Mary has become the ladder by which God came down to us, took on the weakness of our substance, and made of man "a spirit who sees God." Thus Mary brought together what had been separated.[184] The words "a spirit who sees God" are an allusion to Jacob's own words after his struggle: "for I have seen God face to face" (Gen. 32:30), and the name of Israel given to Jacob by the angel has been interpreted by some as meaning "he who saw God." [185] It is also possible that by representing the struggle the artists wanted to recall that Mary, the descendant of Jacob, was the final aim of Israel's mission as the chosen people.

The iconographic scheme of Jacob's vision, represented already during the Early Christian period, varied but little in the course of the centuries. The arc of heaven above the ladder sometimes remains bare; more often, however, in accordance with the wording of Genesis, "and, behold, the Lord stood above it" (28:13), the divine presence is suggested by the Hand of God, or it is represented by the half-figure of Christ, or, as in the bema of the church of St. Sophia in Ohrid, by that of the Ancient of Days.[186] Even when the Marian symbolism was stressed, for instance in the Homilies of the Monk James [187] and in the churches of Prizren and Lesnovo, the painters sometimes continued to place Christ in the arc of heaven. At St. Sophia in Trebizond the upper part of the composition is destroyed; at St. Clement in Ohrid part of the paint has fallen and one can barely distinguish the image in the arc of heaven. At the Holy Apostles in Salonika the small segment of the arc of heaven at the top of the ladder remains bare, but the medallion of the Virgin and Child placed at the summit of the domical vault serves as the crowning image of all the scenes.

At St. Sophia in Trebizond all three angels are ascending; at St. Sophia and St. Clement in Ohrid the angels on the lower steps are ascending and those on the upper steps, descending. The positions are reversed at the Kariye Djami, as they were already in some of the miniatures of the Octateuchs, and this gives a deeper meaning to the composition, for instead of appearing to be turning away from the heaven depicted above, the uppermost angel stretches his hands, in a gesture of adoration, toward the Virgin and Child. At the Holy Apostles in Salonika, as at the Kariye, the two upper angels are ascending and the two lower ones descending, but one detail introduces a new element: Jacob lies on the ground to the left of the ladder; further to the left an angel is seated on a large rectangular stone, his raised right hand points to the central medallion of the Virgin and Child, and he turns his head to look at the reclining Jacob. There is no reference to this angel in the biblical text, but a similar example is to be found in the ninth-century copy of the Homilies of Gregory of Nazianzus, Parisinus gr. 510. Here two angels are ascending the ladder; a third angel stands next to the sleeping Jacob and raises his right hand in a gesture of speech.[188] At St. Sophia in Ohrid, the angel who is on the lowest step of the ladder turns around and seems to be addressing the sleeping figure.[189] At Lesnovo an angel stands next to Jacob.[190]

184 *PG*, 96, col. 713A.

185 St. John of Damascus, *Homélies sur la Nativité et la Dormition*, tr. P. Voulet (Paris, 1961), p. 104, n. 2.

186 Miljković-Pepek, "Matériaux sur l'art macédonien," p. 49 and PL. VIII.

187 Stornajolo, *Omilie*, PL. 7; Omont, *Homélies*, PL. IV, 1.

188 Omont, *Miniatures des plus anciens manuscrits grecs*, PL. XXXVII.

189 Sv. Radojčić and D. Talbot Rice, *Yugoslavia: Mediaeval Frescoes* (UNESCO World Art Series, 4 [Greenwich, Conn.], New York Graphic Society, 1955), PL. V.

190 Okunev, "Lesnovo," PL. XXXIV.

In the representation of the struggle at the Kariye, Jacob and the angel clasp one another bodily; the artist has omitted the typical gesture of the angel's touching the hollow of Jacob's thigh (Gen. 32:25). This has been correctly represented at St. Sophia in Trebizond, and also in manuscripts; for instance, in the Paris manuscript of the Homilies of Gregory of Nazianzus, where this group precedes the representation of Jacob's vision.

MOSES AND THE BURNING BUSH   (PL. 444–52)

The lesson from Exodus 3:1–8 is read twice on the feast of the Annunciation (March 25), during the Great Vespers and in the liturgy. Gregory of Nyssa appears to have been the first to interpret the miracle of the bush that burned with fire but was not consumed as a figure of the virgin birth.[191] From the fourth century on this interpretation recurs frequently in the homilies and hymns.[192] In one of the prayers recited on the feast of the Annunciation, the angel, speaking to Mary, says: "The bush that received the flame without being consumed, O Virgin full of grace, explained to you the ineffable mystery which concerns you: after giving birth, O pure one, you will always remain a Virgin." [193]

The events of the story, which take place at the foot of Mount Horeb, where Moses kept the flock of Jethro, his father-in-law, are developed in three scenes. The first two are grouped in the eastern half of the northern lunette. In the middle ground Moses stands in front of the bush, in the midst of which is a small medallion of the Virgin and Child, and he listens with awe to the words of the angel flying out of the bush. In the next scene Moses, seated on the ground next to his flock, unties the laces of one of his sandals; the other has already been removed.

In the earliest representations only the Hand of God appears above the bush, and even this indication of the divine presence is sometimes omitted. In the Homilies of Gregory of Nazianzus, Paris. gr. 510, the full figure of the angel stands in the bush, in front of which Moses bends to untie his sandal.[194] Two different moments are combined here: in the first, the angel of the Lord appears to Moses (3:2); in the second, God tells Moses to put off the shoes from his feet (3:4–5). These two moments are separately represented in the Octateuchs. There is no angel in the bush of the first scene and the arc of heaven above it remains bare; in the second scene an angel flies toward Moses, who unties his sandal.[195] In the full-page miniature of the Paris and Vatican copies of the Homilies of the Monk James, Moses stands in front of the bush, in the midst of which appears the head of Christ Emmanuel.[196]

The first suggestion of a Marian interpretation of this miracle occurs, as already mentioned, in the Smyrna manuscript of Cosmas Indicopleustes: the Virgin with the Christ Child is depicted above the figure of Moses standing in front of the bush.[197] In the Sinai icon, in which prophets are grouped around the central figure of the Virgin and Child, Moses points to the burning bush (Fig. 1).[198] It is only in the Palaeologan period that the artists identified the Virgin completely with the burning bush by placing her image in the midst of the flames. At St. Clement in Ohrid, as at the Kariye, the medallion of the Virgin and Child appears in the bush, and the angel flies

191 Gregory of Nyssa, *La Vie de Moïse, ou Traité de la perfection en matière de vertu*, tr. J. Daniélou (Paris, 1955), p. 57 and n. 3.

192 Mercenier, *La prière*, II,1, pp. 93, 97–98, 347, 361; II,2, pp. 29–30; *PG*, 96, cols. 689B, 712C; 97, cols. 868–69; Eustratiades, Ἡ Θεοτόκος, s.v. βάθος.

193 Mercenier, *La prière*, II,1, p. 361.

194 Omont, *Miniatures des plus anciens manuscrits grecs.* PL.

XLII.

195 *Miniatures de l'Octateuque grec de Smyrne*, preface by D.-C. Hesseling (Codices Graeci et Latini Palaeographice depicti duce Scatone de Vries . . . Supplementum VI; Leiden, 1909), Fig. 156.

196 Stornajolo, *Omilie*, PL. 21; Omont, *Homélies*, PL. X,1.

197 Strzygowski, *Die Miniaturen*, PL. XXIX.

198 G. and M. Soteriou, *Icônes*, I, PL. 54.

toward Moses. At St. Nicholas Orphanos in Salonika, the angel again addresses Moses, but the bust of the Virgin is orant, in the bush, without the Child.[199] At the churches of Asinou, the Protaton, and Gračanica and in the composition of the Dormition at Staro Nagoričino, the Virgin in the bush is also orant, without the Child, but the angel has been omitted.[200] The painter of Lesnovo (Fig. 14), however, has retained the earlier formula of Christ in the bush,[201] just as in Jacob's vision he depicted Christ in the arc of heaven above the ladder.

The fresco of St. Clement is the earliest one among the monumental compositions known to date which shows the Virgin and Child inside the bush, but a slightly earlier example is to be seen in an Armenian Lectionary illustrated in 1286 in Cilicia. The full-length figure of the Virgin orant, with a medallion of Christ on her breast, stands in the burning bush, in front of which Moses kneels to loosen the strings of his sandal.[202] In Armenian hymns also Mary is hailed as the bush that was not consumed by the divine fire she received in her womb, but it seems probable that the typically Byzantine image of the Blachernitissa has been copied from a Byzantine model. This would suggest that the representation of the burning bush with the image of the Virgin and Child was already known considerably before 1295, when the frescoes of St. Clement were painted.

The fragmentary composition at St. Sophia in Trebizond shows only the full-length figure of the angel standing in the bush; the type, as noted above, had been represented in the ninth century in the Homilies of Gregory of Nazianzus, but here the angel is turned to the right, slightly bent forward, his right hand extended, probably speaking to Moses, whose figure has been destroyed.[203]

The third scene of the Moses cycle is painted in the soffit of the arch adjoining the lunette: Moses stands with head slightly averted next to the bush, which is represented as in the preceding composition with the angel and the medallion of the Virgin and Child. The attitude of Moses agrees with the passage of Exodus inscribed above: "And Moses hid his face; for he was afraid to look upon God" (3:6), but the rod that he holds by its small end suggests a conflation with the episode recounted in Exodus 4:2–4: the rod, cast on the ground, became a serpent, but when the Lord commanded Moses to "take it by the tail . . . it became a rod in his hand."

In the representation of this episode in the Octateuchs, the serpent lies on the ground and Moses looks up to the Hand of God emerging from the arc of heaven.[204] In the miniature of the Homilies of the Monk James, where the miracle of the rod appears on the same page as that of the burning bush, Moses holds the serpent by its tail and looks up to the angel.[205] At Lesnovo, where the two miracles are again depicted side by side, the serpent is erect in front of Moses (Fig. 14).[206] The painting of the Kariye most probably corresponds to the moment when the serpent, held by the tail, becomes again a rod, and the artist has suggested this by making the upper end of the rod narrower than the lower end.

The miracle of the rod has been interpreted by some Church Fathers as a symbol of Christ's incarnation,[207] and as such it could be associated with the scene of the burning bush not merely as a subsequent event in the life of Moses but as a typological scene. At St. Clement in Ohrid

199 Xyngopoulos, Ἅγιος Νικόλαος Ὀρφανός, Fig. 118.
200 Petković, *La peinture serbe*, II, p. 29 and Fig. 31; Millet, *Athos*, PL. 32.
201 Okunev, "Lesnovo," PL. XXXV and Fig. 165.
202 Erevan, *Matenadaran* 979, fol. 229. The image of the Virgin is reproduced in A. Tchobanian, *Armenian Pages* (in Armenian) (Paris, 1912), Fig. 32; the other half of the miniature, Moses removing his sandal, in L. A. Durnovo, *Drevnearmjanskaja miniatjura* (Erevan, 1952), PL. 36.
203 Talbot Rice, *Trebizond*, p. 151, Fig. 112, and PL. 64B.

204 Hesseling, *Octateuque de Smyrne*, Fig. 157 *a*; Th. Uspenskij, *L'Octateuque de la Bibliothèque du Sérail à Constantinople* (Izvestija Russkogo Arxeologičeskogo Instituta v Konstantinopolě, XII), Album (Munich, 1907), Fig. 97; also in the Octateuchs of the Vatican MSS gr. 746 and gr. 747.
205 See n. 196.
206 Okunev, "Lesnovo," p. 238 and Fig. 163.
207 Gregory of Nyssa, *Vie de Moïse*, tr. Daniélou, pp. 39–40. The same interpretation is given by Cyril of Alexandria, *PG*, 99, col. 472A–B.

the painter has represented instead Moses receiving the tables of the law. In his first Homily on the Dormition John of Damascus considers this also as an image of the Virgin, mentioning it at the same time as the burning bush: "The burning bush announced you, the divinely written tables prefigured you";[208] in other homilies, as well as in the hymns, the tables of the law are also mentioned among the types of the Virgin.[209]

THE DEDICATION OF SOLOMON'S TEMPLE (PL. 453–60)

The short lesson from III Kings 8:1–11, read during the Great Vespers at the feast of the Presentation of the Virgin in the Temple (Nov. 21), describes how "the ark of the Lord, and the tabernacle of the congregation, and all the holy vessels that were in the tabernacle" were carried out of the city of David which is Sion, to the temple built by Solomon and "into the oracle of the house, to the most holy place, even under the wings of the cherubim."

The hymns and the homilies dedicated to the Virgin recall how she was introduced into the sacred precinct which the high priest himself could enter only once a year, and how the spiritual temple of God entered into the material temple. Mary is hailed as the temple of God more beautiful than the temple of Solomon, as the ark of the covenant, the tabernacle of the omnipotent God, the spiritual ark enclosing the incomprehensible Logos, and she is identified with each one of the sacred vessels.[210] In his second Homily on the Dormition, John of Damascus, describing the funeral of the Virgin, cites the passages describing the dedication of Solomon's temple and the transfer of the ark, which he compares with the solemn procession accompanying the body of the Virgin. For just as Solomon summoned all the elders of Israel, and the priests brought the ark of the covenant into the Holy of Holies, so also in order to carry to its rest the spiritual ark of the Logos, the new Solomon himself, the Prince of Peace, summoned the celestial host and the chiefs of the New Alliance; that is, the apostles.[211] The Dedication of Solomon's Temple has been more extensively represented than any of the other prefigurations of the Virgin. The first episode of this cycle, the Bearing of the Ark of the Covenant, has been placed in the eastern bay of the parecclesion, which is devoted to the Last Judgment, in the western half of the southern lunette. The story continues with the Bearing of the Sacred Vessels, depicted in the southern half of the adjoining arch, and it culminates in the large composition of the Dedication of the Temple, which fills the entire southern lunette of the western bay.

This detailed cycle has no parallel in other monuments, and only a few of the episodes appear in contemporary and later churches. We also lack the comparative material that illuminated manuscripts provide for the scenes from the life of Jacob and Moses, since in the only extant copy of the Book of Kings, Vaticanus gr. 333, there are very few miniatures for the third book and none of these pertain to Solomon's temple. However, some of the episodes can be compared with representations of similar if not identical events.

The Bearing of the Ark (PL. 453–55) is one of these. The ark of the covenant had been transferred several times before the reign of Solomon, and these transfers have been represented in such manuscripts as the Joshua Roll, the Vatican Bible (Reg. gr. 1), and the Octateuchs.[212]

208 *PG*, 96, col. 712C.

209 Andrew of Crete, *PG*, 97, col. 868C; Eustratiades, 'Η Θεοτόκος, s.v. πλάξ.

210 Mercenier and Bainbridge, *La prière*, II,1, 2nd ed., pp. 91, 102, 147, 154–55, 164, 168, 170, 172–74; Laurentin, *Maria*, pp. 77–83; Congar, *Le mystère du temple*, pp. 302–08.

211 *PG*, 96, cols. 737C–740A.

212 K. Weitzmann, *The Joshua Roll* (Princeton, 1948), Figs. 5–8, 11, 12, 16, 17; *Le miniature della Bibbia cod. Vat. Reg., gr. 1 e del Salterio cod. Vat. Palat. gr. 381* (Collezione paleografica vaticana, I; Rome, 1905), fol. 85v; Hesseling, *Octateuque de Smyrne*, Figs. 272, 274, 277; Uspenskij, *Octateuque du Sérail*, Figs. 226, 233.

With but slight variations these miniatures represent, as at the parecclesion, four priests, in classical dress, carrying the ark on their shoulders. In the Joshua Roll and the illustrations of the Book of Joshua in the Octateuchs the ark is a gabled structure, with sloping top, as at the Kariye, but it rests on a wide slab; whereas in the Vatican Bible and the miniatures of the Octateuchs which illustrate Exodus and Leviticus the top is rounded, as it is also in the *Topography* of Cosmas Indicopleustes. The closest analogy to the composition of the parecclesion is to be seen in one of the miniatures of the Octateuch at Mount Athos, Vatopedi 602, illustrated probably in the thirteenth century (Fig. 15). Except for the wide slab supporting the ark, and the position of the fourth bearer, who is seen slightly in advance of his companion as he should be, instead of behind him as in the fresco, the two compositions are almost identical. This miniature shows how widely the Marian symbolism had spread during the Palaeologan period, for in this narrative scene of the Old Testament the ark of the covenant, carried across the Jordan, is adorned with the medallion figure of the Virgin, painted in the center of the gable [213]—an image which identifies the ark with Mary, "the ark gilded by the Holy Ghost," and which is to be seen in the typological representations of the ark, for instance at Gračanica, Lesnovo, Curtea-de-Argeş, and a small chapel in the monastery of St. Catherine on Mount Sinai.[214] At the parecclesion the surface paint has fallen from the yellow disc on the gable of the ark, but it seems probable that here also there was originally an image of the Virgin. In the composition of the Tabernacle of Moses at the Holy Apostles in Salonika, two medallions adorn the ark, but it is not possible to determine whether or not they contain an image of the Virgin.

The relatively narrow surface of the arch provided room for only two priests bearing the sacred vessels (PL. 456, 457). In contradistinction to the priests who carry the ark, these wear a mantle over their tunics and the Jewish headcloth that falls on the shoulders. The priest at the left holds with both hands the large seven-branched candelabrum, the Menorah. In the paintings of the fourteenth century the Menorah usually has the shape of a circular tray with seven tapers, six of them around the edges of the tray and the seventh in the center.[215] In the Octateuchs and in the Florence manuscript of Cosmas Indicopleustes the candelabrum has foliate branches.[216] At the parecclesion, and also at the Holy Apostles in Salonika, the painters attempted to give a faithful image of the Menorah, as it is described in Exodus 25:31–34 and represented in Jewish art,[217] by showing the "almonds" and the "knops" on the shaft and on the branches, which terminate in sharp spikes projecting from small bowls. There is no image on the rounded element from which the seven branches radiate, but in two frescoes of later date, at Dionysiou and Dochiariou on Mount Athos, we see the bust figure of the Virgin and Child,[218] for the candelabrum is one of the types of the Virgin.[219]

213 In other miniatures of the Vatopedi Octateuch (Weitzmann, *The Joshua Roll*, Figs. 7 [above, Demus' essay, Fig. 58], and 17) and in the Octateuch of Constantinople (Uspenskij, *Octateuque du Sérail*, Fig. 233) the Deesis is represented in the gable of the ark. In the Joshua Roll a man stands in the attitude of prayer in the gable, between two figures bent low in adoration (Weitzmann, *The Joshua Roll*, Figs. 5, 16, 48).

214 Petković, *La peinture serbe*, II, PL. LX; Okunev, "Lesnovo," PL. XXXIV: N. Beljaev, "Le 'Tabernacle du Témoignage' dans la peinture balkanique du XIVᵉ siècle," *L'art byzantin chez les Slaves. Dédié à la mémoire de Théodore Uspenskii*, I: *Les Balkans*, Part 2 (Paris, 1930), pp. 315–24 and PL. XLVI; G. A. Soteriou, Τοιχογραφίαι τῆς Σκηνῆς τοῦ Μαρτυρίου εἰς Παρεκκλησία τοῦ τείχους τῆς Μονῆς Σινᾶ, *Silloge bizantina in onore di Silvio Giuseppe Mercati* (Rome, 1957) =*Studi bizantini e neoellenici, 9*, pp. 389–91 and Fig. 5.

215 Petković, *La peinture serbe*, II, PL. LX,1; Soteriou, Τοιχο-

γραφίαι, Fig. 3; Beljaev, "Le 'Tabernacle du Témoignage'," PL. XLVI.

216 Hesseling, *Octateuque de Smyrne*, Fig. 193; Uspenskij, *Octateuque du Sérail*, Fig. 161. The miniature of the Florence MS is reproduced in P. Bloch, "Siebenarmige Leuchter in christlichen Kirchen," *Wallraf-Richartz-Jahrbuch: Westdeutsches Jahrbuch für Kunstgeschichte*, 23 (1961), pp. 55–90; see p. 72, Fig. 47. In the Smyrna MS the candlestick has yet another shape; Strzygowski, *Die Miniaturen*, PL. XXVIII,1.

217 *The Excavations at Dura-Europos*, Final Report, VIII, Part I; C. H. Kraeling, *The Synagogue* (New Haven, 1956), PL. XVI, LI, LIX; E. R. Goodenough, *Jewish Symbols in the Greco-Roman Period*, IV (New York, 1954), pp. 71–77.

218 Millet, *Athos*, PL. 196,2, 218,2.

219 Laurentin, *Maria*, pp. 36–37, 78–79. John of Damascus, PG, 96, cols. 672A, 712C, 758D. Eustratiades, Ἡ Θεοτόκος, s.v. λυχνία.

The priest at the right carries on his shoulders, holding it with both hands, the golden stamnos containing the manna. As in all contemporary examples, the stamnos has roughly the shape of an amphora with a long neck, but there is, in addition, a cylindrical object with crossed ribbons rising above the opening of the neck. A similar object projecting from the mouth of the stamnos has been represented in the composition of the Tabernacle in the chapel of the monastery of St. Catherine on Mount Sinai (Fig. 16).[220] In Jewish art the Torah scroll is sometimes placed next to the Torah shrine together with the ceremonial vessels.[221] At Gračanica, in the composition of the Tabernacle of Moses, the cylindrical object placed on the altar next to the stamnos must be the Torah scroll, and it is probably this same scroll that at the Kariye and in the chapel of Mount Sinai projects from the mouth of the stamnos. At Gračanica (Fig. 17), and in other paintings as well, the stamnos is adorned with the medallion figure of the Virgin,[222] for she is the golden urn "carrying Christ the celestial manna." [223] At the Kariye no such image is visible.

The final scene of the dedication of the temple built by Solomon, when the ark of the covenant was brought into the Holy of Holies and deposited on the altar, has been given great prominence, for the main theme of the prayers and chants on the feast of the Presentation is that the Virgin, the immaculate tabernacle of the Almighty, the spiritual temple, is offered to the temple of the ancient law to dwell in the Holy of Holies. The dedication of Solomon's temple was represented at the synagogue of Dura-Europos, but unfortunately only a relatively small part of this composition has survived [224] and there are no other early examples with which the scene at the Kariye might be compared. Solomon, nimbed and attired like a Byzantine emperor, holds a lighted taper and swings a censer as he leads the elders of Israel (PL. 459). This part of the composition recalls the representation in Byzantine manuscripts of liturgical processions or other ceremonies in which the emperors took part.[225]

In the right half of the lunette, the bearers deposit on the altar the ark of the covenant (on which the medallion containing the bust of the Virgin can be faintly seen), while the elders of Israel remain outside the sanctuary wall (PL. 460). According to the description given in III Kings 6:27, the cherubim set within the inner house of Solomon's temple stretched their wings "so that the wing of the one touched the one wall, and the wing of the other cherub touched the other wall; and their wings touched one another in the midst of the house."

The representation at the Kariye does not agree with this description, for the wings of the cherubim do not touch "one another in the midst of the house." The cherubim are placed each one next to one of the projecting walls of a low structure raised behind the altar which has the appearance of a rectangular niche; the cherub on the right is fully exposed, but of the one on the left only the tips of the wings are visible. This image agrees better with the description of the cherubim that were made for the tabernacle of Moses and placed on the two ends of the mercy seat, "One cherub on the end on this side, and another cherub on the other end on that side" (Exod. 37:8); this enables us to identify the rectangular niche with the mercy seat. The painter has, however, paid special attention to the "glory of the Lord" that filled the house of the Lord when the ark was deposited in Solomon's temple (III Kings 8:10–11) by drawing a cusped mandorla in the arc of heaven, and a ray of light that descends on the ark, for the glory of the Lord that filled the temple is an image of the Divinity that dwelt in Mary, the spiritual temple.

220 Soteriou, Τοιχογραφίαι, PL. 4.
221 Goodenough, *Jewish Symbols*, I (New York, 1953), Figs. 772, 810, 968, 973.
222 Petković, *La peinture serbe*, II, PL. LX.

223 Laurentin, *Maria*, p. 37, n. 9; Eustratiades, Ἡ Θεοτόκος, s.v. στάμνος.
224 Kraeling, *The Synagogue*, pp. 113–17 and PL. LVIII.
225 *Menologio di Basilio II*, II, PL. 204, 350, 420.

In almost all examples of this scene in other churches of the fourteenth century, instead of Solomon's temple the tabernacle of Moses has been represented, with Moses and Aaron usually standing in the tent housing the ark of the covenant; for instance, at St. Clement, Gračanica, Lesnovo, and Dečani in Yugoslavia, at the Protaton on Mount Athos, in the chapel of Mount Sinai, and in the northern lunette of the southern narthex of the Holy Apostles in Salonika.[226] At Curtea-de-Argeş in Rumania, we find a different interpretation in the composition painted on the semicircular wall of the apse, above the Communion of the Apostles. The central unit is similar to the tabernacle represented in the other churches of the fourteenth century, but from either side six kings—the chiefs of the twelve tribes of Israel—bearing sacred vessels, approach the tabernacle, and the half-figures of Isaiah and Jeremiah, holding open scrolls, appear above the tent.[227]

At the Holy Apostles, Salonika, where the tabernacle of Moses adorned the northern lunette, there is a fragmentary "temple scene" in the dome, in the section above the northwestern pendentive. A large temple, partly effaced but with four columns still visible, fills the background. A man clad in a blue tunic and red mantle stands in the center, in front of the temple, hands raised, and he is approached from the right by a man in classical costume, slightly bent forward, who carries what looks like a ewer and a jug. To the left, at a short distance from the temple, there are fragmentary remains of a man's figure wearing a dark red mantle. Judging from the section that is still visible the temple must have had seven columns; one is reminded of the passage in Proverbs 9:1, "Wisdom hath builded her house, she hath hewn out her seven pillars," the opening words of the lesson read on the feasts of the Birth and the Dormition of the Virgin. Wisdom building her temple has been interpreted as an image of the Incarnation, and representations of the Temple of Holy Wisdom, or the Repast of Holy Wisdom, form part of the biblical prefigurations in several churches of Yugoslavia, each time according to a different iconographic scheme.[228] At St. Clement in Ohrid, Holy Wisdom, represented as an angel with a cruciform nimbus, is seated at a table on which are placed a vase, a bowl containing bread, and an open book inscribed with the words "Come, eat of my bread, and drink" (Prov. 9:5). Three feminine figures, holding bread and a vase, stand on the right, and behind them is a three-aisled basilica with seven columns. The pediment of the temple has a small figure of the Virgin, an indication that she is the true temple in which Christ has come to dwell.[229] At Gračanica, and in the first of the four scenes devoted to the Holy Wisdom at Dečani, the building represented in the background has again seven columns.[230] These examples confirm the identification of the building represented at the Holy Apostles with the temple built by Wisdom, but in the Yugoslav churches mentioned above, as well as in the church of the Virgin Ljeviška at Prizren,[231] Holy Wisdom is represented as an angel, whereas at the Holy Apostles a man stands in front of the temple. Two other examples of the Wisdom scene should also be mentioned. The first is to be seen at the Catholicon of Chilandar, which was repainted in 1804 but retains the iconography of the original compositions of the early fourteenth century. Holy Wisdom, represented as an angel with three heads, is seated at a table placed under a ciborium supported by seven columns; a paten and a ewer are on the table, and behind the table stand two angels holding a chalice and

226 Petković, *La peinture serbe*, II, PL. LX; Okunev, "Lesnovo," PL. XXXIV; Petković and Bošković, *Dečani*, Album, PL. CCLXIX; Millet, *Athos*, PL. 32; Soteriou, Τοιχογραφίαι, PL. 4.
227 Beljaev, "Le 'Tabernacle du Témoignage'," PL. XLVI.
228 Meyendorff, "L'iconographie" (see n. 61), pp. 259–77.

229 Ibid., p. 270 and Fig. 7; Petković, *La peinture serbe*, I, PL. 24 *a*.
230 Meyendorff, "L'iconographie," Fig. 8; Petković, *La peinture serbe*, I, PL. 53 *a*; Petković and Bošković, *Dečani*, Album, PL. CCLXVI.
231 Meyendorff, "L'iconographie," Fig. 4.

a paten. To the right Solomon, carrying a scroll inscribed with the words "Wisdom hath builded her house," points to the Holy Wisdom.[232] In the dome of the narthex of Markov monastery Christ Logos is surrounded by the personifications of the gifts of the Holy Spirit, along with Solomon, who holds a scroll carrying the same inscription. Below are the angels, the attendants whom Wisdom has sent forth, and a table on which are placed the bread and wine that Wisdom invited all men to eat and drink.[233]

Though the figure standing in front of the temple at the Holy Apostles may also represent Solomon, it does not seem to me that the composition is to be connected with the two that have just been mentioned. We have here an ideal image of the Dedication of Solomon's Temple: the figure on the right represents a priest bringing the sacred vessels to the temple, on the left is possibly a pendant figure, rather than one of the attendants sent forth by Wisdom, who are usually depicted as angels.[234] To the temple erected by Solomon the artist has, however, given the form of the temple built by Wisdom, with its seven pillars, a temple which was the image of the Incarnation.

But if no contemporary monuments offer close parallels to the cycle at the Kariye, two of the scenes from the cycle occur in churches of later date. At the Catholicon of Dionysiou, on Mount Athos, decorated in 1547, the Dedication of Solomon's Temple, painted on the lowest register of the eastern arch of the dome, on the north side, is almost identical with the scene at the Kariye. Solomon, nimbed and clad in the Byzantine imperial costume, turns his head slightly toward the elders of Israel who accompany him, and he points to the priests who are depositing the ark of the covenant on the altar.[235] On the south side of the arch, facing this scene, is represented the transfer of the ark by David to Jerusalem.[236] The tabernacle of Moses is painted on the north wall.[237]

At the church of Dochiariou on Mount Athos, on the south end of the bema wall, only the ark deposited by the priests on the altar has been represented, and not Solomon with the elders of Israel, and the scene forms a pendant to the tabernacle of Moses, with Aaron standing behind the altar, painted on the north end of the bema wall.[238]

In view of the iconographic connection of some of these paintings with those at the Kariye, it is important to recall that these scenes do not figure among those that are described in the Painter's Manual of Mount Athos. The three compositions listed there that are connected with the ark, or the tabernacle, are the following. The first subject is the tabernacle of Moses, with Moses and Aaron standing inside the tent,[239] the scene that is most frequently represented in the churches of the fourteenth century and of later date. The second scene illustrates the transfer of the ark to Jerusalem, when "David and all the house of Israel played before the Lord on all manner of instruments." [240] This scene, which illustrates II Kings 6:3–5, is represented, as we have seen, at Dionysiou as a pendant to the Dedication of Solomon's Temple; it also occurs in other churches of Mount Athos, namely at the Catholicon of Lavra, above the Divine Liturgy in the bema, and at the Portaitissa of Lavra, where it is fully developed in the dome of the

232 Millet, *Athos*, PL. 79,2.

233 Sv. N. Radojčić, "Les fresques du monastère de Marko et la vie de St. Basile le Nouveau" (in Serbian with French résumé), *ZRVI*, 49, No. 4 (1956), pp. 215–27 and Figs. 4, 6, 7, 9.

234 In the Septuagint the attendants are called δοῦλοι and the Slavonic version has "maidens," which explains the feminine

figures represented at Ohrid and Gračanica. Cf. Meyendorff, "L'iconographie," pp. 270–72.

235 Millet, *Athos*, PL. 201,1.

236 Ibid., PL. 201,2.

237 Ibid., PL. 196,2.

238 Ibid., PL. 218,2, 219,2.

239 Ἑρμηνεία, pp. 57–58.

240 Ibid., p. 62.

narthex.[241] The third scene describes the building of Solomon's temple: Solomon, holding a book and accompanied by the elders and the soldiers of Israel, watches the workmen busy at their task.[242] I have found no example of this composition which is related to chapter seven of III Kings, rather than to the actual dedication of the temple.

The fact that the Dedication does not figure among the scenes described in the Painter's Manual gives greater significance to the iconographic connection between the compositions of the Kariye and Dionysiou. It does not seem likely that the Athonite painter repeated, more than two centuries later, a composition that had been represented only once at Constantinople. We must suppose that the Dedication scene was fairly well known and that there existed other examples besides the one at the parecclesion. In the Athonite paintings the scenes of the tabernacle and the ark are placed in the bema, close to the Communion of the Apostles or the Divine Liturgy, and thereby their typological meaning is more directly connected with Christ himself, the juxtaposition of these scenes recalling the comparisons made in the ninth chapter of the Epistle to the Hebrews. But the Marian symbolism is not entirely overlooked, for her image adorns the ark, the altar, and the sacred vessels.

ISAIAH PROPHESYING; THE ANGEL SMITING THE ASSYRIANS BEFORE JERUSALEM
(PL. 461–65)

The composition in the southern soffit of the western arch represents the destruction of the armies of Sennacherib, King of Assyria, prophesied by Isaiah to Hezekiah (Isa. 37:21–36; IV Kings 19:20–35). Isaiah, holding a scroll on which were inscribed excerpts from his prophecy, stands on the left, his right hand extended toward the angel, who, with raised sword, "went forth, and smote in the camp of the Assyrians a hundred and fourscore and five thousand" (Isa. 37:36); some of the slain and the wounded lie on the ground. The action takes place in front of the crenellated walls encircling the large city of Jerusalem; the recessed tympanum above the gate contains a small figure of the orant Virgin.

I mentioned above that Metochites' personal devotion to the archangel Michael may explain why this prophecy of Isaiah, which is not read on any of the Marian feasts, was represented at the Kariye, and that by adding the image of the Virgin the painter integrated his composition into the biblical typological cycle. This image, and some of the words inscribed on Isaiah's scroll, "he [Sennacherib] shall not come into this city," [243] suggest a connection with the typological scene of the "closed gate," based on Ezekiel 44:2, "This gate shall be shut, it shall not be opened, and no man shall enter in by it; because the Lord, the God of Israel, hath entered in by it," part of the lesson that is read on all the Marian feasts. But, as we shall see below, in this iconographic theme the Virgin is represented on the door, or in front of it, whereas in the present case the small image in the typanum has no tangible connection with the door itself. The Virgin is here identified with Sion, the inviolate city, an identification already expressed in the ninth century in several miniatures of the Psalters with marginal illustrations.[244] God's promise to Hezekiah, "For I will defend this city to save it for mine own sake, and for my servant David's sake" (Isa. 37:35), could also be interpreted by reference to Mary, the descendant of David.

The image of the Virgin above the gate has also other connotations; it calls to mind that

---

241 Millet, *Athos*, PL. 118,2 118,3, 263. At Lesnovo this scene illustrates Psalm 149; Okunev, "Lesnovo," PL. XL,2.
242 Ἑρμηνεία, p. 63.

243 Underwood, Vol. 1 of this series, p. 233.
244 See above p. 311.

the Virgin was par excellence the protector of Constantinople.[245] In the first ode of a canon sung in honor of the Virgin in time of war it was said that the power of her hand would scatter the forces of the enemy as the armies of Sennacherib had been scattered.[246] The commemoration of the victory over the Avars in 619 was celebrated on June 5, and the lesson from Isaiah 37:21–36 was read during the services.[247] In the sermon attributed to Theodore Synkellos, delivered on this occasion, the deliverance of Constantinople was attributed to the Virgin, and when in 626 the Avars, assisted by the Slavs, again besieged Constantinople, the patriarch Sergius, according to some sources, had images of the Virgin placed on all the western gates of the city.[248] The victory on this occasion, and those over the Arabs in 677 and 717–18, as well as later deliverances of Constantinople were attributed to the miraculous intervention of the Virgin; and they are recalled in the Synaxarion.[249] The proemium of the Akathistos Hymn is addressed to the Virgin as follows:

> To the invincible Leader I, Thy City, freed from danger,
>   I dedicate the thanksgiving for victory, O Mother of God.
>   Since thou hast power unassailable,
>   Free me from all kinds of trials,
>   That I may cry out to Thee: Hail, Bride, unbrided.[250]

Thus the image of the Virgin in the tympanum of the gate of Jerusalem not only is a symbol of the Virgin, identified with Sion, but it no doubt reminded all those who contemplated it that she was the principal defender of Constantinople, the city dedicated to her.

The slaughter of the Assyrian army by Michael had been represented at a very early date on an encaustic icon. A. Xyngopoulos has called attention to the description of this painting contained in one of the homilies of John Chrysostom, quoted at the Second Council of Nicaea, and he has noted that the composition must have been very similar to the fresco at the Kariye, except that David and not Isaiah appeared next to the archangel, who stood above the fallen enemy.[251] The miracle is not represented among the paintings preserved in the chapel of the cathedral of St. Sophia in Kiev, dedicated to the archangel Michael, nor among the apparitions of Michael to men depicted in the diaconicon of the monastery of Mirozh, near Pskov, but a few examples occur elsewhere. On the bronze doors of Monte Sant'Angelo, made in 1076 in Constantinople and decorated with an extensive cycle of the apparitions and miracles of Michael, the second scene in the top row of the left panel shows Michael standing next to the city of Jerusalem and piercing with his lance one of the fallen enemy.[252] This miracle has also been represented on the south door of the cathedral of Suzdal, made in 1230–33,[253] and on a fifteenth-century icon at the cathedral of the Archangel in the Kremlin, at Moscow. Here, thirteen episodes surround the central figure of Michael in military costume. In the last scene but one,

245 A. Frolow, "La dédicace de Constantinople dans la tradition byzantine," *RHR*, 127 (1944), pp. 89–115. For the Virgin's role as protector of Constantinople, see also N. H. Baynes, "The Supernatural Defenders of Constantinople," *Byzantine Studies and Other Essays* (London, 1955), pp. 243–60.

246 J. Goar, Εὐχολόγιον *sive Rituale Graecorum* (Paris, 1647), p. 813.

247 Dmitrievskij, *Opisanie liturgičeskix rukopisej*, I. Τυπικά, pp. 78–79; Frolow, "La dédicace," p. 96.

248 Frolow, "La dédicace," pp. 95–97.

249 H. Delehaye, *Propylaeum ad Acta Sanctorum Novembris: Synaxarium Ecclesiae Constantinopolitanae* (Brussels, 1902), cols.

729–30, 901–04.

250 Translation by C. Mango; cf. E. Wellesz, "The 'Akathistos': A Study in Byzantine Hymnography," *DOP*, 9 and 10 (1956), p. 147.

251 A. Xyngopoulos, Ἡ κηρόχυτος γραφὴ τοῦ Χρυσοστόμου, in Ἐπετηρὶς ἑταιρείας βυζαντινῶν σπουδῶν, 21 (1951), pp. 49–58.

252 H. W. Schulz, *Denkmäler der Kunst des Mittelalters in Unteritalien* (Dresden, 1860), I, pp. 242–51 and PL. XXXIX.

253 Akademiia Nauk SSR, *Istorija Russkogo Iskusstva*, ed. I. E. Grabar, I (Akademija Nauk SSSR, Institut Istorii Iskusstv; Moscow, 1953), pp. 480–84.

on the right, the archangel puts to flight a numerous army on horseback; some of the soldiers have already fallen on the ground.[254]

In these examples, directly connected with the legend of Michael, there was no special reason to recall Isaiah's prophecy by representing him, but he appears in two western manuscripts because the miniatures are related to the Book of Isaiah. In the Gumpert Bible, a German manuscript of the late twelfth century, the composition, painted in a beautiful frame, serves as a frontispiece to Isaiah: Michael, sword in hand, flies down to smite the Assyrians; the city of Jerusalem fills the right half of the quatrefoil, and above this quatrefoil, to the right, Isaiah has been represented speaking to Hezekiah.[255] A miniature in the Bible Moralisée of Paris (Bibl. Nat. lat. 11560) illustrates Isaiah 34:1–5, in which the prophet speaks of the Lord's indignation, his fury at the armies of all nations, which he has delivered to the slaughter. There is no special reference here to the Assyrians or to Michael, but this is the episode depicted by the artist: an angel with bared sword appears above the clouds; Isaiah stands below, on the left, and on the right are the people fallen on the ground.[256]

The miracles performed by Michael, listed in the Painter's Manual of Mount Athos, include the destruction of the Assyrian army—Michael appears in the sky, above the army, but Isaiah is not mentioned; another one, in which Michael again appears in the sky, is the saving of the city of Constantinople when it was attacked by the Persians.[257] At the church of Lesnovo, dedicated to the archangels Michael and Gabriel, one of the scenes painted on the lower register of the nave walls shows Michael repulsing the navy of the Saracens, which was threatening Constantinople.[258] In several Moldavian churches of the sixteenth century, an elaborate composition of an attack against Constantinople, by sea and by land, forms part of the illustration of the Akathistos Hymn; within the city walls the people are seen carrying, in solemn procession, the "Mandylion" and the icon of the Virgin.[259] In his discussion of these representations V. Grecu, referring to the scene of Michael defending Constantinople described in the Painter's Manual, has suggested that the defender's role may have been attributed to Michael through a misunderstanding, the epithet of the Virgin, ὑπέρμαχος στρατηγός, the invincible leader, having been interpreted as designating the archangel.[260] According to one tradition, the Akathistos Hymn was composed on the occasion of the attack on Constantinople in 626. This view is no longer held by modern scholarship,[261] but the representation of the Virgin's icon in the Moldavian frescoes conveys, at a later date and in a different form, the same idea as the small figure of the Virgin in the fresco at the Kariye, that is, of Mary as the protector of the city.

AARON AND HIS SONS BEFORE THE ALTAR (PL. 466–68)

On the northern soffit of the western arch, three priests wearing a chlamys over a short tunic, tight trousers, and boots approach an altar placed in a rectangular niche; each priest car-

254 V. Lazarev [Lasareff] and O. Demus, *USSR: Early Russian Icons* (UNESCO World Art Series, 9 [Greenwich, Conn.], New York Graphic Society, 1958), PL. XXVI.

255 G. Swarzenski, *Die Salzburger Malerei* (Leipzig, 1908–13), p. 133, PL. XL, Fig. 128.

256 A. de Laborde, ed., *La Bible moralisée illustrée*, II (Paris, 1912), PL. 342. The slaughter of the Assyrians, but without the figure of Isaiah, has also been represented in the Farfa Bible—W. Neuss, *Die Katalanische Bibelillustration um die Wende des ersten Jahrtausends und die altspanische Buchmalerei* (Bonn and Leipzig, 1922), PL. 26 and Fig. 86—and on a miniature in a private collection in Basel, published by H. Buchthal, "Some

Sicilian Miniatures of the Thirteenth Century," *Miscellanea Pro Arte: Hermann Schnitzler zur Vollendung des 60. Lebensjahres* (Düsseldorf, 1965), pp. 185–90 and PL. XCVIII. Buchthal also mentions in this connection a fresco in the Painted Chamber of Westminster Palace, p. 188.

257 Ἑρμηνεία, p. 174.

258 Okunev, "Lesnovo," pp. 250–51 and PL. XXX,2.

259 Henry, *Les églises de la Moldavie*, pp. 238–41.

260 V. Grecu, "Eine Belagerung Konstantinopels in der rumänischen Kirchenmalerei," *Byzantion*, 1 (1924), pp. 288–89.

261 Wellesz, "The 'Akathistos,'" pp. 143–56.

ries a small casket, and the first one holds a censer as well. Flame-like "glories" emerge from the arc of heaven above the niche and a ray of light descends on the first priest. A complex structure rises on the left, behind the priests. In a short note published in the *Dumbarton Oaks Papers*, Mrs. Gudrun Engberg has identified the accompanying inscription, of which only a few words are clearly legible, as being a part of Ezekiel 43:27 (rather than as a passage from Exodus 40, as was previously thought): "upon the eighth day, and so forward, the priests shall make your burnt offerings upon the altar." [262] This is the beginning of the lesson from Ezekiel (43:27–44:4) read during the Great Vespers on the feasts of the Birth, the Presentation, and the Dormition of the Virgin as well as on the feast of the Annunciation.

Before discussing this scene, I should like to consider related compositions in contemporary monuments. The fragmentary fresco in the arched niche at the west end of the south façade of St. Mary Pammakaristos (Fethiye Djami) offers the closest parallel (Fig. 18).[263] Three priests, dressed like those in the Kariye painting (except that the third is bare-headed), each one holding a gold box, or bowl, and the second and third a censer as well, approach an altar covered with a red cloth and placed on a marble step. A gold vessel stands on this altar, of which only a small portion remains. An arched building rises in the background, and the Virgin, hands raised palms outwards, stands in front of the closed door. To the scene of the high priests before the altar, the painter has added here the image of the "closed door" based on Ezekiel 44:2, the symbolic interpretation of the virgin birth, for Mary is "the only door of the only Son of God who passing by it left it closed." [264] The closed door has been represented separately in other monuments. On the western arch of the nave of the church of Asinou in Cyprus, Ezekiel gazes at the Virgin orant, standing in front of a closed door.[265] In the outer narthex of the church at Peć, in Yugoslavia, Ezekiel, holding an inscribed scroll, points at a closed door.[266] The image of the Virgin does not appear here, nor in an earlier representation, namely the icon of Mount Sinai (Fig. 1). Ezekiel's portrait is accompanied only by a closed door, just as later, in the Dormition scene in the church of Staro Nagoričino, the closed door is the type painted next to the figure of Ezekiel.[267] In the narthex of Lesnovo we find a slightly different interpretation of Ezekiel's prophecy. The prophet faces Christ, who is seated at a table on which a round loaf of bread has been placed; below, in a separate compartment, one can see an amphora and a candlestick with lighted taper, both vessels adorned with the image of the Virgin.[268] These scenes illustrate Ezekiel 44:3: "the prince, he shall sit in it to eat bread before the Lord; he shall enter by the way of the porch of that gate, and shall go out by the way of the same." In developing the symbolism of Mary as the temple in which God dwelt, the Greek Church Fathers also explained that she is the sanctuary in which God made himself a priest and where he performs his sacerdotal office for all men;[269] the composition at Lesnovo stresses these sacerdotal functions of Christ, recalling at the same time the Marian symbolism through her images on the sacred vessels placed below.

The second composition related to the fresco at the Kariye is of an earlier date; it is located

262 Engberg, "Aaron and His Sons," DOP, 21 (1967) pp. 280–83. Both Professor Underwood, who had connected this scene with Exodus 40 (cf. Vol. 1 of this work, pp. 235 ff.), and I are in agreement with the identification by Mrs. Engberg.

263 Mango and Hawkins, "Report on Field Work . . . 1962–1963," pp. 223–28 and Figs. 10, 11.

264 Mercenier and Bainbridge, *La prière*, II,1, 2nd ed., p. 81— see also pp. 82, 92, 93, 98, 367; Eustratiades, Ἡ Θεοτόκος, s.v. θύρα; *PG*, 96, cols. 665C–D, 692A, 713B; 97, col. 1096C; 99,

col. 728A; and other references in Capelle, "Typologie mariale," pp. 113–14.

265 Seymer et al., "The Church of Asinou," PL. XCIX,1.

266 Babić, "L'image symbolique," Fig. 3.

267 G. and M. Soteriou, *Icônes*, I, pl. 54; Babić, "L'image symbolique," Fig. 2.

268 Okunev, "Lesnovo," p. 238 and PL. XXXVII.

269 Congar, *Le mystère du temple* (see n. 180), p. 306; Laurentin, *Maria* (see n. 38), pp. 65–66.

on the east wall of the south bay of the narthex of St. Clement in Ohrid (Fig. 19).[270] The three priests, carrying incense boxes and censers, are clad in long tunics and ornate mantles; behind them stands Ezekiel, holding a scroll on which are inscribed the words of his prophecy: "This gate shall be shut, it shall not be opened." On the right rises a building with an arched opening; there is no altar on the wide marble step in front of the building, and instead of the full figure of the Virgin, as at the Pammakaristos, her bust figure, enclosed in a medallion, has been painted in the middle of the closed door. Two seraphim flank the building; the one on the right is fully exposed, but only the tips of the wings of the one on the left are visible above the heads of the priests. With some differences, which will be considered below, we find here the same two elements as at the Pammakaristos, namely the high priests and the closed door, but the painter of St. Clement has added a third symbolic image. Behind the precinct walls, on the left, an aged, nimbed figure, turned to the right, holds a book in his raised, veiled hands, and a seraph, flying toward him and holding a coal in a pair of tongs, places it on his lips. The aged figure is obviously Isaiah, and this scene illustrates part of his vision: "Then flew one of the seraphim unto me, having a live coal in his hand, which he had taken with the tongs from off the altar" (Isa. 6:6). The half-effaced inscription refers to this scene. In the first line there remains only the word ΠΡΟΦΗ(της), and in the second line ΤΟΝ ΘΕΙΟΝ 'ΑΝ; this last word can be completed to read ἄνθρακα. In Christian typology the live coal is the type of Christ and the tongs that of the Virgin.[271]

The lesson from Isaiah 6:1–12 is read on the feast of the Presentation of Christ in the Temple, and in the hymns sung on that day, as well as in the homilies, Mary, carrying the Christ Child in her arms, is compared to the seraph sent with the coal to Isaiah, and she is acclaimed as the mystical tongs, having conceived in her womb the live coal that was Christ.[272] Another symbol of Mary, the instrument of the Incarnation, is thus added to that of the closed door in this fresco of St. Clement.

We may have yet a third example of a composition related to the one at the Kariye in one of the badly preserved scenes in the south narthex of the church of the Holy Apostles in Salonika. In the southwestern section of the domical vault three men, one of whom wears the priest's small hat, approach an altar raised on a step and placed in a rectangular niche like the one at the Kariye; one cannot distinguish whether or not the men hold boxes or censers in their hands. A fourth man stands to the right of the altar, and by reference to the composition of St. Clement one may tentatively identify him as the prophet Ezekiel. There is no sign of a door or of the image of the Virgin, and so far as the partly effaced painting enables one to judge, we have in this scene, as at the Kariye, only the high priests before the altar, with, possibly, the addition of the prophet.

We must now return to the painting in the parecclesion and try to determine its exact meaning. As already mentioned above, the inscription, of which only a few words are legible, can be reconstructed as "upon the eighth day, and so forward, the priests shall make your burnt offerings upon the altar," a phrase taken from the opening verses of the lesson read on all the Marian feasts (Ezek. 43:27–44:4). The vision of Ezekiel, from the description of which this passage is excerpted, concerns the New Jerusalem. In Christian exegesis the restoration of the temple of

270 Babić, "L'image symbolique," pp. 145–51.
271 Eustratiades, Ἡ Θεοτόκος, s.v. λαβίς.
272 Mercenier and Bainbridge, La prière, II,1, 2nd ed., pp.

314, 329–30; PG, 18, col. 364B; 96, cols. 677A, 689C; 97, cols. 869D–872A; 98, col. 512B.

Sion has frequently been interpreted as a figure of the spiritual and more perfect temple raised by the Messiah.[273] It will be recalled that on the feast of the Presentation, one of the days on which the lesson from Ezekiel is read during the Great Vespers, the reading for the liturgy is taken from the Epistle to the Hebrews 9:1–7, referring to the tabernacle, the sacred vessels, and the sacrifices of the old dispensation; and these are contrasted with the "greater and more perfect tabernacle, not made with hands" (v. 11) and the sacrifice of Christ, "who through the eternal Spirit offered himself without spot to God" (v. 14).

In order to represent the altar mentioned in Ezekiel's vision, which God commanded him to erect, the painters had to have recourse to the descriptions of the tabernacle and the altar built by Moses, references to which are also to be found in the passages from Exodus read on the feast of the Presentation.[274] There were two altars, in addition to the table of the shewbread. One of these was the altar of burnt offering, made of shittim wood and overlaid with brass, which was placed in the court (Exod. 27:1–8, 38:1–8), and one might suppose that this is the one represented in the frescoes since the verse from Ezekiel also mentions burnt offerings. However, the fact that the priests carry censers and boxes that are manifestly incense boxes suggests that we have here the altar overlaid with pure gold "to burn incense upon," which was "before the vail that is by the ark of the testimony, before the mercy seat that is over the testimony" (Exod. 30:1–6, 37:25–29). The identification with the golden incense altar is further suggested by the fact that it is placed in a rectangular niche, similar to the one drawn behind the altar in the scene of the Installation of the Ark in the Holy of Holies (PL. 460), and may thus be intended to represent the mercy seat. In instructing Moses to place the incense altar before the mercy seat God added "where I will meet with thee"; the presence of the Lord is suggested at the Kariye by the flame-like glories shining above the altar and the ray of light descending upon the priests. At St. Clement in Ohrid the altar has been omitted and the priests appear to be censing the image of the Virgin painted on the door, but the seraphim (instead of cherubim) represented on either side of the door indicate that the action takes place in the Holy of Holies, where two cherubim were placed "in the two ends of the mercy seat" (Exod. 25:18), as in the composition of the Installation of the Ark in the Holy of Holies (PL. 460).

We cannot tell why the painter of the Kariye (and possibly the painter of the Holy Apostles at Salonika) omitted the image of the closed door, which had already been included at an earlier date in this composition at St. Clement and at the Pammacharistos, and which made so clear its Marian symbolism. One reason may be that this symbolism had been suggested in the composition of the Angel Smiting the Assyrians before Jerusalem, where the Virgin is identified with Sion, the inviolable city, even though her image, placed on the tympanum, has no tangible connection with the closed door. In the present scene the only pictorial detail which recalls the Marian symbolism is the altar, one of the principal figures of the Virgin, frequently hailed as the golden incense altar on which the Logos, incarnate, fills the universe with perfume, as the golden altar of incense who carried in her womb the divine coal and perfumed the entire creation.[275] But the text of Ezekiel and its commentaries made this Marian symbolism quite clear, and the symbolism was further strengthened by the excerpts from the Epistle to the Hebrews read on the feast of the Presentation, in particular the reference to "the greater and more perfect tabernacle not made with hands." It does not seem necessary, therefore, to have recourse to the purely formal relationship between the figures of Aaron and his sons and those of the three kings bringing

273 Congar, *Le mystère du temple*, pp. 69–72, 303.
274 Exod. 40:1–5, 9–10, 16, 34–35.

275 George of Nicomedia, *PG*, 100, col. 1424C.

their gifts to the Virgin and to consider, as has been suggested, that the three priests here prefigure the Magi.[276]

* * *

The stylistic affinities between the mosaics and frescoes of the Kariye Djami prove them to be the work of the same atelier, but in content and conception there is a marked difference between them. In the two narthexes, although a definite intent may be discerned in the order and disposition of some of the episodes, and certain elements of the symbolism appear in the decoration of the northern dome of the inner narthex, it is the narrative trend that predominates, whereas in the parecclesion the accent is on the symbolism and the connection with the liturgy.

The biblical prefigurations of the Virgin constitute the most interesting and in many ways the most original part of the paintings of the parecclesion. It is in this category of subjects, which is inspired by and connected with the liturgy, and which also comprises illustrations of psalms and hymns, that the artists of the Palaeologan period made one of their major contributions to the program of church decoration. The extensive Christological cycle, the episodes of the apocryphal life of the Virgin, of which the mosaics of the narthexes offer outstanding examples, the scenes from the lives of saints, represented in other churches, were in part a development of a trend already noticeable in some churches of the eleventh and twelfth centuries, which the painters of the thirteenth and fourteenth centuries further elaborated by the addition of compositions related to the eucharistic cult, such as the representation of the Divine Liturgy. The Old Testament scenes that are types of Christ and of his Passion had already been used in the Early Christian period and occasionally at a later date; the important innovation was the use of other biblical episodes as prefigurations of the Virgin. It is well known that the Marian typology had been greatly developed by the artists of Western Europe ever since the twelfth century. This development lies outside the scope of the present study, focused on the paintings of the parecclesion of the Kariye, but in a more general study of Palaeologan art one should consider whether, and to what extent, acquaintance with the art of Western Europe played a part in this new development of the art of Eastern Europe.

The comparisons made above with the biblical prefigurations represented in other Orthodox churches brought to the fore the marked diversity both in the choice and in the iconography of the individual scenes. The ecclesiastical literature, the homilies, and the hymns offered a variety of types of the Virgin, some of which had already been used by miniaturists and by icon painters from the ninth century on. These simple representations were developed in the mural paintings of the Palaeologan period, each church presenting a somewhat different program. At St. Clement in Ohrid, one of the earliest extant examples of a complete ensemble, the typological scenes, together with single portraits of saints, constituted the sole decoration of the narthex. At the parecclesion of the Kariye the painters, or those who devised the program, had a more difficult problem to solve, but they succeeded in integrating, in a subtle manner, the two main themes: one connected with the funereal function of the building; the other related to the Virgin. In these paintings, as in the art of the fourteenth century in general, the weight of the age–old iconographic tradition may be observed in the Christological scenes—the Anastasis, the two miracles, and the Last Judgment—where the changes from tradition are of a minor order; the typological scenes, on the contrary, show greater freedom and at times result in new creations.

276 Engberg, "Aaron and His Sons," pp. 282–83.

General Index

Churches are indexed under names of places, e.g., Mistra, Peribleptos monastery, or Venice, San Marco. Kariye Djami is an exception. General subjects relating to it are under Kariye Djami, and works of art are indexed by title or grouped under cycles, e.g., Anastasis or Christ, Ministry Cycle.

For manuscripts identified by location and number, see Manuscript Index, which follows this Index.

The index entries referring to the study on Ministry Cycles by the late Professor Paul A. Underwood, editor of the present volume, have been prepared separately and they differ from those of the rest of the index in that they give the footnote numbers.

Aaron, 313, 315, 316, 333, 341, 342; in Genealogy of Christ, 268; and his sons before the altar, 345–49; rod of, 185, 186, 311–13, 315
Abel, 332–33; in Anastasis, 151, 322 and n
Abel, F. M., 308n
Abou Gosh, church, 308 and n
Abraham: Hospitality of, 133, 267, 311, 314; and Isaac, 267, 311; in Last Judgment with Lazarus, 124, 329–31; and Melchizedek, 332–33
Acre, manuscripts, 137
Acts of the Apostles, 104
Adam, 310; in Anastasis, 149, 151
Adam and Eve: in Anastasis, 114–16, 125, 267, 320–21; in Last Judgment, 327; union of, 173n
Adana encolpion (Istanbul Museum), 210n, 227n
Adoration of the Magi, 191n, 197, 198 and n, 200, 209 and n, 214 and n, 215, 216, 217 and n, 218 and n, 220–24, 238n, 240n
Adoration of the Shepherds, 210n
Adra, El, church, 211n
aers, Russian, 169n, 170n
Aeschines, 41
Aeschylus, 30, 38n
Aesclepiades, 42n
Affrodisius, 229 and n
Agathias, 41 and n
Agesilaus, 41n
Ahtala, church, 165 and n
Aïn Qarem chapel, 235n
Ajnalov, D. V., 137 and n, 138n, 173n, 183n, 221n, 325n
Akathistos Hymn, 188, 189n, 190n, 191, 201 and n, 214 and n, 217, 218n, 220, 222n, 223–24, 225n, 226 and n, 227–30, 239–41, 306, 313, 334, 344, 345
Akhmin, silk fragments found at, 211–12
Akindynos, 103, 105
Akropolites, Constantine, 20n, 21n, 23n, 34n
Akropolites, George, 19 and n, 20n, 24n, 36n, 49n
Akropolites, Melchisedek, 23n, 52n
Aktouarios, 23n
Alcibiades, 50n
Aldobrandini Wedding, 175n
Alexander, Romance of, 11
Alexander the Great, 41n, 47; birth of, in Beirut mosaic, 212n
Alexandrian tradition, 239

Alexius I Comnenus, 50n, 95
Almagest, 22n
Alpatov, M., 110n, 127n, 141n, 144n, 154n, 167n, 306n
altar: symbolizing tomb of Christ, 308, 309; symbolizing Virgin, 348
Amann, E., 163n, 180n, 183n, 185n
Ambrose, St., 260, 266 and n.95
Ambrosiana Gospel-Lectionary, see Manuscript Index, Milan
Amelungsborn, stained glass, 182
Amiens cathedral, 156
Amioun, St. Phocas, 308
Amiranašvili, S. J., 155n, 165n, 168n, 169n, 175n, 177n, 184n, 211n, 226n, 325n
Ammonius of Alexandria, 248n.11
Amnos, 319
Amphidromia, 176n
Anagni, mosaics, 138
Ananias, 77, 79
Anastasis (Harrowing of Hell, Christ's Descent into Hell), 114–16, 125, 132, 149–51, 247, 267, 305, 307, 308 and n, 309, 320–22, 324, 326, 331, 349
Anastasius I, 198n
Anatolia, 140
ancestors of Christ, see Christ, Genealogy of
Ancient of Days, 335
Ancona, sarcophagus, 219n
Andreades, A. M., 20n
Andreaš, church, 155
Andrew (Apostle), 252, 272, 274, 277, 283n, 288n
Andrew of Crete, 338n
Andrews ivory diptych (Victoria and Albert Museum), 283n.179, 285, 290n.236
Andronicus II, 19n, 21n, 24n, 25n, 26 and n, 28n, 43, 46n, 52n, 98, 313; art in period of, 145–52; grants to Chora monastery, 32 and n; letters from Athanasius, 29n, 99; Metochites in service of, 25–27, 29–31; Metochites' eulogy of (Logos 5), 40 and n; Metochites related to, by marriage, 27 and n, 54 and n; Palaeologan renaissance and, 23; rebellions against, 29 and n, 30 and n; recolonizing of Tralles, 41n; and restoration of Chora, 54 and n
Andronicus III, 19n, 21n, 25n, 52n; rebellion against Andronicus II, 29–30
Angeli family, 140
Angeli period, style of art, 129

365

Manuscript Index

The Style of the Kariye Djami and its Place in the Development of Palaeologan Art

OTTO DEMUS

Fig. 1. Kurbinovo, church of St. George.
Angel of the Annunciation

Fig. 2. Ohrid, church of St. Sophia. Apostles from the Ascension

[Demus]

Fig. 4. Moscow, Tretiakov Gallery, icon. The Virgin Orant

Fig. 3. Vladimir, church of St. Demetrius. Apostles from the Last Judgment

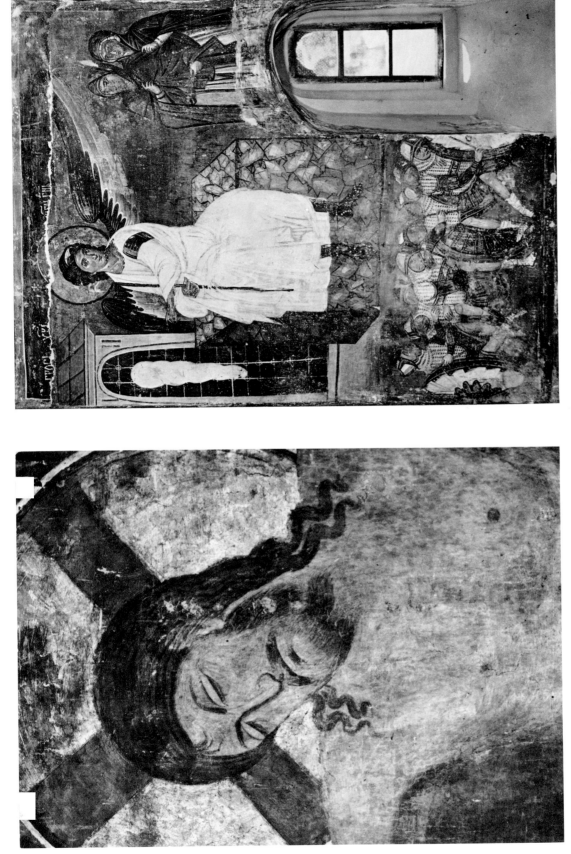

Fig. 6. Mileševo, church of the Ascension.
Holy Women at the Sepulcher

Fig. 5. Studenica, church of the Virgin.
The Crucifixion, detail

Fig. 7. Sopoćani, church of the
Holy Trinity. Prophet

Fig. 8. Sopoćani, church of the Holy Trinity. St. John the Evangelist

Fig. 9. Sopoćani, church of the Holy Trinity. St. Matthew the Evangelist

[Demus]

Fig. 10. Sopoćani, church of the Holy Trinity. The Dormition

Fig. 11. Sopocáni, church of the Holy Trinity.
The Dormition, detail. Bust of Christ

Fig. 12. Sopoćani, church of the Holy Trinity.
The Presentation of the Christ Child in the Temple

Fig. 14. Sopoćani, church of the Holy Trinity.
Old Testament Patriarch, detail

Fig. 13. Sopoćani, church of the Holy Trinity. Christ among the Doctors

Fig. 15. Venice, San Marco, narthex. The Moses dome

Fig. 16. Venice, San Marco, narthex. Third dome of the Joseph cycle

Fig. 17. Vatican Library, gr. 1153.
The Prophet Zephaniah

Fig. 18. Berlin, former Kaiser-Friedrich Museum,
mosaic icon. The Crucifixion

[Demus]

Fig. 20. Istanbul, Hagia Sophia. Deesis mosaic, detail. Head of the Virgin

Fig. 19. Istanbul, Hagia Sophia. Deesis mosaic, detail. Head of Christ

[Demus]

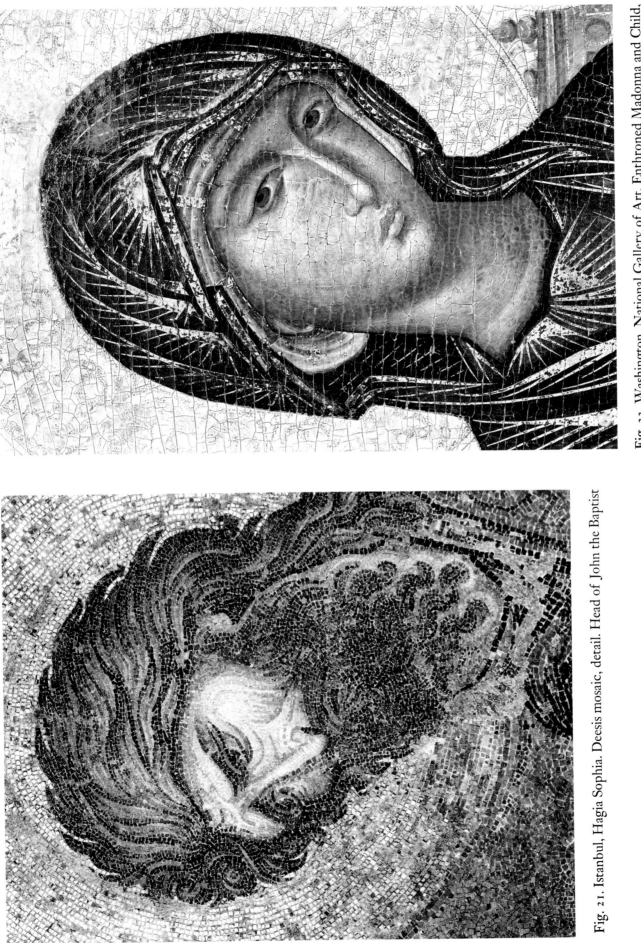

Fig. 22. Washington, National Gallery of Art. Enthroned Madonna and Child, detail (Gift of Mrs. Otto H. Kahn)

Fig. 21. Istanbul, Hagia Sophia. Deesis mosaic, detail. Head of John the Baptist

[Demus]

Fig. 23. Washington, Dumbarton Oaks, mosaic icon. Forty Martyrs, enlarged detail

Fig. 24. Mount Athos, Iviron 5, fol. 218v. St. Luke

Fig. 25. Paris, Bibliothèque Nationale, gr. 54, fol. 173. St. Luke

Fig. 26. Princeton, University Library, gr. Garrett 2,
fol. 270v. St. John

[Demus]

Fig. 27. Vatican Library, gr. 1208, fol. 2. Sts. Peter and John

Fig. 28. Vatican Library, gr. 1158, fol. 196v. St. Luke

[Demus]

Fig. 29. Ohrid, church of St. Clement. Gethsemane

Fig 30. Ohrid, church of St. Clement. The Meeting of Joachim and Anne and the Birth of the Virgin

Fig. 31. Ohrid, National Museum, icon. The Crucifixion

Fig. 32. Moscow, Tretiakov Gallery, icon. The Twelve Apostles

[Demus]

Fig. 33. Ohrid, National Museum, icon. The Annunciation

Fig. 34. Studenica, church of Sts. Joachim and Anne. The Presentation of
the Virgin in the Temple, detail

[Demus]

Fig. 35. Staro Nagoričino, church of St. George. The Betrayal

Fig. 36. Gračanica, church of the monastery. Communion of the Apostles, detail

Fig. 37a. Salonika, church of the Holy Apostles.
The Nativity, detail. Shepherds

Fig. 37b. Salonika, church of the Holy Apostles.
The Nativity, detail. The Bathing of the Infant

Fig. 38. Salonika, church of the Holy Apostles. The Dormition, detail

Fig. 39. Salonika, church of the Holy Apostles.
The Prophet Jeremiah

[Demus]

Fig. 40. Salonika, church of the Holy Apostles. St. Matthew

Fig. 41. Salonika, church of the Holy Apostles.
The Prophet Habakkuk

Fig. 42. Istanbul, Fethiye Djami (church of St. Mary Pammakaristos).
The Prophets Habakkuk and Jonah

[Demus]

Fig. 43. Salonika, church of the Holy Apostles. The Baptism

Fig. 44. Istanbul, Fethiye Djami (church of St. Mary Pammakaristos).
The Baptism

[Demus]

Fig. 45. Peć, church of St. Demetrius. The Birth of the Virgin

Fig. 46. Peć, church of St. Demetrius. Warrior Saints: George, Demetrius, Nestor

[Demus]

Fig. 47. Dečani, monastery church of the Ascension.
The Crucifixion, detail

Fig. 49. London, Victoria and Albert Museum, mosaic icon.
The Annunciation (Crown copyright)

Fig. 48. Mount Sinai, library of the monastery of St. Catherine,
gr. 152, fol. 389v. Christ and St. John

[Demus]

Fig. 50. Venice, San Marco, baptistery. The Baptism

Fig. 51. Ivanovo, cave church. The Washing of the Feet

Fig. 52. Paris, Bibliothèque Nationale, gr. 1242, fol. 92v. The Transfiguration

[Demus]

Fig. 53. Novgorod, church of the Transfiguration.
Head of an Angel

Fig. 54. Tsalendzhikha (Georgia).
Head of an Angel

Fig. 55. Andreaš, church of the monastery. Gethsemane

Fig. 56. Mistra, church of the Pantanassa. The Ascension

[Demus]

Fig. 57. Vatican Library, Joshua Roll (Palat. gr. 431), sheet V.
The Bearing of the Ark of the Covenant

Fig. 58. Mount Athos, Vatopedi 602, fol. 344v.
The Bearing of the Ark of the Covenant

[Demus]

Iconography of the Cycle
of the Life of the Virgin

Iconography of the Cycle of
the Infancy of Christ

JACQUELINE LAFONTAINE-DOSOGNE

Fig. 1. Tiflis Museum, silver icon from Zarzma, detail.
The Rejected Offerings

Fig. 2. Vatican Library, Homilies of the Monk James (gr. 1162),
fol. 8v. The Rejected Offerings

Fig. 3. Homilies of the Monk James, fol. 16v. The Meeting of Joachim and
Anne; Anne's Lament and the Annunciation to Anne

Fig. 4. Bertoubani (Georgia), church. The Return
of Anne and Joachim

Fig. 5. Pelendri (Cyprus), church of the Cross. The Return of Anne and Joachim;
the Annunciation to Anne; the Annunciation to Joachim

Fig. 6. Ohrid, church of St. Clement. The Annunciation to Joachim and Anne

Fig. 7. Daphni, church of the Dormition. The Annunciation to Anne and Joachim

Fig. 8. Rome, church of Sancta Maria de Gradellis
("Tempio della Fortuna Virile").
Joachim and his Shepherds

[Lafontaine-Dosogne]

Fig. 9. Leningrad, Hermitage Museum, ivory.
The Annunciation to Anne

Fig. 10. Vatican Library, Menologion of Basil II (gr. 1613), p. 229. The Meeting of Anne and Joachim

[Lafontaine-Dosogne]

Fig. 11. Studenica, church of Sts. Joachim and Anne. The Birth of the Virgin

Fig. 12. Vatican Library, Menologion of Basil II, p. 22. The Birth of the Virgin

[Lafontaine-Dosogne]

Fig. 13. Daphni, church of the Dormition. The Birth of the Virgin

Fig. 14. Paris, Louvre Museum, "Veil of Antinoë" (printed silk), detail. The Birth of Dionysus

[Lafontaine-Dosogne]

Fig. 15. Ohrid, church of St. Clement. Scenes of the Early Infancy of the Virgin:
the Caresses; the Blessing of the Priests; the First Steps

Fig. 16. Daphni, church of the Dormition. The Virgin
Blessed by the Priests (fragment)

Fig. 17. Daphni, church of the Dormition. The Presentation of the Virgin in the Temple

Fig. 18. Studenica, church of Sts. Joachim and Anne. The Presentation of the Virgin in the Temple

[Lafontaine-Dosogne]

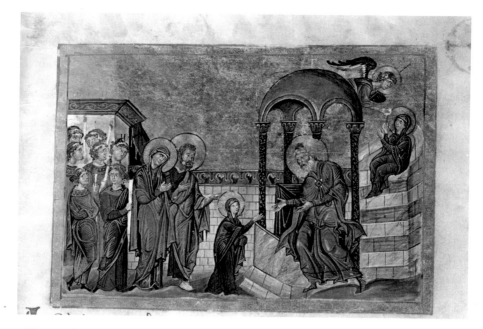

Fig. 19. Vatican Library, Menologion of Basil II, p. 198. The Presentation of the Virgin in the Temple

Fig. 20. Göreme, church of the Theotokos. The Presentation of the Virgin in the Temple

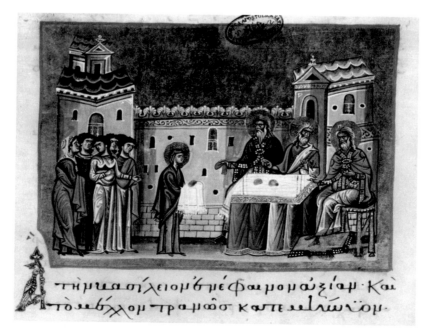

Fig. 21. Vatican Library, Homilies of the Monk James, fol. 109.
The Virgin Receiving the Skein of Purple Wool

[Lafontaine-Dosogne]

Fig. 22. Pelendri (Cyprus), church of the Cross. Scenes of the Life of the Virgin

Fig. 23. Ohrid, church of St. Clement. Scenes of the Marriage

Fig. 24. Vatican Library, Homilies of the Monk James, fol. 97v.
The Election of Joseph

Fig. 25. Homilies of the Monk James, fol. 104. Episodes
following the Marriage

[Lafontaine-Dosogne]

Fig. 26. Homilies of the Monk James, fol. 108. Joseph Taking Leave of the Virgin

Fig. 27. Homilies of the Monk James, fol. 117v. The Annunciation at the Well

[Lafontaine-Dosogne]

Fig. 28. Athens, Byzantine Museum, icon no. 1561. Life of the Virgin

Fig. 29. Paris, Bibliothèque Nationale, gr. 74,
fol. 3. Joseph's Dream

Fig. 30. London, Victoria and Albert Museum, the Werden casket, detail (Crown copyright)

a. Joseph's Dream   *b.* The Journey to Bethlehem

Fig. 31. Kalenić, monastery church

Fig. 32. Paris, Bibliothèque Nationale, gr. 74, fol. 108. The Journey to Bethlehem

Fig. 33. Karanlik Kilisse. The Journey to Bethlehem

Fig. 34. Mount Athos, Dionysiu 587, fol. 129.
The Enrollment for Taxation

Fig. 35. Vatican Library, gr. 1156, fol. 277.
The Enrollment for Taxation

Fig. 36. Curtea-de-Argeş, church of St. Nicholas.
The Enrollment for Taxation

Fig. 37. Beirut Museum, floor mosaic.
The Birth of Alexander

Fig. 38. Vatican Library, Menologion of Basil II (gr. 1613), p. 271.
The Nativity

Fig. 39. Phocis, church of Hosios Loukas. The Nativity

[Lafontaine-Dosogne]

Fig. 40. Mount Sinai, library of the monastery of St. Catherine, icon. The Nativity

Fig. 41. Salonika, church of the Holy Apostles. The Nativity

Fig. 42. Monza, cathedral treasure, phial no. I, obverse.
The Adoration of the Magi and the Annunciation to the Shepherds

a. Fol. 6

b. Fol. 6v
Fig. 43. Florence, Laurentian Library, Plut. VI. 23. Cycle of the Magi

[Lafontaine-Dosogne]

Fig. 44. Curtea-de-Argeş, church of St. Nicholas.
The Journey of the Magi and the Magi before Herod

Fig. 45. Istanbul, building near church of the
Theotokos Chalcopratia. The Arrival of the Magi

a. The Magi before Jerusalem

b. Herod Inquiring of the Priests and Scribes

Fig. 46. Paris, Bibliothèque Nationale, gr. 74, fol. 3v

Fig. 47. Curtea-de-Argeş, church of St. Nicholas. Herod Inquiring of
the Priests and Scribes, detail

Fig. 48. Kalenić, monastery church. The Adoration of the Magi

Fig. 49. Daphni, church of the Dormition. The Adoration of the Magi

a. The Journey of the Magi   *b*. The Adoration of the Magi

Fig. 50. Jerusalem, Greek Patriarchate library, Taphou 14, fol. 99v

Fig. 51. Kalenić, monastery church. The Return of the Magi and Joseph's Dream

Fig. 52. Jerusalem, Greek Patriarchate library,
Taphou 14, fol. 108v. The Departure of the Magi

a. The Return of the Magi

b. The Flight into Egypt

Fig. 53. Matejić, monastery church

Fig. 54. Curtea-de-Argeş, church of St. Nicholas. The Presentation of Christ in the Temple

[Lafontaine-Dosogne]

a. P. 273. Joseph's Dream

b. P. 274. The Flight into Egypt

Fig. 55. Vatican Library, Menologion of Basil II

[Lafontaine-Dosogne]

Fig. 56. Dečani, monastery church of the Ascension. The Flight into Egypt

Fig. 57. Deir Abu Hinnis, church. The Massacre of the Innocents and the Flight of Elizabeth

Fig. 58. Paris, Bibliothèque Nationale, Homilies of Gregory of Nazianzus (gr. 510), fol. 137, middle register.
The Massacre of the Innocents; the Flight of Elizabeth; the Murder of Zacharias

Fig. 59. Istanbul, building near church of the Theotokos
Chalcopratia. The Murder of Zacharias

a. The Massacre of the Innocents

b. The Return of the Holy Family from Egypt

Fig. 60. Paris, Bibliothèque Nationale, gr. 74, fol. 5

Fig. 61. Markov monastery. Rachel Weeping for Her Children

[Lafontaine-Dosogne]

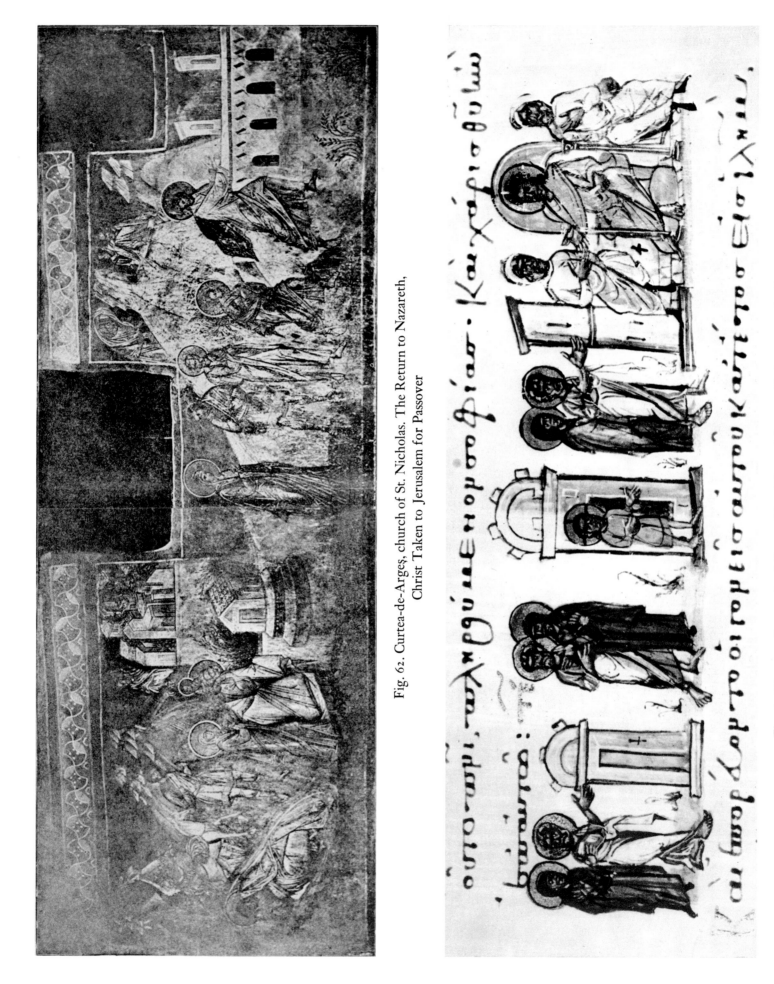

Fig. 62. Curtea-de-Argeş, church of St. Nicholas. The Return to Nazareth, Christ Taken to Jerusalem for Passover

Fig. 63. Florence, Laurentian Library, Plut. VI. 23, fol. 106v. Christ among the Doctors

[Lafontaine-Dosogne]

Some Problems in Programs
and Iconography of Ministry Cycles

PAUL A. UNDERWOOD

Fig. 1. Milan, church of San Nazaro Maggiore, silver reliquary, lid. Christ and Apostles,
Five Baskets of Bread and Six Jars

a.

b.

Fig. 2. Monreale, cathedral, south aisle, east end.
The Healing of the Daughter of the Canaanite Woman

a.

b.

Fig. 3. Monreale, cathedral, north aisle, east end.
The Healing of the Centurion's Son

Fig. 4. Pskov, Mirozh monastery, south arm, south wall. Post-Resurrection scenes (above);
Ministry scenes (below)

Fig. 5. Pskov, Mirozh monastery, south arm, west wall. Miracle scenes (below)

[Underwood]

Fig. 6. Pskov, Mirozh monastery, north arm, north wall. Passion scenes (above), Ministry scenes (below)

Fig. 7. Pskov, Mirozh monastery, north arm, west wall. Miracle scenes (below)

[Underwood]

Fig. 8. Mount Athos, Protaton, nave, south wall. Detail of the Baptism:
John the Baptist Bearing Witness of Christ

Fig. 9. Mount Athos, Chilandar, catholicon, conch of south apse. Baptismal cycle,
General view

Fig. 9*a*. East section

Fig. 9*b*. West section

a. Northeast and southeast quadrants

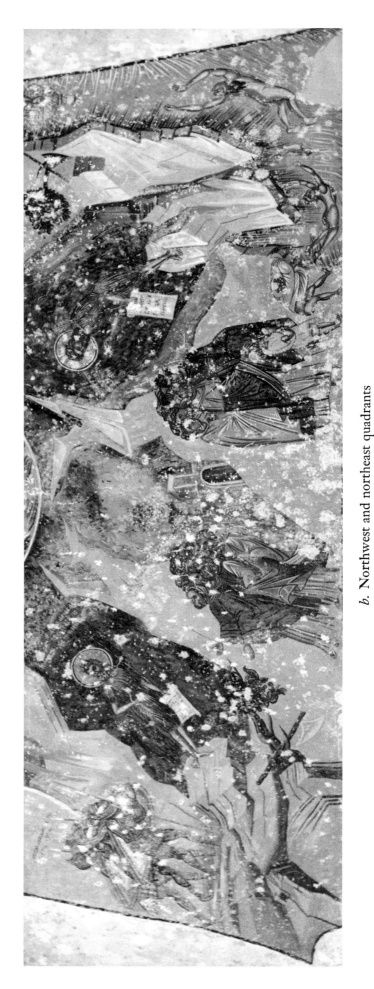

b. Northwest and northeast quadrants

Fig. 10. Prizren, church Bogorodica Ljeviška, outer narthex, central bay, vault. Baptismal cycle

Fig. 12. Moscow, State Historical Museum, Vlad. 146
(Sabba 61), fol. 145. John Baptizing the People in the Jordan

Fig. 11. Mistra, Peribleptos, south transept, vault, west half. The Baptism

[Underwood]

Fig. 13. Sant' Angelo in Formis, church, nave, north wall, upper register. First Temptation

Fig. 14. Sant' Angelo in Formis, church, nave, north wall, upper register. Second Temptation

Fig. 15. Sant' Angelo in Formis, church, nave, north wall, upper register.
Third Temptation

Fig. 16. Venice, San Marco, arch between great and south domes. Temptation scenes

[Underwood]

Fig. 17. Curtea-de-Argeş, church of St. Nicholas, nave, west arm, south wall, second register.
The Marriage Feast and Miracle at Cana

Fig. 18. Mount Athos, Iviron 5, fol. 363v. The Marriage Feast and Miracle at Cana

Fig. 19. Salonika, church of St. Nicholas Orphanos. The Marriage Feast at Cana

[Underwood]

Fig. 20. Church of St. Nikita, near Čučer. The Marriage Feast at Cana

Fig. 21. Dečani, monastery church of the Ascension, south arm, northwest pier, north face. The Marriage Feast at Cana

Fig. 22. Curtea-de-Arges, church of St. N
The Multiplica

icholas, nave, north wall, upper register.
:ion of Loaves

Fig. 23. Paris, Bibliothèque Nationale, gr. 74, fol. 29v. The Multiplication of Loaves

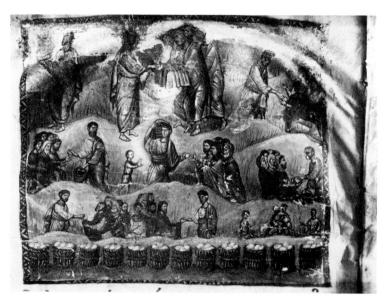

Fig. 24. Mount Athos, Iviron 5, fol. 63v.
The Multiplication of Loaves

Fig. 25. Paris, Bibliothèque Nationale, gr. 54, fol. 55.
The Multiplication of Loaves

Fig. 26. Kalenić monastery church. The Multiplication of Loaves

Fig. 27. Mount Athos, Iviron 5, fol. 377v. The Healing of the Paralytic at Bethesda

Fig. 28. Ravanica, church. The Healing of the Paralytic at Bethesda

Fig. 29. Church of St. Nikita, near Čučer.
The Healing of the Paralytic at Bethesda

Fig. 30. Monreale, cathedral, south transept, south wall,
zone 2. The Healing of the Paralytic at Bethesda

Fig. 31. Rome, San Saba, lower church, nave, right wall. The Healing of the Paralytic at Capernaum

[Underwood]

Fig. 32. Monreale, cathedral, north aisle. The Healing of the Paralytic at Capernaum;
The Healing of the Blind and Lame

Fig. 33. Venice, San Marco, arch between great and north domes, detail.
The Healing of the Paralytic at Capernaum

Fig. 34. Dečani, monastery church of the Ascension,
north arm, northeast pier, south face. The
Healing of Two Blind and Lame Men

Fig. 35. Dečani, monastery church of the Ascension, apse wall, second register. The Healing of a Multitude

Program and Iconography of the Frescoes
of the Parecclesion

SIRARPIE DER NERSESSIAN

Fig. 1. Mount Sinai, monastery of St. Catherine, icon. Enthroned Virgin and Child Surrounded by Prophets

Fig. 2. Prizren, church Bogorodica Ljeviška outer narthex, north bay, lunette.
Jacob's Vision of the Ladder and Jacob Wrestling with the Angel

Fig. 3. Salonika, church of the Holy Apostles, outer narthex, east bay, north lunette.
The Tabernacle of Moses

Fig. 4. Staro Nagoričino, church of St. George,
iconostasis. The Virgin Pelagonitissa

Fig. 5. Studenica, church of Sts. Joachim and Anne, nave, north wall, tympanum,
east half. The Anastasis

Fig. 7. Kalenić, monastery church, south apse, west side.
The Raising of Jairus' Daughter

Fig. 6. Kalenić, monastery church, nave, west wall.
The Raising of the *Widow's* Son

[Der Nersessian]

Fig. 8. Athens, Byzantine Museum, icon no. 2162. The Archangel Michael

Fig. 9. Cyprus, monastery of St. Neophytos, bema. Neophytos between the
Archangels Michael and Gabriel

Fig. 10. Manasija, monastery church, nave, soffit of arch above tympanum of west door.
The Hand of God between Solomon and David

Fig. 11. Trebizond, church of St. Sophia, north porch, lunette, detail.
Jacob's Vision of the Ladder and Jacob Wrestling with the Angel

Fig. 12. Ohrid, church of St. Clement, narthex, north bay,
west section. Jacob's Vision of the Ladder and
Jacob Wrestling with the Angel

Fig. 13. Lesnovo, monastery church.
Jacob Wrestling with the Angel

[Der Nersessian]

Fig. 14. Lesnovo, monastery church.
Moses and the Burning Bush

Fig. 15. Mount Athos, Vatopedi 602 (Octateuch), fol. 344v. The Bearing of the Ark of the Covenant

Fig. 16. Mount Sinai, monastery of St. Catherine, chapel

Fig. 17. Gračanica, monastery church, bema, north wall. The Tabernacle of Moses

Fig. 19. Ohrid, church of St. Clement, narthex, south bay, east section. The "Closed Door"

Fig. 18. Istanbul, Fethiye Djami (church of St. Mary Pammakaristos), south façade, west end, arched niche. The Three Priests before the Altar, and the "Closed Door" (fragment)

[Der Nersessian]

Plans and Sections

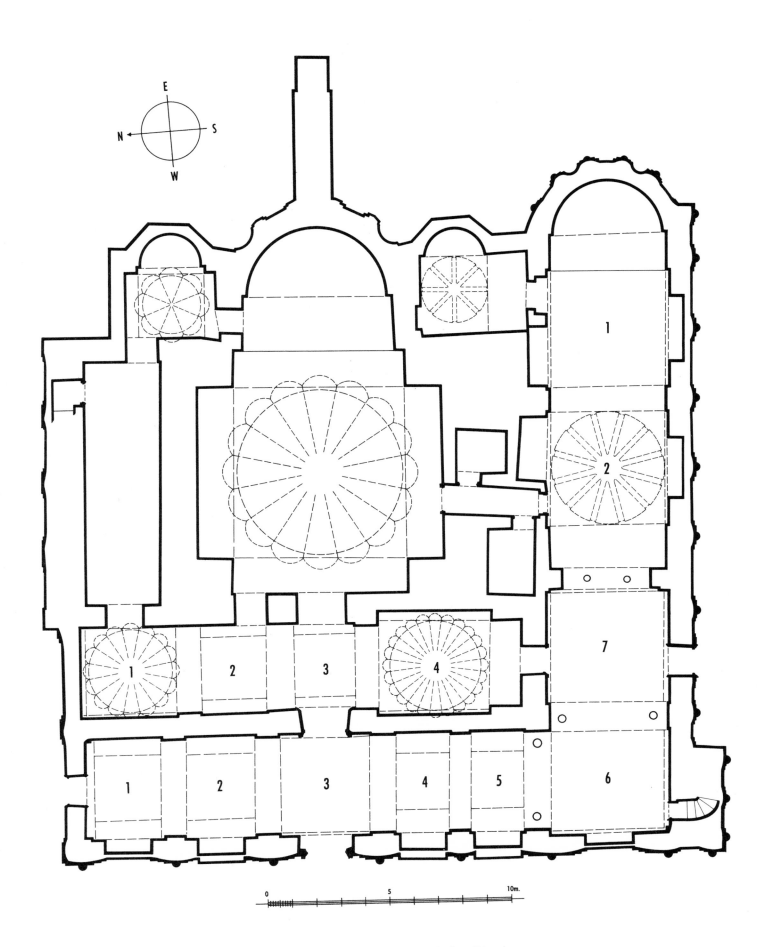

Fig. 1. General plan of the Kariye Djami

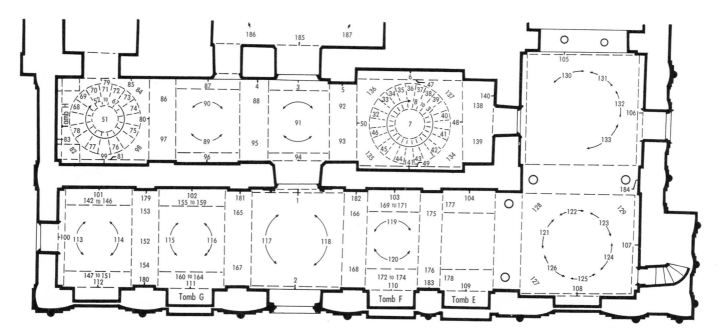

Fig. 2. Plan of the outer and inner narthexes

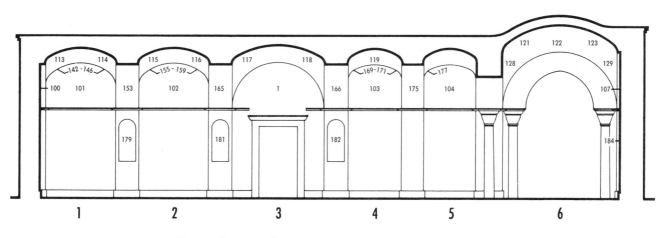

Fig. 3. Section of outer narthex, Bays 1–6, looking east

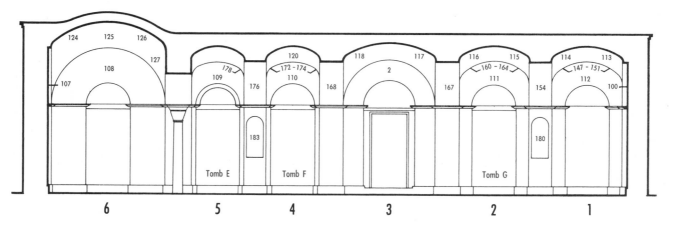

Fig. 4. Section of outer narthex, Bays 1–6, looking west

THE NARTHEXES

Key numbers in red indicate location of mosaics

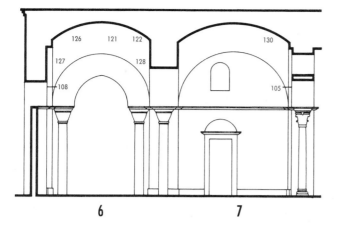

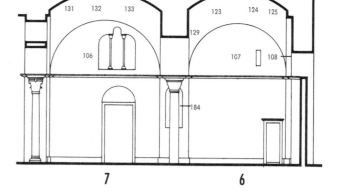

Fig. 5. Section of outer narthex, Bays 6 and 7, looking north

Fig. 6. Section of outer narthex, Bays 6 and 7, looking south

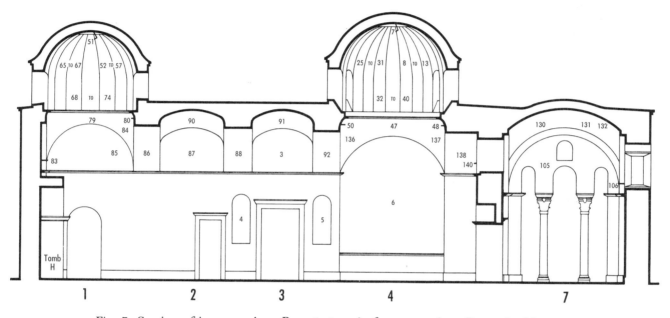

Fig. 7. Section of inner narthex, Bays 1–4, and of outer narthex, Bay 7, looking east

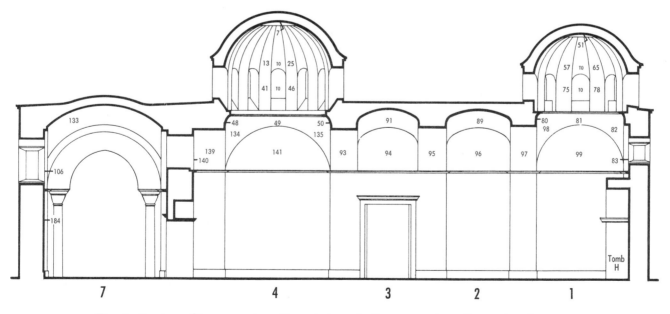

Fig. 8. Section of inner narthex, Bays 1–4, and of outer narthex, Bay 7, looking west

THE NARTHEXES

Key numbers in red indicate location of mosaics

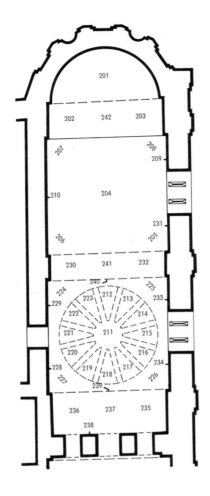

Fig. 9. Plan of the upper zone

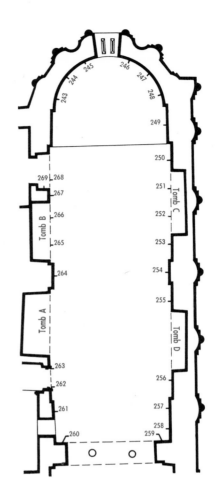

Fig. 10. Plan of the lower zone

THE PARECCLESION

Key numbers in red indicate location of frescoes

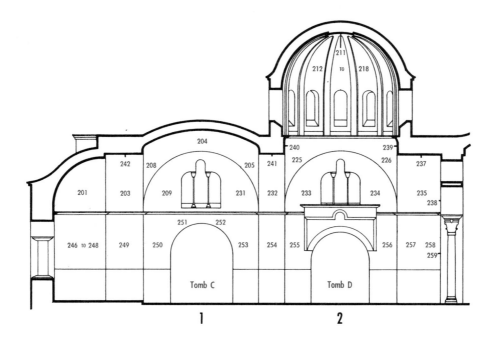

Fig. 11. Section, looking south

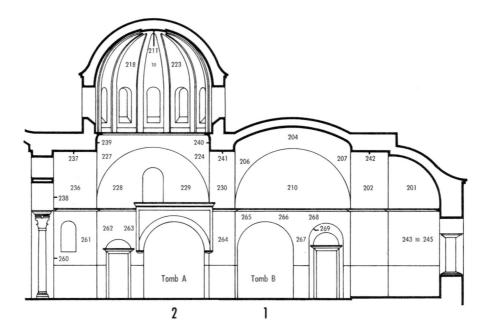

Fig. 12. Section, looking north

THE PARECCLESION

Key numbers in red indicate location of frescoes